Theory and Novel Applications of Machine Learning

Theory and Novel Applications of Machine Learning

Edited by

Meng Joo Er

and

Yi Zhou

Theory and Novel Applications of Machine Learning
Editors: Meng Joo Er and Yi Zhou

CBS, Edition **2017**

Published by InTech

Janeza Trdine 9, 51000 Rijeka, Croatia

Additional hard copies can be obtained from orders@intechopen.com

Theory and Novel Applications of Machine Learning,
Editors: Meng Joo Er and Yi Zhou
p. cm.

ISBN 978-3-902613-55-4

Preface

Even since computers were invented many decades ago, many researchers have been trying to understand how human beings learn and many interesting paradigms and approaches towards emulating human learning abilities have been proposed. The ability of learning is one of the central features of human intelligence, which makes it an important ingredient in both traditional Artificial Intelligence (AI) and emerging Cognitive Science.

Machine Learning (ML) draws upon ideas from a diverse set of disciplines, including AI, Probability and Statistics, Computational Complexity, Information Theory, Psychology and Neurobiology, Control Theory and Philosophy. ML involves broad topics including Fuzzy Logic, Neural Networks (NNs), Evolutionary Algorithms (EAs), Probability and Statistics, Decision Trees, etc. Real-world applications of ML are widespread such as Pattern Recognition, Data Mining, Gaming, Bio-science, Telecommunications, Control and Robotics applications.

Designing an intelligent machine involves a number of design choices, including the type of training experience, the target performance function to be learned, a representation of this target function and an algorithm for learning the target function from training. Depending on the resources of training, ML is always categorized as Supervised Learning (SL), Unsupervised Learning (UL) and Reinforcement Learning (RL). It is interesting to note that human beings adopt more or less these three learning paradigms in our learning process.

This books reports the latest developments and futuristic trends in ML. New theory and novel applications of ML by many excellent researchers have been organized into 23 chapters.

SL is a ML technique for creating a function from training data with pairs of input objects and desired outputs. The task of a SL is to predict the value of the function for any valid input object after having seen a number of training examples (i.e. pairs of inputs and desired outputs). Towards this end, the essence of SL is to generalize from the presented data to unseen situations in a "reasonable" way. The key characteristic of SL is the existence of a "teacher" and the training input-output data. The primary objective of SL is to minimize the system error between the predicated output from the system and the actual output. New developments of SL paradigms are presented in Chapters 1-3.

UL is a ML methodology whereby a model is fit to observations by typically treating input objects as a set of random variables and building a joint density model. It is distinguished from SL by the fact that there is no a *priori* output required. Novel clustering and classification approaches are reported in Chapters 4 and 5.

Distinguished from SL, Reinforcement Learning (RL) is a learning process without explicit teacher for any correct instructions. The RL methodology is also different from other UL approaches as it learns from an evaluative feedback of the system. RL has been accepted as a fundamental paradigm for ML with particular emphasis on computational aspects of learning.

The RL paradigm is a good ML framework to emulate human way of learning from interactions to achieve a certain goal. The learner is termed an agent who interacts with the environment. The agent selects appropriate actions to interact with the environment and the environment responses to these actions and presents new states to the agent and these interactions are continuous. In this book, novel algorithms and latest developments of RL have been included. To be more specific, the proposed methodologies for enhancing Q-learning have been reported in Chapters 6-11.

Evolutionary approaches in ML are presented in Chapter 12-14 and real-world applications of ML have been reported in the rest of the chapters.

Editors

Meng Joo Er
School of Electrical and Electronic Engineering,
Nanyang Technological University
Singapore

Yi Zhou
School of Electrical and Electronic Engineering,
Singapore Polytechnic
Singapore

Contents

In Eqs.(3) and (4), a is a damping factor, *TH* denotes a threshold parameter, and *min* denotes a minimum operation. As Eq.(2) shows, different from the conventional method, the proposed method can alleviate the influence of involuntary motions continuously. Figure 3 shows an example of the weight function. When a sudden action arises, the value of $D_x(t)$ (or $D_y(t)$) becomes large as shown in Eq.(4). Therefore, the weight $W_x(D_x(t))$ (or $W_y(D_y(t))$) becomes small when the sudden action arises. As Eqs.(2) and (3) show, the influence of a sudden action can be alleviated according to the decrease of $W_x(D_x(t))$ (or $W_y(D_y(t))$). However, the optimal shape of the weight functions depends on the condition of the handicapped student. Thus the shape of the weight function is determined by using supervised learning based on a fuzzy scheme.

The learning algorithm will be described in the following subsection.

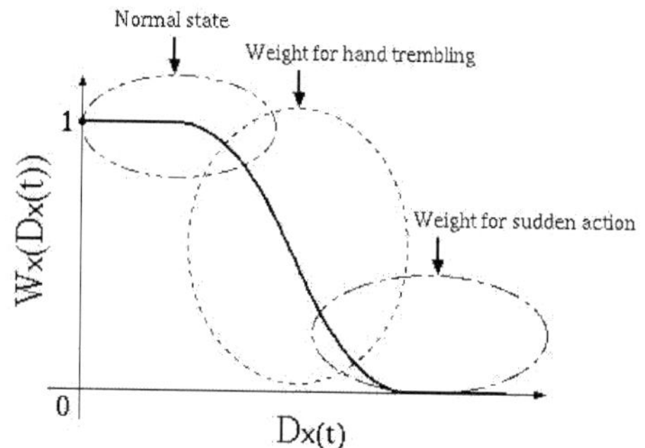

Fig. 3. Weight function.

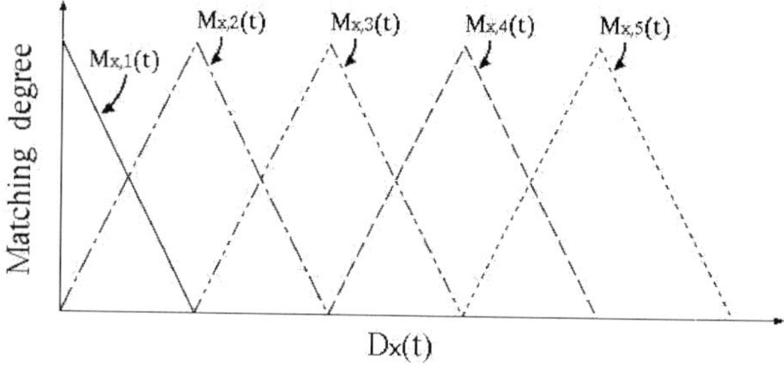

Fig. 4. Examples of triangular membership functions.

3.2 Determination of weight function

Weight functions are approximated as piecewise-linear functions. For inputs $D_x(t)$ and $D_y(t)$, matching degrees $M_{x,n}(t)$ and $M_{y,n}(t)$ are determined by the following equations:

$$M_{x,n}(t) = \mu_{x,n}\left(D_x(t)\right) \quad \text{and} \quad M_{y,n}(t) = \mu_{y,n}\left(D_y(t)\right), \tag{5}$$

respectively, where the parameter n (=1, 2, ... ,k) denotes the fuzzy label (Zadeh, 1965)for inputs $D_x(t)$ and $D_y(t)$, and $\mu_{x,n}(D_x(t))$ and $\mu_{y,n}(D_y(t))$ are triangular membership functions (Zadeh, 1968). Figure 4 shows an example of the triangular membership function when n=5. The output fuzzy sets

$$\frac{M_{x,1}(t)}{S_{x,1}(t)} + \cdots + \frac{M_{x,k}(t)}{S_{x,k}(t)} \quad \text{and} \quad \frac{M_{y,1}(t)}{S_{y,1}(t)} + \cdots + \frac{M_{y,k}(t)}{S_{y,k}(t)},$$

are defuzzified by the centre-of-gravity method (Zadeh, 1973), where $S_{x,n}(t)$ and $S_{y,n}(t)$ are singleton's elements [17-18], / is Zadeh's separator, and + is a union operation. The defuzzified outputs $W_x(D_x(t))$ and $W_y(D_y(t))$ corresponding to the weight functions are given by

$$W_x\big(D_x(t)\big) = \frac{\sum_{n=1}^{k} S_{x,n}(t)M_{x,n}(t)}{\sum_{n=1}^{k} M_{x,n}(t)} \quad \text{and} \quad W_y\big(D_y(t)\big) = \frac{\sum_{n=1}^{k} S_{y,n}(t)M_{y,n}(t)}{\sum_{n=1}^{k} M_{y,n}(t)}, \tag{6}$$

respectively. To simplify the above-mentioned operations, the membership functions are chosen such that the summation of the matching degrees becomes 1. Thus, Eq.(6) can be rewritten as

$$W_x\big(D_x(t)\big) = \sum_{n=1}^{k} S_{x,n}(t)M_{x,n}(t) \quad \text{and} \quad W_y\big(D_y(t)\big) = \sum_{n=1}^{k} S_{y,n}(t)M_{y,n}(t). \tag{7}$$

As Eqs.(6) and (7) show, the weight functions are approximated as piecewise-linear functions. Figure 5 shows an example of the piecewise-linear function. In Fig.5, $B_{x,n}$ and $B_{y,n}$ denote sample inputs which correspond to the coordinate values of the horizontal axis of boundary points. The shape of the piecewise-linear functions depends on $S_{x,n}(t)$ and $S_{y,n}(t)$.

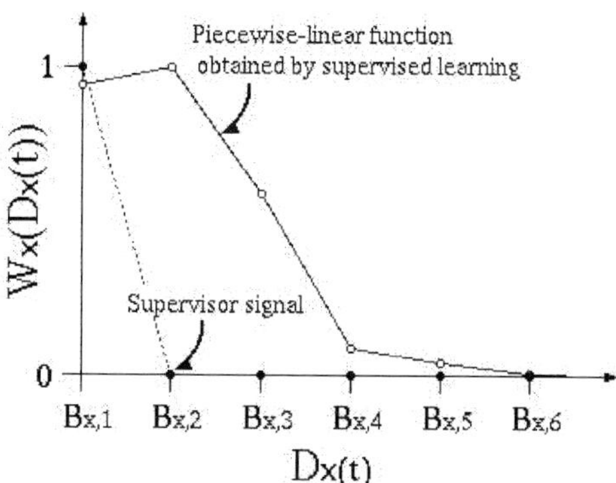

Fig. 5. Weight function obtained by supervised learning.

The singleton's elements $S_{x,n}(t)$ and $S_{y,n}(t)$ are determined by supervised learning. The learning dynamics for $S_{x,n}(t)$ and $S_{y,n}(t)$ are given by

$$S_{x,n}(t+1) = \begin{cases} S_{x,n}(t) + \eta_1 M_{x,n}(t) & \big(if \ M_{x,n}(t) \neq 0\big), \\ S_{x,n}(t) + \eta_2 \big\{H_{x,n} - S_{x,n}(t)\big\} & \big(if \ M_{x,n}(t) = 0\big), \end{cases}$$

$$S_{y,n}(t+1) = \begin{cases} S_{y,n}(t) + \eta_1 M_{y,n}(t) & \big(if \ M_{y,n}(t) \neq 0\big), \\ S_{y,n}(t) + \eta_2 \big\{H_{y,n} - S_{y,n}(t)\big\} & \big(if \ M_{y,n}(t) = 0\big), \end{cases} \tag{8}$$

where $S_{x,n}(t)$ and $S_{y,n}(t)$ satisfy

$$S_{x,n}(t) = \begin{cases} 1 & (if \quad S_{x,n}(t) > 0) \\ 0 & (if \quad S_{x,n}(t) < 0) \end{cases} \quad and \quad S_{y,n}(t) = \begin{cases} 1 & (if \quad S_{y,n}(t) > 0) \\ 0 & (if \quad S_{y,n}(t) < 0) \end{cases} \tag{9}$$

respectively. In Eq.(8), η_1 (<1) and η_2 (<1) denote learning parameters, and $H_{x,n}$ and $H_{y,n}$ are supervisor signals. The initial values of $S_{x,n}(t)$ and $S_{y,n}(t)$ are set to $S_{x,n}(0)=0.5$ and $S_{y,n}(0)=0.5$, respectively, because the optimal shape of the weight function changes according to the condition of the handicapped student.

When all the matching degrees $M_{x,n}(t)$'s and $M_{y,n}(t)$'s satisfy $M_{x,n}(t)\neq0$ and $M_{y,n}(t)\neq0$, respectively, Eq.(8) can be rewritten as

$$S_{x,n}(t+1) = S_{x,n}(t) + \eta_1 M_{x,n}(t) \quad and \quad S_{y,n}(t+1) = S_{y,n}(t) + \eta_1 M_{y,n}(t). \tag{10}$$

To save space, let us consider only the behaviour of $S_{x,n}(t)$. Since $S_{x,n}(t)$ is expressed by

$$S_{x,n}(1) = S_{x,n}(0) + \eta_1 M_{x,n}(0)$$

$$S_{x,n}(2) = S_{x,n}(1) + \eta_1 M_{x,n}(1)$$

$$\cdots$$

$$S_{x,n}(I-1) = S_{x,n}(I-2) + \eta_1 M_{x,n}(I-2)$$

$$S_{x,n}(I) = S_{x,n}(I-1) + \eta_1 M_{x,n}(I-1),$$

the following equation can be obtained:

$$S_{x,n}(I) = S_{x,n}(0) + \eta_1 \sum_{t=0}^{I-1} M_{x,n}(t). \tag{11}$$

As Eqs.(9) and (11) show, the singleton's elements $S_{x,n}(t)$ and $S_{y,n}(t)$ become $S_{x,n}(t)=1$ and $S_{y,n}(t)=1$, respectively, when $I\rightarrow\infty$. Hence, $S_{x,n}(t)$ (or $S_{y,n}(t)$) becomes large when $D_x(t)$'s (or $D_y(t)$'s) are close values.

On the other hand, when all the matching degrees $M_{x,n}(t)$'s and $M_{y,n}(t)$'s satisfy $M_{x,n}(t)=0$ and $M_{y,n}(t)=0$, respectively, Eq.(8) is rewritten as

$$S_{x,n}(t+1) = S_{x,n}(t) + \eta_2 \{H_{x,n} - S_{x,n}(t)\}$$
$$and \quad S_{y,n}(t+1) = S_{y,n}(t) + \eta_2 \{H_{y,n} - S_{y,n}(t)\}. \tag{12}$$

From Eq.(12), the learning dynamics can be expressed by

$$S_{x,n}(t+1) - H_{x,n} = (1-\eta_2)\{S_{x,n}(t) - H_{x,n}\}$$
$$and \quad S_{y,n}(t+1) - H_{y,n} = (1-\eta_2)\{S_{y,n}(t) - H_{y,n}\}. \tag{12}$$

Since $S_{x,n}(t)$ of Eq.(13) is expressed by

$$S_{x,n}(1) - H_{x,n} = (1-\eta_2)\{S_{x,n}(0) - H_{x,n}\}$$

$$S_{x,n}(2) - H_{x,n} = (1-\eta_2)\{S_{x,n}(1) - H_{x,n}\}$$

$$\cdots$$

$$S_{x,n}(I-1) - H_{x,n} = (1-\eta_2)\{S_{x,n}(I-2) - H_{x,n}\}$$

$$S_{x,n}(I) - H_{x,n} = (1-\eta_2)\{S_{x,n}(I-1) - H_{x,n}\},$$

the following equation can be obtained:

$$S_{x,n}(I) - H_{x,n} = (1-\eta_2)^I \{S_{x,n}(0) - H_{x,n}\}. \tag{14}$$

As Eq.(14) shows, the singleton's elements $S_{x,n}(t)$ and $S_{y,n}(t)$ become $S_{x,n}(t)=H_{x,n}$ and $S_{y,n}(t)=H_{y,n}$, respectively, when the conditions obtain that $0<\eta_2<1$ and $I\to\infty$. Hence, $S_{x,n}(t)$ and $S_{y,n}(t)$ approach $H_{x,n}$ and $H_{y,n}$, respectively, when $D_x(t)$'s (or $D_y(t)$'s) are not close values. From Eqs.(11) and (14), the singleton's elements satisfy the following conditions:

$$S_{x,n}(t) \in \lfloor H_{x,n}, \ 1 \rfloor \quad \text{and} \quad S_{y,n}(t) \in \lfloor H_{y,n}, \ 1 \rfloor. \tag{15}$$

For the sample inputs $B_{x,n}$ and $B_{y,n}$ which correspond to the boundary points of piecewise-linear functions, the supervisor signals $H_{x,n}$ and $H_{y,n}$ are chosen as

$$H_{x,n}(t) = \begin{cases} 1 & (if \ n=1), \\ 0 & (if \ n\neq 1), \end{cases} \quad \text{and} \quad H_{y,n}(t) = \begin{cases} 1 & (if \ n=1), \\ 0 & (if \ n\neq 1), \end{cases} \tag{16}$$

respectively (see Fig.5). The weight functions which satisfy $S_{x,n}(t)=H_{x,n}$ and $S_{y,n}(t)=H_{y,n}$ are the worst case.

4. Numerical simulation

To confirm the validity of the proposed algorithm, numerical simulations were performed by assuming a screen with 8,000×8,000 pixels.

Figure 6 (a) shows the simulation result of the moving average method incorporated with the compulsory elimination method. The simulation of Fig.6 (a) was performed under the conditions where the number of the averaged points $N=20$ and the threshold value is 5

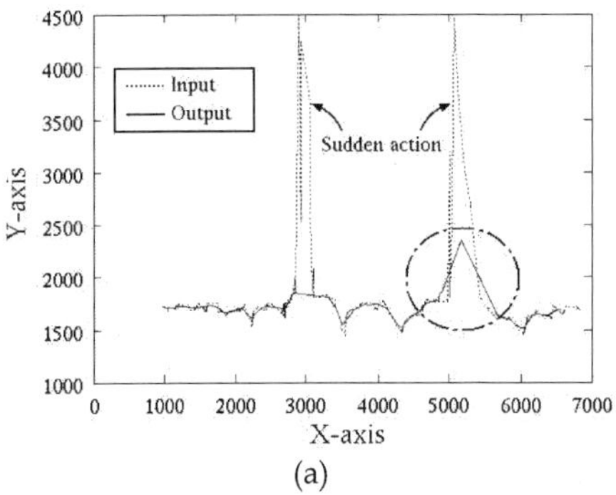

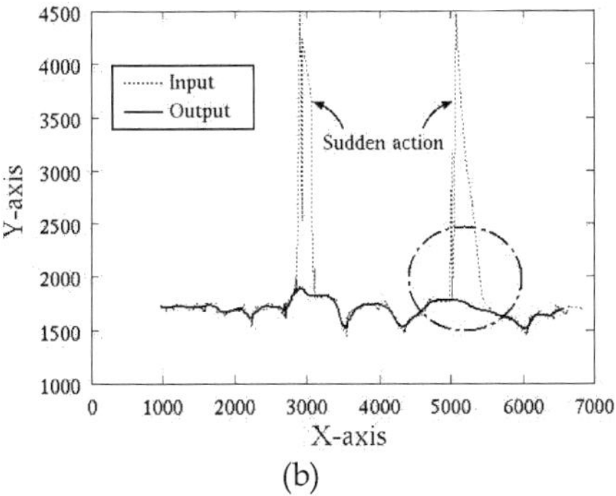

Fig. 6. Simulation results. (a) Conventional method. (b) Proposed method.

pixels (Nawate et al., 2004). As Fig.6 shows, preliminary experiments are necessary for the conventional method in order to determine the threshold value.

Figure 6 (b) shows the simulation result of the proposed method. The simulation shown in Fig.6 (b) was performed under conditions where the number of averaged points N=20, the number of singleton's elements k=8, and the learning parameter η_1=0.1 and η_2=0.01. The number of boundary points in the weight function depends on the parameter k. In proportion to the increase of k, the flexibility of the weight function is improved. However, the flexibility of the function has the relation of a trade-off with computational complexity. In the meaning of an approximation of the sigmoid function of Fig.3, parameter k must be larger than 4.

The membership functions $\mu_{x,n}(D_x(t))$ and $\mu_{y,n}(D_y(t))$ used in the simulation shown in Fig.6 (b) are

$$\mu_{x,n}(D_x(t)) = \begin{cases} 1 - |D_x(t) - 50(n-1)|/50 & \left(if \quad 1 > |D_x(t) - 50(n-1)|/50\right) \\ 0 & \left(if \quad 1 \le |D_x(t) - 50(n-1)|/50\right) \end{cases}$$

$$\text{and} \quad \mu_{y,n}(D_y(t)) = \begin{cases} 1 - |D_y(t) - 50(n-1)|/50 & \left(if \quad 1 > |D_y(t) - 50(n-1)|/50\right) \\ 0 & \left(if \quad 1 \le |D_y(t) - 50(n-1)|/50\right) \end{cases} \tag{17}$$

$$(n = 1,\ldots,8),$$

respectively. As Fig.6 (b) shows, the proposed method can alleviate the influence of sudden actions effectively. For the input image of Fig.6 (b), the weight functions shown in Fig.7 were obtained by supervised learning. Figure 8 shows the behaviour of singleton's elements. As Fig.8 shows, to adjust the shape of the weight functions, the values of the singleton's elements change dynamically. In Figs.7 and 8, the values of $S_{x,3}(t)$ - $S_{x,8}(t)$ and $S_{y,3}(t)$ - $S_{y,8}(t)$ are very small. This result means that the influence of involuntary action is alleviated when $D_x(t)$>100 or $D_y(t)$>100. Of course, depending on the condition of handicapped students, the values of $S_{x,n}(t)$ and $S_{y,n}(t)$ are adjusted automatically by supervised learning. As Fig.8 shows, the rough shape of the weight function is almost determined within t=100.

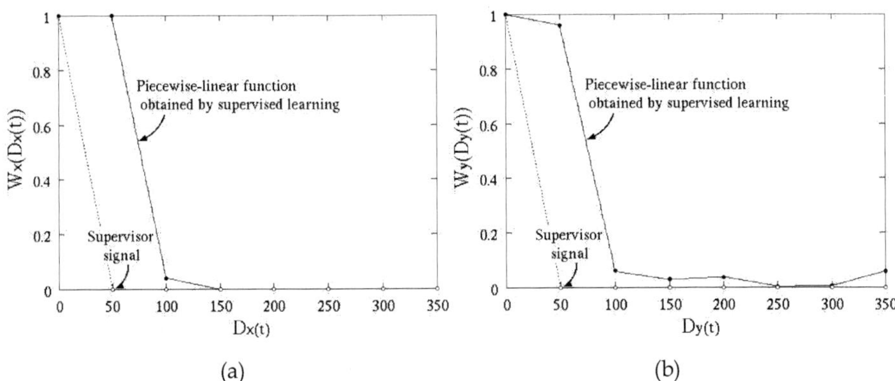

Fig. 7. Weight functions obtained by supervised learning. (a) $W_x(D_x(t))$. (b) $W_y(D_y(t))$.

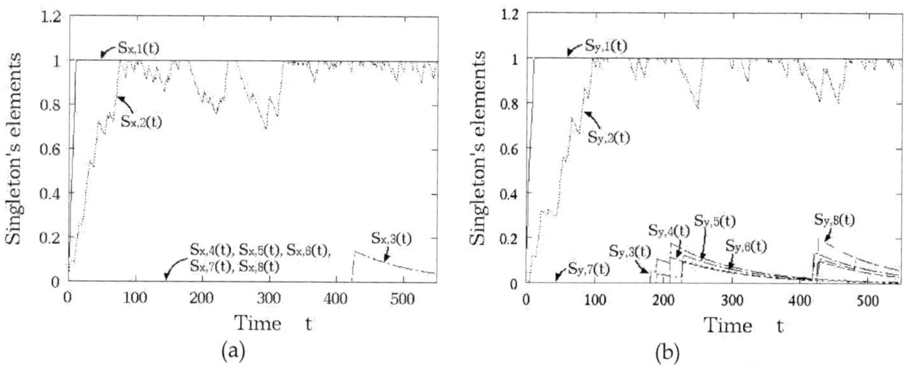

Fig. 8. Learning processes of singleton's elements. (a) $S_{x,n}(t)$. (b) $S_{y,n}(t)$.

5. Conclusion

A drawing-aid system to support handicapped students with nerve paralysis has been proposed in this paper. By using the weight functions which are determined by supervised learning, the proposed method continuously alleviates the influence of involuntary motions of the hand.

The characteristics of the proposed algorithm were analyzed theoretically. Furthermore, numerical simulations showed that the proposed method can alleviate the influence of hand trembling and sudden action without preliminary experiments.

Hardware implementation of the proposed algorithm is left to a future study.

6. References

Fujioka, H. ; Kano, H. ; Egerstedt, M. & Martin, C.F. (2006). Skill-assist control of an omni-directional neuro-fuzzy systems using attendants' force input, *International Journal of Innovative Computing, Information and Control*, Vol.2, No.6, pp.1219-1248, ISSN 1349-4198

Uesugi, K. ; Hattori, T. ; Iwata, D. ; Kiyota, K. ; Adachi, Y. & Suzuki, S. (2005). Development of gait training system using the virtual environment simulator based on bio-information, *Journal of International Society of Life Information Science*, Vol.23, No.1, pp.49-59, ISSN 1341-9226

Ezaki, N. ; Minh, B.T. ; Kiyota, K. ; Bulacu, M. & Schomaker, L. (2005a). Improved text-detection methods for a camera-based text reading system for blind persons, *Proceedings of the 8th International Conference on Document Analysis and Recognition*, pp.257-261, Korea, September, IEEE Computer Society, Gyeongju

Ezaki, N. ; Kiyota, K. ; Nagano, K. & Yamamoto, S. (2005b). Evaluation of pen-based PDA system for visually impaired, *Proceedings of the 11th International Conference on Human-Computer Interaction*, CD-ROM, USA, July 2005, Lawrence Erlbaum Associates, Inc., Las Vegas

Kiyota, K. ; Hirasaki, L. K. & Ezaki, N. (2005). Pen-based menu system for visually impaired, *Proceedings of the 11th International Conference on Human-Computer Interaction*, CD-ROM, USA, July 2005, Lawrence Erlbaum Associates, Inc., Las Vegas

Burke, E. ; Paor, A.D. & McDarby, G. (2004). A vocalisation-based drawing interface for disabled children, *Advances in Electrical and Electronic Engineering (Slovakia)*, Vol.3, No.2, pp.205-208, ISSN 1336-1376

Ito, E. (2004). Interface device for the user with diversity function (in Japanese), *Journal of the Japanese Society for Artificial Intelligence*, Vol.19, No.5, pp.588-592, ISSN 0912-8085

Nawate, M. ; Morimoto, D. ; Fukuma, S. & Honda, S. (2004). A painting tool with blurring compensation for people having involuntary hand motion, *Proceedings of the 2004 International Technical Conference on Circuits/Systems Computers and Communications*, pp.TD1L-2-1 - 4, Japan, July, Miyagi

Nawate, M. ; Fukuda, K. ; Sato, M. & Morimoto, D. (2005). Upper limb motion evaluation using pointing device operation for disabled, *Proceedings of the First International Conference on Complex Medical Engineering*, CD-ROM, Japan, May, Takamatsu

Morimoto, D. & Nawate, M. (2005). FFT analysis on mouse dragging trajectory of people with upper limb disability, *Proceedings of the First International Conference on Complex Medical Engineering*, CD-ROM, Japan, May, Takamatsu

Igarashi, T. ; Matsuoka, S. ; Kawachiya, S. & Tanaka, H. (1997). Interactive beautification: a technique for rapid geometric design, *Proceedings of ACM Annual Symposium on User Interface Software and Technology*, pp.105-114, Canada, October, ACM, Banff

Yu, B. (2003). Recognition of freehand sketches using mean shift, *Proceedings of the 8th International Conference on Intelligent User Interface*, pp.204-210, USA, January, ACM, Miami

Fujioka, H. ; Kano, H. ; Egerstedt, M. & Martin, C.F. (2005). Smoothing spline curves and surfaces for sampled data, *International Journal of Innovative Computing, Information and Control*, Vol.1, No.3, pp.429-449, ISSN 1349-4198

Zadeh, L.A. (1965). Fuzzy sets, *Information Control*, Vol.12, Issue 2, pp.94-102, ISSN 0019-9958

Zadeh, L.A. (1968). Fuzzy algorithm, *Information Control*, Vol.8, Issue 3, pp.338-353, ISSN 0019-9958

Zadeh, L.A. (1973). Outline of a new approach to the analysis of complex systems and decision process, *IEEE Transactions on Systems, Man, and Cybernetics*, Vol.SMC-3, pp.28-44, ISSN 0018-9472

2

Supervised Learning with Hybrid Global Optimisation Methods. Case Study: Automated Recognition and Classification of Cork Tiles

Antoniya Georgieva[1] and Ivan Jordanov[2]
University of Oxford
University of Portsmouth
United Kingdom

1. Introduction

Supervised Neural Network (NN) learning is a process in which *input* patterns and known *targets* are presented to a NN while it *learns* to recognize (classify, map, fit, etc.) them as desired. The *learning* is mathematically defined as an optimisation problem, i.e., an error function representing the differences between the desired and actual output, is being minimized (Bishop, 1995; Haykin, 1999). Because the most popular *supervised learning* techniques are gradient based (Backpropagation - BP), they suffer from the so-called Local Minima Problem (Bishop, 1995). This has motivated the employment of Global Optimisation (GO) methods for the supervised NN learning. Stochastic and heuristic GO approaches including Evolutionary Algorithms (EA) demonstrated promising performance over the last decades (Smagt, 1994; Sexton et al., 1998; Jordanov & Georgieva, 2007; etc.). EA appeared more powerful than BP and its modifications (Sexton et al., 1998; Alba & Chicone 2004), but hybrid methods that combine the advantages of one or more GO techniques and local searches were proven to be even better (Yao, 1999; Rocha et al., 2003; Alba & Chicano, 2004; Ludemir et al., 2006).

Hybrid methods were promoted over local searches and simple population based techniques in Alba & Chicone (2004). The authors compared five methods: two BP implementations (gradient descent and Levenberg-Marquardt), Genetic Algorithms (GA), and two hybrid methods, combining GA with different local methods. The methods were used for NN learning applied to problems arising in medicine. Ludemir et al. (2006) optimized simultaneously NN weights and topology with a hybrid method combining Simulated Annealing (SA), Tabu Search (TS) and BP. A set of new solutions was generated on each iteration by TS rules, but the best solution was only accepted according to the probability distribution as in conventional SA. Meanwhile, the topology of the NN was also optimized and the best solution was kept. Finally, BP was used to train the best NN topology found in the previous stages. The new methodology compared favorably with SA and TS on four classification and one prediction problems.

Plaginakos et al. (2001) performed several experiments to evaluate various training methods – six Differential Evolution (DE) implementations (with different mutation operators), BP, BPD (BP with deflection), SA, hybridization of BP and SA (BPSA), and GA. They reported poor performance for the SA method, but still promoted the use of GO methods instead of standard BP. The reported results indicated that the population based methods (GA and DE) were promising and effective, although the *winner* in their study was their BPD method. Several methods were critically compared by Rocha et al. (2003) as employed for the NN training of ten classification and regression examples. One of the methods was a simple EA, two others were combinations of EA with local searches in *Lamarckian* approach (differing in the adopted mutation operator), and their performance was compared with BP and modified BP. A hybridization of local search and EA with random mutation (*macro-mutation*) was found to be the most successful technique in this study.

Lee et al. (2004) used a deterministic hybrid technique that combines a local search method with a mechanism for escaping local minima. The authors compared its performance with five other methods, including GA and SA, when solving four classification problems. The authors reported worst training and testing results for GA and SA, and concluded that their method proposed in the paper was substantially faster than the other methods.

Yao (1999) discussed hybrid methods combining EA with BP (or other local search), suggested references to a number of papers that reported encouraging results, and pointed out some controversial results. The author stated that the best optimizer is generally problem dependant and there was no overall winner.

In our recent research (Jordanov & Georgieva, 2007; Georgieva & Jordanov, 2008a; Georgieva & Jordanov, 2008c) we investigated, developed and proposed a hybrid GO technique called Genetic $LP\tau$ Search ($GLP\tau S$), able to solve high dimensional multimodal optimization problems, which can be used for local minima free NN learning. $GLP\tau S$ benefits from the hybridization of three different approaches that have their own specific advantages:

- $LP\tau$ Optimization ($LP\tau O$): a GO approach proposed in our earlier work (Georgieva & Jordanov, 2008c) that is based on meta-heuristic rules and was successfully applied for the optimization of low dimensional mathematical functions and several benchmark NN learning tasks of moderate size (Jordanov & Georgieva, 2007);
- Genetic Algorithms: well known stochastic approaches that solve successfully high dimensional problems (De Jong, 2006);
- Nelder-Mead Simplex Search: a derivative-free local search capable of finding quickly a solution with high accuracy, once a region of attraction has been identified by a GO method (Nelder & Mead, 1965).

In this chapter, we investigate the basic properties of $GLP\tau S$ and compare its performance with several other algorithms. In Georgieva & Jordanov (2008a) the method was tested on multimodal mathematical functions of high dimensionality (up to 150), and results were compared with findings of other authors. Here, a summary of these results is presented and subsequently, the method is be employed for NN training of benchmark pattern recognition problems. In addition, few of the more interesting benchmark problems are discussed here.

Finally, a case study of machine learning in practice is presented: the NNs trained with $GLP\tau S$ are employed to recognize and classify seven different types of cork tiles. This is a challenging real-world problem, incorporating computer vision for the automation of production assembly lines (Georgieva & Jordanov, 2008b). Reported results are discussed and compared with similar approaches, demonstrating the advantages of the investigated method.

2. A novel global optimisation approach for training neural networks

2.1 Introduction and motivation

In Georgieva & Jordanov (2007) we proposed a novel heuristic, population-based GO technique, called *LPτ Optimization (LPτO)*. It utilizes *LPτ* low-discrepancy sequences of points (Sobol', 1979), in order to uniformly explore the search space. It has been proven numerically that the use of low-discrepancy point sequences results in a reduction of computational time for small and moderate dimensionality problems (Kucherenko & Sytsko, 2005). In addition, Sobol's *LPτ* points have very useful properties for higher dimensionality problems, especially when the objective function depends strongly on a subset of variables (Kucherenko & Sytsko, 2005; Liberti & Kutcherenko, 2005). In *LPτO* are incorporated novel, complete set of logic-based, self-adapting heuristic rules (meta-heuristics) that guide the search through the iterations. The *LPτO* method was further investigated in Georgieva & Jordanov (2008c) while combined with the Nelder-Mead Simplex search to form a hybrid *LPτNM* technique. It was compared with other methods, demonstrating promising results and strongly competitive nature when tested on a number of multimodal mathematical functions (2 to 20 variables). It was successfully applied and used for training of neural networks with moderate dimensionalities (Jordanov & Georgieva, 2007). However, with the increase of the dimensionality, the method experienced greater computational load and its performance worsened. This led to the development of a new hybrid technique – *GLPτS* that combines *LPτNM* with evolutionary algorithms and aims to solve efficiently problems of higher dimensionalities (up to a 150).

GAs are known for their very good exploration abilities and when optimal balance with their exploitation ones is found, they can be powerful and efficient global optimizers (Leung and Wang, 2001; Mitchell, 2001; Sarker et al., 2002). Exploration dominated search could lead to excessive computational expense. On the other hand, if the exploitation is favourable, the search is in danger of premature convergence, or simply of turning into a local optimizer. Keeping the balance between the two and preserving the selection pressure relatively constant throughout the whole run is important characteristic of any GA technique (Mitchell, 2001; Ali et al., 2005). Other problems associated with GA are their relatively slow convergence and low accuracy of the found solutions (Yao et al., 1999; Ali et al., 2005). This is the reason why GA are often combined with other search techniques (Sarker et al., 2002), and the same approach is adopted in our hybrid method, aiming to tackle these problems effectively by complementing GA and *LPτO* search.

The *LPτO* technique can be summarized as follows: we *seed* the whole search region with *LPτ* points, from which we select *several* promising ones to be centres of regions in which we *seed* new *LP_τ* points. Then we choose few promising points from the new ones and again *seed* in the neighbourhood of each one and so on, until a halting condition is satisfied. By combining *LPτO* with GA of moderate population size, the aim is to explore the search space and improve the initial *seeding* with *LPτ* points by applying genetic operators in a few generations. Subsequently, a heuristic-stochastic rule is applied in order to select some of the individuals and to start *LPτO* search in the neighbourhood of each of the chosen ones. Finally, we use a local Simplex Search to refine the solution and achieve better accuracy.

2.2 *LPτ* low-discrepancy points

Low-discrepancy sequences (LDS) of points are deterministically generated uniformly distributed points (Niederreiter, 1992). *Uniformity* is an important property of a sequence which guarantees that the points are *evenly* distributed in the whole domain. When comparing two uniformly distributed sequences, features as *discrepancy* and *dispersion* are used in order to quantify their uniformity. Two different uniform sequences in three dimensions are shown in Fig. 1. The advantage of the low-discrepancy sequences is that they avoid the so called shadow effect, i.e., when projections of several points on the projective planes are coincident.

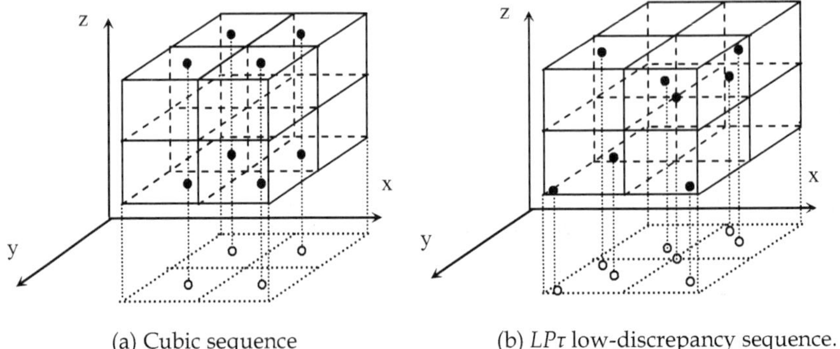

(a) Cubic sequence   (b) $LP\tau$ low-discrepancy sequence.

Fig. 1. Two different uniform sequences.

As it can be seen from Fig.1, the projections of the cubic sequence give four different points on the projective plane, each of them repeated twice, while the $LP\tau$ sequence gives eight different projection points. Therefore, the low-discrepancy sequence would describe the function behaviour in this plane much better than the cubic one; this advantage is enhanced with the increase of the dimensionality and the number of points. This feature is especially important when the function at hand is weakly dependent on some of the variables and strongly dependent on the rest of them (Kucherenko & Sytsko, 2005).

The application of LDS in GO methods was investigated in Kucherenko & Sytsko (2005), where the authors concluded that the Sobol's $LP\tau$ sequences are superior to the other LDS. Many useful properties of $LP\tau$ points have been shown in Sobol', (1979) and tested in Bratley & Fox (1988), Niederreiter (1992), and Kucherenko & Sytsko (2005). The properties of LDS could be summarized as follows:

- retain their properties when transferred from a unit hyper-cube to a hyper-parallelepiped, or when projected on any of the sides of the hyper-cube;
- explore the space better avoiding the *shadowing effect* discussed earlier. This property is very useful when optimising functions that depend weakly on some of the variables, and strongly on the others;
- unlike the conventional random points, successive LDS have *memory* and *know* about the positions of the previous points and try to fill the gaps in between (this property is true for all LDS and is demonstrated in Fig. 2);
- it is widely accepted (Sobol', 1979; Niederreiter, 1992) that no infinite sequence of N points can have discrepancy ρ that converges to zero with smaller order of magnitude than $O(N^{-1}\log^n(N))$, where n is the dimensionality. The $LP\tau$ sequence satisfies this estimate. Moreover, due to the way $LP\tau$ are defined, for values of $N = 2^k$, $k = 1, 2, ..., 31$, the discrepancy converges with rate $O(N^{-1}\log^{n-1}(N))$ as the number of points increases (Sobol', 1979).

2.3 The *LPτO* meta-heuristic approach

Stochastic techniques depend on a number of parameters that play decisive role for the algorithm performance assessed by speed of convergence, computational load, and quality of the solution. Some of these parameters include the number of initial and subsequent trial points, and a parameter (or more than one) that defines the speed of convergence (cooling temperature in SA, probability of mutation in GA, etc.). Assigning values to these parameters (*tuning*) is one of the most important and difficult parts from the development of a GO technique. The larger the number of such decisive parameters, the more difficult (or sometimes even impossible) is to find a set of parameter values that will ensure an algorithm's good performance for as many as possible functions. Normally, authors try to reduce the number of such *user defined* parameters, but one might argue that in this way, the technique becomes less flexible and the search depends more on random variables.

The advantage of the *LPτO* technique is that the values of these parameters are selected in a meta-heuristic manner – depending on the function at hand, while guided by the user. For example, instead of choosing a specific number of initial points N, in *LPτO*, a range of allowed values (N_{min} and N_{max}) is defined by the user and the technique adaptively selects (using the *filling-in the gaps* property of *LPτ* sequences) the smallest allowed value that gives enough information about the landscape of the objective function, so that the algorithm can continue the search effectively. Therefore, the parameter N is exchanged with two other user-defined parameters (N_{min} and N_{max}), which allows flexibility when N is selected automatically, depending on the function at hand. Since the method does not assume a priori knowledge of the global minimum (GM), all parts of the parameter space must be equally treated, and the points should be uniformly distributed in the whole region of initial searched. The *LPτ* low-discrepancy sequences and their properties fulfill this issue satisfactorily. We also use the property of *LPτ* sequences that additional points *fill the gaps* between the other *LPτ* points. For example, if we have an *LPτ* sequence with four points and we would like to double their number, the resulting sequence will include the initial four points plus the new four ones positioned in-between them. This property of the *LPτ* sequences is demonstrated in Fig. 2.

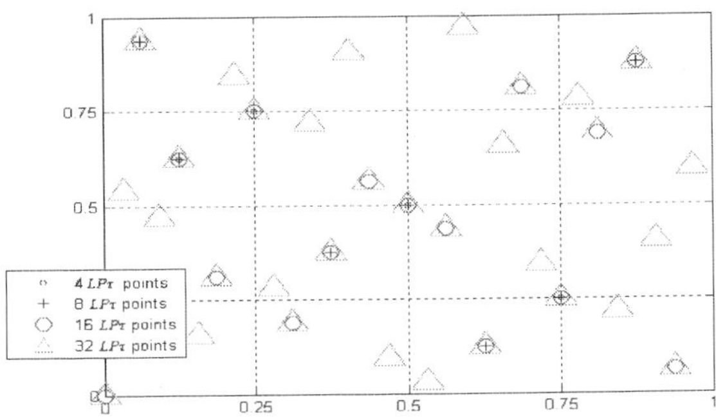

Fig. 2. *Fill in the gaps* property of the *LPτ* sequences.

As discussed above, when choosing the initial points of *LPτO*, a range of allowed values (N_{min} and N_{max}) is defined and the technique adaptively selects the smallest possible value that gives enough information about the landscape of the objective function, so that the algorithm can continue the search effectively. Simply said, after the minimal possible number of points is selected, the function at hand is investigated with those points, and if there are not *enough promising points*, additional ones are generated and the process is repeated until an *appropriate* number of points is selected, or the maximal of the allowed values is reached.

Another example of the meta-heuristic properties of *LPτO* is the parameter that allows switching between exploration and exploitation and, thus, controls the convergence of the algorithm. In *simulating annealing* (SA), this is done by the *cooling temperature* (decreased by *annealing shedule*); in GA - by the *probability of mutation*, etc. These parameters are user-defined at the beginning of the search. In the *LPτO* method, the convergence speed is controlled by the size of future regions of interest, given by a radius R, and, in particular, the *speed* with which R decreases (Georgieva & Jordanov, 2008c). If R decreases slowly, then the whole search converges slowly, allowing more time for exploration. If R decreases quickly, the convergence is faster, but the risk of omitting a GM is higher. In the *LPτO*, the decrease/increase step of R is not a simple user-defined value. It is determined adaptively on each iteration and depends on the current state of the search, the *importance* of the region of interest, as well as the complexity of the problem (dimensionality and size of the searched domain). The convergence speed depends also on a parameter M, which is the maximum allowed number of future regions of interest. M is a user defined upper bound of the number of future regions of interest M_{new}, while the actual number is adaptively selected at each iteration within the interval $[1, M]$. The GO property of *LPτO* to escape local minima is demonstrated in Fig. 3, where the method locates four regions of interest and after a few iterations detects the GM.

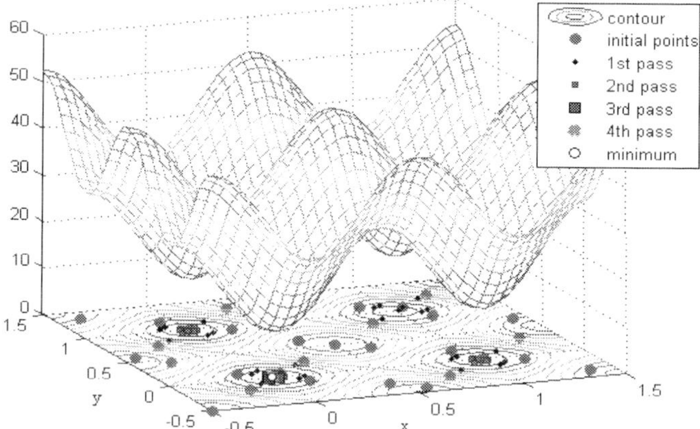

Fig. 3. Two-dimensional Rastrigin function with three local and one global minima, optimized with *LPτO*.

The convergence stability of *LPτO* with respect to these parameters (in particular M and N_{max}), the stability of the method with respect to the initial points and the searched domain, the analytical properties of the technique and the results from testing on a number of benchmark functions are further analysed and discussed in Georgieva & Jordanov (2008c).

2.4 GA and Nelder-Mead simplex search

General information for GA and their properties can be found in Mitchell (2001). We use conventional one-point recombination and our mutation operator is the same as in (Leung & Wang, 2001). We keep constant population size, starting with G individuals. The general form of the performed GA is:

Step 1. From the current population $p(G)$, each individual is selected to undergo recombination with probability P_r. If the number of selected individuals is odd, we dispose of the last one selected. All selected individuals are randomly paired for *mating*. Each pair produces two new individuals by recombination;

Step 2. Each individual from the current population $p(G)$ is also selected to undergo mutation with probability P_m;

Step 3. From the *parent* population and the *offspring* generated by recombination and mutation, the best G individuals are selected to form the new generation $p(G)$.

Step 4. If the halting condition is not satisfied, the algorithm is repeated from step 1.

Further details of the adopted GA can be found in Georgieva & Jordanov (2008a). The Nelder-Mead (NM) simplex method for function optimization is a fast local search technique (Nelder & Mead, 1965), that needs only function values and requires continuity of the function. It has been used in numerous hybrid methods to refine the obtained solutions (Chelouah & Siarry, 2003; 2005), and for coding of GA individuals (Hedar & Fukushima, 2003). The speed of convergence (measured by the number of function evaluations) depends on the function values and the continuity, but mostly, it depends on the choice of the initial simplex - its coordinates, form and size. We select the initial simplex to have one vertex in the best point found by the $LP\tau O$ searches and another n vertices distanced from it in a positive direction along each of its n coordinates, with a coefficient λ. As for the choice of the parameter λ, we connect it with the value of R_1, which is the average distance between the testing points in the region of attraction, where the best solution is found by $LP\tau O$.

2.5 The *GLPτS* technique: hybridization of GA, *LPτO* and Nelder-Mead search

Here, we introduce in more detail the hybrid method called *Genetic LPτ and Simplex Search* (*GLPτS*), which combines the effectiveness of GA during the early stages of the search with the advantages of *LPτO*, and the local improvement abilities of NM search (further discussion of the method can be found in Georgieva & Jordanov (2008a).

Based on the complexity of the searched landscapes, most authors intuitively choose population size for their GA that could vary from 100s to 1000s (De Jong, 2006). We employ smaller number of points that leads to a final population with promising candidates from regions of interest, but not necessarily to a GM. Also, our initial population points are not random (as in a conventional GA), but uniformly distributed $LP\tau$ points.

Generally, the technique could be described as follows:

Step 1. Generate a number I of initial $LP\tau$ points;

Step 2. Select G points, ($G < I$), that correspond to the best function values. Let this be the initial population $p(G)$ of the GA;

Step 3. Perform GA until a halting condition is satisfied;

Step 4. From the population $p(G)$ of the last GA generation, select g points of future interest $(1 \leq g \leq G/2)$;

Step 5. Initialize the $LP\tau O$ search in the neighbourhood of each selected point;

Step 6. After the stopping conditions of the $L P \tau O$ searches are satisfied, initialize a local NM search in the best point found by all $L P \tau O$ searches.

To determine the number g of subsequent $L P \tau O$ searches (**Step 4**), the following rule is used (illustrated in Fig. 4):

Let $p(G)$ be the population of the last generation found by the GA run. Firstly, all G individuals are sorted in non-descending order using their fitness values and then rank r_i is associated to the first half of them by using formula (1):

$$r_i = \frac{f_{\max} - f_i}{f_{\max} - f_{\min}}, \ i = 2, \ldots, G/2. \tag{1}$$

In (1), $f_{\max}$ and $f_{\min}$ are the maximal and minimal fitness values of the population and the rank r_i is given with a linear function which decreases with the growth of f_i, and takes values within the range [0, 1].

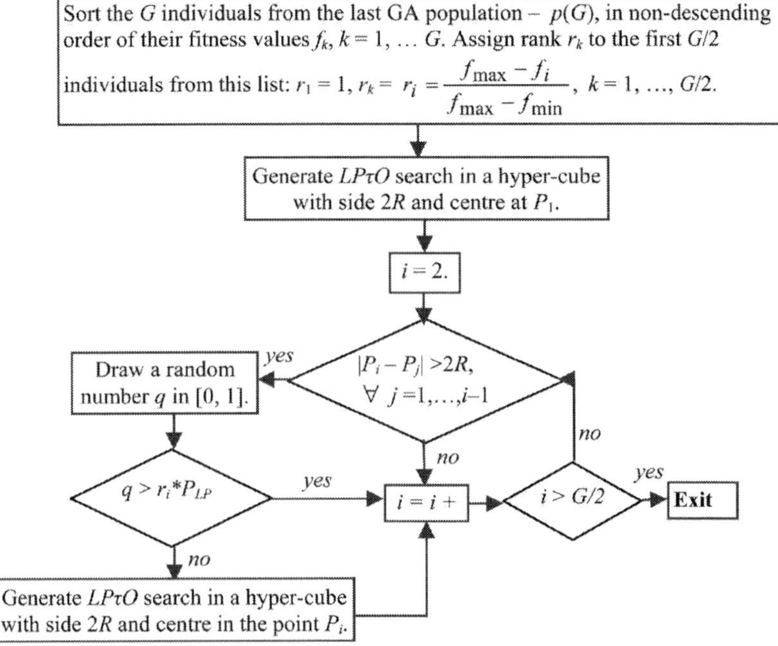

Fig. 4. Algorithm for adaptive selection of points of future interest from the last population of the GA run.

The best individual of the last population $p(G)$ has rank $r_1 = 1$ and always competes. It is used as a centre for a hyper-cube (with side $2R$), in which the $L P \tau O$ search will start. The parameter R is heuristically chosen with formula (2)

$$R = 50/G + \text{int}_{\max} * 0.001, \tag{2}$$

where int_{max} is the largest of all initial search intervals. This parameter estimates the trade-off between the computational expense and the probability of finding a GM. The greater the population size G, the smaller the intervals of interest that are going to be explored by the $LP\tau O$ search. The next individual P_i, $i = 2, ..., G/2$ is then considered, and if all of the Euclidean distances between this individual and previously selected ones are greater than $2R$ (so that there is no overlapping in the $LP\tau O$ search regions), another $LP\tau O$ search will be initiated with a probability $r_i P_{LP}$. Here P_{LP} is a user-defined probability constant in the interval [0, 1]. In other words, individuals with higher rank (that corresponds to lower fitness) will have greater chance to initiate $LP\tau O$ searches. After the execution of the $LP\tau O$ searches is completed, Nelder-Mead Local Simplex Search is applied to the best function value found in all previous stages of $GLP\tau S$.

3. Testing *GLPτS* on mathematical optimisation problems and benchmark NN learning tasks

3.1 Mathematical testing functions

Detailed testing results of $GLP\tau S$ on multi-dimensional optimization functions are reported in Georgieva & Jordanov (2008a). Here, we only demonstrate the results of testing $GLP\tau S$ on 30 and 100 dimensional problems for which a comparison with several other GO approaches was possible. The results, in terms of average (over 100 runs) number of function evaluations, are scaled logarithmically for better visualization and are shown in Fig. 5.

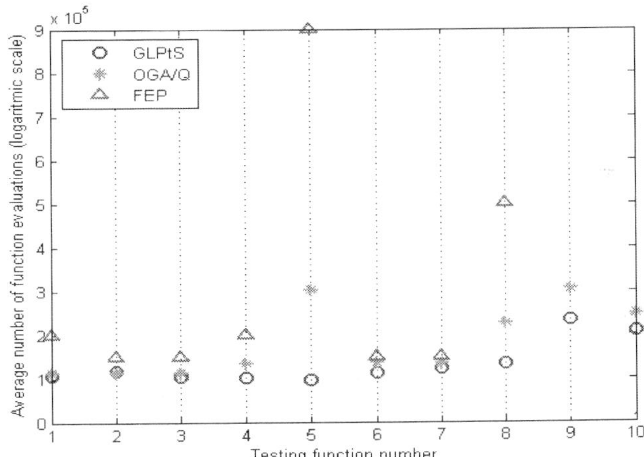

Fig. 5. Average number of function evaluations for ten test functions: comparison of *GLPτS* with needed Orthogonal Genetic Algorithm with Quanitsation (OGA/Q, Leung & Wang, 2001) and FEP (Yao et al., 1999).

When compared to the other evolutionary approaches, it can be seen from Fig. 5 that *GLPτS* performed very efficiently. In addition, the comparison with Differential Evolution in Georgieva & Jordanov (2008a) for lower dimensional problems helped us conclude that *GLPτS* is a promising *state-of-the-art* GO approach solving equally well both low and high-dimensional problems.

3.2 NN learning benchmark problems

Subsequently, we employed the *GLPτS* for minimizing the error function in NN learning problems and the results were reported in Georgieva & Jordanov, (2006). Here, we present only few interesting examples of using *GLPτS* for NN training.

The architectures of the investigated NNs comprise static, fully connected between the adjacent layers topologies with a standard sigmoidal transfer functions. The training is performed in a batch-mode, i.e., all of the training samples are presented to the NN at one go. The NN weight vector is considered an n-dimensional real Euclidean vector $\overline{W}$, obtained by concatenating the weight vectors for each layer of the network. The *GLPτS* global optimisation algorithm is then employed to minimize the objective function (the NN error function) and to perform optimal training. The proposed algorithm is tested on well-known benchmark problems with different dimensionalities. For comparison, a BP (Levenberg-Marquardt) is also employed and performed using Matlab NN Toolbox. Both methods are ran 50 times and their average values are reported.

Classification of XOR Problem

For the classification of the XOR, which is a classical toy problem (Bishop, 1995), the minimal configuration of a NN with two inputs, two units in the hidden layer, and one output is employed. The network also has a bias, contaches 9 connection weights, and therefore, defines $n = 9$ dimensional optimization problem. There are $P = 4$ input-target patterns for the training set. It can be seen from the Fig. 6 that after the 20th epoch, BP did not improve the error function, while our method continued minimizing it. To assess the ability of the trained NN to generalize, tests with 100 random samples of noisy data are performed, where the noise is up to 15%. Obtained optimal results from the training and testing are given in Table 1 (Georgieva & Jordanov, 2006).

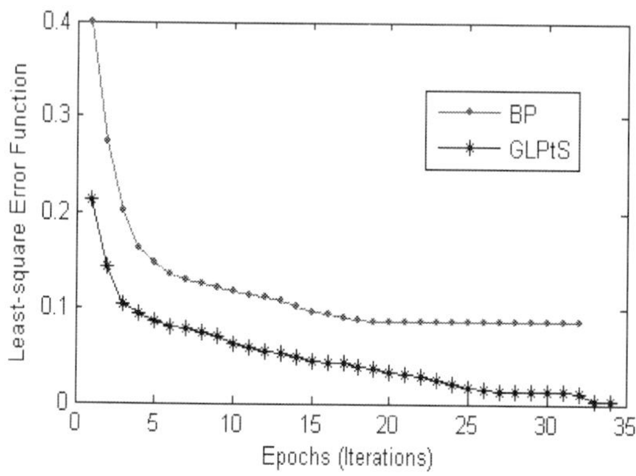

Fig. 6. Error function for the XOR problem when BP and *GLPτS* are used.

Predicting the rise time of a servo mechanism

The Servo data collection represents an extremely non-linear phenomenon (Quinlan, 1993; Rocha et al., 2003) – predicting the rise time of a servomechanism, depending on four attributes: two gain settings and two mechanical linkages. The database consists of 167 different samples with continuous output (the time in seconds). In order to avoid

Criterion Method	Error Function (Std. Dev.)	Mean Test Error (Std. Dev.)
BP	0.08 (0.09)	0.1987 (0.0290)
GLPτS	7.6e-08 (7e-08)	8.3e-07 (3.3e-7)

Method: BP – Backpropagation with Levenberg-Marquardt optimisation (the source of Matlab NN Toolbox is used).

Table 1. Optimal errors for the *GLPτS* and BP (XOR problem).

computational inaccuracies, we normalized the set of outputs to have a zero mean and unit standard deviation. A network with a 4-4-1 architecture (25-dimensional problem) is employed to produce a continuous output. The dataset is divided into two parts – one batch of 84 training samples and second batch of 83 testing ones. In this case, the transfer function in the output layer is changed to a linear function (instead of a sigmoidal one) in order to be able to produce output outside the [0, 1] interval. Obtained optimal solutions for the train and test errors are given in Table 2 and Fig. 7 illustrates the average values of the errors for each testing sample for both BP and *GLPτS*. One can see from the figure that there are more outliers in the case of BP and that overall, a smaller mean test value is achieved by the *GLPτS* method.

Criterion Method	Error Function (Std. Dev.)	Mean Test Error (Std. Dev.)
BP	0.0474 (0.06)	0.4171 (0.5515)
GLPτS	0.0245 (0.005)	0.2841 (0.4448)

Table 2. Optimal errors for the *GLPτS* and BP (*Servo* problem).

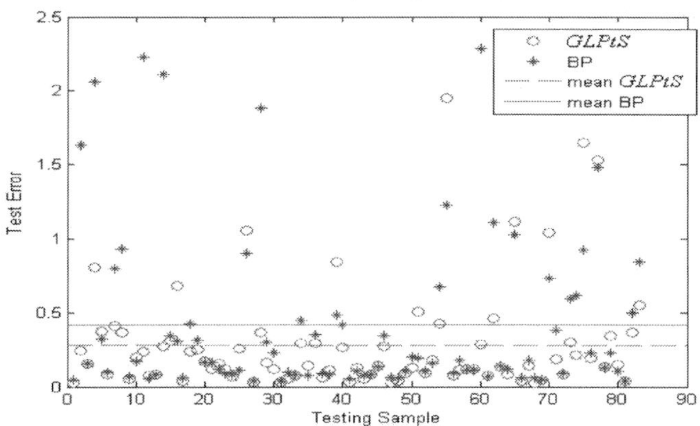

Fig. 7. Test errors and mean test errors for BP and *GLPτS*.

Classification of Pima Indians Diabetes Database
In the *Diabetes* data collection, the investigated, binary-valued variable is used to diagnose whether a patient shows signs of diabetes or not (Rocha et al., 2003). All patients are females of at least 21 years old and of Pima Indian heritage. The data set comprises 500 instances

that produce an output 0 (non-positive for diabetes), and 268 with output 1 (positive for diabetes). Each sample has 8 attributes: number of times pregnant, age, blood test results, etc. In order to avoid computational inaccuracies, in our experiment all attributes are normalized to have a zero mean and a unit standard deviation. A network with 8-8-1 architecture (81-dimensional problem) is adopted to produce continuous output in the range [0, 1]. The dataset is divided into two parts – training subset of 384 samples (145 of which correspond to output 1), and testing subset of the same number of patterns. Table 3 shows the obtained optimal solutions for the training and testing errors.

Criterion Method	Error Function (Std. Dev.)	Mean Test Error (Std. Dev.)
BP	0.0764 (0.07)	0.2831 (0.2541)
GLPτS	0.001 (0.005)	0.2619 (0.3861)

Table 3. Optimal errors for the *GLPτS* and BP (*Diabetes* problem)

Function Fitting Regression Example

We also performed a function fitting example, for which the network is trained with noisy data. The function to be approximated is the Hermit polynomial:

$$G(x) = 1.1(1\text{-}x+2x^2)\exp(\text{-}x^2/2).$$

The set up of the experiment is the same as reported in Leung *et al.* (2001), with the only difference that we use batch-mode instead of on-line training. The test results from 2000 testing samples and 20 independent runs of the experiment are shown in Table 4. It can be seen from the table that our results improve slightly the best ones reported in Leung *et al.* (2001). Fig. 8 graphically illustrates the results and shows the Gaussian noise that we used for training, the function to be approximated, and the NN output.

Criterion Method	Average	Max	Min	Std. Dev.
RLS	0.1901	0.2567	0.1553	0.0259
IPRLS	0.1453	0.1674	0.1207	0.0076
TWDRLS	0.1472	0.1711	0.1288	0.0108
GLPτS	0.1349	0.1602	0.1184	0.01

Method: By Leung et al. (2001): RLS – Recursive Least Squares; IPRLS – Input Perturbation RLS; TWDRLS – True Weight Desay RLS.

Table 4. Test results for the *GLPτS* and the methods in Leung et al. (2001).

The results from the classification experiments (Table 1, Table 2, and Table 3) show that the achieved by *GLPτS* least-square errors are at   least twice better than the BP ones. The multiple independent runs of our method also show that the obtained solutions are stable with small deviations. As it can be seen from Table 1, in the case of XOR, the *GLPτS* method outperforms BP considerably (BP with mean error of 0.08, in comparison with 7.6e-8 for the proposed here method). For this task Wang et al. (2004), also reported low success rate for BP with frequent entrapment in local minima. In the case of *Servo* problem, the superiority of our method is not so dominant (as in the case of XOR), but still the results in Table 2 show better standard deviation of both measures – 0.005 against 0.06 for the error function, and 0.44 against 0.55 for the test error. This indicates a better and more stable solution for our method. The reported in Rocha et al. (2003) results from five different methods for the same task and architecture are also with worse error function values compared to ours. Those observations indicate that further improvement of the solution could not be found for the investigated 4-4-1 NN architecture, nevertheless, experiments with different architectures could lead to better results. The comparison of the training results for *Diabetes* given in Rocha et al. (2003), also confirms the advantages of the *GLPτS* method.

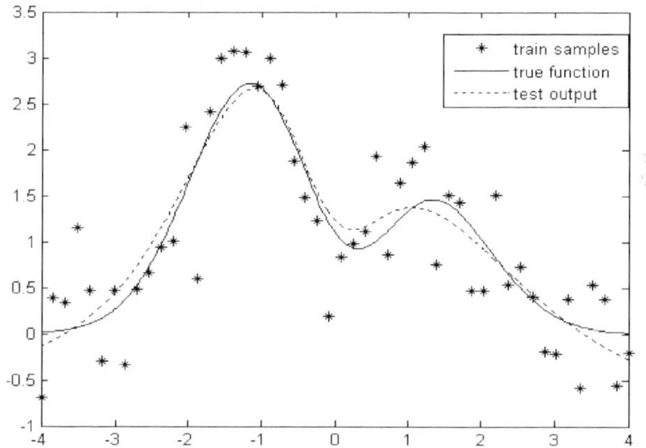

Fig. 8. Output of the network trained with *GLPτS* for the function fitting example.

4. Machine learning in practise: an intelligent machine vision system

4.1. Introduction and motivation

In (Georgieva & Jordanov, 2008b) we investigate an intelligent machine vision system that uses NNs trained with *GLPτS* for pattern recognition and classification of seven types of cork tiles with different texture. Automated visual inspection of products and automation of product assembly lines are typical examples of application of machine vision systems in manufacturing industry (Theodoridis & Koutroumbas, 2006). At the assembly line, the objects of interest must be classified in *a priori* known classes, before a robot arm places them in the right position or box. In the area of automated visual inspection, where decisions about the adequacy of the products have to be made constantly, the use of pattern recognition provides an important background (Davies, 2005).

Cork is a fully renewable and biodegradable sustainable product obtained from the bark of the cork oak tree. Although the primary use of cork is in the wine stoppers production (70% of the total cork market), cork floor and wall covering give about 20% of the total cork business (WWF, 2006). Cork oak plantations have proven biodiversity, environmental and economical values. Recent increase of alternative wine stoppers arises serious attention and concerns, since this is reducing the economical value of cork lands and might lead to abandonment, degradation and loss of irreplaceable biodiversity (WWF, 2006). On the other hand, in the past several years of technological advancement, cork has become one of the most effective and reliable natural materials for floor and wall covering. Some of the advantages of the cork tiles are their durability, ability to reduce noise, thermal insulation, and reduction of allergens. Many of the cork floors installed during the "golden age" of cork flooring (Frank Lloyd Wright's *Fallingwater*; *St. Mary of the Lake* Chapel in Mundelein (USA); US Department of Commerce Building, etc.) are actually still in use, which is the best proof of their durability and ever-young appearance.

Image analysis techniques have been applied for automated visual inspection of cork stoppers in (Chang et al., 1997; Radeva et al., 2002; Costa & Pereira, 2006), and according to the authors, the image-based inspection systems have high production rates. Such systems are based on a line-scan camera and a computer, embedded in an industrial sorting machine which is capable of acquiring and real-time processing of the product surface image.

4.2 Database and features extraction

The aim of this case study was to design, develop and investigate an intelligent system for visual inspection that is able to automatically classify different types of cork tiles. Currently, the cork tiles are sorted "by hand" (e.g., see www.expanko.com), and the use of such a computerized system could automate this process and increase its efficiency. We experimented with seven types of cork wall tiles with different texture. The tiles used in this investigation are available on the market by www.CorkStore.com and samples of each type are shown in Fig. 9.

Fig. 9. Images taken with our system: samples from the seven different types of wall cork tiles.

The functionality of our visual system is based on four major processing stages: image acquisition, features extraction (generation and processing), NN training, and finally NN testing. For the image acquisition stage, we used a Charge-Coupled Device (CCD) camera with a focal length 5-50 mm that is capable of capturing fine details of the cork texture. For all cork types we used grayscale images of size 230x340 pixels and, in total, we collected 770 different images for all classes. Fig. 10 shows the percentage distribution of each type of cork tiles. We used 25% of all images for testing (not shown to the NN during training) and assessing the generalization abilities of the networks.

The first step of the features generation stage was to reduce the effects of illumination. Subsequently, we used two classical approaches to generate image texture characteristics: the Haralick 'sco-occurrence method (Haralick et al., 1973) and the Laws' filter masks (Laws, 1980). Both methods were employed and the obtained features were used to generate one dataset, without taking into account the feature generation technique. This approach resulted in obtaining 33 features for each image (8 co-occurrence characteristics and 25 Laws' masks). These features were further processed statistically with Principal Component Analysis (PCA) and Linear Discriminent Analysis (LDA) in order to extract the most valuable information and to present it in a compact form, suitable for NN training (Bishop, 1995). Before processing the data, we took out 120 samples to be used later as a testing subset, therefore, this data was not involved in the feature analysis stage. All additional details of this case study, can be found in Georgieva & Jordanov (2008b).

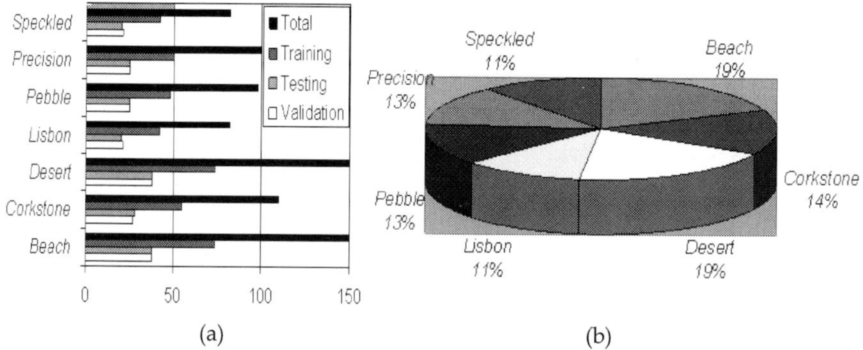

(a)   (b)

Fig. 10. Dataset sample distribution (50% training, 25% testing, 25% validation): (a) Number of samples from each cork type; (b) The percentage distribution of each cork type.

4.3 Neural network training and testing

NNs with three different topologies (with biases) were employed and different coding of the seven classes of interest was used. In the first case, a NN with three neurons in the output layer (with *Heaviside* transfer function) was employed. The seven classes were coded as binary combinations of the three neurons ('*1-of-c*' coding, as proposed in Bishop, 1995), e.g., *Beach* was coded as (0, 0, 0), *Corkstone* as (1, 0, 0), etc. The last, (8th) combination (1, 1, 1) was simply not used. In the second designed topology, the output layer contained only one neuron (with *Tanh* transfer function and continuous output). Since the *Tanh* function has values in [-1, 1], the seven classes were coded as (-0.8571, -0.5714, -0.2857, 0, 0.2857, 0.5741, 0.8571) respectively. When assessing the system generalization abilities, we considered each testing sample as correctly classified if |output – target| < 0.14. For the last topology was used an output layer with seven neurons and a *Heaviside* transfer function. Each class was coded as a vector of binary values where only one output is 1, and all others are 0. For example, *Beach* was coded as (1, 0, 0, 0, 0, 0, 0), *Corkstone* as (0, 1, 0, 0, 0, 0, 0), etc.

The number of neurons in the input layer depends on the number of features (K) that characterize the problem samples. Utilizing the *rules of thumb* given by Heaton (2005) and after experimenting, the number of neurons in the hidden layer was chosen to be $N = 7$. The three different architectures were employed for both datasets, obtained by the PCA and LDA respectively, processing: K-7-3 (3-binary coding of the targets), K-7-1 (continuous coding of the targets), and K-7-7 (7-binary coding), where K is the number of features. At the system evaluation stage, 25% of the total data were used as a testing set, only 1/3 of which was present at the feature analysis phase (used in the preprocessing with PCA and LDA) and the remaining 2/3 of the test set were kept untouched. Further on, we considered the testing results as average test errors for both testing subsets. Rigorous tests when a validation set is used were performed and the results can be found in Georgieva & Jordanov (2008b).

Feature Set	Measure	Three outputs (*binary coding*)	One output (*continuous coding*)
PCA	MSE (std), [min, max]	0.052 (0.0094) [0.03, 0.074]	0.014 (0.0044) [0.011, 0.036]
	Test rate, [min, max]	86% [79%, 94%]	66% [41%, 77%]
LDA	MSE (std), [min, max]	0.0038 (0.0029) [0, 0.014]	0.0037 (0.0022) [0.0005, 0.0113]
	Test rate, [min, max]	95% [88%, 99%]	88% [74%, 98%]

Feature set: Principal Component Analysis (PCA) and Linear Discriminant Analysis – discussed in Georgieva & Jordanov, 2008b.

Table 5. Neural Network Training with *GLPτS* and Performance Evaluation: two different datasets with binary and continuous output.

Table 5 shows training and testing results for both topologies with $K = 7$ for the PCA dataset and $K = 6$ for the LDA dataset. In Table 5 the MSE (mean squared error) and standard deviation (given in parentheses) for 50 runs are independently reported for each dataset. The minimal and maximal values obtained for the different runs are also shown in this table. The system was evaluated with the testing rate, given by the percentage of correctly classified samples from the test set. Similarly, Table 6 shows results for the same topologies and datasets, with the only difference being the NN training technique. For the training of the NNs in Table 5, *GLPτS* was used, and for Table 6 – the Matlab implementation of gradient-based *Levenberg-Marquardt* minimisation, denoted here as *Backpropagation* (BP). All test results are jointly illustrated in Fig. 11. The analysis of the results given in Table 5, Table 6, and Fig. 11, led to the following conclusions:

- The generalisation abilities of the NNs trained with *GLPτS* were strongly competitive when compared to those trained with BP. The best testing results of 95% were obtained for NN trained with *GLPτS*, LDA dataset, and three binary outputs;
- In general, the BP results were not as stable as the *GLPτS* ones, having significantly larger differences between the attained minimal and maximal testing rate values. This is due to entrapment of BP in local minima that resulted in occasional very poor solutions;
- The LDA dataset results had better testing rate and smaller MSE than those corresponding to the PCA dataset. In our view this advantage is due to the LDA property to look for optimal class separability;
- The three-output binary coding of the targets led to a NN architecture with higher dimensionality, but gave better results than the continuous one. This is not surprising, since the binary coding of the targets provided linearly independent outputs for the different classes, which is more suitable for classification tasks compared to continuous

coding (Bishop, 1995). However, in the case of seven binary outputs, the NN performance deteriorated, since the dimensionality was increased unnecessarily.

Feature Set	Measure	Three outputs (*binary coding*)	One output (*continuous coding*)
PCA	MSE (std), [min, max]	0.025 (0.053) [0.001, 0.245]	0.0489 (0.1473) [0.0113, 0.9116]
	Test rate, [min, max]	85% [39%, 94%]	71% [0%, 85%]
LDA	MSE (std), [min, max]	0.022 (0.06) [0, 0.244]	0.0049 (0.027) [0, 0.1939]
	Test rate, [min, max]	89% [40%, 98%]	90% [45%, 98%]

Table 6. Neural Network Training with BP and Performance Evaluation: two different datasets with binary and continuous output.

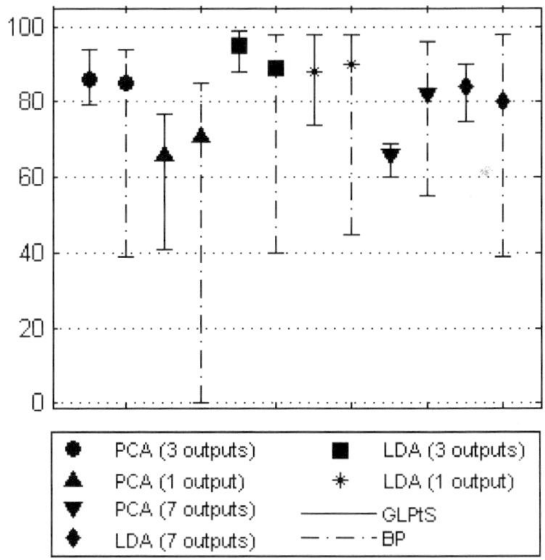

Fig. 11. Mean, min, and max test success rate (Table 5 and Table 6) for the experiments with different datasets, NN topologies, and learning approaches.

Further on, we considered only the two cases with 3-binary and 1-continuous coding (as well as NN trained with *GLPτS*), as the most interesting and successful ones. Fig. 12 illustrates the testing success rate for the two NN topologies for both datasets (PCA and LDA) with respect to the increasing number of training samples. The idea was to assess whether the number of used samples and features gave comprehensive and reliable information for the different cork classes. We used 25% of the whole data as an unseen testing subset and started increasing the percentage of used samples when training, keeping the NN topology unchanged. If the success rate increases proportionally to the increase of the training set size, then the features can be considered to be reliable (Umbaugh, 2005). The results illustrated in Fig. 12 were averaged over 20 runs. One can see from Fig. 12 that for both NN architectures, LDA gives better generalisation results than PCA. It can also be seen that for all combinations (datasets and coding), the test rate graphs are ascendant, but the increased of number of training samples above 60% hardly brings any improvement of the test error success rate (with the exception of the LDA – binary architecture).

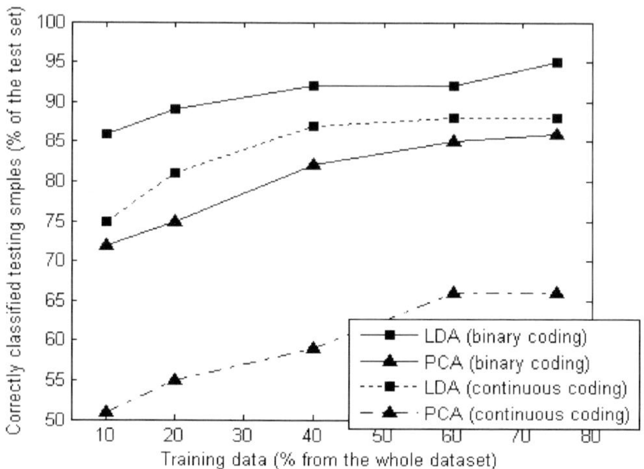

Fig. 12. Test success rate for increasing number of samples in the training set. PCA and LDA feature sets are considered with binary and continuous coding of the classes.

4.4 Comparison with results of other authors

Straightforward comparison of our results with findings for similar cork classification systems (Chang et al., 1997; Radeva et al., 2002; Costa & Pereira, 2006) is a difficult task, because of the many differences in the parameters and techniques. Some of the main differences can be listed as follows:

- Automated systems for cork products inspection have been developed only for cork stoppers and planks, but not for cork tiles;
- While natural cork stoppers are manufactured by punching a one-piece cork strip (which may have cracks and insect tunnels), cork tiles consist of various sizes of granules compressed together under high temperature, and cracks are not likely to be expected to appear. In (Chang et al., 1997; Radeva et al., 2002; Costa & Pereira, 2006), the authors are looking mostly for pores, cracks and holes (and their sizes) in cork stoppers, whereas in our case, gray density (texture) changes and overall appearance is of interest. We use feature generation techniques that capture the images texture information, while in (Chang et al., 1997; Radeva et al., 2002; Costa & Pereira, 2006) the authors use features that aim to identify cracks and holes;
- In Costa & Pereira (2006) the authors employ only LDA as a classifier and in (Chang et al., 1997) the investigation does not include any feature analysis techniques at all. In our

experiment, after using LDA and PCA to reduce the dimensionality of the problem space, we used $GLP\tau S$ method for optimal NN learning. Other authors relay on different classifiers (Nearest Neighbor, Maximal likelihood, Bayesian classifier (Radeva et al., 2002), Fuzzy-neural networks (Chang et al., 1997), LDA (Costa & Pereira, 2006);

- The size of training and testing datasets and the size of the investigated images vary significantly.

In our study, we showed that LDA could reach up to 95% success rate for a task with seven classes, providing that the classifier is well designed and combined with NN (trained with $GLP\tau S$ method). We claim that LDA is computationally efficient and very useful technique when the other stages of the system process – feature generation and appropriate classifier design are thoroughly thought and investigated. On the other hand, ICA is not suitable for all types of data, because it imposes independence conditions on the features and also involves additional computational cost (Theodoridis & Koutroumbas, 2006; Radeva et al., 2002). Considering the above-mentioned results, we can conclude that the intelligent classification system investigated has very good and strongly competitive generalization abilities (Table 7).

System	Costa & Pareira	Radeva et al.	Chang et al.	This Experiment BP training	This Experiment $GLP\tau S$ training
Test Rate	46% –58%	46% –98%	93.3%	71% –90%	66% –95%

Table 7. Neural Network testing: comparison of our system with other intelligent visual systems employed for cork stoppers classification.

6. Conclusions

Here has been presented an overview of our recent research findings. Initially, a novel Global Optimisation technique, called $LP\tau O$, has been investigated and proposed. The method is based on $LP\tau$ Low-discrepancy Sequences and novel heuristic rules for guiding the search. Subsequently, $LP\tau O$ has been hybridized with Nelder-Mead local search, showing very good results for low-dimensional problems. Nevertheless, with the increase of problems dimensionality, method's computational load increases considerably. To tackle this problem, a hybrid Global Optimisation method, called $GLP\tau S$, that combines Genetic Algorithms, $LP\tau O$ method and Nelder-Mead simplex search, has been studied, discussed and proposed. When compared with Genetic Algorithms, Evolutionary Programming, and Differential Evolution, $GLP\tau S$ has demonstrated strongly competitive results in terms of both number of function evaluations and success rate. Subsequently, $GLP\tau S$ has been applied for supervised NN training and tested on a number of benchmark problems. Based on the reported and discussed findings, it can be concluded that the investigated and proposed $GLP\tau S$ technique is very competitive and demonstrates reliable performance when compared with similar approaches from other authors.

Finally, an Intelligent Computer Vision System has been designed and investigated. It has been applied for a real-world problem of automated recognition and classification of industrial products (in our case study – cork tiles). The classifier, employing supervised

Sobol', I.M. (1979). On the systematic search in a hypercube. *SIAM Journal of Numerical Analysis*, Vol. 16, No. 5, pp. 790-792.

Theodoridis, S. & Koutroumbas, K. (2006). *Pattern Recognition*, Academic Press, 3rd edition.

Umbaugh, S. (2005). *Computer imaging: digital image analysis and processing*, The CRC Press.

Wang, X.; Tang, Z.; Tamura, H.; Ishii, M.; & Sun, W. (2004). An improved backpropagation algorithm to avoid the local minima problem", *Neurocomputing*, vol. 56, pp. 455-460.

WWF/MEDPO, (2006). A WWF Report, Cork Screwed? Environmental and economic impacts of the cork stoppers market. .

Yao, X. (1999). Evolving artificial neural networks. *Proceedings of IEEE*, Vol. 87, No. 9, pp. 1423-1447.

Yao, X.; Liu, Y. & Lin, G. (1999). Evolutionary programming made faster. *IEEE Transactions on Evolutionary Computation*, Vol. 3, No. 2, pp. 82-102.

3

Supervised Rule Learning and Reinforcement Learning in A Multi-Agent System for the Fish Banks Game

Bartłomiej Śnieżyński
AGH University of Science and Technology
Poland

1. Introduction

Environment of multi-agent systems is often very complex. Therefore it is sometimes difficult, or even impossible, to specify and implement all system details a priori. Application of machine learning algorithms allows to overcome this problem. One can implement an agent that is not perfect, but improves its performance.

There are many learning methods that can be used to generate knowledge or strategy in a multi-agent system. Choosing an appropriate one, which fits a given problem, can be a difficult task. *The aim of the research presented here was to test applicability of reinforcement learning and supervised rule learning strategies in the same problem.*

Reinforcement learning is the most common technique in multi-agent systems. It allows to generate a strategy for an agent in a situation, when the environment provides some feedback after the agent has acted.

Symbolic, supervised learning is not so widely used in multi-agent systems. There are many methods belonging to this class that generate knowledge from data. Here a rule induction algorithm is used. It generates a rule-based classifier, which assigns a class to a given example. As an input it needs examples, where the class is assigned by some teacher. We show how observation of other agents' actions can be used instead of the teacher.

As an environment the Fish Banks game is used. It is a simulation, in which agents run fishing companies and its main task is to decide how many ships send for fishing, and where to send them. Four types of agents are created. Reinforcement learning agent and supervised learning agent improve their allocation performance using appropriate learning strategy. As a reference two additional types of agents are introduced: random agent, which chooses allocation action randomly, and predicting agent, which assumes that fishing results will be the same as in previous round, and allocates ships using this simple prediction.

In the next section related research on learning in multi-agent systems is briefly presented. The third section explains details of the environment, architecture and behaviours of the agents. Next, results of several experiments, which were performed to compare mentioned learning methods, are presented and discussed. Results show that both of them give good results. However; both of them have some advantages and disadvantages. In the last two sections conclusions and further research are presented.

This work is an extended version of the paper (Śnieżyński, 2007), in which initial results are published.

2. Learning in multi-agent systems

The problem of learning in multi-agent systems may be considered as a union of research on multi-agent systems and on machine learning. Machine learning focuses mostly on research on isolated process performed by one intelligent module. The multi-agent approach concerns the systems composed of autonomous elements, called agents, whose actions lead to the realization of given goals. In this context, learning is based on the observation of the influences of activities, performed to achieve the goal by an agent itself or by other agents. Learning may proceed in a traditional – centralized (one learning agent) or decentralized manner. In the second case more than one agent is engaged in the learning process (Sen & Weiss, 1999). A good survey on machine learning in the context of multi-agent systems can be found in (Stone & Veloso, 2000).

So far agent-based systems with learning capabilities were applied in many domains: to train agents playing in RoboCup Challenge (Kitano et.al, 1997), adapt user interfaces (Lashkari et.al, 1994), take part in agent-based computational economics simulations (Tesfatsion, 2001), analyze distributed data (Stolfo et.al, 1997), and to discover intrusions (Servin & Kudenko, 2008).

The learning process is strictly associated with reasoning and decision making aspects of agents. The most popular learning technique in multi-agent systems is reinforcement learning. Other techniques can be also applied. Learning process can be based on the symbolic knowledge representation (e.g. rules, decision trees), neural networks, models coming from game theory as well as optimization techniques (like the evolutionary approach, tabu search, etc.).

Reinforcement learning allows to generate a strategy for an agent in a situation, when the environment provides some feedback after the agent has acted. Feedback takes the form of a real number representing reward, which depends on the quality of the action executed by the agent in a given situation. The goal of the learning is to maximize estimated reward.

Supervised learning is not so popular in multi-agent systems. However; there are some works with use of this strategy. Sugawara is using this technique for improving plan coordination. Gehrke is using rule induction for route planning (Gehrke & Wojtusiak, 2008). However; rule induction is done offline. Szita and Lorincz apply global optimization algorithm to select set of rules used by the agent playing Pac-Man game (Szita & Lorincz 2007). Airiau adds learning capabilities into BDI model. Decision tree learning is used to support plan applicability testing (Airiau et. al 2008).

Universal architecture for learning agent can be found in (Russell & Norvig, 1995). It fits mainly reinforcement learning. Sardinha et. al, propose a learning agent design pattern, which can be used during system implementation (Sardinha et. al, 2004). More abstract architecture is presented in (Śnieżyński, 2008).

3. Multi-agent system for fish banks game

3.1 Environment

Fish Banks game is designed for teaching people effective cooperation in using natural resources (Meadows et.al, 1993). It may be also used in multi-agent systems. In this research the game is a dynamic environment providing all necessary resources, action execution procedures, and time flow, which is represented by game rounds. Each round consists of the following steps:

- ships and money update,
- ship auctions,
- trading session,
- ship orders,
- ship allocation,
- fishing,
- fish number update.

Agents represent players that manage fishing companies. Each company aims at collecting maximum assets expressed by the amount of money deposited at a bank account and the number of ships. The company earns money by fishing at fish banks.

Environment provides two fishing areas: coastal and a deep-sea. Agents can also keep their ships at the port. Cost of fishing at the deep-sea is the highest. Cost of staying at port is the lowest but such ship does not catch fish.

Initially, it is assumed that the number of fish in both banks is close to the bank's maximal capacity (equal to 4000 for a deep sea, and 2000 for a coastal area). During the game the number of fish in every bank changes according to the following equation:

$$f_{t+1} = f_t + bf_t\left(1 - \frac{f_t}{f_{max}}\right) - C_t \tag{1}$$

where f_t is a fish number at a time t, b is a birth rate (value 0.05 was used in experiments), f_{max} is a maximum number of fish in the bank, $C_t = n\, c_t$ is a total fish catch: n is a number of ships of all players sent to the bank, and c_t is a fish catch for one ship at the time t:

$$c_t = c_{max} w_t \sqrt{\frac{f_t}{f_{max}}} \tag{2}$$

where c_{max} is a maximal catch (equal to 25 for a deep sea, and 15 for a coastal area), and w_t is a weather factor at a time t. Weather factor is a random number between 0.8 and 1.0.

As we can see, at the beginning of game, when f_t is close to f_{max}, fishing at the deep sea is more profitable. Parameters are set in such a way that exploration overcomes birth, and after several rounds the number of fish can decrease to zero. It is a standard case of "the tragedy of commons" (Hardin, 1968). It is more reasonable to keep ships at the harbor then, therefore companies should change their strategies.

In the original game, fishing companies may order new ships to be built as well as they may cross-sell their ships. The ships may be also sold at the auction organized by the game manager. In the current version of the system ship auctions and trading sessions are not supported.

The costs of building a ship, costs of its maintenance and use and the price of sold fish are fixed for the whole game. At the end of the game the value of the ships owned by the companies is estimated (number of ships is multiplied by a constant) and added tho the money balance.

3.2 Architecture of the agents

Four types of agents are implemented: reinforcement learning agent, rule learning agent, predicting agent, and random agent. The first one uses learned strategy to allocate ships, the second one uses rules induced from the experience to classify actions and chose the best one, agent of the third type uses previous fishing results to estimate values of different allocation actions, the last one allocates ships randomly.

All types of agents may observe the following aspects of the environment:

- arriving of new ships bought from a shipyard,
- money earned in the last round,
- ship allocations of all agents,
- fishing results (c_i) for deep sea and inshore area.

All types of agents can execute the following two types of actions: order ships, allocate ships.

Order ships action is currently very simple. It is implemented in all types of agents in the same way. At the beginning of the game every agent has 10 ships. Every round, if it has less then 15 ships, there is 50% chance that it orders two new ships.

Ships allocation is based on the method used in (Koźlak et.al, 1999). The allocation action is represented by a triple (h, d, c), where h is the number of ships left in a harbour, d and c are numbers of ships sent to a deep sea, and a coastal area, respectively. Agents generate a list of allocations for h=0%, 25%, 50%, 75%, and 100% of ships that belong to the agent. The rest of ships (s) is partitioned; for every h the following candidates are generated:

1. All: ($h, 0, s$), ($h, s, 0$) – send all remaining ships to a deep sea or coastal area,
2. Check: ($h, 1, s$-1), (h, s-1, 1) – send one ship to a deep sea or coastal area and the rest to the other,
3. Three random actions: (h, x, s-x), where $1 \leq x < s$ is a random number – allocate remaining ships in a random way,
4. Equal: ($h, s/2, s/2$) – send equal number of ships to both areas (one more ship is sent to a deep sea if s is odd.)

The random agent allocates ships using one of the action candidates chosen by random. Predicting agent uses the following formula to estimate the value of each action candidate a:

$$v(a)=\text{income}(a)+\varepsilon\,\text{ecology}(a), \tag{3}$$

where income(a) represents the prediction of the income under the assumption that in the current round fishing results will be the same as in the previous round, ecology(a) represents ecological effects of the action a (the value is low if fishing is performed in the area with low fish population), and ε represents importance of the ecology factor.

3.3 Learning agents details

Both learning agents have the same general architecture, which is based on one proposed in (Snieżyński, 2008). It is presented in Fig. 1. Processing module is responsible for analyzing percepts, buying ships, preparing training data, executing learning, and calling a learning module to chose appropriate action in the current situation. To specify details of the learning process and using the learned knowledge, we need the following four-tuple: (*Learning algorithm, Training data, Problem, Answer*). *Learning algorithm* represents a way, in which *Training data* is transformed into the internal knowledge representation. This knowledge is used to give an *Answer* to a given *Problem*. Below specifications for both learning agents are presented.

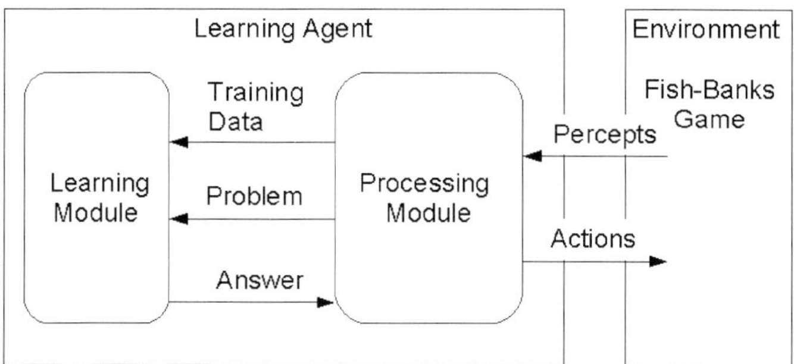

Fig. 1. Architecture of learning agents used in the system implemented for Fish-Banks Game

Agent using reinforcement learning strategy gets description of the current state and using its current strategy chooses an appropriate action from a defined set. Next, using reward from the environment and next state description it updates its strategy. Several methods of choosing the action and updating the strategy have been developed so far. In Q-learning developed by Chris Watkins (Watkins, 1989) Q is a function that estimates value of the action in a given state:

$$Q: A \times X \rightarrow \Re, \tag{4}$$

where A is a set of actions, and X is a set of possible states. Q function is updated after action execution:

$$Q(a, x) := Q(a, x) + \beta \Delta. \tag{5}$$

Δ represents change of the Q function value that should be applied according to the last reward. It is defined in the following way:

$$\Delta = \gamma Q_{max} + r - Q(a, x), \tag{6}$$

$$Q_{max} = \max_a Q(a, x'), \tag{7}$$

where $x, x' \in X$ are subsequent states, $a \in A$ is an action chosen, r is a reward obtained from the environment, $\gamma \in [0,1]$ is a discount rate (importance of the future rewards), and $\beta \in (0,1)$ is a learning rate.

Reinforcement learning agent chooses action by random in the first round. In the following rounds, reinforcement learning module is used, and an action with the highest predicted value (Q) is chosen. Set of possible actions contains ship allocation triples: $A = \{(h, d, c)\}$ such that $h, d, c \in \{0\%, 25\%, 50\%, 75\%\ 100\%\}$, $d+c=1$. Set of possible states $X = \{(dc, cc)\}$, where $dc \in \{1, 2, \ldots 25\}$ represent catch in a deep-sea area, and $cc \in \{1, 2, \ldots, 15\}$ represents catch in a coastal area in the previous round. Therefore *Problem* is a pair (dc, cc) and *Answer* is a triple (h, d, c). The *Training data* consists of a pair (dc', cc'), which is a catch in the current round, and a reward that is equal to the income (money earned by fishing decreased by ship maintenance costs). *Learning algorithm* applied is the Q-Learning algorithm. In the current implementation, Q function has tabular representation.

At the beginning Q is initialized as a constant function 0. To provide sufficient exploration, in a game number g a random action is chosen with probability $1/g$ instead of using Q function (all actions have the same probability then).

Generally, supervised learning allows to generate an approximation of a function $f: D \rightarrow C$ from labelled examples, which consist of pairs of arguments and function values. This approximation is called a hypothesis h. If the size of the set C is small (like in this application), we call C a set of classes, and hypothesis is called a classifier.

Elements of D (called examples) are described by set of attributes $Attr = (a_1, a_2, \ldots, a_n)$, where $a_i: D \rightarrow V_i$. Therefore $x^{Attr} = (a_1(x), a_2(x), \ldots, a_n(x))$ is used instead of x.

In a general case, supervised learning module have *Training data* in a form of a set $\{(x^{Attr}, f(x))\}$, and generates hypothesis h. *Problem* is a x^{Attr}, and the *Answer* is $h(x^{Attr})$.

The simplest solution in our system would be to learn a classifier, in which classes represent allocation actions, and attributes describe a current situation. Unfortunately, there is no a direct way, in which agent could prepare a training data for such a classifier. Another problem is a big size of C in such a solution. To overcome this problem the following work-around is used. Thank to comparison of income of all agents after action execution, the learning agent has information about quality of actions executed in the current situation and can use it for training. Learning module is used to classify action in the given situation as good or bad. Such classifier may be used to give ranks to action candidates.

More precisely, the *Problem* is defined as a five-tuple: (dc, cc, h, d, c), it consists of catch in the both areas during the previous round and a ship allocation action parameters. The *Answer* is an integer, which represents the given allocation action rating. The agent collects ratings for all generated allocation action candidates and for execution chooses the action with the highest rating.

Training examples are generated from agent observations. Every round the learning agent stores ship allocations of all agents, and the fish catch in the previous round. The action of an agent with the highest income is labelled as *good*, and the action of an agent with the lowest income is labelled as *bad*. If in some round all agents get the same income, none action is classified, and as a consequence, none of them is used in learning. *Training data* consists of the following pairs: $((dc, cc, h, d, c), q)$, where q is equal to *good* or *bad*. At the end of each game the agent uses training examples, which were generated during all games played so far, to learn a new classifier, which is used in the next game.

Rating v of the action a is calculated according to the formula:

$$v(a) = \alpha \, \mathrm{good}(a) - \mathrm{bad}(a), \tag{4}$$

where $\mathrm{good}(a)$ and $\mathrm{bad}(a)$ are numbers of rules, which match the action and current environment parameters, with consequence *good* and *bad*, respectively, and α is a weight representing a relative importance of rules with consequence *good*.

Learning algorithm used for supervised learning is AQ algorithm. More specifically, AQ21 program is executed. It is the last implementation of the AQ algorithm (Wojtusiak, 2004). This algorithm was developed by Ryszard Michalski (Michalski & Larson, 1975). Hypothesis is represented by a set of attributional rules, which have tests on attribute values in the premise part, and a class in the conclusion. Rules are generated using sequential covering: the best rule (e.g. giving an appropriate answer for the most examples) is constructed by a beam search, examples covered by this rule are eliminated from a training set, and the procedure repeats. What is important for this system, the rule set produced is not ordered

(rules can be applied in any order). Therefore we can simply count the number of matching
rules during action rating calculation.

3.4 Implementation

The software used in experiments is written in *Prolog*, using *Prologix* compiler (Majumdar &
Tarau, 2004). Every agent is a separate process. It can be executed on a separate machine.
Agents communicate with the environment using Linda blackboard.
Prologix is an extension of *BinProlog* that has many powerful knowledge-based extensions
(e.g. agent language *LOT*, Conceptual Graphs and *KIF* support).
Table 1 contains predicates, its argument domains, and predicate descriptions, which are
used in supervised learning module knowledge base. They appear in the training data and
rules induced by the AQ algorithm.

Predicate	Argument domains	Description
`rate(R)`	good, bad	Rating of the allocation strategy
`harbor(N)`	100%, 75%, 50%, 25%, 0	Fraction of ships left in a harbour
`alloc(A)`	100%-0%, 75%-25%, 50%-50%, 25%-75%, 0%-100%	Allocation: ship fraction sent to a deep sea, and ship fraction sent to a coastal area
`prevCatchDeep(D)`	integer numbers	Number of fish caught by every ship on a deep sea
`prevCatchCoastal(C)`	integer numbers	Number of fish caught by every ship on a coastal area

Table 1. Predicates and its arguments used in the rules build in the supervised learning
module

4. Experimental results

To compare reinforcement and supervised learning strategies during controlling ship
allocation action of agents, four experiments were performed. Four agents took part in every
experiment. Each experiment consisted of 20 repetitions of the sequences of ten games.
Knowledge of learning agents was passing along consecutive games in one sequence, but
was cleared between sequences. The performance of agents was measured as a balance at
the end of every game. In the figures we see average values of balances from repetitions.
In the first experiment there were three random agents and one reinforcement learning
agent (with $\gamma=1$ and $\beta=0.1$). Results are presented in Fig.2-(a).
In the second series there were three random agents and one supervised rule learning agent
(with weight $\alpha=1$). The performance of these agents is presented in Fig.2-(b).
In the third experiment both types of learning agents (with parameters as above) and two
random agents were examined. Results are presented in Fig. 3-(a). Stability of performance
(measured by the standard deviation of the balance at the end of games) is presented in
Fig. 4.
In the fourth series one supervised learning ($\alpha=1$), one predicting and two random agents
were used. The performance of agents is presented in Fig.3-(b).
In all experiments average balance of both types of learning agents increases with the
agent's experience, while the performance of the predicting and random agents decreases

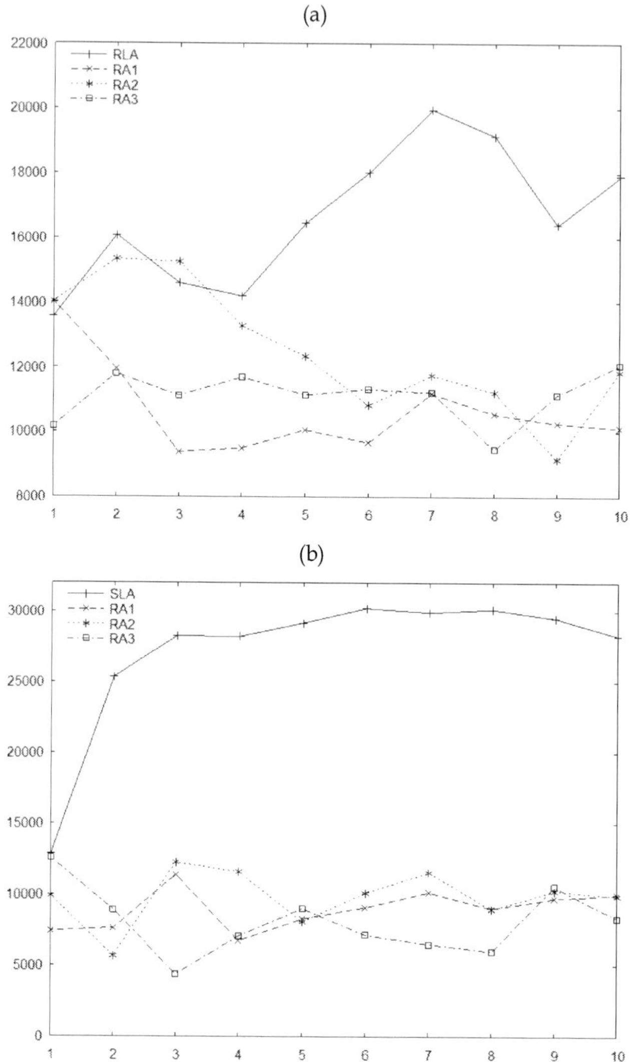

Fig. 2. Comparison of performance of reinforcement learning agent (RLA), supervised rule learning agent (SLA) and agents using random strategy of ship allocation (RA1, RA2, RA3). Horizontal axis represents number of a game in the sequence. Vertical axis represents an average balance of an agent at the end of the game

slightly (because of the learning agents competition). Reinforcement learning agent was worse then a rule learning agent, but tuning of its parameters and taking into account actions of other agents during learning should increase its performance. Also change of the

Q function representation (e.g. into neural-network based approximator) should improve the performance.

Results of reinforcement learning agent were also less stable (had higher standard deviation).

(a)

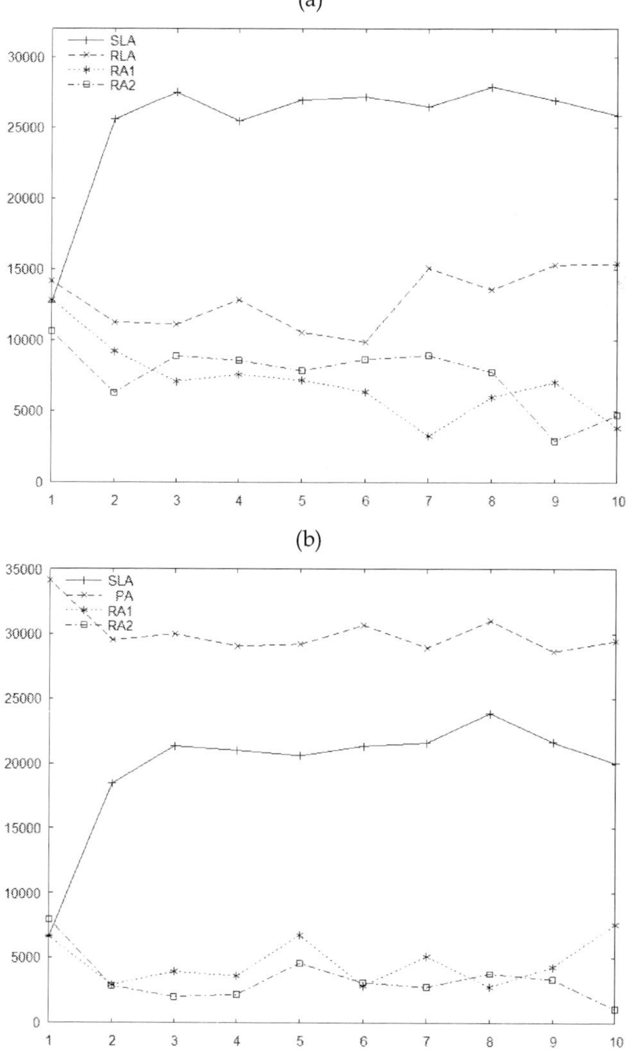

(b)

Fig. 3. Comparison of performance of reinforcement learning agent (RLA), supervised rule learning agent (SLA), agents using random strategy of ship allocation (RA1, RA2), and predicting agent (PA). Horizontal axis represents number of a game in the sequence. Vertical axis represents an average balance of an agent at the end of the game

Experimental results show that the supervised rule learning agent performance increases rapidly at the beginning of the learning process, when generated rules are used instead of a random choice. Next it increases slowly, because new examples do not contain any significant new knowledge. The performance stabilizes at the end of the process.
As we can see in Fig.3-(b), the predicting agent performs better then the supervised learning agent. It suggests, that there is a space for improvement of the learning method. Further research is necessary to check if it is possible to learn such a good strategy.

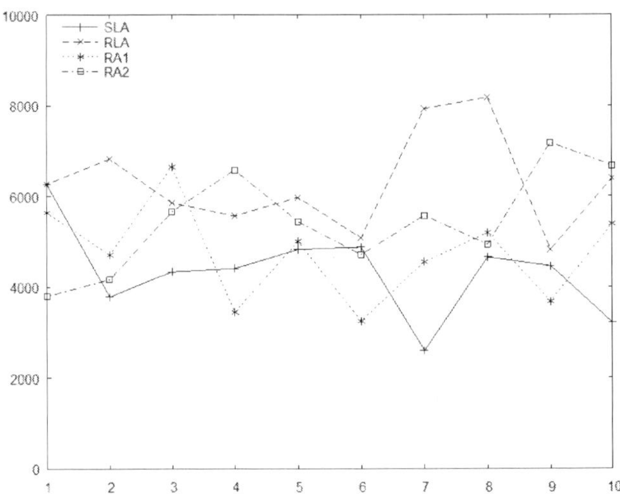

Fig. 4. Stability of performance of agents taking part in the third experiment: reinforcement learning agent (RLA), supervised rule learning agent (SLA) and agents using random strategy of ship allocation (RA1, RA2). Horizontal axis represents number of a game in the sequence. Vertical axis represents standard deviation of an agent performance at the end of the game

Examples of rules learned are presented in Fig. 5. They are in the form of *Prolog* clauses. Capital letters represent variables that can be unified with any value. Predicate member checks if its first argument belongs to the list that is a second argument. It is used to represent an internal disjunction (expression of the form $x = v_1$ or v_2 or … or v_n). Remaining predicates are presented in Table 1. These rules can be interpreted in the following way:
Clause (a): it is a bad decision to keep at a harbour 25, 50, or 75 percent of ships if the previous catch at a deep-sea is greater or equal to 16, and the previous catch at a coastal area is 10.
Clause (b): it is a good decision to send 100% ships to a deep sea or 75% to a deep sea and 25% to a coastal area if previous catch at a deep-sea is greater or equal to 18, and smaller or equal to 21, and previous catch at a coastal area is smaller or equal to 10.

5. Conclusion

As we can see, both learning algorithms can be applied for learning resource allocation in a multi-agent system. Their performance is much better then a random strategy, but there is still a space for improvement.

(a)   (b)

```
rate(bad) :-                    rate(good) :-
    harbor(B),                      deep_coastal_ratio(B),
    member(B,[25,50,75]),           member(B,[100%-0%,75%-25%]),
    prevCatchDeep(C),               prevCatchDeep(C),
    C >= 16,                        C >= 18,
    prevCatchCoastal(10).           C =< 21,
                                    prevCatchCoastal(D),
                                    D =< 10.
```

Fig. 5. Examples of rules in the form of *Prolog* clauses learned by the supervised learning
agent

This work shows also that it is possible to use supervised learning method in a case, in
which there is no direct training data. It is enough that agent has some qualitative
information about action that was executed in a given state.

Both of the considered learning strategies have some advantages and disadvantages. These
two methods use different knowledge representation. Reinforcement learning uses the
action value function, which is difficult to analyze especially in a case of a large domain.
Rules are usually much easier to interpret (unless there are too many of them). Therefore, if
learned knowledge is analyzed by a human, rule induction seems to be a better choice.

A disadvantage of reinforcement learning is necessity of tuning its parameters (γ, β, and
exploration method). The choice has a high impact on the results. What is more, due to
necessary exploration, the algorithm's performance is less stable.

On the other hand, reinforcement learning works well even if the reward is delayed.
Additionally, it does not need information about other agents' actions. Hence it is more
universal.

6. Further research

Currently the architecture of agents supports centralized learning only. In the future it should
be extended to cover distributed learning (communication and cooperation during learning).
Future works will concern applying other learning algorithms and also other strategies (e.g.
unsupervised learning).
Additionally, agents with more then one learning module for different aspects of their
activity should be studied and the possibility of interaction between learning modules in the
same agent should be examined.

7. Acknowledgements

The author is grateful to Arun Majumdar, Vivomind Intelligence Inc. for providing Prologix
system (used for implementation), and for help with using it, Janusz Wojtusiak, MLI
Laboratory for AQ21 software and assistance, and last but not least Jaroslaw Koźlak, AGH
University of Science and Technology for help with the Fish Bank Game.

8. References

Airiau, S., Padham, L., Sardina, S. and Sen, S. (2008). Incorporating Learning in BDI Agents,
In: *Proceedings of the ALAMAS+ALAg Workshop*, Estoril, Portugal

Gehrke, J.D., Wojtusiak J. (2008). Traffic Prediction for Agent Route Planning, In: *Computational Science - ICCS 2008*, part III, Bubak, M., van Albada, G.D., Dongarra, J., Sloot P.M.A. (Eds.), Lecture Notes in Computer Science 5103, pp. 692-701, Springer

H.Kitano, M.Tambe, P.Stone, M.Veloso, S.Coradeschi, Osawa, E., Matsubara, H., Noda, I., Asada, M. (1997). The RoboCup synthetic agent challenge 97, In: *International Joint Conference on Artificial Intelligence (IJCAI97)*, pp. 24–29, Nagoya, Japan

Hardin, G. (1968). The tragedy of commons, *Science*, Vol.162, 1243–1248

Koźlak, J., Demazeau, Y., Bousquet, F. (1999). Multi-agent system to model the Fishbanks game process. In: *The First International Workshop of Central and Eastern Europe on Multi-agent Systems (CEEMAS'99)*, St. Petersburg

Lashkari, Y., Metral, M., Maes, P. (1994). Collaborative interface agents. *Proceedings of AAAI 1994*, pp. 444–449

Majumdar, A., Tarau, P. (2004). *Prologix: Users guide*, Technical Report, VivoMind LLC

Meadows, D., Iddman, T., Shannon, D. (1993). *Fish Banks, LTD: Game Administrator's Manual.* Laboratory of Interactive Learning, University of New Hampshire, Durham, USA

Michalski, R.S., Larson, J. (1975). Aqval/1 (aq7) user's guide and program description. *Technical Report 731*, Department of Computer Science, University of Illinois, Urbana, USA

Russell, S., Norvig, P. (1995). Artificial Intelligence – A Modern Approach. Prentice-Hall, Englewood Cliffs

Sardinha, J.A.R.P., Garcia, A.F., Milidiú, R.L., Lucena, C.J.P. (2004). The Agent Learning Pattern, *Fourth Latin American Conference on Pattern Languages of Programming, SugarLoafPLoP'04*, Fortaleza, Brazil

Sen, S., Weiss, G. (1999). Learning in multiagent systems, In: *A Modern Approach to Distributed Artificial Intelligence*, Weiss, G., (Ed.), The MIT Press, Cambridge, Massachusetts

Servin, A., Kudenko, D. (2008). Multi-Agent Reinforcement Learning for Intrusion Detection: A case study and evaluation, *Eighth Workshop on Adaptive Agents and Multi-Agent Systems (ALAMAS-ALAg)*

Śnieżyński, B. (2007). Resource Management in a Multi-agent System by Means of Reinforcement Learning and Supervised Rule Learning, In: *Computational Science - ICCS 2007*, Part II, Shi, Y., van Albada, G.D., Dongarra, J., Sloot P.M.A. (Eds.), Lecture Notes in Computer Science 4488, pp. 864-871, Springer

Śnieżyński, B. (2008). An Architecture for Learning Agents, In: *Computational Science - ICCS 2008*, part III, Bubak, M., van Albada, G.D., Dongarra, J., Sloot P.M.A. (Eds.), Lecture Notes in Computer Science 5103, pp. 722-730 , Springer

Stolfo, S.J., Prodromidis, A.L., Tselepis, S., Lee, W., Fan, D.W., Chan, P.K. (1997). Jam: Java agents for meta-learning over distributed databases, *Proceedings of KDD 1977*, pp. 74–81

Stone, P., Veloso, M. (2000). Multiagent systems: A survey from a machine learning perspective, *Autonomous Robots*, Vol. 8, No. 3, July

Sugawara, T., Lesser, V. (1993). On-line learning of coordination plans, *Proceedings of the 12th International Workshop on Distributed Artificial Intelligence*, 335-345, 371-377

Szita, I., Lorincz, A. (2007) Learning to Play Using Low-Complexity Rule-Based Policies: Illustrations through Ms. Pac-Man, *J. Artif. Intell. Res. (JAIR)*, Vol. 30, 659-684

Tesfatsion, L. (2001). Agent-based computational economics: Growing economies from the bottom up. *Artificial Life*, Vol. 8, No. 1, 55–82

Watkins, C.J.C.H. (1989). *Learning from Delayed Rewards*, PhD thesis, King's College, Cambridge

Wojtusiak, J. (2004). AQ21 User's Guide. *Reports of the Machine Learning and Inference Laboratory*, MLI 04-3. George Mason University, Fairfax, VA, USA

4

Clustering, Classification and Explanatory Rules from Harmonic Monitoring Data

Ali Asheibi, David Stirling, Danny Sutanto and Duane Robinson
The University of Wollongong
Australia

1. Introduction

With the increased use of power electronics in residential, commercial and industrial distribution systems, combined with the proliferation of highly sensitive micro-processor controlled equipment, a greater number of distribution customers are becoming sensitive to excessive harmonics in the supply system. In industrial systems for example, harmonic losses can increase the operational cost and decrease the useful life of the system equipment (Lamedica, et al., 2001). For these reasons, large industrial and commercial customers are becoming proactive with regards to harmonic monitoring. The deregulation in the utility industry makes it necessary for some utilities to carry out extensive harmonic monitoring programs to retain current customers and targeted new customers by ensuring disturbance levels remain within predetermined limits (Dugan, et al. 2002). This will lead to a rapid escalation of harmonic data that needs to be stored and analysed.

Utility engineers are now seeking new tools in order to extract information that may otherwise remain hidden within this large volume of data. Data mining tools are an obvious candidate for assisting in such analysis of large scale data. Data mining can be understood as a process that uses a variety of analysis tools to identify hidden patterns and relationships within data. Classification based on clustering is an important unsupervised learning technique within data mining, in particular for finding a variety of patterns and anomalies in multivariate data through machine learning techniques and statistical methods. Clustering is often used to gain an initial insight into complex data and particularly in this case, to identify underlying classes within harmonic data. Many different types of clustering have been reported in the literature, such as: hierarchical (nested), partitioned (un-nested), exclusive (each object assigned to a cluster), non-exclusive (an object can be assigned to more than one cluster), complete (every object should belong to a cluster), partial (one or more objects belong to none), and fuzzy (an object has a membership weight for all clusters) (Pang, et al., 2006).

A method based on the successful AutoClass (Cheeseman & Stutz, 1996) and the Snob research programs (Wallace & Dowe, 1994); (Baxter & Wallace, 1996) has been chosen for our research work on harmonic classification. The method utilizes mixture models (McLachlan, 1992) as a representation of the formulated clusters. This research is principally based on the formation of such mixture models (typically based on Gaussian distributions) through a Minimum Message Length (MML) encoding scheme (Wallace & Boulton, 1968). During the formation of such mixture models the various derivative tools (algorithms) allow for the automated selection of the number of clusters and for the calculation of means, variances and relative abundance of the member clusters. In this work a novel technique has been developed using the MML method to determine the optimum number of clusters (or mixture model size) during the clustering process. Once the optimum model size is determined, a supervised learning algorithm is employed to identify the essential features of each member cluster, and to further utilize these in predicting which ideal clusters any new observed data may best described by.

This chapter first describes the design and implementation of the harmonic monitoring program and the data obtained. Results from the harmonic monitoring program using both unsupervised and supervised learning techniques are then analyzed and discussed.

2. Harmonic monitoring program

A harmonic monitoring program (Gosbell et al., 2001); (Robinson, 2003) was installed in a typical 33/11kV MV zone substation in Australia that supplies ten 11kV radial feeders. The zone substation is supplied at 33kV from the bulk supply point of a transmission network. Fig. 1 illustrates the layout of the zone substation and feeder system addressed with this harmonic monitoring program.

Seven monitors were installed; a monitor at each of the residential, commercial and industrial sites (sites 5-7), a monitor at the sending end of the three individual feeders (sites 2-4) and a monitor at the zone substation incoming supply (Site ID 1). Sites 1-4 in Fig. 1 are all within the substation at the sending end of the feeders identified as being of a predominant load type. Site 5 was along the feeder route approximately 2km from the zone substation, feeds residential area. Site 6 supplies a shopping centre with a number of large supermarkets and many small shops. Site 7 supplies factory manufacturing paper products such as paper towels, toilet paper and tissues.

Based on the distribution customer details, it was found that Site 2 comprises 85% residential and 15% commercial, Site 3 comprises 90% commercial and 10% residential and Site 4 comprises 75% industrial, 20% commercial and 5% residential.

The monitoring equipment used is the EDMI Mk3 Energy Meter from Electronic Design and Manufacturing Pty. Ltd. (EDMI, 2000). Three phase voltages and currents at sites 1-4 were recorded at the 11kV zone substation and at the 430V sides of the 11kV/430V distribution transformers at sites 5-7, as shown in Fig. 1. The memory capabilities of the above meters, at the time of purchase limited recordings to the fundamental current and voltage in each phase, the current and voltage Total Harmonic Distortion (THD) in each phase, and three other individual harmonics in each phase.

For the harmonic monitoring program, the harmonics selected for recording were the 3rd, 5th and 7th harmonic currents and voltages at each monitoring site, since these are typically the most significant harmonics. The memory restrictions of the monitoring equipment dictated that the sampling interval would be constrained to 10 minutes. This follows the suggested measurement time interval by the International Electrotechnical Commission (IEC) standard as given in IEC61000-4-30 for harmonic measurements, inter-harmonic and unbalances waveforms. The standard is regarded as best practice for harmonic measurement and it recommends 10 minute aggregation intervals for routine harmonic survey. Each 10 minute data sample represents the aggregate of the 10-cycle rms (root mean squared) magnitudes over the 10 minutes period. A recent study (Elphick, et al., 2007) suggested that statistically, sampling at faster rate will not provide additional significant extra insight.

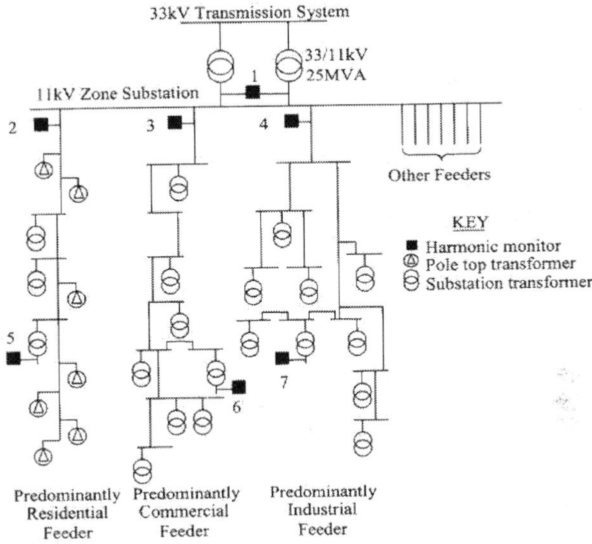

Fig. 1. Single line diagram illustrating the zone distribution system.

The data retrieved from the harmonic monitoring program spans a period from August 1999 to December 2002. Figs. 2 and 3, show a typical output data from the monitoring equipment of the fundamental, 3rd, 5th and 7th harmonic currents in Phase 'a' at sites 1 and 2, taken on 12 - 19 January 2002 showing a 10-min maximum fundamental current of 1293 Amps and minimum fundamental current of 435 Amps. It is obvious that for the engineers to realistically interpret such large amounts of data, it will be necessary to cluster the data into meaningful segments.

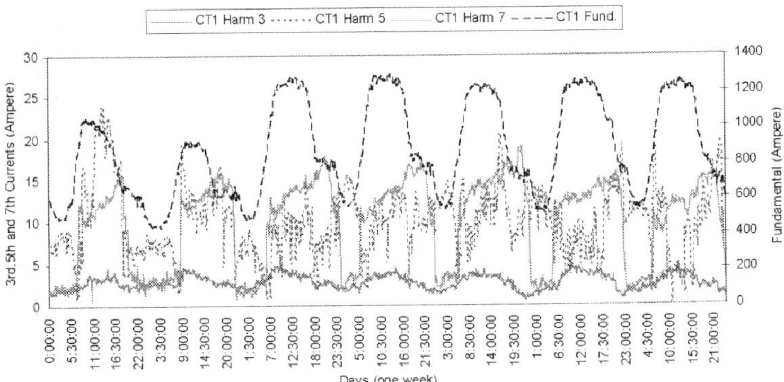

Fig. 2. Zone substation (Site 1) weekly harmonic current data from the monitoring equipment.

3. Minimum Message Length (MML) technique in mixture modelling method

The MML technique and mixture modelling was initially developed by Wallace and Boulton in 1968 through their classification program called Snob (Wallace & Boulton, 1968). The program was successfully used to classify groups of six species of fur seals. Since then, the program has been extended and utilised in different areas, such as psychological science, health science, bioinformatics, protein and image classification (Agusta, 2004). Mixture Modelling Methods using MML technique have also been applied to other real world problems such as human behaviour recognition and the diagnosis of complex issues in industrial furnace control (Zulli & Stirling, 2005).

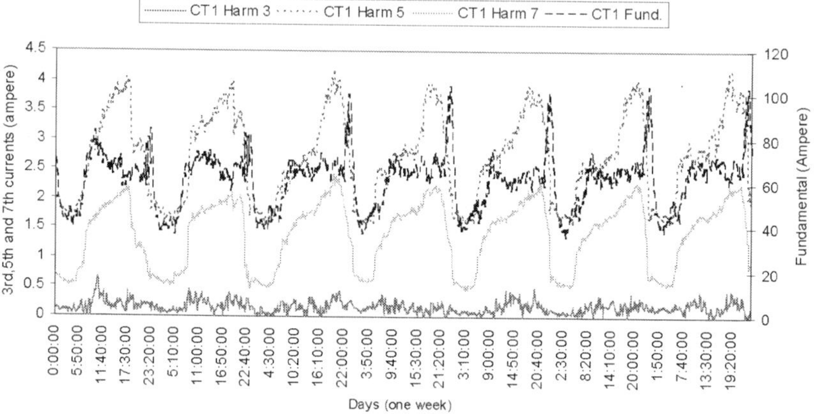

Fig. 3. Residential feeder (Site 2) weekly harmonic Current data from the monitoring equipment.

The Minimum Message Length inductive inference methodology seeks to identify efficient models by evaluating the size of a hypothetical message that describes each model together with any data which does not fit to the supposed model (exceptions). By evaluating this message length, the algorithm is able to identify, from a sequence of plausible models, those that yield an incrementally improving efficiency, or reducing size. The general concept here is that the most efficient model, describing the data will also be the most compact. Compression methods generally attain high densities by formulating efficient models of the data to be encoded.

The encoded message here consists of two parts. The first of these describes the model and the second describes the observed data given that model. The model parameters and the data values are first encoded using a probability density function (pdf) over the data range and assume a constant accuracy of measurements (Aom) within this range. The total encoded message length for each different model is then calculated and the best model (shortest total message length) is selected. The MML expression is given as:

$$L(D, K) = L(K) + L(D/K) \tag{1}$$

where:

K   : mixture of clusters in model

L (K)   : the message length of model K

L(D/K)   : the message length of the data given the model K

L (D, K)   : the total message length

Initially given a data set D, the range of measurement and the accuracy of measurement for the data set are assumed to be available. The message length of a mixture of clusters each assuming to have Gaussian distributions with their own mean (μ) and variance (σ) can be calculated as follows: (Oliver & Hand, 1994).

$$L\,(K) \;=\; \log_2 \frac{range_\mu}{AOPV_\mu} + \log_2 \frac{range_\sigma}{AOPV_\sigma} \tag{2}$$

where:

$range_\mu$: range of possible μ values

$range_\sigma$: range of possible σ values

$AOPV_\mu$: accuracy of the parameter value of μ

$$AOPV_\mu \;=\; \bar{s}\sqrt{\frac{12}{N}} \, L\,(D,K) \;=\; L\,(K) + L\,(D/K) \tag{3}$$

$\bar{s}$: unbiased sample standard deviation

$$\bar{s} \;=\; \sqrt{\frac{1}{(N-1)} \sum_{i=1}^{n}(x_i - \bar{x}\,)^2} \tag{4}$$

N : number of data samples
$\bar{x}$: the sample mean
x_i : data points
AOPVσ: accuracy of the parameter value of σ

$$AOPV_\sigma \;=\; \bar{s}\sqrt{\frac{6}{N-1}} \tag{5}$$

The message length of the data using Gaussian distribution model can be calculated from the following equation (Oliver & Hand, 1994):

$$L(D/K) \;=\; N\log_2 \frac{\bar{s}\sqrt{2\pi}}{Aom} + N\,\frac{s^2 + \dfrac{\bar{s}^2}{N}}{2\bar{s}^2}\,\log_2(e) \tag{6}$$

where:
    Aom: accuracy of measurement
    s : sample standard deviation

$$s = \sqrt{\frac{1}{N}\sum_{i=1}^{n}(x_i - \overline{x})^2} \tag{7}$$

An example of how the Mixture Modelling Method using MML technique works, can be illustrated by applying the method to a small data set that contained five distinct distributions of data points (D's) each of which were randomly generated (D1, D2, ..., D5), with its own mean and standard deviation. The generated clusters that were subsequently correctly identified through the MML algorithm are shown in Table 1 and the normal distributions of these clusters are superimposed on the data as shown in Fig. 4.

Cluster	Mean (μ)	SD (σ)
s0	1.021899	0.278162
s1	4.00873	0.616833
s2	7.910658	0.980416
s3	11.86431	1.146317
s4	16.05827	1.446599

Table 1. The parameters (μ and σ) of the five generated clusters.

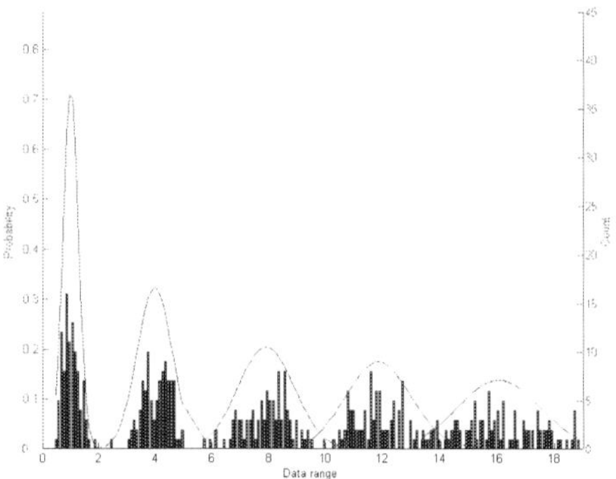

Fig. 4. Five randomly generated clusters each with its own mean and standard deviation.

This mixture modelling approach using the MML technique was used for harmonics classification to discover similar groups of records in the harmonic database; this included clustering the harmonic data from the test system described in section 2. ACPro, a specialised data mining software tool for the automatic segmentation of databases, was primarily used in this work. The preparation of the harmonic data and clustering process are explained in the next section.

3.1 Data preparation and clustering

The dominant harmonic currents and voltages attributes identified in Section 2 (3rd, 5th, 7th and THD) were selected from the four different sites; Substation (Site 1), residential (Site 5), commercial (Site 6) and industrial (Site 7) — as per Fig. 1. The resulting data set used in this application is one file of 8064 instances which consists of four combined files (4×2016) from the selected sites taken from 12-25 January 2002 inclusive. This data was normalised by dividing each data point by the typical values of each corresponding attribute. The suggested typical value for the harmonic currents is the maximum value whereas for the harmonic voltage is the average value. The maximum value of the harmonic current attributes and the average value of harmonic voltage after normalisation is one. The normalised attributes were selected as input features to the MML algorithm with a given accuracy of measurement (Aom) for each attribute. The number of clusters obtained was automatically determined based on the significance and confidence placed in the measurements, which can be estimated using the entire set of measured data. Each cluster contains a collection of data instances that have been so assembled according to an inferred (learnt) pattern, and the abundance of each group is calculated over the full data range. The abundance value for each cluster represents the proportion of data that is contained in the cluster in relation to the total data set. If for example, only one cluster was formed then the single cluster abundance value will be 100%. Each generated cluster can therefore be considered as a profile of the twelve variables (being the 3rd, 5th, 7th and THD for each of 3 phases) within an acceptable variance. If new data lies beyond the clusters associated variance, another cluster is created. Using a basic spreadsheet tool the clusters are subsequently ordered inversely proportional to the actual abundance, i.e. the most abundant cluster is seen as, *s0*, and those that are progressively rarer have a high value type numbers.

4. Results and outcomes

The following section provides an array of results and outcomes relating to the mixture modelling afforded by the MML clustering algorithm, as well as other associated techniques. These include the detection of anomalous patterns within the harmonic data and, the simplification or transforming of the mixture model through an abstraction process. Without knowing in advance the appropriate size for a mixture model, i.e. its ideal number of clusters, abstraction to a fewer number of super groups, often assists in perceiving the associated contexts each super group. A range of detail applications illustrates this approach. Subsequent insights arising from these operations have lead to a novel outcome allowing for the prior identification of the correct model size for the harmonic data. Further inspection of interesting clusters or super groups is also facilitated through the use of supervised learning, wherein an essential (or minimal) set of influencing factors behind each is derived in a symbolic form.

4.1 Anomaly detection and pattern recognition

Initially six clusters were specified as input parameters to the MML data mining program, with cluster *s5* having the least abundance at 6%. However, the value (mean) of the fifth harmonic in this cluster is at its maximum for all of the data. This cluster (*s5*) acquires its importance from both the high value of the fifth harmonic current (CT1_Harm_5) and its least number of occurrences. The second highest value of the fifth harmonic current is associated with cluster *s1* at 0.78 of the maximum value an abundance of 22%. This cluster might be as important as *s5* because it has high fifth harmonic current with a high frequent rate nevertheless the fundamental current (CT1_Fund) is very low.

The concept of rare clusters may also be used to identify the most significant distorting loads at different customer sites. Fig. 6 illustrates a mosaic of patterns of the six clusters (see

Fig. 5) over the period of one week at sites 1, 5, 6 and 7 that are represented in Fig. 1. Here, all clusters are represented as a certain shades of grey in proportion to the abundance of each cluster, i.e. the least abundant cluster ($s5$) will appear as black and the most abundant cluster ($s0$) will be the lightest shade of grey. Noticeable characteristics from Fig. 6 include the two distinctive darker patterns towards the left hand side of the Medium Voltage

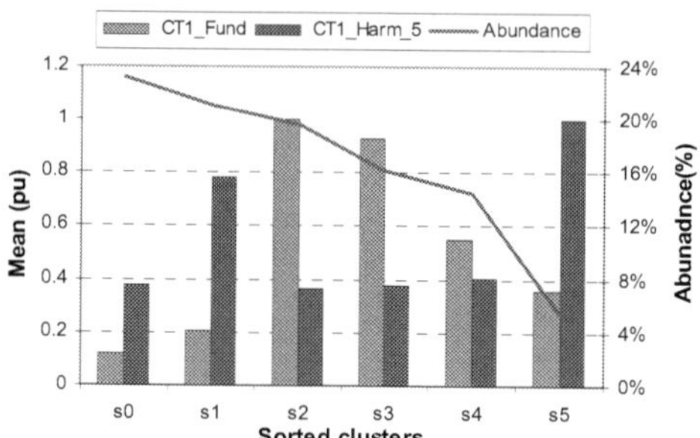

Fig. 5. Fundamentals and 5th harmonic current clusters in a single phase.

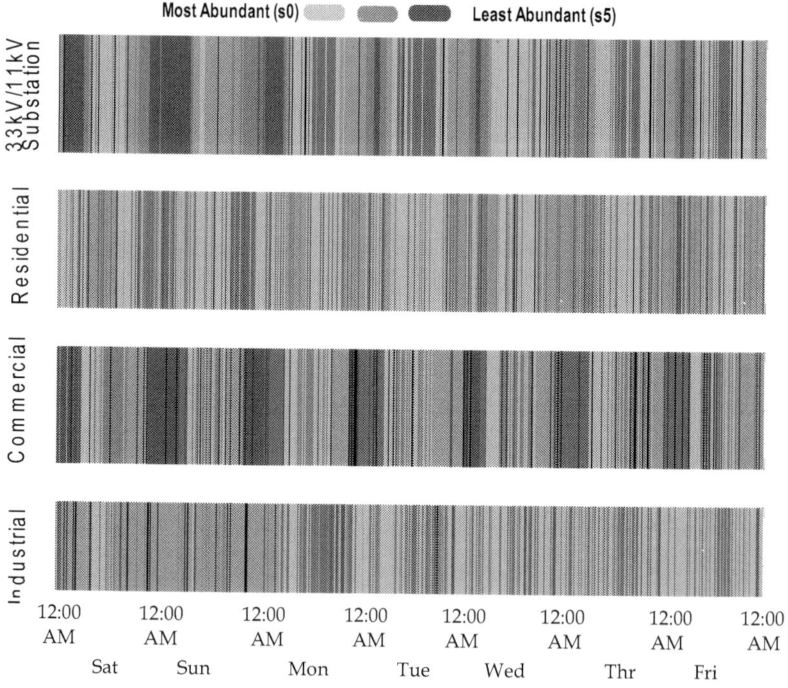

Fig. 6. Clusters of harmonic emissions from the different customer loads and system overall for a one week period.

(MV) 33/11 kV substation data (Site 1). This indicates that the least abundant occurrences appear during the mornings of the weekend days. Also the commercial site, Site 6, exhibits a recurring pattern of harmonics over each day, noting that the shopping centre is in operation seven days a week. The industrial site (site 7) shows that there is a distinctly different pattern on weekend than during weekdays. The residential customer clusters (site 5) are somewhat more random than the other sites, suggesting that harmonic emission levels in this site follow no well defined characteristics.

4.2 Abstraction of super groups

From the results from the previous section it can be observed that data mining can become a useful tool for identifying additional information from the harmonic monitoring data, beyond that which is obtained from standard reporting techniques.

Further additional information can be retrieved by using the Kullback-Lieber (KL) distance (Duda et al., 2001)which is a measure of similarities and dissimilarities between any two distributions (clusters). A multidimensional scaling algorithm (MDS) is utilised to process the resultant KL distances. This enables the generation a 2D geometric visualization (interpretation) in conjunction with an interactive link analysis, which can ultimately suggest what combinations of clusters, and neighbourhoods of clusters, could be merged to form various (fewer) super–groups.

To explain the concept of super–groups, a subset of the harmonic data described in Section 2 being (3rd, 5th, and 7th) from different sites (1, 5, 6, 7) was used as selected attributes for the MML segmentation. This time ACPro was allowed to determine the number of clusters itself resulting in eleven clusters (*s0, s1, s2... s10*). A detail of the abundances, means and standard deviations of the 5th harmonic current across these 11 clusters is illustrated in Fig. 7. The Kullback-Lieber tool in ACPro is applied on the model to generate the lower triangular 11×11 matrix of KL–distances shown in Table 2.

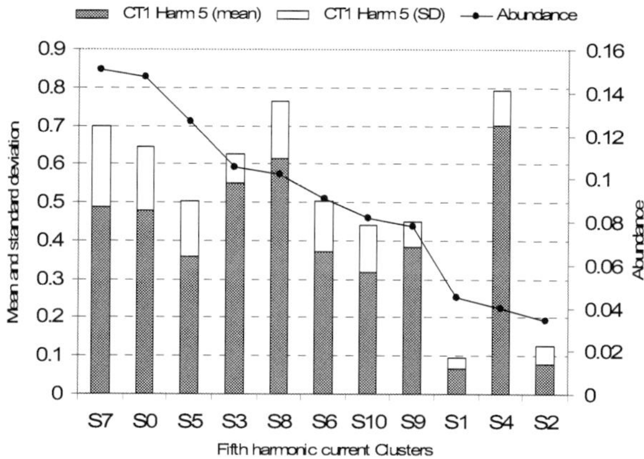

Fig. 7. Abundance, mean and standard deviation for each cluster of 5th harmonic current in phase 'a'.

	s0	s1	s2	s3	s4	s5	s6	s7	s8	s9	s10
s0											
s1	**2674**										
s2	832	232									
s3	62	**3186**	**1157**								
s4	181	2486	941	178							
s5	59	1077	358	185	127						
s6	51	1277	361	173	169	**37**					
s7	51	2518	871	107	155	58	142				
s8	102	2773	1003	113	169	145	201	39			
s9	450	1486	612	519	649	194	234	471	365		
s10	115	867	332	233	153	**34**	107	**36**	70	116	
	s0	s1	s2	s3	s4	s5	s6	s7	s8	s9	s10

Table 2. Kullback-Lieber distances between components of the 11 cluster mixture model.

The highlighted distance values represent the three largest and the three smallest distance values. For example, the distance between *s3* and *s1* is given as 3186, which is the largest distance, which suggests that there is a considerable difference between these two clusters, while on the other hand the distance between *s10* and *s5* is only 34, which suggests that there is a lot of similarity between these two clusters.

The links between all clusters, based on the KL–distances, were visualized using a multi dimensional scaling (MDS) program (Interlink, 2007), which effectively reduces an 11–dimensional model into a two dimensional representational graph. The resulting super-groups were subsequently formed by removing any link whose distance exceeds a certain threshold. The obtained super-groups (A, B, C, D and E) are shown in Fig. 8.

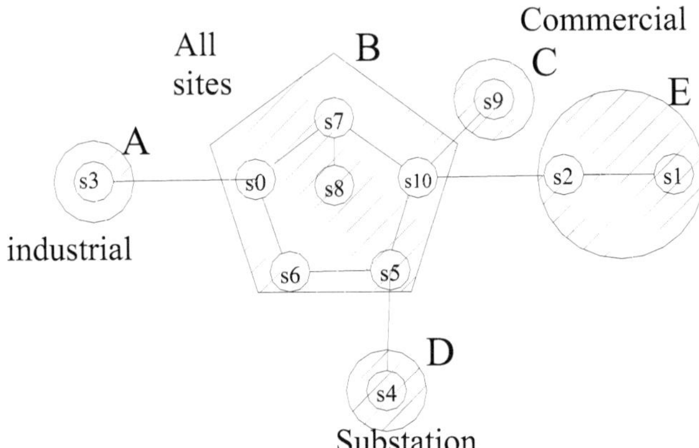

Fig. 8. Super-group abstraction by MDS.

Most of the super–group abstractions are formed based on the site type, for example supergroup A covers the industrial site, supergroup D covers the substation site, supergroup C and E covers the commercial sites, with supergroup C being separated because the distances between *s9* with *s2* and *s9* with *s1* are larger than the distance between *s1* with *s2*. Super-group B is formed from clusters containing data from all sites. The residential site does not seem to have a particular supergroup which means that the influence of harmonic emission (or participation) from this site is very low. The concurrences of two or more of these super-groups at different sites indicate that there is a mutual harmonic effect between those sites at that particular time. For example, a temporal correspondence of super-group A at the industrial site can be observed with both super–group D at the substation site and super–group E at the commercial site early in the morning of each day as shown in Fig. 9. The associated pattern of harmonic factors that might exist in the formation of these super–groups can, in future, be extracted using the classification techniques of supervised learning.

4.3 Detection of harmonic events

The number of the clusters in the previous sections was either specified as input parameters to the MML data mining program or automatically generated by the program itself given a data set D and its accuracy of measurement, Aom. In this section, however, the message length criterion of the MML is utilized to choose the model (number of clusters) that best represent the data. The smaller the encoded message length the better the model fits the data. Therefore the program was controlled to produce a series of models each with an increasing number of clusters for the same fixed values of Aom, and the message lengths of these models have been plotted against the number of clusters as shown in Fig. 10.

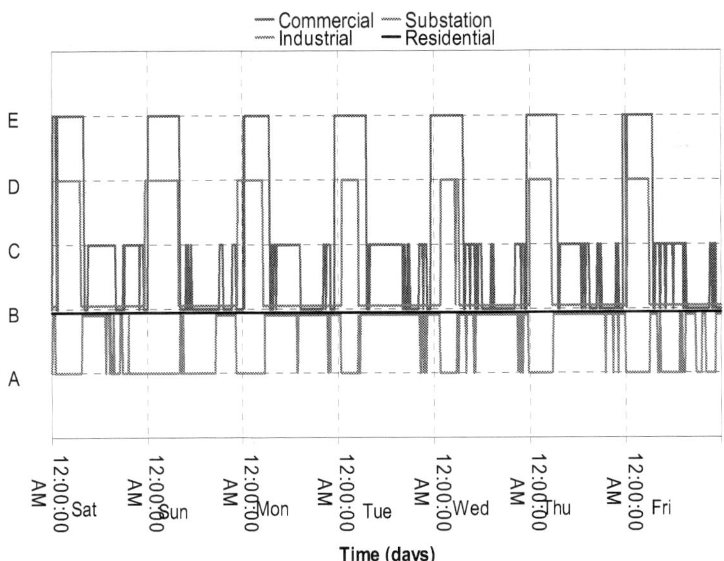

Fig. 9. Super-groups in all sites over one week.

In this case, the best model to represent the data was identified as that with six clusters. The reasoning behind selecting this number of clusters is that the decline in the message length significantly decreases when the model size reaches 6 clusters, and the message length is comparatively constant afterward as shown in Fig. 10. In other words, this can be considered to represent the first point of minimum sufficiency for the model.

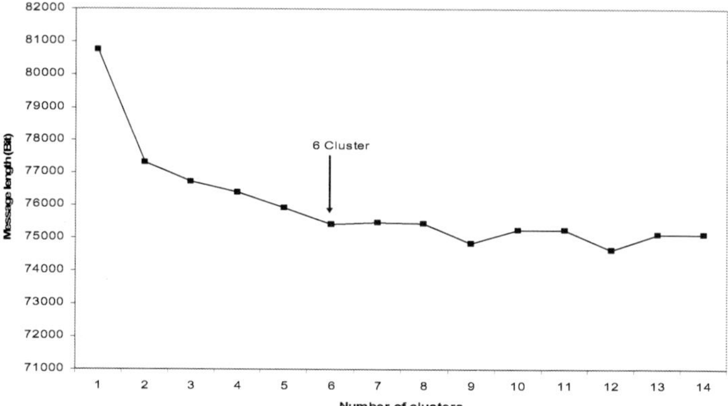

Fig. 10. Message length vs. number of generated clusters.

Using a basic spreadsheet tool the clusters are subsequently sorted in ascending order (*s0, s1, s2, s3, s4* and *s5*) based on the mean value of the fundamental current, such that cluster *s0* is associated with the lighter off peak loads period whilst cluster *s5* related to the heavier on-peak load periods as shown in Fig. 11. The mean value (μ) of the fundamental, 5th and 7th currents along with the standard deviation (σ) and the abundance (π) of each model cluster are detailed in Table 3.

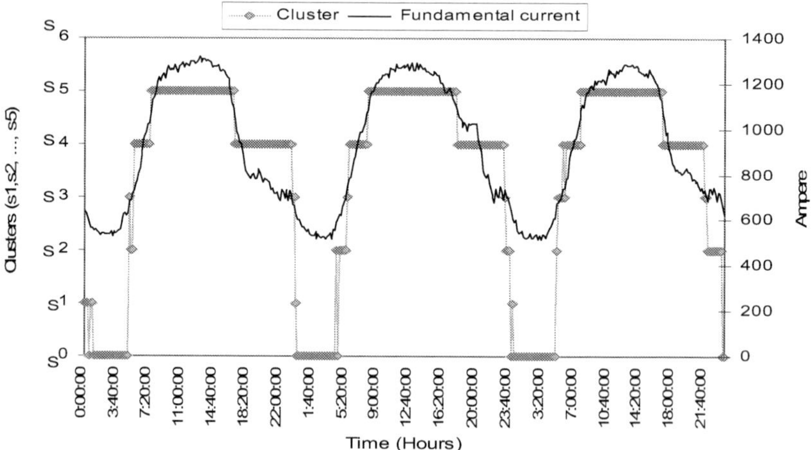

Fig. 11. Clusters obtained superimposed on the phase 'a' fundamental waveform at substation site.

Cluster	Abundance (π)	Fundamental current		5th Harmonic current		7th Harmonic current	
		Mean (μ)	*SD* (σ)	*Mean* (μ)	*SD* (σ)	*Mean* (μ)	*SD* (σ)
s0	0.068386	0.096571	0.041943	0.165865	0.130987	0.062933	0.022882
s1	0.155613	0.106102	0.061533	0.445056	0.123352	0.250804	0.127779
s2	0.056779	0.1694	0.093434	0.300385	0.14996	0.115216	0.028599
s3	0.090994	0.35053	0.132805	0.308374	0.120799	0.330834	0.142327
s4	0.342654	0.38735	0.123757	0.524376	0.193181	0.604311	0.18195
s5	0.285559	0.728608	0.095226	0.5218	0.191722	0.516901	0.149544

Table 3. Generated model detailing the abundance value (π) of the six cluster a long with the mean (μ) and standard deviation (σ).

Each generated cluster can therefore be considered as a profile of the three variables (fundamental, 5th and 7th harmonic currents) within an acceptable variance. If new data lies beyond this variance, additional clusters are created until all of the data is enclosed within the generated model as shown in Fig. 12.

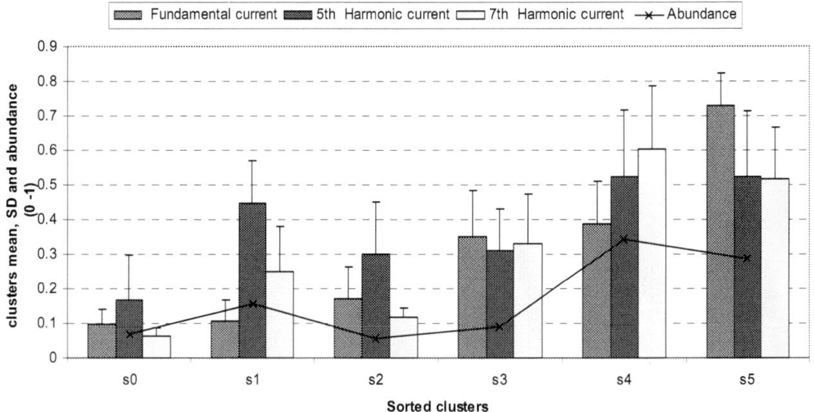

Fig. 12. Graphical profile view of model clusters indicating the statistical parameters mean (μ), standard deviation (σ) and abundance (π).

Despite the cluster labels having no specific meaning when initially generated, one can appreciate the benefit of their visual profiles in conjunction with previous sorting process, in particular one can see that cluster *s5* not only has the highest fundamental current, but also the highest 5th harmonic current. This infers that the high 5th harmonic currents are due to an overloading condition. Fig. 12 also highlights that cluster *s2* (and to a lesser extent s0) have a very low abundance. These may be viewed as anomalous, and potentially problematic clusters as described later. Two of these clusters (*s5, s2*) are further examined to identify different operating conditions based on the various attributes used in the data (fundamental, 5th and 7th harmonic currents) as follows:

4.3.1 Cluster s5 at residential site

Fig. 13 illustrates the difference in harmonic clusters at residential site between the normal weather days and the hot days. In this polar coordinate plot the variable magnitude represented by the length of the radius vector of the circle whereas the angle from the x-axis to the radius vector represents the time of the day. It is evident that the MML has identified *s5* cluster occurring more often at daytime during the hot period compared to the days when the temperature is relatively mild. It can also be observed from Fig. 13, that there is a period of peak load (cluster *s5*) around midnight, and following discussion with the utility engineer, we were informed that this is related to turning-on of the off-peak water heaters.

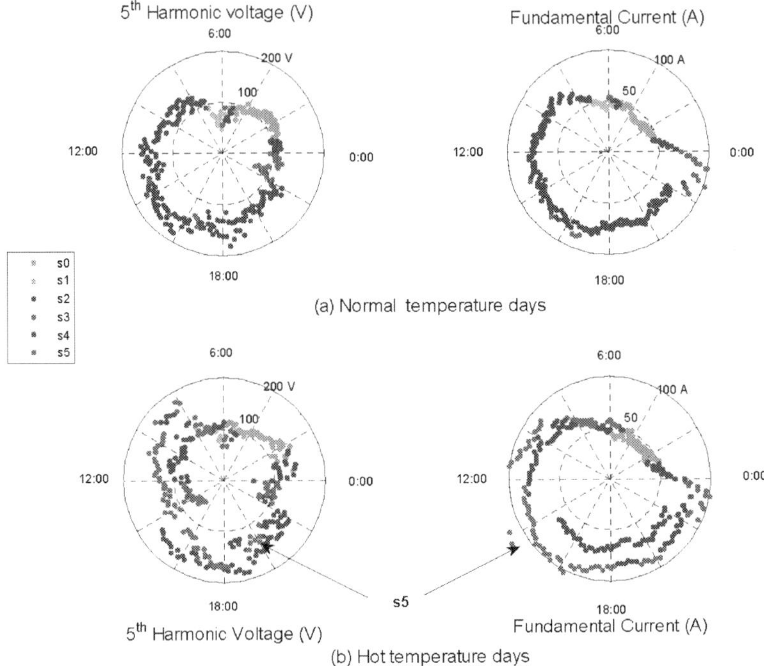

Fig. 13. Normal and hot days at residential site (Site 2).

4.3.2 Cluster s5 at industrial site

The 5th harmonic current at industrial site (Site 4) in different days of the week is shown in Fig. 14. On Saturday, for example, cluster *s5* is only present from early morning to early in the afternoon which may indicate that an industrial process that could produce the levels of 5th harmonic current, that characterize this cluster, has been terminated at around 2 pm.

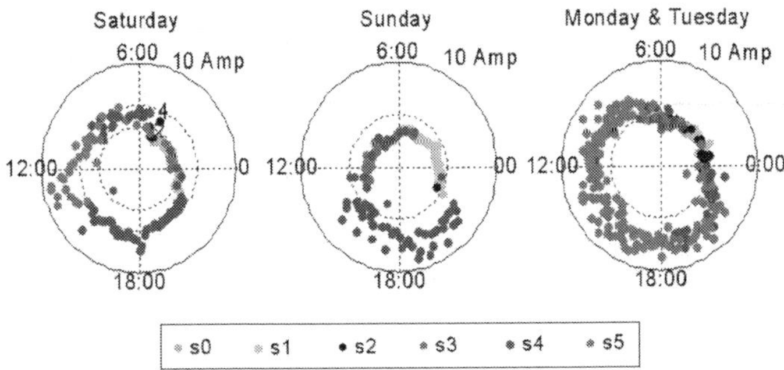

Fig. 14. 5th harmonic current clusters at industrial site for different week days.

On Sunday however, the cluster *s5* has disappeared inferring that these loads were off. These loads were on again during the weekday at day and night time showing the long working hours in this small factory at the weekdays. Similar results of the 5th harmonic current can be seen at the commercial site, see Fig. 15.

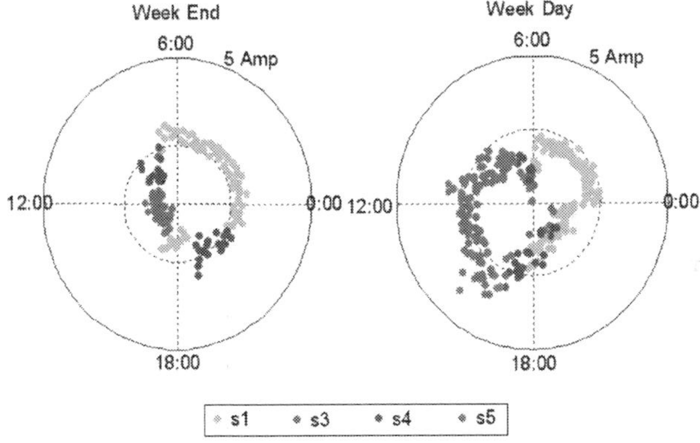

Fig. 15. 5th harmonic current clusters at commercial site for two different week days.

4.3.3 Cluster s2 at substation site.

Generally by examining the behaviour of MML model classifications (based on the recorded data) one is able to attribute further meaning to each of its cluster components(Asheibi, 2006). For example, it is noted that there are several sudden changes to cluster *s2* at particular time instances during the day. It appears from Fig. 16(b) that this is due to sudden changes in the 7th harmonic current. After further investigation of the reactive power (MVAr) measurement at the 33kV side of the power system shown in Fig. 16(c), it can be deduced that the second cluster (*s2*) is related to a capacitor switching event. Early in the morning, when the system MVAr demand is high as shown in Fig. 16(c), the capacitor is switched on in the 33kV side to reduce bus voltage and late at night when the system MVAr demand is low, the capacitor is switched off to avoid excessive voltage rise. By just observing the fundamental current, it is difficult to understand why the second cluster has been generated. The 7th harmonic current and voltage plots as shown in Fig. 16(b) provides a clue that something is happening during cluster *s2*, in that the 7th harmonic current increases rapidly and 7th harmonic voltage decreases, although the reason is still unknown. In this case, the clustering process correctly identified this period as a separate cluster compared to other events, and this can be used to alert the power system operator of the need to understand the reasoning for the generation of such a cluster, particularly when considering the fact that the abundance value for *s2* is quite low (5%). When contacted, the operator identified this period as a capacitor switching event which can be verified from the MVAr plot of the system (which was not used in the clustering algorithm). The capacitor switching operation in the 33kV side can also be detected at the other sites (sites 2, 3 and 4) at the 11kV side.

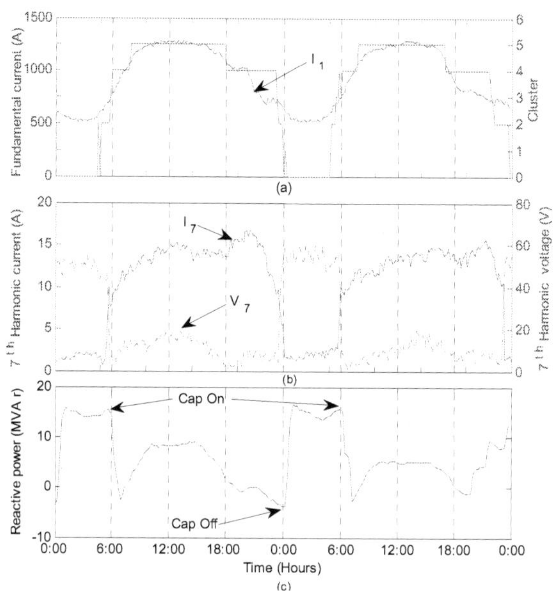

Fig. 16. Clusters at substation site in two working days (a) Clusters superimposed on the fundamental current waveform, (b) 7th harmonic current and voltage data. (c) MVAr load at the 33kV.

4.4 Determination of the optimum number of clusters in harmonic data

Determining the optimum number of clusters becomes important since overestimating the number of clusters will produce a large number of clusters each of which may not necessarily represent truly unique operating conditions, whereas underestimation leads to only small number of clusters each of which may represent a combination of specific events. A method is developed to determine the optimum number of clusters, each of which represents a unique operating condition. The method is based on the trend of the exponential difference in message length when using the MML algorithm. The MML states that the best theory or model K is the one that produces the shortest message length of that model and data D given that model. From information theory, minimizing the message length in an MML technique is equivalent to maximizing the posterior probability in Bayesian theory (Oliver, et al. , 1996). This posterior probability of Bayes' theorem is given by:

$$Prob(D\,|\,K) = \frac{Prob(K)*L(D/K)}{Prob(D)} \qquad (8)$$

Since the minimum message length in (1), is equivalent to the maximum posterior probability in (8), this yields:

$$L(D\,|\,K) = Prob(D\,|\,K) \qquad (9)$$

This suggests that the message length declines as more clusters are generated and hence the difference between the message lengths of two consecutive mixture models is close to zero as it approaches its optimum value and stays close to zero. A series of very small values of the difference of the message length of two consecutive mixture models can then be used as an indicator that an optimum number of clusters has been found. Further, this difference can be emphasised by calculating the exponential of the change in message length for consecutive mixture models, which in essence represents the probability of the model correctness $prob(D\,|\,K)$. If this value remains constant at around 1 for a series of consecutive mixture models then the first time it reaches this value can be considered to be the optimum number of clusters.

To illustrate the use of the exponential message length difference curve on determining the optimal number of clusters for the harmonic monitoring system described in Section 2, the measured fundamental, 5th and 7th harmonic currents from sites 1, 2, 3 and 4 in Fig.1 (taken on 12 -19 January 2002) were used as the input attributes to the MML algorithm (here ACPro). The trend in the exponential message length difference for consecutive pairs of mixture models is shown in Fig. 17.

Here, the exponential of the message length difference does not remain at 1 after it initially approaches it, but rather oscillates close to 1. This is because the algorithm applies various heuristics in order to avoid any local minima that may prevent it from further improving the message length. Once the algorithm appears to be trapped at the local minima, ACPro tries to split, merge, reclassify and swap the data in the clusters found so far to determine if by doing so it may result in a better (lower) message length. This leads to sudden changes to the message length and more often than not, the software can generate large number of clusters which are generally not optimum.

This results in the exponential, message length difference deviating away from 1 to a lower value, after which it gradually returns back to 1. To cater for this, the optimum number of clusters is chosen when the exponential difference in message length first reaches its highest value. Using this method, it can be concluded that the optimum number of cluster is 16, because this is the first time it reaches its highest value close to 1 at 0.9779. With the help of the operation engineers, the sixteen clusters detected by this exponential method were interpreted as given in Table 4. It is virtually impossible to obtain these 16 unique events by visual observation of the waveforms shown in Fig. 18.

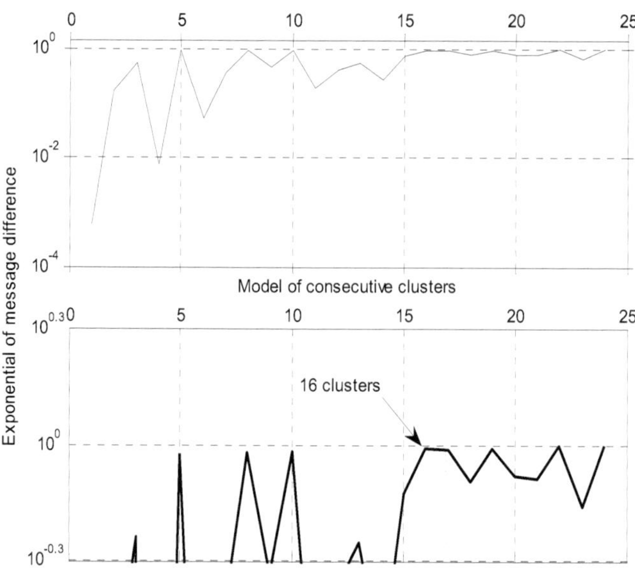

Fig. 17. Exponential curve detect sixteen clusters of harmonic data.

Cluster	Event
s0	5th harmonic loads at Substation due to Industrial site
s1	Off peak load at Substation site
s2	Off peak load at Commercial site
s3	Off peak at load Commercial due to Industrial
s4	Off peak at Industrial site
s5	Off peak at Substation site
s6 and s7	Switching on and off of capacitor at Substation site
s8	Ramping load at industrial site
s9	Switch on harmonic load at Industrial
s10	Ramping load at Residential site
s11	Ramping load at Commercial site
s12	Switching on TV's at Residential site
s13	Switching on harmonic loads at Industrial and Residential
s14	Ramping load at Substation due to Commercial
s15	On peak load at Substation due to Commercial

Table 4. The 16 clusters by the method of exponential difference in message length.

4.5 Classification of the optimal number of clusters in harmonic data

The C5.0 algorithm classification tool was applied to the measured data set and the sixteen generated clusters, obtained from the previous section, as class labels to this data. The C5.0 algorithm is an advanced supervised learning tool with many features that can efficiently induce plausible decision trees and also facilitate the pruning process. The resulting models can either be represented as tree-like structures, or as rule sets, both of which are symbolic and can be easily interpreted. The usefulness of decision trees, unlike neural networks, is that it performs classification without requiring significant training, and its ability to generate a visualized tree, or subsequently expressible and understandable rules.

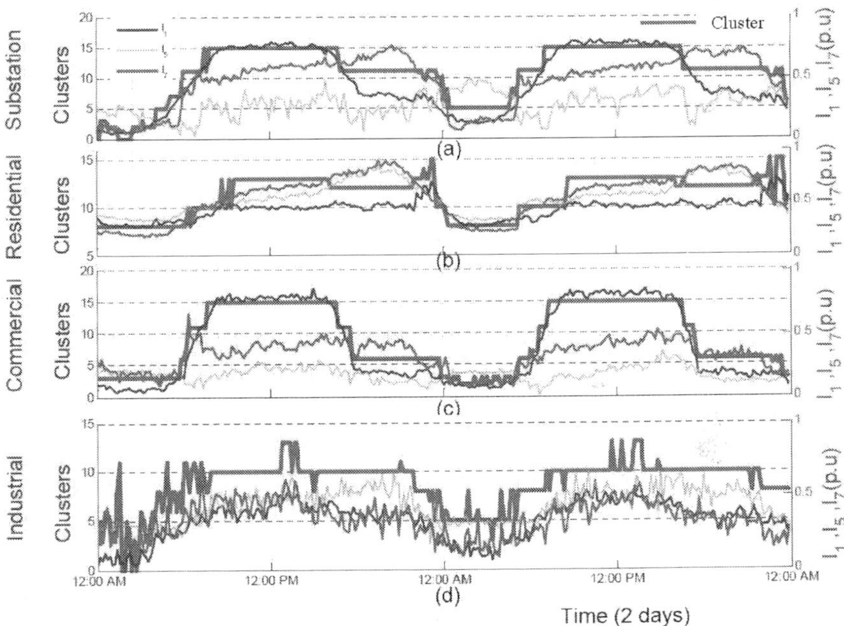

Fig. 18. Sixteen clusters superimposed on four sites (a) Substation, (b) Residential, (c) Commercial and (d) Industrial.

Two main problems may arise when applying the C5.0 algorithm on continuous attributes with discrete symbolic output classes. Firstly, the resulting decision tree may often be very large for humans to easily comprehend as a whole. The solution to this problem is to transform the class attribute, of several possible alternative values, into a binary set including the class to be characterised as first class and all other classes combined as the second class. Secondly, too many rules might be generated as a result of classifying each data point in the training data set to belong to which recognized cluster. To overcome this problem, the data is split into ranges instead of continuous data. These ranges can be built from the average parameters (mean (μ), standard deviation (σ)) of data distributions as listed in Table 5 and visualised in Fig. 19.

Range	Range Name
[0 , μ–2*σ]	Very Low (VL)
[μ–2*σ, μ–σ]	Low (L)
[μ–σ , μ+σ]	Medium (M)
[μ+σ , μ+2*σ]	High (H)
[μ+2*σ, 1]	Very High (VH)

Table 5. The continuous data is grouped into five ranges.

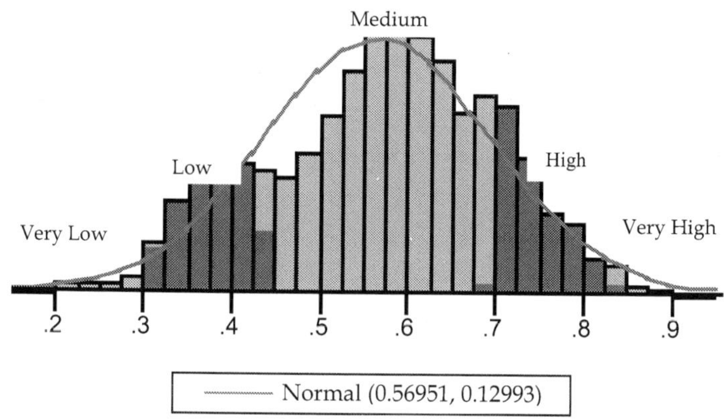

Fig. 19. The five regions of Gaussian distribution used to convert the numeric values.

4.6 Rules discovered from the optimum clusters using decision tree

Using the symbolic values (VL, L, M, H and VH) of input attributes (fundamental, 5th and 7th harmonic current) and the binary sets of classes {(*s0*, other), (*s1*, other).... (*s15*, other)} the C5.0 algorithm has been applied to as much times as the number of clusters (16 times) to uncover and define the minimal expressible and understandable rules behind each of the harmonic-level contexts associated with each of the sixteen cluster described in Section 4.4. Samples of these rules is shown in Table 6 for both *s12* which has been identified as the cluster associated with switching on TV's at the residential site and *s13* which is a cluster encompassing the engagement of other harmonic loads at both industrial and residential sites. The quality measure of each rule is described by two numbers (m, n) shown in Table 6, in brackets, preceding the description of each rules, where:

m: the number of instances assigned to the rule and
n: the proportion of correctly classified instances.

For this process some 66% of the data has been used as the training set and the rest (33%) was used as test set, as generally the larger proportion of data used in training the better the result will be, however care needs to be exercised to avoid overtraining. The accuracy of the test data was reasonably close to that of the training data for most of the clusters. The full data set was also tested and resulted in the same accuracy level as sample data. Table 7 shows the accuracy levels for cluster *s7*, *s8*, *s9* and *s10*. The utilization of these rules on new data sets is explained in the next section.

Rules for *s12* - contains 3 rule(s)		
Rule 1 for s12 (513, 0.891)	Rule 2 for s12 (523, 0.874)	Rule 3 for s12 (10, 0.583)
if Fund_I = M and 5th_I = VH then s12	if 5th_I = VH then s12	if 5th_I = H and 7th_I = VH then s12
Rules for *s13* - contains 1 rule(s)		
Rule 1 for s13 (1,572, 0.622) if Fund_I = M and 5th_I = H then s13		

Table 6. The generated Rules by C 5.0 for clusters 12 and 13.

	Data sets (January-April)		
Cluster ID	Training (66%)	Testing (33%)	Full data
s7	92.52	91.67	90.91
s8	92.11	91.67	91.46
s9	79.04	80.22	79.50
s10	94.55	95.36	94.04

Table 7. Model accuracy levels of training, test data and data sets for the cluster s7-s10.

4.7 The C5.0 rules for prediction of harmonic future data

The generated rules of the C5.0 algorithm used for classifying the optimum clusters have also been used for prediction. Several available harmonic data from different dates were used for this purpose. Data of the same period from another year (Jan-Apr 2001) and data from different time of the year (May-Aug 2002) were used to test the applicability of the generated rules. The model accuracy (see Fig. 20) for the similar data was considerably high whereas in different period data it was not always the case. This is due to fact that the algorithm performs well when the range of training data and test data are the same, but when these ranges are mismatched then the model will perform poorly and hence the accuracy of the future data (unseen data during training) will be low.

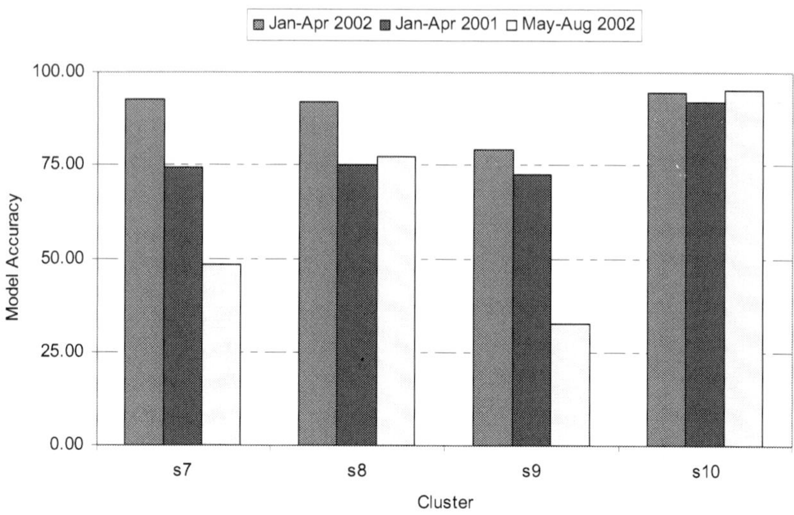

Fig. 20. Prediction Model accuracy levels for the clusters s7-s10 on training and future data.

5. Conclusion

Harmonic data from a harmonic monitoring program in an Australian medium voltage (MV) distribution system containing residential, commercial and industrial customers has been analyzed using data mining techniques. Unsupervised learning, and in particular,cluster analysis using MML, which searches for the best model describing the data using a metric of an encoded message, has been shown to be able to detect anomalies and identify useful patterns within the monitored harmonic data set. The output of the clustering process has to be appropriately displayed and interpreted in relation to the problem domain so that utility engineers can provide the relevant information. The technique presented in this work allows utility engineers to detect unusual harmonic events from monitored sites, using clustering, and then to subsequently characterize the obtained clusters using the classification techniques to infer information about future harmonic performance at the monitored sites.

The C5.0 algorithm has been used to generate expressible and understandable rules characterising each cluster without requiring significant data training. The optimal number of clusters in different types of data sets was investigated using a proposed method based on the trend of the exponential difference in message length between two consecutive mixture models. Testing this method using various two-weekly data sets from the harmonic monitoring data over three year period show that the suggested method is effective in determining the optimum number of clusters in harmonic monitoring data. The continuous data has been split into ranges to avoid too many rules that might be generated. The C5.0 algorithms were then used to generate considerable number of rules for classification and prediction of the optimum clusters.

6. References

Agusta, Y. (2004). Minimum Message Length Mixture Modelling for Uncorrelated and Correlated Continuous Data Applied to Mutual Funds Classification, *PhD Thesis*, Monash University, Clayton, Victoria, Australia.

Asheibi, A., Stirling, D. and Soetanto, D. (2006). *Analyzing Harmonic Monitoring Data Using Data Mining*. In Proc. Fifth Australasian Data Mining Conference (AusDM2006), Sydney, Australia. CRPIT, 61. Peter, C., Kennedy, P.J., Li, J., Simoff, S.J. and Williams, G.J., Eds., ACS. 63-68.

Cheeseman, P.; Stutz, J. (1996). Bayesian Classification (AUTOCLASS): Theory and Results, In *Advances in Knowledge Discovery and Data Mining*, Fayyad, U.; Piatetsky-Shapiro, G.; Smyth, P.; Uthurusanny, R., eds, pp. 153-180, AAAI press, Menlo Park, California.

Elphick, S.; Gosbell, V. & Perera, S. (2007). The Effect of Data Aggregation Interval on Voltage Results, *Proceedings of Australasian Universities Power Engineering Conference AUPEC07*, Dec. 2007, Perth, Australia, Paper 15-02

Gosbell, V.; Mannix, D.; Robinson, D. ; Perera, S. (2001) Harmonic Survey of an MV distribution system, *Proceedings of Australasian Universities Power Engineering Conference*, pp. 338-342, 23-26 September 2001, Perth, Australia.

Interlink, Knowledge Network Organising Tool (2007), KNOT, 24 August, 2007. *http://www.interlinkinc.net/KNOT.html*,

Lamedica, R.; Esposito, G.; Tironi, E.; Zaninelli, D. & Prudenzi, A. (2001) A survey on power quality cost in industrial customers. *Proceedings of IEEE PES Winter Meeting*, Vol 2, pp. 938 – 943.

McLachlan, G. (1992). *Discriminant Analysis and Statistical Pattern Recognition*, Wiley, New York.

Oliver, J.; Baxter, R. & Wallace, C. (1996). Unsupervised Learning using MML, *Proceedings of the 13th Int. Conf in Machine Learning:(ICML-96)*, pp. 364-372.

Oliver, J. J. & Hand, D. J. (1994) Introduction to Minimum Encoding Inference, [TR 4-94] Dept. Statistics. Open University. Walton Hall, Milton Keynes,UK.

Pang, T.; Steinbach, M. & Kumar V. (2006). *Introduction to Data Mining*, Pearson Education, Boston.

Robinson, D., "Harmonic Management in MV Distribution System" *PhD Thesis*, University of Wollongong, 2003.

Wallace, C.; Boulton D.M. (1968). An information measure for classification *The Computer Journal*, Vol 11, No 2, August 1968, pp185-194.

Wallace, C.; Dowe D. (1994). Intrinsic classification by MML – the Snob program, *proceeding of 7th Australian Joint Conf. on Artificial Intelligence*, World Scientific Publishing Co., Armidale, Australia,1994.

Wallace, C. (1998). Intrinsic Classification of Spatially Correlated Data, *The Computer Journal*, Vol. 41, No. 8.

Zulli, P.; Stirling, D. (2005) "Data Mining Applied to Identifying Factors Affecting Blast Furnace Stave Heat Loads," *Proceedings of the 5th European Coke and Ironmaking Congress.*

5

Discriminative Cluster Analysis

Fernando De la Torre and Takeo Kanade
Robotics Institute, Carnegie Mellon University
5000 Forbes Avenue Pittsburgh
USA

1. Introduction

Clustering is one of the most widely used statistical methods in data analysis (e.g. multimedia content-based retrieval, molecular biology, text mining, bioinformatics). Recently, with an increasing number of database applications that deal with very large high dimensional datasets, clustering has emerged as a very important research area in many disciplines. Unfortunately, many known algorithms tend to break down in high dimensional spaces because of the sparsity of the points. In such high dimensional spaces not all the dimensions might be relevant for clustering, outliers are difficult to detect, and the curse of dimensionality makes clustering a challenging problem. Also, when handling large amounts of data, time complexity becomes a limiting factor.

There are two types of clustering algorithms: partitional and hierarchical (Jain et al., 1999). Partitional methods (e.g. k-means, mixture of Gaussians, graph theoretic, mode seeking) only produce one partition of the data; whereas hierarchical ones (e.g single link, complete link) produce several of them. In particular, k-means (MacQueen, 1967) is one of the simplest unsupervised learning algorithms that has been extensively studied and extended (Jain, 1988). Although k-means is a widely used technique due to its ease of programming and good performance, it suffers from several drawbacks. It is sensitive to initial conditions, it does not remove undesirable features for clustering, and it is optimal only for hyper-spherical clusters. Furthermore, its complexity in time is $O(nkl)$ and in space is $O(k)$, where n is the number of samples, k is the number of clusters, and l the number of iterations. This degree of complexity can be impractical for large datasets.

To partially address some of these challenges, this papers proposes Discriminative Cluster Analysis (DCA). DCA jointly performs clustering and dimensionality reduction. In the first step, DCA finds a low dimensional projection of the data well suited for clustering by encouraging preservation of distances between neighboring data points belonging to the same class. Once the data is projected into a low dimensional space, DCA performs a "soft" clustering of the data. Later, this information is feedback into the dimensionality reduction step until convergence. Clustering in the DCA subspace is less prone to local minima, noisy dimensions that are irrelevant for clustering are removed, and clustering is faster to compute (especially for high dimensional data). Recently, other researchers (Ding & Li., 2007), (Ye et al., 2007) have further explored advantages of discriminative clustering methods versus generative approaches.

2. Previous work

This section reviews previous work on k-means, spectral methods for clustering, and linear discriminant analysis in a unified framework.

2.1 *k*-means and spectral graph methods: a unified framework

k-means (MacQueen, 1967; Jain, 1988) is one of the simplest and most popular unsupervised learning algorithms used to solve the clustering problem. Clustering refers to the partition of n data points into c disjoint clusters. k-means clustering splits a set of n objects into c groups by maximizing the between-cluster variation relative to within-cluster variation. In other words, k-means clustering finds the partition of the data that is a local optimum of the following energy function:

$$J(\mathbf{m}_1, ..., \mathbf{m}_c) = \sum_{i=1}^{c} \sum_{j \in C_i} \|\mathbf{d}_j - \mathbf{m}_i\|_2^2 \qquad (1.1)$$

where $\mathbf{d}_j$ (see notation[1]) is a vector representing the jth data point and $\mathbf{m}_i$ is the geometric centroid of the data points for class i. The optimization criterion in eq. (1.1) can be rewritten in matrix form as:

$$E_1(\mathbf{M}, \mathbf{G}) = \|\mathbf{D} - \mathbf{M}\mathbf{G}^T\|_F \;\; subject\;to\; \mathbf{G}\mathbf{1}_c = \mathbf{1}_n \;\; and \;\; g_{ij} \in \{0,1\} \qquad (1.2)$$

where $\mathbf{G}$ is an indicator matrix, such that $\Sigma_j g_{ij} = 1$, $g_{ij} \in \{0,1\}$ and g_{ij} is 1 if $\mathbf{d}_i$ belongs to class j, c denotes the number of classes and n is the number of samples. $\mathbf{M} \in \mathfrak{R}^{d \times c}$ is the matrix containing all the means for each cluster. The columns of $\mathbf{D} \in \mathfrak{R}^{d \times n}$ contain the original data points, and refers to the number of features. The equivalence between the k-means error function of eq. (1.1) and eq. (1.2) is only valid if $\mathbf{G}$ strictly satisfies the constraints.

The k-means algorithm performs coordinate descent in $E_1(\mathbf{M}, \mathbf{G})$. Given the actual value of the means $\mathbf{M}$, the first step finds, for each data point $\mathbf{d}_j$, the value of $\mathbf{g}^j$ minimizing eq. (1.2) subject to the constraints. The second step optimizes $\mathbf{M} = \mathbf{D}\mathbf{G}(\mathbf{G}^T\mathbf{G})^{-1}$, which effectively computes the mean of each cluster. Although it can be proven that alternating these two steps will always converge, the k-means algorithm does not necessarily find the optimal configuration of all possible assignments. The algorithm is significantly sensitive to the

---

[1] Bold capital letters denote matrices $\mathbf{D}$, and bold lower-case letters signify a column vector $\mathbf{d}$. $\mathbf{d}_j$ represents the jth column of the matrix $\mathbf{D}$. $\mathbf{d}^j$ is a column vector that designates the j-th row of the matrix $\mathbf{D}$. All non-bold letters refer to scalar variables. d_{ij} corresponds to the scalar in the row i and column j of the matrix $\mathbf{D}$, as well as the i-th element of a column vector $\mathbf{d}_j$. *diag* is an operator that transforms a vector into a diagonal matrix or transforms the diagonal of a matrix into a vector. *vec* vectorizes a matrix into a vector. $\mathbf{1}_k \in \mathfrak{R}^{k \times 1}$ is a vector of ones. $\mathbf{I}_k \in \mathfrak{R}^{k \times k}$ denotes the identity matrix. $\|\mathbf{d}\|_2^2$ denotes the norm of the vector $\mathbf{d}$. $tr(\mathbf{A}) = \Sigma_i a_{ii}$ is the trace of the matrix $\mathbf{A}$, and $|\mathbf{A}|$ denotes the determinant. $\|\mathbf{A}\|_F = tr(\mathbf{A}^T\mathbf{A}) = tr(\mathbf{A}\mathbf{A}^T)$ designates the Frobenious norm of matrix $\mathbf{A}$. $N_d(\mathbf{x};\mu,\Sigma)$ indicates a d-dimensional Gaussian on the variable $\mathbf{x}$ with mean μ and covariance Σ. $\circ$ denotes the Hadamard or point-wise product.

initial randomly selected cluster centers. It is typically run multiple times, and the solution with less error is chosen. Despite these limitations, the algorithm is used frequently as a result of its easiness of implementation and effectiveness.

After optimizing over $\mathbf{M}$, eq. (1.2), can be rewritten as:

$$E_2(\mathbf{G}) = ||\mathbf{D} - \mathbf{D}\mathbf{G}(\mathbf{G}^T\mathbf{G})^{-1}\mathbf{G}^T||_F = tr(\mathbf{D}^T\mathbf{D})$$
$$-tr((\mathbf{G}^T\mathbf{G})^{-1}\mathbf{G}^T\mathbf{D}^T\mathbf{D}\mathbf{G}) \geq \sum_{i=c+1}^{min(d,n)} \lambda_i \tag{1.3}$$

where λ_i are the eigenvalues of $\mathbf{D}^T\mathbf{D}$. Minimizing $E_2(\mathbf{G})$, eq. (1.3), is equivalent to maximizing $tr((\mathbf{G}^T\mathbf{G})^{-1}\mathbf{G}^T\mathbf{D}^T\mathbf{D}\mathbf{G})$. Ignoring the special structure of $\mathbf{G}$ and considering g_{ij} in the continuous domain, the optimum $\mathbf{G}$ value is given by the eigenvectors of the Gram matrix $\mathbf{D}^T\mathbf{D}$. The error of E_2 with the optimal continuous $\mathbf{G}$ is $E_2 = \sum_{i=c+1}^{min(d,n)} \lambda_i$. A similar reasoning has been reported by (Ding & He, 2004; Zha et al., 2001), demonstrating that a lower bound of $E_2(\mathbf{G})$, eq. (1.3), is given by the sum of residual eigenvalues. The continuous solution of $\mathbf{G}$ lies in the $c-1$ subspace, spanned by the first $c-1$ eigenvectors with highest eigenvalues (Ding & He, 2004) of $\mathbf{D}^T\mathbf{D}$.

Finally, it is worthwhile to point out the connections between k-means and standard spectral graph algorithms (Dhillon et al., 2004), such as Normalized Cuts (Shi & Malik, 2000), by means of kernel methods. The kernel trick is a standard method for lifting the points of a dataset to a higher dimensional space, where points are more likely to be linearly separable (assuming that the correct mapping is found). Consider a lifting of the original points to a higher dimensional space, $\Gamma = [\ \phi(\mathbf{d}_1)\ \phi(\mathbf{d}_2)\ ...\phi(\mathbf{d}_n)\ ]$ where ϕ represents a high dimensional mapping. The kernelized version of eq. (1.2) is:

$$E_3(\mathbf{M},\mathbf{G}) = ||(\Gamma - \mathbf{M}\mathbf{G}^T)\mathbf{W}||_F \tag{1.4}$$

in which we introduce a weighting matrix $\mathbf{W}$ for normalization purposes. Eliminating $\mathbf{M} = \Gamma\mathbf{W}\mathbf{W}^T\mathbf{G}(\mathbf{G}^T\mathbf{W}\mathbf{W}^T\mathbf{G})^{-1}$, it can be shown that:

$$E_3 \propto tr((\mathbf{G}^T\mathbf{W}\mathbf{W}^T\mathbf{G})^{-1}\mathbf{G}^T\mathbf{W}\mathbf{W}^T\Gamma^T\Gamma\mathbf{W}\mathbf{W}^T\mathbf{G}) \tag{1.5}$$

where $\Gamma^T\Gamma$ is the standard affinity matrix in Normalized Cuts (Shi & Malik, 2000). After a change of variable $\mathbf{Z} = \mathbf{G}^T\mathbf{W}$, the previous equation can be expressed as $E_3(\mathbf{Z}) \propto tr((\mathbf{Z}\mathbf{Z}^T)^{-1}\mathbf{Z}\mathbf{W}^T\Gamma^T\Gamma\mathbf{W}\mathbf{Z}^T)$. Choosing $\mathbf{W} = diag(\Gamma^T\Gamma\ \mathbf{1}_n)^{-\frac{1}{2}}$ the problem is equivalent to solving the Normalized Cuts problem. This formulation is more general since it allows for arbitrary kernels and weights. In addition, the weight matrix can be used to reject the influence of pairs of data points with unknown similarity (i.e. missing data).

2.2 Linear discriminant analysis

The aim of LDA is to find a low dimensional projection, where the means of the classes are as far as possible from each other, and the intra-class variation is small. LDA can be computed in closed form using the following covariance matrices, conveniently expressed in matrix form (de la Torre & Kanade, 2005):

$$f\mathbf{S}_t = \sum_{j=1}^{n}(\mathbf{d}_j - \mathbf{m})(\mathbf{d}_j - \mathbf{m})^T = \mathbf{DP}_1\mathbf{D}^T$$

$$f\mathbf{S}_w = \sum_{i=1}^{c}\sum_{\mathbf{d}_j \in C_i}(\mathbf{d}_j - \mathbf{m}_i)(\mathbf{d}_j - \mathbf{m}_i)^T = \mathbf{DP}_2\mathbf{D}^T$$

$$f\mathbf{S}_b = \sum_{i=1}^{c}n_i(\mathbf{m}_i - \mathbf{m})(\mathbf{m}_i - \mathbf{m})^T = \mathbf{DP}_3\mathbf{D}^T$$

where $f = n-1$, and $\mathbf{P}_i$'s are projection matrices (i.e. $\mathbf{P}_i^T = \mathbf{P}_i$ and $\mathbf{P}_i^2 = \mathbf{P}_i$) with the following expressions:

$$\mathbf{P}_1 = \mathbf{I} - \frac{1}{n}\mathbf{1}_n\mathbf{1}_n^T \quad \mathbf{P}_2 = \mathbf{I} - \mathbf{G}(\mathbf{G}^T\mathbf{G})^{-1}\mathbf{G}^T \quad \mathbf{P}_3 = \mathbf{G}(\mathbf{G}^T\mathbf{G})^{-1}\mathbf{G}^T - \frac{1}{n}\mathbf{1}_n\mathbf{1}_n^T \tag{1.6}$$

$\mathbf{S}_b$ is the between-class covariance matrix and represents the average distance between the mean of the classes. $\mathbf{S}_w$ is the within-class covariance matrix and it is a measure of the average compactness of each class. Finally, $\mathbf{S}_t$ is the total covariance matrix. Through these matrix expressions, it can be easily verified that $\mathbf{S}_t = \mathbf{S}_w + \mathbf{S}_b$. The upper bounds on the ranks of the matrices are $min(c-1,d)$, $min(n-c,d)$, $min(n-1,d)$ for $\mathbf{S}_b, \mathbf{S}_w$, and $\mathbf{S}_t$ respectively.

LDA computes a linear transformation of the data $\mathbf{B} \in \Re^{d \times k}$ that maximizes the distance between class means and minimizes the variance within clusters. Rayleigh like quotients are among the most popular LDA optimization criterion (Fukunaga, 1990). For instance, LDA can be obtained by minimizing:

$$E_2(\mathbf{B}) = tr((\mathbf{B}^T\mathbf{S}_1\mathbf{B})^{-1}\mathbf{B}^T\mathbf{S}_2\mathbf{B}) \tag{1.7}$$

where several combinations of $\mathbf{S}_1$ and $\mathbf{S}_2$ matrices lead to the same LDA solution (e.g. $\mathbf{S}_1 = \{\mathbf{S}_b, \mathbf{S}_b, \mathbf{S}_t\}$ and $\mathbf{S}_2 = \{\mathbf{S}_w, \mathbf{S}_t, \mathbf{S}_w\}$). The Rayleigh quotient of eq.(1.7) has a closed-form solution in terms of a Generalized Eigenvalue Problem (GEP), $\mathbf{S}_2\mathbf{B} = \mathbf{S}_1\mathbf{B}\Lambda$ (Fukunaga, 1990). In the case of high-dimensional data (e.g. images) the covariance matrices are not likely to be full rank due to the lack of training samples and alternative approaches to compute LDA are needed. This is the well-known small sample size (SSS) problem. There are many techniques to solve the GEP when $\mathbf{S}_1$ and $\mathbf{S}_2$ are rank deficient, see (Zhang & Sim, 2007; Ye, 2005) for a recent review. However, solving LDA with standard eigensolvers is not efficient (neither space or nor time) for large amounts of high dimensional data. Formulating LDA as a leastsquares problem suggests efficient methods to solve LDA techniques. Moreover, a least-squares formulation of LDA facilitates its analysis and generalization.

Consider the following weighted between-class covariance matrix $\hat{\mathbf{S}}_b = \mathbf{DGG}^T\mathbf{D}^T = \sum_{i=1}^{c}(\frac{n_i}{n})^2\mathbf{m}_i\mathbf{m}_i^T$, that favors classes with more samples. $\mathbf{m}_i$ is the mean vector for class i, and we assume zero mean data (i.e. $\mathbf{m} = \frac{1}{n}\mathbf{D1}_n$). Previous work on neural networks (Gallinari et al., 1991; Lowe & Webb, 1991) have shown that maximizing $J_4(\mathbf{B}) = tr((\mathbf{B}^T\hat{\mathbf{S}}_b\mathbf{B})(\mathbf{B}^T\mathbf{S}_t\mathbf{B})^{-1})$ is equivalent to minimizing:

$$E_4(\mathbf{B},\mathbf{V}) = ||\mathbf{G}^T - \mathbf{VB}^T\mathbf{D}||_F \propto -tr((\mathbf{B}^T\mathbf{DD}^T\mathbf{B})^{-1}\mathbf{B}^T\mathbf{DGG}^T\mathbf{D}^T\mathbf{B}) \tag{1.8}$$

This approach is attractive because (Baldi & Hornik, 1989) have shown that the surface of eq. (1.8) has a unique local minima, and several saddle points.

3. Discriminative cluster analysis

In the previous section, we have provided a least-squares framework for LDA (supervised dimensionality reduction) and k-means (unsupervised clustering). The aim of DCA is to combine clustering and dimensionality reduction in an unsupervised manner. In this section, we propose a least-squares formulation for DCA.

3.1 Error function for LDA and DCA

The key aspect to simultaneously performing dimensionality reduction and clustering is the analysis of eq. (1.8). Ideally we would like to optimize eq. (1.8) w.r.t. $\mathbf{B}$ and $\mathbf{G}$. However, directly optimizing eq. (1.8) has several drawbacks. First, eq. (1.8) biases the solution towards classes that have more samples because it maximizes $\hat{\mathbf{S}}_b = \mathbf{DGG}^T\mathbf{D}^T = \sum_{i=1}^{c}\left(\frac{n_i}{n}\right)^2$ $(\mathbf{m}_i)(\mathbf{m}_i)^T$. Secondly, eq. (1.8) does not encourage sparseness in $\mathbf{G}$ if $g_{ij}> 0$. That is, assuming that $\mathbf{C} = \mathbf{B}^T\mathbf{D} \in \Re^{k\times n}$, then eq. (1.8) is equivalent to $E_4 = tr(\mathbf{G}^T\mathbf{G})-tr(\mathbf{G}^T\mathbf{C}^T(\mathbf{CC}^T)^{-1}\mathbf{CG})$. If $g_{ij}\ \forall$ i,j is positive, minimizing the first term, $tr(\mathbf{G}^T\mathbf{G})$, does not encourage sparseness in $\mathbf{g}^i\ \forall i$ ($\mathbf{g}^i$ represents the ith row of $\mathbf{G}$, see notation).

In this section, we correct eq. (1.8) to obtain the unbiased LDA criterion by normalizing E_4 as follows:

$$E_5(\mathbf{B},\mathbf{V},\mathbf{G}) = ||(\mathbf{G}^T\mathbf{G})^{-\frac{1}{2}}(\mathbf{G}^T - \mathbf{VB}^T\mathbf{D})||_F \tag{1.9}$$

where $(\mathbf{G}^T\mathbf{G})^{-\frac{1}{2}}$ is the normalization factor. After eliminating $\mathbf{V}$, eq. (1.9) can be written as:

$$\begin{aligned}E_5(\mathbf{B},\mathbf{G}) &= ||(\mathbf{G}^T\mathbf{G})^{-\frac{1}{2}}\mathbf{G}^T(\mathbf{I}_n - \mathbf{C}^T(\mathbf{CC}^T)^{-1}\mathbf{C})||_F \\ &\propto tr((\mathbf{B}^T\underbrace{\mathbf{DD}^T}_{f\mathbf{S}_t}\mathbf{B})^{-1}\mathbf{B}^T\underbrace{\mathbf{DG}(\mathbf{G}^T\mathbf{G})^{-1}\mathbf{G}^T\mathbf{D}^T}_{f\mathbf{S}_b}\mathbf{B})\end{aligned} \tag{1.10}$$

If $\mathbf{G}$ is known, eq. (1.10) is the exact expression for LDA.

Eq. (1.10) is also the basis for DCA. unlike LDA, DCA is an unsupervised technique and $\mathbf{G}$ will be a variable to optimize, subject to the constraints that $g_{ij} \in \{0,1\}$, and $\mathbf{G1}_c = \mathbf{1}_n$. DCA jointly optimizes the data projection matrix $\mathbf{B}$ and the indicator matrix $\mathbf{G}$.

3.2 Updating B

The optimal $\mathbf{B}$ given $\mathbf{G}$ can be computed in closed form by solving the following GEP:

$$\mathbf{DRD}^T\mathbf{B} = \mathbf{DD}^T\mathbf{B}\Lambda_1 \quad where \quad \mathbf{R} = \mathbf{G}(\mathbf{G}^T\mathbf{G})^{-1}\mathbf{G}^T \tag{1.11}$$

There are many methods for efficiently solving the GEP in the case of highdimensional data when $(d >> n)$ (de la Torre et al., 2005; Zhang & Sim, 2007; Ye, 2005). In this section, we propose a regularized stable closed form solution. Assuming $\mathbf{D}^T\mathbf{D}$ is full rank, computing $(\mathbf{D}^T\mathbf{D})^{-1}$ can be a numerically unstable process, especially if $\mathbf{D}^T\mathbf{D}$ has eigenvalues close to zero. A common method to solve ill-conditioning is to regularize the solution by factorizing $\Sigma = \mathbf{D}^T\mathbf{D}$ as the sum of the outer products plus a scaled identity matrix, i.e. $\Sigma \approx \mathbf{V}\Lambda\mathbf{V}^T + \sigma^2\mathbf{Id}$. $\mathbf{V} \in \Re^{n\times k}$, $\Lambda \in \Re^{k\times k}$ is a diagonal matrix. The parameters σ^2, $\mathbf{V}$ and Λ are estimated by minimizing:

$$E_c(\mathbf{V}, \Lambda, \sigma^2) = ||\Sigma - \mathbf{V}\Lambda\mathbf{V}^T - \sigma^2\mathbf{I}_n||_F \qquad (1.12)$$

After optimizing over $\mathbf{V}, \Lambda, \sigma^2$, it can be shown (de la Torre & Kanade, 2005) that: $\sigma^2 = tr(\Sigma - \mathbf{V}\hat{\Lambda}\mathbf{V}^T)/d - k$, $\Lambda = \hat{\Lambda} - \sigma^2\mathbf{I}_d$, where $\hat{\Lambda}$ is a matrix containing the eigenvalues of the covariance matrix Σ and $\mathbf{V}$ the eigenvectors. This expression is equivalent to probabilistic PCA (Moghaddam & Pentland, 1997; Roweis & Ghahramani, 1999; Tipping & Bishop, 1999). After the factorization, the matrix inversion lemma (Golub & Loan, 1989) $(\mathbf{A}^{-1} + \mathbf{V}\mathbf{C}^{-1}\mathbf{V}^T)^{-1} = \mathbf{A} - \mathbf{A}\mathbf{V}(\mathbf{C} + \mathbf{V}^T\mathbf{A}\mathbf{V})^{-1}\mathbf{V}^T\mathbf{A}$ is applied to invert $(\mathbf{V}\Lambda\mathbf{V}^T + \sigma^2\mathbf{I}_n)^{-1}$, which results in:

$$(\mathbf{V}\Lambda\mathbf{V}^T + \sigma^2\mathbf{I}_n)^{-1} = \frac{1}{\sigma^2}(\mathbf{I}_n - \frac{1}{\sigma^2}\mathbf{V}(\Lambda^{-1} + \frac{\mathbf{I}_n}{\sigma^2})^{-1}\mathbf{V}^T)$$

Now, solving $(\mathbf{I}_n - \frac{1}{\sigma^2}\mathbf{V}(\Lambda^{-1} + \frac{\mathbf{I}_n}{\sigma^2})^{-1}\mathbf{V}^T)\mathbf{R}\mathbf{D}^T\mathbf{D}\alpha = \alpha\Lambda$ becomes a better conditioned problem.

The number of bases (k) are bounded by the number of classes (c), because the $rank(\mathbf{D}\mathbf{R}\mathbf{D}^T)$ = c. We typically choose $c-1$ to be consistent with LDA. Moreover, the best clustering results are achieved by projecting the data into a space of $c-1$ dimensions. Also, observe that there is an ambiguity in the result, because for any invertible matrix $\mathbf{T}_1 \in \mathbf{R}^{k \times k}$, $E_5(\mathbf{B}) = E_5(\mathbf{B}\mathbf{T}_1)$.

3.3 Optimizing G

Let $\mathbf{A} = \mathbf{C}^T(\mathbf{C}\mathbf{C}^T)^{-1}\mathbf{C} \in \Re^{n \times n}$, where $\mathbf{C} = \mathbf{B}^T\mathbf{D}$, then eq. (1.10) can be rewritten as:

$$E_5(\mathbf{G}) \propto tr((\mathbf{G}^T\mathbf{G})^{-1}\mathbf{G}^T\mathbf{A}\mathbf{G}) \qquad (1.13)$$

Optimizing eq. (1.13) subject to $g_{ij} \in \{0,1\}$ and $\mathbf{G}\mathbf{1}_c = \mathbf{1}_n$ is an NP complete problem. To make it tractable, we relax the discrete constraint on g_{ij} allowing to take values in the range $(0,1)$. To use a gradient descent search mechanism, we parameterize $\mathbf{G}$ as the Hadamard (pointwise) product of two matrices $\mathbf{G} = \mathbf{V} \circ \mathbf{V}$ (Liu & Yi, 2003), and use the following updating scheme:

$$\mathbf{V}^{n+1} = \mathbf{V}^n - \eta\frac{\partial E_5(\mathbf{G})}{\partial\mathbf{V}}$$
$$\frac{\partial E_5(\mathbf{G})}{\partial\mathbf{V}} = (\mathbf{I}_c - \mathbf{G}(\mathbf{G}^T\mathbf{G})^{-1}\mathbf{G}^T)\mathbf{A}\mathbf{G}(\mathbf{G}^T\mathbf{G})^{-1} \circ \mathbf{V} \qquad (1.14)$$

The increment of the gradient, η, in eq. (1.14) is determined with a line search strategy (Fletcher, 1987). To impose $\mathbf{G}\mathbf{1}_c = \mathbf{1}_n$ in each iteration, $\mathbf{V}$ is normalized to satisfy the constraint. Because eq. (1.14) is prone to local minima, this method starts from several random initial points and selects the solution with smallest error.

This optimization problem is similar in spirit to recent work on clustering with non-negative matrix factorization (Zass & Shashua, 2005; Ding et al., 2005; Lee & Seung, 2000). However, we optimize a discriminative criterion rather than a generative one. Moreover, we simultaneously compute dimensionality reduction and clustering, using a different optimization technique.

3.4 Initialization

At the beginning, neither $\mathbf{G}$ nor $\mathbf{B}$ are known, but the matrix $\mathbf{G}(\mathbf{G}^T\mathbf{G})^{-1}\mathbf{G}^T$ can be estimated from the available data. Similar to previous work (He & Niyogi, 2003), we compute an estimate of a local similarity matrix, $G(G^TG)^{-1}G^T \in \Re^{n\times n}$, from data. We assume that $(G^TG) \approx sI_c$, so that all classes are equally distributed and s is the number of samples per class. $R = \frac{1}{s}GG^T$ is a hard-affinity matrix, where r_{ij} will be 1 if d_i and d_j are considered neighbors (i.e. belong to the same class). R can be estimated by simply computing the k nearest neighbors for each data point using the Euclidian distance. To make R symmetric, if d_i is within the k-neighborhood of d_j, but not the contrary, then its similarity is set to zero. Figure 1.5.b shows an estimate of R for 15 subjects in the ORL database. Each subject (class) has ten samples and for each sample the nearest nine neighbors are selected. The samples are ordered by class. After factorizing $R = U\Sigma U^T$, we normalize R as $\hat{R} \approx U_c U_c^T$, where $U^c \in R^{n\times c}$ are the first c eigenvectors of R. $\hat{R}$ is the initial neighbor matrix.

3.5 Interpreting the weighted covariance matrix

A key aspect to understand DCA is the interpretation of the weighted covariance matrix $DRD^T = \sum_{i=1}^n \sum_{j=1}^n r_{ij} d_i d_j^T$. Principal Component Analysis (PCA) (Jolliffe, 1986) computes a basis B that maximizes the variance of the projected samples, i.e. PCA finds an orthonormal basis that maximizes $tr(B^T DD^T B) = \sum_{i=1}^n \|B^T d_i\|_2^2$. The PCA solution B is given by the eigenvectors of DD^T. Finding the leading eigenvectors of DRD^T is equivalent to maximizing $tr(B^T DRD^T B) = \sum_{i=1}^n \sum_{j=1}^n r_{ij} d_i^T BB^T d_j$. If $R = I$, it is equivalent to standard PCA. However, if R is $G(G^TG)^{-1}G^T$, where G is the indicator matrix (or an approximation), the weighted covariance only maximizes the covariance within each cluster. This effectively maximizes the correlation between each pair of points in the same class. Figure 1.1 shows a toy problem with two oriented Gaussian classes. The first eigenvector in PCA finds a direction of maximum variance that does not necessarily correspond to maximum discrimination. In fact, by projecting the data into the first principal component, the clusters overlap. If R is the initial matrix of neighbors, the first step of DCA finds a more suitable projection that maximizes class separability (see fig. 1.1).

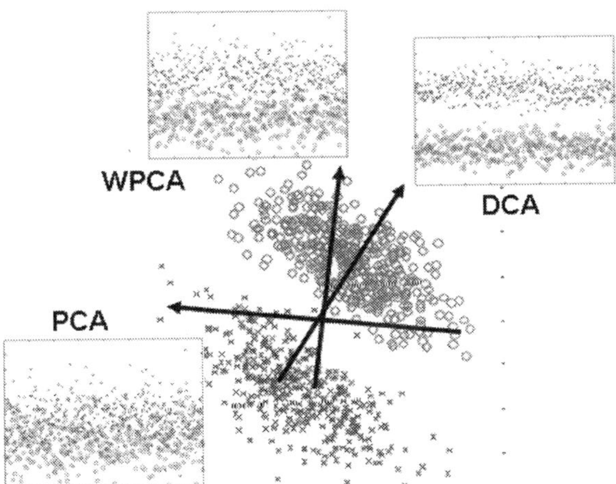

Fig. 1.1 Two class toy problem. PCA, WPCA, and DCA projections in one dimensional space.

4. Experiments

This section describes three experiments using synthetic and real data that demonstrate the effectiveness of DCA for clustering.

4.1 Clustering with DCA

In the first experiment, we show how the DCA error function is able to correctly cluster oriented clusters.

Consider the DCA optimization expression, eq. (1.10), when $\mathbf{B} = \mathbf{I}_d$ (i.e. no projection); in this case, eq. (1.10) becomes $tr((\mathbf{G}^T\mathbf{G})^{-1}\mathbf{G}^T\mathbf{D}^T (\mathbf{DD}^T)^{-1}\mathbf{DG})$. This error function, due to the term $(\mathbf{DD}^T)^{-1}$, provides affine invariance to clustering. To illustrate this property, we have generated three examples of three two-dimensional random Gaussian clusters. Figure 1.2.a shows three clusters of 300 samples each, generated from three two-dimensional Gaussians: $N_2(\mathbf{x};\ [-4;3],0.25\mathbf{I}_2)$, $N_2(\mathbf{x};-[4;2],0.25\mathbf{I}_2)$ and $N_2(\mathbf{x};\ [7;3],0.25\mathbf{I}_2)$. Similarly, fig. 1.2.b illustrates 300 samples generated from three two-dimensional Gaussians $N_2(\mathbf{x};\ [-10;-10],0.25\mathbf{I}_2)$, $N_2(\mathbf{x};\ [-10;-5],0.25\mathbf{I}_2)$ and $N_2(\mathbf{x};\ [30;15],0.25\mathbf{I}_2)$. Analogously, fig. 1.2.c shows $N_2(\mathbf{x};-[4;3],2[1\ 0.8;0.1\ 1])$, $N_2(\mathbf{x};-[4;2],0.25[1\ 0.8;0.1\ 1])$ and $N_2(\mathbf{x};\ [3;3],0.25[1\ 0.8;0.1\ 1])$.

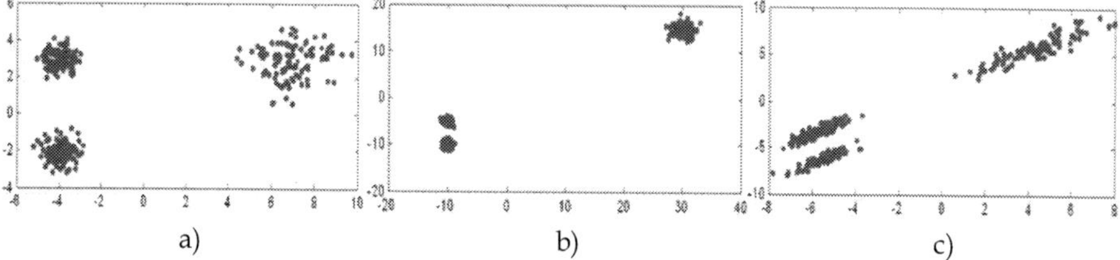

a)b)c)

Fig. 1.2 Three examples of three two-dimensional Gaussian clusters.

We run DCA and k-means with the same random initialization and let both algorithms converge. To compute the accuracy of the results for a c cluster case, we compute a c-by-c confusion matrix $\mathbf{C}$, where each entry c_{ij} is the number of data points in cluster i that belong to class j. It is difficult to compute the accuracy by strictly using the confusion matrix $\mathbf{C}$, because it is unknown which cluster matches with which class. An optimal way to solve this problem is to compute the following maximization problem (Zha et al., 2001; Knuth, 1993):

$$\max\ tr(\mathbf{CP}) \mid \mathbf{P} \textit{ is a permutation matrix} \tag{1.15}$$

To solve eq. (1.15), we use the classical Hungarian algorithm (Knuth, 1993). Table (1.2) shows the clustering accuracy for the three examples described above. We run the algorithms 1000 times from different random initializations (same for k-means and DCA).

	k-means	DCA
Fig. 1.2.a	0.713±0.23%	0.990±0.05%
Fig. 1.2.b	0.526±0.07%	0.959±0.09%
Fig. 1.2.c	0.594±0.13%	0.974±0.06%

Table 1.1 Comparison of clustering accuracy for DCA and k-means.

As we can see from the results in table 1.1, DCA is able to achieve better clustering results starting from the same initial condition as k-means. Moreover, DCA results in a more stable (less variance) clustering. k-means clustering accuracy largely degrades when two clusters are closer together or the clusters are not spherical. DCA is able to keep the accuracy even with oriented clusters (fig. 1.2.c).

4.2 Removing undesirable dimensions

The second experiment demonstrates the ability of DCA to deal with undesired dimensions not relevant for clustering. A synthetic problem is created as follows: 200 samples from a two-dimensional Gaussian distribution with mean [−5,−5] and another 200 samples from another Gaussian distribution with mean [5,5] are generated (x and y dimensions). We add a third dimension generated with uniform noise between [0,35] (z dimension). Figure 1.3 shows 200 samples of each class in the original space (fig. 1.3.a), as well as the projection (fig. 1.3.b) onto x and y. The k-means algorithm is biased by the noise (fig. 1.4.a). Similarly, projecting the data into the first two principal components also produces the wrong clustering because PCA preserves the energy of the uniform noise, which is not relevant for clustering. However, DCA is able to remove the noise and achieve the correct clustering as evidenced in fig. 1.4.b. In this particular example 15 neighbors were initially selected and $\mathbf{B} \in \mathfrak{R}^{3 \times 2}$.

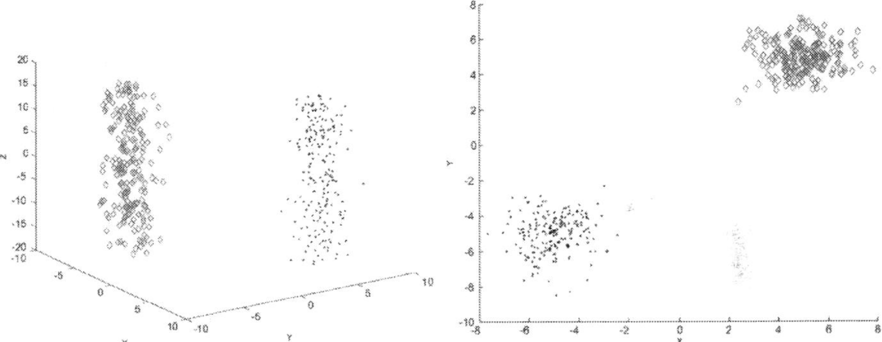

Fig. 1.3 a) 2 classes of 3 dimensional data. b) Projection onto XY space.

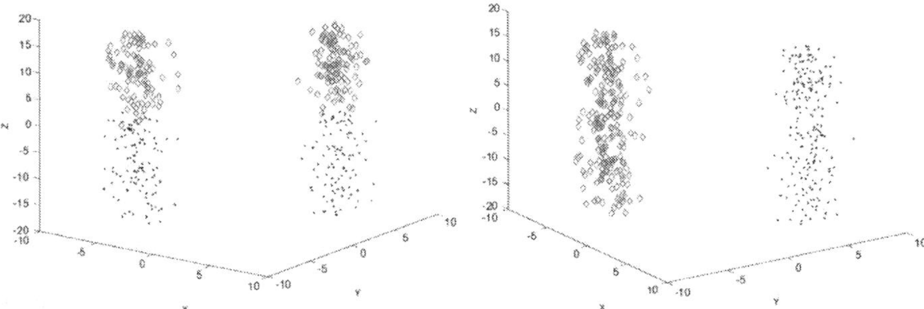

Fig. 1.4 a) k-means clustering. b) DCA clustering.

4.3 Clustering faces

The final experiment shows results on clustering faces from the ORL face database (Samaria & Harter, 1994). The ORL face database is composed of 40 subjects and 10 images per subject.We randomly selected c subjects from the database and add the 10 images for each subject to $\mathbf{D} \in \mathfrak{R}^{d \times 10c}$ (e.g. fig. 1.5.a). Afterwards, we compute PCA, weighted PCA (WPCA), PCA+LDA (preserving 95% of the energy in PCA), and DCA. After computing PCA, WPCA (with the initial matrix $\mathbf{R}$), and PCA+LDA, we run the k-means algorithm 10 times and the solution with smallest error is chosen. This procedure is repeated 40 times for different number of classes (between 4 and 40 subjects). To perform a fair comparison, we project the data into the number of classes minus ones $(c-1)$ dimensions for all methods.

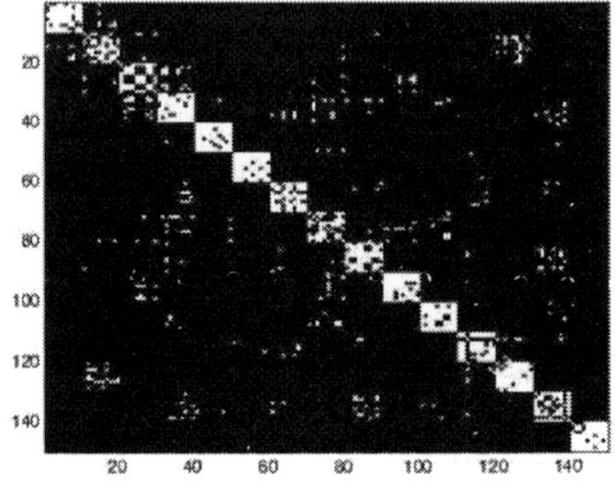

Fig. 1.5 a) Some faces of the ORL data base. b) Estimate of $\mathbf{R}$ for 15 clusters (people), each cluster has 10 samples. The samples are ordered by clusters.

c	PCA	WPCA	DCA	PCA+LDA
4	73±0%	1±0%	87±2%	1±0%
10	88±6%	95±6%	**97±4%**	88±8%
15	86±5%	88±4%	**96±1%**	82±6%
20	80±4%	84±4%	**87±2%**	83±4%
25	77±3%	80±4%	**87±2%**	80±4%
30	75±3%	79±3%	**81±3%**	81±4%
35	73±4%	77±3%	78±4%	**81±3%**
40	71±2%	74±3%	73±3%	**80±4%**

Table 1.2 Comparison of the clustering accuracy for several projection methods (same number of bases).

Fig. 1.6 shows the accuracy in clustering for PCA+k-means versus DCA. For a given number of clusters, we show the mean and variance over 40 realizations. DCA always outperforms PCA+k-means. Table 1.2 shows some numerical values for the clustering accuracy. DCA outperforms most of the methods when there are between 5 and 30 classes. For more classes, *PCA+LDA* performs marginally better. In addition, the accuracy of the PCA+k-means method drops as the number of classes increases (as expected).

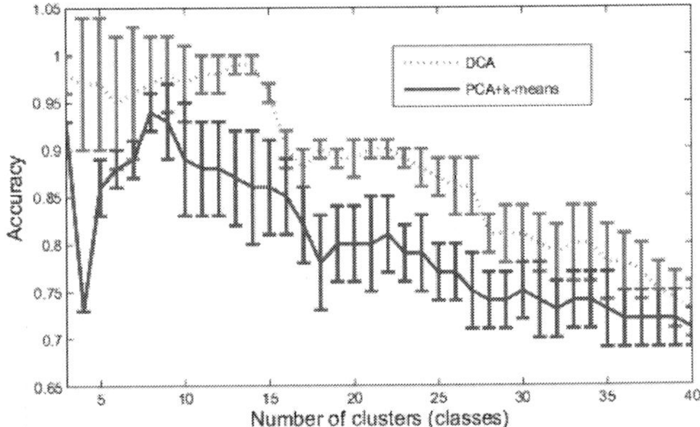

Fig. 1.6 Accuracy of clustering versus the number of classes. Blue PCA and red DCA (dotted line).

5. Discussion and future work

In this paper, we have proposed DCA, a technique that jointly performs dimensionality reduction and clustering. In synthetic and real examples, DCA outperforms standard k-means and PCA+k-means, for clustering high dimensional data. DCA provides a discriminative embedding that minimizes cluster separation and is less prone to local minima. Additionally, we have proposed an unbiased least-squares formulation for LDA.
Although DCA has shown promising preliminary results, several issues still need to be addressed. It remains unclear how to select the optimal number of clusters. Several model order selection (e.g. Minimum Description Length or Akaike information criterion) could be applied towards this end. On the other hand, DCA assumes that all the clusters have the same orientation (not necessarily spherical). This limitation could be easily address by using kernel extensions of eq. (1.10) to deal with non-Gaussian clusters.

6. Acknowledgements

This work has been partially supported by NIH R01 51435 from the National Institute of Mental Health, N000140010915 from the Naval Research Laboratory, the Department of the Interior National Business Center contract no. NBCHD030010, and SRI International subcontract no. 03-000211.

7. References

Baldi, P., & Hornik, K. (1989). Neural networks and principal component analysis: Learning from examples without local minima. *Neural Networks, 2,* 53–58.

de la Torre, F., Gross, R., Baker, S., & Kumar, V. (2005). Representational oriented component analysis for face recognition with one sample image per training class. *Computer Vision and Pattern Recognition.*

de la Torre, F., & Kanade, T. (2005). Multimodal oriented discriminant analysis. *International Conference on Machine Learning* (pp. 177–184).

Dhillon, I. S., Guan, Y., & Kulis, B. (2004). A unified view of kernel k-means, spectral clustering and graph partitioning. *UTCS Tech. Report TR-04-25.*

Ding, C., & He, X. (2004). K-means clustering via principal component analysis. *International Conference on Machine Learning* (pp. 225–232).

Ding, C., He, X., & Simon, H. (2005). On the equivalence of nonnegative matrix factorization and spectral clustering. *Siam International Conference on Data Mining (SDM).*

Ding, C., & Li., T. (2007). Adaptive dimension reduction using discriminant analysis and k-means clustering. *International Conference on Machine Learning.*

Fletcher, R. (1987). *Practical methods of optimization.* John Wiley and Sons.

Fukunaga, K. (1990). *Introduction to statistical pattern recognition, second edition.* Academic Press.Boston, MA.

Gallinari, P., Thiria, S., Badran, F., & Fogelman-Soulie, F. (1991). On the relations between discriminant analysis and multilayer perceptrons. *Neural Networks, 4,* 349–360.

Golub, G., & Loan, C. F. V. (1989). *Matrix computations.* 2nd ed. The Johns Hopkins University Press.

He, X., & Niyogi, P. (2003). Locality preserving projections. *Neural Information Processing Systems.*

Jain, A., Murty, M., & Flynn, P. (1999). Data clustering: A review. *ACM Computing Surveys.*

Jain, A. K. (1988). *Algorithms for clustering data.* Prentice Hall.

Jolliffe, I. T. (1986). *Principal component analysis.* New York: Springer-Verlag.

Knuth, D. E. (1993). *The standford graphbase.* Addison-Wesley Publishing Company.

Lee, D., & Seung, H. (2000). Algorithms for non-negative matrix factorization. *Neural Information Processing Systems* (pp. 556–562).

Liu, W., & Yi, J. (2003). Existing and new algorithms for nonnegative matrix factorization. *University of Texas at Austin.*

Lowe, D. G., & Webb, A. (1991). Optimized feature extraction and the bayes decision in feed-forward classifier networks. *IEEE Transactions on Pattern Analysis and Machine Intelligence,* 355–364.

MacQueen, J. B. (1967). Some methods for classification and analysis of multivariate observations. *5-th Berkeley Symposium on Mathematical Statistics and Probability. Berkeley, University of California Press.* (pp. 1:281–297).

Moghaddam, B., & Pentland, A. (1997). Probabilistic visual learning for object representation. *Pattern Analysis and Machine Intelligence, 19,* 137–143.

Roweis, S., & Ghahramani, Z. (1999). A unifying review of linear gaussian models. *Neural Computation, 11,* 305–345.

Samaria, F., & Harter, A. (1994). Parameterization of a stochastic model for human face identification. *Proceedings of the 2nd IEEE Workshop on Applications of Computer Vision.*

Shi, J., & Malik, J. (2000). Normalized cuts and image segmentation. *IEEE Transactions on Pattern Analysis and Machine Intelligence, 22,* 888–905.

Tipping, M., & Bishop, C. M. (1999). Probabilistic principal component analysis. *Journal of the Royal Statistical Society B, 61,* 611–622.

Ye, J. (2005). Generalized low rank approximation of matrices. *Machine Learning.*

Ye, J., Zhao, Z., &Wu., M. (2007). Discriminative k-means for clustering. *Advances in Neural Information Processing Systems.*

Zass, R., & Shashua, A. (2005). A unifying approach to hard and probabilistic clustering. *International Conference on Computer Vision. Beijing.*

Zha, H., Ding, C., Gu, M., He, X., & Simon., H. (2001). Spectral relaxation for k-means clustering. *Neural Information Processing Systems* (pp. 1057–1064).

Zhang, S., & Sim, T. (2007). Discriminant subspace analysis: A fukunaga-koontz approach. *PAMI, 29,* 1732–1745.

6

Influence Value Q-Learning: A Reinforcement Learning Algorithm for Multi Agent Systems[1]

Dennis Barrios-Aranibar and Luiz M. G. Gonçalves
Universidade Federal do Rio Grande do Norte
Brazil

1. Introduction

The idea of using agents that can learn to solve problems became popular in the artificial intelligence field, specifically, in machine learning technics. Reinforcement learning (RL) is part of a kind of algorithms called *Reward based learning*. The idea of these algorithms is not to say to the agent what the best response or strategy, but, indicate what the expected result is, thus, the agent must discover what is the best strategy for obtaining the desired result.

Reinforcement learning algorithms calculate a value function for state predicates or for state-action pairs, having as goal the definition of a policy that best take advantage of these values.

Q-learning (Watkins, 1989) is one of the most used reinforcement learning algorithms. It was widely applied in several problems like learning in robotics (Suh et al., 1997; Gu & Hu, 2005), channel assignment in mobile communication systems (Junhong & Haykin, 1999), in the block-pushing problem (Laurent & Piat, 2001), creation of electricity supplier bidding strategies (Xiong et al. 2002), design of intelligent stock trading agents (Lee et al., 2004), design of a dynamic path guidance system based on electronic maps (Zou et al., 2005), mobile robots navigation (Barrios-Aranibar & Alsina, 2004; Tanaka et al., 2007), energy conservation and comfort in buildings (Dalamagkidis et al., 2007), resource allocation (Usaha & Barria, 2007; Vengerov, 2007), and others.

In the other hand, the use of multi-agent systems became popular in the solution of computacional problems like e-commerce (Chen et al., 2008), scheduling in transportation problems (Mes et al., 2007), estimation of energy demand (Toksari, 2007), content based image retrieval (Dimitriadis et al., 2007), between others; and in the solution of problems involving robots like mail sending using robots (Carrascosa et al., 2008), rescue missions (Rooker & Birk, 2005), mapping of structured environments (Rocha et al., 2005), and others.

Also, Q-learning and derived algorithms were applied in multi-agent problems too. For example a fuzzy Q-learning was applied to a multi-player non-cooperative repeated game (Ishibuchi et al., 1997), a hierarchical version of Q-learning (HQL) was applied to learn both the elementary swing and stance movements of individual legs as well as the overall coordination scheme to perform forward movements on a six legged walking machine

---

[1] This work is supported by Conselho Nacional de Desenvolvimento Científico e Tecnológico CNPq/Brasil

(Kirchner, 1997), a modular Q-learning was applied to multi-agent cooperation in robot soccer (Park et al., 2001), Q-learning was independently applied in a group of agents making economic decisions (Tesauro & Kephart, 2002), and others.

However, when applying Q-Learning to a multi-agent system (MAS), it is important to note that this algorithm was developed for single agent problems. Thus, application of it in MAS problems can be made in several forms. They can be grouped in four paradigms: Team learning, independent learning, joint action learning and influence value learning. The last proposed by authors in previous works (Barrios-Aranibar & Gonçalves, 2007a; Barrios-Aranibar & Gonçalves, 2007b; Barrios-Aranibar & Gonçalves, 2007c).

In this work authors explain the so called IVQ-learning algorithm, which is an extension of the Q-learning algorithm using the concepts of the influence value learning paradigm. In this sense, this chapter is organized as follows: In section 2 we explain the Q-learning algorithm and analyse some extension to it, in section 3 we discuss the four paradigms of application of reinforcement learning in MAS, specially focused in the extensions to Q-learning algorithm, in section 4 we present our algorithm called IVQ-learning and, in section 5 all results of using this algorithm obtained until now are resumed. Finally, conclusions and trends for future works are discussed in section 6.

2. Q-learning

Q-learning is a temporal difference algorithm, where the agent learn independently the action selection policy it is executing. It is important to note that the policy still has an effect in that it determines which state-action pairs are visited and updated. However, all that is required for correct convergence is that all pairs continue to be updated. (Sutton and Barto, 1998). The basic form of the equation for modifying state-action pair value is given by equation 1.

$$Q(s(t), a(t)) \leftarrow Q(s(t), a(t)) + \alpha(r(t+1) +$$
$$\gamma \max_{a \in A}[Q(s(t+1), a)] - Q(s(t), a(t)))$$

(1)

where $Q(s(t),a(t))$ is the value of action $a(t)$ executed by the agent, α is the learning rate $(0 \leq \alpha \leq 1)$, γ is the discount rate $(0 \leq \gamma \leq 1)$, $r(t+1)$ is the instantaneous reward obtained by the agent and A is the set of actions agent can execute.

In equation 1 can be observed that algorithm updates states action pairs using the maximum of the values of actions of possible next state. The last can be verified in the backup diagram showed in figure 1. Q-learning algorithm is showed in algorithm 1.

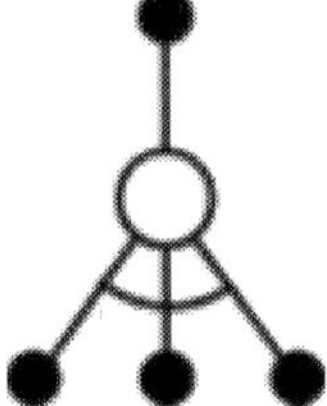

Fig. 1. Backup Diagram of the Q-Learning Algorithm (Source: Sutton & Barto, 1998)

Algorithm 1. Q-learning algorithm

Require: Initialize $Q(s,a)$ with arbitrary values
for all episodes **do**
    Initialize $s(0)$
    $t \leftarrow 0$
    repeat
        Choose action $a(t)$ in state $s(t)$, using a policy derived from Q
        Execute action $a(t)$, observe $r(t+1)$ and $s(t+1)$

$$Q(s(t),a(t)) \leftarrow Q(s(t),a(t)) + \alpha(r(t+1) +$$
$$\gamma \max_{a \in A}[Q(s(t+1),a)] - Q(s(t),a(t)))$$

        $t \leftarrow t+1$
    until $s(t)$ being a terminal state
end for

Watkins and Dayan proved the convergence of this algorithm when the sequence of episodes that forms the basis of learning include an infinite number of episodes for each starting state and action (Watkins & Dayan, 1992). Also, Tsitsiklis proved its convergence over more general conditions (Tsitsiklis, 1994).

Several extensions of this algorithm were proposed. Extensions generally aim to overpass some drawbacks that appear when Q-learning algorithms are applied to specific fields or kind of problems. Some of this extensions include, but are not limited to:

1. The FQ-Learning (Berenji, 1994), which is a Fuzzy Q-Learning algorithm for decision processes in which the goals and/or the constraints, but not necessarily the system under control, are fuzzy in nature.
2. The QLASS algorithm (Murao & Kitamura, 1997), which is a Q-learning algorithm with adaptive state segmentation specially created for learning robots that need to construct a suitable state space without knowledge of the sensor space.
3. The Region-based Q-learning (Suh et al., 1997), which was developed for using in continuous state space applications. the method incorporates a region-based reward assignment being used to solve a structural credit assignment problem and a convex clustering approach to find a region with the same reward attribution property.
4. The Bayesian Q-learning (Dearden et al., 1998), which is a learning algorithm for complex environments that aims to balance exploration of untested actions against exploitation of actions that are known to be good.
5. The kd-Q-learning (Vollbrecht, 2000), which is an algorithm for problems with continuous state space. It approximates the quality function with a hierarchic discretization structure called kd-tree.
6. The SQ-learning (Kamaya et al., 2000), which is memoryless approach for reinforcement learning in partially observable environments.
7. The Continuous-Action Q-Learning (Millán et al., 2002), a Q-learning method that works in continuous domains. It uses an incremental topology preserving map (ITPM) to partition the input space, and incorporates a bias to initialize the learning process.
8. The SA-Q-learning (Maozu et al. 2004), where the Metropolis criterion of simulated annealing algorithm is introduced in order to balance exploration and exploitation of Q-learning.

3. Q-learning in multi agent systems

As explained in section 2, sometimes it is necessary to extend the Q-learning algorithm in order to overpass some problemas that appear when developers try to apply it in some fields. When applying it in multi-agent systems the same occurs.

Specifically, two problems appear, the size of the state space and the convergence capacity of the algorithm. The first problem is related to the fact that agents position in the environment must be part of the state in the system. Thus, when the number of agents increase, the size of the state space increase too and the problem can became computationally intractable. The second problem is related to the fact that Q-learning algorithm and almost all traditional reinforcement learning algorithms were created for problems with one agent, thus, convergence is not assured when these algorithms are applied to MAS problems.

For solving the first problem, three general approaches could be identified: State abstraction, function approximation and hierarchic decomposition (Morales & Sammut, 2004). One example of these efforts for solving this problem is the work of Ono et al., which developed an architecture for modular Q-learning agents, which was designed for reducing each agent's intractably enormous state space caused by the existence of its partners jointly working in the same environment (Ono et al., 1996).

However, the second problem can be considered a critical one. For this reason, this chapter is devoted to it. Two trends can be distinguished: The first one relies in the construction of hybrid algorithms by combining Q-learning or other RL algorithms with other technics like k-neighbours algorithm (Ribeiro et al., 2006) or by combining it with concepts or other fields like pheromone concept from swarm intelligence (Monekosso & Remagnino, 2004).

The pheromone-Q-learning algorithm (phe-Q) deserves especial attention because in this algorithm agents "influence", in certain way, behaviour of other agents. This algorithm was developed to allow agents to communicate and jointly learn to solve a problem (Monekosso and Remagnino, 2004). Equation for modifying state-action pair value for an i agent using this algorithm is given by equation 2.

$$Q(s(t), a_i(t)) \leftarrow Q(s(t), a_i(t)) + \alpha(r(t+1) +$$
$$\gamma \max_{a_i \in A_i}[Q(s(t+1), a_i) + \xi B(s(t+1), a_i)] - Q(s(t), a_i(t))) \tag{2}$$

where $Q(s(t),a_i(t))$ is the value of action $a_i(t)$ executed by agent i, α is the learning rate ($0 \leq \alpha \leq 1$), γ is the discount rate ($0 \leq \gamma \leq 1$), $r(t+1)$ is the instantaneous reward obtained by agent i, ξ is a sigmoid function of time epochs, and $B(s(t),a_i(t))$ is defined by equation 3

$$B(s(t), a_i(t)) = \frac{\sum_{s \in Na} \Phi(s)}{\sum_{\sigma \in Na} \Phi_{max}(\sigma)} \tag{3}$$

where $\Phi(s)$ is the pheromone concentration at a point, s in the environment and Na is the set of neighbouring states for a chosen action a. The belief factor is a function of the synthetic pheromone $\Phi(s)$, a scalar value that integrates the basic dynamic nature of the pheromone, namely aggregation, evaporation and diffusion.

The second trend of application of RL algorithms relies in the application of algorithms without combining it with any other technic or concept. Thus, agents will use only the information existing in the traditional algorithms. As an example, if developers use Q-learning, agents will trust only in Q values and immediate rewards.

In this sense, there exist four paradigms for applying algorithms like Q-learning in multi-agent systems: Team learning, independent learning, joint action learning and influence value reinforcement learning.

The paradigm where agents learn as a team is based in the idea of modelling the team as a single agent. The great advantage of this paradigm is that the algorithms do not need to be modified (For Q-learning implementations, the algorithm 1 is used). But, in robotics and distributed applications, it can be difficult to implement because we need to have a centralized learning process and sensor information processing.

An example of this paradigm using reinforcement learning is the work of Kok and Vlasis (2004) that model the problem of collaboration in multi-agent systems as a Markov Decision Process. The main problem in their work and other similar works is that the applicability becomes impossible when the number of players increases because the number of states and actions increases exponentially.

The problems reported in learning as a team can be solved by implementing the learning algorithms independently in each agent. Thus, in the case of Q-learning, each agent will implement the algorithm 1 without modifications. Several papers show promising results when applying this paradigm (Sen et al., 1994; Kapetanakis & Kudenko, 2002; Tumer et al., 2002). However, Claus and Boutilier (1998) explored the use of independent learners in repetitive games, empirically showing that the proposal is able to achieve only sub-optimal results. The above results are important when analyzed regarding the nature of the used algorithms. It may be noted that the reinforcement learning algorithms aim to take the agent to perform a set of actions that will provide the greatest utility (greater rewards). Below that, in problems involving several agents, it is possible that the combination of optimal individual strategies not necessarily represents an optimal team strategy. In an attempt to solve this problem, many studies have been developed. An example is the one of Kapetanakis & Kudenko (2002) which proposes a new heuristic for computing the reward values for actions based on the frequency that each action has maximum reward. They have shown empirically that their approach converges to an optimal strategy in repetitive games of two agents. Also, they test it in repetitive games with four agents, where, only one agent uses the proposed heuristic, showing that the probability of convergence to optimal strategies increases but is not guaranteed (2004). Another study (Tumer et al., 2002) explores modifications for choosing rewards. The problem of giving correct rewards in independent learning is studied. The proposed algorithm uses collective intelligence concepts for obtaining better results than by applying algorithms without any modification and learning as a team. Even achieving good results in simple problems such as repetitive games or stochastic games with few agents, another problem in this paradigm, which occurs as the number of agents increase, is that traditional algorithms are designed for problems where the environment does not change, that is, the reward is static. However, in multi-agents systems, the rewards may change over time, as the actions of other agents will influence them.

In the current work, although independent learning uses the algorithm 1 without modifications, we will call this algorithm as IQ-Learning.

One way for solving the problem of the independent learning model is learn the best response to the actions of other agents. In this context, the joint action learning paradigm appears. Each agent should learn what the value of executing their actions in combination with the actions of others (joint action) is. By intuits a model for other agents, it must calculate the best action for actions supposed to be executed by colleagues and/or adversaries (Kapetanakis et al., 2003; Guo et al., 2007). Claus & Bouitilier (1998) explored the use of this paradigm in repetitive games showing that the basic form of this paradigm does not guarantee convergence to optimal solutions. However, the authors indicate that, unlike the independent learning algorithms, this paradigm can be improved if models of other agents are improved.

Other examples include the work of Suematsu and Hayashi that guarantee convergence to optimal solutions (Suematsu & Hayashi, 2002). The work of Banerjee and Sen (Banerjee & Sen, 2007) that proposes a conditional algorithm for learning joint actions, where agents learn the conditional probability of an action be executed by an opponent be optimal. Then, agents use these probabilities for choosing their future actions. The main problem with this paradigm is the number of combinations of states and actions that grows exponentially as the number of states, actions and/or agents grows.

A modified version of the traditional Q-Learning, for joint action learning, the so called JAQ-Learning algorithm (algorithm 2), is defined by the equation 4.

$$Q_i(s(t), a1(t), ..., aN(t)) \leftarrow Q_i(s(t), a1(t), ..., aN(t)) +$$
$$\alpha(r(t+1) + \gamma \max_{a1,...,aN} Q_i(s(t+1), a1, ..., aN) - Q_i(s(t), a1(t), ..., aN(t))) \tag{4}$$

where ai_t is the action performed by the agent i at time t; N is number of agents, $Q_i(s(t),a1(t),...,aN(t))$ is the value of the joint action $(a1(t),...,aN(t))$ for agent i in the state $s(t)$. $r(t+1)$ is the reward obtained by agent i as it executes action $ai(t)$ and as other agents execute actions $a1(t),...,ai-1(t),ai+1(t),...,aN(t)$ respectively, α is the learning rate $(0 \leq \alpha \leq 1)$, γ is the discount rate $(0 \leq \gamma \leq 1)$.

An agent has to decide between its actions and not between joint actions. For this decision, it uses the expected value of its actions. The expected value includes information about the joint actions and the current beliefs about other agent that is given by (Equation 5):

$$EV(s(t), ai) \leftarrow \sum_{a_{-i} \in A_{-i}} Q(s(t), a_{-i} \cup ai) * \prod_{j \neq i} Pr_t(a_{-i}j) \tag{5}$$

where ai is an action of agent i, $EV(s(t),ai)$ is the expected value of action ai in state $s(t)$, a_{-i} is a joint action formed only by actions of other agents, A_{-i} is the set of joint actions of other agents excluding agent i, $Q(s(t),a_{-i} \cup ai)$ is the value of a joint action formed by the union of the joint action a_{-i} of all agents excluding i with action ai of agent i in state $s(t)$ and $Pr_t(a_{-i}j)$ is the probability of agent j performs action aj that is part of joint action a_{-i} in state s_t.

Finally, the learning by influence value paradigm proposed by authors in previous work (Barrios-Aranibar & Gonçalves, 2007a; Barrios-Aranibar & Gonçalves, 2007b) is based on the idea of influencing the behaviour of each agent according to the opinion of others. The value of state-action pairs will be a function of the reward of each agent and the opinion that the other players have on the action that the agent execute individually. This opinion should be a function of reward obtained by the agents. That is, if an agent affects the other players pushing their reward below than the previously received, they have a negative opinion for the actions done by the first agent.

Algorithm 2. JAQ-learning algorithm for an agent i

Require: Initialize $Q_i(s,a1,...,aN)$ with arbitrary values
for all episodes **do**
　　Initialize $s(0)$ (the same initial state for all agents)
　　$t \leftarrow 0$
　　repeat
$$EV_i(s(t),ai) \leftarrow \sum_{a_{-i} \in A_{-i}} Q_i(s(t),a_{-i} \cup ai) * \prod_{j \neq i} Pr_i(a_{-i}j)$$

　　　　Choose action $ai(t)$ in state $s(t)$, using a policy derived from EV_i
　　　　Execute action $ai(t)$, observe $r(t+1)$ and $s(t+1)$
　　　　Observe actions of all agents in the system $(a1(t),...,ai-1(t),ai+1(t),...,aN(t))$
$$Q_i(s(t),a1(t),...,aN(t)) \leftarrow Q_i(s(t),a1(t),...,aN(t)) +$$
$$\alpha(r(t+1) + \gamma \max_{a1,...,aN} Q_i(s(t+1),a1,...,aN) - Q_i(s(t),a1(t),...,aN(t)))$$

　　　　$t \leftarrow t+1$
　　until $s(t)$ being a terminal state
end for

From the theoretical point of view, the model proposed does not have the problems related to the paradigms of team learning and joint action learning about the number of actors, actions and states. Finally, when talking about possible changes of rewards during the learning process and that the agent must be aware that the rewards may change because of the existence of other agents, authors conjecture that this does not represent a problem for this paradigm, based on experiments conducted until now.

This paradigm is based on social interactions of people. Some theories about the social interaction can be seen in theoretical work in the area of education and psychology, such as the work of Levi Vygotsky (Oliveira & Bazzan, 2006; Jars et al., 2004).

Based on these preliminary studies on the influence of social interactions in learning, we conjecture that when people interact, they communicate each other what they think about the actions of the other, either through direct criticism or praise. This means that if person A does not like the action executed by the person B, then A will protest against B. If the person B continue to perform the same action, then A can become angry and protest angrily. We abstract this phenomenon and determined that the strength of protests may be proportional to the number of times the bad action is repeated.

Moreover, if person A likes the action executed by the person B, then A must praise B. Even if the action performed is considered as very good, then A must praise B vehemently. But if B continues to perform the same action, then A will get accustomed, and over time it will cease to praise B. The former can be abstracted by making the power of praise to be inversely proportional to the number of times the good action is repeated.

More importantly, we observe that protests and praises of others can influence the behaviour of a person. Therefore, when other people protest, a person tries to avoid actions that caused these protests and when other people praise, a person tries to repeat actions more times.

4. IVQ-learning

Inspired in the facts explained before, in influence value paradigm, agents estimate the values of their actions based on the reward obtained and a numerical value called influence value. The influence value for an agent i in a group of N agents is defined by equation 6.

$$IV_i \leftarrow \sum_{j \in (1:N), j \neq i} \beta_i(j) * OP_j(i) \tag{6}$$

Where $\beta_i(j)$ is the influence rate of agent j over agent i, $OP_j(i)$ is the opinion of agent j about the action executed by agent i.

The influence rate β determine whether or not an agent will be influenced by opinions of other agents. OP is a numerical value which is calculated on the basis of the rewards that an agent has been received. Because in reinforcement learning the value of states or state-action pairs is directly related to rewards obtained in the past, then the opinion of an agent will be calculated according to this value and reward obtained at the time of evaluation (Equation 7).

$$OP_j(i) \leftarrow \begin{cases} RV_j * Pe(s(t), a_i(t)) & If \quad RV_j \leq 0 \\ RV_j * (1 - Pe(s(t), a_i(t))) & In \quad other \quad case \end{cases} \tag{7}$$

Where

$$RV_j \leftarrow r_j + \max_{a_j \in A_j} Q(s(t+1), a_j) - Q(s(t), a_j(t)) \tag{8}$$

For the case to be learning the values of state-action pairs. $Pe(s(t), a_i(t))$ is the occurrence index (times action a_i is executed by agent i in state $s(t)$ over times agent i have been in state $s(t)$). $Q(s(t), a_j(t))$ is the value of the state-action pair of the agent j at time t. And, A_j is the set of all actions agent j can execute. Thus, in the IVQ-learning algorithm based on Q-Learning, the state-action pair value for an agent i is modified using the equation 9.

$$\begin{aligned} Q(s(t), a_i(t)) \leftarrow Q(s(t), a_i(t)) + \alpha(r(t+1) + \\ \gamma \max_{a_i \in A_i} Q(s(t+1), a_i) - Q(s(t), a_i(t)) + IV_i) \end{aligned} \tag{9}$$

where $Q(s(t), a_i(t))$ is the value of action $a_i(t)$ executed by agent i, α is the learning rate $(0 \leq \alpha \leq 1)$, γ is the discount rate $(0 \leq \gamma \leq 1)$. And, $r(t+1)$ is the instantaneous reward obtained by agent i.

In this sense, the IVQ-Learning algorithm that extends the Q-learning algorithm by using equations 6 to 9 is presented in algorithm 3.

Algorithm 3. IVQ-learning algorithm for an agent i

Require: Initialize $Q(s, ai)$ with arbitrary values
for all episodes **do**
    Initialize $s(0)$ (the same initial state for all agents)
    $t \leftarrow 0$
    repeat
        Choose action $ai(t)$ in state $s(t)$, using a policy derived from Q
        Execute action $ai(t)$, observe $r(t+1)$ and $s(t+1)$

$$RV_i \leftarrow r_i + \max_{a_i \in A_i} Q(s(t+1), a_i) - Q(s(t), a_i(t))$$

        Observe actions of all agents in the system $(a1(t),...,ai-1(t),ai+1(t),...,aN(t))$
        for j = all agents except i **do**

$$OP_i(j) \leftarrow \begin{cases} RV_i * Pe(s(t), a_j(t)) & If \quad RV_i \leq 0 \\ RV_i * (1 - Pe(s(t), a_j(t))) & In \quad other \quad case \end{cases}$$

---

       end for

Observe opinions of all agents in the system ($OP_1(i),...,\ OP_{i-1}(i),\ OP_{i+1}(i),...,\ OP_N(i)$)

$$IV_i \leftarrow \sum_{j\in(1:N),j\neq i} \beta_i(j)*OP_j(i)$$

$$Q(s(t),a_i(t)) \leftarrow Q(s(t),a_i(t)) + \alpha(r(t+1) +$$

$$\gamma \max_{a_i\in A_i} Q(s(t+1),a_i) - Q(s(t),a_i(t)) + IV_i)$$

$$t \leftarrow t+1$$

    until $s(t)$ being a terminal state

End for

5. Experimental results

This section summarizes results obtained by using IVQ-learning algorithm in comparison with the IQ-learning ang JAQ-Learning algorithms (Barrios-Aranibar & Gonçalves, 2007a; Barrios-Aranibar & Gonçalves, 2007b; Barrios-Aranibar & Gonçalves, 2007c).

Before talking about our results, it is important to know that when talking about cooperative agents or robots, it is necessary that agents cooperate on equality and that all agents receive equitable rewards for solving the task. Is in this context that a different concept from the games theory appears in multi-agent systems. This is the concept of the Nash equilibrium.

Let be a multi-agent system formed by N agents. σ^*_i is defined as the strategy chosen by the agent i, σ_i as any strategy of the agent i, and Σ_i as the set of all possible strategies of i. It is said that the strategies $\sigma^*_i,...,\ \sigma^*_N$ constitute a Nash equilibrium, if inequality 10 is true for all $\sigma_i \in \Sigma_i$ and for all agents i.

$$r_i(\sigma_1^*,...,\sigma_{i-1}^*,\sigma_i,\sigma_{i+1}^*,...,\sigma_N^*) \leq r_i(\sigma_1^*,...,\sigma_{i-1}^*,\sigma_i^*,\sigma_{i+1}^*,...,\sigma_N^*) \tag{10}$$

Where r_i is the reward obtained by agent i.

The idea of Nash equilibrium, is that the strategy of each agent is the best response to the strategies of their colleagues and/or opponents (Kononen, 2004). Then, it is expected that learning algorithms can converge to a Nash equilibrium, and it is desired that can converge to the optimal Nash equilibrium, that is the one where the reward for all agents is the best.

We test and compare all paradigms using two repetitive games (The penalty problem and the climbing problem) (Barrios-Aranibar & Gonçalves, 2007a) and one stochastic game for two agents (Barrios-Aranibar & Gonçalves, 2007b). The penalty problem, in which IQ-Learning, JAQ-Learning and IVQ-Learning can converge to the optimal equilibrium over certain conditions, is used for testing capability of those algorithms to converge to optimal equilibrium. And, the climbing problem, in which IQ-Learning, JAQ-Learning can not converge to optimal equilibrium was used to test if IVQ-Learning can do it. Also, a game called the grid world game was created for testing coordination between two agents. Here, both agents have to coordinate their actions in order to obtain positive rewards. Lack of coordination causes penalties. Figure 2 shows the three games used until now.

In penalty game, k < 0 is a penalty. In this game, there exist three Nash equilibriums ((a0,b0), (a1,b1) and (a2,b2)), but only two of them are optimal Nash equilibrums ((a0, b0) and (a3, b3)). When k = 0 (no penalty for any action in the game), the three algorithms (IQ-Learning, JAQ-Learning and IVQ-Learning) converge to the optimal equilibrium with probability one. However, as k decrease, this probability also decrease.

	a0	a1	a2
b0	10	0	k
b1	0	2	0
b2	k	0	10

(a)

	a0	a1	a2
b0	11	-30	0
b1	-30	7	6
b2	0	0	5

(b)

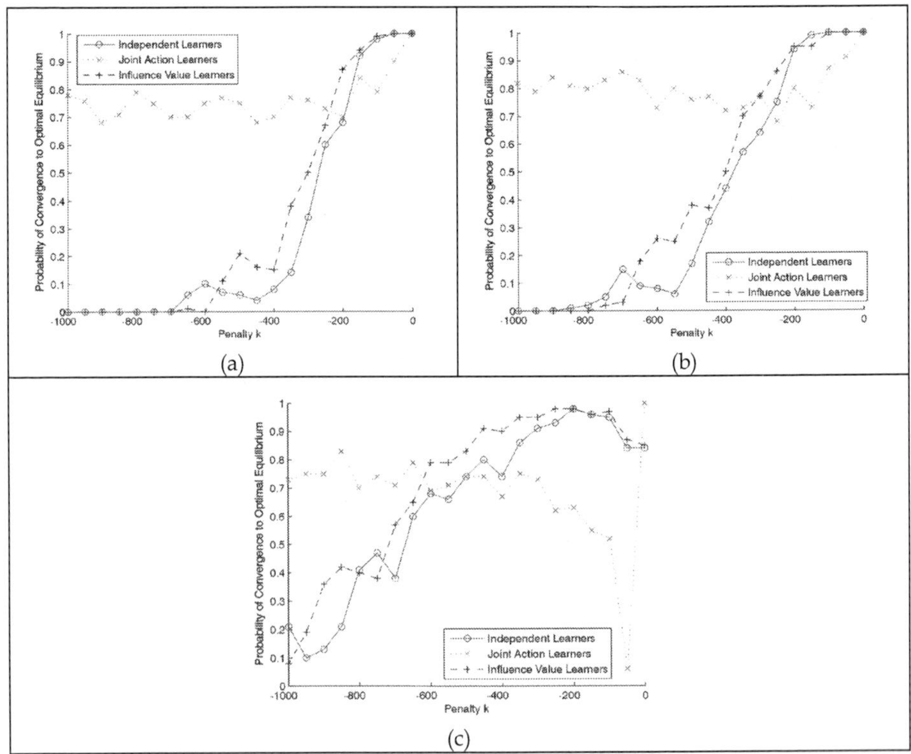

(c)

Fig. 2. Games used for testing performance of paradigms for applying reinforcement learning in multi-agent systems: (a) Penalty game, (b) Climbing game, (c) Grid world game.

Figure 3 compiles results obtained by these three algorithms in the penalty game, all of them was executed with the same conditions: A Boltzman action selection strategy with initial temperature T = 16, λ = 0.1 and in the case of IVQ-Learning β = 0.05. Also, a varying decaying rate for T was defined and each algorithm was executed 100 times for each decaying rate.

Fig. 3. Probability of convergence to optimal equilibrium in the penalty game for λ = 0.1, β = 0.05 and (a) T = 0.998^t * 16, (b) T = 0.999^t * 16, and (c) T = 0.9999^t * 16.

In this problem JAQ-Learning has the best perform. But, it is important to note also that for values of k near to zero, IVQ-Learning and IQ-Learning performs better than the JAQ-

Learning, and for those values the IVQ-Learning algorithm has the best probability to converge to the optimal equilibrium.

The climbing game problem is specially difficult for reinforcement learning algorithms because action a2 has the maximum total reward for agent A and action b1 has the maximum total reward for agent B. Independent learning approaches and joint action learning was showed to converge in the best case only to the (a1, b1) action pair (Claus and Boutilier, 1998). Again, each algorithm was executed 100 times in the same conditions: A Boltzman action selection strategy with initial temperature T = 16, λ = 0.1 and in the case of IVQ-Learning β = 0.1 and a varying temperature decaying rate.

In relation to the IQ-Learning and the JAQ-Learning, obtained results confirm that these two algorithms can not converge to optimal equilibrium. IVQ-Learning is the unique algorithm that has a probability different to zero for converging to the optimal Nash equilibrium, but this probability depends on the temperature decaying rate of the Boltzman action selection strategy (figure 4). In experiments, the best temperature decaying rate founded was 0.9997 on which probability to convergence to optimal equilibrium (a0, b0) is near to 0.7.

The grid world game starts with the agent one (A1) in position (5; 1) and agent two (A2) in position (5; 5). The idea is to reach positions (1; 3) and (3; 3) at the same time in order to finish the game. If they reach these final positions at the same time, they obtain a positive reward (5 and 10 points respectively). However, if only one of them reaches the position (3; 3) they are punished with a penalty value k. In the other hand, if only one of them reaches position (1; 3) they are not punished.

This game has several Nash equilibrium solutions, the policies that lead agents to obtain 5 points and 10 points, however, optimal Nash equilibrium solutions are those that lead agents to obtain 10 points in four steps.

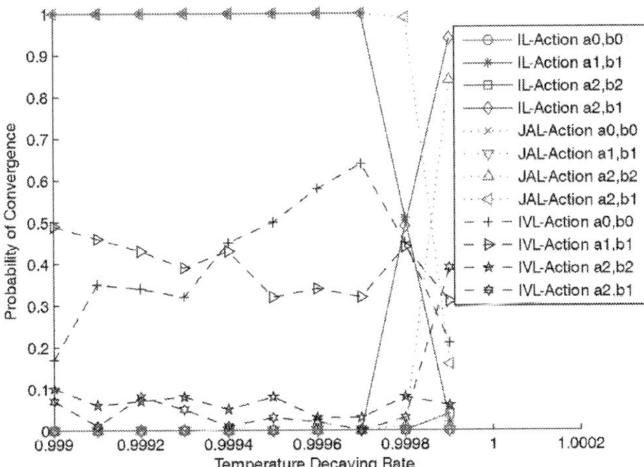

Fig. 4. Probability of Convergence in Climbing Game with λ = 0.1, β = 0.1 and Variable Temperature Decaying Rate

The first tested algorithm (Independent Learning A) considers that the state for each agent is the position of the agent, thus, the state space does not consider the position of the other agent. The second version of this algorithm (Independent Learning B) considers that the state space is the position of both agents. The third one is the JAQ-Learning algorithm and the last one is the IVQ-Learning.

In the tests, each learning algorithm was executed three times for each value of penalty k ($0 \leq k \leq 15$) and using five different decreasing rates of temperature T for the softmax policy (0:99t; 0:995t; 0:999t; 0:9995t; 0:9999t). Each resulting policy (960 policies, 3 for each algorithm with penalty k and a certain decreasing rate of T) was tested 1000 of times.

Figure 5 shows the probability of reaching the position (3; 3) with $\alpha=1$, $\lambda=0.1$, $\beta=0:1$ and T = 0:99t. In this figure, was observed that in this problem the joint action learning algorithm has the smaller probability of convergence to the (3; 3) position. This behavior is repeated for the other temperature decreasing rates. From the experiments, we note that the Independent Learning B and our approach have had almost the same behavior. But, when the exploration rate increases, the probability of convergence to the optimal equilibrium decreases for the Independent Learners and increase for our paradigm.

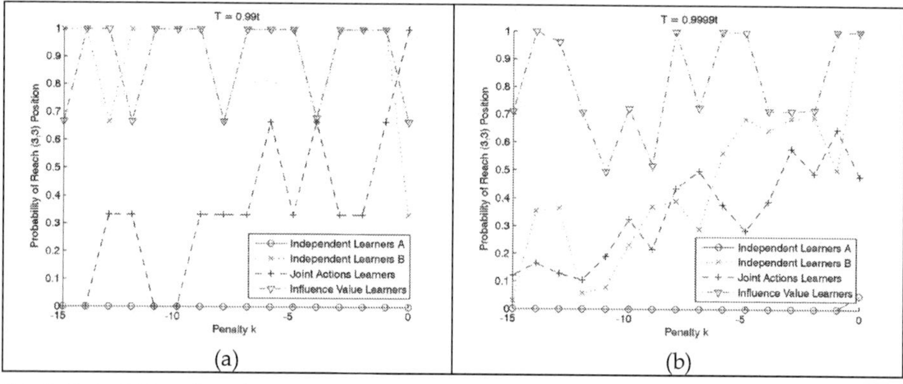

Fig. 5. Probability of reaching (3,3) position for (a) T = 0.99t and (b) T = 0.9999t

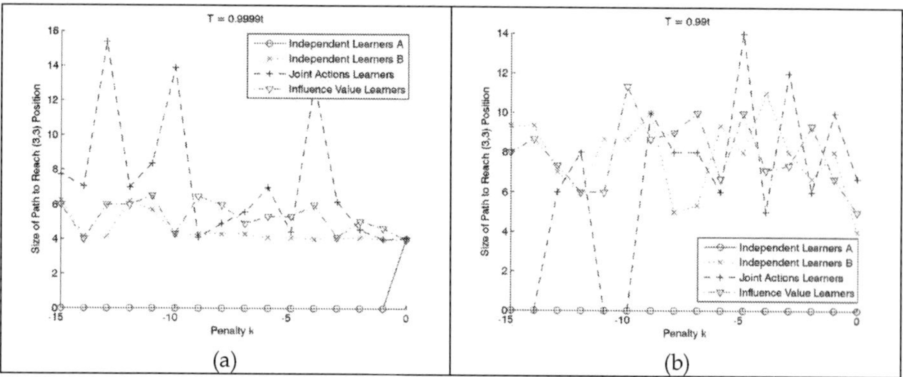

Fig. 6. Size of path for reaching (3,3) position for (a) T = 0.99t and (b) T = 0.9999t

As shown in figure 6, as more exploratory the action selection policy is, smaller is the size of the path for reaching (3; 3) position. Then, it can concluded that when exploration increases, the probability of the algorithms to reach the optimal equilibrium increases too. It is important to note that our paradigm has the best probability of convergence to the optimal equilibrium. It can be concluded by joining the probability of convergence to the position (3; 3) and the mean size of the path for reaching this position.

In order to test collaboration and self organization (automatic task assignment) in a group of reinforcement learning agents, authors created the foraging game showed in figure 7 (Barrios-Aranibar and Gonçalves, 2007c). In this game, a team of agents have to find food in the environment and eat it. When food in the environment no more exists, then, the game finishes. Initially, agents do not know that by reaching food they are going to win the game, then, they have to learn that eat food is good for them and also they have to learn to find it in the environment in order to win the game.

IQ-Learning, JAQ-Learning and IVQ-Learning were implemented in this problem with *20000* learning epochs. Also each algorithm was trained 10 times, and 3 different values of parameter α (*0.05, 0.1, 0.15*) were used. Because our approach (IVQ-Learning) has an extra parameter (β), it was trained with six different values: β=*{0.05, 0.1, 0.15, 0.2, 0.25, 0.3}*. Thus, we constructed 8 algorithms and trained it 10 times each one. For all algorithms, the parameter γ was chosen to be *0.05*.

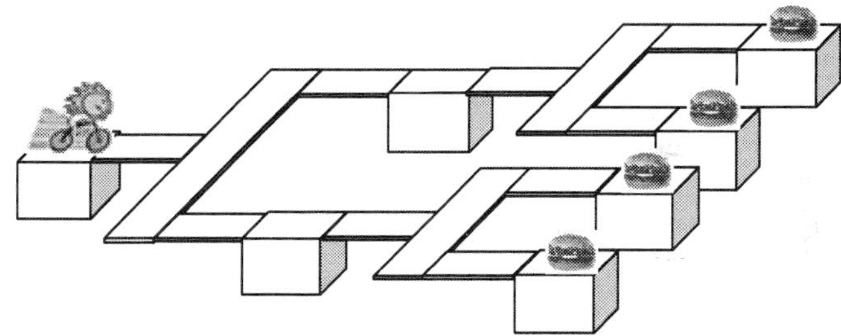

Fig. 7. Foraging game for testing collaboration between agents.

In figure 8.a, a comparison of these eight algorithms is showed. This comparison is based on the number of steps needed by the two agents to solve the problem. This value is calculated considering the mean of *100* tests for each algorithm and parameter α. In the optimal strategy the number of steps must be four. In this context, it was observed that our approach with parameters β=*0.15* and α=*0.15* had the best performance.

Figure 8.a shows the mean of number of steps need for each algorithm to solve the problem. But, in certain tests, the algorithms could converge to the optimal strategy (four steps). Then it is important to analyze the number of times each algorithm converge to this strategy. This analysis is showed in figure 8.b. In this figure, the percentage of times each algorithm converge to the optimal solution is showed. Again, it could be observed that our approach performs better. Also, the best IVQ-Learning was the one with parameters β=*0.15* and α=*0.15*.

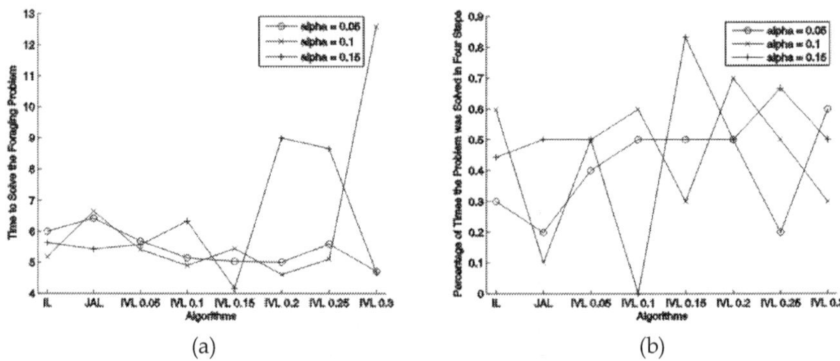

(a)   (b)

Fig. 8. Comparison between three paradigms when applyied to the foraging game.

6. Conclusion and future works

In this work, we explain the extension made to the Q-learning algorithm by using the influence value reinforcement learning paradigm. Also, we present a summary of all results obtained by comparing our approach with the IQ-learning and JAQ-learning algorithms. After analyse these results it is possible to note that our approach had advantages over the traditional paradigms and encourage authors to continue researching in this paradigm.

Also, our paradigm is an intend to solve the problem of convergence generated when applying Q-learning in multi-agent systems but in future works it is necessary to explore solutions for the problem related to the size of the state space.

7. References

Banerjee, D. and Sen, S. (2007). Reaching pareto-optimality in prisoner's dilemma using conditional joint action learning. *Autonomous Agents and Multi-Agent Systems* 15(1), 91–108.

Barrios-Aranibar, D. and Alsina, P. J. (2004), Reinforcement Learning-Based Path Planning for Autonomous Robots. In *I ENRI - Encontro Nacional de Robótica Inteligente no XXIV Congresso da Sociedade Brasileira de Computação*, Salvador, BA, Brazil, 08/2004.

Barrios-Aranibar, D. and Gonçalves, L. M. G. (2007a). Learning Coordination in Multi-Agent Systems using Influence Value Reinforcement Learning. In: *7th International Conference on Intelligent Systems Design and Applications (ISDA 07)*, 2007, Rio de Janeiro. Pages: 471-478.

Barrios-Aranibar, D. and Gonçalves, L. M. G. (2007b). Learning to Reach Optimal Equilibrium by Influence of Other Agents Opinion. In: *Hybrid Intelligent Systems, 2007. HIS 2007. 7th International Conference on*, 2007, Kaiserslautern. pp. 198-203.

Barrios-Aranibar, D. and Gonçalves, L. M. G. (2007c). Learning to Collaborate from Delayed Rewards in Foraging Like Environments. In: *VI Jornadas Peruanas De Computación - JPC 2007*.

Berenji, H. R. (1994), Fuzzy Q-learning: a new approach for fuzzy dynamic programming. In *Fuzzy Systems, 1994. IEEE World Congress on Computational Intelligence., Proceedings of the Third IEEE Conference on.* 26-29 June 1994. 1:486-491.

Carrascosa, C.; Bajo, J.; Julian, V.; Corchado, J. M. and Botti, V. (2008). Hybrid multi-agent architecture as a real-time problem-solving model. *Expert Systems with Applications.* 34(1):2-17.

Chen, D.; Jeng, B.; Lee, W. and Chuang, C. (2008). An agent-based model for consumer-to-business electronic commerce. *Expert Systems with Applications.* 34(1): 469-481.

Claus, C. and Boutilier, C. (1998). The dynamics of reinforcement learning in cooperative multiagent systems. In *Proceedings of the 15th National Conference on Artificial Intelligence -AAAI-98.* AAAI Press., Menlo Park, CA, pp. 746-752.

Dalamagkidis, K.; Kolokotsa, D.; Kalaitzakis, K. and Stavrakakis, G. S. (2007), Reinforcement learning for energy conservation and comfort in buildings. *Building and Environment.* 42(7):2686-2698.

Dearden, R.; Friedman, N. and Russell, S. (1998). Bayesian Q-learning. In *(1998) Proceedings of the National Conference on Artificial Intelligence.* 761-768.

Dimitriadis, S.; Marias, K. and Orphanoudakis, S. C. (2007). A multi-agent platform for content-based image retrieval. *Multimedia Tools and Applications.* 33(1):57-72.

Gu D. and Hu H. (2005). Teaching robots to plan through Q-learning. *Robotica.* 23: 139-147 Cambridge University Press.

Guo, R., Wu, M., Peng, J., Peng, J. and Cao, W. (2007). New q learning algorithm for multi-agent systems, *Zidonghua Xuebao/Acta Automatica Sinica,* 33(4), 367-372.

Ishibuchi, H.; Nakashima, T.; Miyamoto, H. and Chi-Hyon Oh (1997), Fuzzy Q-learning for a multi-player non-cooperative repeated game. In *Fuzzy Systems, 1997., Proceedings of the Sixth IEEE International Conference on.* 1-5 July 1997. 3:1573-1579.

Jars, I., Kabachi, N. and Lamure, M. (2004). Proposal for a vygotsky's theory based approach for learning in MAS. In *AOTP: The AAAI-04 Workshop on Agent Organizations: Theory and Practice.* San Jose, California. http://www.cs.uu.nl/virginia/aotp/papers/AOTP04IJars.Pdf.

Junhong N. and Haykin, S. (1999), A Q-learning-based dynamic channel assignment technique for mobile communication systems. *Vehicular Technology, IEEE Transactions on.* 48(5):1676-1687. Sept. 1999.

Kamaya, H.; Lee, H. and Abe, K. (2000), Switching Q-learning in partially observable Markovian environments. In *Intelligent Robots and Systems, 2000. (IROS 2000). Proceedings. 2000 IEEE/RSJ International Conference on.* 31 Oct.-5 Nov. 2000, 2:1062-1067.

Kapetanakis, S. and Kudenko, D. (2002). Reinforcement learning of coordination in cooperative multi-agent systems. In *Proceedings of the National Conference on Artificial Intelligence.* pp. 326-331.

Kapetanakis, S. and Kudenko, D. (2004). Reinforcement learning of coordination in heterogeneous cooperative multi-agent systems. In *Proceedings of the Third International Joint Conference on Autonomous Agents and Multiagent Systems, AAMAS 2004.* Vol. 3, pp. 1258-1259.

Kapetanakis, S., Kudenko, D. and Strens, M. J. A. (2003). Reinforcement learning approaches to coordination in cooperative multi-agent systems. *Lecture Notes in Artificial Intelligence (Subseries of Lecture Notes in Computer Science) 2636*, 18–32.

Kirchner, F. (1997), Q-learning of complex behaviours on a six-legged walking machine. In *Advanced Mobile Robots, 1997. Proceedings., Second EUROMICRO workshop on.* 22-24 Oct. 1997. 51 – 58.

Kononen, V. (2004). Asymmetric multiagent reinforcement learning. *Web Intelligence and Agent System* 2(2), 105 – 121.

Kok, J. R. and Vlassis, N. (2004). Sparse cooperative q-learning. In *Proceedings of the twenty-first international conference on Machine Learning.* Banff, Alberta, Canada, p. 61.

Laurent, G. and Piat, E. (2001), Parallel Q-learning for a block-pushing problem. In *Intelligent Robots and Systems, 2001. Proceedings. 2001 IEEE/RSJ International Conference on.* 29 Oct.-3 Nov. 2001. 1:286-291.

Lee, J.W.; Hong, E. and Park, J.(2004), A Q-learning based approach to design of intelligent stock trading agents. In *Engineering Management Conference, 2004. Proceedings. 2004 IEEE International.* 18-21 Oct. 2004. 3:1289–1292.

Mes, M.; van der Heijden, M. and van Harten, A. (2007). Comparison of agent-based scheduling to look-ahead heuristics for real-time transportation problems. *European Journal of Operational Research.* 181(1):59–75.

Maozu G.; Yang L. and Malec, J. (2004), A new Q-learning algorithm based on the metropolis criterion. *Systems, Man, and Cybernetics, Part B, IEEE Transactions on.* Oct. 2004. 34(5):2140-2143.

Millán, J. R.; Posenato, D. and Dedieu, E. (2002), Continuous-Action Q-Learning. *Machine Learning.* November, 2002. 49(2-3): 247-265.

Monekosso, N. and Remagnino, P. (2004), The analysis and performance evaluation of the pheromone-Q-learning algorithm. *Expert Systems* 21(2):80-91.

Morales , E. F. and Sammut, C. (2004), Learning to fly by combining reinforcement learning with behavioural clonning. In *Twenty-first international conference on Machine Learning,* ACM International Conference Proceeding Series. ACM Pres New York, NY, USA.

Murao, H.; Kitamura, S. (1997), Q-Learning with adaptive state segmentation (QLASS). In *Computational Intelligence in Robotics and Automation, 1997. CIRA'97., Proceedings., 1997 IEEE International Symposium on.* 10-11 July 1997. 179 – 184.

Oliveira, D. De and Bazzan, A. L. C. (2006). Traffic lights control with adaptive group formation based on swarm intelligence. *Lecture Notes in Computer Science (including subseries Lecture Notes in Artificial Intelligence and Lecture Notes in Bioinformatics) 4150 LNCS,* 520-521.

Ono, N.; Ikeda, O. and Fukumoto, K. (1996), Acquisition of coordinated behavior by modular Q-learning agents. In *Intelligent Robots and Systems '96, IROS 96, Proceedings of the 1996 IEEE/RSJ International Conference on.* 4-8 Nov. 1996. 3:1525-1529.

Park, K. H.; Kim, Y. J. and Kim, J. H. (2001), Modular Q-learning based multi-agent cooperation for robot soccer, *Robotics and Autonomous Systems.* 31 May 2001, 5(2): 109-122.

Ribeiro, R.; Enembreck, F. and Koerich, A. L. (2006). A hybrid learning strategy for discovery of policies of action. *Lecture Notes in Computer Science (including subseries Lecture Notes in Artificial Intelligence and Lecture Notes in Bioinformatics)*. 4140 LNAI: 268–277.

Rocha, R.; Dias, J. and Carvalho, A. (2005). Cooperative multi-robot systems: A study of vision-based 3-d mapping using information theory. *Robotics and Autonomous Systems*. 53(3-4):282–311.

Rooker, M. N. and Birk, A. (2005). Combining exploration and ad-hoc networking in robocup rescue. *Lecture Notes in Artificial Intelligence (Subseries of Lecture Notes in Computer Science)*. 3276:236–246.

Sen, S., Sekaran, M. and Hale, J. (1994). Learning to coordinate without sharing information. In *Proceedings of the National Conference on Artificial Intelligence*. Vol. 1, pp. 426–431.

Suematsu, N. and Hayashi, A. (2002), A multiagent reinforcement learning algorithm using extended optimal response. In *Proceedings of the International Conference on Autonomous Agents*. number 2, pp. 370–377.

Suh, I. H.; Kim, J. H. and Oh, S. R. (1997), Region-based Q-learning for intelligent robot systems. In *Computational Intelligence in Robotics and Automation, 1997. CIRA'97., Proceedings., 1997 IEEE International Symposium on*. 10-11 July 1997. 172-178.

Sutton, R. and Barto, A. (1998), *Reinforcement learning: an introduction*. MIT Press, Cambridge, MA, 1998.

Tanaka, T.; Nishida, K. and Kurita, T. (2007). Navigation of mobile robot using location map of place cells and reinforcement learning. *Systems and Computers in Japan*. 38(7), 65–75.

Tesauro, G. and Kephart, J. O. (2002), Pricing in Agent Economies Using Multi-Agent Q-Learning. *Autonomous Agents and Multi-Agent Systems*. September, 2002. 5(3): 289–304.

Toksari, M. D. (2007). Ant colony optimization approach to estimate energy demand of turkey. *Energy Policy*. 35(8):3984–3990.

Tsitsiklis, J. N. (1994), Asynchronous Stochastic Approximation and Q-Learning. *Machine Learning*. Kluwer Academic Publishers, Boston. 16(3): 185-202.

Tumer, K., Agogino, A. K. and Wolpert, D. H. (2002). Learning sequences of actions in collectives of autonomous agents. In *Proceedings of the International Conference on Autonomous Agents*. número 2, pp. 378–385.

Usaha, W. and Barria, J. A. (2007), Reinforcement learning for resource allocation in leo satellite networks. *IEEE Transactions on Systems, Man, and Cybernetics, Part B: Cybernetics*. 37(3): 515–527.

Vengerov, D. (2007), A reinforcement learning approach to dynamic resource allocation. *Engineering Applications of Artificial Intelligence*. 20(3): 383–390.

Vollbrecht, H. (2000), Hierarchic function approximation in kd-Q-learning. In *Knowledge-Based Intelligent Engineering Systems and Allied Technologies, 2000. Proceedings. Fourth International Conference on*. 30 Aug.-1 Sept. 2000, 2:466-469.

Watkins, C. J. C. H. (1989), *Learning from Delayed Rewards*. PhD thesis, Cambridge University, Cambridge, England.

Watkins, C. J. C. H. and Dayan, P. (1992), Q-Learning. *Machine Learning*. Kluwer Academic Publishers, Boston. 8(3-4): 279-292.

Xiong, G.; Hashiyama, T. and Okuma, S. (2002), An electricity supplier bidding strategy through Q-learning. In *(2002) Proceedings of the IEEE Power Engineering Society Transmission and Distribution Conference*. 3 (SUMMER): 1516-1521.

Zou L.; Xu, J. and Zhu, L. (2005). Designing a dynamic path guidance system based on electronic maps by using Q-learning. In *Proc. SPIE*. 5985, 59855A. International Conference on Space Information Technology. DOI:10.1117/12.658569,.

7

Reinforcement Learning in Generating Fuzzy Systems

Yi Zhou[1] and Meng Joo Er[2]

[1]School of Electrical and Electronic Engineering, Singapore Polytechnic
[2]School of Electrical and Electronic Engineering, Nanyang Technological University
Singapore

1. Introduction

Fuzzy-logic-based modelling and control is very efficient in dealing with imprecision and nonlinearity [1]. However, the conventional approaches for designing Fuzzy Inference Systems (FISs) are subjective, which require significant human's efforts. Other than time consuming, the subjective approaches may not be successful if the system is too complex or uncertain. Therefore, many researchers have been seeking automatic methods for generating the FIS [2].

The main issues for designing an FIS are structure identification and parameter estimation. Structure identification is concerned with how to partition the input space and determine the number of fuzzy rules according to the task requirements while parameter estimation involves the determination of parameters for both premises and consequents of fuzzy rules [3]. Structure identification and input classification can be accomplished by Supervised Learning (SL), Unsupervised Learning (UL) and Reinforcement Learning (RL). SL is a learning approach that adopts a supervisor, through which, the training system can adjust the structure and parameters according to a given training data set. In [4], the author provided a paradigm of acquiring the parameters of fuzzy rules. Besides adjusting parameters, self-identified structures have been achieved by SL approaches termed Dynamic Fuzzy Neural Networks in [3] and Generalized Dynamic Fuzzy Neural Networks in [5]. However, the training data are not always available especially when a human being has little knowledge about the system or the system is uncertain. In those situations, UL and RL are preferred over SL as UL and RL are learning processes that do not need any supervisor to tell the learner what action to take. Through RL, those state-action pairs which achieve positive reward will be encouraged in future selections while those which produce negative reward will be discouraged. A number of researchers have applied RL to train the consequent parts of an FIS [6.8]. The preconditioning parts of the FIS are either predefined as in [6] or through the ε-completeness and the squared TD error criteria in [7] or through the "aligned clustering" in [8]. Both DFQL and CQGAF methods achieve online structure identification by creating fuzzy rules when the input space is not well partitioned. However, both methods cannot adjust the premise parameters except when creating new rules. The center position and width of fuzzy neurons are allocated by only considering the input clustering. Moreover, both methods cannot delete fuzzy rules once they are generated even when the rules become redundant.

Since RL has been utilized as a good approach to generate well-matched state-action pairs for the consequent parts of an FIS, it is possible to train the premises and generate the structure of an FIS by RL as well. Thus, a novel algorithm termed Dynamic Self-Generated Fuzzy Q-learning (DSGFQL) which is capable of automatically generating and pruning fuzzy rules as well as tuning the premise parameters of an FIS by RL is presented.

2. Architecture of the fuzzy controlling system

The architecture of the fuzzy controlling system is based on extended Ellipsoidal Basis Function (EBF) neural networks, which are functionally equivalent to a simple Takagi-Sugeno-Kan (TSK) fuzzy systems [4]. The neural networks structure of the DSGFQL system is depicted in Figure 1.

Layer one is an input layer and layer two is a fuzzification layer which evaluates the Membership Functions (MFs) of the input variables. Layer one takes in the senor information and normalizes the value to be in range [0,1]. The MF is chosen as a Gaussian function and each input variable x_i (i = 1, 2, ...,N) has L MFs given by

$$\mu_{ij}(x_i) = exp[-\frac{(x_i - c_{ij})^2}{\sigma_{ij}^2}] \quad i = 1, 2...N, j = 1, 2..., L \tag{1}$$

where μ_{ij} is the jth MF of x_i, while c_{ij} and σ_{ij} are the center and width of the jth Gaussian MF of x_i respectively. Layer three is a rule layer which decides controlling rules. The output of the jth rule R_j(j = 1, 2, ...L) in layer 3 is given by

$$f_j(x_1, x_2, ..., x_N) = exp[-\sum_{i=1}^{N} \frac{(x_i - c_{ij})^2}{\sigma_{ij}^2}] \quad j = 1, 2, ..., L \tag{2}$$

if multiplication is adopted for the T-norm operator.

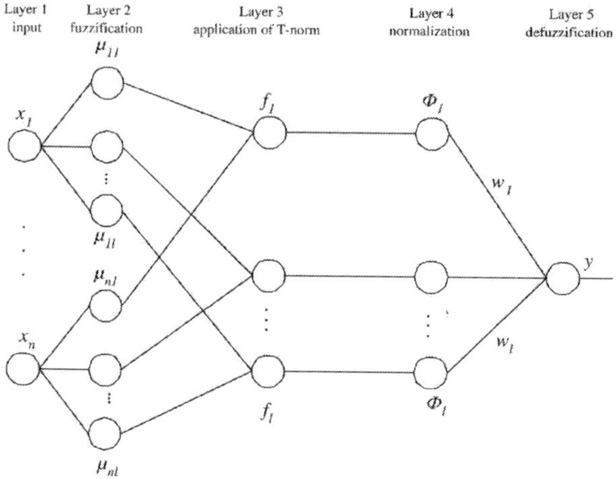

Fig. 1. Structure of the Fuzzy Controlling System

Normalization takes place in layer 4 and we have

$$\phi_j = \frac{f_j}{\sum_{i=1}^{L} f_i} \quad j = 1, 2, ..., L \tag{3}$$

Lastly, nodes of layer five define output variables. If the Center-Of-Gravity (COG) method is performed for defuzzification, the output variable, as a weighted summation of the incoming signals, is given by

$$y = \sum_{j=1}^{L} \phi_j \omega_j \tag{4}$$

where $\omega_j = a_j$ for the Q-learning-based FIS and a_j is the action selected through Q-learning in rule R_j.

Here, the antecedent parts of the fuzzy inference systems are regarded as states and the consequent parts are local actions of each controlling rules. Gaussian MFs are utilized to convert discrete states and actions to continuous ones.

Remark: It should be highlighted that the number of rules does not increase exponentially with the number of inputs as the EBF structure is adopted.

3. Fixed fuzzy Q-learning

We first consider the Fuzzy Q-Learning (FQL) approach of [6] that has a fixed number of fuzzy rule sets and the consequents of the rules can be adjusted based on the FQL. The local actions are selected through competitions based on local q-values which indicate the quality of actions at different states (in different fuzzy rule).

3.1 Local action exploration and selection

Here, we simply use the undirected exploration method employed in [6] to select a local action a from possible discrete action vector A, as follows:

$$a_\pi = \Pi_{a \in A}(q(S, a)) = argmax_{a \in A}(q(S, a) + \eta(S, a)) \tag{5}$$

The term of exploration η stems from a vector of random value ψ (exponential distribution) scaled up or down to take into account the range of q values as follows:

$$s_f = \begin{cases} 1 & if\ max(q) = min(q) \\ \frac{s_p(max(q) - min(q))}{max(\psi)} & otherwise \end{cases} \tag{6}$$

$$\eta = s_f \psi \tag{7}$$

where s_p is the noise size and s_f is the corresponding scaling factor. Decreasing the s_p factor implies reducing the undirected exploration. Details of the exploration-exploitation strategy can be found in [6].

3.2 Generation of global actions

As a learner may visit more than one fuzzy states, the system output/global action is determined by weighting all the local actions. Assume that L fuzzy rules have been generated. At time step t, the input state is X_t and the normalized firing strength vector of each rule is ϕ. Each rule R_i has M possible discrete actions and the local action of each rule is selected from the action set A by competing with each other based on their q-values. The winning local action a_i of every rule cooperates to produce the global action based on the rule's normalized firing strength ϕ. Therefore, the global action is given by

$$U_t(X_t) = \sum_{i=1}^{L} \pi_A(q_t)\phi_t^i = \sum_{i=1}^{L} \phi_i^t a_i^t \tag{8}$$

where a_i^t is the selected action of rule R_i at time step t and U_t is the global action which is the same as y in Eq (2).

3.3 Update of Q-value

As defined before, local q-value presents the action quality with respect to the state. In the FQL, global Q-values are also obtained similarly as the global actions and they are weighted value of the local q-values of those local winning actions. The global Q function is given by

$$Q_t(X_t, U_t) = \sum_{i=1}^{L} q_t(S_i, a_i^t)\phi_i^t \tag{9}$$

where U_t is the global action, a_i^t is the selected action of rule R_i and q_t is the q-value associated with the fuzzy state S_i and action a_i^t at time step t.

Q-learning is a type of Temporal Difference (TD) learning [9]. Based on the TD learning, the value function corresponding to the rule optimal actions is defined as follows:

$$V_t(X_t) = \sum_{i=1}^{L} (max_{a \in A} q_t(S_i, a))\phi_i^t \tag{10}$$

and the global TD error is given by

$$TD_{t+1} = r_{t+1} + \gamma V_t(X_{t+1}) - Q_t(X_t, U_t) \tag{11}$$

where r_{t+1} is the reinforcement signal received at time $t + 1$ and γ is the discounted factor utilized to determine the present value of future TD errors. Note that this TD error term only needs to be estimated with quantities available at time step $t + 1$.

This TD error can be used to evaluate the action just selected. If the TD error is positive, it suggests that the quality of this action should be strengthened for future use; whereas if the TD error is negative, it suggests that the quality should be weakened. The learning rule is given by

$$q_{t+1}(S_i, a_i^t) = q_t(S_i, a_i^t) + \alpha TD_{t+1}\phi_i^t, \quad i = 1, 2, ..., L \tag{12}$$

where α is the learning rate.

3.4 Eligibility traces

In order to speed up learning, eligibility traces are used to memorize previously visited stateaction pairs, weighted by their proximity at time step t [6, 7]. The trace value indicates how state-action pairs are eligible for learning. Thus, it permits not only tuning of parameters used at time step t, but also those involved in past steps.

Let $Tr_t(S_i, a_j)$ be the trace associated with the discrete action a_i of rule R_i at time step t

$$Tr_t(S_i, a_j) = \begin{cases} \lambda Tr_{t-1}(S_i, a_j) + \phi_i^t & if\ a_j = a_i^t \\ \lambda Tr_{t-1}(S_i, a_j) & otherwise \end{cases} \tag{13}$$

where the eligibility rate λ is used to weight time steps. For all rules and actions, the parameter updating law given by Eq (12) becomes

$$q_{t+1}(S_i, a_j) = q_t(S_i, a_j) + \alpha TD_{t+1} Tr_t(S_i, a_j), \quad i = 1, 2, ..., L, \ j = 1, 2, ..., M \tag{14}$$

and the traces are updated between action computation and its applications.

4. Dynamic self-generated fuzzy Q-learning

In this chapter, a Dynamic Self-Generated Fuzzy Q-Learning (DSGFQL) is presented to automatically determine fuzzy controllers based on reinforcement learning. In the DSGFQL method, fuzzy rules are to be created, adjusted and deleted automatically and dynamically according to the system performance and the contributions of each fuzzy rules.

4.1 ε-Completeness criterion for input space partitioning

In the DSGFQL approach, the input variable fuzzy sets are used to represent appropriate high-dimensional continuous sensory spaces.

First of all, the ε-completeness criterion for judging clustering of the input space is adopted as in [3, 7, 8, 10]. As pointed out by the author of [8], a rule in a fuzzy controlling system corresponds to a cluster in the input space geometrically. An input data with higher firing strength of a fuzzy rule means that its spatial location is closer to the cluster center compared to those with smaller strengths. The definition of the ε-completeness of fuzzy rules is given in [10] as:

For any input in the operating range, there exists at least one fuzzy rule so that the match degree (or firing strength) is no less than ε.

The ε-completeness criterion is to check whether the whole input space has been completely covered with a certain degree (ε). If the criterion is not satisfied, it means more fuzzy rules should be created to accomplish the input space.

4.2 Allocation of newly generated rules
4.2.1 Assignment of membership functions

If the existing system does not satisfy the ε-completeness criterion, a new rule should be considered. If the existing fuzzy system passes a similarity test [5, 7], a new Gaussian MF is allocated whose center is with

$$c_{i(L+1)} = x_i \tag{15}$$

and the widths of MFs in the ith input variable are adjusted as follows:

$$\sigma_{ik} = \frac{max(|c_{ik} - c_{i(k-1)}|, |c_{i,(k+1)} - c_{ik}|)}{\sqrt{ln(1/\epsilon)}}, \quad k = 1, ..., L+1 \tag{16}$$

where $c_{i(k-1)}$ and $c_{i(k+1)}$ are the two centers of adjacent MFs of the middle MF whose center is c_{ik}. Note that only the new MF and its neighboring MFs need to be adjusted. The main result concerning adjusting MFs to satisfy the ε-completeness of fuzzy rules has been proved in [2, 5]

4.2.2 Novel sharing mechanism for initialization of new q-values

Instead of randomly assigning q-values for the newly created rules, a novel initialization approach is presented here. In order to reduce the training time, the initial q-values for the newly generated fuzzy rule are set by the nearest neighbors. By this means, the newly generated rules learn/share the training experience from the neighboring rules. For instance, if rules R_m and R_n are the two nearest neighbors to the newly generated rule R_i, then

$$q(S_i, a_j) = \frac{q(S_m, a_j) f_m(C_i) + q(S_n, a_j) f_n(C_i)}{f_m(C_i) + f_n(C_i)}, \quad j = 1, 2, \cdots M. \tag{17}$$

where $f_m(C_i)$ and $f_n(C_i)$ stand for the firing strengths of the newly generated center C_i to rules R_m and R_n, which can be obtained from Eq (2).

4.3 Global TD error evaluation

The objective of RL is to maximize the expected value function. Q-learning is a TD-based approach which utilizes the TD error for updating the estimated reward value function. In TD-based methods, the estimated value function is updated, as in [9], as follows:

$$V(s) \longleftarrow V(s) + \alpha[r + \gamma V(s') - V(s)] \tag{18}$$

where $TD = r + \gamma V(s') - V(s)$ and $V(s)$ is the value function of state s.
Thus, we have

$$V(s) \longleftarrow V(s) + \alpha TD \tag{19}$$

If the initial value of $V(s, 0)$ is 0, the value function can be regarded as

$$\begin{aligned} V(s, k) &= \alpha \sum_{t=0}^{k} [r(t) + \gamma V(s', t+1) - V(s, t)] \\ &= \alpha \sum_{t=0}^{k} TD(t) \end{aligned} \tag{20}$$

It can be seen that the TD error estimates the value function and it becomes a criterion for measuring the learning system as well the performance of fuzzy controller. The bigger the TD error is, the greater the value function will be. Therefore, TD error can be considered as a criterion for measuring the system performance in RL.

As a criterion of system performance, the TD error is to be checked periodically, e.g. a number of training steps or an episode. At the end of each training episode or after several steps, the performance of the fuzzy system is examined by the TD error obtained during that period. Average TD error is adopted if the training environment is static. However, discounted TD error is to be considered for dynamic environment, i.e.

$$TD_{avg} = \begin{cases} \dfrac{\sum_{t=0}^{t=T} TD(t)}{T} & Static\ environment \\[2ex] \dfrac{\sum_{t=0}^{t=T} \gamma^t TD(t)}{T} & Dynamic\ enviroment \end{cases} \tag{21}$$

where T is the training time of each episode, $TD(t)$ is the TD error at time t and is the discounted factor which is less than 1.

By this means, the averaged system TD error is adopted as an index of the system performance.

4.4 Local TD error evaluation

Besides evaluation of system performance via reinforcement signals, contributions of each fuzzy rules are also measured through reinforcement signals in the DSGFQL system. In order to evaluate the individual contributions of each fuzzy rules, a local TD error criterion is adopted. By this means, contributions or significance of each fuzzy rules are evaluated through the local TD errors. Inspired from the TD error sharing mechanism in [11], a local TD error scheme is adopted here to share the reinforcement with each local rule according to its contributions. The local TD error for each fuzzy rule is given, similarly as in [11], as follows:

$$TD_j^{local}(t) = \phi_j^t r(t+1) + \gamma \phi_j^{t+1} \max_{a_j \in A_j} q_j^t(s^t, a_j) - \phi_j^t q_j^t(s^t, a_j^t) \tag{22}$$

where $j = 1, 2, ...,L$, and a_j^t is the action selected at time t.

Remarks: The local TD error adopted here is different from that in [11] in that the original form is multiplied by the firing strength of the corresponding fuzzy rule. In [11], the local TD error is used for selecting local actions while the local TD error is adopted as an evaluation criterion of individual rules in this thesis.

4.5 Reinforcement learning on input space partitioning

In the DSGFQL approach, the system/global TD error is selected as a measurement of system performance, the local TD error is adopted as an evaluation for individual contributions, while an averaged firing strength is adopted as a measurement for participation. If the averaged firing strength is lower than a threshold value, it means the significance of that rule is too low. Therefore, the rule can be eliminated to reduce the computational cost.

If the global TD error is less than a threshold value, it means that the overall performance of the entire system is unsatisfactory. Therefore, the FNNs need to be adjusted.

4.6 Restructure of FNNs via reinforcement learning

In the DSGFQL system, if the global average TD error is too negative e.g. it is less than a threshold value k_g, the overall performance is considered unsatisfactory. If the FNN passes the ε-completeness criterion but fails the average TD error test, it means that the input space is well partitioned but the overall performance needs to be improved.

To resolve this problem, the weights of some good rules should be increased which means that the system will be modified by promoting the rule with the best performance, e.g. the best local TD error, to a more important position. As a result, the overall performance is improved as the rules with good contributions participate more in the system while those rules with poor contributions participate less, correspondingly. In this case, the width of the jth fuzzy rule's MF (the one with the best local TD error) will be increased as follows

$$\sigma_{ij} \longleftarrow \kappa\sigma_{ij}, \qquad i = 1, 2...N \quad if \ \kappa\sigma_{ij} \leq \sigma_{max}$$
$$\longleftarrow \sigma_{max}, \qquad\qquad\qquad if \ \kappa\sigma_{ij} > \sigma_{max} \tag{23}$$

where κ is slightly larger than 1 and σ_{max} is the maximum width allowed for Gaussian MFs, which can be set to 1.2 if ε is chosen as 0.5 $\frac{1}{\sqrt{ln(1/\varepsilon)}}$).

Remarks: The restructuring is only adopted when the system under-performs. Enlarging the MF of the rule will increase the firing strength of the rule. As a result, the global action is improved by becoming closer to the best local action.

On the other hand, if the local TD error is larger than a heavy threshold value k_{lh}, but smaller than a light threshold value k_{ll}, a punishment will be given to the rule by decreasing its width of the MF as follows:

$$\sigma_{ik} \longleftarrow \tau\sigma_{ik}, \qquad i = 1, 2...N \tag{24}$$

where τ is a positive value less than 1.

Remarks: This is a performance-oriented approach, in which fuzzy rules with the best local TD error values are to be promoted and those with unsatisfactory local TD error are to be demoted or even removed from the system.

4.7 Pruning of redundant fuzzy rules

The local TD error criterion offers a direct evaluation of contributions of fuzzy rules. The more negative the local TD error is, the worse result is offered by the fuzzy rule and vice versa. Therefore, a fuzzy rule should be punished if the local TD error is extremely poor. If the local TD error of a fuzzy rule is less than a heavy threshold value k_{lh} ($k_{lh} < k_{ll}$), the individual contributions are unsatisfactory and the fuzzy rule will be deleted as a serious punishment.

Removing problematic fuzzy rules can help to improve the overall performance of the FNN and new rules may be generated if the ε-completeness criterion fails due to the elimination of rules at the next step. By this means, performance can be improved as "black sheep" has been eliminated and it is better to restart the learning rather than staying in the problematic region.

Besides the TD error, firing strength should also be considered for system evaluation as it is a measurement for participation. If a fuzzy rule has very low firing strength during the entire episode or a long period of time recently, it means that this rule is unnecessary for the system. As more fuzzy rules mean more computation and longer training time, the rule whose mean firing strength over a long period of time is less than a threshold value, k_f, should be deleted.

Remarks: If a fuzzy rule keeps failing the light local TD error check, its firing strength will be reduced by decreasing width of its MF. When the width is reduced to a certain level, it will fail the firing strength criterion and will be deleted. The light local test gives a certain tolerance, which means the fuzzy rule is not deleted due to one slight fault. However, the fuzzy rule which does not provide satisfactory result is still punished by being demoted and it will be deleted if it keeps failing the light local test.

4.8 Gradualism of learning

The values of the thresholds for the TD error criteria are set according to the expection of the task. At the early stage of training, each fuzzy rule needs time to adjust its own performance. For a training system, it is natural to set the demanding requirement small at the beginning and increase it later when the training becomes stable. Thus, the idea of gradualism learning in [12], which uses coarse learning in the early training stage and fine learning in the later stage, is adopted here. Moreover, the elimination process is frozen in the early stage and rules are only pruned after a certain period of time.

In this chapter, a linear gradualism learning is introduced and the values of the thresholds for global and local TD error are set as follows:

$$k_g = k_g^{min} + (k_g^{max} - k_{gr}^{min})\frac{episodes}{episodes + K_r} \tag{25}$$

$$k_{lh} = k_{lh}^{min} + (k_{lh}^{max} - k_{lh}^{min})\frac{episodes}{episodes + K_r} \tag{26}$$

$$k_{ll} = k_{ll}^{min} + (k_{ll}^{max} - k_{ll}^{min})\frac{episodes}{episodes + K_r} \tag{27}$$

where k_g^{min} and k_g^{max} are the minimal and maximal values for the global TD error threshold values respectively, k_{lh}^{min} and k_{lh}^{max} are the minimal and maximal values for the heavy local TD error threshold values respectively, and k_{ll}^{min} and k_{ll}^{max} are the minimal and maximal values for the light TD error threshold values respectively. The term *episodes* is the number of training episodes or periods and Kr is a controlling constant which can be set according to the number of training episodes. Those threshold values are set according to the target of the training system. If the total TD error (value function) is expected to be V in T training steps, the values of thresholds of the TD error criterion should be set around the value V/T. The maximal threshold values should be slightly bigger than the minimal ones as the system trained by the DSGFQL is supposed to obtain better results via the training. Another suggested guidance is to check the performances of some classical controllers (such as basic fuzzy Controller and FQL controller) and set the results as the minimal threshold values.

Remarks: The gradualism learning is optional for applying the DSGFQL method. The DSGFQL can also be applied with unique threshold values throughout the training, if users do not like to adjust the thresholds. Gradualism learning offers a framework or guideline in case that users are keen on adjusting the thresholds during the learning process.

5. The Khepera robot

The robot employed in this chapter is a miniature mobile robot called Khepera [13] shown in Figure 2. The Khepera mobile robot is cylindrical in shape, with 55 mm in diameter and 30 mm in height weighting only 70g. Its small size allows experiments to be performed in a small work area. The robot is supported by two lateral wheels that can rotate in both directions and two rigid pivots in the front and back.

Fig. 2. The miniature mobile robot: Khepera

The basic configuration of Khepera is composed of the CPU and the sensory/motor boards. The micro-controller includes all the features needed for easy interfacing with memories, with I/O ports and with external interrupts.

The sensory/motor board includes two DC motors coupled with incremental sensors, eight analogue infra-red (IR) proximity sensors denoted by $(S_0, ..., S_7)$ in Figure 3, and an on-board power supply. Each IR sensor is composed of an emitter and an independent receiver. The dedicated electronic interface uses multipliers, sample/holds and operational amplifiers. This allows absolute ambient light and estimation, by reflection, of the relative position of an object to the robot to be measured. By this estimation, the distance between the robot and the obstacle can be derived. This estimation gives, in fact, information about the distance between the robot and the obstacle. The sensor readings are integer values in the range of [0, 1023]. A sensor value of 1023 indicates that the robot is very close to the object, and a sensor value of 0 indicates that the robot does not receive any reflection of the IR signal.

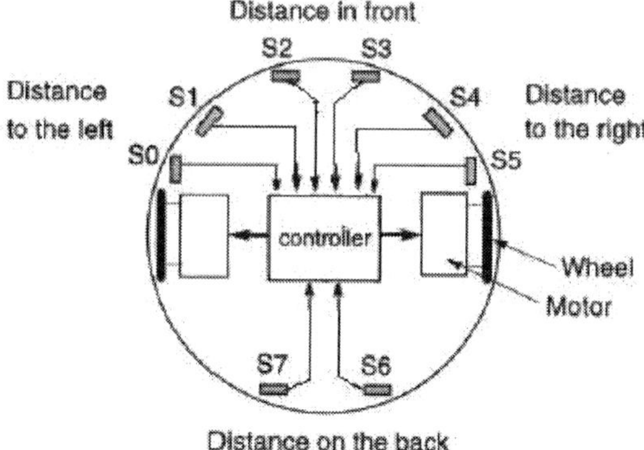

Fig. 3. Position and orientation of sensors on the Khepera

Simulation version of the Khepera [14] is used for carrying out a comprehensive numerical comparison of different approaches. The program simulates Kheperas in the MATLAB environment. Simulated Kheperas are controlled in the same way as real physical Kheperas. Simulation studies on a wall following task are presented in the following sections.

6. Wall following task for Khepera robot

In this chapter, the Khepera robot is to be applied for a wall-following task. The aim of the experiment is to design a controller for wall following. In order to simplify the problem, we only consider robots moving in clockwise direction at a constant speed as that in [7]. Thus, we only need to deal with four input variables, which are the values of sensor S_i (i = 0, 1, 2, 3). All these sensor values can be normalized within the interval [0, 1]. The output of the controller is the steering angle of the robot. In order for the robot to follow a wall, it must keep the distance from the wall while staying between a maximum distance, d_+, and a minimum distance, d_-. The distance to the wall being followed, d, can be calculated via the sensor values. The robot receives a reward evaluation after performing every action U. The reward function depends on this action and the next situation as given in [7]:

$$
r = \begin{cases} 0.1, & if (d_- < d < d_+) \; and \; (U \in [-8^o, +8^o]) \\ -3.0, & if (d \leq d_-) \; or \; (d_+ \leq d) \\ 0.0, & otherwise. \end{cases}
\tag{28}
$$

Here, d_- = 0.15 and d_+ = 0.85, which are normalized values, and U is the steering angle of the robot. These values are the same as the settings used in [7].

The training environment with lighted shaped walls used for simulation studies is shown in Figure 4.

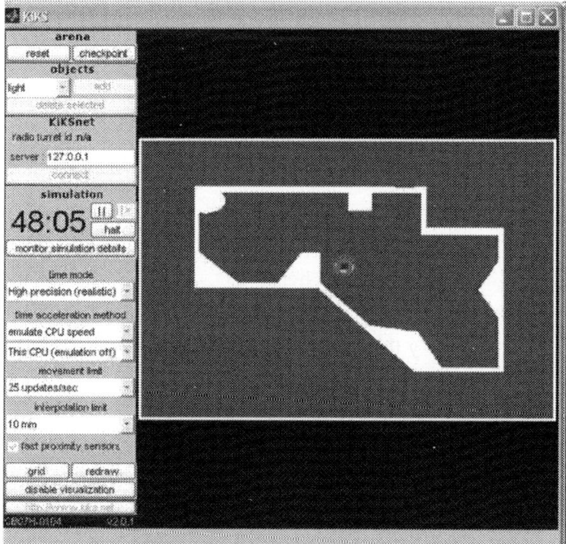

Fig. 4. MATLab simulation environment for wall-following experiments

The performances of different approaches are evaluated at every episode of 1000 control steps according to two criteria, namely the number of failures which correspond to the total number of steps the robot has left the "lane" and rewards which are accumulated. In order to compare the different approaches systematically and find appropriate parameters, we have done a number of comparison studies of these methods on simulations.

7. Simulation results and comparison studies

7.1 Basic fuzzy controller

First, a fuzzy controller based on intuitive experiences is designed. For each input linguistic variable, we define two linguistic values: *Small* and *Big*, whose MFs cover the region of the input space evenly with the match degree set to 0.5. This means that there are 16 (2^4) fuzzy rules. Through trial and error, 16 fuzzy rules are obtained as a special case of the TSK fuzzy controller, whose consequents are constant, as in [7]. The 16 fuzzy rules are listed in Table 1.

Rule	S_0	S_1	S_2	S_3	Steering angle
1	Small	Small	Small	Small	30
2	Small	Small	Small	Big	30
3	Small	Small	Big	Small	30
4	Small	Small	Big	Big	15
5	Small	Big	Small	Small	30
6	Small	Big	Small	Big	15
7	Small	Big	Big	Small	15
8	Small	Big	Big	Big	15
9	Big	Small	Small	Small	30
10	Big	Small	Small	Big	15
11	Big	Small	Big	Small	0
12	Big	Small	Big	Big	0
13	Big	Big	Small	Small	30
14	Big	Big	Small	Big	-15
15	Big	Big	Big	Small	-15
16	Big	Big	Big	Big	-15

Table 1. Basic fuzzy control rules for wall following

If the robot only uses the basic fuzzy controller, it can actually follow the wall, but along inefficient trajectories. When only the basic fuzzy controller is used, the robot encounters 79 failures and -164.0 of reward value per episode on average. Certainly, we can provide finer partitioning of the input space or tune the parameters of the MFs and consequents so as to obtain better performances. However, the number of rules will increase exponentially with increase in the number of input variables. Furthermore, tuning consequents of rules is time consuming because of the risk of creating conflicts among the rules. It is almost impossible or impractical to design an optimal fuzzy controller by hand due to a great number of variables involved. Therefore, automatic tuning and determination of fuzzy controlling rules are desired.

7.2 Simulation results for the FQL controller

The set of discrete actions is given by A = [-30, -25, -20, -15, -10, -5, 0, 5, 10, 15, 20, 25, 30]. The initial q-values for incorporated fuzzy rules are set as, k_q = 3.0. Other parameters in the learning algorithm are: Discounted factor, γ = 0.95; Trace-decay factor, λ = 0.7; TD learning rate, α = 0.05. The controller with 81 (3^4) fuzzy rules whose MFs is with 0.5 match degree of the input space is also considered. Average performances of the two controllers during 40 episodes over 30 runs are shown in Figures 5 and 6.

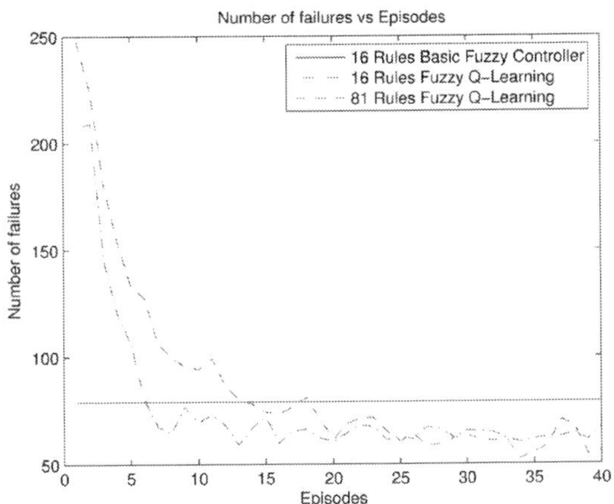

Fig. 5. Number of failures for comparison of performances of fuzzy controllers for (a)Basic fuzzy controller with 16 fuzzy rules, (b)16 fuzzy rules based on FQL, (c)81 fuzzy rules based on FQL

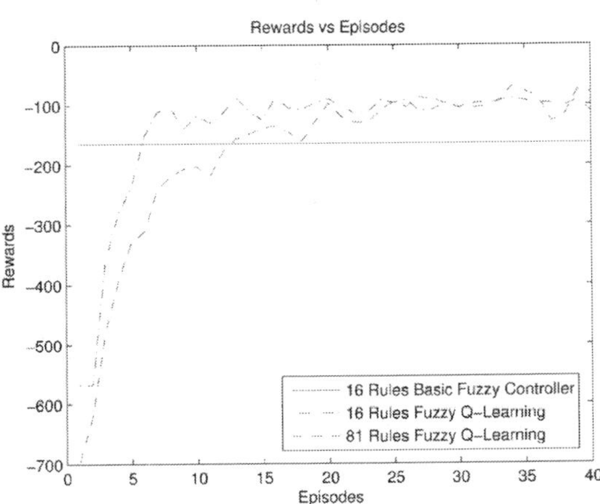

Fig. 6. Reward values for comparison of performances of fuzzy controllers for (a)Basic fuzzy controller with 16 fuzzy rules, (b)16 fuzzy rules based on FQL, (c)81 fuzzy rules based on FQL

At the very beginning, performances of the two controllers based on the FQL are worse than that of the basic fuzzy controller due to the exploration feature of RL. The robot has to explore different actions in order to ensure that better actions are selected in the future. However, the performance of the robot is improved gradually and is better than that of the basic fuzzy controller. Therefore, it can be concluded that performance can be improved by explorations in the action set and tuning consequent parameters.

To assess the effectiveness of finer partitioning of the input space, we compare the performances of the FQL using 16 rules and 81 rules. The speed of learning 81 rules is slower than that of 16 rules because a lot more parameters need to be explored. However, asymptotic performances of these two methods are almost the same. It is impractical to partition the input space further due to the curse of dimensionality. Therefore, automatic generation of premises of fuzzy controllers and automatic partitioning of input space are desired.

7.3 Simulation results of the DSGFQL controller

The DSGFQL is presented as a novel approach of determining premise parts of fuzzy controllers. In this section, the performance of the DSGFQL approach is to be assessed. The parameter values for consequents training are the same as those used in the FQL approach. Other learning parameters for rule generation are ε-completeness, $\varepsilon = 0.5$ and similarity of MF, $k_{mf} = 0.3$. The training aim is to limit the number of failures to 60; therefore, the threshold values of the TD error criterion should be set around $(-3 \times 60/1000) = -0.18$. If it requires each rule to be active at least with an average firing strength for 10 times in the 1000 training steps among about 50 rules, the firing strength threshold value is set as 10.(1000 $\times$ 50) = 0.0002. Therefore, the global TD error threshold values are $k_g^{max} = -0.05$ and $k_{lh}^{min} = -$ 0.45; heavy local threshold values are $k_{lh}^{max} = -0.10$ and $k_{lh}^{min} = -0.30$; light local TD error threshold values are $k_{ll}^{max} = 0$ and $k_{ll}^{min} = -0.20$; the firing strength threshold values are $k_f = 0.0002$ and $K_r = 20$, $\kappa = 1.05$ and $\tau = 0.95$. These values give good performances of the algorithms in an initial phase. However, it should be pointed out that we have not searched the parameter space exhaustively.

The performances of the DSGFQL approach shown in Figures 7 and 8 which are also the mean values during 40 episodes over 30 runs.

As expected, the DSGFQL performs better than the FQL with respect to both number of failures and reward values. The number of fuzzy rules generated at every episode is shown in Figure 9. The MFs produced by the DSGFQL after learning input variables at one run are shown in Figure 10. The number of rules can be generated automatically online and does not increase exponentially with the increase in the number of input variables. At the same time, MFs can be adjusted dynamically according to the performance of controlling rules. Thus, a compact and excellent fuzzy controller can be obtained online.

The reason why the DSGFQL method outperforms the FQL method is that the DSGFQL approach is capable of online self-organizing learning. Besides the input space partitioning, both overall and local performances have been evaluated to determine the structure of a fuzzy system. The common approach of conventional input-space partitioning is the socalled grid-type partitioning. The FQL with 16 rules partitions the state space coarsely, on the other hand, the speed of learning 81 rules is slow because a lot more parameters need to be explored. The DSGFQL does not need to partition the input space a *priori* and is suitable for RL. It partitions the input space online dynamically according to both the accommodation boundary and the reinforcement criteria. The compact fuzzy system considers sufficient rules in the critical state space which requires high resolution and does not include redundant rules in unimportant or unvisited state space so that learning is rapid and efficient.

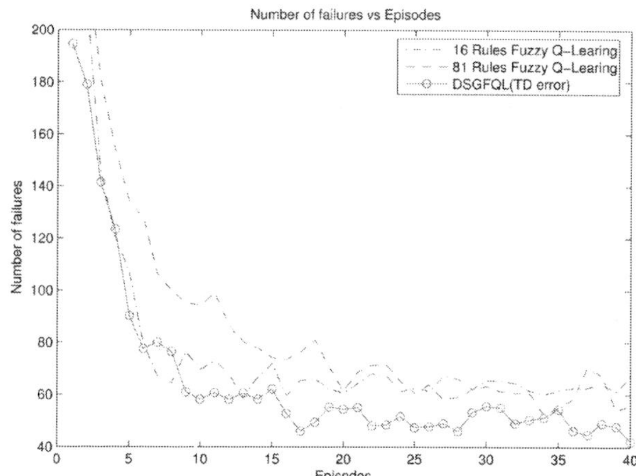

Fig. 7. Number of failures for comparison of performances of fuzzy controllers for (a) 16 fuzzy rules based on FQL, (b) 81 fuzzy rules based on FQL, (c) DSGFQL

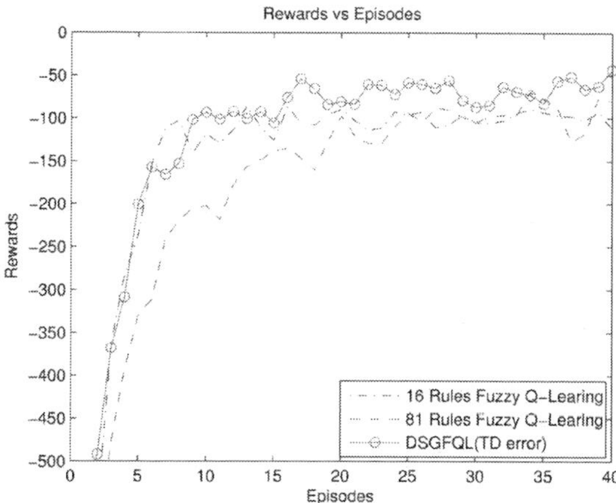

Fig. 8. Reward values for comparison of performances of fuzzy controllers for (a) 16 fuzzy rules based on FQL, (b) 81 fuzzy rules based on FQL, (c) DSGFQL

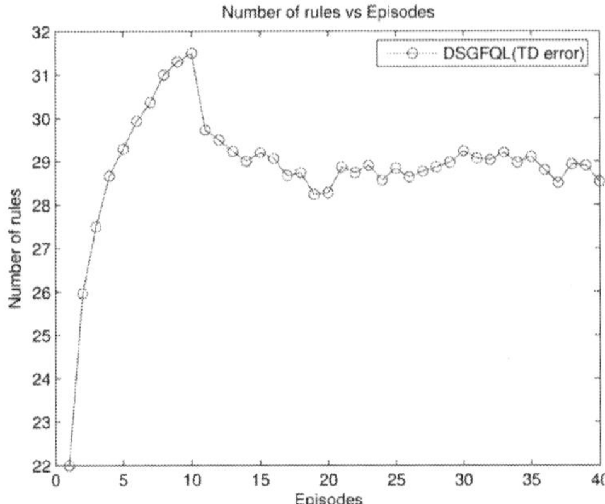

Fig. 9. Number of rules generated by the DSGFQL approach

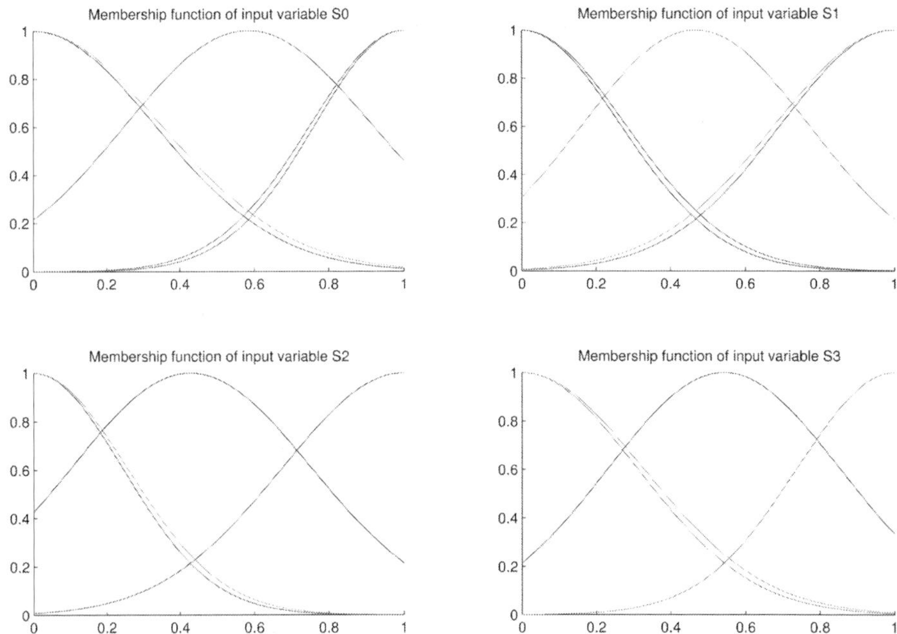

Fig. 10. Membership functions after learning at one run

8. Conclusions

In this chapter, a novel reinforcement learning method termed (DSGFQL) is introduced for navigation tasks of mobile robots. In the DSGFQL approach, continuous sensory states and action space for mobile robots can be self-generated. Controlling rules are expressed in fuzzy logic and the rules can be generated, adjusted and pruned automatically and dynamically without a priori knowledge or supervised learning. Online clustering method is adopted for partitioning the input space (sensory space of robots) and fuzzy rules are generated automatically by reinforcement learning. In the DSGFQL, new rules are created if system fails the ε-completeness criterion. At the same time, contributions of existing rules are to be determined through a reinforcement sharing mechanism. When the performance of the control system is poor, controlling rules are adjusted according to reinforcement signals. Q-learning is adopted in selecting optimal local actions in each fuzzy rule and the system action is a weighted continuous action via fuzzy reasoning. Comparative studies with other fuzzy controllers on mobile robot navigation demonstrate that the DSGFQL method is superior.

9. References

[1] L. X. Wang, Universal approximation by hierarchical fuzzy systems, *Fuzzy sets and systems*, vol. 93, no. 22, pp. 223-230, 1998.

[2] M. J. Er, S. Wu, and Y. Gao, *Dynamic fuzzy neural networks: architectures, algorithms and applications*, McGraw-Hill, New York, 2003.

[3] S. Wu and M.J. Er, Dynamic fuzzy neural networks: A novel approach to function approximation, *IEEE Trans. on Systems, Man and Cybernetics, Part B*, vol. 30, no. 2, pp. 358-364, 2000.

[4] J. S. R. Jang, Anfis: Adaptive-network-based fuzzy inference system, *IEEE Trans. System, Man and Cybernetics*, vol. 23, no. 3, pp. 665-684, 1993.

[5] S. Wu, M.J. Er, and Y. Gao, A fast approach for automatic generation of fuzzy rules by generalized dynamic fuzzy neural networks, *IEEE Trans. on Fuzzy Systems*, vol. 5, no. 4, pp. 578-594, 2001.

[6] L. Jouffe, Fuzzy inference system learning by reinforcement methods, *IEEE Trans. Systems, Man, and Cybernetics, Part C*, vol. 28, no. 3, pp. 338-335, 1998.

[7] M. J. Er and C. Deng, Online tuning of fuzzy inference systems using dynamic fuzzy q-learning, *IEEE Trans on Systems, Man and Cybernetics, Part B*, vol. 34, no. 3, pp. 1478-1489, 2004.

[8] C. F. Juang, Combination of online clustering and q-value based ga for reinforcement fuzzy systems, *IEEE Trans on Fuzzy Systems*, vol. 13, no. 3, pp. 289-302, 2005.

[9] R. S. Sutton and A. G. Barto, *Reinforcement learning: an introduction*, The MIT Press, Cambridge, Massachusetts., 1998.

[10] C. C. Lee, Fuzzy logic in control systems: fuzzy logic controller, *IEEE Trans. System, Man and Cybernetics*, vol. 20, no. 2, pp. 404-435, Mar 1990.

[11] P. Ritthiprava, T. Maneewarn, D. Laowattana, and J. Wyatt, A modi_ed approach to fuzzy-q learning for mobile robots, in *Proc. IEEE International Conference on Systems, Man and Cybernetics*, 2004, vol. 3, pp. 2350 - 2356.

[12] K. B. Cho and B. H. Wang, Radial basis function based adaptive fuzzy systems and their applications to system identification and prediction, *Fuzzy Sets Syst.*, vol. 83, no. 3, pp. 325-339, 1996.

[13] S. A. K-Team, Switzerland, *Khepera 2 user manual*, 2002.
[14] T. Nilsson, [online]. avaiable: http://www.kiks.f2s.com.

8

Incremental-Topological-Preserving-Map-Based Fuzzy Q-Learning (ITPM-FQL)

Meng Joo Er[1], Linn San[1] and Yi Zhou[2]

[1]School of Electrical and Electronic Engineering, Nanyang Technological University
[2]School of Electrical and Electronic Engineering, Singapore Polytechnic
Singapore

1. Introduction

Reinforcement Learning (RL) is thought to be an appropriate paradigm to acquire policies for autonomous learning agents that work without initial knowledge because RL evaluates learning from simple "evaluative" or "critic" information instead of "instructive" information used in Supervised Learning. There are two well-known types of RL, namely Actor-Critic Learning and Q-Leaning. Among them, Q-Learning (Watkins & Dayan, 1992) is the most widely used learning paradigm because of its simplicity and solid theoretical background. In Q-Learning, Q-vectors are used to evaluate the performance of appropriate actions which are selected by choosing the highest Q-value in the Q-vectors. Unfortunately, the conventional Q-Learning approach can only handle discrete states and actions. In the real-world, the learning agent needs to deal with continuous states and actions. For instance, in robotic applications, the robot needs to respond to dynamically changing environmental states with the smoothest action possible. Furthermore, the robot's hardware can be damaged as a result of inappropriate discrete actions.

In order to handle continuous states and actions, many researchers have enhanced the Q-learning methodology over the years. Continuous Action Q-Learning (Millan et al., 2002) is one of the Q-Learning methodologies which can handle continuous states and actions. Although this approach is better than the conventional Q-Learning technique, it is not as popular as the Fuzzy Q-Learning (FQL) (Jouffe, 1998) because the former is not based on solid theoretical background. Whereas CAQL considers neighboring actions of the highest Q-valued action in generating continuous actions, the FQL uses theoretically sound Fuzzy Inference System (FIS). On the contrary, the FQL approach is more favorable than the CAQL. Thus, our proposed approach is based on the FQL technique.

The FIS identification can be carried out in two phases, namely structure identification phase and parameter identification phase. The structure identification phase defines how to generate fuzzy rules while the parameter identification phase determines premise parameters and consequent parts of the fuzzy rules. The FQL approach mainly focuses to handle parameter identification automatically while structure identification still remains an open issue in FQL. To circumvent the issue of structure identification, the Dynamic Fuzzy Q-Learning (DFQL) (Er & Deng, 2004) is proposed. The salient feature of the DFQL is that it can generate fuzzy rules according to the ε-completeness and Temporal Difference criteria so that a FIS can be tuned automatically. From the point of view of structure identification and parameter identification, the DFQL is one of the promising approaches for online learning. The drawback of the DFQL is that the fuzzy rules cannot be adjusted according to the input distribution changes. Once a fuzzy rule has been generated, the rule will remain at its initial position and the position of the rule is no longer adjusted. As a consequence, the DFQL can generate inappropriate and redundant rules. To circumvent this problem, the authors of Dynamic Self-Generated Fuzzy Q-Learning (DSGFQL) (Er & Zhou, 2008) proposed to modify membership functions of each rule and delete redundant rules after a certain amount of training process. However, the adjustment of fuzzy rules positions is not discussed in (Er & Zhou, 2008). In fuzzy clustering, the position of a fuzzy rule is also regarded as an important factor that governs the performance of a fuzzy rule. A further development of the DSGFQL termed Enhanced Dynamic Self-Generated Fuzzy Q-Learning (EDSGFQL) (Er & Zhou) uses the Extended SOM algorithm to overcome the deficiency of (Er & Zhou, 2008).

In this chapter, the Incremental-Topological-Preserving-Map-Based Fuzzy Q-Learning (ITPM-FQL) approach is presented. Structure identification is based on the ITPM approach so that fuzzy rules will relocate to their appropriate positions after rule generation. The ITPM approach is originally inspired by limitations of the SOM algorithm (Kohonen, 1982). The early development of online SOM algorithm is the Growing Neural Gas (GNG) (Fritzke, 1995). But, GNG inserts a neuron only after some fixed training steps. Thus, it is not suitable for online learning. In vain of this, the ITPM is developed for online learning and is used in CAQL of (Millan et al., 2002). Using the convergence property of SOM, the ITPM can automatically generalize the fuzzy rules. In addition, an adaptive learning rate is used to adjust the convergence rate of each rule. In the original GNG (Fritzke, 1995), the author used a constant learning rate. But constant learning rate for all neurons is found to be not suitable in many cases. In our context, some rules might be placed initially far from their appropriate locations and some are placed very near to their suitable positions. The rules which are far from their right positions should converge with a large learning rate while the rules which are near to their appropriate positions should be tuned with a smaller learning rate. Thus, we further employ the adaptive learning rate for each rule so that all the positions of fuzzy rules can be adjusted adaptively. Similar to (Er & Deng, 2004), (Er & Zhou, 2008) and (Er & Zhou), the ε-completeness criterion is adopted in order to generate the fuzzy rules when the input space is not well clustered.

2. Structure of ITPM-FQL

Similar to the DFQL (Er & Deng, 2004) , the architecture of ITPM-FQL system is also based on extended EBF neural networks which are functionally equivalent to Takagi-Sugeno FIS system which is shown in Figure 1.

Layer one is the input layer and it transmits the input variable x_i (i=1,2,…,n) to the next layer and Layer two carries out fuzzification of each input variable. The membership functions are chosen as a Gaussian function of the following form:

$$\mu_{ij}(x_i) = \exp\left[-\frac{(x_i - c_{ij})^2}{\sigma_{ij}^2}\right]$$

$$i = 1,2,…,n, \quad j = 1,2,…,l$$

(1)

where x_i is the input state at ith time, μ_{ij} is the jth membership function of x_i, c_{ij} is the centers and σ_{ij} is the width of the jth Gaussian membership function of x_i. Layer three is the rule layer. The number of nodes in this layer represents the number of fuzzy rules. The output of the jth rule R_j (j=1,2,... l) in Layer three is given by

$$f(x_1, x_2, ..., x_n) = \exp\left[-\sum_{i=1}^{n} \frac{(x_i - c_{ij})^2}{\sigma_{ij}^2}\right]$$

(2)

$$i = 1,2,...,n, \quad j = 1,2,...,l$$

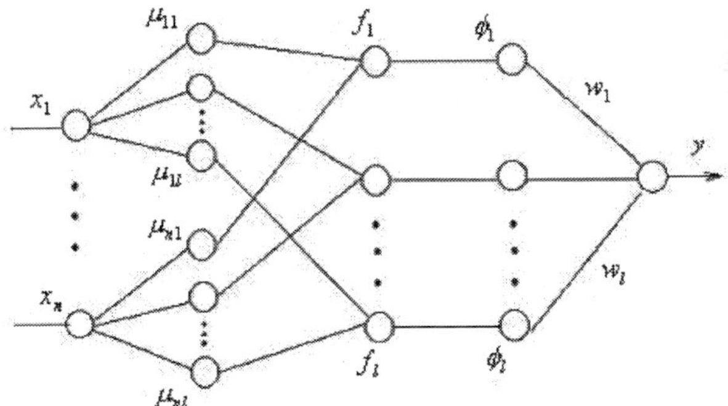

Fig. 1.1. Structure of fuzzy rule sets of ITPM-FQL.

Normalization takes place in Layer four and can be expressed as follows:

$$\phi_j = \frac{f_j}{\sum_{i=1}^{n} f_i} \qquad j = 1,2,....l$$

(3)

Layer five defines output variables by using the center-of-gravity method for defuzzificaiton.

$$y = \sum_{j=1}^{l} \phi_j w_j$$

(4)

where y denotes the value of an output variable and w_j is the consequent parameter of the jth rule. For the Q-learning based FIS, $w_j = a_j$ is the action selected through Q-learning in R_j.

3. Complete algorithm of ITPM-FQL

In order to understand the proposed ITPM-FQL algorithm, the readers should refer to the CAQL (Millan et al., 2002) and the GNG (Fritzke, 1995) and (Holmstrom) because the ITPM-FQL is an extension of the CAQL technique. Based on CAQL, we make some modifications to the ITPM so that it can be combined with the FQL approach. The complete algorithm of the ITPM-FQL is as follows:

1. Perceive the initial situation X_0, adopt the first fuzzy rule from the immediate input sensory data and initialize the width and Q-values according to initial built-in knowledge. Compute the action $U_0(X_0)$ based on its current knowledge.
2. Loop: Take computed action $U_{t-1}(X_{t-1})$.
3. Receive reward z_{t-1} and observe the next situation X_t.
4. Find the nearest M-distance unit (best matching fuzzy rule) b' for any X_t.
5. Compute the firing strength $f_j(X_t)$ for each rule.
6. Compute the TD error, update $V_t(X_t)$ and update Q-values of the previous action $U_{t-1}(X_{t-1})$ reward z_{t-1}.
7. If the ε-completeness is not satisfied (X_t is outside the Membership Function (MF) of unit b'), then
    a. If the MF similarity is not satisfied, the new unit u to the ITPM center on X_t and initialize the Q-values according to the built-in knowledge.
    b. Adjust the MF functions.
    c. Find the second nearest unit b'' to X_t and create the edge from newly added unit u to b' and b''. Remove the edge between b' and b'' if it exists.
    d. Find the best matching rule b' (i.e. $b' \leftarrow u$) and compute the firing strength $f_j(X_t)$ for each rule based on the new FIS structure.
    e. Reduce the local error K_{jt} of each rule with a very small factor (i.e. $K_{jt}= K_{jt} \times e_f$).
8. Use the Q-values and firing strength $f_j(X_t)$ of each rule, compute the global action $U_t(X_t)$.
9. Update the local error $K_{b't}$ and number of winning time $wt_{b't}$ of the nearest unit b' as follows:
    a. $K_{b't}=K_{b'(t-1)}+E\text{-}distance(b', X_t)$
    b. $wt_{b't}=wt_{b'(t-1)}+1$
10. Reinforcement Learning: Estimate the Q-value $Q(U_t,X_t)$ for global action $U_t(X_t)$ based on the firing strength $f_j(X_t)$.
11. Self Organization: Update the connectivity of the nearest unit b'.
    a. Find the second nearest unit b'' of X_t.
    b. Connect the edge between b' and b''. If it exists, set the age of this edge to zero.
    c. Increase the age of the rest of the edges to b' by one.
12. Move the sensory components of b' and its topological neighbors h to X_t'.
    a. Compute the learning rate $\eta_{b'}$ of unit b'.
    b. Move the sensory components of b'.

$$C_{b'}(t+1) = C_{b'}(t) + \eta_{b'}(t)\varphi_{b'}(X_t - C_{b'}(t))$$

    c. Compute the learning rate of the neighbour η_h.
    d. Move the sensory components of h.

$$C_h(t+1) = C_h(t) + \eta_h(t)\varphi_h(X_t - C_h(t))$$

13. Update the eligibility trace.
14. Remove the edges which are greater than the maximum age (a_{max}).
15. $X_{t-1} \leftarrow X_t$; $U_{t-1}(X_{t-1}) \leftarrow U_t(X_t)$; Go to step 2 if the training process is not finished.

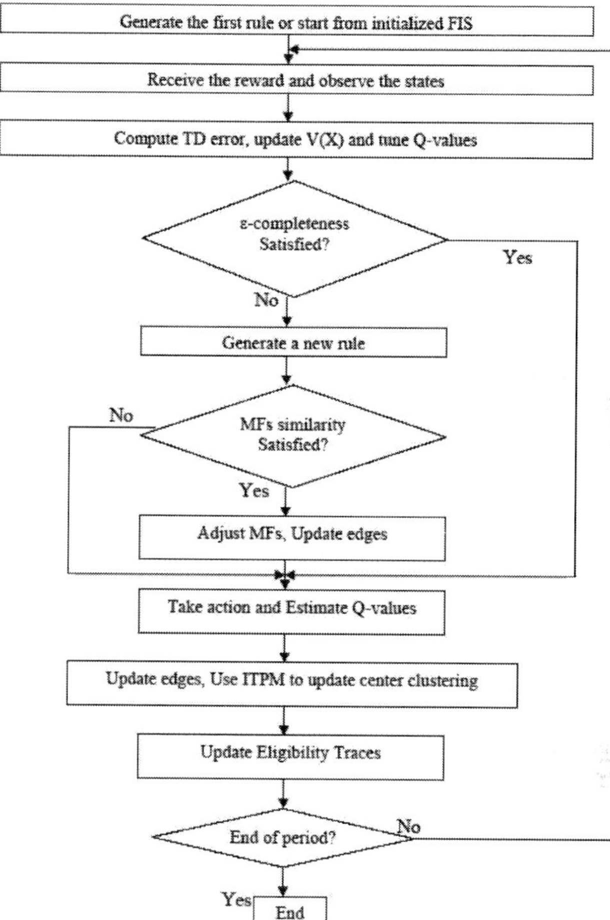

Fig. 2. Flowchart of ITPM-FQL algorithm.

3.1 ε- Completeness Criterion for Rules Generation

Generation of fuzzy rules in ITPM is only based on the ε-completeness and does not consider the performance index, which makes it difficult to obtain suitable values and is not applicable for non-TD-based RL methods. The generated fuzzy rules are later adjusted by means of the ITPM to their appropriate positions.

According to the ε-completeness, when an input vector $X \in R^{N}$ enters the system, the firing strength and M-distance between the current observation state X and centers C_j (j = 1, 2, 3,..., l) of the existing fuzzy rules can be calculated as follows:

$$f(J) = \phi_j = \exp(-md^2(j)) \tag{5}$$

Where

$$\sqrt{(X - C_j)^T \sum_j^{-1} (X - C_j)} \tag{6}$$

is the M-distance, $X = [x_1 \cdots x_n]^T \in \Re^n$, $C_j = [c_{1j}, c_{2j} \cdots c_{nj}]^T \in \Re^n$ and Σ_j^{-1} is defined as follows:

$$\Sigma_j^{-1} = \begin{bmatrix} \dfrac{1}{\sigma_{1j}^2} & 0 & \cdots & 0 \\ 0 & \dfrac{1}{\sigma_{2j}^2} & 0 & 0 \\ 0 & 0 & \ddots & 0 \\ 0 & \cdots & 0 & \dfrac{1}{\sigma_{nj}^2} \end{bmatrix} \qquad j = 1,2,\ldots,l \tag{7}$$

Next, find

$$J = \arg\min_{1 \le j \le l}(md(j)) \tag{8}$$

If

$$md_{min} = md(j) > k_d \tag{9}$$

where k_d is the predefined threshold of ε-completeness and is given by:

$$k_d = \sqrt{\ln(1/\varepsilon)} \tag{10}$$

and

$$f(J) < \exp(-k_d^2) = \exp(-(\sqrt{\ln(1/\varepsilon)})^2) = \varepsilon \tag{11}$$

This implies that the existing system does satisfy the ε- completeness criterion and a new rule should be considered. If the Euclidean distance does not pass the similarity test as mentioned in (Jouffe, 1998), no new rules will be created. Otherwise, a new fuzzy rule with Gaussian MFs is allocated with

$$C_{i(l+1)}(t) = x_i^t$$
$$\sigma_{ij} = \frac{\max(|C_{ij}(t) - C_{i(j-1)}(t)|, |C_{i(j+1)}(t) - C_{ij}(t)|)}{\sqrt{\ln(1/\varepsilon)}} \tag{12}$$
$$j = 1,2,3,\ldots,l+1$$

The basic idea of similarity process used in (Er & Deng, 2004) is to generate only one rule for a predefined topological area. This assumption is only suitable for low density data areas and not suitable for those areas which have high density data. High density data areas should be covered with more than one rule to get better performance. So, similarity restrictions should be relaxed on these areas. By applying the ITPM structure in FQL, the ITPM can adjust centre locations of the rules to their appropriate locations and also solve the similarity restriction problems.

3.2 Adaptive learning rate

The original ITPM algorithm (Millan et al., 2002) uses the constant learning rate which is not suitable in many real-world situations. The fuzzy rules will be generated according to the incoming sensory data when the ε-completeness and similar matching criteria failed. So, some of the fuzzy rules are initially located near to their appropriate locations while some are located far from their designated positions as mentioned in Section 1.1. Each rule should have an appropriate learning rate according to their initial positions.

A rule which is initially in a wrong location starts to be adjusted with a larger learning rate first and follows by a small learning rate when it is located in the neighborhood of its appropriate location. Similarly, a rule which is initially located in the neighborhood area of its appropriate position starts with a small learning rate to ensure that the rule can be finely tuned to its desired place. To circumvent the learning problem of the fuzzy rules, an adaptive learning scheme is proposed as follows:

$$\eta_{b'}(t) = \exp\left(-k_1\left(1 - \frac{\Lambda_{b'}(t)}{\Lambda_{\max}}\right)\right)k_2 \tag{13}$$

$$\eta_h(t) = \exp\left(-k_1\left(1 - \frac{\Lambda_h(t)}{\Lambda_{\max}}\right)\right)k_3 \tag{14}$$

where b' is the best matching fuzzy rule, h denotes the neighboring fuzzy rules of b' and $\eta_{b'}(t)$ and $\eta_h(t)$ are the individual learning rates of the best matching fuzzy rule and its neighboring rules at a particular time instance t. The terms k_2 and k_3 are the maximum adaptive learning rate and k_1 denotes the rate of change of the learning rate. The term $\Lambda_{\max}$ is the maximum error radius of a rule, the term $\Lambda_{b'}(t)$ and $\Lambda_h(t)$ is the error radius of b' and h fuzzy rules respectively and the error radius of each rule, as in (15), can be formulated as follows:

$$\Lambda_j(t) = \frac{\kappa_j(t)}{wt_j(t)} \qquad 1 \le j \le l \tag{15}$$

where $\kappa_j(t)$ is the accumulated local error and $wt_j(t)$ is the number of times won by the fuzzy rule at the time instant t. The terms $\kappa_j(t)$ and $wt_j(t)$ are computed as follows:

$$K = ed(b') \tag{16}$$

$$\kappa_{b'}(t+1) = \kappa_{b'}(t) + K \tag{17}$$

$$wt_{b'}(t+1) = wt_{b'}(t) + 1 \tag{18}$$

where b' is the best matching fuzzy rule.

The neighboring learning rate k_3 is usually used 100 times less than k_2 in order to favor the best matching rule. Similar to the Self Organizing Map, the adaptation process can be divided into self-organizing (rough-tuning) phase and convergence (fine-tuning) phase. At the convergence phase, the learning rate should be 20 times less than the maximum learning rate. Whether the fuzzy rules are in the convergence phase are decided by an error radius threshold Λ_{th} as shown in Figure 3. The term k_1 is computed according to (13) using Λ_{th}.

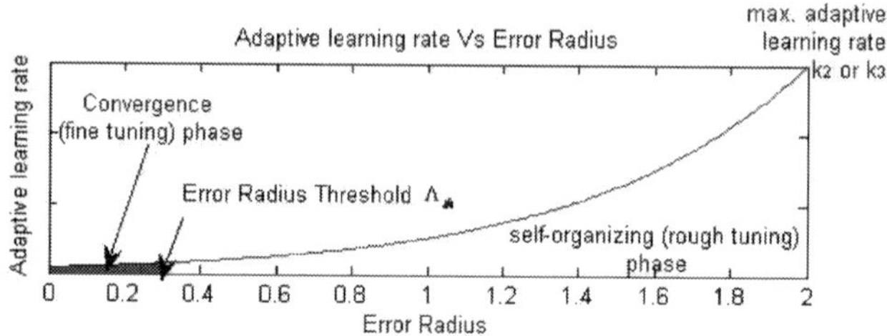

Fig. 3. Error-radius-based adaptive learning rate.

The proposed learning rate of the rule is based on the error radius of each rule because the error radius indicates the clustering ability of the rules.

3.3 Generation of global continuous action

In order to explore the set of possible actions and acquire experiences through reinforcement signals, the local action a_j for each rule R_j is selected using exploration-exploitation strategy as in (Jouffe, 1998), (Er & Deng, 2004), (Er & Zhou, 2008) and (Zhou & Er, 2008) from possible discrete actions set A as follows:

$$\pi_A(q) = \arg\max_{a \in A}\left(q(S,a) + \eta(S,a)\right) \tag{19}$$

where η denotes exploration, S is the state situation and a is the action in the action set A, and $q(S,a)$ is the q-value of action a at state S. Readers can refer to (Jouffe, 1998) and (Sutton, 1988) for details of the exploration-exploitation strategy. At time step t, the input state is X_t. Assume that l fuzzy rules have been generated and the normalized firing strength vector of rules is ϕ_t^j. Each rule R_j has m possible discrete actions A. Local actions selected from A compete with each other based on their q-values while the winning local action $U_t^j = a_t^j$ of every fuzzy rule cooperates to produce the global action $(U_t(X_t) = a_t)$ based on the rule's normalized firing strength, ϕ_j. The global action is given by

$$U_t(X_t) = \sum_{j=1}^{l} \pi_A(q_t)\phi_t^j = \sum_{j=1}^{l} a_t^j \phi_t^j \tag{20}$$

where a_t^j is the selected action of rule R_j at time step t.

3.4 Update of Q-values

Q-values are also obtained by the FIS outputs, which are inferred from the quality of local discrete actions that constitute the global continuous action. The Q function for global action $Q_t(X_t, U_t)$ is computed with the same assumption as that for generation of global continuous action, i.e.

$$Q_t(X_t, U_t) = \sum_{j=1}^{l} q_t\left(S_i, a_t^j\right)\phi_t^j \tag{21}$$

where U_t is the global action, a_t^j is the selected action of rule R_j at time step t and q_t is the q-value associated with the fuzzy state, state situation, S_i and action, a_t^j.

Based on TD learning, the Q-values corresponding to the rule optimal actions which defined as follows:

$$V_t(X_t) = \sum_{j=1}^{l}\left(\max_{a \in A} q_t(S_i, a)\right)\phi_t^j \tag{22}$$

The Q-values are used to estimate the following TD error:

$$\tilde{\varepsilon}_{t+1} = r_{t+1} + \gamma V_t(X_{t+1}) - Q_t(X_t, U_t) \tag{23}$$

where r_{t+1} is the reinforcement signal received at time $t+1$ and γ is the discount factor used to determine the present value of future rewards. Note that we have to estimate this error only with quantities available at time step $t+1$.

The learning rule based on the TD error is, as in (Jouffe, 1998) and (Er & Deng, 2004) , given by

$$q_{t+1}\left(S_i, a_t^j\right) = q_t\left(S_i, a_t^j\right) + \alpha\tilde{\varepsilon}_{t+1}\phi_t^j \qquad j = 1, 2, \ldots, l \tag{24}$$

where α is the learning rate.

3.5 Eligibility traces

In order to speed up learning, eligibility traces are used to memorize previously visited rule-action pairs weighted by their proximity to time step t. Let $Tr_t(S_i, a_j)$ be the trace associated with discrete action a_j of rule R_j at time step t. We have

$$Tr_t(S_i, a_j) = \begin{cases} \gamma\lambda Tr_{t-1}(S_i, a_j) + \phi_t^i & if \quad a_j = a_t^j \\ \gamma\lambda Tr_{t-1}(S_i, a_j) & otherwise \end{cases} \tag{25}$$

where the eligibility rate λ is used to weight time steps.

The parameter updating law given by Eq. (24) becomes, for all rules and actions,

$$q_{t+1}(S_i, a_j) = q_t(S_i, a_j) + \alpha\tilde{\varepsilon}_{t+1}Tr_t(S_i, a_j)$$
$$i = 1, 2, \ldots, n, \quad j = 1, 2, \ldots, l \tag{26}$$

and the traces are updated between action computation and its application.

4. Simulation studies and results

In order to compare the ITPM-FQL with other methodologies, an experimental study has been carried out on a Khepera II mobile robot (Nilsson, Online). The aim of the experiment is to design a controller for the mobile robot in order to follow the wall within the range of $[d_-, d_+]$. The environment which is exactly the same as in (Zhou & Er, 2008) is adopted and depicted in Figure 4. The same reward system, as in (Er & Deng, 2004), (Er & Zhou, 2008), (Er & Zhou) and (Zhou & Er, 2008) , has been adopted here and the reinforcement signal, r is given by

$$r = \begin{cases} 0.1, & if\,(d_- < d < d_+)\ and\ (U \in [-8°, +8°] \\ -3.0 & if\,(d \le d_-)\ or\ (d_+ \le d) \\ 0.0, & otherwise. \end{cases} \tag{27}$$

where $d_-=0.15$ and $d_+=0.85$ which are the same as in (Er & Deng, 2004) , (Er & Zhou, 2008) and (Zhou & Er, 2008).

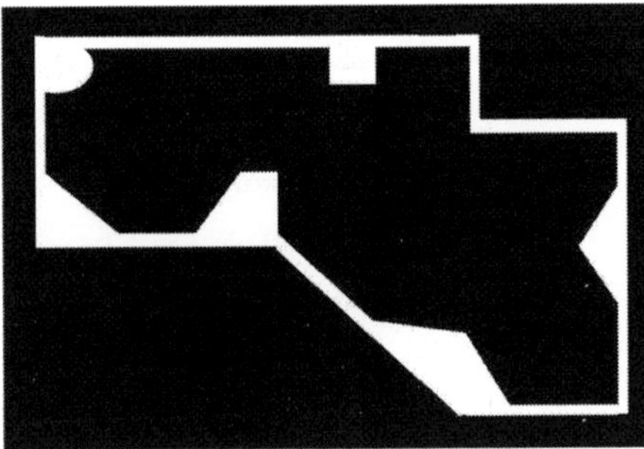

Fig. 4. The testing environment.

The performances of all methodologies are evaluated based on the number of failures and reward values at every episode of 1000 control steps as in (Er & Deng, 2004),), (Er & Zhou, 2008), (Er & Zhou) and (Zhou & Er, 2008) . In order to compare the performances, we use the mean values during 40 runs over 10 episodes. The same parameter settings, as in (Er & Deng, 2004) and (Zhou & Er, 2008) , are adopted, i.e. the FQL controller with 81 rules, whose MFs satisfy the 0.5 ε-completeness; initial Q value, $k_q = 3.0$; exploration rate, $S_p = 0.001$; discount factor, $\gamma = 0.95$; learning rate $\alpha = 0.05$; the specific distance range $[d_-,d_+] = [0.15,0.85]$ and set of discrete actions $A = [-30,-25,-20,-15,-10,-5,0,5,10,15,20,25,30]$. For CAQL, the width of the receptive field, k_r is set to 0.35, learning rate (winning unit) $\delta = 0.01$, learning rate (neighboring units) $\delta_r = 0.0001$ and the rest are the same as that of FQL-81 rules. For DFQL, the parameters are set as follows: $\varepsilon = 0.5$; similarity of membership, $k_{mf} = 0.3$ and the rest of the parameter settings are similar to FQL-81 rules. In the DSGFQL and EDSGFQL approaches, the global reward thresholds are set as $k_g^{max} = -0.05$ and $k_g^{min} = -0.45$; heavy local thresholds set as $k_{lh}^{max} = -0.10$ and $k_{lh}^{min} = -0.30$; light local reward thresholds values set as $k_{ll}^{max} = 0$ and $k_{ll}^{min} = -0.20$; firing threshold value is $k_f = 0.0002$; $K_r = 20$, $\kappa = 1.05$ and $\tau = 0.95$. Readers can refer to (Er & Deng, 2004), (Zhou & Er, 2008) and (Millan et al., 2002) for parameter settings in details. For the ITPM-FQL approach, the following parameters are set: the maximum age $a_{max} = 100$; similarity of membership, k_{mf} = 0.32 because it needs a larger value than the DFQL algorithm so that the fuzzy rules can be adjusted without causing many similarity matching rules; the maximum error radius Λ_{max}= 2; the error radius threshold Λ_{th} = 0.3 ($\Lambda_{th} \leq k_{mf}$) so that the fuzzy rule, which has the error radius less than k_{mf}, undergoes convergence phase; the rate of change of learning rate, k_1 = 3.5; the maximum adaptive learning rates are k_2 = 0.03 and k_3 = 0.0001; the error reducing factor e_f=0.995 and the rest of the parameters are the same as in (Er & Deng, 2004).

Figures 5 and 6 compare the performances of the robot during direct training by ITPM-FQL, DFQL, DSGFQL, EDSGFQL, CAQL and FQL-81 rules. Judging from the simulation results, we can conclude that the proposed approach of ITPM-FQL can produce better performance than the FQL-81 rules, CAQL and similar performances to the DFQL in terms of failures and

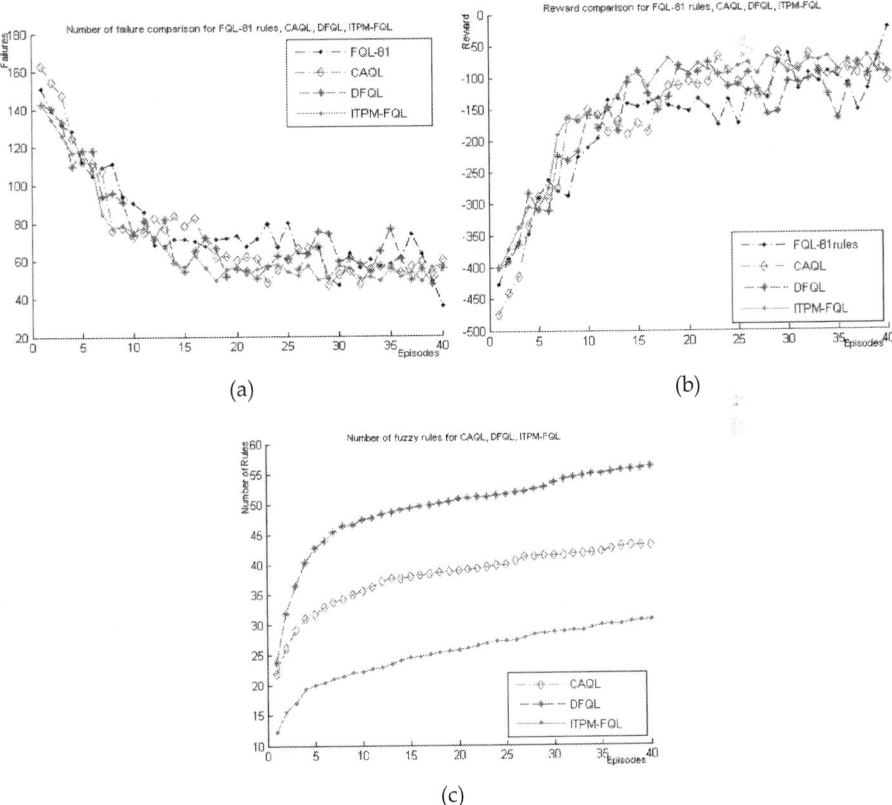

(a)

(b)

(c)

Fig. 5. Performance comparisons of ITPM-FQL, DFQL, CAQL and FQL-81 rules (a) Number of failures versus episodes (b) Reward values versus episodes (c) Number of generated fuzzy rules versus episodes.

reward criteria. From the point of number of generated fuzzy rules, the ITPM-FQL approach is better than other methodologies which do not have pruning capability because it uses not only the ε-completeness to generate the rules but also the convergence property for generalization of the rules. Comparing with the approaches which adopt pruning mechanism, especially EDSGFQL, the performance of ITPM-FQL is not desirable because it does not have the ability to fine tune fuzzy membership functions of the fuzzy rules and pruning mechanism. The main advantage of EDSGFQL is that it can delete unnecessary rules and maintain the requirement of rules within a certain region. But, the ITPM-FQL method achieves the same performance with significantly fewer numbers of rules than the DFQL.

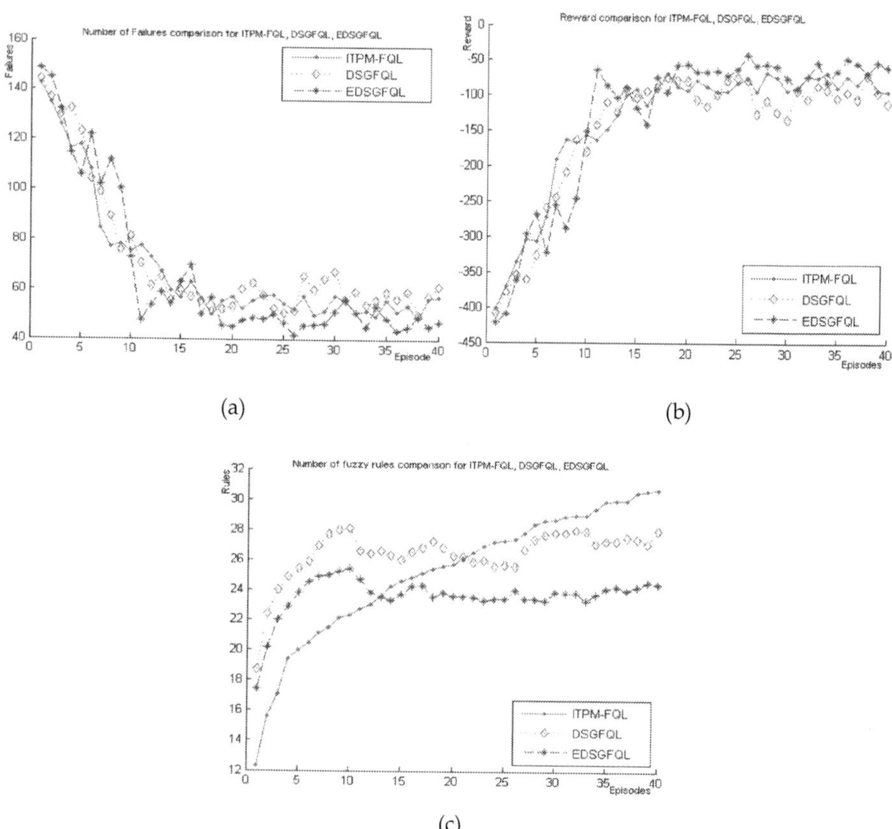

Fig. 6. Performance comparisons of ITPM-FQL, DSGFQL and EDSGFQL (a) Number of failures versus episodes (b) Reward values versus episodes (c) Number of generated fuzzy rules versus episodes.

5. Conclusions

In this study, a new Q-learning-based approach termed ITPM-FQL which can automatically generate and tune fuzzy rules based on the online SOM algorithm (ITPM) with ε-completeness criterion is proposed. Compared with the original CAQL approach, the ITPM-FQL uses the ε-completeness criterion instead of predefined Euclidean distance and fuzzy reasoning to generate continuous actions. To improve the generalizing ability, adaptive learning rate has also been adopted in the ITPM-FQL. Therefore, the ITPM-FQL is theoretically superior to the CAQL. Compared to the DFQL, the ITPM-FQL has convergence ability in generalizing fuzzy rules, which is lacking in the former approach. Comparative studies in the wall-following task show that the proposed method produces more desirable overall performance than the DFQL, CAQL and FQL approaches.

6. References

Chapter 15 Kohonen Network, Available: http://page.mi.fu-berlin.de/rojas/neural/.

Er M. J. & Deng C. (2004). Online Tuning of Fuzzy Inference Systems Using Dynamic Fuzzy Q-Learning, *IEEE Trans. on Systems, Man and Cybernetics*, vol. 34, no. 3, part B.

Er M.J. & Zhou Y. (2008). A Novel Framework for Automatic Generation of Fuzzy Neural Networks, *Neurocomputing*, Vol. 71, pp. 584-591.

Er M.J. & Zhou Y. Automatic Generation of Fuzzy Inference Systems via Unsupervised Learning Neural Networks, accepted for publication in *Neural Networks*.

Fritzke B. (1995). A Growing Neural Gas Network Learns Topologies, *Advances in Neural Information Processing Systems 7(NIPS)*, MIT Press, Cambridge MA, pp. 625-632.

Furao S. & Hasegawa O. (2006). An Incremental network for on-line unsupervised classification and topology learning, *Neural Networks*, vol.19, pp. 90-106.

Holmstrom J. Growing Neural Gas Experiments with GNG, GNG with Utility and Supervised GNG, *Uppsala Univ., Master's thesis*, Uppsala, Sweden.

Jouffe L.(1998) Fuzzy Inference System Learning by Reinforcement Methods, *IEEE Trans. on System, Man and Cybernetics*, vol. 28, no. 3, pp 338-355.

Kohonen T. (1982). Self-organized formation of topologically correct feature maps, *Biological Cybernetics*, vol 43, pp. 59 – 69.

K-Team S. A. (2002). Khepera II user manual, Switzerland.

Millan J. D. R.; Posenato D. & Dedieu E. (2002). Continuous-action learning, *Machine Learning*, vol. 49, no. 2-3, pp.247-265.

Nilsson T. (Online). Available: http://www.kiks.f2s.com.

Sutton R. S. (1988). Learning to predict by the methods of temporal differences, *Machine Learning*, vol. 3, pp 9-44.

Sutton, R. S. & Barto A. G .(1998). *Reinforcement learning: An Introduction.* The MIT Press,Cambridge, Massachusetts.

Watkins, C. J. C. H. & Dayan, P. (1992). Q-learning, *Machine Learning*, vol. 8, pp. 279-292.

Zhou Y. & Er M.J. (2008). A Reinforcement Learning Approach Towards Automatic Generation of Fuzzy Inference Systems, accepted for publication in *IEEE Trans on Systems, Man and Cybernetics, Part B, Special Issue on Adaptive Dynamic Programming/Reinforcement Learning.*

9

A Q-learning with Selective Generalization Capability and its Application to Layout Planning of Chemical Plants

Yoichi Hirashima
Osaka Institute of Technology
Japan

1. Introduction

Under environments that the criteria to achieve a certain objective is unknown, the reinforcement learning is known to be effective to collect, store and utilize information returned from the environments. Without a supervisor, the method can construct criteria for evaluation of actions to achieve the objective. However, since the information received by a learning agent is obtained through an interaction between the agent and the environment, the agent must move widely around the environment and keep vast data for constructing criteria when complex actions are required to achieve the objective. To conqure these drawbacks, function approximation methods that have generalization capability have had the attention as one of effective methods. The challenge of this chapter is focused on improving learning performances of the rainforcement learning by using a function approximation method, a modefied version of Cerebellar Model Articulation Controller (CMAC) (Albus, 1975a; Albus, 1975b), used in the reinforcement learning.

CMAC is a table look-up method that has generalization capabilities and is known as a function learning method without using precise mathematical models for nonlinear functions. Thus, CMAC is used to approximate evaluation functions in reinforcement learning in order to improve learning performance (Sutton & Barto, 1999; Watkins, 1989). In the CMAC, the numerical information is distributively stored at memory locations as weights. Each weight is associated with a basis function which outputs a non-zero value in a specified region of the input. The CMAC input is quantized by a lattice constructed by basis functions. In order to speed up learning and increase the information spread to adjacent basis functions, the CMAC updates a group of weights associated with basis functions that are close to a given point, and thus yields generalization capability. The concept of closeness stems from the assumption that similar inputs will require similar outputs for well-behaved systems. The structure of lattice determines how the CMAC input space is quantized and how the generalization works. However, the conventional CMAC has a fixed lattice and a fixed shape of region covered by the effects of generalization. Although the size of the region can be changed by adjusting the quantization intervals for lattice, the shape of the region is not adjustable. The required size and shape of the regions are not same for different cases, and thus, the CMAC has difficulties to obtain appropriate generalization for each case.

To conquer the drawback, a design method of CMAC that has a selective generalization capability is introduced. In this method, several CMACs are selected by extended input that can adjust the shape and size of region covered by the effects of CMAC generalization. The extended input is generated by a function obtained by using a priori knowledge of the addressed problem. By the proposed method, appropriate generalization can be obtained for cases that the conventional CMAC is not efficacious. The proposed method is applied to a allocation problem of a plant based on the fictitious chemical production plant as a case study. In chemical plants, layout of plant-elements should be determined considering at least the accessibility for maintenance and fire fighting, operability, and construction cost. From a pure safety perspective, tanks and reactors should be placed as far as possible from each other, in order to minimize the effect of a fire or explosion which a tank or reactor have on adjuscent equipment. But a larger distance between these elements of chemical plant, such as tanks and reactors, requires a larger pipe-length for connecting these elements and the efficiency of production and operation get worse. Hence in the layout of the chemical plant, there is a problem to minimize risk due to fires and explosions and maximize efficiency of production and operation simultaneously. Thus, the element allocation in a chemical plant is a multi-objective optimization problem. This problem was approached by using mathematical programming (Ceorgiadis et al, 1999; Vecchietti & Montagna, 1998). Or it may be considered to use Neural Network or Genetic Algorithm. But the problem has so many variables and freedoms to be chosen and also so many constraints among variables. Hence solving the problem by using those methods may take too much time and is not adequately efficient. Recently, a new reinforcement learning method has been proposed in order to solve allocation problem (Hirashima et al, 2002). The method is derived based on Q-learning (Watkins, 1989; Watkins, 1992) and hybrid-cordination that only a certain part of the plant-layout is recognized by the distance and rotational angle of each element measured from a `basis element'. In this method, rotated and/or shifted plants that have the same layout are identically recognized (Hirashima et al, 2005). The CMAC with selective generalization capability is integrated to this method, and effectiveness of the new CMAC is shown by computer simulations.

The remainder of this chapter is organized as follows: section 2 gives a detailed explanation of the CMAC that has selective generalization capabilities. Section 3 explains allocation problem of chemical plants. Section 4 presents a Q-learning method for plant allocation problem. Section 5 depicts and compares several results of computer simulations for a plant allocation problem. Finally, section 6 concludes the chapter.

2. CMAC

In this section, CMAC that has Selective Generalization capability (SG-CMAC) is explained. Assume the SG-CMAC has n inputs and 1 output. Define the input of SG-CMAC as

$$\mathbf{s} = (\mathbf{s}_I, s_z), \ \mathbf{s}_I = \{s_i\} \ (0 \le s_i < \Delta_i, i = 1, \cdots, n-1; 0 \le s_z < \Delta_z), \quad \text{where} \quad s_z = f(\mathbf{s}_I). \ s_z \ \text{is}$$

quantized with m areas and a corresponding CMAC module is assigned to each quantized area. CMAC modules used by the proposed method are same as the conventional CMAC. In the next subsection, the structure of CMAC modules is explained.

2.1 CMAC modules

Consider a basis function whose output is 1 when the input lies in its *support* and 0 otherwise. We define the size of the support as ρ for each axis. A set of k overlays is formed so that each of the module inputs is covered by k supports. The overlays are displaced by ρ relative to each other. Each overlay consists of the union of adjacent non-overlapping supports. Edges of supports generate knots, and the subset of knots constructs a square lattice of size ρ which quantizes the whole input space. The quantization interval ρ is determined by the size of the interval of neighboring knots, and it controls the degree of generalization.

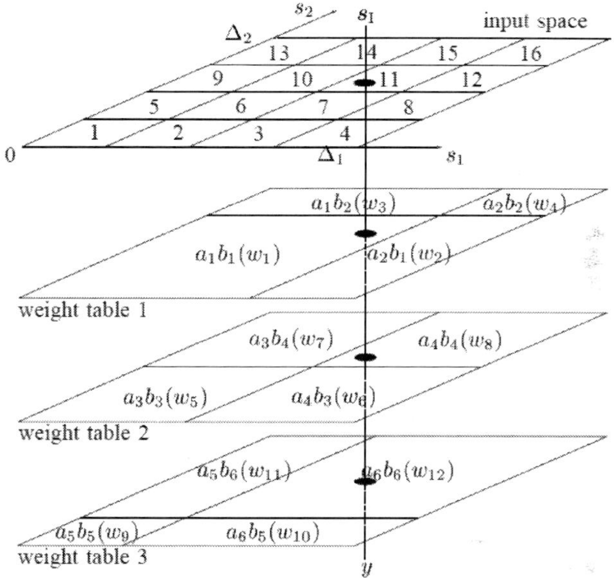

Fig. 1. Structure of a CMAC module

Fig.1 shows a CMAC module for the 2-dimensional input and 1-dimensional output consisting of 3 overlays and 12 basis functions. The lattice cells are numbered from 1 to 16. Assume the input to the CMAC module as $\mathbf{s}_I = \{s_1, s_2\}$ and the input space as $S = \{(s_1, s_2) \mid 0 \leq s_1 \leq \Delta_1,\ 0 \leq s_2 \leq \Delta_2\}$. Then s_1 and s_2 are quantized quantization interval ρ in the lattice. In the first overlay, s_1 is quantized into a_1 or a_2, and s_2 is quantized into b_1 or b_2, respectively. The pairs of $a_1 b_1$, $a_2 b_1$, $a_1 b_2$, $a_2 b_2$ express basis functions, and $a_2 b_2 (w_4)$ implies that the basis function $a_2 b_2$ has the weight w_4.

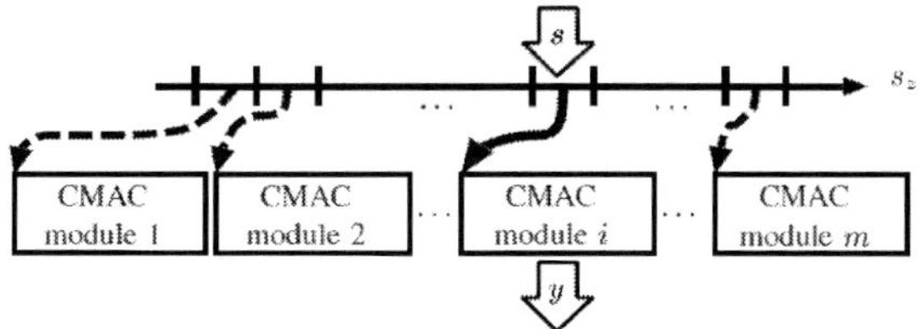

Fig. 2. Output of a SG-CMAC

2.2 Output of a SG-CMAC

The output of a module u is formed from a linear combination of basis functions. Given an input $\mathbf{s}=(\mathbf{s}_I, s_z)$ to the SG-CMAC, the input is quantized, the corresponding CMAC module is selected, a basis function is specified for each overlay in the selected module, and the weight value associated with the specified basis function is output from the overlay. The outputs of all the overlays are then summed up to yield the SG-CMAC output y, that is,

$$y = \sum_{j=1}^{k} w_j , \cdot \tag{1}$$

where w_j is the weight value associated with the basis function specified in the jth overlay.

In Fig.2, the input $(\mathbf{s}_I, s_z)$ is given to the SG-CMAC. Quantized value of s_z corresponds to the ith CMAC module. Then, $\mathbf{s}_I$ specifies a certain lattice cell in the CMAC module, for example the 11th cell as shown in Fig.1. In the figure, $\mathbf{s}_I$ specifies $a_1 b_1$, $a_4 b_4$ and $a_6 b_6$. Then, the module outputs $w_1 + w_8 + w_{12}$ as the output of SG-CMAC.

Suppose that the desired signal for the input $\mathbf{s}_I$ is d and the learning rate is g. The SG-CMAC is then learned by adding the following correction factor δ to all weights corresponding to $\mathbf{s}_I$ in the CMAC module specified by s_z:

$$e = d - y . \tag{2}$$

$$\delta = g \frac{e}{k} . \tag{3}$$

When giving two similar inputs to the CMAC module, several basis functions are commonly specified. The existence of such common basis functions yields generalization capability. Since the weights corresponding to the input $\mathbf{s}_I$ are only in the CMAC module specified by s_z, the degree of generalization is adjustable by the quantization intervals for s_z. In addition, the shape of the region covered by the effects of generalization can be determined by the shape of function $s_z = f(s_I)$.

2.3 Numerical examples

Effects of CMAC generalization are explained by numerical examples. An input $(\mathbf{s}_I, s_z)$ is given to CMACs that each module has the 2-dimensional input and 1-dimensional output consisting of 3 overlays and 27 basis functions. Here, $\Delta_1 = \Delta_2 = 7$, $\rho = 1$, $g = 0.1$, $\mathbf{s}_I = (3.5, 3.5)$, $d = 1.0$, and $m = 20$. After giving $\mathbf{s}$ once, generalizations of following 3 CMACs are compared:

(A) Conventional CMAC.

(B) Proposed SG-CMAC, $s_z = s_2 - s_1 \big|_{S_z = 0}$

(C) Proposed SG-CMAC, $s_z = s_2 - 1 - (s_1 - 2)^2 \big|_{S_z = 0}$

After k and ρ are determined, the shape of the region covered by the effects of generalization for an input is fixed in the CMAC (A) as shown in Fig.3. In this case, 3 weights specified by $\mathbf{s}_I$ are updated, so that the effect spreads over colored area in the right figure of Fig. 3. While, in CMACs (B) (C), the region that the effects of generalization spread

is restricted in the CMAC module specified according to the value of s_z, as illustrated in
Figs.4, 5. Thus, the shape and the quantization interval of s_z determins the degree of
generalization in the SG-CMAC.

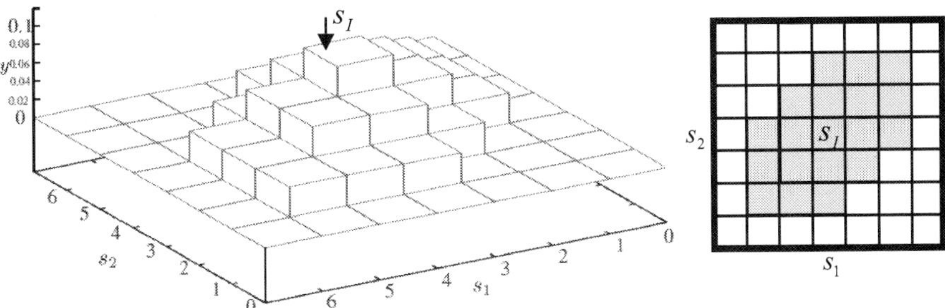

Fig. 3. Output of a CMAC (A)

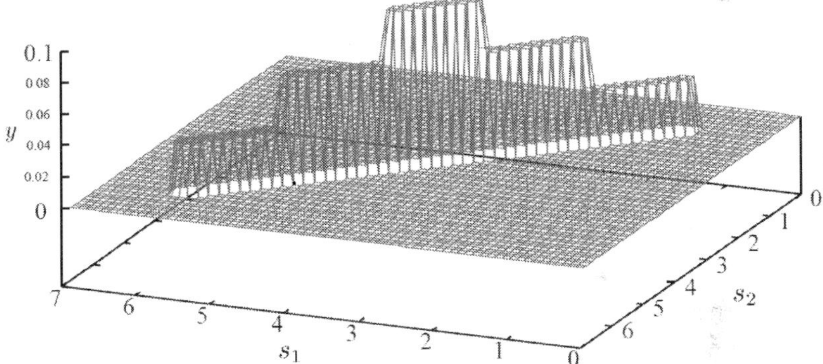

Fig. 4. Output of a SG-CMAC (B)

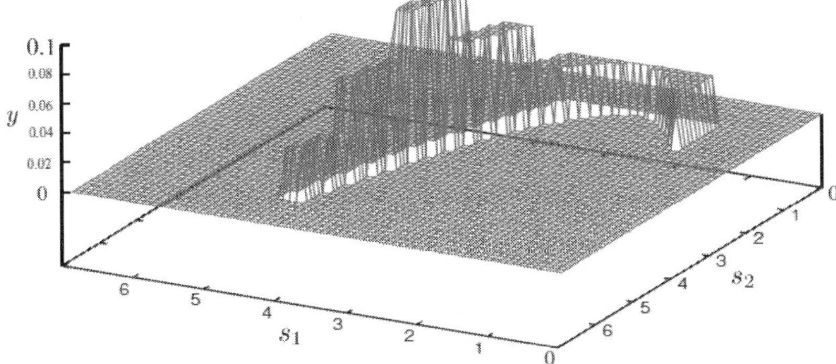

Fig. 5. Output of a SG-CMAC (C)

3. Allocation problem of chemical plant

As an application example, SG-CMAC explained above is used to solve an allocation problem of chemical plant. The objective of the problem is to minimize the total distance of the links under the constraint that the distance of two elements cannot be set smaller than a certain value in order to avoid influence of explosions. Precise roles of the elements included in the original plant are omitted in the simplified problem and every element is called ``unit''. Now, the allocation space is assumed to be normalized into square field, and quantized by square cells that have the same quantization interval. Also, assuming that the number of units is k_c, the number of lattice cells is m_c, each unit is recognized by an unique name c_j $(j=1,\cdots k_c)$ and the position where a unit is placed is discriminated by discrete position number $1,\cdots m_c$, then, the position of the unit c_j is described by d_j, $(j=1,\cdots k_c, 1 \le d_j \le m_c)$. The state of the allocation space is determined by $x = \left[d_1, \cdots, d_{k_c} \right]$. Here, if c_j is not allocated, $d_j = 0$. Since units are allocated into a lattice cell, the maximum number of candidate positions where a units can be allocated is m_c. The unit to be allocated is defined as c_T $(T = 1, \cdots k_c)$ and a position u that c_T is to be allocated is selected from candidate positions $(1, \cdots m_c)$. c_T must be allocated into a position where the distance $l_{Tj} (1 \le j \le k_c, T \ne j)$ between c_T and every other unit is larger than certain distances $L_{Tj} (1 \le j \le k_c, T \ne j)$. Then, the plant is described as $x' = f(x,u)$, where $f(\cdot)$ denotes that allocation of c_T is processed.

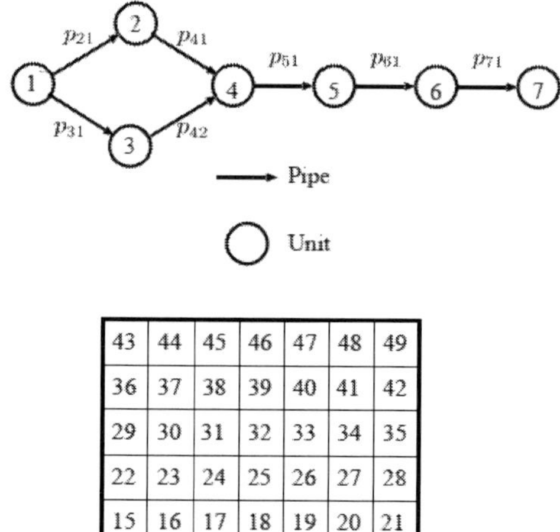

43	44	45	46	47	48	49
36	37	38	39	40	41	42
29	30	31	32	33	34	35
22	23	24	25	26	27	28
15	16	17	18	19	20	21
8	9	10	11	12	13	14
1	2	3	4	5	6	7

Unit allocation space

Fig. 6. Plant for allocation problem

Fig.6 shows an example of a plant, where m_c =49, k_c =7. In the figure, positions of units are discriminated by integer $1,\cdots,49$. p_{ij} $(i=1,\cdots,7;\ j=1,\cdots,n_T)$ denotes a length of jth intake pipe of ith unit, where n_T is the number of intake pipe to the ith unit. n_T is determined according to product process. In this example, the first unit is a mixer in which some raw materials are mixed before reaction in either of the two reactors (unit 2 or 3). These two reactors produce to intermediate products, which then react to produce the desired product in the next reactor (unit 4). After this reactor follows some purification steps. The first is a simple settler, which separates solids and liquids (unit 5). The desired product is assumed to be in the liquid phase, and is isolated in the crystallizers (unit 6 and 7). Two crystallization steps are needed to get the desired purity of the final product.

The objective of the proposed method is to find the plant layout that can reduce the total length of pipe with minimized risk.

4. A Q-Learning for plant allocation problem

In the conventional Q-learning algorithm, Q-table has to store evaluation-values for all the plant state. In unit allocation problems, the state of the allocation space is described by the positions of all the units x and c_T. Since units are allocated by predetermined order, c_T can be determined by units that have already allocated. A Q-value is thus stored for each pair $x = \lfloor d_1,\cdots,d_{k_c} \rfloor$ and u_i $(i=1,\cdots m_c)$. In this case, the number of states and Q-value is $\prod_{i=0}^{k_c}(m_c - i)$ that increases by the exponential rate with increase of k_c. Moreover, in realistic situations, the number of lattice cells is often large, then required memory size to store information for all the state of the allocation space also becomes large (Baum, 1999).

4.1 Update rules

The proposed learning procedure consists of 3 update rules: (1) to update Q_1 for evaluation of the position of unit 1, (2) to update Q_2 for evaluation of the position of units 1 and 2, (3) to update Q_T for evaluation of the positions of unit T ($T=3,\cdots k_c$). In the update rule (1), the input is the position of each unit u_i $(i=1,\cdots,m_c)$. $Q_1(u_i,x)$ is updated by eq. (4).

$$Q_{1_t}(u_i,x) = (1-\alpha)Q_{1_{t-1}}(u_i,x) + \alpha\gamma \max_{u\in U} Q_{2_{t-1}}(u,x). \tag{4}$$

In the update rule (2), $Q_2(u_i,x)$ is updated when all the units are successfully allocated to the space by using the following rule:

$$Q_{2_t}(u_i,x) = (1-\alpha)Q_{2_{t-1}}(u_i,x) + \alpha\gamma R. \tag{5}$$

In the update rule (3), the state is redefined by using the relative position of the rth unit pos_r $(r=2,\cdots k_c)$ measured from the position of unit 1 and the angle ϑ_r between the line that links units 1,2 and the line that link unit 1 and rth unit ($r=2,\cdots k_c, \vartheta_2=0$). That is, $x_R = \{x_r\}$ $(r=3,\cdots k_c)$ is the state of the allocation space for the update rule (3), where $x_r = [pos_r, \vartheta_r]$. Also, u_i is redefined as the relative position on the basis of x_R. Then $Q_T(u_i, x_R)$ is updated by eq. (6).

$$Q_{T_{t+1}}(u_i, x_R) = (1-\alpha)Q_{T_t}(u_i, x_R) + \alpha[R + \gamma \max_{u \in U} Q_{T_t}(u, x_R'), (T = 3, \cdots, k-1). \quad (6)$$

In plant allocation problems, the objective is to reduce the total pipe length in the allocation space. Thus, in the proposed system, Q-values reflect the pipe length by adjusting the discount factor γ according to the pipe length. In the following, $L_{ij}(i = 1, \cdots, k_c; j = 1, \cdots, n_T)$ is defined as the minimum length of the jth intake pipe of ith unit, and U is defined as a set of positions that satisfy constraints $l_{Tj} > L_{Tj}$ in the allocation space. Then, γ is calculated by using the following equations :

$$\gamma = \begin{cases} 1 & \text{(for update rule (1))} \\[2ex] \dfrac{\displaystyle\sum_{i=1}^{k_c}\sum_{j=1}^{n_T} L_{ij}}{\displaystyle\sum_{i=1}^{k_c}\sum_{j=1}^{n_T} l_{ij}} & \text{(for update rule (2))}. \\[4ex] \dfrac{\displaystyle\sum_{j=1}^{n_T} L_{ij}}{\displaystyle\sum_{j=1}^{n_T} l_{ij}}, (1 \le i \le k_c, i \ne 2) & \text{(for update rule (3))} \end{cases} \quad (7)$$

where n_T is the number of pipes that link c_T and allocated units, and $l_{ij}(j = 1, \cdots, n_T)$ is the length of the pipe that links c_T and the allocated unit. Here, R is given only when all the units has been allocated. Propagating Q-values by eqs.(4)-(6) as update rules, Q-values are discounted according to the pipe length. In other words, by selecting a position that has the larger Q-value, the length of pipe can be reduced. Each u_i is selected by the following probability (Sutton & Barto, 1999; Watkins, 1989) :

$$P(u_i, x_j) = \frac{\exp(Q_{t-1}(u_i, x_j)/C}{\displaystyle\sum_{u \in U} \exp(Q_{t-1}(u, x_j)/C}. \quad (8)$$

where C is a thermo constant. The learning algorithm is depicted in Fig.7.

4.2 Q-tables

In realistic problems the number of lattice cells is large, so that huge memory size is required in order to store Q-values for all the states. Therefore, in the proposed method, only Q-values corresponding states that have been searched are stored for unit i $(i = 3, \cdots k_c)$. Binary tree is constructed dynamically (Hirashima et al., 2005) during the course of the learning for storing Q-values.

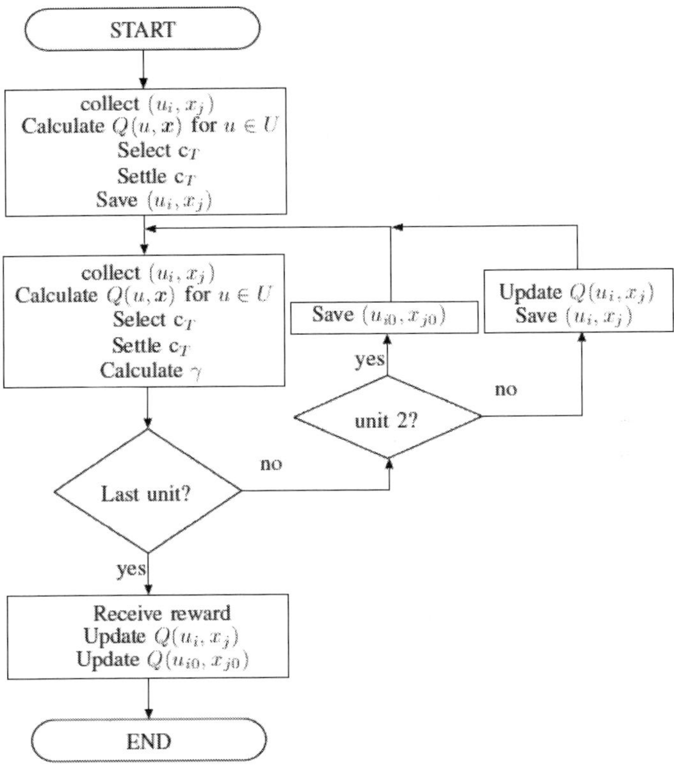

Fig. 7. Flowchart of the learning algorithm

Since similar layouts of the plant have similar evaluations, that is, difference of pipe lengths between such layouts is small, the learning performance can be improved by using appropriate generalization for evaluation of pipe length. By using CMAC as Q-tables for units 1,2, an evaluation for one input (for example, a position of unit 1) can be spread over adjacent inputs. However, the conventional CMAC has fixed shape of region covered by the generalization effects. Then, in Q-table for unit 2, the same evaluation is given to the layout that has longer pipe length and the one that has shorter pipe length when a similar layout is updated in the course of learning. Giving comparable evaluation to longer pipe length as compared to shorter pipe length is not appropriate, and thus, conventional CMAC can spoil the learning performance of the system.

In the proposed method, the CMAC that has selective generalization (SG-CMAC) is used as the Q-table for unit 2. Now, define positions of units 1,2, d_1, d_2 as $d_1 = (d_{1_x}, d_{1_y}), d_2 = (d_{2_x}, d_{2_y})$ by the x-y coordinate. The input of the SG-CMAC is $\mathbf{s} = (\mathbf{s}_I, s_z)$, where $\mathbf{s}_I = x$, $s_z = \sqrt{(d_{1_x} - d_{2_x})^2 + (d_{1_y} - d_{2_y})^2}$. s_z describes the distance between unit 1 and unit 2. Values of s_z are calculated based on quantized values of s_1, s_2. Corresponding CMAC module is assigned to each value of s_z, so that only the positions that have the same pipe length as the position specified by an input are affected by the generalization.

An example of generalization of SG-CMAC is illustrated in Fig.8. In the figure, $\Delta_1 = \Delta_2 = 7$, $\rho = 1, g = 0.1$, $d=1.0$. The position of unit 1 is $(d_{1_x}, d_{1_y}) = (2,3)$ that is blue colored position in the right figure of Fig. 8. The result is obtained after $s_l=(4.0,4.0)$ is given once. Only positions that the distance from unit 1 is same as the input are updated by the generalization of SG-CMAC. These positions are colored by yellow in the right figure of Fig. 8.

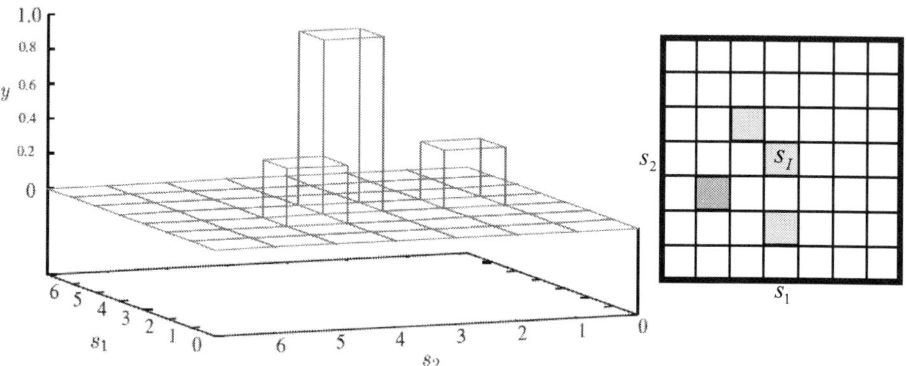

Fig. 8. Generalization of SG-CMAC

The outputs of all the weight tables are summed up to yield the output of the CMAC. For example, the output of the CMAC according to u_i and x is

$$q_t(u_i, x_j) = \sum_{p=1}^{k} w_{p,t}^{\text{ref}} \cdot \tag{9}$$

where $w_{p,t}^{\text{ref}}$ $(p = 1, \cdots, k)$ are weights specified by the input u_i for the Q-table at time t. $q_t(u_i, x_j)$ is updated by the update law of the CMAC. In other words, defining the output error at time t as e_t, the desired signal at time t as Q_t and learning rate as g, weights are updated as follows:

$$e_t(u_i, x) = Q_t(u_i, x) - q_t(u_i, x) \cdot \tag{10}$$

$$w_{p,t+1}^{\text{ref}} = w_{p,t}^{\text{ref}} + g \frac{e_t(u_i, x)}{k} \quad (p = 1, \cdots, k) \cdot \tag{11}$$

Then the desired signal $Q_t(u_i, x_j)$ is calculated by the Q-learning algorithm eqs.(4)-(6).

5. Computer simulations

Computer simulations are conducted for the same plant described in Fig.6. That is, $k_c = 7$, $m_c = 49$. Minimum pipe lengths between two units are set as

$$L_{Tj} = \begin{cases} 2.0\,(T = 2,3,5;\, j = 1) \\ 1.5\,(T = 6,7;\, j = 1) \\ 2.5\,(T = 4;\, j = 1,2) \end{cases}$$

Then, learning performance of the following 3 methods are compared:
(A) proposed method that Q-tables for Q_2 are SG-CMAC,
(B) a method that conventional CMACs are used for Q-tables to store Q_1, Q_2,
(C) a method that conventional table look-up method without generalization is used to construct Q-tables for Q_2.

In CMAC modules in method (A) and CMACs in method (B) for storing Q_2, $\rho = 3, k = 3$. In CMACs in methods (A), (B) and (C) for Q_q, $\rho = 8, k = 6$. Parameters used in the proposed method are set as $\alpha = 0.8, g = 0.6, C = 0.1$. Reward $R=1.0$ is given only when all the units has been allocated. A trial starts from a initial state and ends when all the units are allocated. Fig.8 shows examples of plant-layout obtained by method (A). For each unit c_T ($T = 1, \cdots k_c$), lengths of intake pipes l_{Tj} are

$$l_{Tj} = \begin{cases} \sqrt{5}\,(T = 2,3,5;\, j = 1) \\ 2.0\,(T = 6,7;\, j = 1) \\ 2\sqrt{2}\,(T = 4;\, j = 1,2) \end{cases}$$

They are best values that satisfy constrains $L_{Tj} < l_{Tj}$, so that the total pipe length of the optimal layout is $3\sqrt{5} + 4\sqrt{2} + 4 \approx 16.37$.

Fig. 8 shows simulation results. The proposed method could find several optimal solutions, and 4 results that have shortest pipe length are shown in the figure. In the figure, results (I),(II),(III) and (IV) have different layouts, and thus the state x for each solution is different to each other. While, the solution in result (I) is identical to solution (II) with horizontal shift. Also, the solution in result (II) is identical to solution (IV) with rotation, horizontal shift and vertical shift. Therefore, results (I) has the same x_R as result (II) after unit 2 is allocated, and thus, the same Q-value is referred for the layout in the course of learning and input-selecting phase. In the same way, results (III) and (IV) are obtained by using the same Q-values. Once, a good layout is obtained, then, the corresponding Q-value is used for several layouts that are rotated/shifted from the original layout. Moreover, the information of a good layout is spread over adjacent positions of second unit by the generalization capabilities of SG-CMAC. Therefore, the learning performance of the proposed method can be improved as compared to conventional methods that have fixed generalization capabilities. A simulation requires about 5 minutes as runtime and 500KBytes memory on a personal computer that has Pentium4 3GHz CPU.

Fig.9 depicts simulation results where the vertical axis shows the shortest pipe length that is found in the past trials and horizontal axis shows the number of trials. Each result is averaged over 10 independent simulations. In the figure, the proposed method (A) finds optimal solutions that have 16.37 as total pipe length in all simulations, whereas methods (B),(C) cannot. The learning performance of the conventional method (C) is better as compared to method (B) especially in early stages of learning. In method (B), by generalization of the conventional CMAC, inappropriate evaluations are spread over the region adjacent to inputs, so that the learning performance has been spoiled.

6. Conclusions

A design method for CMAC that has selective generalization (SG-CMAC) has been proposed. Also, a Q-learning system using SG-CMAC is proposed, and the proposed system is applied to allocation problem of chemical plant. In the computer simulations, the proposed method could obtain optimal solutions with feasible computational cost, and the learning performance was improved as compared to conventional methods.

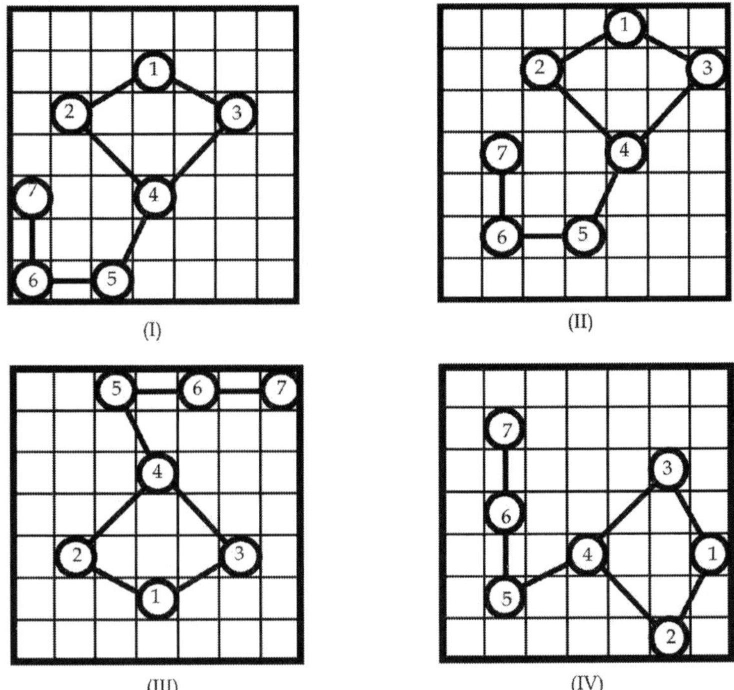

Fig. 8. Optimal lyaouts obtained by method (A)

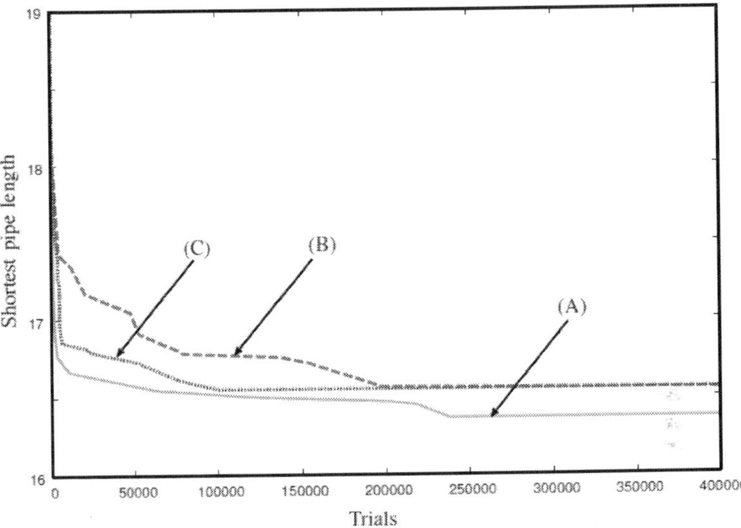

Fig. 9. Performance comparison

6. References

Albus, J. S. (1975a). A New Approach to Manipulator Control : The Cerebellar Model Articulation Controller (CMAC), Trans. ASME J. Dynam. Syst., Meas., Contr., Vol. 97, 220-227

Albus, J. S. (1975b). Data Storage in the Cerebellar Model Articulation Controller (CMAC), Trans. ASME J. Dynam. Syst., Meas., Contr., Vol. 97, 228-233

Baum, E. B. (1999). Toward a model of intelligence as an economy of agents, *Machine Learning*, Vol. 35, 155–185.

Ceorgiadis, M. C., Schilling, G., Rotstein, G. E. and Macchietto (1999). S. A General Mathematical Programming Approach for Process Plant Layout, Comput. Chem. Eng., Vol. 23, No. 7, pp.823-840.

Hirashima, Y., Deng, M., Inoue, A. (2005). An Intelligent Layout Planning Method for Chemical Plants Considering   I/O Connections, Proceedings of SICE Annual Conference, pp.2021--2024.

Hirashima, Y., Inoue, A. and N. Jensen, A Method Placing Tanks and Reactors in a Chemical Plant to Minimize Risk Due to Fires and Explosions Using Reinforcement learning, Proc. International Symposium on Advanced Control of Industrial Processes, pp.381-386, 2002.

Sutton, R.S. and Barto (1999). A.G. Reinforcement Learning, MIT Press

Vecchietti, A. R. and Montagna, J. (1998). Alternatives in the Optimal Allocation of Intermediate Storage Tank in Multiproduct Batch Plants, Comput. Chem. Eng., Vol. 22,No. suppl.issue, pp.S801-4.

Watkins, C. J. C. (1989). Learning from Delayed Rewards, Ph.D. Thesis, Cambridge University, Cambridge, England.

Watkins, C. J. C. H. and Dayan, P. (1992). Q-learning, *Machine Learning*, 8:279–292.

10

A FAST-Based Q-Learning Algorithm

Kao-Shing Hwang[2], Yuan-Pao Hsu[1] and Hsin-Yi Lin[2]
[1]Department of Computer Science and Information Engineering National Formosa University Yunlin,
[2]Department of Electrical Engineering National Chung-Cheng University Chiayi,
Taiwan

1. Introduction

Q-learning is a stochastic dynamic programming algorithm that doesn't need to have the interactive model of machine-environment [1] [2]. Taking action 'a' according to state 's', the algorithm measures the feedback rewards and updates its Q values from rewards step by step. In a reasonable period of learning process, the Q-learning obtains outstanding performance and has been successfully applied on collision-avoidance, homing, and robots cooperation [3] [4].

Traditionally, in Q-learning algorithm, a decoder pre-partitions the input space into grid called boxes that map input vectors into activated boxes. However, the way of pre-partitioning the input space might not be suitable for all systems, especially for unknown systems. Therefore, theorems such as CMAC, ART, FAST, etc. have been suggested to replace the box decoder for clustering input vectors [5]-[7]. Input vectors then can be mapped into more suitable clusters for the purpose of getting better state-action values to meet the desirable control effect.

The ART [6] is one kind of unsupervised learning artificial neural networks possessing the advantage of solving the stability-plasticity dilemma. The FAST [7] [8] algorithm merges the advantage of variable vigilance value of the ART and the pruning mechanism of the GAR (Grow and Represent Model) [9] theorem, amending the disadvantage of the boxes method which maps only one activated box for each input vector. It dynamically adjusts the size and location of the sensitivity region for activated neurons, and makes boundaries between categories to be changeable, resulting in producing more suitable input for increasing the system learning speed. Furthermore, when an input pattern activates more than one neuron, the pruning mechanism of the FAST appropriately prunes one of the neurons with overlapped sensitivity region for preserving neurons to accommodate more categories in the cause of resource reservation.

The article aims at combining a FAST-based algorithm and Q-learning algorithm into a reinforcement learning algorithm called ARM Q-learning algorithm that improves Q-learning algorithm on learning speed and learning stability. The article is organized in four sections; the first Section being this introduction. In Section 2 we discuss the theories of clustering and reinforcement learning. Section 3 presents the simulation results and results analysis. Finally, a discussion is drawn in Section 4.

2. Theory

2.1 Adaptive resonance theory

ART is a dynamic neural network structure. With a feedback mechanism the ART produces a top-down expectation. Not only must a neuron win the competition but also should it match this expectation before it is qualified to learn. As the interaction between the feed-forward path and the feedback path is established, the winning neuron will output the same pattern iteratively. This state is so called the resonant state and that is why the theorem is named to be Adaptive Resonance Theory.

2.2 Flexible adaptable-size topology

FAST is developed from the concept of ART algorithm with the dynamic categorization function. Merging with the dynamic vigilance parameter and online pruning mechanism, the FAST is able to realize the clustering efficiently.

Each FAST neuron j maintains an n-dimensional reference vector C_j, and a threshold, T_j, determining its sensitivity region. At the beginning, input patterns are presented and the network adapts through application of the FAST algorithm (Figure 1). If a new input vector P_j doesn't lie within any sensitivity region of any neuron, a new neuron is generated by setting its reference vector C_j centered on the input vector pattern P_j. On the other hand, the C_j and T_j of a neuron are dynamically updated if P_j lies within its sensitivity region. There is another scenario that P_j may activate more than one neuron. This implies the FAST network has redundant neurons with overlapped sensitivity regions. The pruning function is then executed to delete one of these neurons to decrease the network size. The operations can be described as the following steps:

1. Initialize the system.
2. Present an input pattern P and compute $D(P, C_j)$ for every operational neuron j. Where $D(P, C_j)$ is the Manhattan distance, a distance between two points measured along axes at right angles, e.g., on a plane with two points, p_1 at (x_1, y_1) and p_2 at (x_2, y_2), their Manhattan distance is $|x_1 - x_2| + |y_1 - y_2|$.
3. If $D(P, C_j) > T_j$ for all j, activate a new neuron j^* by initializing its reference vector to C_j^* $= P$, its threshold to $T_j^* = T_{ini}$, and its deactivation parameter to $Pr_j^* = 1$.
4. If $D(P, C_j) < T_j$, where j is an active neuron, and T_j is its threshold, update C_j and T_j as follows:

$$C_{ji}(t+1) = C_{ji}(t) + \alpha T_j \left(P_i - C_{ji}(t) \right) \tag{1}$$

$$T_j(t+1) = T_j(t) - \gamma \left(T_j(t) - T_{\min} \right) \tag{2}$$

where α, γ, and T_{min} are learning constants. Update the global T_{ini} parameter to $T_{ini} = T_{ini}(t+1) - \gamma(T_{ini}(t) - T_{min})$.

5. If several neurons are activated in step 3, deactivate one of the neurons if $rnd(\ ) > Pr_j$, where Pr_j is the deactivation parameter, and $rnd(\ )$ is a uniformly distributed random number in the range (0, 1). Increase the activated neurons' probability of deactivation as follows:

$$Pr_j(t+1) = Pr_j(t) - \eta(Pr_j(t) - Pr_{min}), \tag{3}$$

Where η and Pr_{min} are pruning constants.

6. Goto step 2.

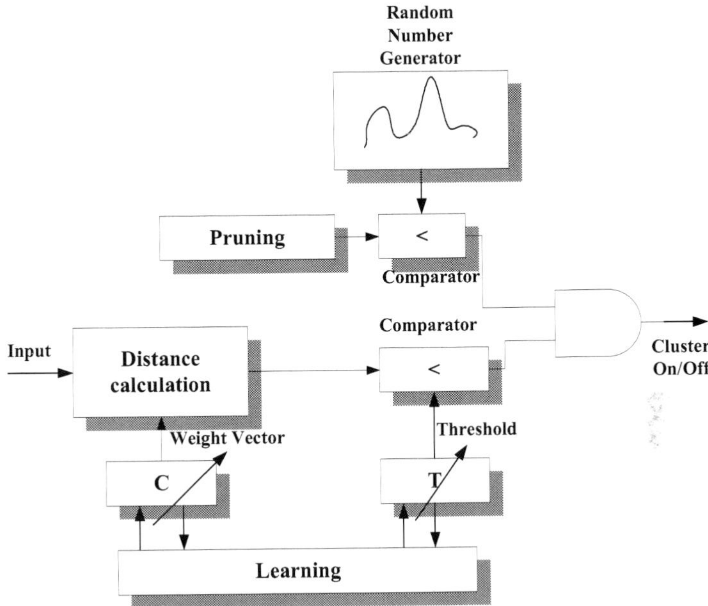

Fig. 1. Block diagram of an FAST neuron.

2.3 Q-learning algorithm

Q-learning is one of reinforcement learning algorithms (figure 2). The algorithm selects an action with max Q value (or by ε-greedy) from the Q table basing on the clustered result of current state. A feedback reinforcement signal (reward) is then read for the system to update its Q value and the system enters the next state at the same time. At the next state, the system goes again the selection of the action, and receives the reward, and enters the following state. The operations are periodically performed for reaching the ultimate purpose that the best action of each state can be trained to get the optimal Q value (Q^*).

The procedure of the algorithm is list as follows.

- Initialize the system. All $Q(s, a)$ are set to be zero.
- Repeat (for each episode):
  - Repeat (for each step of episode):
    - Observe current state s.
    - Select an action a with max Q value from Q table (or select an action by ε-greedy policy).
    - Take action a, read reward r caused by action a, and observe next state s'.
    - Update Q value corresponding to state s and action a as equation (4).

$$Q(s,a) = Q(s,a) + \beta(r + \gamma Max(Q(s',a)) - Q(s,a)) \tag{4}$$

Where r is reinforcement signal (reward), s' is all possible states t hat state s can visit, and β and γ are coefficients lie between 0 and 1.

- • Replace s with s'.
- • Until s is terminal or stop condition has been met.

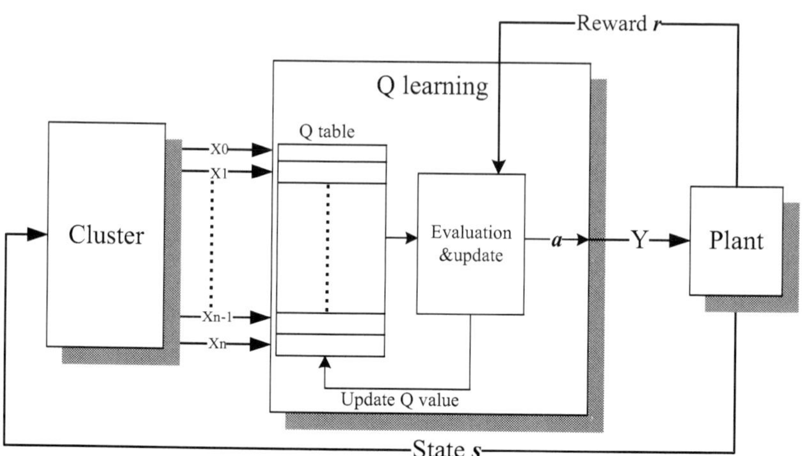

Fig. 2. Q-learning block diagram.

2.4 Adaptive resonance method

The ARM architecture modified from FAST is developed to provide more suitable clustered results to the Q-learning architecture for achieving the purpose of improving the learning speed and learning stability. The modification involves three parts: normalization, weight update, and pruning mechanism.

2.4.1 Normalization

The FAST compares an input vector with each neuron's center point to calculate the Manhattan distances D. However, the variation of the input vector in its distinct dimension may not have the same scale. Consequently, in the system input space, a slightly changing of a parameter in some dimension of an input vector might make the calculated D larger than T value causing a new neuron being generated. For another parameter, on the other hand, even having a great deal of change, the D is still unable to exceed the T value to generate a new neuron. Therefore, a normalization mechanism should be added in front of the FAST to normalize each dimension's value of the input vector into the same scale, so as to appropriately categorize the input vectors and to generate new neurons.

2.4.2 Weight update

When a neuron has been activated repeatedly, its center point moves following the successive new input vectors. The more number of times of a neuron has been activated, the larger moving distance of the neuron will have. This causes the FAST encoding the same input vector into different cluster and the Q-learning will receive erroneous clusters.

As shown in figure 3, (a) represents that the system generates a neuron centered by C_0 for the input vector P_1; (b) shows that the center point C_0 has been moved to C_0' for the input

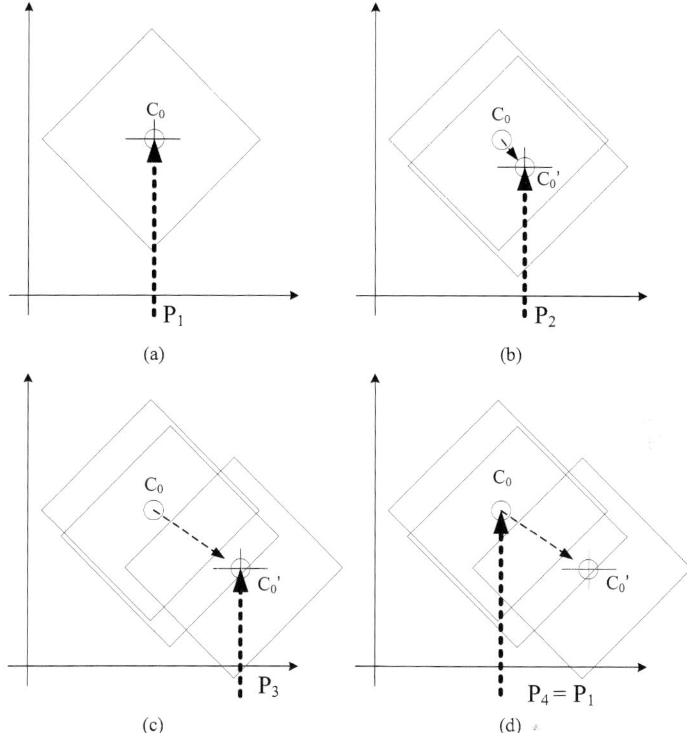

Fig. 3. Center adjustment of a FAST neuron.

vector P_2 which lies within the sensitive region of C_0, but P_2 is different from P_1; (c) represents that the center point C_0 has been moved farther away from its original center in (a) because of the input P_3; (d) points out that the input vector P_4 lies outside of the sensitive region of C_0 and will be categorized as another cluster which is different from the cluster of the P_1, even P_4 is the same as P_1. The system would not be able to refer to the learned experiences for this reason and jeopardize its performance significantly. To resolve this difficulty, the learning rate α should be limited under some small value in order that the FAST can cluster input vectors stably.

2.4.3 Pruning mechanism

The original concept of pruning mechanism of the FAST is depended upon the pruning probability, whereas the pruning probability is determined by the number of times of a neuron being activated. From this concept, a neuron is prone to be pruned when its times of being activated is relatively larger than other neurons. However, it is also possible that similar input vectors are easily to repeatedly present on the input making the FAST regenerates new neurons for the input vectors that they might have just caused some neurons to be pruned. The system will be stuck on the unstable situation of switching between pruning and generating. Moreover, neurons that were generated by input vectors appeared only once will stay in the system and unreasonably never have the chance of being pruned. This leads us to modify the pruning mechanism that keeps neurons that are having high probability of being activated, deletes neurons which have low probability of being re-activated.

The pruning mechanism is modified to be: when a neuron is activated, its Pr value is set to be 1, while the Pr values of other un-activated neurons are updated basing on (3). The neuron number is limited to be K. When the number of generated neurons of the system reaches K, the pruning mechanism is triggered to check the Pr values of each neuron. Those neurons with Pr values smaller than a random number $rnd()$ will be pruned.

The algorithm of the modified FAST is listed as the following steps.

1. Normalize input vector P.
2. Calculate Manhattan distance $D(P, C_j)$ between input vector P and neurons j.

3. If $D(P, C_j) > T_j$, input vector P doesn't belong to any existing clusters, generate the $(j + 1)$th new neuron and initialize its weight value being $C_{j+1} = P$, and $T_{j+1} = T_{ini}$, and $Pr_{j+1} = 1$.

4. If $D(P, C_j) < T_j$, categorize input vector P being the cluster of the jth neuron, set $Pr_j = 1$, update Cj and T_j according to (1) and (2). Update Pr value of each un-activated along (3).

5. If generated neurons reaching K, compare each neuron's Pr_j with a random number $rnd()$ (between 0 and 1), delete one of the neurons when their Pr are larger than $rnd()$.

6. Get next input vector P, go to step 1。

These modifications of the FAST give birth to the ARM. The ARM replaces the cluster module in figure 2 to encode input vectors for the Q-learning. Section 3 will demonstrate its performance.

2.4.4 Modified Q-learning

The original Box Q-learning selects the action with the biggest Q value from the Q table referred to by the box that triggered by input state. But, in our architecture, we calculate the Manhattan distances between the center point of current state and triggered neurons. These distances determine the percentage of each activated neurons that contribute to the calculation of Q value. If a triggered neuron is near the current state, then their Manhattan distance would be small, so that neuron provides a large share of the Q value. The proportion scale that each activated neuron contributes to the Q value is shown in equation (5).

$$w_i = \begin{cases} \dfrac{\sum distance - distance_i}{(n-1) \times \sum distance}, & when\ n \neq 1\ ; \\ 1.0 & ,\ when\ n = 1\ . \end{cases} \tag{5}$$

Where w_j represents the proportion that activated neuron j contributes; n denotes the number of activated neurons; $\sum distance$ stands to be the summation distance of all activated neurons; $distance_j$ denotes the total distance of neuron j.

Expected value V is calculated as follows:

$$V_t = \max_a \sum w_j Q_j(s, a), \tag{6}$$

where V_t is expected value at time t.

Q is updated according to equation (7).

$$Q_j(s_t,a) = Q_j(s_t,a) + \beta(r_t + \gamma V_t \times w_j - Q_j(s_t,a)) \tag{7}$$

3. Simulation

3.1 Cart-Pole simulation

The well-known cart-pole simulation having been used in verification of the performance of reinforcement learning algorithms is simulated here to check if the proposed architecture works. A typical mathematical model of a cart-pole system can be represented by forms as (8) and (9). We use fourth order Runge-Kutta to simulate the cart-pole model by a personal computer [10].

$$\ddot{\theta}_t = \frac{g\sin\theta_t + \cos\theta_t[\dfrac{-F_t - ml\dot{\theta}_t^2 \sin\theta_t + \mu_c \operatorname{sgn}(\dot{x})}{m_c + m}] - \dfrac{\mu_p \dot{\theta}_t}{ml}}{l[\dfrac{4}{3} - \dfrac{m\cos^2\theta_t}{m_c + m}]}, \tag{8}$$

$$\ddot{x}_t = \frac{F_t + ml[\dot{\theta}_t^2 \sin\theta_t - \ddot{\theta}_t \cos\theta_t] - \mu_c \operatorname{sgn}(\dot{x}_t)}{m_c + m}. \tag{9}$$

Where g is the gravity constant, 9.8 m/s²; m_c is the mass of cart, 1 kg; m_p is the mass of pole, 0.1kg; l is the half length of pole, 0.5 m; μ_p is the friction coefficient of the pole on the cart; μ_c is the friction coefficient of the cart on the track; F_t is the applied force generated by the controller. The dynamics of the systems are assumed to be unknown but the states are measurable. In the simulation, frictions are eliminated. Hence μ_p and μ_c are set to be zero.

The cart travels left or right along a one dimensional track. The pole is hinged to the top of the cart and is free to move in the vertical plane along with the track. The objective is to learn to drive the cart left or right so as to keep the pole balanced vertically above the cart, and to keep the cart from colliding with the ends of track. The learner accesses the state vector $(x,\dot{x},\theta,\dot{\theta})$ at each time step and selects one of two actions, a rightward or leftward force on the cart. The cart-pole system begins with $x=0$, $\dot{x}=0$, $\theta=0$, and $\dot{\theta}=0$. If the pole falls over more than 12 degrees from vertical, or if the cart hits the track boundary (track length 2.4m), a failure occurs. All immediate rewards are zero except that when a failure is occurred a reward of negative one is received. When a failure occurs, the cart-pole system is reset to the initial state, and begins a new attempt to balance the pole.

3.2 Simulation results

The simulation includes 10 experiments. There are 500 trials in one experiment. One trail is said to be ended if an attempt of balancing the pole is failed. When an attempt is lasting over 100,000 sampling steps, a successful trial occurs, and a new attempt is restarted by initializing the cart and pole. Sampling interval is set as 0.02 second.

Parameters of the ARM are: learning constant α=0. 000001, $\gamma = 0.007$, $\eta = 0.045$, $T_{ini} = 2.0$, $T_{min} = 1.8$, $Pr_{ini} = 1.0$, and $Pr_{min} = 0.09$; whereas parameters of the Q-learning are set to be: learning rate $\alpha = 0.2$, discount rate $\gamma = 0.999$.

	Best	Worse
BOX Q	351	>500
ARM Q	7	82

Table 1. Summary of simulation results

ARM Q-learning and Box Q-learning are simulated for manifesting the improvement of the proposed method. Average results of 10 experiments of the both algorithms are depicted in figure 4. The ARM Q-learning method balances the pole within about 100 trials, while the Box Q-learning method needs more than 500 trials to learn to balance the pole. The stability of the ARM Q-learning also shows in the figure. The pole can be balance again quickly even if it should fall after a long time of balancing. The ARM Q-learning keeps its learned experiences well to equip it with superior stability.

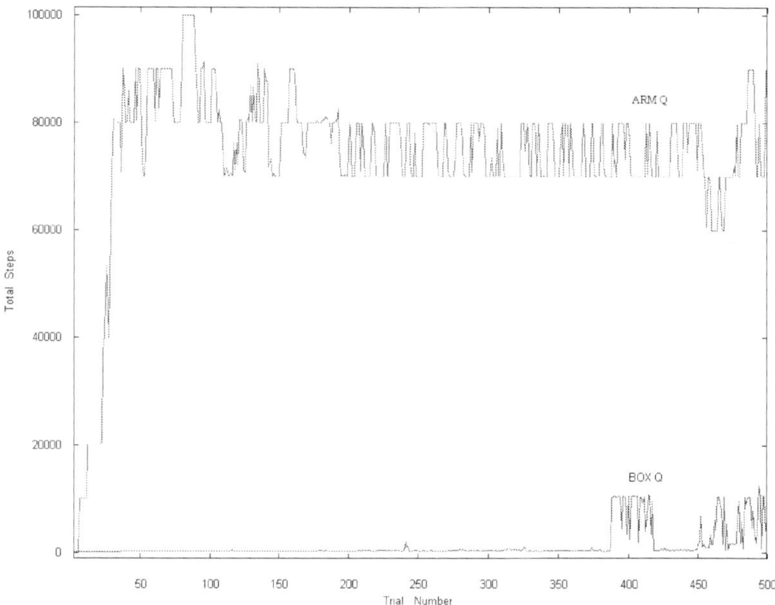

Fig. 4. Performance of ARM Q-learning and Box Q-learning system.

Table 1 demonstrates that the modified ARM Q took only 7 trails for the first time that it can successfully balance the pole for the best case. To accomplish the same job, the Box Q took 351 trials. Furthermore, the ARM generated 7 to 10 neurons to categorize the states. The Box instead pre-partitioned the input state space into 162 boxes.

In accordance with the above observation, for a plant like the cart-pole system, the ARM Q-learning method needed only a small amount of neurons to learn to balance the pole within much shorter time than the Box Q-learning method did.

4. Discussion

This article proposed a reinforcement learning architecture that combines ARM, a FAST-based algorithm, and Q-learning algorithm. The ARM, at the front end, is featured with multi-neuron triggering and dynamically adjusting its sensitive region as well, providing the Q-learning, at the back end, with more suitable clustered input states. In such a way, the Q-learning learns quick and stable.

There are future work can be tried to enhance the Q-learning for constructing more efficient reinforcement learning architecture, such as replaces the Q-learning in our architecture with the $Q(\lambda)$-learning [11] or SARSA [12].

5. Acknowledgment

The authors are grateful for financial support from the National Science Council of Taiwan, the Republic of China, under Grant NSC94-2213-E-150-025-.

6. Reference

[1] Watkins, C. J. C. H., and Dayan, P., Technical note: Q-Learning, *Machine Learning*, 8(3-4): pp. 279-292, 1992.

[2] Claude F. Touzet, "Q-Learning for Robot," in M. A. Arbib, editor, *Handbook of Brain Theory and Neural Networks*, pp. 934-937, 2003.

[3] L. E. Parker, C. Touzet and F. Fernandez, "Techniques for learning in multi-robot teams," in *Robot Teams: From Diversity to polymorphism* (T Balch and L. E. Parker, Eds.), Natick, MA: A. K. Peters, 2001.

[4] K.-S. Hwang, S.-W. Tan; C.-C. Chen, "Cooperative strategy based on adaptive Q-learning for robot soccer systems," *IEEE Transactions on Fuzzy Systems*, Vol. 12, Issue: 4, pp. 569-576 Aug. 2004.

[5] G. A. CARPENTER and S. GROSSBERG, "The ART of adaptive pattern recognition by a self-organizing neural network," *IEEE Computer*, 21(3), pp77-88, March 1988.

[6] J. S. Albus, "A New Approach to Manipulator Control: The Cerebellar Model Articulation Controller (CMAC)," Trans. ASME, J. Dynamic Syst. Meas., Contr., Vol. 97, pp. 220-227, Sept. 1975.

[7] A. Pérez-Uribe, *Structure-adaptable digital neural networks*, PhD Thesis 2052, Swiss Federal Institute of Technology-Lausanne, Lausanne, 1999.

[8] A. Perez and E. Sanchez, "The FAST architecture: a neural network with flexible adaptable-size topology," *Proceedings of Fifth International Conference on Microelectronics for Neural Networks*, pp. 337–340, 12-14 Feb. 1996

[9] A. E. Alpaydin, *Neural models of incremental supervised and unsupervised learning*. PhD thesis, Swiss Federal Institute of Technology-Lausanne, Lausanne, DPFL, 1990. Thesis 863.

[10] Barto, Andrew G., Sutton, Richard S. and Anderson, Charles W., "Neuronlike adaptive elements that can solve difficult learning control problems." *IEEE Transactions on System, Man, and Cybernetics* SMC-13: 834-846. 1983.

[11] Peng, J. and Wiliams, R.J., "Incremental Multi-Step Q Learning," *Machine Learning, 22,* pp. 283-290, 1996.

[12] R. S. Sutton and A. G. Barto, *Reinforcement Learning An Introduction*, Cambridge, Mass., MIT Press, 1998.

Constrained Reinforcement Learning from Intrinsic and Extrinsic Rewards

Eiji Uchibe and Kenji Doya
Okinawa Institute of Science and Technology
Japan

1. Introduction

The main objective of the learning agent is usually determined by experimenters. In the case of reinforcement learning (Sutton & Barto, 1998), it is defined as maximization of a scalar reward function which should be designed for each task through a trial-and-error process. It is still important to implement learning algorithms that can efficiently improve the learning capabilities, but the principles for designing the appropriate reward functions become important more and more in the future. Reward functions are categorized into two types: extrinsic and intrinsic rewards. In many cases, extrinsic rewards are zero everywhere except for a few important points that correspond to the important events. Although designing such a sparse reward function is easier than designing a dense one, the sparse rewards prevent the learning agent to learn efficiently. On the contrary, the intrinsic reward is regarded as dense reward functions which give non-zero rewards most of the time because it is usually computed from the agent's internal information such as sensory inputs. Although the intrinsic reward is generally task-independent, it plays an important role for designing an open-ended system.

Recently, learning algorithms with intrinsic rewards have been studied by several researchers. Barto and his colleagues (Barto et al., 2004; Singh et al., 2005; Stout et al., 2005) proposed an algorithm for intrinsically motivated reinforcement learning based on the theory of options (Sutton, et al., 1999). Meeden *et al.* realized that a simulated robot tracked a moving decoy robot with the rewards based on the error of its own prediction (Meeden et al., 2004). Oudeyer and his collegues adopted progress of prediction learning as intrinsic rewards and showed that behavior evolution of the Sony's four-legged robot, AIBO, were realized by step-by-step learning (Oudeyer & Kaplan, 2004; Oudeyer et al., 2007). However, most previous studies did not discuss the negative effects of extrinsic rewards on intrinsically motivated learning suggested by (Deci and Flaste, 1996). It is still unclear how extrinsic rewards can help or hinder the learning process.

As the first step towards this problem, this chapter deals with the interaction between intrinsic and extrinsic rewards from a viewpoint of constrained optimization problems. The learning agent tries to maximize the long-term average intrinsic reward under the inequality constraints given by extrinsic rewards. We propose a new framework termed the *Constrained Policy Gradient Reinforcement Learning* (CPGRL) consisting of a Policy Gradient Reinforcement Learning (PGRL) algorithm (Baxter & Bartlett, 2001; Konda & Tsitsiklis, 2003;

Morimura et al., 2005) and a gradient projection method (Rosen, 1960). Since The PGRL algorithms can estimate the gradients of the expected average rewards with respect to the policy parameters, they are nicely integrated with the gradient projection method. Although constrained Markov Decision Process (MDP) problems are previously studied based on linear programming techniques (Feinberg & Shwartz,1999; Dolgov & Durfee, 2005), their methods do not suit our case because the state transition probabilities are known, and because it cannot be easily extended to continuous state and action spaces. In order to evaluate the CPGRL we conduct two simulations: a simple MDP problem with three states and a control task of a robotic arm.

2. Constrained policy gradient reinforcement learning

2.1 Formulation

At each time step, an agent observes a state $x \in X$ and executes an action $u \in U$ with probability $\mu_\theta(x,u)$: $X \times U \to [0, 1]$ that represents a stochastic policy parameterized by an n-dimensional vector $\theta \in R^n$. The agent calculates an intrinsic reward r_t^1 and extrinsic rewards r_t^2 (i=2, 3,..., m) at time t, which depend on the state and the action. Let $r_t^i = r^i(x_t, u_t)$ and $r_t = [r_t^1 \ r_t^2 \ ... \ r_t^m]^T$ denote respectively the immediate reward at time t and the vectorized representation. The operation a^T means the transpose of vector/matrix a.

The objective for the agent is to find the policy parameter θ that maximizes an average reward

$$g^1(\theta) = \lim_{T \to \infty} E_\theta \left[\frac{1}{T} \sum_{t=1}^{T} r_t^1 \right] \tag{1}$$

under the constraints determined by the extrinsic rewards given by

$$g^i(\theta) = \lim_{T \to \infty} E_\theta \left[\frac{1}{T} \sum_{t=1}^{T} r_t^i \right] \geq G^i, \quad i = 2, \ldots, m, \tag{2}$$

where G^i is a threshold for controlling a level of the constraint. It is noted that the inequality constraints on extrinsic rewards are also the functions of the average rewards.

Fig.1 illustrates the CPGRL system based on the actor-critic architecture (Sutton & Barto, 1998). It consists of one actor, multiple critics, and a gradient projection module that computes a projection onto a feasible region, which is the set of points satisfying all the inequality constraints. Based on the immediate reward r^i, each critic produces an estimate of the long-term average reward ρ^i and its gradient Δ^i with respect to the policy parameters. Actor selects the action u according to the stochastic policy $\mu_\theta(x,u)$. The procedure of the CPGRL is listed below:

while $k < N_K$

    1.   Set $z_0 = 0$ and $\Delta^i = 0$ for all i.

    2.   **while** $t < N_T$

        i.   Observe x_t and execute u_t.

        ii.   Receive the rewards r_t.

        iii.   Estimate the average rewards and their gradients.

    3.   Store the estimated average rewards.

    4.   Update the policy parameter,

where N_K and N_T denote the number of episode and the maximum time step, respectively.

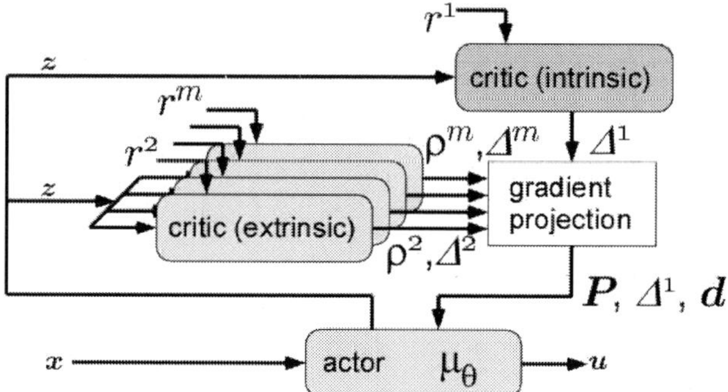

Fig. 1. Block diagram of the actor-critic architecture for learning behaviours from intrinsic and extrinsic rewards.

2.2 Gradient estimates by policy gradient reinforcement learning

The PGRL algorithms have recently been re-evaluated since they are well-behaved with function approximation. As opposed to the action value function based reinforcement learning such as Q-learning, the PGRL algorithms are naturally integrated with function approximators, and therefore they can deal with continuous actions. There exist several methods to compute the gradient of the average reward Δ^i. In the current implementation, we choose the GPOMDP algorithm (Baxter and Bartlett, 2001) and the actor-critic method (Konda and Tsitsiklis, 2003). At first, we briefly introduce the GPOMDP algorithm when the reward depends on the action as well as the state. According to the current state and action, the function ψ_t is defined by

$$\psi_t(x_t, u_t) \triangleq \frac{1}{\mu_\theta(x_t, u_t)} \frac{\partial \mu_\theta(x_t, u_t)}{\partial \theta}.$$

The learning agent interacts with the environment, producing a state, action, reward sequence. After receiving experiences $(x_t, u_t, x_{t+1}, u_{t+1}, r_{t+1})$, the GPOMDP updates an eligibility traces $z_t \in R^n$

$$z_{t+1} = \beta z_t + \psi_t(x_t, u_t)$$

where $\beta \in [0, 1)$ is a discount rate that controls the variance of the gradient estimate. Since z_t is independent of the reward functions, z_t can be used for estimating gradients of different average rewards. Then, all the gradients are updated in the same manner. That is, the gradient of the long-term average reward is approximated by

$$\Delta^i_{t+1} = \Delta^i_t + \frac{1}{t+1} \left[r^i_{t+1} \left(z_{t+1} + \psi_{t+1}(x_{t+1}, u_{t+1}) \right) - \Delta^i_t \right] \tag{3}$$

for all $i = 1, ..., m$. The estimate of the average reward r^i is updated by

$$\rho^i_{t+1} = \rho^i_t + \alpha_r (r^i_{t+1} - \rho^i_t), \tag{4}$$

where α_r is a positive step-size meta-parameter. It is noted that $\rho_{i,t+1}$ gives an estimate of $g_i(\theta)$ and plays an important role for finding active constraints. Although the GPOMDP can estimate the gradient with less number of parameters, it has a large variance as $\beta \to 1$.

We also use a simplified method based on the actor critic method (Konda & Tsitsiklis, 2003) that exploits a value function. The gradient of the long-term average reward is calculated by

$$\Delta_{t+1}^{i} = \Delta_{t}^{i} + \frac{1}{t+1}\left[Q^{i}(\boldsymbol{x}_t, \boldsymbol{u}_t)\psi(\boldsymbol{x}_t, \boldsymbol{u}_t) - \Delta_{t}^{i}\right], \tag{5a}$$

$$Q^{i}(\boldsymbol{x}, \boldsymbol{u}) = (\boldsymbol{w}^{i})^{\top}\psi(\boldsymbol{x}, \boldsymbol{u}). \tag{5b}$$

where $Q^i(x, u)$ and w^i denote an approximated state-action value function and a parameter vector, respectively. In order to train w^i, the standard temporal difference method is carried out

$$\boldsymbol{w}_{t+1}^{i} = \boldsymbol{w}_{t}^{i} + \alpha_r \delta_t^i \boldsymbol{z}_{t+1},$$

where the temporal difference δ_t^i is defined by

$$\delta_t^i = r_{t+1}^i - \rho_{t+1}^i + (\boldsymbol{w}_t^i)^{\top}\left[\psi_{t+1}(\boldsymbol{x}_{t+1}, \boldsymbol{u}_{t+1}) - \psi_t(\boldsymbol{x}_t, \boldsymbol{u}_t)\right].$$

Although Konda's actor-critic requires an additional learning mechanism to approximate the state-action value function, it can utilize the Markov property.

2.3 Gradient projection

As described in section 2.2, the average rewards and their gradients are obtained at the end of each episode. Next, we apply a gradient projection method to solve the maximization problem with inequality constraints. In order to derive a modified learning rule, a set of indices of the active inequality constraints is defined by

$$\mathcal{A} = \left\{i \mid \rho^i - G^i \le 0, \ i = 2, \ldots, m\right\}$$

and let $a = |A|$ denote the number of active constraints in which A is called an active set. If no constraints are active (the case $a = 0$), the solution lies at the interior of the feasible region. A standard learning rule can be applied in the case of $a = 0$, the case $a \neq 0$ is considered hereafter. With the outputs from the multiple critics, we define

$$\boldsymbol{g}_A \triangleq \left[\rho^{i_1} - G^{i_1} \quad \cdots \quad \rho^{i_a} - G^{i_a}\right]^{\top},$$

$$N_A \triangleq \left[\Delta^{i_1} \quad \cdots \quad \Delta^{i_a}\right],$$

where i_a is an index to count the element in A. Fig.2 illustrates the basic idea of gradient projection based on the nonlinear programming. The gray are represents the feasible region and therefore the policy parameter vector at the k-th episode must approach the feasible region while move into the direction Δ_1. Suppose that the policy parameter is modified without considering a restoration move d. When the k-th episode ends, the update rule is given by

$$\theta_k' = \theta_k + \alpha_1 \boldsymbol{s},$$

where s is the steepest ascent direction.

By using the estimated gradients, the set of active constraints can be approximated by the following linear equation:

$$N_A^\top \theta + b \approx 0,$$

where b is an appropriate vector. Since the gradient projection method (Rosen, 1960) assumes that θ lies in the subspace tangent to the active constraints, both θ_k' and θ_k should satisfy the above equations. Then, we obtain an equality constraints $N^\top s = 0$. Since the steepest ascent direction s satisfying the above constraints is required, we can pose this problem as

$$\max\ s^\top \Delta^1\quad \text{s.t.}\quad N_A^\top s = 0\ \text{and}\ s^\top s = 1.$$

The second constraint is required to normalize s. In order to solve this problem with equality constraints, the Lagrange multiplier method is applied. Now, the Lagrangian function is defined as

$$\mathcal{L}(s, \lambda, \kappa) = s^\top \Delta^1 - s^\top N_A \lambda - \kappa(s^\top s - 1),$$

where λ and κ are Lagrange multipliers. The condition for L to be stationary is given by:

$$\frac{\partial \mathcal{L}}{\partial s} = \Delta^1 - N_A \lambda - 2\kappa s = 0.$$

By pre-multiplying $N_A^\top$ into the above equaiton, we obtain

$$N_A^\top \Delta^1 - N_A^\top N_A \lambda = 0. \tag{6}$$

It should be noted that $N_A^\top s = 0$. If $N_A^\top N_A$ is invertible, the Lagrange multipliers λ can be represented by

$$\lambda = \left(N_A^\top N_A\right)^{-1} N_A^\top \Delta^1. \tag{7}$$

From Equations (6) and (7), s is derived as

$$s = \frac{1}{2\kappa}\left[I - N_A \left(N_A^\top N_A\right)^{-1} N_A^\top\right] \Delta^1,$$

where the scalar Lagrange multiplier κ remains unknown. However, this parameter is not important because we are interested in the modified direction of the gradient Δ^1. As a result, when k-th episode ends, the policy parameters are update as follows:

$$\theta_{k+1} = \theta_k + \alpha_1 P \Delta^1 - \alpha_e d \tag{8}$$

where $\alpha_1, \alpha_e \in [0, 1)$ are learning rates, P is a matrix that projects Δ^1 into the subspace tangent to the active constraints, and is a restoration move for the violating constraints. The projection matrix P and restoration move d are given by

$$P = I - N_A \left(N_A^\top N_A\right)^{-1} N_A^\top, \tag{9}$$
$$d = N_A \left(N_A^\top N_A\right)^{-1} g_A. \tag{10}$$

It should be noted that $Pd = 0$. If the active set A is empty, P and d are set to the identity matrix and zero vector, respectively.

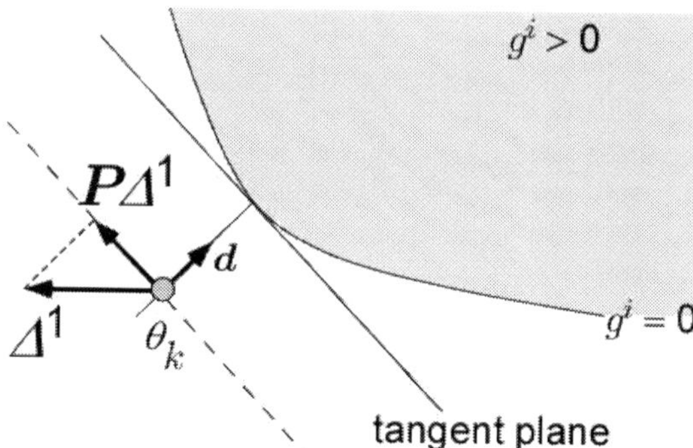

Fig. 2. Graphical interpretation of gradient projection. The gray area represents the feasible region in the policy parameter space. θ_k, Δ^1, and d are the current policy parameter, the policy gradient of the average reward r^1, and the restoration vector, respectively. P is a projection matrix which maps the vector into the subspace tangent to the feasible region.

Here, we should note two points when P and d are computed in the program. At first, it must be noted that the matrix $N_A^T N_A$ in (9) and (10) is not invertible if the set of active constraint gradients $\{\Delta^{ij} \,|\, j = 1, ..., a\}$ is linearly dependent. In practice, rank deficiency of $N_A^T N_A$ is sometimes observed due to the accuracy of numerical computation and/or biased samples. The pseudo-inverse of $N_A^T N_A$ should be used if it is not full-rank. In addition we must consider the situation where $P\Delta^1 = 0$ because it may be possible to modify the parameters. This situation can be detected by using Lagrange multipliers (7). If λ has no negative components, we have a solution and terminate. Otherwise, the constraint with maximum Lagrange multiplier is calculated by

$$r = \arg \max_{i \in A} \lambda_i,$$

and then it is removed from the active set as $A \leftarrow A \backslash \{r\}$. After deleting one constraint from the active set, P and d are evaluated again by using (9) and (10).

2.4 Backups of the long-term average rewards

Since the CPGRL uses ρ^i ($i = 2,..., m$) to determine the set of active constraints A, these estimates directly specify the feasible region in the policy parameter space.

3. Computer simulation in a simple MDP task

3.1 MDP setting

In order to evaluate the performance of the CPGRL from a viewpoint of constrained optimization problems, we apply the CPGRL to a simple three-state Markov Decision Problem shown in Fig.3. The sets of states and actions are $\{s_1, s_2, s_3\}$ and $\{a_1, a_2, a_3\}$, respectively. Let s and a denote the original state and action in this MDP problem while the variables x and u represent the state and action at each time step. Therefore, $x_t \in \{s_1, s_2, s_3\}$

and $u_t \in \{a_1, a_2, a_3\}$. Each action achieves the intended effect with probability 0.8, but it makes a random transition otherwise. For example, from the state s_1 the action a_1 moves the agent to s_2, s_3, s_1 with probabilities 0.8, 0.1, 0.1, respectively.

One intrinsic reward r^1 and three extrinsic rewards r^2, r^3, r^4 are prepared in this problem;

$$r^1 = \begin{bmatrix} 1 & 0 & -1 \\ 1 & 0 & 2 \\ 1 & 0 & -1 \end{bmatrix}, \ r^2 = \begin{bmatrix} 0 & -1 & 0 \\ 0 & 0 & 1 \\ 0 & 0 & 0 \end{bmatrix}, \ r^3 = \begin{bmatrix} 0 & 0 & 0 \\ 0 & 0 & -1 \\ 0 & 0 & 1 \end{bmatrix}, \ r^4 = \begin{bmatrix} 0 & 1 & 0 \\ 0 & 0 & 0 \\ 0 & 0 & -1 \end{bmatrix},$$

where $r^i = (r_{jk})$ is a reward value of r^i when the action a_k is selected at the state s_j. For instance, the reward vector is $r = [2 \ 1 \ -1 \ 0 \ ]^T$ when the agent selects the action a_3 at the state s_2. Under these settings, the optimal policy is to select a_1 in each state, and the corresponding long-term average reward vector is $[1 \ 0 \ 0 \ 0]^T$. It should be noted that the extrinsic rewards are competitive with each other. As the stochastic policy, we use a lookup table with softmax distribution

$$\mu_\theta(x_t, u_t) = \frac{\exp(\theta_{x_t, u_t})}{\sum_{u'} \exp(\theta_{x_t, u'})},$$

yielding a total of nine policy parameters. That is, the policyparameters are assigned such that $\theta_1 = \theta_{s_1, a_1}$, $\theta_2 = \theta_{s_1, a_2}$, and so on.

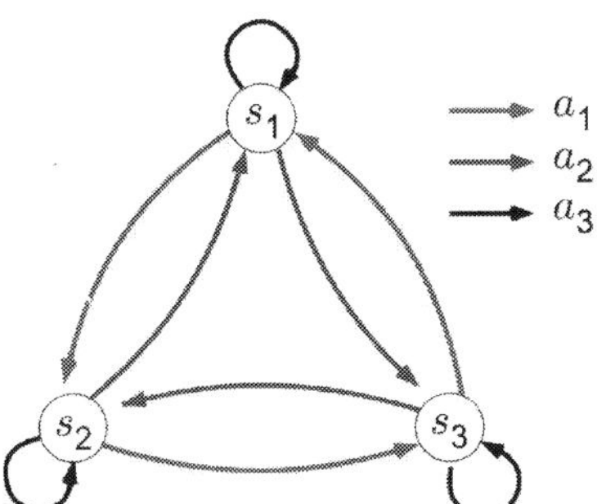

Fig. 3. Simple MDP with three states, three actions, and four reward functions.

The GPOMDP algorithm is adopted for estimating the policy gradient. Each policy parameter is randomly initialized with a uniform distribution over the interval $[0, 1]$. Thresholds used in inequality constraints are set as $G^2 = G^3 = G^4 = 0$. Other meta-parameters are set as follows: $\alpha_\rho = 0.02$, $\beta = 0.99$, $\alpha_1 = \alpha_e = 0.02$. These values are determined by trial and error. In order to compare the performance, we consider two different approaches named the CONstraints-Based (CONB) and the SUM method. The CONB switches the policy gradient of each reward according to the following condition:

$$\Delta = \begin{cases} \Delta^1 & \text{if } g^i - G^i > 0 \text{ for } i = 2, \dots, m \\ \Delta^j & \text{otherwise}, \quad j = \arg\min_{i \in A}(\rho^i - G^i). \end{cases}$$

to maximize the average reward of r^1 and to satisfy the constraints. The SUM learns to maximize the average reward of the summation of all rewards

$$r^{\mathrm{sum}} = r^1 + r^2 + r^3 + r^4$$

based on the standard policy gradient method. However, it is expected that the learned parameters does not satisfy the constraints since the SUM does not consider the constraints at all. The agent starts at the state $x_0 = s_1$. The number of episodes and steps are $N_T = 100$ and $N_K = 10000$, respectively. We perform 20 simulation runs.

3.2 Experimental results

Fig.4 shows the means and the standard deviations of 20 simulation runs obtained by the CPGRL, CONB, and SUM, respectively. The CPGRL found the parameters that satisfy the inequality constraints at the very early stage of learning, and the standard deviations of the average rewards of constraints were very small after 1×10^3-th episode. The CONB also obtained the policy parameters satisfying constraints, but it took a longer time than the CPGRL. The long-term average reward of r^1 was gradually increased by the CPGRL. Interestingly, the CONB failed to maximize the average reward of r^1. In addition, we found that the standard deviation estimated by the CONB was larger than that of the CPGRL. The performance of the SUM was different from those of the CPGRL and the CONB because the constraint on r^3 was violated at all. Although the SUM obtained the best average reward on r^1, it failed to find the policy parameters satisfying the constraint on r^3.

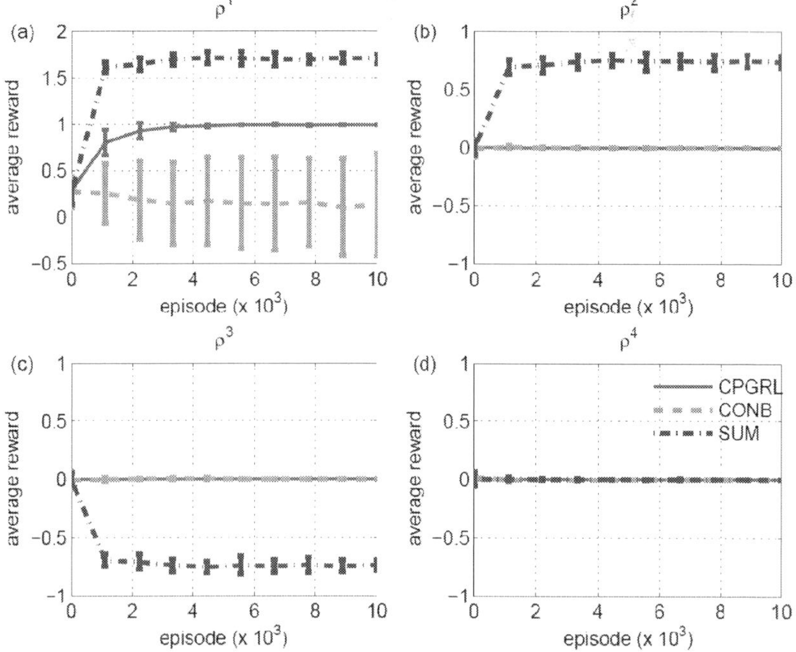

Fig. 4. Transition of the estimated average rewards. (a) ρ^1, (b) ρ^2, (c) ρ^3, and (d) ρ^4, respectively. These figures show the means and standard deviations of 20 independent runs.

Then, we checked the stochastic policy during the learning process. Fig.5 shows the evolution of the policy parameters of the CPGRL, CONB, and SUM, respectively. In this figure, all policies lie in the lower-left triangle, and gray-colour represents the average reward of r^1. Although all methods could obtain appropriate action at the state s_1 ($\Pr(a_1 \mid s_1)$ = 1 is optimal), the CONB and SUM obtained inappropriate actions at the states s_2 and s_3. For example, the SUM leaned to select a_3 at s_2 because the large positive reward (2 + 1 - 1 + 0 = 2) was received in this case. Obviously, this violated the constraints on r^3. The CONB failed to obtain the appropriate action at s_3. It should be noted that both of a_1 and a_2 did not generate negative rewards in this state. However, the CONB failed to improve the average reward of r^1 because the gradient of r^1 was rarely selected. Since the estimated average reward by (4) is not deterministic, some constraints were violated suddenly. On the contrary, the CPGRL successfully obtained the optimal policy that satisfied all constraints in this simulation.

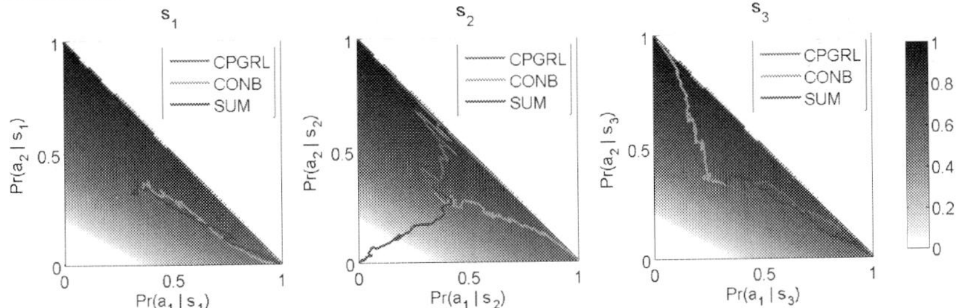

Fig. 5. Evolution of probabilities for action selection calculated from the policy parameters. Each lower triangle shows a feasible region of the values of the probabilities.

4. Control task of a robotic arm

4.1 Simulation setting

Then we conduct a control task of a robotic arm to investigate how the thresholds G^i used in the inequality constraints affect the learning processes in the CPGRL framework. Fig.6 (a) shows a simulated environment. There exists a typical two-link arm that can interact with four objects (circle, star, square, and triangle). These four objects are fixed in the environment. The intrinsic reward r^1 is computed from the distance between the position of the end-effector of the arm and the nearest objects. Fig.6 (b) shows a distribution of r^1. This dense reward function enables the robotic arm to learn touching behaviours actively. Then, two extrinsic rewards r^2 and r^3 are introduced in this task. The first extrinsic reward gives upper and lower bounds on the joint angles ϕ_1 and ϕ_2 while the second extrinsic reward depends on whether the touched object is appetitive or aversive:

$$r^2 = \begin{cases} 0 & \frac{\pi}{10} \leq \phi_1 \leq \frac{\pi}{2},\ \frac{\pi}{4} \leq \phi_2 \leq \frac{3\pi}{4}, \\ -1 & \text{otherwise,} \end{cases}$$

$$r^3 = \begin{cases} 1 & \text{if the object is appetitive,} \\ -1 & \text{if the object is aversive,} \\ 0 & \text{otherwise.} \end{cases}$$

It should be noted that zero reward is given when the robotic arm touches the circular and triangular objects.

The continuous state is $x = [\phi_1, \phi_2]^T$ while the continuous action consists of desired joint velocities, $u = [\Delta\phi_1, \Delta\phi_2]^T$. To represent the stochastic policy, we use a normalized Gaussian network,

$$\mu_\theta(x_t, u_t) = \eta_1 \exp\left[-\eta_2 \left\| u_t - \theta^\top n(x_t) \right\|\right],$$

where η_1, η_2 and $n(x)$ denote the constant values and the vector of the basis function. The number of basis functions is 40, determined by trial and error. In this experiment, Konda's actor-critic method is used to compute the policy gradient.

This simulation does not consider dynamics of the arm. The initial joint angles are initialized randomly. The same meta-parameters such as learning rates are used in section 3. When the arm touches one of the objects or $N_T = 1000$ time steps are expired, the episode terminates. One episode lasts for $N_K = 10000$ episodes and we perform 20 simulation runs.

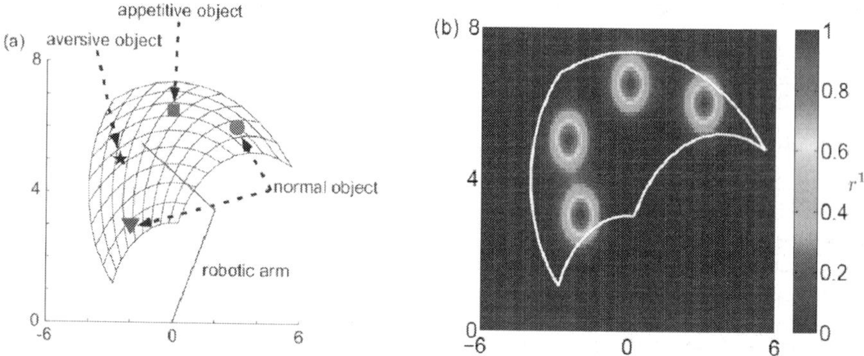

Fig. 6. Control task of a robotic arm. (a) Simulated environment where a mesh represents a reachable region of the end-effector of the arm. (b) Distribution of the intrinsic reward r^1.

4.2 Experimental results

Fig.7 (a) shows the number of touches on the objects in each 100 episodes and a typical learned behaviour at the end of episodes when the robotic arm is motivated only by the intrinsic reward. Since r^1 was a dense reward function, it was not hard to obtain touching behaviours. Then we introduce two constraints by extrinsic rewards with thresholds $G^2 = G^3 = 0$. Fig.7 (b) shows the experimental results. At the early stage of learning, the robotic arm touched the aversive star object. Then, it learned to avoid the aversive star object after about 1×10^3 episodes. The bottom of Fig.7 (b) shows a typical learned behaviour. The end-effector of the robot arm was initially located in the neighbourhood of the aversive star object, but the arm touched the triangular object.

Finally, we strengthen the constraint by setting $G^3 = 0.5$ and observe the behaviours shown in Fig.7 (c). Since the robotic arm has to touch the square object in order to obtain a positive r^2, the number of touches on the square objects increases while those on other objects are gradually reduced to zero. It is revealed that G^2 is a sensitive threshold that affects the resultant behaviours. The obtained behaviour at the end of episode is shown in the bottom of Fig.7 (c).

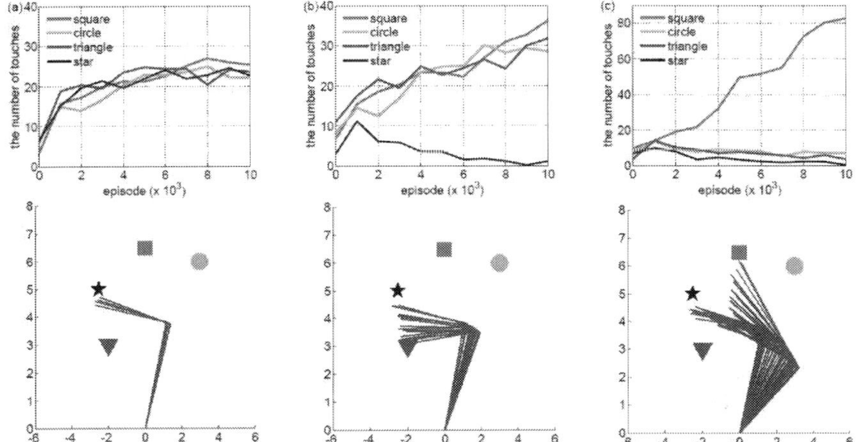

Fig. 7. Number of touches on the objects and learned behaviours. (a) No constraints. (b) Normal constraints: $G^2 = G^3 = 0$. (c) Tight constraints: $G^2 = 0$ and $G^3 = 0.5$.

5. Conclusion

In this chapter we have proposed the CPGRL that maximizes the long-term average reward under the inequality constraints that define the feasible policy space. Experimental results encourage us to conduct the robotic experiments because one of our interests is to design the developmental learning methods for real hardware systems. Although we could not discuss the design principles of intrinsic and extrinsic rewards to establish a sustainable and scalable learning progress, this is very important. We think that the CPGRL gives the first step towards developmental learning. We develop the experimental setup that integrates the CPGRL and the technique of the embodied evolution in our multi-robot platform named "Cyber Rodents" (Doya & Uchibe, 2005). In this case, the intrinsic reward is computed from sensor outputs while the extrinsic rewards are given according the external events such as collisions with obstacles, capturing a battery pack, and so on. We have reported that good exploratory reward is acquired as the intrinsic reward through the interaction among three mobile robots (Uchibe and Doya, to appear). We also plan to test other types of intrinsic rewards used in previous studies (Singh et al., 2005; Oudeyer & Kaplan, 2004).

Finally, we describe three foreseeable extensions of this study. At first, we improve the efficiency of numerical computation. It is known that the learning speed of standard PGRL can be slow due to high variance in the estimate. Then, the Natural Policy Gradient (NPG) method (Morimura et al., 2005) supported by the theory of information geometry is implemented to accelerate the speed of learning. Secondly, we develop a method to tune the thresholds used in the inequality constraints during learning processes. As shown in section 4, the learned behaviours were strongly affected by the setting of the thresholds. From a viewpoint of constrained optimization problems, G^i is just a meta-parameter given by the experimenters. However, the learning agent will show a variety of behaviours by changing these thresholds. We think that CPGRL has a potential to create new behaviours through the interaction between intrinsic and extrinsic rewards.

6. References

Barto, A.G.; Singh, S. & Chentanez, N. (2004). Intrinsically Motivated Learning of Hierarchical Collections of Skills, *Proceedings of International Conference on Developmental Learning*

Baxter, J. & Bartlett, P.L. (2001). Infinite-horizon gradient-based policy search. *Journal of Artificial Intelligence Research*, Vol. 15, pages 319-350

Deci, E.L. & Flaste, R. (1996). *Why we do what we do: understanding self-motivation*, Penguin books

Dolgov, D. & Durfee, E. (2005). Stationary deterministic policies for constrained MDPs with multiple rewards, costs, and discount factors, *Proceedings of the 19th International Joint Conference on Artificial Intelligence*, pp. 1326-1331

Doya, K. & Uchibe, E. (2005). The Cyber Rodent Project: Exploration of adaptive mechanisms for self-preservation and self-reproduction. *Adaptive Behavior*, Vol. 13, pages 149-160

Feinberg, E. & Shwartz, A. (1999). Constrained dynamic programming with two discount factors: Applications and an algorithm. *IEEE Transactions on Automatic Control*, Vol. 44, pages 628-630

Konda, V.R. & Tsitsiklis, J.N. (2003). Actor-critic algorithms. *SIAM Journal on Control and Optimization*, Vol. 42, No. 4, pages 1143-1166

Meeden, L.A.; Marshall, J.B. & Blank, D. (2004). Self-Motivated, Task-Independent Reinforcement Learning for Robots, *Proceedings of 2004 AAAI Fall Symposium on Real-World Reinforcement Learning*

Morimura, T.; Uchibe, E. & Doya, K. (2005). Utilizing the natural gradient in temporal difference reinforcement learning with eligibility traces, *Proceedings of the 2nd International Symposium on Information Geometry and its Application*, pp. 256-263

Oudeyer, P.-Y. & Kaplan, F. (2004). Intelligent adaptive curiosity: A source of self-development, *Proceedings of the 4th International Workshop on Epigenetic Robotics*, pp. 127-130

Oudeyer, P.-Y., Kaplan, F. & Hafner, V. (2007). Intrinsic motivation systems for autonomous mental development. *IEEE Transactions on Evolutionary Computation*, Vol. 11, No. 2, pages 265-286

Rosen, S.A. (1960). The gradient projection method for nonlinear programming --- part I: linear constraints. *Journal of the Society for Industrial and Applied Mathematics*, Vol. 8, No. 1, pages 181-217

Singh, S.; Barto, A.G. & Chentanez, N. (2005). Intrinsically motivated reinforcement learning, *Advances in Neural Information Processing Systems 17*, pp. 1281-1288, MIT Press

Stout, A.; Konidaris, G.D. & Barto, A.G. (2005). Intrinsically motivated reinforcement learning: A promising framework for developmental robot learning, *Proceedings of the AAAI Spring Symposium Workshop on Developmental Robotics*

Sutton, R.S. & Barto, A.G. (1998). *Reinforcement Learning: An Introduction*, MIT Press

Sutton, R.S.; Precup, D. & Singh, S. (1999). Between MDPs and semi-MDPs: A framework for temporal abstraction in reinforcement learning. *Artificial Intelligence*, Vol. 112, pages 181-211

Uchibe, E. & Doya, K. (to appear). Finding Intrinsic Rewards by Embodied Evolution and Constrained Reinforcement Learning. *Neural Networks*

12

TempUnit: A Bio-Inspired Spiking Neural Network

Olivier F. L. Manette

Unité de Neurosciences Intégrative et Computationnelle (UNIC), CNRS
France

1. Introduction

Formal neural networks have many applications. Applications of control of tasks (motor control) as well as speech generation have a certain number of common constraints. We are going to see seven main constraints that a system based on a neural network should follow in order to be able to produce that kind of control. Afterwards we will present the TempUnit model which is able to give some answers for all these seven criteria.

1.1 Learning

Neural networks show usually a certain level of learning abilities, (Hornik, 1991). In the case of systems of motor control or of speech generation those learning skills are particularly important. Indeed they enable the system to establish the link between the motor command and the act as it has been achieved. In real systems (not simulated), biological or machines, the effector could evolve for all sort of reasons such as limb growth or injury for biological systems; For artificial systems, the reason could be some breakage or a subsystem malfunction. It has also been demonstrated that the motor command is directly related to the characteristics of the effector (Bernstein, 1967; Hogan & Flash, 1987; Gribble & Ostry, 1996). Thus learning capabilities should be permanently maintained: it is necessary that the neural network is able to evolve its transfer function. In this case, because the aim is to learn the link between a desired output (the effector activity) and a given input (the motor command), it is called supervised learning.

1.2 Inverse model

Several models of motor control exist but we can globally group them into two categories: reactive (Sherrington, 1906/1947) and predictive (Beevor, 1904). Reactive models usually work as a closed loop, in which a very imprecise motor command is sent and is then updated using sensory feedbacks. For most movements, for instance, the basket ball throw (Seashore, 1938; Keele, 1968; Bossom, 1974; Taub, 1976), sensory feedback is simply too slow to enable efficient motor control. In this chapter, we will focus particularly on predictive models. Predictive models imply the calculation of a forward function which gives, from a given motor command, a prediction of the effector activity (Desmurget & Grafton, 2000). This type of function can be very useful because it enables the result of a given command to be simulated without the need to effectively carry it out. However, the inverse function is much more useful because it enables determination of the motor command from a desired motor output. Theory of motor control predicted the need for an inverse model (Berthoz, 1996) in the brain to enable calculation of the motor command (Shadmehr & Mussa-ivaldi, 1994; Wolpert et al., 1995; Kawato, 1999). The use of an inverse function enables the system to calculate by itself the motor command that leads to a specific desired result, which is a great advantage.

1.3 Syntax

In linguistics, syntax is the group of rules that defines the chain of words to form sentences. In control of speech production, it is easy to understand why the system needs to be able to respect those syntax rules. But it should also be the case in control of movements and it is even more important than in speech generation. Indeed, while a limb is in a particular position, it is simply impossible to immediately reach any other arbitrary position. From a given position of a limb, only a few other positions are accessible, otherwise some bad command could possibly damage the system if those rules are not respected. The neural network in charge of the overall control of the system should therefore necessarily respect scrupulously those chaining rules from one state to another state of the system.

1.4 Decision node

The lack of flexibility is generally the main problem in a feed-forward system: a system should be able to interrupt the execution of a motor program to change direction in order to, for example, ward off an unexpected disruption. Hence, a process able to manage decision nodes at every single time step, with the aim of enabling the system to evolve in different directions, should be integrated.

1.5 Respect of the range limits

Keeping the system in the range of possible values is another important constraint for a task control system. Also, some mechanism able to handle aberrant values has to be integrated in order to avoid damage to the system.

1.6 Complexity

The choice of the neural network architecture is also an important issue since it is absolutely necessary to use an architecture adapted to the problem to be solved. An under-sized network will not be able to obtain the expected results with the desired level of performance. Conversely, an over-sized network can show problems such as over-learning, i.e. an inability to correctly generalize the data, possibly even to the point of learning the noise. It is therefore important to obtain a system adapted to the desired task and a clear way to find the best fit architecture.

1.7 Parsimony

In a predictive model, the system includes a feed-forward module that gives the predicted motor activity from a motor command. It is then equivalent to encoding the motor activity in the command domain. A well designed system should limit the command size at its maximum. It does mean maximize the information compression rate.

1.8 Suggested solution

The choice of a transfer function is generally a problem for formal neural networks, because they should be determined "by hand" after several trials. After having been chosen, the transfer function does not evolve anymore and limits the future neural network abilities in a decisive behavior. Furthermore, there exist only empirical solutions to determination of the number of neurons or the size of the hidden layer (Wierenga & Kluytmans, 1994; Venugopal & Baets, 1994; Shepard, 1990).

The behavior of the TempUnit model presented below enables us to give some solutions to these problems found in common formal neural network models. TempUnit does not have a fixed transfer function but is able to learn the best adapted one to fit the desired signal. The basic principle is quite simple because it is only based on the principle of temporal summation such as has been observed in biological neurons. In order to keep thinking at a biologically inspired level, the input of each TempUnit neuron is a spikes train: only binary values. We will now develop in the following the reasons why TempUnit is a particularly well-adapted model for satisfying all the constraints previously discussed.

2. The tempUnit model

2.1 Temporal summation and straight forward function

The TempUnit model is based on the mechanism of the temporal summation of post-synaptic potentials as observed in biological neurons (e.g. Rieke et al, 1996). TempUnit means simply 'Temporal summation unit'. When a spike arrives at a synaptic bouton it triggers a local potential in the soma of the post-synaptic neuron. If many spikes arrive at a fast enough rate, the triggered potentials are summed in the post-synaptic neuron to shape a global membrane activity. This new global temporal activity of the post-synaptic neuron depends only on the structure of the input spikes train from the pre-synaptic neurons. In fact, this principle, as noticed in biological neurons, can be generalized to any serial system where the output is only correlated to the input. A TempUnit network can be considered in this form as a binary-analog converter whose output is totally deterministic, as we shall see later. Furthermore, biological neurons have, in common with TempUnit, a deterministic behavior, as shown by empirical (Mainen & Sejnowski, 1995).

In the simplest case, a TempUnit network is composed of only a single pre-synaptic neuron which is the input and a post-synaptic neuron which is the location of the temporal summation. r is the result of the temporal summation, the membrane activity, x is the spiking activity of the pre-synaptic neuron and v is the post-synaptic potential or basis function. To simplify we will work on a discrete time level. The potential v lasts p time steps. p will define for the rest of this article the size of the vector v. It is then possible from those parameters to write the membrane potential r of the post-synaptic neuron as a function of time t:

$$r(t) = \sum_{i=1}^{p} x_{t-p+i} v_i \tag{1}$$

The u^t vector can define the sequence of values from x_{t-p} to x_t, which means the sequence of the input activity x from time step $t - p$ to time step t. It implies that the u vector is also of size p like the v vector. We can hence simplify equation 1 in this manner:

$$r(t) = \sum_{i=1}^{p} u_i^t v_i = u^t v \tag{2}$$

2.2 Supervised learning

The learning skills of the TempUnit neurons have been already demonstrated in Manette and Maier, 2006 but the learning equations have not been explicitly published. Let $f(t)$ be a temporal function that we wish to learn with TempUnit. The learning algorithm should make $r(t)$ reach $f(t)$ by modifying the weights v_i of the basis function vector. For every i from 1 to p, it is possible to follow this rule:

$$\forall i \ de \ 1 \ \grave{a} \ p : \ \frac{dv_i(t)}{dt} = \gamma(f(t) - r(t))x_{t-p+i} \tag{3}$$

This equation gives very good results and a very good convergence; see Manette & Maier, 2006, for more details.

2.3 Evolution of r analysis

Let us see how the output signal evolves as a function of the time and as a function of the basis function v:

$$\frac{dr(t)}{dt} = x_{t+1}v_p + \left[\sum_{i=2}^{p} u_i^t(v_{i-1} - v_i)\right] - u_1^t v_1 \tag{4}$$

We observe in equation 4 that $dr(t)/dt$ shows an evolution depending only on the new input value: x_{t+1}, which indicates that this is a decision node depending on the new binary value x_{t+1}. Thus the next spike is able to define if the following time activity of the TempUnit will follow one direction or another.

2.4 The graph of the neural activity

Equation 4 shows that the output of the TempUnit neuron can at every time step takes two different directions depending on the new binary input, i.e. whether a new spike arrives at instant t+1 or not. According to this principle, it is thus possible to build a graph that represents the entire neuron activity. We can define, F as a vector space and $(c_1, \cdots, c_n)$ a basis of F. In the current case with only one input (pre-synaptic neuron) and only one TempUnit (post-synaptic neuron), $n = 2$. We can, using this vector space, project the entire set of input vector u^t by calculating the coordinates c_1 and c_2 as follows:

$$u^t = \begin{cases} c_1 = \sum_{i=1}^{p} 2^{i-1} u_i^t \\ \\ c_2 = \sum_{i=1}^{p} 2^{p-i} u_i^t \end{cases} \tag{5}$$

Given that every u vector is of size p, as defined earlier, and contains only binary data, there exist exactly 2^p different input vectors. Our vector space contains thus this exact amount of nodes. Every vector u^t is thus represented in the vector space by a point with coordinates (c_1^t, c_2^t). According to equation (4), every single point in this vector space is a decision node from where it is possible to follow two different paths on the graph through two different nodes. We can calculate the coordinates of the vertices that connect the nodes to each other:

$$a^t = \begin{cases} 2^{p-1}x_{t+1} - \sum_{i=2}^{p} 2^{i-1}u_i^t - u_1^t \\ \\ x_{t+1} + \sum_{i=2}^{p} 2^{p-i}u_i^t - 2^{p-1}u_1^t \end{cases} \tag{6}$$

The coordinates of vertices a^t depend only on u^t, i.e. directly from the previous node in the vector space, and on the presence or absence of a spike at the next time step $t+1$. As a consequence, at every node in the space F as defined by the basis (c_1, c_2), there exist only two vertices reaching two other nodes of this space. Thus there exist 2^{p+1} vertices in the space F.

(c_1, c_2) makes a basis because every vector u^t can be associated with only a unique pair of coordinates in space F. It is therefore easy to move from a vector u^t to the coordinates of a particular node of the graph and vice versa. In reality, c_1 and c_2 are both a basis and it is unnecessary to know both coordinates of a specific node to be able to identify the related vector u^t. Let us take the case of the calculation of vector u^t using only c_2:

$$\text{for i=1}: \qquad \begin{cases} u_1^t = 1 \ si \ c_2^t \geq 2^{p-1} \\ u_1^t = 0 \ else \end{cases}$$

$$\forall i \ from \ 2 \ to \ p: \qquad \begin{cases} u_i^t = 1 \ si \ c_2^t \geq \left(2^{p-i} + \sum_{j=1}^{i-1} 2^{p-j}u_j^t \right) \\ u_i^t = 0 \ else \end{cases} \tag{7}$$

Example:
To illustrate this, we will calculate the coordinates of the node in F of the vector $u^t = [0010]$. In this case, $u_3^t = 1$ while $u_1^t = u_2^t = u_4^t = 0$, so that, taking into account equation (5), we can calculate the coordinates c_1 and c_2 which are: $u^t = (2^{3-1}, 2^{4-3}) = (4,2)$. From equation (6), we can calculate also the two vertices a_1^t and a_2^t from this node: $a_1^t = [-2,2]$ and $a_2^t = [6,3]$. We know then that from the original node u^t it is possible to reach the next node of coordinates $u^{t+1} = (2,4)$ or the other node $u^{t+1} = (10,5)$. Using equation (7) we can determine the corresponding input vectors $u^{t+1} = [0100]$ and $u^{t+1} = [0101]$ respectively.

Graphical representation:
In the case of only one TempUnit with only one binary input, it is still possible to make a graphical representation of the graph of the neural activity. It is then easier to understand how information is organized on the graph. Figure 1 presents in a schematic fashion a very small graph of neuronal activity containing only 16 nodes.

Figure 2, by contrast, is drawn using the exact coordinates c_1 and c_2 as calculated from equation (5), with vertices as calculated from equation (6).

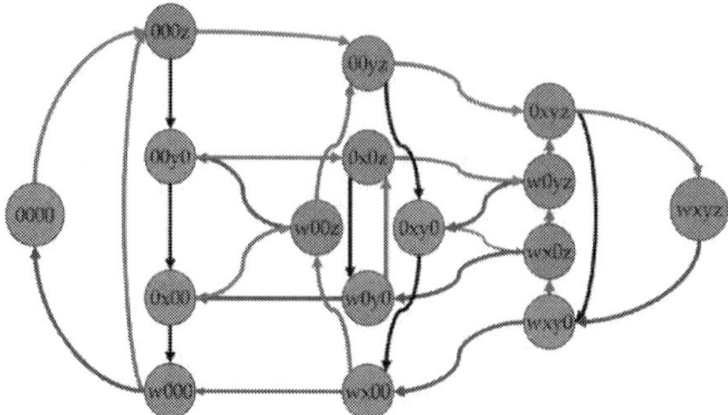

Fig. 1. This diagram illustrates the organization of a graph of neural activity for a TempUnit which has a basis function of four time steps in length. This makes, therefore sixteen different combinations of the inputs which are represented by a colored circle, red or blue as a function of the presence or absence of a spike in the bin at the extreme left respectively. Absence of a spike in a bin is represented with a '0' in the 4-element code in every circle. Presence of a spike is symbolized with one of the letters w, x, y or z depending on the position of this specific spike within the train of four time steps. Vertices are drawn with a colored arrow. Red arrows indicate an increase in the global number of spikes in the input train u^t ; blue arrows indicate the decrease of one spike in the input vector; black color typify that there is no global modification in the amount of spike but there are no spikes in the next time step t+1. Pink arrows indicate that there is no modification of the global number of spikes but a spike will arrive at the next time step.

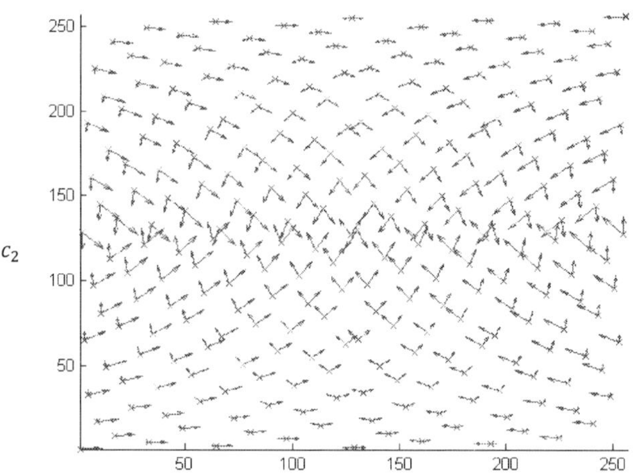

Fig. 2. Graph of the neural activity calculated with Matlab® for 256 nodes. Each node is represented by an 'x' and the beginning of each vertex by an arrow. We clearly observe trends in orientation related to the localization of the vertices.

2.5 Inverse function

It is possible to draw on the same graph of neural activity both the input and the output of the TempUnit neuron with a particular color code. As well as in figure 2 where we can see trends in the vertex directions and positions, in figure 3 & 4 we can observe that outputs values are not organized on a randomly but on contrary as a function of their intensity. Of course, the organization of the outputs on the graph is directly based on the basis function v. Nevertheless, in spite of great difference that can be observed from one basis function v (e.g. fig. 3) to another (e.g. fig. 4), it is still possible to establish some similarities which enable us to calculate an inverse function.

An inverse function enables calcultation of the input corresponding to a desired output. The inverse of the function in equation (2) is a surjective function for the most of the sets of weights in the basis function v and this is the main problem. Because a surjective function means that for a specified value there can exists more than one possible answer and it is difficult to determine which of all those possible answers is the one that is needed. Indeed in figure 3 there are areas of the same color including many input nodes, which means of the same output values. The graph of neural activity gives a way to determine which of those possible values is the good one.

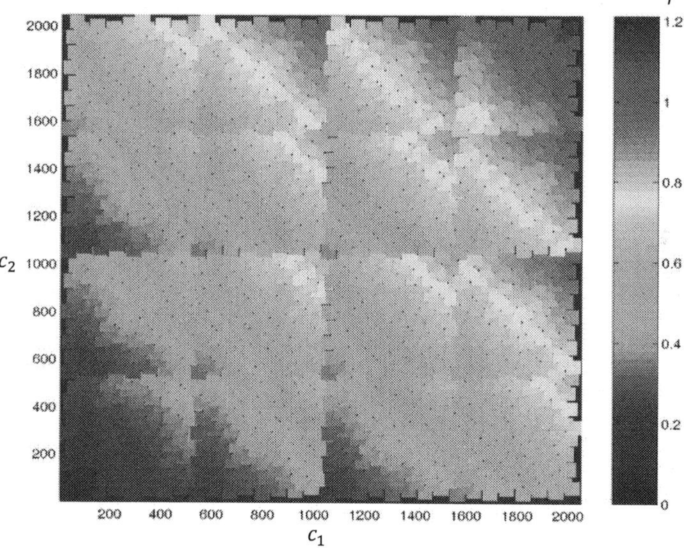

Fig. 3. Graph of neural activity showing all the possible outputs of a TempUnit neuron using the same system of coordinates of the input from equation (5). The input u and the basis function v are in this case of size $p = 11$ time steps, thus there are 2048 nodes in the graph. The basis function v is an inverted Gaussian function: $v_i = 0.2 - e^{i-(p/2)^2/2(p/5)^2} / p\sqrt{2\pi}/5$.

The color code represents the intensity of the output value. Red indicates higher values while blue indicates lower values.

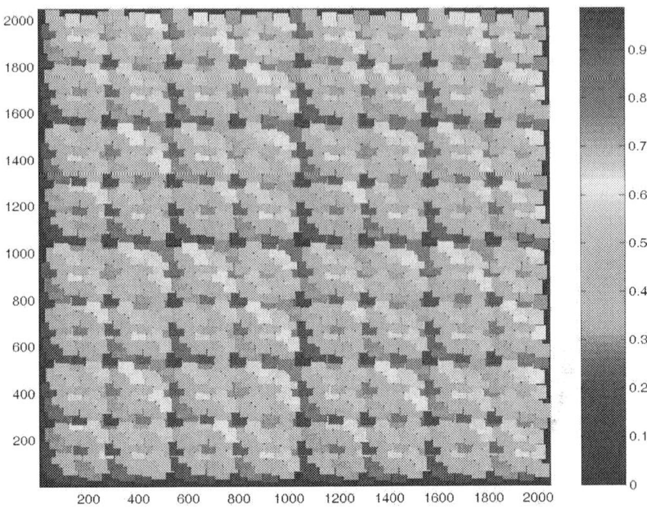

Fig. 4. Graph of neural activity showing the output using a color code. The basis function v is a Gaussian function: $v_i = 0.2 - e^{i-(p/2)^2/2(p/5)^2} / {p\sqrt{2\pi}/5}$ which is compatible with the

"value" type of neural coding (Salinas & Abbott, 1995, Baraduc & Guigon, 2002).

In brief, the inverse function algorithm which from a sequence of temporal desired output values gives back the path on the graph of the neural activity and then the temporal sequence of the related input, is composed of five steps:

1. Determine the set of coordinates on the graph associated with a given output at time t.
2. From the set of the selected nodes in 1), calculate the set of nodes for time step t+1.
3. In the set of nodes for time step t+1 delete all the nodes which do not correspond to the desired output value at time t+1 and delete as well all the nodes in the subset corresponding to time step t which are not reaching any of the remaining nodes of the subset t+1.
4. Start again from step 1 while in the subset t there is more than one possible solution. Instant t+1 becomes instant t and instant t+2 becomes instant t+1.
5. From the sequence of coordinates on the graph, calculate the corresponding binary input using equation (7).

Why to try to determine on the graph the set of nodes leading to a particular output value? Simply because on the graph the output values are organized as a function of their intensity, we will see in the following that only a simple calculation is necessary to find out all the researched nodes. Another important point is that it is also possible to use the links between the nodes in order to reduce the indeterminacy of the multiple possible results.

How are the output values organized on the graph?
Studying the relationship between the coordinates of the nodes on the graph $r = g(c_1)$, one observes that it is a periodic function containing multiple imbricated periods and generally growing especially if v is growing. Periods of g are always the same and are completely independent of the function v but only depend on p: $T_1 = 2^{p-1}, T_2 = 2^{p-2}$, etc. ... It is hence easy from a small amount of data to deduce the complete set of possible output values because of this known property of periodic functions:

$$\forall i \; 1 \leq i \leq p - 1 : \qquad g(c_1 + T_i) = g(c_1) + m_i \tag{8}$$

For instance, if p=5, the graph contain 2^5=32 nodes. The function $r = g(c_1)$ has hence 5-1=4 imbricated periods: $T_1 = 2^{5-1} = 16, T_2 = 8, T_3 = 4, T_4 = 2$. To infer all the 32 possible output values on the graph, one should first calculate $r = g(1)$, $r = g(2)$ then $r = g(3)$ which following equation (8), allow one to calculate $m_4 = g(3) - g(1)$. $m_3 = g(5) - g(1)$, $m_2 = g(9) - g(1)$ and $m_1 = g(17) - g(1)$. Thus, from only these six values we can deduce the complete set of the 32 values of the graph. The search algorithm in the output values could be similar to already known algorithm of search in an ordered list.
Figure 5 shows an example of the function $r = g(c_1)$ for a basis function $v_i = i^3$. Of course, the function $r = g(c_1)$ varies as a function of v. But, as in figure 4, it is always a periodic function. Drawing a horizontal line at the level of the desired output value on the y-axis gives a graphical solution of the point 1) in the inverse function algorithm. The set of searched-for nodes corresponds to all the coordinates on the x-axis every time the horizontal line crosses the function $r = g(c_1)$. In the case of the example shown in figure 4, one can see that a specified output value (r) is observed only a few times (maybe 3 or 4 times at maximum), but depending on the shape of the function v it could be much more.

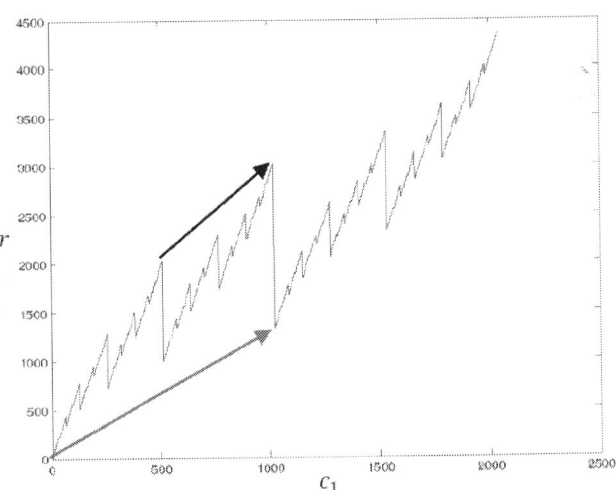

Fig. 5. Example of function $r = g(c_1)$ with p=11 giving 2048 nodes in the graph of neural activity. The basis function is $v_i = i^3$. The red vector indicates the vector m_2 while the black one indicates the vector m_3.

Once all the nodes have been selected according to a desired output value, one can search the connected nodes at the next time step. Equation 6 enables us to calculate these connected nodes at the next time step. All the nodes of the subset selected for time t+1 which are not associated with the next desired output value at time t+1 are deleted. In addition, all the nodes from the subset for time t which are after this no longer linked with any other node of the subset t+1 are also deleted. It is possible to continue with the same principle of deleting independent nodes which are not linked with any other node of a following subset. The algorithm finishes when it obtains only one possible pathway on the graph, which should represent the searched-for input command. Obviously this algorithm gives the exact inverse function. If there could be some imprecision on the desired output value, this method should not change except that nodes associated with close values should also be selected and not only nodes with the exact desired value.

Partial inverse function

In some cases of motor control, it may be better to only ask for the final desired position and let the system determine by itself all the intermediate steps. On the graph it is easy to determine all the intermediate values. It is particularly simple to determine all the intermediate values with the help of the graph. Indeed, the initial state as well as the final state should be defined by nodes on the graph and the path between those nodes is an already well known problem because it is equivalent to an algorithm for finding the shortest path on a graph, about which it is unnecessary to give more details.

2.6 Complexity

Since so far we have only investigated the capacity of a single TempUnit with a single input, we will next investigate the capacities of other TempUnit network architectures. We will see in the following that the signal generator abilities of a specified TempUnit network depends directly on its architecture. Each type of TempUnit network architecture corresponds to a particular kind of graph with very precise characteristics. The complexity of the neural network can be calculated based on the complexity of the emergent graph because the graph represents exactly the way the TempUnit network behaves. This gives a means of determining in a very precise fashion the kind of neural network architecture needed for a given type of generated temporal function characteristics.

One TempUnit with many inputs

Taking account all the Sk binary inputs of the TempUnit, equations 1 and 2 become:

$$r(t) = \sum_{i=1}^{p} \sum_{s=1}^{Sk} x_{s,t-p+i} v_i = \sum_{s=1}^{Sk} u_{t,s} v_i \qquad (9)$$

Figure 6 gives in a schematic fashion the architecture of equation 9.

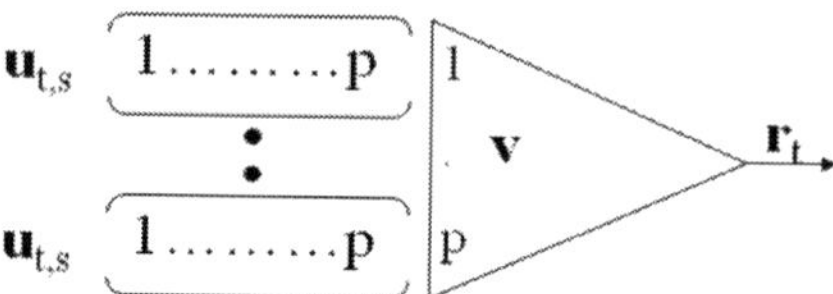

Fig. 6. Schema of one TempUnit with several binary inputs.

All the inputs can be summed equally to create a new global u vector and a new global x vector that contain all the summed input. This architecture is still biologically compatible; in particular, the resulting potential is much larger for near coincident arrival of spikes (Abeles, 1991; Abeles et al 1995). The evolution of the output r is then equivalent as what has been written in equation 4 but encoded with more than 1 bit of information. In this case every decision node can be connected with more than two other nodes. The global number of nodes in the graph is: $(Sk + 1)^p$

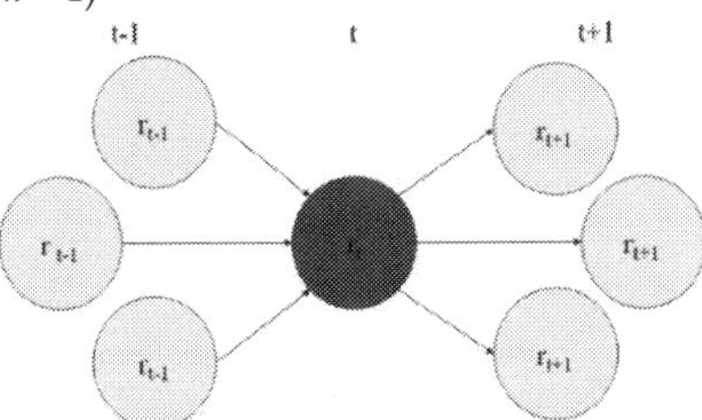

Fig. 7. Because all the inputs are equivalent, the degree of the graph is equal at $Sk + 1$. In this example is represented a node at time t with its previous and following connected nodes at times $t - 1$ and $t + 1$ respectively. In the case of one TempUnit with two different binary inputs, the graph becomes of vertex degree 3.

Many TempUnits with one input

In this case inputs are not equivalent because every input connects to different TempUnit. In a network of N TempUnits, there are 2^N vertices going from and to every node and the graph contains 2^{Np} nodes. Equation 10 shows the calculation of the output in this TempUnit architecture.

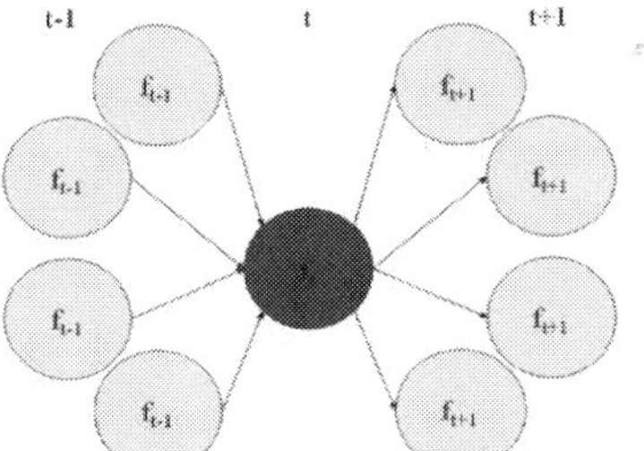

Fig. 8. Example of a node with its connected nodes at time $t - 1$ and at time $t + 1$ for a network of $N = 2$ TempUnits. In this case the graph of the global neural activity is of vertex degree $2^2 = 4$.

$$r(t) = \sum_{i=1}^{p} \sum_{j=1}^{N} x_{j,t-p+i} v_{i,j} = \sum_{j=1}^{N} u_{t,j} v_{i,j} \tag{10}$$

We have seen in this section that the evolution of the graph of neural activity depends directly on the TempUnit network architecture. The complexity of the graph could be defined by the number of elementary vertices that it contains, in other word, the number of nodes that multiply the vertex degree of the graph.

3. Conclusion

We have seen in this chapter the central role played by the graph of neural activity helping to understand the behavior of the TempUnit model. The graph gives the possibility of calculating the inverse function as well; it is also because of the graph that we can better understand the relationship between the TempUnit network architecture and its signal generator abilities. The graph of neural activity represents very clearly the behavior of the entire TempUnit network. The graph is not really implemented, only the TempUnit model is as defined on equation 1 or 9. Additionally, the graph of neural activity can be seen as the "software" while the TempUnit network would be the "hardware". In any case, a great advantage of the graph is that all the already-known algorithms in graph theory can then be applied to TempUnits.

A first use of the graph has been to solve the inverse function problem. Relationship between the nodes give us a mean to avoid any ambiguity produced by this surjective function.

In the control of task context, the existence of Central Pattern Generators (CPG) in the brain has been suggested based on work showing complex movements in deafferented animals (Brown, 1911; Taub, 1976; Bossom, 1974, Bizzi et al, 1992). Even if couples of "motor command"/"specific movement" are hardly credible, suggestions of motor schemes (Turvey, 1977) able to generate sets of specific kinds of movements (Pailhous & Bonnard, 1989) are more appealing. At the same time other data show that the motor activity depends also on sensory feedback (Adamovich et al, 1997). It would seem that instead of having two opposite theories, one more predictive using only CPGs and another completely reactive using mainly reflexes triggered by sensory feedback, a compromise could be found. Indeed, in considering the neural activity graphs of TempUnit networks one can see that TempUnit can work as a feedforward function generator. The entire graph could represent a complete set of a kind of movement while a path in the graph could constitute a particular execution of this movement. Furthermore, at every time step TempUnit is at a decision corner and the new direction depends on the inputs. We can imagine a sensory input that can then influence the TempUnit behavior to be able to adapt the movement command as a function of the sensory parameters. The TempUnit activity cannot escape from the path defined on the graph; hence these kinds of networks are naturally shaped to follow constrained rules like syntax. As well, since it is impossible to reach any arbitrary node from a given specific node, these kinds of networks are well suited for speech generation or motor control where it should not be possible to ask the system to reach any arbitrary position of the limb from another defined position.

4. Acknowledgements

This work was supported by research grant EC-FET-Bio-I3 (Facets FP6-2004-IST-FETPI 15879).

5. References

Abeles M., Corticonics: *Neural Circuits of the Cerebral Cortex*. Cambridge: Cambridge University Press., 1991.

Abeles M., H. Bergman, I. Gat, I. Meilijson, E. Seidenmann, N. Tishby, and E. Vaadia, "Cortical Activity Flips among quasi-Stationary States.," *Proc. Natl. Acad. Sci.*, vol. 92, pp. 8616-8620, 1995.

Adamovich S.V., Levin M.F, Feldman, A.G. (1997) Central modification of reflex parameters may underlie the fastest arm movement. Journal of Neurophysiology 77: 1460-1469.

Baraduc P. and E. Guigon, "Population computation of vectorial transformations.," *Neural Computation*, vol. 14, pp. 845–871, 2002.

Bernstein N.A. (1967) *The Coordination and Regulation of Movements*. London, Pergamon Press.

Berthoz A. (1996) *Le sens du mouvement*. Paris : Odile Jacob

Beevor C.E. (1904). *The croonian lectures on muscular movements and their representation in the central nervous system*. London: Adlar

Bizzi E., Hogan N., Mussa-Ivaldi F. A., Giszter S. (1992) Does the nervous system use equilibrium-point control to guide sigle and multiple joint movements? *Behavioral and Brain Sciences* 15: 603-613

Bossom J. (1974). Movement without proprioception. *Brain Research* 71: 285-296.

Brown T.G. (1911) The intrinsic factors in the act of progression in the mammal. *Proceeding Royal Society*, London, Series B, 84: 308-319.

Desmurget M, Grafton S. Forward modeling allows feedback control for fast reaching movements. *Trends Cogn Sci*. 4: 423-431, 2000.

Gribble P.L., Ostry, D. J. (1996) Origins of the power law relation between movement velocity and curvature: modeling the effects of muscle mechanics and limb dynamics. *Journal of Neurophysiology* 6: 2853-2860.

Hogan N., Flash T. (1987). Moving gracefully: quantitative theories of motor coordination. *Trends in Neuroscience* 10: 170-174.

Hornik K. (1991). Approximation capabilities of multilayer feedforward networks. *Neural Networks* 4(2): 251-257

Kawato, M. (1999). Internal models for motor control and trajectory planning. *Current Opinion in Neurobiology*, 9, 718-727.

Keele S.W. (1968). Movement control in skilled motor performance. *Psychology Bulletin* 70: 387-403.

Manette, O.F.; Maier, M.A. (2006). TempUnit: A bio-inspired neural network model for signal processing. *Neural Networks, 2006. IJCNN 06. International Joint Conference on.* Page(s):3144 – 3151

Mainen Z. F. and T. J. Sejnowski, "Reliability of spike timing in neocortical neurons," *Science*, vol. 268, pp. 1503–1506, 1995.

Pailhous J, Bonnard M (1989) Programmation et contrôle du mouvement. In : *Traité de psychologie cognitive*, C. Bonnet, R. Ghiglione, J-F Richard. (Eds) . Paris : Dunod, 129-197

Rieke F, Warland D, De Ruyter Van SteveninkR, Bialek W,Characterizing the neural response in: *Spikes: Exploring the Neural Code* . Cambridge, MA: MIT Press, 1996.

Salinas E. and L. Abbott, "Transfer of coded information from sensory to motor networks," *Journal of Neuroscience*, vol. 15, pp. 6461–6474, 1995.

Seashore C.E. (1938) *Psychology of music*. New York: Academic Press.

Shadmehr R, Mussa-Ivaldi F. (1994) Adaptive representation of dynamics during learning of a motor task. *Journal of Neurosciences* 14: 3208-3224.

Shepherd, G. M. (1990). The Significance of Real Neuron Architectures for Neural Network Simulations. In: *Computational Neuroscience*, E. L. Schwartz, ed., chapter 8, pages 82--96. A Bradford book, MIT Press.

Sherrington C.S. (1906/1947) *The integrative action of the nervous system.* Yale University Press.

Taub E. (1976) Movement in nonhuman primates deprived of somatosensory feedback. *Exercise and sports Science Review* 4: 335-374

Turvey M.T. (1977) Preliminaries to a theory of action with reference to vision. In: *Perceiving, acting and knowing: toward an ecological psychology*, R. Shaw, J. Bransford (Eds.),. Hillsdale, (N.J.) Lawrence Erlbaum Ass.

Venugopal, Venu, Walter R.J. Baets, (1994). "Neural networks and statistical techniques in marketing research : a conceptual comparison." *Marketing Intelligence & Planning* 12.7: 30-38.

Wierenga, B. & J. Kluytmans (1994). Neural nets versus marketing models in time series analysis: A simulation study in: Bloemer, J. e.a., Marketing: its Dynamics and Challenges, *Proceedings 23 rd. EMAC Conference*, Maastricht 17-20 May, pp. 1139-1153.

Wolpert D.M., Gharamani Z, Ardan, M.J. (1995). An internal model for sensorimotor integration. *Science* 269: 1179-1182

13

Proposal and Evaluation of the Improved Penalty Avoiding Rational Policy Making Algorithm

Kazuteru Miyazaki[1], Takuji Namatame[2] and Hiroaki Kobayashi[3]

[1]National Institution for Academic Degrees and University Evaluation
[2]MAZDA
[3]Meiji University
Japan

1. Introduction

Reinforcement learning (RL) is a kind of machine learning. It aims to adapt an agent to a given environment with a reward and a penalty. Traditional RL systems are mainly based on the *Dynamic Programming* (DP). They can get *an optimum policy* that maximizes an expected discounted reward in *Markov Decision Processes (MDPs)*. We know *Temporal Difference learning* (Sutton, 1988) and *Q-learning* (Watkins, 1992) as a kind of the *DP-based RL systems*. They are very attractive since they are able to guarantee the optimality in MDPs. We know that *Partially Observable Markov Decision Processes* (POMDPs) classes are wider than MDPs. If we apply the DP-based RL systems to POMDPs, we will face some limitation. Hence, a heuristic *eligibility trace* is often used to treat a POMDP. We know TD(λ) (Sutton, 1988), Sarsa(λ) (Singh & Sutton, 1996), (Sutton & Barto, 1998) and Actor-Critic (Kimura & Kobayashi, 1998) as such kinds of RL systems.

The DP-based RL system aims to optimize its behavior under given reward and penalty values. However, it is difficult to design these values appropriately for the purpose of us. If we set inappropiate values, the agent may learn unexpected behavior (Miyazaki & Kobayashi, 2000). We know the *Inverse Reinforcement Learning* (IRL) (Ng & Russell, 2000) as a method related to the design problem of reward and penalty values. If we input an expected policy to the IRL systems, it can output a *reward function* that can realize just the same policy. IRL has several theoretical results, i.e. *apprenticeship learning* (Abbeel & Ng, 2005) and *policy invariance* (Ng et.al., 1999).

On the other hand, we are interested in the approach where a reward and a penalty are treated independently. As examples of RL systems that we are proposed on the basis of the viewpoint, we know the rationality theorem of *Profit Sharing* (PS) (Miyazaki et.al., 1994), the *Rational Policy Making algorithm* (RPM) (Miyazaki & Kobayashi, 1998) and *PS-r** (Miyazaki & Kobayashi, 2003). They are restricted to the environment where the number of types of a reward is one. Furthermore, we know the *Penalty Avoiding Rational Policy Making algorithm* (PARP) (Miyazaki & Kobayashi, 2000) and the *Penalty Avoiding Profit Sharing* (PAPS) (Miyazaki et.al., 2002) as examples of RL systems that are able to treat a penalty, too. We call these systems *Exploitaion-oriented Learning (XoL)*.

XoL have several features: (1) Though traditional RL systems require appropriate reward and penalty values, XoL only requires *an order of importance* among them. In general, it is easier than designing their values. (2) They can learn more quickly since they trace successful experiences very strongly. (3) They are not suitable for pursuing an optimum policy. The optimum policy can be acquired with *multi-start method* (Miyazaki & Kobayashi, 1998) but it needs to reset all memories to get a better policy. (4) They are effective on the classes beyond MDPs since they are a *Bellman-free method* (Sutton & Barto, 1998) that do not depend on DP.

We are interested in XoL since we require quick learning and/or learning in the class wider than MDPs. We focus on PARP and PAPS especially because they can treat a reward and a penalty at the same time. The application of PARP to a real world is difficult since it requires $O(MN^2)$ memories where N and M are the number of types of a sensory input and an action. Though PAPS only require $O(MN)$ memories, it may learn an irrational policy. In this paper, we aim to reduce the memories of PARP to $O(MN)$ by updating a reward and a penalty in each episode and also selecting an action depending on the degree of a penalty. We show the effectiveness of this approach through a soccer game simulation and its real world experimentation.

2. The domain

2.1 Notations

Consider an agent in some unknown environment. For each discrete time step, after the agent senses the environment as a pair of a discrete attribute and its value, it selects an action from some discrete actions and executes it. In usual DP-based RL systems and PS, a scalar weight, that indicates the importance of a rule, is assigned to each rule. The environment provides a reward or a penalty to the agent as a result of some sequence of actions. In this paper, we foucus on the class where the numbers of types of a reward and a penalty are at most ones, respectively, as same as PARP and PAPS. We give the agent a reward for achievement of our purpose and a penalty for violation of our restriction.

We term the sequence of rules selected between the rewards as an *episode*. For example, when the agent selects *xb*, *xa*, *ya*, *za*, *yb*, *xa*, *za*, and *yb* in Fig. 1 a), there are two episodes (*xb·xa·ya·za·yb*) and (*xa·za·yb*), as shown in Fig. 1 b). Consider a part of an episode where the sensory input of the first selection rule and the sensory output of the last selection rule are the same although both rules are different. We term it as a *detour*. For example, an episode (*xb·xa·ya·za·yb*) has two detours (*xb*) and (*ya·za*), as shown in Fig. 1 b).

The rules on a detour may not contribute to obtain a reward. We term a rule as *irrational* if and only if it always exist on detours in any episodes. Otherwise, a rule is termed as *rational*. After obtaining the episode 1 of Fig. 1 b), rule *xb,ya* and *za* are irrational rules and rule *xa* and *yb* are rational rules. When the episode 2 is experienced furthermore, rule *za* changes to a rational rule. We term a rule *penalty* if and only if it has a penalty or it can transit to a *penalty state* in which there are penalty or irrational rules only.

The function that maps sensory inputs to actions is termed a *policy*. The policy that maximizes an expected reward per an action is termed as an *optimum policy*. We term a policy *rational* if and only if the expected reward per an action is larger than zero. We term a rational policy a *penalty avoiding rational policy* if and only if it has no penalty rule. Furthermore, the policy that outputs just one action for each sensory input is termed a *deterministic policy*.

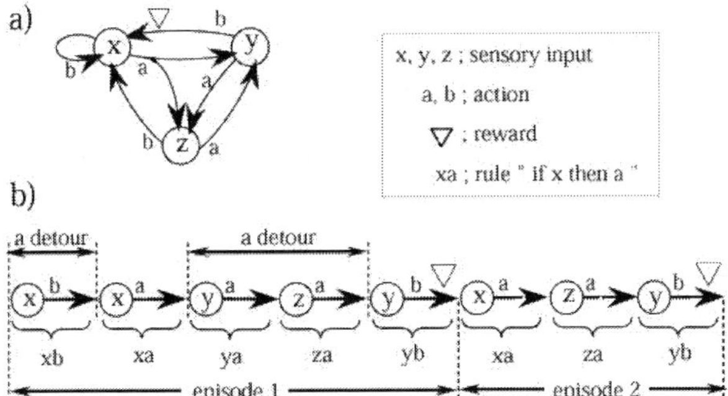

Fig. 1. a) An environment of 3 sensory inputs and 2 actions. b) An example of an episode and a detour

2.2 Previous works

The Penalty Avoiding Rational Policy Making algorithm

We know the *Penalty Avoiding Rational Policy Making algorithm* (PARP) as XoL that can make a penalty avoiding rational policy. To avoid all penalties, PARP suppresses all penalty rules in the current rule sets with the *Penalty Rule Judgment algorithm* (PRJ) in Fig. 2. After suppressing all penalty rules, it aims to make a deterministic rational policy by PS, RPM and so on.

> **procedure** The penalty Rule Judgement (PRJ)
> **begin**
>   Put the mark in the rule that has been got a penalty directly
>   **do**
>   Put the mark in the following state;
>   *there is no rational rule* or
>   *there is no rule that can transit to non-marked state*
>   Put the mark in the following rule;
>   *there are marks in the states that can be transited by it*
>   **while** (there is a new mark on some state)
> **end**

Fig. 2. The Penalty Rule Judgment algorithm (PRJ); We can regard the marked rule as a penalty rule. We can find all penalty rules in the current rule set through continuing PRJ

Furthermore, PARP avoids a penalty stochastically if there is no deterministic rational policy. It is realized by selecting the rule whose penalty level is the least in all penalty levels at the same sensory input. The penalty level is estimated by *interval estimation* of transition probability to a penalty state of each rule. If we can continue to select only rational rule, we can get a penalty avoiding rational policy. On the other hand, if we have to refer to the penalty level, we get a policy that has a possibility to get a penalty.

PARP uses PRJ. PRJ has to memorize all rules that have been experienced and descendant states that have been transited by their rules to find a penalty rule. It requires $O(MN^2)$ memories where N and M are the number of types of a sensory input and an action. Furthermore, PARP requires the same memory to suppress all penalties stochastically. In applying PRJ to large-scale problems, we are confronted with the curse of dimensionality.

The Penalty Avoiding Profit Sharing

We know PAPS as XoL to make a penalty avoiding rational policy with $O(MN)$ memories that is the same memory to storage all rules. The original PRJ requires $O(MN^2)$ memories since it scans all of the known rules. On the other hand, PAPS uses *PRJ on episode* (PRJ[episode]) where the scanning is restricted within each episode. Therefore it can find a penalty rule with $O(MN)$ memories.

Furthermore, PAPS uses PS[+] and PS[-] to avoid a penalty stochastically with $O(MN)$ memories. PS[+] is the same as PS whose weights are reinforced only by a reward. It is used in the case where there is a non-penalty rule in a current state. If there is no non-penalty rule in a current state, PAPS selects an action that is the least reinforced by PS[-] whose weights are reinforced by a penalty only.

PAPS aims to make a penalty avoiding rational policy with $O(MN)$ memories. However there is a serious problem in the action selection based on PS[-]. Originally, PS aims to learn a rational policy that reaches to a reward. In the same way, we can get a policy that reaches to a penalty, if we select an action that is the most reinforced by PS[-] in each state. However, we cannot know how rules except for the most reinforced rule are reinforced. Therefore we may select an action that will get a penalty with rather high possiblity, even if we select the least inforced rule in the current state.

3. Improvement of the penalty avoiding rational policy making algorithm

3.1 Basic ideas

We aim to make a penalty avoiding rational policy with $O(MN)$ memories. A penalty rule is found by PRJ[episode] as well as PAPS. Therefore, we can find a penalty rule with $O(MN)$ memories.

If we cannot select any non-penalty rules in a current state, we should avoid a penalty stochastically. It is realize with penalty level of each rule as PARP. PARP has to memorize all state transitions in order to calculate the penalty level. It means that it requires $O(MN^2)$ memories. In order to reduce the memory to $O(MN)$, we aim to calculate the penalty level by each episode.

3.2 Approximation of the penalty level

We do not memorize all state transitions but memorize only state transitions of each episode to estimate the penalty level of each rule. It only requires $O(MN)$ memories. The penalty level of rule S_1a, $PL(S_1a)$, is calculated by the following equation:

$$PL(S_1a) = \frac{N_p(S_1a)}{N(S_1a)} \tag{1}$$

where $N_p(S_1a)$ is the number of times that rule S_1a has judged as a penalty rule, and $N(S_1a)$ is the number of times that the rule has been selected so far. We show examples of $N_p(S_1a)$ and $N(S_1a)$ at a rectangle of Fig. 3 (b) and ellipses of Fig. 3 (a)(b), respectively.

The range of $PL(S_1a)$ is $1.0 \geq PL(S_1a) \geq 0.0$. If $PL(S_1a)$ is close to 1.0, we can regard that the possibility of getting a penalty by the action a in the state S_1 is high. On the other hand, if $PL(S_1a)$ is close to 0.0, we can regard that the possibility is low. We can calculate $PL(S_1a)$ every episodes. It requires the following two types memories only. One is the number of times where each rule has been selected until now. The other is that where each rule has been judged to a penalty rule. They only require $O(MN)$ memories.

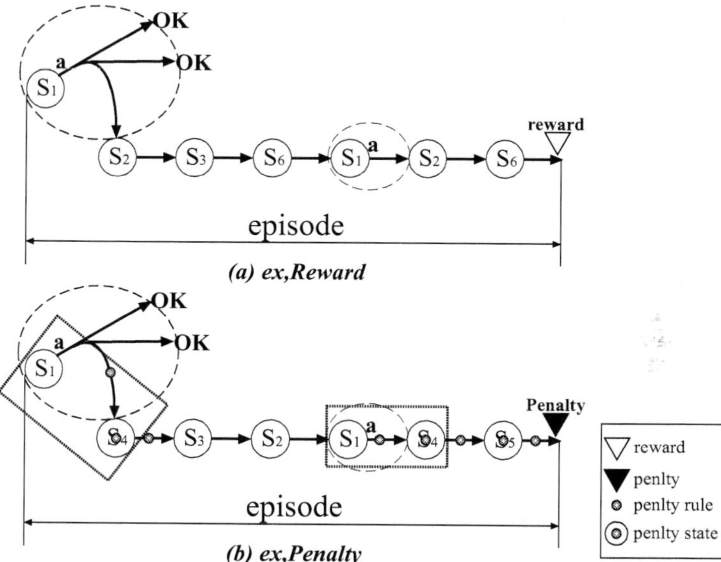

(a) ex,Reward

(b) ex,Penalty

Fig. 3. Approximation of the penalty level

3.3 The action selection based on the penalty level

If there is a rational rule in the current rule set after excluding all penalty rules, we should select the rule to make a penalty avoiding rational policy. It is realized by PS(PS[+]) or RPM. On the other hand, if we cannot select such rule, we select an action in the rule whose penalty level calculated by equation (1) is the least in order to reduce the probability of getting a penalty.

From section 2.1, the rule that has a possibility to get a penalty is defined as a penalty rule. This definition has a possibility of regarding all rules as penalty rules. We introduce the cutting parameter γ $(1.0 \geq \gamma \geq 0.0)$ to reduce the number of penalty rules. If $PL(S_1a)$ is larger than γ, the rule S_1a is a penalty rule. Otherwise, it is not a penalty rule.

It means that the rule is not regarded as a penalty rule if the possibility of getting a penalty is low. If we set $\gamma=0.0$, the rule that has been given a penalty even once is regarded a penalty rule. It is coincident to the case where we do not introduce the parameter γ to PARP. On the other hand, if γ is closed to 1.0, the number of penalty rules will decrease, and in turn, the number of rules that can be selected by PS(PS[+]) or RPM will increase significantly. If we set $\gamma=1.0$, it is coincident to PS(PS[+]) or RPM that do not avoid any penalty. We can control the number of rules that can be selected with γ.

3.4 Features

We call the proposal method *Improved PARP*. Improved PARP has the following features.

- We can avoid a penalty stochastically with $O(MN)$ memories through combining of both PRJ[episode] and the approximation of a penalty level.
- We can cotrol the number of penalty rules with the cutting parameter γ.

4. Numerical experimentation

We use the simulator shown in Fig. 4 that is based on the Small Size Robot League on RoboCup. There are two learning agents for one side. One agent puts a pass out for the other agent. The other agent aims to receive it. There is an opponent agent for the other side. The agent aims to cut off the pass. We show the initial positions of these agents in Fig. 4. We know the *keepaway task* (Stone et.al. 2005) as another soccer game. The performance of the keepaway task strongly depneds on the designing of a reward and a penalty (Tanaka & Arai, 2006). In the future, we will challenge to the keepaway task, too.

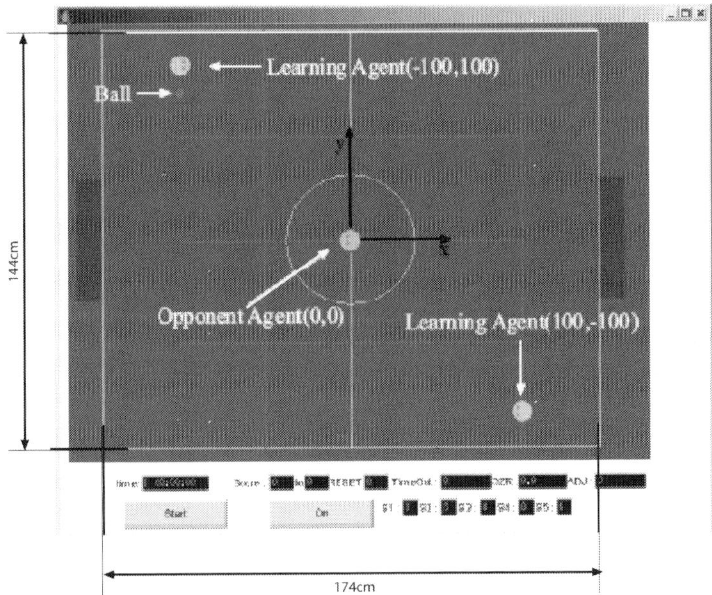

Fig. 4. Soccer game simulator

4.1 Detail design of the task
The learning agents
The state spaces of a learning agent is classified to the following five cases; 9 states of a ball from the learning agent (Fig. 5 a)), 10 states of an opponent agent from the learning agent (Fig. 5 b)), 5 states of the other learning agent from the learning agent (Fig. 5 c)), 4 states of destination between two learning agents (Fig. 5 d)) and 5 states of the learning agent from the other learning agent (Fig. 5 c)).
There are the following seven actions; stop, go forward, turn by five degrees to direction of a ball, turn right by five degrees, turn left by five degrees, kick for dribble and kick for pass.

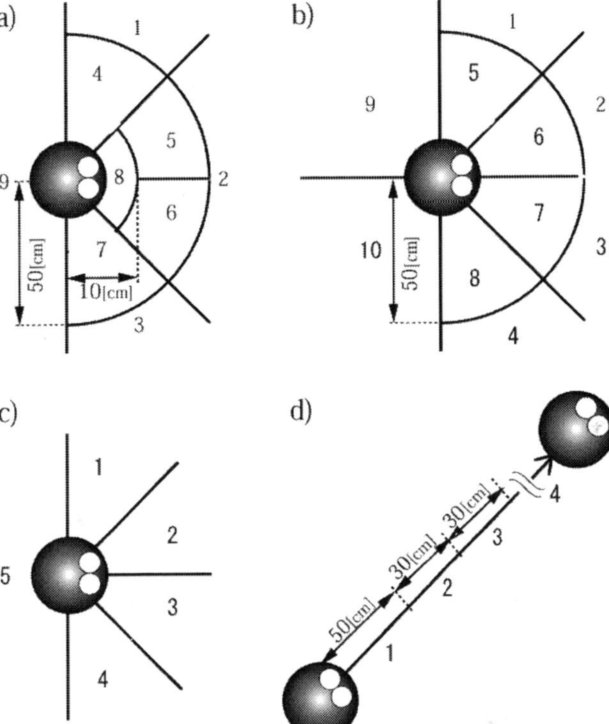

Fig. 5. a) 9 states of a ball from the learning agent. b) 10 states of an opponent agent from the learning agent. c) 5 States between two learning agents. d) 4 states of destination between two learning agents

A reward and a penalty
The learning is judged to *success* when a ball in a learning agent had reached to the other learning agent and the distance between two learning agents is larger than 40cm. A reward is given to two learning agents when the condition for success is achieved. A penalty is given to two learning agents when a ball had reached to an opponent agent, the learning time had exceeded 12000 msec that is called *TimeOut*, or a ball in a learning agent had reached to the other learning agent but the distance between two learning agents is not larger than 40cm. Though there are three types of penalties, learning agents do not distinguish them, that is, they are treated as the same penalty. In the future, we will try to the case where these penalties are treated independently.

The opponent agent
There are two policies in the opponent agent. One policy aims to reach to a ball. The other policy aims to reach to the middle position of two learning agents to block the pass. The former is selected when the distance from the agent to a ball is closer than the distance from the agent to the middle position of two learning agents. Otherwise, the latter policy is selected.

Setting of the experiment

The learning agents sense the environment each 3 msec. When they had received a reward or a penalty, the trial has been ended and new trial begins with the initial position. We take 100 experiments with different random seeds.

We introduce two noises to simulate a stochastic state transition. One is added to the movements of all agents and a ball. The maximum value is $\pm1/10$ [mm/s]. The other is added to the angles of the turn actions of learning agents and the direction of a ball when agents kicked it. The maximum value is $\pm1/100$ [deg].

4.2 Results and discussion

About the setting of γ

We have compared our proposed method called Improved PARP with PAPS. On the other hand, PARP cannot apply to this task since it requires many memories. We have changed γ every 0.1 from 0.5 up to 1.0. Fig. 6 and Fig. 7 are the results of success rates of pass behaviors of PAPS and Improved PARP, respectively. The horizontal axis is the number of trials and the vertical axis is the percentage of the success rate. One trial includes a pair of sensing the environment and selecting an action. The plots are shown every 100 trials. The initial point of these plots are the results of random walk.

Fig. 6 shows that PAPS cannot learn. It comes from the fact that the penalty avoiding by PS[-] does not function properly. On the other hand, we can conclude that Improved PARP gets high performance than PAPS from these figures.

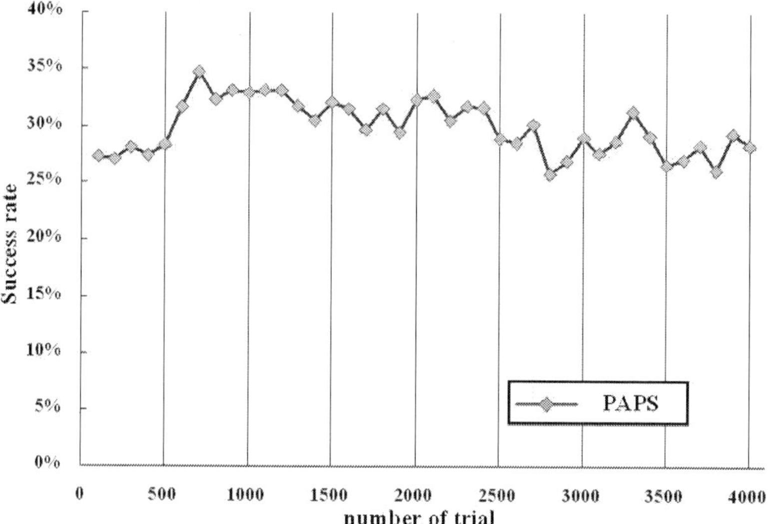

Fig. 6. Success rate (%) of pass behavior by PAPS

If we decrease γ, the number of penalty rules of Improved PARP increases. It means that the penalty avoiding is more important than the reward getting. Therefore, if we decrease γ, the action selection based on PS(PS[+]) decreases, and the success rates become bad as shown in Fig. 7. On the other hand, if we increase γ until *0.8*, the success rates become good. It comes from the fact that the action selection based on PS(PS[+]) increases because of decreasing the number of penalty rules. However, the results of γ=*0.9* and *1.0* show bad. It means that if we set γ excessively largely, the learning agents regard an important penalty rule as a non-penalty rule.

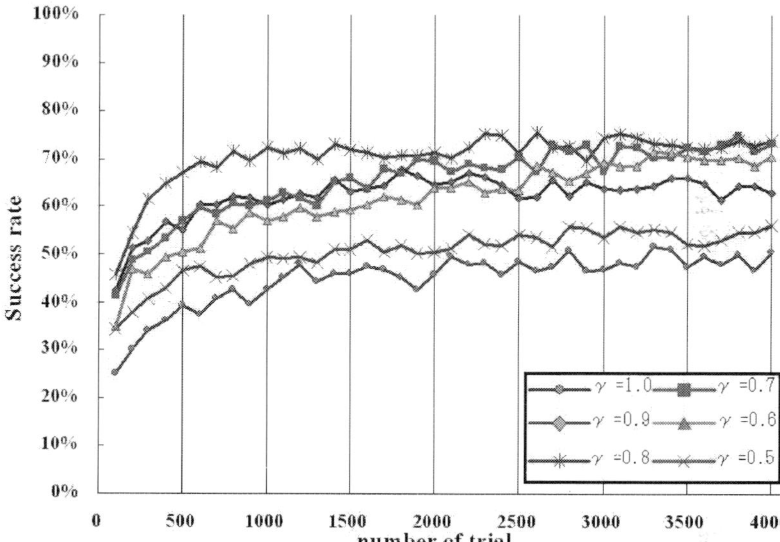

Fig. 7. Success rate (%) of pass behavior by Improved PARP

The result of Improved PARP depends on γ. If we set γ small, we can get a policy that is focused on a penalty avoiding. If we set γ large, we can get a policy that is focused on a reward getting. Therefore, we should change γ dynamically. For example, we should set γ large to get a goal in the initial phase of a game or in the situation where the game may lose. On the other hand, we should set γ small to protect our goal when our score being more than the other.

About the setting of penalties

We give a learning agent the same penalty when the learning reaches TimeOut, a ball had reached to an opponent agent, or a ball in a learning agent had reached to the other learning agent but the distance between two learning agents is not larger than 40cm. We confirm the effects of first two penalties. Fig. 8 shows the TimeOut rate plotted against the number of trials. Fig. 9 shows miss rate of pass behavior plotted against the number of trials.

Though we can confirm the effect of learning in Fig. 8, we cannot do it in Fig. 9. It comes from the fact that the policy that is specialized in TimeOut has been learned than the other policies, since TimeOut occurs frequently than the others. Therefore, we should not give the same penalty to the different types of behaviors. In the future, we aim to combine Improved

PARP with the method in the paper (Miyazaki & Kobayashi, 2004) that can treat several types of rewards and penalties at the same time.

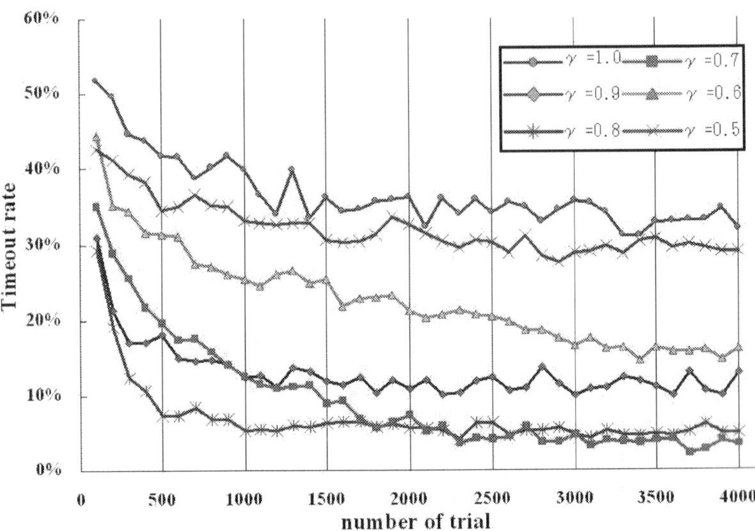

Fig. 8. Timeout rate (%) by Improved PARP

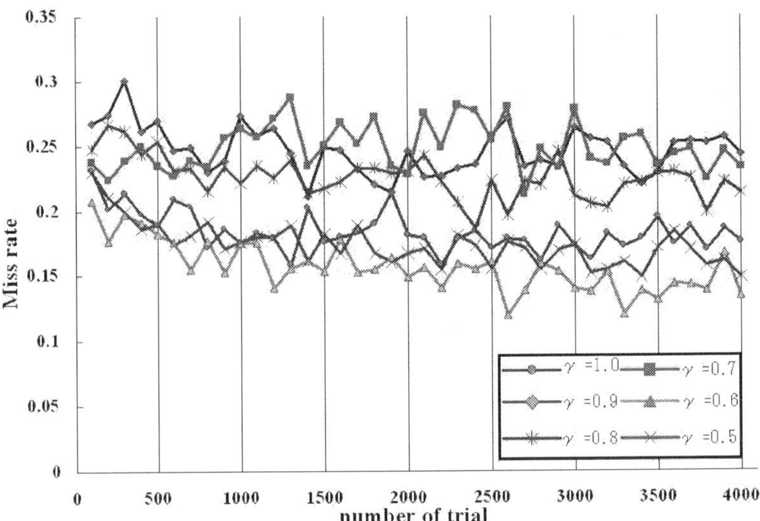

Fig. 9. Miss rate of pass behavior by Improved PARP

5. Real world experimentation

5.1 The soccer robot system

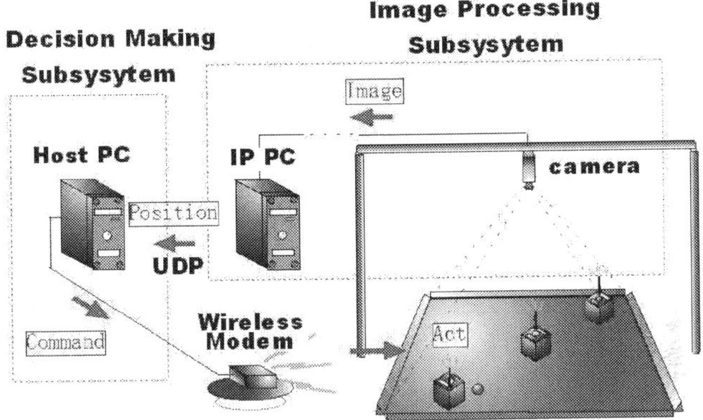

Fig. 10. The soccer robot system

We have developed a soccer robot system (Fig.10) to evaluate impoved PARP. It has the decision making subsystem and the image processing subsystem. The former is to decide an action and the latter is to process images from camera. It can adapt on the reguration of Robo Cup Small Size Robot League excet for the field size.

5.2 Soccer robot

We use three robots called Robo-E (Fig. 11). It has 12 light sensors. They are used to escape from clashing with a wall or another robots. Each robot has different markers each other to distinguish each robot. We show the combinations of colors for robots in table.1.

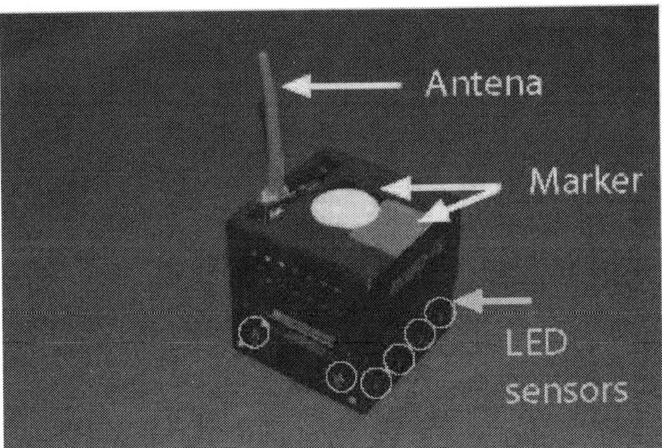

Fig. 11. Soccer Robot Robo-E

Robot 1	Yellow and light green
Robot 2	Yellow and Cyan
Robot 3	Blue and light green

Table 1. Combinations of colors for robots

5.3 Host system

The host system is consturcted by two computers, that is, Host and Image Processing (IP) PCs. IP and Host PCs are connected by TCP/IP. We use UDP (User Datagram Protocol) as the protocol on IP.

Host PC is to decide an action. We have impremented Improved PARP on Host PC. The decision of Host PC is transmitted by willess modem.

Fig. 12. 3CCD Camera

On the other hand, IP PC is to process images from camera. It calculates positions of robots and a ball. Their images are given by the camera (SONY XC-003; Fig. 12). We had the camera mounted at the top of the field to get global vision. We use machine vision tool *HALCON* with its *Hdevelop* programming environment to get robots and a ball positions. The positions of each robots are calculated with markers on Table. 1 and their body color (black). We use RGB parameter to distinguish each color. Table 2 shows these threshholds.

Color	R	G	B
Field (green)	10-40	75-100	40-65
Robot (black)	0-20	0-55	0-220
Wall (white)	255	255	255
Ball (orange)	125-200	95-125	45-85
Yellow	170-255	180-255	110-190
Blue	30-110	40-30	80-200
Light green	40-130	130-230	60-180
Cyan	100-170	140-240	140-240

Table 2. RGB parameter of each color

The position of the robot is the center of gravity of two markers. It is (X_{robot}, Y_{robot}) on Fig. 13 (a). The position of a ball is the center of ball marker (orange). It is (X_{ball}, Y_{ball}) on Fig. 13 (b).

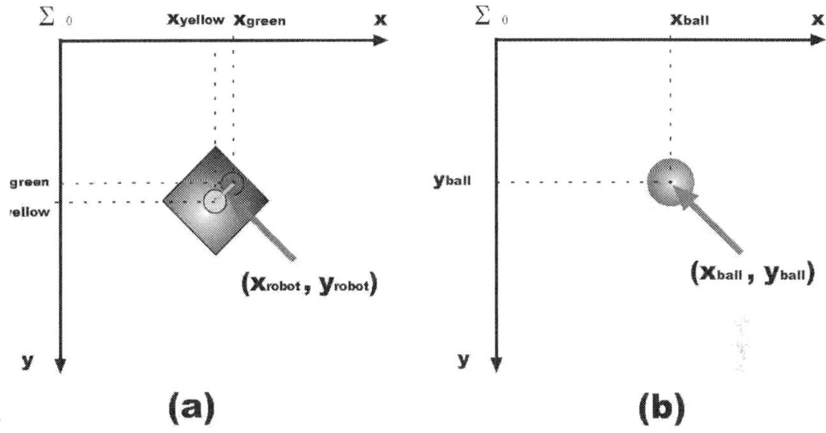

Fig. 13. Positions of robots and a ball

The orientation of the robot is calculated by the center of gravity of two markers (Fig. 14). If we set the center of gravity of center marker (X_{center}, Y_{center}) and it of another marker $(X_{outside}, Y_{outsde})$, we can get the angrle θ is as the following,

$$\theta = \text{atan2}(d_y, d_x), \quad (180° < \theta < 180°) \tag{2}$$

where dx, dy is $d_x = x_{outside} - x_{center}, d_{y=}y_{outside} - y_{center}$.

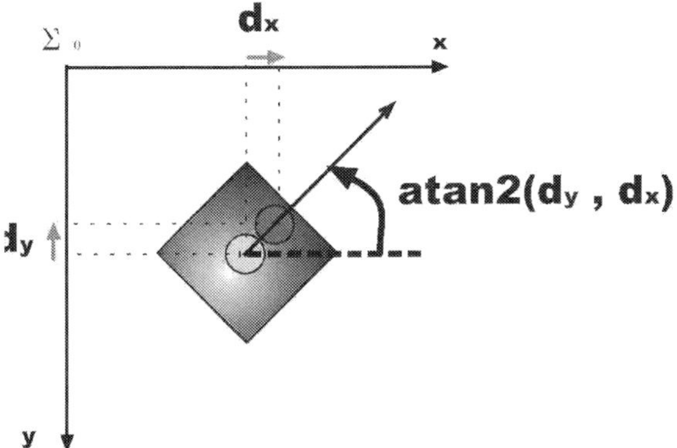

Fig. 14. Orientation of a robot

5.4 Experimental results

We use three Robo-E type robots in our real world experimentation. One is an opponent agent and the others are learning agets. Three robots and a ball are set on the field in Fig.15.

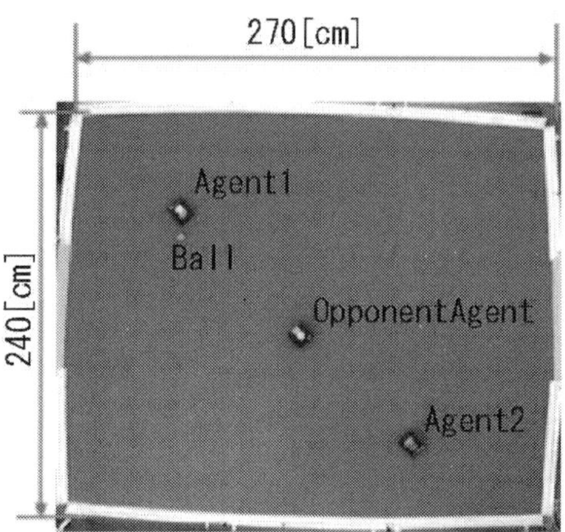

Fig. 15. Real world field

Fig. 16 shows the results of success rates of pass behavior of Improved PARP, the Q-learning and random agets. Improved PARP has 4 experiments with different random seeds from SEED_1 to SEED_4. We set γ=0.8. We can confirm the effectiveness of Improved PARP as same as numerical experimentation. Especially, it can learn very quickly than Q-learning agent that is the most famous DP-based RL system.

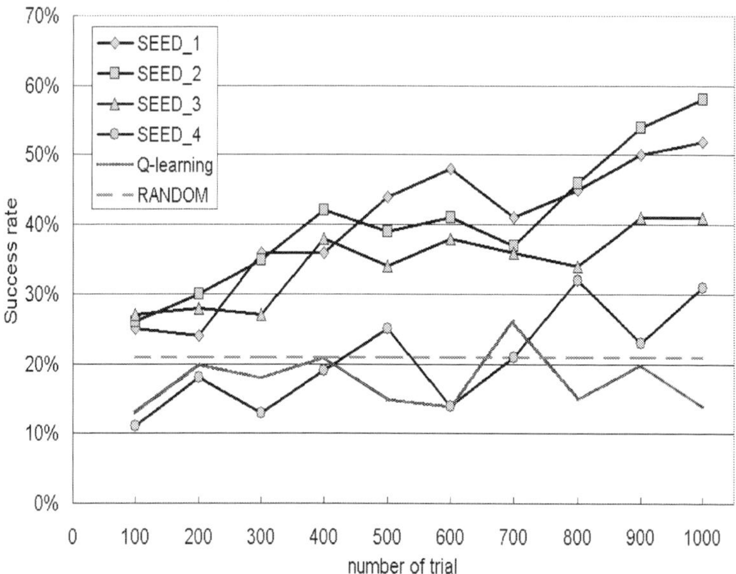

Fig. 16. Success rate (%) of pass behavior in real world experimentation

6. Conclusion

As examples of XoL that use both a reward and a penalty simultaneously, we know PARP and PAPS. The application of PARP to real worlds is difficult since it requires $O(MN^2)$ memories where N and M are the number of types of a sensory input and an action. Though PAPS only requires $O(MN)$ memories, it may learn unexpected behavior.

In this paper, we have proposed *Improved PARP* in order to overcome the difficulty by updating a reward and a penalty in each episode and selecting actions depending on the degree of a penalty. We have shown the effectiveness of this approach through a soccer game simulation and its real world experimentation.

Improved PARP cannot treat multiple rewards and penalties. In the future, we try to combine Improved PARP with the method in the paper (Miyazaki & Kobayashi, 2004) to treat several types of rewards and penalties at the same time. Furthermore, we will apply Improved PARP to the *keepaway task* (Stone et.al. 2005) and the other real world applications.

7. References

Abbeel, P. & Ng., A. Y. (2005). Exploration and apprenticeship learning in reinforcement learning. Proceedings of the 21th International Conference on Machine Learning, pp.1-8

Kimura, H. & Kobayashi, S. (1998). An analysis of actor/critic algorithms using eligibility traces: reinforcement learning with imperfect value function. Proceedings of the 15th International Conference on Machine Learning, pp. 278-286.

Miyazaki, K. & Kobayashi, S. (1998). Learning Deterministic Policies in Partially Observable Markov Decision Processes. Proceedings of the International Conference on Intelligent Autonomous System 5, pp. 250-257.

Miyazaki, K. & Kobayashi, S. (2000). Reinforcement Learning for Penalty Avoiding Policy Making. In Proceeding of the 2000 IEEE International Conference on Systems, Man and Cybernetics, pp. 206-211.

Miyazaki, K. & Kobayashi, S. (2003). An Extension of Profit Sharing to Partially Observable Markov Decision Processes: Proposition of PS-r* and its Evaluation. Journal of the Japanese Society for Artificial Intelligence, Vol.18, No.5, pp. 166-169. (in Japanese).

Miyazaki, K. & Kobayashi, S. (2004). Reinforcement Learning in Multiple Rewards and Penalties Environments. Proceedings of Joint 2nd International Conference on Soft Computing and Intelligent Systems and 5th International Symposium on Advanced Intelligent Systems.

Miyazaki, K., Yamamura, M. & Kobayashi, S. (1994). On the Rationality of Profit Sharing in Reinforcement Learning. Proceedings of the Third International Conference on Fuzzy Logic, Neural Nets and Soft Computing, pp. 285-288.

Miyazaki, K, Saitou, J. & Kobayashi, H. (2002). Reinforcement Learning for Penalty Avoiding Profit Sharing and its Application to the Soccer Game. Proceedings of the 4th Asia-Pacific Conference on Simulated Evolution and Learning, pp. 335-339.

Ng, A. Y. & Russell, S. J. (2000). Algorithms for Inverse Reinforcement Learning. Proceedings of the 17th International Conference on Machine Learning, pp. 663-670.

Ng, A. Y., Harada, D. & Russell, S. J. (1999). Policy Invariance Under Reward Transformations: Theory and Application to Reward Shaping Proceedings of the 17th International Conference on Machine   Learning, pp. 278-287.

Singh, S. P. & Sutton, R. S. (1996). Reinforcement Learning with Replacing Eligibility Traces. Machine Learning, Vol.22, pp. 123-158.

Stone. P., Sutton, R. S. & Kuhlmann, G. (2005). Reinforcement Learning for RoboCup Soccer Keepaway. Adaptive Behavior, Vol.13, No.3, pp. 165-188.

Sutton, R. S. & Barto, A. (1998). Reinforcement Learning: An Introduction. A Bradford Book, The MIT Press.

Sutton, R. S. (1988). Learning to Predict by the Methods of Temporal Differences. Machine Learning, Vol.3, pp. 9-44.

Tanaka, N. & Arai, S. (2006). Teamwork Formation for Keepaway in Robotics Soccer (Reinforcement Learning Approach), Pacific Rim International Workshop on Multi-Agents, Lecture Notes in Computer Science, Vol.4088, pp. 279-292.

Watkins, C. J. H. & Dayan, P. (1992). Technical note: Q-learning.Machine Learning, Vol.8, pp. 55-68.

14

A Generic Framework for Soft Subspace Pattern Recognition

Dat Tran, Wanli Ma, Dharmendra Sharma, Len Bui and Trung Le
University of Canberra, Faculty of Information Sciences and Engineering
Australia

1. Introduction

In statistical pattern recognition, hidden Markov model (HMM) is the most important technique for modelling patterns that include temporal information such as speech and handwriting. If the temporal information is not taken into account, Gaussian mixture model (GMM) is used. This GMM technique uses a mixture of Gaussian densities to model the distribution of feature vectors extracted from training data. When little training data are available, vector quantisation (VQ) technique is also effective (Tran & Wagner 2002). In fuzzy set theory-based pattern recognition, fuzzy clustering techniques such as fuzzy c-means and fuzzy entropy are used to design re-estimation techniques for fuzzy HMM, fuzzy GMM, and fuzzy VQ (Tran & Wagner 2000).

The first stage in pattern recognition is data feature selection. A number of features that best characterises the considering pattern is extracted and the selection of features is dependent on the pattern to be recognised and has direct impact on the recognition results. The above-mentioned pattern recognition methods cannot select features automatically because they treat all features equally. We propose that the contribution of a feature to pattern recognition should be measured by a weight that is assigned to the feature in the modelling process. This method is called soft subspace pattern recognition. There have been some algorithms proposed to calculate weights for soft subspace clustering (Huang et al. 2005, Jing et al. 2007). However a generic framework for the above-mentioned modelling methods has not been built.

A generic framework for soft subspace pattern recognition will be proposed in this chapter. A generic objective function will be designed for HMM and maximizing this function will provide an algorithm for calculating weights. Other weight calculation algorithms for GMM and VQ will also be determined from the algorithm for HMM.

The proposed soft subspace pattern recognition methods will be evaluated in network intrusion detection. Some preliminary experiments have been done and experimental results showed that the proposed algorithms could improve the recognition rates.

2. Continuous hidden Markov model

The underlying assumption of the HMM is that the speech signal can be well characterised as a parametric random process, and that the parameters of the stochastic process can be estimated in a precise, well-defined manner. The HMM method provides a reliable way of recognizing speech for a wide range of applications (Juang 1998, Furui 1997, Rabiner et al. 1996).

There are two assumptions in the first-order HMM. The first is the Markov assumption, i.e. a new state is entered at each time t based on the transition probability, which only depends on the previous state. It is used to characterise the sequence of the time frames of a speech pattern. The second is the output-independence assumption, i.e. the output probability depends only on the state at that time regardless of when and how the state is entered (Huang et al. 1990). A process satisfying the Markov assumption is called a Markov model (Kulkarni 1995). An observable Markov model is a process where the output is a set of states at each instant of time and each state corresponds to an observable event. The hidden Markov model is a doubly stochastic process with an underlying Markov process which is not directly observable (hidden) but which can be observed through another set of stochastic processes that produce observable events in each of the states (Rabiner & Juang 1993).

Let $S = \{s_1, s_2, ..., s_T\}$ and $\mathbf{X} = \{\mathbf{x}_1, \mathbf{x}_2, ..., \mathbf{x}_T\}$ be a sequence of states and a sequence of continuous feature vectors, respectively. The compact notation $\Lambda = \{\pi, A, B\}$ indicates the complete parameter set of the HMM where

- $\pi = \{\pi_i\}$, $\pi_i = P(s_1 = i \mid \Lambda)$: the initial state distribution
- $A = \{a_{ij}\}$, $a_{ij} = P(s_t = j \mid s_{t-1} = i, \Lambda)$: the state transition probability distribution, and
- $B = \{b_j(\mathbf{x}_t)\}$, $b_j(\mathbf{x}_t) = P(\mathbf{x}_t \mid s_t = j, \Lambda)$: the output probability distribution of feature vector $\mathbf{x}_t$ in state j.

The following constraints are applied:

$$\sum_{i=1}^{N} \pi_i = 1, \quad \sum_{j=1}^{N} a_{ij} = 1, \quad \text{and} \quad \int b(\mathbf{x}_t)d\mathbf{x}_t = 1 \tag{1}$$

The HMM parameters are estimated such that in some sense, they best match the distribution of the feature vectors in $\mathbf{X}$. The most widely used training method is the maximum likelihood (ML) estimation. For a sequence of feature vectors $\mathbf{X}$, the likelihood of the HMM is

$$P(\mathbf{X} \mid \Lambda) = \prod_{t=1}^{T} P(\mathbf{x}_t \mid \Lambda) \tag{2}$$

The aim of ML estimation is to find a new parameter model $\overline{\Lambda}$ such that $P(\mathbf{X} \mid \overline{\Lambda}) \geq P(\mathbf{X} \mid \Lambda)$. Since the expression in (2) is a nonlinear function of parameters in Λ, its direct maximisation is not possible. However, parameters can be obtained iteratively using the expectation-maximisation (EM) algorithm (Dempster 1977). An auxiliary function Q is used

$$Q(\Lambda, \overline{\Lambda}) = \sum_{t=1}^{T-1} \sum_{i=1}^{N} \sum_{j=1}^{N} P(s_t = i, s_{t+1} = j \mid \mathbf{X}, \Lambda) \log[\overline{a}_{ij}\overline{b}_{ij}(\mathbf{x}_{t+1})] \tag{3}$$

where $\overline{\pi}_{s_1=j}$ is denoted by $\overline{a}_{s_0=i\,s_1=j}$ for simplicity. Setting derivatives of the Q function with respect to $\overline{\Lambda}$ to zero, the following reestimation formulas are found

$$\overline{\pi}_i = \gamma_1(i) \qquad \overline{a}_{ij} = \frac{\displaystyle\sum_{t=1}^{T-1}\xi_t(i,j)}{\displaystyle\sum_{t=1}^{T-1}\gamma_t(i)} \tag{4}$$

where

$$\gamma_t(i) = \sum_{j=1}^{N}\xi_t(i,j), \quad \xi_t(i,j) = P(s_t = i, s_{t+1} = j \mid \mathbf{X}, \Lambda) \tag{5}$$

The most general representation of the output probability distribution is a mixture of Gaussians

$$b_j(\mathbf{x}_t) = P(\mathbf{x}_t \mid s_t = j, \Lambda) = \sum_{k=1}^{K} P(k \mid s_t = j, \Lambda)P(\mathbf{x}_t \mid k, s_t = j, \Lambda)$$

$$b_j(\mathbf{x}_t) = \sum_{k=1}^{K} c_{jk} N(\mathbf{x}_t, \boldsymbol{\mu}_{jk}, \boldsymbol{\Sigma}_{jk}) \tag{6}$$

where $c_{jk} = P(k \mid s_t = j, \Lambda)$, $j = 1,\ldots, N$, $k = 1,\ldots, K$ are mixture coefficients, and $N(\mathbf{x}_t, \boldsymbol{\mu}_{jk}, \boldsymbol{\Sigma}_{jk})$ is a Gaussian with mean vector $\boldsymbol{\mu}_{jk}$ and covariance matrix $\boldsymbol{\Sigma}_{jk}$ for the kth mixture component in state j. The following constraints are satisfied

$$c_{jk} > 0 \quad \text{and} \quad \sum_{k=1}^{K} c_{jk} = 1 \tag{7}$$

The mixture coefficients, mean vectors and covariance matrices are calculated as follows

$$\overline{c}_{jk} = \frac{1}{T}\sum_{t=1}^{T} P(k \mid \mathbf{x}_t, s_t = j, \Lambda) \qquad \overline{\boldsymbol{\mu}}_{jk} = \frac{\displaystyle\sum_{t=1}^{T} P(k \mid \mathbf{x}_t, s_t = j, \Lambda)\mathbf{x}_t}{\displaystyle\sum_{t=1}^{T} P(k \mid \mathbf{x}_t, s_t = j, \Lambda)}$$

$$\overline{\boldsymbol{\Sigma}}_{jk} = \frac{\displaystyle\sum_{t=1}^{T} P(k \mid \mathbf{x}_t, s_t = j, \Lambda)(\mathbf{x}_t - \boldsymbol{\mu}_{jk})(\mathbf{x}_t - \boldsymbol{\mu}_{jk})'}{\displaystyle\sum_{t=1}^{T} P(k \mid \mathbf{x}_t, s_t = j, \Lambda)} \tag{8}$$

where the prime denotes vector transposition, and

$$P(k \mid \mathbf{x}_t, s_t = j, \Lambda) = \frac{c_{jk} N(\mathbf{x}_t, \boldsymbol{\mu}_{jk}, \boldsymbol{\Sigma}_{jk})}{\sum_{n=1}^{K} c_{jn} N(\mathbf{x}_t, \boldsymbol{\mu}_{jn}, \boldsymbol{\Sigma}_{jn})} \tag{9}$$

In the M-dimensional feature space, the Guassian function can be written as follows

$$N(\mathbf{x}_t, \boldsymbol{\mu}_{jk}, \boldsymbol{\Sigma}_{jk}) = P(\mathbf{x}_t \mid k, s_t = j, \Lambda) = \prod_{m=1}^{M} P(x_{tm} \mid k, s_t = j, \Lambda) \tag{10}$$

where

$$P(x_{tm} \mid k, s_t = j, \Lambda) = \frac{1}{\sqrt{2\pi\sigma_{jkm}^2}} e^{-\frac{(x_{tm} - \mu_{jkm})^2}{2\sigma_{jkm}^2}} \tag{11}$$

2. Fuzzy subspace continuous hidden Markov model

It can be observed in (10) that features are treated equally in the HMM. In order to differentiate the contribution of features, we propose to assign a weight to each feature as follows

$$N(\mathbf{x}_t, \boldsymbol{\mu}_{jk}, \boldsymbol{\Sigma}_{jk}) = \prod_{m=1}^{M} \left[P(x_{tm} \mid k, s_t = j, \Lambda) \right]^{w_{jkm}^{\alpha}} \tag{12}$$

where w_{jkm}^{α}, $m = 1, 2, \ldots, M$ are components of an M-dimensional weight vector $\mathbf{w}_{jm}^{\alpha}$, and α is a parameter weight for w_{jkm}^{α}. Weight values satisfy the following conditions:

$$0 \le w_{jkm} \le 1 \quad \forall m, \quad \sum_{m=1}^{M} w_{jkm} = 1 \tag{13}$$

The weight values can be determined by considering the following function which is part of the Q function in (3):

$$Q_j(\Lambda, \overline{\Lambda}) = \sum_{k=1}^{K} \sum_{t=1}^{T} P(k \mid \mathbf{x}_t, s_t = j, \Lambda) \log[\overline{c}_{jk} N(\mathbf{x}_t, \overline{\boldsymbol{\mu}}_{jk}, \overline{\boldsymbol{\Sigma}}_{jk})] \tag{14}$$

where

$$\log N(\mathbf{x}_t, \overline{\boldsymbol{\mu}}_{jk}, \overline{\boldsymbol{\Sigma}}_{jk}) = \sum_{m=1}^{M} w_{jkm}^{\alpha} \log P(x_{tm} \mid k, s_t = j, \overline{\Lambda}) \tag{15}$$

The basic idea of this approach is to maximize the function $Q_j(\Lambda,\overline{\Lambda})$ over the variable w_{jkm}^α on the assumption that the weight vector $\mathbf{w}_{jm}^\alpha$ identifies a good contribution of the features. Maximizing the function $Q_j(\Lambda,\overline{\Lambda})$ in (14) using (13) and (15) gives

$$w_{jkm} = \frac{1}{\sum_{n=1}^{M}(D_{jkm}/D_{jkn})^{1/(\alpha-1)}} \tag{16}$$

where $\alpha \neq 1$ and $D_{jkm} = -\sum_{t=1}^{T}P(k\,|\,\mathbf{x}_t,s_t = j,\Lambda)\log P(x_{tm}\,|\,k,s_t = j,\overline{\Lambda})$

The advantage of this approach is that it does not change the structure of the HMM listed in (4) through (11). This means that these equations are still applied in fuzzy subspace HMM. Therefore, this approach can be considered as a generic framework and can extend to other models that relate to the HMM such as Gaussian mixture model (GMM) and Vector Quantization (VQ). Fuzzy subspace GMM can be obtained by setting the number of states in fuzzy subspace continuous HMM to one. The VQ will be considered in the next section.

3. Fuzzy subspace vector quantization

3.1 Vector quantization

The VQ modelling is an efficient data reduction method, which is used to convert a feature vector set into a small set of distinct vectors using a clustering technique. Advantages of this reduction are reduced storage and computation. The distinct vectors are called code vectors and the set of code vectors that best represents the training set is called the codebook. Since there is only a finite number of code vectors, the process of choosing the best representation of a given feature vector is equivalent to quantizing the vector and leads to a certain level of quantization error. This error decreases as the size of the codebook increases, however the storage required for a large codebook is non-trivial. The VQ codebook can be used as a model in pattern recognition. The key point of VQ modelling is to derive an optimal codebook which is commonly achieved by using a clustering technique.

In VQ modeling, the model Λ is a set of cluster centers $\Lambda = \{\mathbf{c}_1,\mathbf{c}_2,...,\mathbf{c}_K\}$ where $\mathbf{c}_k = (c_{k1},c_{k2},...,c_{kM})$, $k = 1, 2, ..., K$ are code vectors. Each code vector $\mathbf{c}_k$ is assigned to an encoding region R_k in the partition $\Omega = \{R_1,R_2,...,R_K\}$. Then the source vector $\mathbf{x}_t$ can be represented by the encoding region R_k and expressed by

$$V(\mathbf{x}_t) = \mathbf{c}_k \quad \text{if} \quad \mathbf{x}_t \in R_k \tag{17}$$

Let $U = [u_{kt}]$ be a matrix whose elements are memberships of x_t in the nth cluster, $k = 1, 2, ..., K$, $t = 1, 2, ..., T$. A K-partition space for $\mathbf{X}$ is the set of matrices U such that

$$u_{kt} \in \{0,1\}\ \forall k,t, \quad \sum_{k=1}^{K}u_{kt} = 1\ \forall t, \quad 0 < \sum_{t=1}^{T}u_{kt} < T\ \forall k \tag{18}$$

where $u_{kt} = u_k(\mathbf{x}_t)$ is 1 or 0, according to whether $\mathbf{x}_t$ is or is not in the kth cluster,

$\sum_{k=1}^{K} u_{kt} = 1 \; \forall t$ means each $\mathbf{x}_t$ is in exactly one of the K clusters, and $0 < \sum_{t=1}^{T} u_{kt} < T \; \forall k$

means that no cluster is empty and no cluster is all of $\mathbf{X}$ because of $1 < K < T$.

3.2 Fuzzy subspace VQ

The fuzzy subspace VQ method is based on minimization of the $Q_j(\Lambda, \overline{\Lambda})$ function in (14) considered as the following sum-of-squared-errors function (the index j for state is omitted)

$$J(U,W,\Lambda) = \sum_{k=1}^{K}\sum_{t=1}^{T} u_{kt} \sum_{m=1}^{M} w_{km}^{\alpha} d_{ktm} \tag{19}$$

where $\overline{\Lambda}$ is included in d_{ktm}, which is the Euclidean norm of $(\mathbf{x}_t - \mathbf{c}_k)$. Applying the equations (8) through (16), we obtain the following equations for fuzzy subspace VQ

$$\mathbf{c}_k = \sum_{t=1}^{T} u_{kt}\mathbf{x}_t \left/ \sum_{t=1}^{T} u_{kt} \right. , \quad 1 \leq k \leq K \tag{20}$$

$$u_{kt} = \begin{cases} 1: & d_{kt} < d_{jt}, \quad j = 1,...,K, j \neq k \\ 0: & otherwise \end{cases} \tag{21}$$

$$w_{km} = \frac{1}{\sum_{n=1}^{M}(D_{km}/D_{kn})^{1/(\alpha-1)}} , \quad D_{km} = \sum_{t=1}^{T} u_{kt}d_{ktm} \tag{22}$$

where

$$d_{ktm} = (c_{km} - x_{tm})^2 , \quad d_{kt} = \sum_{m=1}^{M} w_{km}^{\alpha} d_{ktm}^2 \tag{23}$$

The fuzzy subspace VQ modeling algorithm is summarized as follows:
1. Given a training data set $\mathbf{X} = \{\mathbf{x}_1, \mathbf{x}_2,..., \mathbf{x}_T\}$, where $\mathbf{x}_t = (x_{t1}, x_{t2},..., x_{tM})$, $t = 1, 2,..., T$.
2. Initialize memberships u_{kt} , $1 \leq t \leq T$, $1 \leq k \leq K$, at random satisfying (18)
3. Initialize weight values w_{km} , $1 \leq k \leq K$, $1 \leq m \leq M$ at random satisfying (13)
4. Given $\alpha \neq 1$ and $\varepsilon > 0$ (small real number)
5. Set $i = 0$ and $J^{(i)}(U,W,\Lambda) = 0$. Iteration:

     a. Compute cluster centers using (20)

     b. Compute distance components d_{ktm} and distances d_{kt} using (23)

     c. Update weight values using (22)

d. Update membership values using (21)

e. Compute $J^{(i+1)}(U,W,\Lambda)$ using (19)

f. If

$$\frac{J^{(i+1)}(U,W,\Lambda) - J^{(i)}(U,W,\Lambda)}{J^{(i+1)}(U,W,\Lambda)} > \varepsilon \tag{24}$$

set $J^{(i)}(U,W,\Lambda) = J^{(i+1)}(U,W,\Lambda)$, $i = i + 1$ and go to step (a).

4. Network anomaly detection

Assuming Λ is the *normal* model. Given an unknown network feature vector $\mathbf{x}$, the task is to determine $\mathbf{x}$ is normal or intrusive. The following algorithm is proposed

1. Given an unknown network feature vector $\mathbf{x}$ and the *normal* model Λ
2. Set a threshold value θ
3. Calculate the minimum distance between $\mathbf{x}$ and Λ

$$d_{\min} = \min_{k} d(\mathbf{x}, \mathbf{c}_k) \tag{25}$$

where $d(.)$ is defined in (23) and $\mathbf{c}_k$ is the kth code vector in Λ.

4. If $d_{\min} < \theta$ then $\mathbf{x}$ is normal else $\mathbf{x}$ is intrusive

It can be seen that when the threshold value increases, the anomaly detection rate and the false alarm rate also increase. If the false alarm rate is fixed, we can determine the corresponding values for the threshold value and the anomaly detection rate.

5. Experimental results

5.1 Network data and attack types

We consider a sample dataset which is the KDD CUP 1999 dataset. This dataset was based on MIT Lincoln Lab intrusion detection dataset, also known as DARPA dataset (DARPA, KDD CUP 1999). The data was produced for "The Third International Knowledge Discovery and Data Mining Tools Competition", which was held in conjunction with the Fifth International Conference on Knowledge Discovery and Data Mining. The raw network traffic records have already been converted into vector format. Each feature vector consists of 41 features. The meanings of these features can be found in (Tran et al. 2007). In this paper, we ignore features with symbolic values.

The attacks listed in feature vectors of KDD CUP 1999 dataset come from MIT Lincoln intrusion detection dataset web site (KDD CUP 1999). The labels are mostly the same except a few discrepancies. The MIT Lincoln lab web site lists 2 types of buffer overflow attack: *eject* and *ffb*. The former explores the buffer overflow problem of *eject* program of Solaris, and the later explores the buffer overflow problem of *ffb* config program. Guessing user logon names and passwords through remote logon via telnet session is labeled as *guess_passwd* in the KDD CUP 1999 dataset, but listed as *dict* on the MIT Lincoln lab web site. Finally, we cannot find the counterparts of *syslog* and *warez* in the KDD CUP 1999 dataset. In addition to the attack labels, the KDD CUP 1999 dataset has also the label *normal*, which means that the traffic is normal and free from any attack.

5.2 Anomaly detection and false alarm results

The proposed method for network intrusion detection was evaluated using the KDD CUP 1999 data set for training and the *Corrected* data set for testing. For training, the number of feature vectors for training the *normal* model was set to 5000. For testing, there were not sufficient data for all attack types, so we selected the *normal* network pattern and the 5 attacks which were *ipsweep, neptune, portsweep, satan,* and *smurf.* The testing data set contains 60593 feature vectors for the *normal* network pattern, and 306, 58001, 354, 1633 and 164091 feature vectors for the five attacks, respectively.

We also conducted a set of experiments for the network data using the normalization technique as follows

$$x'_{tm} = \frac{x_{tm} - \mu_m}{\sigma_m}, \quad \sigma_m = \frac{1}{T} \sum_{t=1}^{T} |x_{tm} - \mu_m| \tag{26}$$

where x_{tm} is the *m*th feature of the *t*th feature vector, μ_m the mean value of all T feature vectors for feature m, and σ_m the mean absolute deviation.

Anomaly detection rates versus false alarm rates are presented in Tables 1, 2, 3, and 4, where the codebook size is set to 4, 8, 16, and 32, respectively. The value of α was set to 4. All network data were normalised. We chose 5 false alarm rates (in %) which were 0.0, 0.1, 1.0, 10.0, and 100.0 to compare the corresponding anomaly detection rates for the standard VQ modelling and the proposed fuzzy subspace VQ modeling method. The ideal value for false alarm rate is 0.0, and from the 4 tables, we can see that the fuzzy subspace VQ performed outperformed the standard VQ modeling even with the smallest codebook size.

All the considered methods could not achieved the highest anomaly detection rate of 100% even though we changed the threshold value to accept all attack patterns (i.e., the false alarm rate is 100%). With codebook size of 32, the fuzzy subspace VQ modeling achieved very good results even with the lowest false alarm rate. The training data set contained 5000 feature vectors. If all training data for the *normal* pattern were used to train the model, the result would be better.

Modelling	False Alarm Rate (in %)				
	0.0	0.1	1.0	10.0	100.0
VQ	45.6	46.1	46.7	48.4	77.4
Fuzzy Subspace VQ	98.1	98.1	98.3	98.4	98.8

Table 1. Anomaly detection results (in %). Codebook size = 4

Modelling	False Alarm Rate (in %)				
	0.0	0.1	1.0	10.0	100.0
VQ	45.9	50.8	54.2	60.3	79.6
Fuzzy Subspace VQ	98.2	98.3	98.3	98.5	98.9

Table 2. Anomaly detection results (in %). Codebook size = 8

Modelling	False Alarm Rate (in %)				
	0.0	0.1	1.0	10.0	100.0
VQ	64.9	81.2	82.1	83.3	94.8
Fuzzy Subspace VQ	98.8	98.9	98.9	98.9	99.2

Table 3. Anomaly detection results (in %). Codebook size = 16

Modelling	False Alarm Rate (in %)				
	0.0	0.1	1.0	10.0	100.0
VQ	83.5	84.7	86.5	87.0	95.0
Fuzzy Subspace VQ	98.9	99.0	99.0	99.0	99.3

Table 4. Anomaly detection results (in %). Codebook size = 32

5. Conclusion

We have proposed a generic framework for soft subspace pattern recognition. The framework has been designed for continuous hidden Markov model. The framework for fuzzy subspace Gaussian mixture model has been extracted by setting the number of states in continuous hidden Markov model to one. With an assumption on covariance matrix and density, a fuzzy subspace model for vector quantization has been determined. The proposed methods are based on fuzzy c-means modeling to assign fuzzy weight values to features depending on which subspace they belong to. We have also applied the vector quantization model to anomaly network detection problem. We have used the KDD CUP 1999 dataset as the sample data to evaluate the proposed methods. The fuzzy subspace vector quantization method outperformed the standard vector quantization model.

6. References

Anderson R. and Khattak A. (1998). The use of Information Retrieval Techniques for Intrusion Detection, in First International Workshop on Recent Advances in Intrusion Detection (RAID'98), Louvain-la-Neuve, Belgium

Balasubramaniyan, J. S., Garcia-Fernandez, J. O. et al. (1998). An Architecture for Intrusion Detection using Autonomous Agents, in Proceedings of the 14th IEEE ACSAC, Scottsdale, AZ, USA, pp. 13-24

Caruso C. and Malerba D. (2004). Clustering as an add-on for firewalls, Data Mining, WIT Press

Chan, P. K., Mahoney, M. V., and Arshad, M. H. (2003). A Machine Learning Approach to Anomaly Detection, Technical Report CS-2003-06

DARPA Intrusion Detection Evaluation Data Sets 1999, available at http://www.ll.mit.edu/IST/ideval/data/data_ index.html

Dempster, A. P., Laird, N. M., and Rubin, D. B. (1997). Maximum Likelihood from Incomplete Data via the EM algorithm, *Journal of the Royal Statistical Society*, Ser. B, 39: pp. 1-38

Eskin, E. (2000). Anomaly Detection over Noisy Data Using Learned Probability Distributions, in the 17th International Conference on Machine Learning, Morgan Kaufmann, San Francisco, USA, pp. 255-262

Furui, S. (1997). Recent advances in speaker recognition, *Patter Recognition Lett.*, vol. 18, pp. 859-872

Huang, J.Z., Ng, M.K., Rong, H., and Li, Z. (2005). Automated Variable Weighting in k-means Type Clustering, *IEEE Trans. Pattern Analysis and Machine Intelligence*, vol. 27, no. 5, pp. 657-668

Huang, X., Acero, A., Alleva, F., Huang, M., Jiang, L., and Mahajan, M. (1996). From SPHINX-II to WHISPER: Making speech recognition usable, chapter 20 in *Automatic Speech and Speaker Recognition, Advanced Topics*, edited by Chin-Hui Lee, Frank K. Soong, and Kuldip K. Paliwal, Kluwer Academic Publishers, USA, pp. 481-508

Jing, L., Ng., M. K., Huang, J. Z., (2007). An entropy weighting k-means algorithm for subspace clustering of high-dimensional sparse data, *IEEE Transactions on Knowledge and Data Engineering*, vol. 19, no. 6, pp. 1026-1041

Juang, B.-H. (1998). The Past, Present, and Future of Speech Processing, *IEEE Signal Processing Magazine*, vol. 15, no. 3, pp. 24-48

KDD CUP 1999 Data Set, http://kdd.ics.uci.edu/databases/kddcup99/kddcup99.html

Stanifor, Hoagland and McAlerney (2002). Practical Automated Detection of Stealthy PortScans, *Journal of Computer Security*, vol. 10, no. 1, pp. 105-136

Kulkarni. V. G. (1995). *Modeling and analysis of stochastic systems*, Chapman & Hall, UK

Li X. and Ye N. (2004). Mining Normal and Intrusive Activity Patterns for Computer Intrusion Detection, in Intelligence and Security Informatics: Second Symposium on Intelligence and Security Informatics, Tucson, USA, Springer-Verlag, vol. 3073, pp. 1611-3349

Lee W. and Xiang D. (2001). Information theoretic measures for anomaly detection, in IEEE Synposium on Security and Privacy, pp. 130-143

Mahoney, M. V. and Chan, P.K. (2001). PHAD: Packet Header Anomaly Detection for Identifying Hostile Network Traffic, Technical report, Florida Tech., CS-2001-4

Mahoney, M. (2003). Network Traffic Anomaly Detection Based on Packet Bytes, Proc. ACM. Symposium on Applied Computing, pp. 346-350

Ourston, D., Matzner, S., et al. (2004). Coordinated Internet attacks: responding to attack complexity, *Journal of Computer Security*, vol. 12, pp. 165-190

Paxson, V. (1998). Bro: A system for detecting network intruders in real-time, in Proceedings of the 7th USENIX Security Symposium, Texas, USA, pp. 3-7

Portnoy, L., Eskin, E., and Stolfo, S. (2001). Intrusion detection with unlabeled data using clustering, in Proceedings of ACM CSS Workshop on Data Mining Applied to Security (DMSA-2001), Philadelphia, USA, pp. 333-342

Rabiner, L. R., Juang B. H., and Lee, C. H., (1996). An Overview of Automatic Speech Recognition, chapter 1 in *Automatic Speech and Speaker Recognition, Advanced Topics*, edited by Chin-Hui Lee, Frank K. Soong, and Kuldip K. Paliwal, Kluwer Academic Publishers, USA, pp. 1-30

Rabiner, L. R. and Juang, B. H. (1993). *Fundamentals of speech recognition*, Prentice Hall PTR, USA

Sherif, J.S., Ayers, R. and Dearmond, T. G. (2003). Intrusion Detection: the art and the practice, Part 1. *Information Management and Computer Security*, vol. 11, no. 4, pp. 175-186

Sherif J.S. and Ayers R. (2003). Intrusion detection: methods and systems, Part II. *Information Management and Computer Security*, vol. 11, no. 5, pp. 222-229

Stolfo, S.J. , Fan, W., Lee, W., Prodromidis, A. and Chan, P.K. (2000). Cost-based Modeling and Evaluation for Data Mining With Application to Fraud and Intrusion Detection: Results from the JAM Project, in Proceedings of DARPA Information Survivability Conference and Exposition, 2000, pp. 1130-1144

Taylor C. and Alves-Foss, J. (2002). An Empirical Analysis of NATE: Network Analysis of Anomalous Traffic Events, in 10th New Security Paradigms Workshop, Virginia Beach, Virginia, USA, pp. 18-26

Taylor C. and Alves-Foss J. (2001). NATE: Network Analysis of Anomalous Traffic Events, a low-cost approach, in Proceedings of New Security Paradigms Workshop, Cloudcroft, New Mexico, USA, pp. 89-96

Tran D., Ma W., Sharma D. and Nguyen T. (2007). Fuzzy Vector Quantization for Network Intrusion Detection, IEEE International Conference on Granular Computing, Silicon Valley, USA

Tran D., Ma W., and Sharma D. (2008). Automated Feature Weighting for Network Anomaly Detection, *IJCSNS International Journal of Computer Science and Network Security*, Vol. 8 No. 2 pp. 173-178

Tran D. and Wagner M. (2002). Generalised Fuzzy Hidden Markov Models for Speech Recognition, *Lecture Notes in Computer Science: Advances in Soft Computing* - AFSS 2002, N.R. Pal, M. Sugeno (Eds.), pp. 345-351, Springer-Verlag.

Tran D. and Wagner M. (2000). A General Approach to Hard, Fuzzy, and Probabilistic Models for Pattern Recognition, *Advances in Intelligent Systems: Theory and Applications*, M. Mohammadian (ed.), pp. 244-251, IOS Press, Netherlands

Yasami, Y., Farahmand, M., Zargari, V. (2007). An ARP-based Anomaly Detection Algorithm Using Hidden Markov Model in Enterprise Networks, Second International Conference on Systems and Networks Communications, pp. 69 - 75

Yang, H., Xie, F. and Lu, Y. (2006). Clustering and Classification Based Anomaly Detection, Lecture Notes in Computer Science, vol. 4223, pp. 1611-3349

Data Mining Applications in Higher Education and Academic Intelligence Management

Vasile Paul Bresfelean
Babes-Bolyai University of Cluj-Napoca, Faculty of Economics,
Romania

1. Introduction

Higher education institutions are nucleus of research and future development acting in a competitive environment, with the prerequisite mission to generate, accumulate and share knowledge. The chain of generating knowledge inside and among external organizations (such as companies, other universities, partners, community) is considered essential to reduce the limitations of internal resources and could be plainly improved with the use of data mining technologies.

Data mining has proven to be in the recent years a pioneering field of research and investigation that faces a large variety of techniques applied in a multitude of areas, both in business and higher education, relating interdisciplinary studies and development and covering a large variety of practice. Universities require an important amount of significant knowledge mined from its past and current data sets using special methods and processes. The ways in which information and knowledge are represented and delivered to the university managers are in a continuous transformation due to the involvement of the information and communication technologies in all the academic processes.

Higher education institutions have long been interested in predicting the paths of students and alumni (Luan, 2004), thus identifying which students will join particular course programs (Kalathur, 2006), and which students will require assistance in order to graduate. Another important preoccupation is the academic failure among students which has long fuelled a large number of debates. Researchers (Vandamme et al., 2007) attempted to classify students into different clusters with dissimilar risks in exam failure, but also to detect with realistic accuracy what and how much the students know, in order to deduce specific learning gaps (Piementel & Omar, 2005).

The distance and on-line education, together with the intelligent tutoring systems and their capability to register its exchanges with students (Mostow et al., 2005) present various feasible information sources for the data mining processes. Studies based on collecting and interpreting the information from several courses could possibly assist teachers and students in the web-based learning setting (Myller et al., 2002). Scientists (Anjewierden et al., 2007) derived models for classifying chat messages using data mining techniques, in order to offer learners real-time adaptive feedback which could result in the improvement of learning environments. In scientific literature there are some studies which seek to classify students in order to predict their final grade based on features extracted from logged data in educational web-based systems (Minaei-Bidgoli & Punch, 2003). A combination of multiple classifiers led to a significant improvement in classification performance through weighting the feature vectors.

The author's research directions through the data mining practices consist in finding feasible ways to offer the higher education institutions' managers ample knowledge to prepare new hypothesis, in a short period of time, which was formerly rigid or unachievable, in view of large datasets and earlier methods. Therefore, the aim is to put forward a way to understand the students' opinions, satisfactions and discontentment in the each element of the educational process, and to predict their preference in certain fields of study, the choice in continuing education, academic failure, and to offer accurate correlations between their knowledge and the requirements in the labor market. Some of the most interesting data mining processes in the educational field are illustrated in the present chapter, in which the author adds own ideas and applications in educational issues using specific data mining techniques.

The organization of this chapter is as follows. Section 2 offers an insight of how data mining processes are being applied in the large spectrum of education, presenting recent applications and studies published in the scientific literature, significant to the development of this emerging science. In Section 3 the author introduces his work through a number of new proposed directions and applications conducted over data collected from the students of the Babes-Bolyai University, using specific data mining classification learning and clustering methods. Section 4 presents the integration of data mining processes and their particular role in higher education issues and management, for the conception of an Academic Intelligence Management. Interrelated future research and plans are discussed as a conclusion in Section 5.

2. Data mining applications in the large spectrum of education

Data mining is an important data analysis methodology that has been successfully employed in many domains, with numerous applications in educational issues and was identified as one of the ten emergent technologies of the 21st century by the MIT Technology Review. It is an innovative field of research and study which is being implemented in education with several promising areas for data mining suggested and partially put into practice in the academic world. The educational data mining was defined as "the process of converting raw data from educational systems to useful information that can be used to inform design decisions and answer research questions" (Heiner et al., 2006)

A main concern of each institution of higher education is to predict the paths of students and alumni (Luan, 2004). They would like to identify which students will join particular course programs, and which students will require assistance in order to graduate. At the same time institutions want to learn whether some students more likely to transfer than others, and what groups of alumni are most likely to offer pledges. In addition to this challenge, traditional issues such as enrolment management and time-to-degree continue to motivate higher education institutions to search for better solutions.

The prediction of class configuration based on the course prerequisites and the prior courses taken by the students is another research illustration of educational data mining. Equipped with this information (Kalathur, 2006), the instructor can undertake remedial measures by supplementing the lecture material with the required topics which the students were lacking from their previous courses. After acquiring real data and building the database about the students and their course history, the model is trained with students' data and the system could provide immediate feedback to the student upon enrolling in a course how their profile fits with the course requirements.

Various studies are based on students' present "knowledge luggage", detecting with realistic accuracy what and how much the students know, in order to deduce specific learning gaps. This set of information could be obtained during an ongoing learning assessment process that makes possible to specify, with reasonable precision, which subject the student is better suited to learn at that moment, and requires automatic or semi-automatic procedures for treatment and analysis for acquisition of new knowledge. Pimentel and Omar (2005) presented a model for organizing and measuring knowledge upgrade in systems of education and learning with the support of data mining tools.

Academic failure among freshmen has long inspired a large number of questions , many psychologists seeking to comprehend and explicate it, and many statisticians have tried to predict it. Vandamme and collaborators (2007) attempted to classify, as early in the academic year as possible, students into three groups: the 'low-risk' students, with a high probability of succeeding; the 'medium-risk' students, who may succeed thanks to the measures taken by the university; and the 'high-risk' students, with a high probability of failing (or dropping out). They present the results of their application of discriminant analysis, neural networks, random forests and decision trees aiming to predict those students' academic success.

Another motivating issue in educational data mining is finding the reasons why students abandon school or certain courses before concluding the subjects required. One methodology (Antunes, 2008) consisted of discovering the frequent sequential patterns among the recorded behaviors, keeping the discovery limited to the sequences that are approximately in accordance to the existing background knowledge. The methodology assumes that the existing background knowledge can be represented by a context-free language, which plays the role of a constraint in the sequential pattern mining process. The curriculum knowledge was represented as a finite automaton, which established the order of subjects that a student should attend to finish his graduation.

Since universities courses progressively oblige students to use online tools in their studies, there are numerous prospects to mine the resultant large quantity of student learning data for hidden valuable information. Several approaches in scientific literature try to classify students in order to predict their final grade based on features extracted from logged data in educational web-based systems (Minaei-Bidgoli & Punch, 2003). A combination of multiple classifiers led to a significant improvement in classification performance through weighting the feature vectors; by using a Genetic Algorithm researchers could optimize the prediction accuracy and got a marked improvement over raw classification.

Intelligent tutoring systems' capability to register its exchanges with students is an important challenge and an opportunity (Mostow et al., 2005). A central matter in mining data from an intelligent tutoring system is "What happened when...?". In comparison to individual observation of live or videotaped tutoring, logs can be more far-reaching in the number of students, more comprehensive in the number of sessions, and exquisite in details, avoiding thus observer effects, costing less to obtain, and easier to analyze. Mostow and collaborators describe (2005) an educational data mining tool to support such case analysis by exploiting three simple but powerful ideas: first, a student, computer, and time interval suffice to specify an event; second, a containment relation between time intervals defines a hierarchical structure of tutorial interactions; third, the first two ideas make it possible to implement a generic but flexible tool for mining tutor data with minimal dependency on tutor-specific details.

A number of data mining studies were founded on distance and on-line education, which presents some probable information sources for data mining processes. These studies based on collecting and interpreting the information from several courses may assist teachers and students in the web-based learning setting. This information could be applied for assigning varied groups in programming courses or projects and to evaluate the actual learning (Myller et al., 2002).

On-line collaborative discussions have significant role in distance education and web-enhanced courses. Automatic tools for assessing student activities and promoting collaborative problem solving can offer an improved learning practice for students and also offer useful assistance to teachers. Researchers developed a specific mining tool for making the configuration and execution of data mining techniques easier for instructors and in order to be of use for decision making, using real data from on-line courses (Romero et al., 2008). Others (Anjewierden et al., 2007) derived models for classifying chat messages using data mining techniques, tested them and established the reliability of the classification of chat messages comparing the models performance to that of humans. (Ravi et al., 2007) presented an approach that could be used to scaffold undergraduate student discussions by retrieving useful information from past student discussions and an instructional tool that profiled student contributions with respect to student genders and the roles that students play in discussion.

3. Experiments in education based data mining at Babes-Bolyai University

The quality of an institution of higher education is specified among other concerns by its adapting know-how to the continuous varying requirements of the socio-economic background, the quality of the managerial system based on a high level of professionalism and on applying the latest technologies (Bresfelean, 2007).

The author's recent experiments at the Babes-Bolyai University of Cluj-Napoca were focused mostly on two of the main learning methods in data mining: classification learning and data clustering. The main objectives for the data mining practices were to offer the higher education institutions' managers ample knowledge to prepare new hypothesis, in a short period of time, which was precedently rigid or unachievable, in view of large datasets and earlier methods. It was aimed to put forward a way to understand the students' opinions, satisfactions and discontentment in every element of the educational process, and to predict their preference in certain fields of study, the choice in continuing their education and also the understanding, prediction and prevention of the academic failure. Building a profile for the students, and their grouping based on exam failure risk is a very motivating approach which could help both institution and students. Universities could learn students content/discontent regarding its education processes, curricula, courses, endowment, and figure out specific learning gaps and which students might require assistance in order to graduate. The student, which is the main focus of a student-based education, could benefit from the institution's know-how and support.

There are two keys to success in data mining (Edelstein, 1999). First is coming up with an exact formulation of the problem to solve. A focused report usually results in the best payoff. The second key is using the right data. After choosing from the data available, or perhaps buying external data, one may need to transform and combine it in significant ways.

As presented in the next table (Table 1.), the research was based on questionnaires' collected data from Romanian senior undergraduate students and master degree students from The Faculty of Economics and Business Administration, Babes-Bolyai University of Cluj-Napoca, using on-line and written surveys in order to evaluate their motivation in continuing education and the accomplishment regarding the educational process (Bresfelean et al., 2006), and included multiple choice questions and a few questions requiring written answers. There were also important data collected from faculty's databases, such as: tuition database, students' scholastic situation database, etc. The information collected consists of: general data on the subject (gender etc.), scholastic situation (grades, failed exams), several types of gained scholarships, interruption of study, exams absence, tuition, and also students' opinion (on courses, materials, curricula, research, teachers, laboratories technical novelty, knowledge gained, continuing education) etc.

Weka and RapidMiner workbenches, which are collections of machine learning algorithms and data preprocessing tools, were used to analyze the data, and proved to be valuable tools in order to gain insight into how certain processes are handled within higher education institutions. Weka workbench is an open source software issued under the GNU General Public License, a collection of machine learning algorithms for data mining tasks. It is currently developed at the University of Waikato in New Zealand, and the name stands for Waikato Environment for Knowledge Analysis. Weka contains tools for data pre-processing, classification, regression, clustering, association rules, and visualization. RapidMiner is another important open-source system for knowledge discovery and data mining, providing more than 400 operators for all main machine learning procedures, including input and output, and data preprocessing and visualization. It is written in the Java programming language and therefore can work on all popular operating systems.

3.1 Classification learning experiments

In classification learning, the learning design is offered with a set of classified examples from which it is estimated to learn a way of classifying unseen examples (Witten & Frank, 2005). Decision trees represent a supervised approach to classification and the models are commonly used in data mining to examine the data and induce the tree and its rules that will be used to make predictions (Edelstein, 1999). A "divide-and-conquer" approach (Witten & Frank, 2005) to the problem of learning from a set of independent instances leads naturally to a style of representation called decision tree.

There is a significant number of different algorithms that can be used for building decision trees including CHAID (Chi-squared Automatic Interaction Detection), CART (Classification And Regression Trees), Quest, C4.5 and C5.0 etc. Decision trees are grown through an iterative splitting of data into discrete groups, where the goal is to maximize the "distance" between groups at each split. Leaf nodes give a classification that applies to all instances that reach the leaf or a set of classifications, or a probability distribution over all possible classifications (Witten & Frank, 2005).

For the classification learning experiments the J48 method was chosen (based on the C4.5 algorithm from the machine learning), for being one of the most used Weka classification algorithms that offers a superior stability between precision, speed and interpretability of results. The basic algorithm for decision tree induction is a greedy algorithm that generates decision trees in a top-down recursive divide-and-conquer manner.

Data subjects	Instruments of collecting data	Information collected	Data mining method	Results of data mining/ Knowledge obtained
Undergraduate senior students	Questionnaires, Faculty's databases: -tuition database, -students scholastic situation database, etc.	•General information (gender etc.); •Opinions on: -fundamental knowledge gained, -books, course materials, case studies, -curricula, practical activities, -participation to research, grants, -recommending the specialization to future students, -courses teaching methods in each of the years of study; -continuing education; •Gained scholarships; •Parents' material support; •Scholastic situations and degrees. etc.	*Classification Learning (based on C4.5 algorithm)*	☺ Prediction of the students' choice in continuing their education with post university studies (master degree, Ph.D. studies etc.); and their preference in certain fields of study. ☺ Prediction of students failing to pass their exams
			Data Clustering (based on K-means algorithm)	☺ Grouping students in clusters with dissimilar behavior, the students from the same cluster embrace the closest behavior, and the ones from different clusters have the most different one. ☺ Drawing up the students profile based on their choice to continue their education. ☺ Grouping students in clusters based on the probability of: -passing their exams, -obtaining a scholarship
Alumni – presently master degree students	Questionnaires	•General information (gender etc.); •Opinions on: -contentment in the graduated and in chosen master degree specialization, -fundamental knowledge gained, -books, course materials, case studies, -curricula, practical activities, -participation to research, grants, -recommending specialization, -courses teaching methods in each of the years of study; -continuing education; -undergraduate/master degree courses considered important or outdated; •Details on present job; •Gained scholarships; •Competences obtained; •Parents' material support; •Scholastic situations, degrees etc.	*Classification Learning (based on C4.5 algorithm)*	☺ Prediction of the students' choice in continuing their education (Ph.D. studies etc.); and their preference in certain fields of study.
			Data Clustering (based on K-means algorithm)	☺ Grouping students in clusters with dissimilar behavior, the students from the same cluster embrace the closest behavior, and the ones from different clusters have the most different one. ☺ Drawing up the students profile based on: - their present choice to continue their education. -present job field (Does it correspond to the graduated or the master degree specialization?)

Table 1. Author's experiments in education based data mining at Babes-Bolyai University, after (Bresfelean et al., 2008b)

A general approach[1] to the decision tree algorithm can be summarized as following:
1. Choose an attribute that best differentiates the output attribute values.
2. Create a separate tree branch for each value of the chosen attribute.
3. Divide the instances into subgroups so as to reflect the attribute values of the chosen node.
4. For each subgroup, terminate the attribute selection process if:
    a. All members of a subgroup have the same value for the output attribute, terminate the attribute selection process for the current path and label the branch on the current path with the specified value.
    b. The subgroup contains a single node or no further distinguishing attributes can be determined. As in (a), label the branch with the output value seen by the majority of remaining instances.
5. For each subgroup created in (3) that has not been labeled as terminal, repeat the above process.

The purpose of the first classification learning experiments (Bresfelean, 2007) was to predict of the students' choice in continuing their education with post university studies (master degree, Ph.D. studies etc.) and their preference in certain fields of study. The results consist in several decision trees generated upon the initial data set, then on a number of filtered instances, corresponding to the students belonging to certain specializations. There were generated values of several performance measures for the classification problems described in the previous table: Kappa statistic, MAE (mean absolute error), RMSE (root mean square error), RAE(relative absolute error, %), RRSE (root relative squared error,%).

An illustration of a decision tree resulted from 409 instances (2007-2008 senior students from all specializations of the Faculty of Economics and Business Administration), has as a central root joint the Curricula attribute (opinions about whether the curriculum was relaxed and gave time to individual studying). The next levels of ramification are based on the futureJob attribute (the confidence in finding a job appropriate to their specialization after graduating) and 1st_year attribute (students' evaluation of courses teaching methods of the 1st year of study, this year being a test for the freshmen).

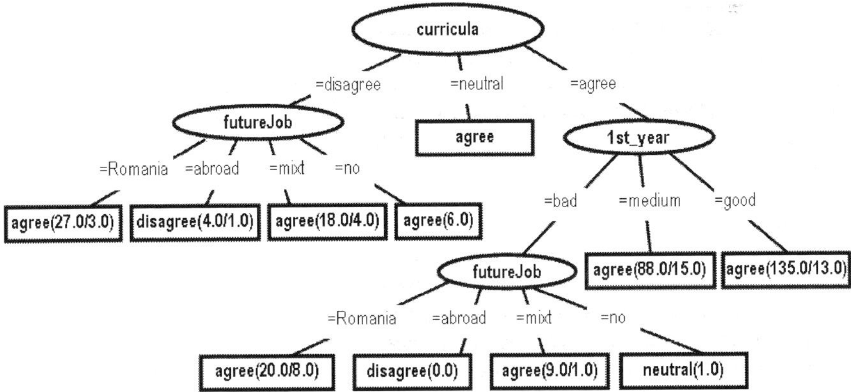

Fig. 1. Decision tree for predicting the students' choice in continuing their education

---

[1] Minnesota State University, http://grb.mnsu.edu/grbts/doc/manual/J48_Decision_Trees.html

Examples of interpretation of the decision tree's branches:
"If the students agreed they had relaxed curricula which allowed time for individual studying, and had a good opinion about the quality of courses teaching methods in the 1st year of study, then they would agree to continue their education with post university studies".
"If the students disagreed they had relaxed curricula which didn't allow time for individual studying, and were confident to find a job abroad appropriate to their specialization after graduation, then they would not agree to continue their education with post university studies".
The classification learning was also used to predict the students' failure/success to pass the academic exams based on their present behavioral profile. For the J48 classification learning based on the training set, there was a 75,79% success rate (the correctly classified instances), and for the cross-validation experiment we acquired a 72,86% success rate. The Laplace estimator was used with J48, which initiated all numbering starting with 1 as a substitute of 0, a standard technique named after the great mathematician of the 18th century Pierre Laplace. In the next figure (Fig.2) the first ramifications appear at entering_degree numerical attribute (students admittance grade in the Romanian 1-10 numerical grading systems, based on baccalaureate, high school final degree, etc.), and for next levels the ramification is based on expectations attribute (the fulfillment of their prior expectations regarding their present specialization) and the parents_sup attribute (the financial support received from their parents).

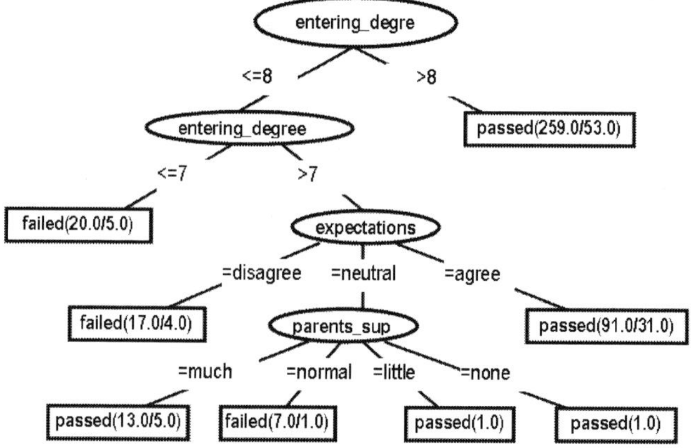

Fig. 2. Decision tree for predicting academic failure/success

Here are examples of interpretation of the decision tree's branches:
"If students' admittance grade was above 8, then they would pass all their exams"
"If students' admittance grade was in the (7,8] interval, were neutral that their expectations regarding the present specialization were fulfilled, believed the financial support from their parents was normal, then they would fail one or more exams".
"If students' admittance grade was in the (7,8] interval, did not agree that their expectations regarding the present specialization were fulfilled, then they would fail one or more exams".

The previous experiments were conducted over significant data collected from senior undergraduate students from all specializations of the Faculty of Economics and Business Administration. Several analogous experiments utilized data also from previous years senior students (currently master degree students or alumni), and were concentrated on certain specializations such as Business Information Systems (IE – Informatica economica), Marketing, Management, or Accounting (CIG – Contabilitate si informatica de gestiune) with different results to some extent from one specialization to another (Bresfelean et al., 2008a), (Bresfelean, 2007).

3.2 Data clustering experiments

The clustering process is a practice in which a set of data is replaced with clusters, which symbolize collections of data points belonging together, its success often being measured subjectively in terms of how useful the result appears to be to a human user (Witten & Frank, 2005). Clustering has been extensively used to partition data into groups so that the level of association is high between members of the same group and low between members of dissimilar groups (Jung et al., 2004).

The clustering algorithms generally follow hierarchical or partitional approaches. Several algorithms have been proposed in the literature for clustering, among which K-means clustering algorithm is the most commonly used because it can be easily implemented (Hung et al., 2005). For the partitional approach, the K-means and its variants, such as the fuzzy c-means algorithm, are the most popular algorithms.

In the recent data mining research (Bresfelean et al., 2006), (Bresfelean et al., 2007), we applied the clustering method called FarthestFirst which implements the transversal algorithm of Hochbaum and Shmoys, a simple, fast, approximation method based on the K-means algorithm. The idea (Dasgupta & Long, 2005) is to pick any data point to start with, then choose the point furthest from it, then the point furthest from the first two (the distance of a point x from a set S is the usual min $\{d(x, y) : y \in S\}$), and soon until k points are obtained. These points are taken as cluster centers and each remaining point is assigned to the closest center. If the distance function is a metric, the resulting clustering is within a factor two of optimal.

One of the main goals in applying the data clustering methods was to group students in clusters with dissimilar behavior; the students from the same cluster embrace the closest behavior, and the ones from different clusters have the most different one (Bresfelean et al., 2006), (Bresfelean et al., 2007). At the same time this process facilitates the drawing up the students profile based on their choice to continue their education, but also on the academic failure risk. We used the analysis based on data clustering with the purpose to classify students founded on their present job field, made a number of correlations, and tried to answer an important question: "Does it correspond to the graduated or to the master degree specialization?". In this way, we tried to get a feed-back from our alumni and/or master degree students, resulting in some important information for the higher education managers, a part of a superior sequence: "Are the current specializations competitive on the labor market?"

The next study was conducted over senior undergraduates and master degree students from one of the last generations of the four-years undergraduate first cycle (one-year Master, 4-years doctorate) during 2006-2008, before the full implementation of Bologna declaration (first degree of three years, two-years Master, 3-years doctorate). Using the FarthestFirst clustering method based on K-means algorithm (Bresfelean et al., 2006), (Bresfelean et al., 2007), we initialized the k cluster centers to k randomly chosen points from the data, which was partitioned based on the minimum squared distance criterion (Maulik & Bandyopadhyay, 2002). In our experiment, the k parameter is 3, corresponding to students' 3 choices in continuing their post university studies: disagree, neutral, agree. The cluster centers were then updated to the mean or the centroid of the points belonging to them. This entire process was repeated until either the cluster centers did not alter or there was no major change in the J values of two successive iterations. At this point, the clusters were stable and the clustering process ended. The clustering process proved to be particularly useful in dividing the students in segments with different behavioral models, the students from the same segment have the closest behavior, and the ones from different segments have the most different one.

Based on the students' choice to continue their education we divided them into 3 groups (Bresfelean et al., 2006), each presenting specific centroids, with an optimistic result after Weka validation (27.4151 % of the instances were incorrectly clustered):

Group 0: Students agree to continue their post university studies;

Group 1: Students do not agree to continue their post university studies;

Group 2: Students are neutral to continue their post university studies.

As a result of applying the FarthestFirst algorithm, we obtained 3 clusters with the following centroids:

Attributes (*Information/Opinion*):	Cluster 0 Agree	Cluster 1 Disagree	Cluster 2 Neutral
Gender	Male	Female	F
Specialization	IE-Business Information systems	Marketing	Management
Graduated High school	Other (mainly theoretical)	Agricultural profile	Economical profile
Their expectations regarding the specialization were fulfilled	Agree	Disagree	Neutral
Gained important knowledge	Neutral	Disagree	Agree
Were offered high quality courses, materials	Agree	Disagree	Agree
The curriculum was relaxed	Agree	Disagree	Neutral
The faculty had a good technical endowment	Agree	Neutral	Agree
Participated in practical activities	Agree	Disagree	Disagree
Participated in research/grants	Neutral	Disagree	Neutral
Would recommend the specialization	Agree	Disagree	Neutral
Teaching quality in the 1'st year	Good	Very bad	Medium
Teaching quality in the 2nd year	Good	Very bad	Medium

Teaching quality in the 3rd year	Good	Very bad	Excellent
Teaching quality in the 4th year	Good	Very bad	Excellent
Present job	none	Part time	Part time
Benefited from parents' financial support	Very much	No	Much
Expect to find a future job	In Romania	In Romania	No
Failed exams	none	3 or 4 failed	1 or 2 failed

Table 2. FarthestFirst clusters based on students' choice to continue their education, adapted from (Bresfelean et al., 2006)

The needed information is extracted from the clusters' centroids. Following this, it was determined that there were no common values fields for the three clusters, and as a result all the fields contain relevant information for the segmentation process.

The opinion on relaxed curriculum plays a substantial part in differentiating the clusters population:

cluster 0 - Agree
cluster 1 - Disagree
cluster 2 - Neutral

The same situation is observed in the case of the following: opinion on expectations' fulfillment regarding the specialization, and the opinion on recommending the specialization to future students.

The failed exams attribute (scholastic situation at the end of last academic year) also contains significant information in differentiating the cluster population:

cluster 0 - none (passed all exams at the end of last academic year)
cluster 1 - 3 or 4 failed exams
cluster 2 - 1 or 2 failed exams

Moreover, the opinion on the quality of courses teaching methods in the 1st and the last years of study (4th year) plays an important role in defining the clusters as seen in Table 2.

To fundament the decisions regarding the managerial strategies the faculty leaders can approach in order to fulfill all students' expectations, and enhance their competiveness on the labor market, it is compulsory to correlate the information extracted from terminal year students' questionnaires with graduate students' data, currently master degree students. Starting from the information mined in the undergraduate and master degree questionnaires, the following correlations and analysis were concluded:

- correlation and percentage relation between the graduated specialization and the master degree specialization;
- correlation and percentage relation between the current job and the graduated specialization;
- correlation and percentage relation between the current job and the master degree specialization.

The following table (Table 3) presents the data extracted from the questionnaires filled up by master degree students from the Faculty of Economics and Business Administration, Cluj-

Napoca, filtered to include only the students from Business Information Systems -IE, Marketing -Mk and Management –Mng master specializations.

Cathegories	Master degree students		
	IE	Mk	Mng
Total master degree students in the above specialization	11	40	15
First degree specialization similar to master specialization	10	16	6
First degree specialization different from master specialization	1	24	9
Job in other areas than the graduated specialization	4	11	5
Similar job to the graduated specialization	5	9	2
Job in other areas than the master degree specialization	5	13	6
Similar job to the master degree specialization	4	7	1
Unemployed IE master degree students	2	20	8

Table 3. Master degree students - Jobs and specializations, from (Bresfelean et al., 2006)

In the next tables and diagrams I present the correlations and percentage relations between different attributes suggestive to this study.

Master degree specialization	First degree specialization similar to master specialization (%)	First degree specialization different from master specialization (%)
IE	90,9%	9,09%
Mk	40%	60%
Mng	40%	60%

Table 4. Percentage relation between graduated specialization and the master degree specialization

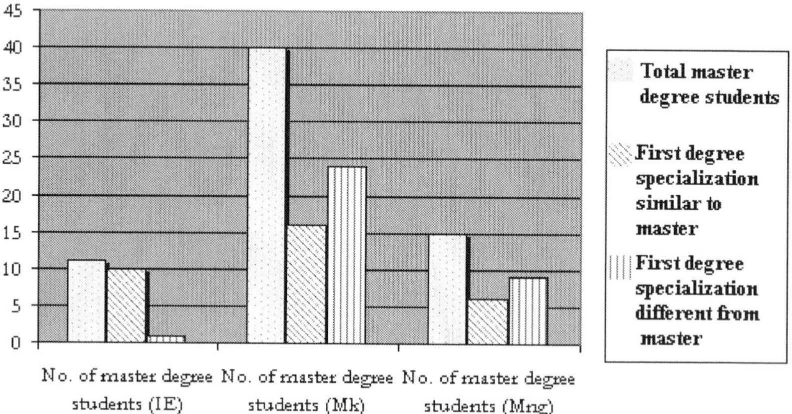

Fig. 3. Correlation between the graduated specialization and master degree specialization

Graduated specialization	Job in other area than the graduated specialization (%)	Similar job to the graduated specialization (%)	Unemployed master degree students of the present specialization (%)
IE	36,36%	45,45%	18,18%
Mk	27,5%	22,5%	50%
Mng	33,33%	13,33%	53,33%

Table 5. Percentage relation between the current job and the graduated specialization

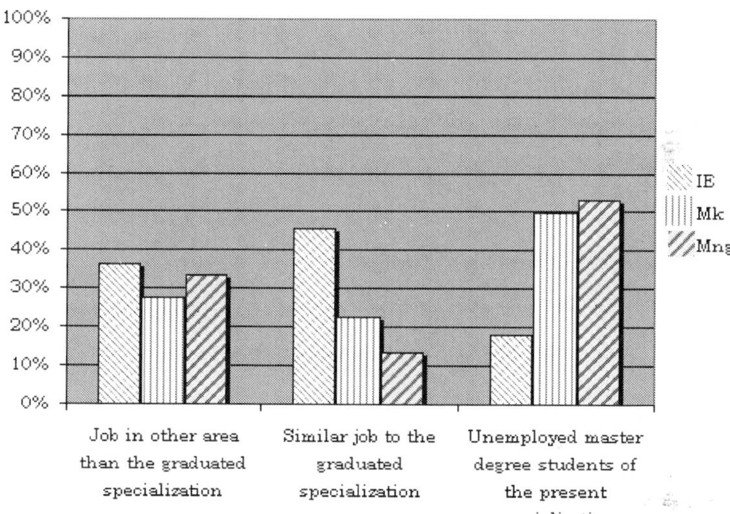

Fig. 4. Graphical representation of the percentage relation between the current job and the graduated specialization

Master degree specialization	Job in other areas than the master degree specialization (%)	Similar job to the master degree specialization (%)	Unemployed IE master degree students (%)
IE	45,45%	36,36%	18,18%
Mk	32,5%	17,5%	50%
Mng	40%	6,66%	53,33%

Table 6. Percentage relation between the current job and the master degree specialization

From the data analysis, correlation and percentage relations presented in this study, and based on other detailed research included in (Bresfelean et al., 2006) and (Bresfelean et al., 2007), we can conclude that:

- The majority of the undergraduate IE students were keen on continuing their education with master degree studies, while the undergraduate Mng students formed an important segment with neutral opinions on continuing education, and the undergraduate Mk students formed another segment with negative opinions on continuing education.

- The great majority of IE master degree students (approximate 90,9%) were formed by former IE graduate students, and only a small percent of other than IE graduates (approx. 9,09%);
- The majority of Mk and Mng master degree students (approx. 60%) were formed by students that didn't previously graduate the same specialization;
- An important percent (45,45%) of the IE master degree students found a similar job to the graduated specialization, and 36,36% of IE master degree students had an occupation similar to the master specialization;
- A small percent (22,5%) of the Mk master degree students found a similar job to the graduated specialization, and 17,5% of Mk master degree students had an occupation similar to the master specialization;
- A very small percent (13,33%) of the Mng master degree students found a similar job to their graduated specialization, and 6,66% of Mng master degree students had an occupation similar to the master specialization;
- Only a small percent (18,18%) of the IE master degree students were unemployed, but half of Mk (50%) and the majority of Mng (53,33%) master degree students were unemployed for different reasons, not mentioned in the questionnaires.
- Due to the financial support obtained from different companies, banks etc. we observed an increased number of students to other than IE master degree specializations; Mk and Mng master degree specializations attracted a large number of graduate students from other areas.

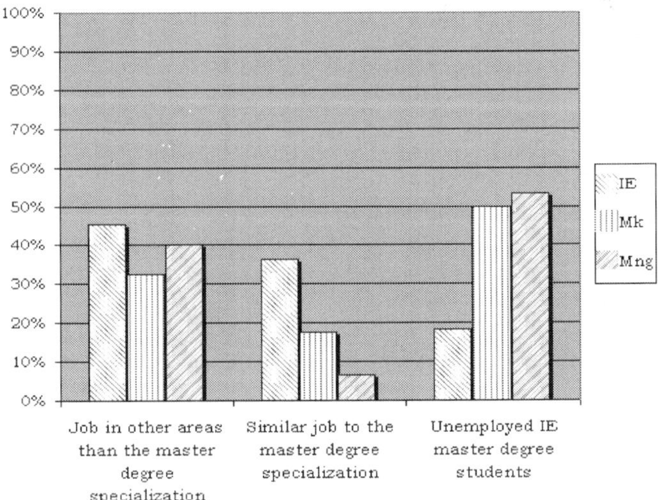

Fig. 5. Graphical representation of the percentage relation between the current job and the master degree specialization

4. The integration of data mining processes in higher education topics

The higher education institutions represent dissimilar and complex environments which involve links to communication and collaboration among its various departments and the society. In the situation of a state-financed higher education, the society manifests as the main partner of a university, and is represented at the purveyor-client interface by central or local governmental institutions, companies and organizations, labor management institutions etc. (Rusu & Bresfelean, 2006).

The European Council stated in Lisbon 2000 that the Europe should became by 2010, "the most competitive and dynamic knowledge-based economy in the world, capable of sustainable economic growth with more and better jobs and great social cohesion". The continuous change in European educational expectations due to Bologna Process and the demands for an EU area of educational collaboration have been gradually replacing the old-fashioned routine management with ICT-based knowledge management, leading to the emergence of an Academic Intelligence Management.

The Academic Intelligence Management includes all higher education institution's processes utilized to acquire, generate and spread knowledge in order to accomplish its objectives and strategies, based on the latest ICT (Information and Communication Technologies) and collaborative practices. It is tied to organizational goals such as improved performance, competitive advantage, innovation, research and development, which derive from technologies and applications providing historical, present, and predictive analysis of all academic activities. The ways in which information and knowledge are represented and delivered to the university managers are in a continuous transformation due to the involvement of the information and communication technologies in all the higher education processes.

The Bologna Declaration imposed a motivating process of change for a large and diversified number of countries to work together in order facilitate the quality assurance in the creation of a European Higher Education Area. Consequently, an integration of the latest research results involving these technologies, in terms of their contents and impact, is an issue that should be vital, while taking into account the fundamental role of a university as a knowledge creator and facilitator of teaching and research. Such is the case of all Romanian higher education institutions involved in complex processes of evaluation and accreditation: the traditional universities, which aim to develop their activities to include new areas, or the recently established private institutions aspirant to achieve university status.

The university is progressively regarded as a collaborative organization whose mission is to foster knowledge creation and knowledge diffusion among communities of students, scholars and researchers (Rodrigues & Barrulas, 2003). In the case of higher education institutions, the designing circuits of a managerial system (Rusu & Bresfelean, 2006) aiming an academic intelligent/intelligence management (Fig. 6) must be closely tied to:

- educational process activities: structure design and curricula content must be token of labor market requests and institution's capability; quality and freshness of courses information; adequate teaching/learning and evaluation methods; appropriate performance of educational processes etc.
- scientific research activities: thematic originality and opportunity; consistency of results; scientific probity; ethic experimenting; ways of utilizing the results etc.
- internal organization: authority and responsibility delegation; transparency and efficiency in the utilization of human and material resources; equity and performance encouragement in personnel promotion; continuous personnel training etc.
- external relations with local, national and international community; relations with other educational institutions and companies from different activity sectors; alumni etc.

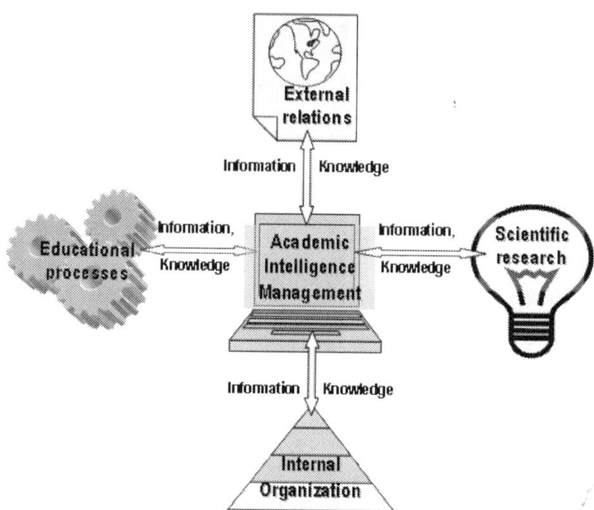

Fig. 6. Academic Intelligence Management, the hub of higher education activities

The higher education institutions' objectives answer the needs of the society and of the labor market and can surpass them, playing an important part in demand's generation (Rusu & Bresfelean, 2006). They serve as reference values for the adjusting circuits between the university-external partners' levels. Starting from this point, university managers set the strategic objectives, which would supply reference values for the lower levels, playing a parameter part in levels' correction. Based on it, in a designing stage, the strategies for developing a coherent academic offer would be implemented for quality management, strategic management, scientific research management and the "must" values for the lower levels: elaboration of education curricula and analytic programmes; scholastic management; school taxes management; accounting; human resource administration etc. The results, amount features of lower levels, are transmitted to the superior ones in a continuous communication within a managerial collaborative system (Fig.7), based on the latest ICT and knowledge management.

The data mining process integrated in the managerial system has two objectives: knowledge discovery, for offering explicit information, and a prediction objective for the forecast of future evolutions and events. By contrast with the normal interrogations addressed to current databases, using an interrogation language, the data mining process classifies and groups different systems data, eventually incompatible, searching for new associations. The decision support (DS) provides a variety of data analysis, simulation, visualization and data modeling techniques, and software such as decision support systems, executive support systems, databases and data warehouses.

Data mining and decision support are two disciplines aimed at solving difficult practical problems, and in many ways they are complementary (Bohanec & Zupan, 2001). To solve a particular problem, DS tends to rely on knowledge acquired from experts, while data mining attempts to extract it from data. Their combination would result in important benefits in solving real-life decision and data-analysis problems:

- Data mining has the prospective of solving decision support problems, when earlier decision support answers was recorded as analysis data to be used with mining tools.
- DS methods typically products a decision model, proving the expert knowledge of decision makers.

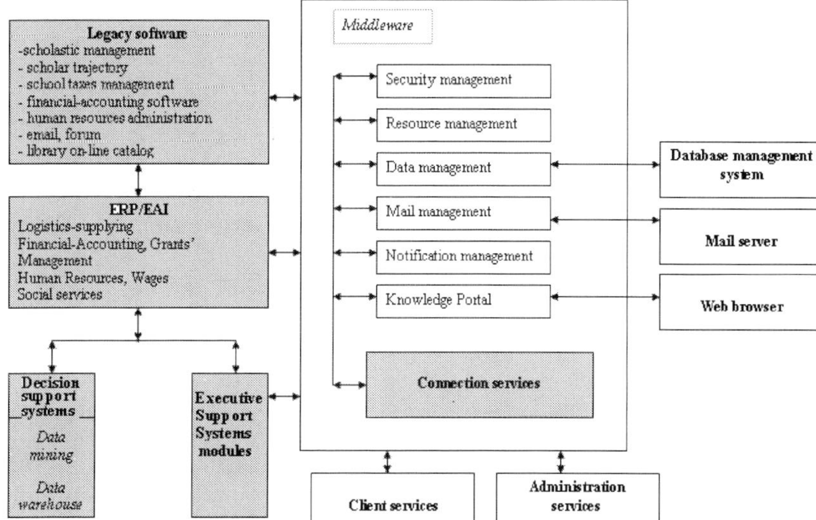

Fig. 7. Conceptual scheme of a collaborative managerial information system, from (Rusu & Bresfelean, 2006), (Dustdar, 2004)

An important step for successful combination will be the switch from the current data mining software tools to a data mining application systems approach (Rupnik et al, 2006) which introduces the possibility to develop decision support systems which use data mining methods and do not demand expertise in data mining for business users. It is an approach which focuses on users and decision makers, enabling them to view data mining models which are presented in a user-understandable manner through a user friendly and intuitive GUI using standard and graphical presentation techniques. Through the use of data mining application systems approach, data mining can become better integrated in business environments and their decision processes.

The exploitation of data mining processes for decision support is based on the CRISP European standard[2] (CRoss Industry Standard Process for Data Mining) proposed in mid 90's by a European consortium of companies as an industry- and tool-neutral data mining process model. The CRISP methodology provides guidelines and a sequence of steps to be followed in the applied knowledge discovery process. The life cycle of a data mining project consists of six phases:

1. Business Understanding (in our case – academic understanding) phase focuses on understanding the project objectives and requirements from a business perspective, and then converting this knowledge into a data mining problem definition.

---

[2] CRISP, http://www.crisp-dm.org/Process/index.htm

2. Data Understanding phase starts with an initial data collection and proceeds with activities in order to get familiar with the data, to identify data quality problems, to discover first insights into the data, or to detect interesting subsets.
3. Data Preparation phase covers all activities to construct the final dataset from the initial raw data. Tasks include table, record, and attribute selection as well as transformation and cleaning of data for modeling tools.
4. In the Modeling phase, various modeling techniques are selected and applied, and their parameters are calibrated to optimal values.
5. At the Evaluation stage in the project the user has built a model that appears to have high quality, from a data analysis perspective. At the end of this phase, a decision on the use of the data mining results should be reached.
6. Deployment phase. Creation of the model is generally not the end of the project. Depending on the requirements, the deployment phase can be as simple as generating a report or as complex as implementing a repeatable data mining process, expanding the obtained model and its results at the level of managerial information system of the higher education institution.

5. Conclusions

The data mining experiments from this chapter are a component of a larger research which is to be used to make several correlations, analysis in order to integrate data mining process in the managerial system for optimal decision support. I offered an insight of how data mining processes are being applied in the large spectrum of education by presenting recent applications and studies published in the scientific literature, considered to be relevant to the development of this emerging science. I presented my work through a number of experiments conducted over questionnaires data and scholastic databases at Faculty of Economics and Business Administration Cluj-Napoca, using classification learning and data clustering methods. In the last part of the chapter I introduced the concept of Academic Intelligence Management, and illustrated the integration of data mining processes and their particular role in higher education management and decision support.
The studies will continue with deeper mining of educational topics, such as performance in scientific research, correlations between the students' knowledge and the competences demanded on the labor market, academic failure, to perceive what and how much the students know, to realize learning gaps, and also improve teaching methods and educational management processes.

6. Acknowledgements

The research included in the present article is a part of Romanian CNCSIS TD-329 Grant "Contributii la perfectionarea managementului institutiilor universitare prin aplicarea de tehnologii informatice moderne" (Contribution to improving universities' management using modern IT technologies).

7. References

Antunes C., Acquiring Background Knowledge for Intelligent Tutoring Systems, Proceedings of Educational Data Mining 2008, The 1st International Conference on Educational Data Mining Montreal, Quebec, Canada, June 20-21, 2008 pp.18-27

Anjewierden A., Kollöffel B., Hulshof C., Towards educational data mining: Using data mining methods for automated chat analysis to understand and support inquiry learning processes. ADML 2007, Crete, September 2007. pp. 27-36.

Bohanec, M., Zupan, B., Integrating decision support and data mining by hierarchical multi-attribute decision models, IDDM-2001: ECML/PKDD-2001 Workshop Integrating Aspects of Data Mining, Decision Support and Meta-Learning, Freiburg, 2001, pp. 25-36.

Bresfelean, V.P., Bresfelean, M., Ghisoiu, N., Comes, C.-A., Determining Students' Academic Failure Profile Founded on Data Mining Methods, 30th International Conference Information Technology Interfaces, ITI 2008, 23-26 June 2008 Cavtat, Croatia (a)

Bresfelean, V.P., Bresfelean, M., Ghisoiu, N., Comes, C.-A., Development of universities' management based on data mining researches, INTED 2008, International Technology, Education and Development Conference, March 3-5 2008 Valencia, Spain (b)

Bresfelean V.P., Analysis and predictions on students' behavior using decision trees in Weka environment, 29th International Conference Information Technology Interfaces, ITI 2007, Cavtat, Croatia, June 2007, pp. 51-56

Bresfelean V.P, Bresfelean M, Ghisoiu N, Comes C-A., Data mining clustering techniques in academia, 9th International Conference on Enterprise Information Systems, 12-16, June 2007, Funchal, Portugal, pp. 407-410

Bresfelean V.P, Bresfelean M, Ghisoiu N, Comes C-A., Continuing education in a future EU member, analysis and correlations using clustering techniques, Proceedings of EDU'06 International Conference, Tenerife, Spain, December 2006, pp. 195-200

Dasgupta S., Long P.M., Performance Guarantees for Hierarchical Clustering, Journal of Computer and System Sciences, Volume 70 , Issue 4, June 2005, Special issue on COLT 2002, pp. 555 - 569

Dustdar, S., Caramba—A Process-Aware Collaboration System Supporting Ad hoc and Collaborative Processes in Virtual Teams, Distributed and Parallel Databases, 15, Kluwer Academic Publishers, 2004

Edelstein H., Introduction to Data Mining and Knowledge Discovery. Third Edition. Two Crows Corporation, Potomac, MD, USA, 1999

Heiner, C., Baker, R., Yacef, K.: Preface. In: Workshop on Educational Data Mining at the 8th International Conference on Intelligent Tutoring Systems (ITS 2006), Jhongli, Taiwan. 2006

Hung, M. C., Wu, J., Chang, J.H., Yang, D. L., 2005. An Efficient K-Means Clustering Algorithm Using Simple Partitioning. Journal of Information Science and Engineering 21, 1157-1177, 2005

Jung, Y.; Park, H.; Du, D.Z.; Drake, B. (2003) A Decision Criterion for the Optimal Number of Clusters in Hierarchical Clustering, Journal of Global Optimization 25: 91–111, Kluwer Academic Publishers 2003

Kalathur S. An Object-Oriented Framework for Predicting Student Competency Level in an Incoming Class, Proceedings of SERP'06 Las Vegas , 2006, pp. 179-183

Luan Jing, Data Mining Applications in Higher Education, SPSS Exec. Report, 2004. http://www.spss.com/home_page/wp2.htm

Maulik, U., Bandyopadhyay, S., 2002. Performance Evaluation of Some Clustering Algorithms and Validity Indices, IEEE Transactions on Pattern Analysis and Machine Intelligence, Vol. 24, No. 12, December 2002

Minaei-Bidgoli B., Punch W.F., Using Genetic Algorithms for Data Mining Optimization in an Educational Web-based System, GECCO 2003 Conference, Springer-Verlag, Vol 2, Chicago, USA; July 2003. pp. 2252-2263.

Mostow J., Beck J., Cen H., Cuneo A., Gouvea E., Heiner C. ,An educational data mining tool to browse tutor-student interactions: Time will tell! Proceedings of the Workshop on Educational Data Mining, Pittsburgh, USA; 2005. pp.15-22.

Myller N., Suhonen J, Sutinen E. Using data mining for improving web-based course design, Proceedings ICCE'02 of the International Conference on Computers in Education, Auckland, New Zealand vol.2; December, 2002. pp.959 – 963.

Pimentel E.P., Omar N., Towards a model for organizing and measuring knowledge upgrade in education with data mining, The 2005 IEEE International Conference on Information Reuse and Integration, Las Vegas, USA; August 15-17, 2005. pp. 56-60

Ravi S., Kim J., Shaw E., Mining On-line Discussions: Assessing Technical Quality for Student Scaffolding and Classifying Messages for Participation Profiling, Workshop of Educational Data Mining, Supplementary Proceedings of the 13th International Conference of Artificial Intelligence in Education. Marina del Rey, CA. USA. July 2007, pp. 70-79

Rodrigues, J.P.C., Barrulas, M. J. (2003), Towards Web-Based Information and Knowledge Management in Higher Education Institutions, Lecture Notes in Computer Science, Volume 2720, Sep 2003, pp. 188-197

Romero C., Ventura S., Espejo P. and Hervas C., Data Mining Algorithms to Classify Students, Proceedings of Educational Data Mining 2008, The 1st International Conference on Educational Data Mining Montreal, Quebec, Canada, June 20-21, 2008 pp. 8-17

Rupnik R., Kukar, M., Bajec M., Krisper, M., DMDSS: Data mining based decision support system to integrate data mining and decision support, 28th International Conference Information Technology Interfaces, ITI 2006, Cavtat, Croatia, June 2006, pp.225-230

Rusu, L., Breşfelean, V.P., Management prototype for universities. Annals of the Tiberiu Popoviciu Seminar, Supplement: International Workshop in Collaborative Systems, Volume 4, 2006, Mediamira Science Publisher, Cluj-Napoca, Romania, pp. 287-295

Universitatea Babes-Bolyai Cluj-Napoca, Romania. Programul Strategic al Universitatii Babes-Bolyai (2007-2011), Nr.11.366; 1 august 2006.

Vandamme J.P., Meskens N., Superby J.F., Predicting Academic Performance by Data Mining Methods, Education Economics, Volume 15, Issue 4 December 2007 , pp. 405 - 419

Witten I.H., Frank E., Data Mining: Practical Machine Learning Tools and Techniques, 2nd ed., Morgan Kaufmann series in data management systems, Elsevier Inc., 2005.

16

Solving POMDPs with Automatic Discovery of Subgoals

Le Tien Dung, Takashi Komeda and Motoki Takagi
Shibaura Institute of Technology
Japan

1. Introduction

Reinforcement Learning (RL) is the problem faced by an agent that must learn behavior through trial-and-error interactions with a dynamic environment (Kaelbling et al., 1996). At any time step, the environment is assumed to be at one state. In Markov Decision Processes (MPDs), all states are fully observable in which the agent can choose a good action based only on the current sensory observation. In Partially Observable Markov Decision Processes (POMDPs), any state can be a hidden state in which the agent doesn't have sufficient sensory observation and the agent must remember the past sensations to select a good action. Q-learning is the most popular algorithm for learning from delayed reinforcement in MDPs, and RL with Recurrent Neural Network (RNN) can solve deep POMDPs.

Several methods have been proposed to speed up learning performance in MDPs by creating useful subgoals (Girgin et al., 2006), (McGovern & Barto, 2001), (Menache et al., 2002), (Simsek & Barto, 2005). Subgoals are actually states that have a high reward gradient or that are visited frequently on successful trajectories but not on unsuccessful ones, or that lie between densely-connected regions of the state space. In MDPs, to attaint a subgoal, we can use a plain table based policy, named a skill. Then these useful skills are treated as options or macro actions in RL (Barto & Mahadevan, 2003), (McGovern & Barto, 2001), (Menache et al., 2002), (Girgin et al., 2006), (Simsek & Barto, 2005), (Sutton et al., 1999). For example, an option named "going to the door" helps a robot to move from any random position in the hall to one of two doors. However, it is difficult to apply directly this approach to RL when a RNN is used to predict Q values. Simply adding one more unit into output layer to predict Q values for an option doesn't work because updating any connection's weight will affect all previous Q values and because it is easy to lose the Q values when the option can't be executed for a long time.

In this chapter, a method named Reinforcement Learning using Automatic Discovery of Subgoals is presented towards this approach but in POMDPs. We can reuse existing algorithms to discover subgoals. To obtain a skill, a new policy using a RNN is trained by experience replay. Once useful skills are obtained by RNNs, these learned RNNs are integrated into the main RNN as experts in RL. Results of experiment in two problems, the E maze problem and the virtual office problem, show that the proposed method enables an agent to acquire a policy, as good as the policy acquired by RL with RNN, with better learning performance.

2. Reinforcement learning and recurrent neural network

RL is learning what to do to maximize a numerical reward signal. The learner is not told which actions to take, as in supervised learning, but instead must discover which actions yield the most reward by trying them (Sutton & Barto, 1998). RL allows a software agent to automatically determine its behavior within a specific context, in order to maximize its performance. Simple reward feedback is required for the agent to learn its behavior; this is known as the reinforcement signal. This automated learning scheme implies that there is little need for a human expert who knows about the domain of application. Much less time will be spent designing a solution, since there is no need for hand-crafting complex sets of rules as with expert systems (Champandard, 2007). Beyond the agent and the environment, four main sub-elements of a reinforcement learning system are a policy, a reward function, a value function, and, optionally, a model of the environment.

In the general case of a reinforcement learning problem, the agent's actions determine not only its immediate reward, but also the next state of the environment. The agent has to be able to learn from delayed reinforcement: it may take a long sequence of actions, receiving insignificant reinforcement, and then finally arrive at a state with high reinforcement. I.e., the agent must be able to learn which of its actions are desirable based on reward that can take place arbitrarily far in the future.

2.1 Q learning

When a model of fully observable environment is not available, the most widely used RL is Q-learning (Sutton & Barto, 1998), (Watkins, 1989). Q-learning iteratively approximates the state-action value function by updating its plain table based Q values as

$$Q(s,a) = Q(s,a) + \alpha[r + \gamma \max_{a'} Q(s',a') - Q(s,a)] \tag{1}$$

where $Q(s,a)$ is the state-action value for action a in state s, α is learning rate, and γ is the factor of discount.

Based on Q values, the agent selects an action to execute using a standard exploration method. A simple selection rule, ε-greedy method, is to behave greedily most of the time. The agent selects the action with highest estimated action value with a big probability. But sometimes, the agent selects an action at random with small probability. An alternative solution, softmax selection rule, is to vary the action probabilities as a graded function of estimated value (Sutton & Barto, 1998).

2.2 Perceptual aliasing

In a real world environment, not all states are fully observable, named hidden states. I.e., in some world states, the observation is same, but the optimal actions are different. These problems are called POMDPs. Fig. 1 shows an example of POMDPs (Ohta et al., 2003). If the agent selects the same action at a hidden state, it may not reach the goal. To solve this kind of problems, some researchers propose memory-less approach. This method is simply to avoid passing through hidden states or uses stochastic action selection rule at hidden states (Littman, 1994), (Ohta et al., 2003). However, this approach doesn't fit well when there are many perceptual aliasing states in the optimal policy. Memory based approach uses past sensations to predict optimal actions (McCallum, 1995), (Whitehead, 1995).

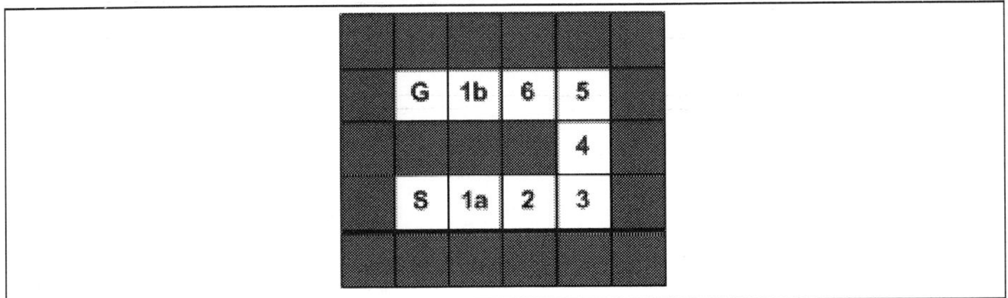

Fig. 1. A maze including perceptual aliasing.

2.3 RL with RNN

A number of researchers use a RNN to predict Q values to solve POMDPs (Bakker, 2002), (Ballini, 2001), (Gomez et al., 2005), (Gomez & Schmidhuber, 2006), (Le et al., 2007), (Le et al., 2008), (Lin & Mitchell, 1993), (Lin, 1993), (Ho & Kamel, 1994), (Onat et al., 1998), (Schafer & Udluft, 2005). The number of input unit is equal to the dimension of the sensory inputs from the environment. The number of output units is equal to the number of possible actions. Each output represents the Q-value of the associated action. For the output units, a linear activation function is used to cope with the required range of Q values. At a time step, RNN inputs are the sensations of the current state and RNN outputs are approximated Q values for that state. Similar as plain table based Q learning, the agent selects an action based on Q values and observes new Q values. However, the agent doesn't update the Q values as in (1). It updates the RNN connections' weights to predict the Q values.

RNN architecture can be Time-Delayed Neural Network, Elman Network, Recurrent Neurofuzzy Network, or Long Short Term Memory Network (LSTM). The RNN used in this chapter is LSTM which has been proved to have a strong ability to solve many difficult tasks (Gers et al., 2000), (Gers et al., 2002), (Hochreiter & Schmidhuber, 1997), (Schmidhuber et al., 2007). The basic element in LSTM is memory cell (Fig. 2), which contains a recurrently self-connected liner unit called the "Constant Error Carousel" or CEC (Hochreiter & Schmidhuber, 1997). A multiplicative input gate unit is employed to protect the memory contents from perturbation by irrelevant inputs. Likewise, a multiplicative output gate unit is used to protect other units from perturbation by currently irrelevant memory contents. F. A. Gers improves the limitation of traditional LSTM by adding a forget gate to memory cell (Gers et al., 2000). Standard LSTM (or LSTM for short) with forget gates can learn to reset the memory contents that are out of date.

The activations are computed as follows:

For each unit i in hidden layer at time t, the net input is

$$net_i(t) = \sum_m w_{im} y_m(t-1) \tag{2}$$

where w_{im} is the weights of the connection from unit m to unit i.

The hidden unit activation y_h, input gate activation y_{in}, output gate activation y_{out}, and the forget gate activation y_φ is calculated by

$$y_i = f(net_i(t)) \tag{3}$$

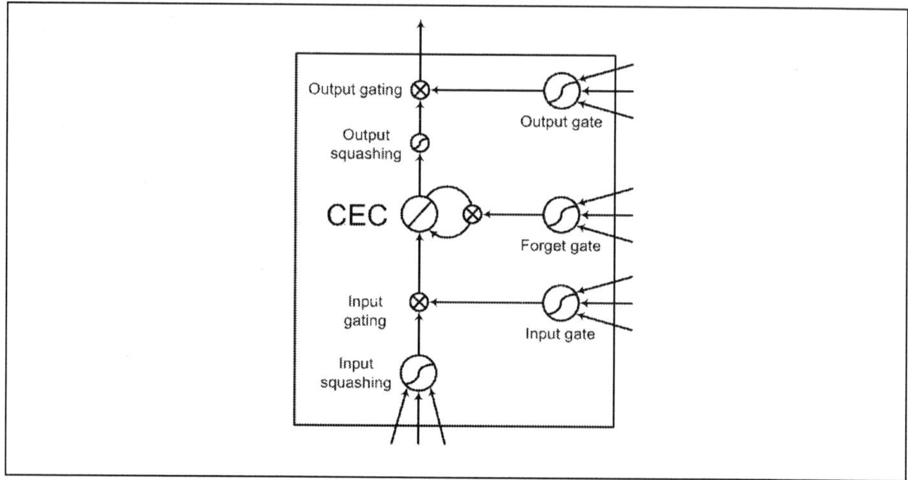

Fig. 2. A memory cell with its gates

where f is the standard logistic sigmoid function

$$f = \frac{1}{1+e^{-x}} \tag{4}$$

The CEC activation s_{c_j} is calculated by

$$s_{c_j}(t) = y_\varphi(t)s_{c_j}(t-1) + y_{in}(t)g(net_{c_j}(t)) \tag{5}$$

where g is the logistic sigmoid function scaled to [-2, 2]

$$g = \frac{4}{1+e^{-x}} - 2 \tag{6}$$

The memory cell output activation y_{c_j} is calculated by

$$y_{c_j}(t) = y_{out_j}(t)h(s_{c_j}(t)) \tag{7}$$

where h is the logistic sigmoid function scaled to [-1, 1]

$$h = \frac{2}{1+e^{-x}} - 1 \tag{8}$$

Finally, the output unit activation y_k is calculated by

$$y_k = f_k(net_k(t)) \tag{9}$$

where f_k is the standard logistic sigmoid function or the identity function.

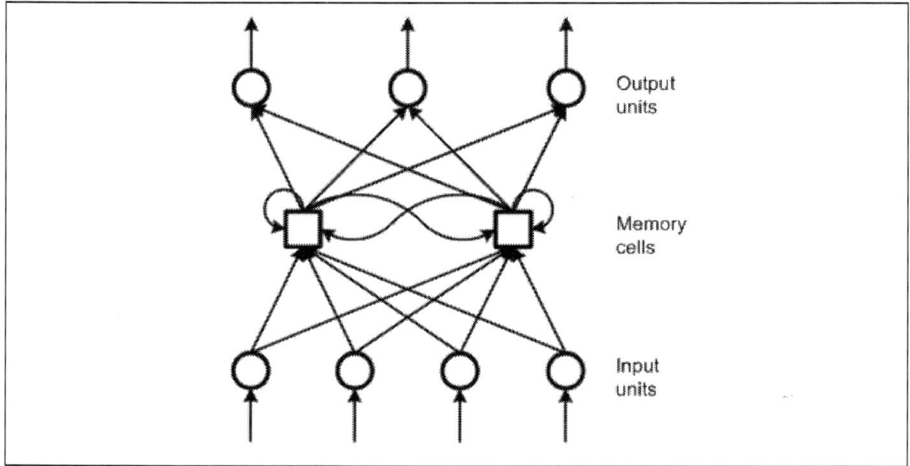

Fig. 3. A typical LSTM network with 4 input units, 2 memory cells, and 3 output units.

Several LSTM network topologies are proposed to solve some particular problems (Gers et al., 2000), (Gers et al., 2002), (Hochreiter & Schmidhuber, 1997), (Schmidhuber et al., 2007). Fig. 3 shows a typical LSTM network architecture with 4 input units, 2 memory cells, and 3 output units.

3. Solving POMDPs with automatic discovery of subgoals

Reinforcement Learning using Automatic Discovery of Subgoal (RLSG) is a framework to accelerated learning ability in non-Markovian problems. There are two phases in RLSG. The first phase is to obtain online generated sub-policies. One sub-policy is a useful skill to attain subgoals. Each sub-policy has its own RNN which plays a role of Recurrent Neural SubNetwork (RSN) in RLSG. The second phase in RLSG is to integrate online generated RSNs into the main RNN. The new RNN will be trained to predict the Q values for the original problem.

3.1 Automatic discovery of subgoal
Several methods have been proposed to discover subgoals (Girgin et al., 2006), (McGovern & Barto, 2001), (Menache et al., 2002), (Simsek & Barto, 2005). Subgoals are actually states that have a high reward gradient or that lie between densely-connected regions of the state space. In our system, a state will be considered as a subgoal if it is visited frequently on successful trajectories but not on unsuccessful trajectories. A simple method to find a subgoal is to calculate the probability of being a subgoal for all states by:

$$P(s) = P(s \in B^{+}) * \left[1 - P(s \in B^{-}) \right] \tag{10}$$

where B^{+} and B^{-} are successful bag and unsuccessful bag. The states with high probability and not surrounding the starting and ending states are considered as subgoals.

3.2 Learning a skill

After finding a subgoal, a new policy should be trained to attain it. Most of previous researchers assume that the environment is observable therefore they can use a plain table to store Q values for the new policy (Girgin et al., 2006), (McGovern & Barto, 2001), (Menache et al., 2002), (Simsek & Barto, 2005). However, it can't be done in POMDPs. In our system, a policy using a RNN is trained to attain this subgoal by experience replay as described in (Lin, 1992) with a pseudo reward function once we can find a subgoal.

3.3 Integration

In full observable environments, we can use skills as options in RL by adding these options to the action set of the agent. These options are considered as macro actions. New elements are inserted into the table to predict Q values of these macro actions. Update one value in a table doesn't affect the others. However, it is hard to apply directly these methods in RL with RNN because update a neural network connection's weight will affect all other previous Q values. Furthermore, only in some parts of the whole state space, we can execute an option. That means if we add one more output unit for an option, it is very easy to lose the previous learned Q values for that option.

In this chapter, our proposed method Reinforcement Learning using automatic discovery of SubGoals (RLSG) doesn't use generated skills as options but as components of the RNN to predict Q value for the main policy. All elements of previous learned neural networks except input and output units are integrated into the main RNN. Our previous works show that it is possible to speed up learning performance by reuse previous policies in similar tasks (Le et al., 2007). Similar as in supervised learning, the new RNN is composed from all learned RNNs with or without new hidden units (Carroll & Peterson, 2002), (Carroll et al., 2001), (Kirschning et al., 1995), (Jordan et al., 1994). The previous connections can be frozen or trainable. Our previous work (Le et al., 2007) also shows that Mixture of Experts System (MES) is the best among several integration methods. After integration, the agent continues to learn to accomplish its task using the new policy.

3.5 Mixture of Experts System (MES)

In MES, we merge the original network and all learned sub-networks in order to make a new network as shown in Fig. 4. Learned connections are considered as experts in the new network to speed up learning performance (Jordan et al., 1994). All connections are trainable. I.e., we can change the weight of any connection.

4. Experiment

In order to examine the learning ability of RLSG, we performed two experiments in the E maze problem and in the Virtual Office problem. In the first and the second experiments, RLSG uses online generated RSNs with one and two useful skills respectively.

4.1 E maze problem

An agent must learn to move from a starting position S to a goal position G. Observation at each position is shown in Fig. 5. The agent can choose one of four actions: North, East, South, and West. Executing any action, the agent receives a reward -1. If the agent can reach the goal it receives a reward 10. An episode is terminated when the agent reaches the goal or the agent has executed 100 actions.

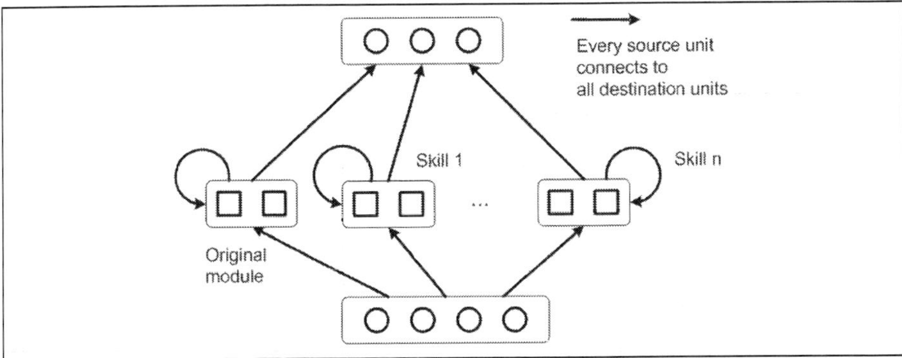

Fig. 4. Mixture of Expert System.

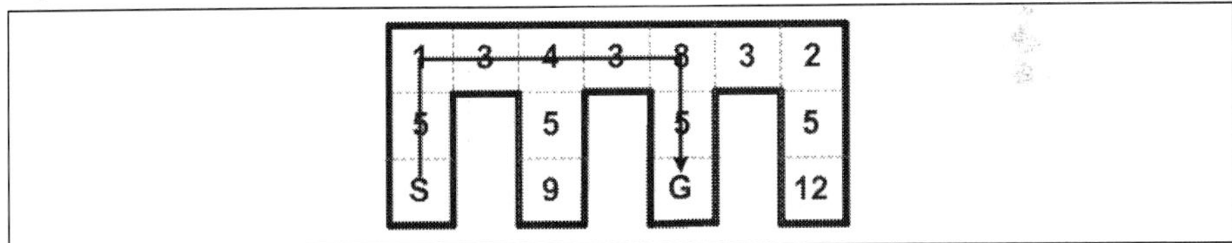

Fig. 5. E Maze Problem: The agent must learn to move from S to G.

We executed RLSG and RL with RNN using softmax exploration method to compare the learning performance. The following parameters were used: discount factor γ = 0.98, exploration temperature τ = 1, RNN learning rate α = 0.1, 4 input units, 6 memory cells, 4 output units. After every 10 episodes, the system evaluates the current RNN. Learning process is terminated when the agent can reach the goal in 10 moves using greedy method. In this experiment, only one subgoal was allowed to create after 100 first learning episodes. For each method, 5 runs were performed.

Results

In some runs, state 8 is detected as a subgoal. In the others, state 2 is considered as a subgoal. We found that even if the subgoal discovery process wasn't very perfect, it didn't affect the learning ability. All runs were convergent giving a good policy. Learning performance of two methods is shown in Fig. 6. The figure shows RLSG outperforms RL with RNN.

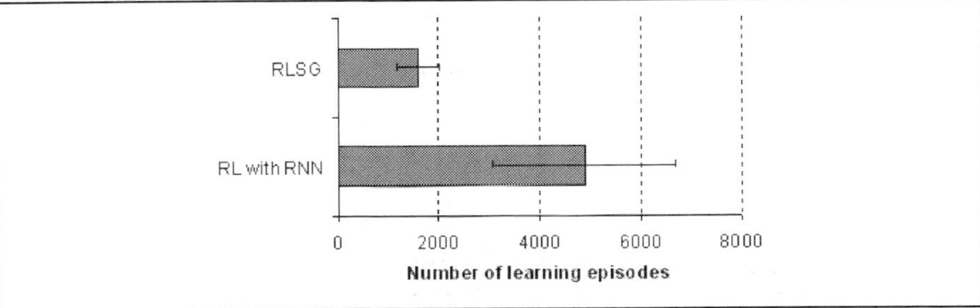

Fig. 6. Learning Performance in the E Maze Problem.

4.2 The virtual office problem

An agent must learn to move from the any random starting position in the hall H (the left room) to one of the goals in the right rooms (Fig. 7). Observations in the upper right room are same as observations in the lower right room except the goal positions. Four actions are available: North, East, South, and West. If the agent reaches the goal, it receives a reward 10. An episode is terminated when the agent reaches the goal or it has executed 100 actions.

Again, we executed RLSG and RL with RNN using softmax exploration method to compare the learning performance. The following parameters were used: discount factor $\gamma = 0.98$, exploration temperature $\tau = 1$, RNN learning rate $\alpha = 0.1$, 6 input units, 6 memory cells, 4 output units. After every 10 episodes, the system evaluates the current RNN. Learning process is terminated when the agent can reach one goal from any starting position in 10 moves using greedy method. Two subgoals were allowed to create after 30 first learning episodes. For each method, 10 runs were performed.

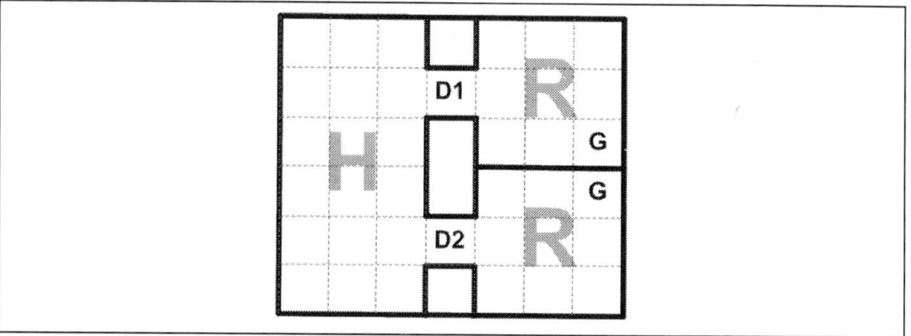

Fig. 7. Virtual Office Problem: D1, D2 are doors between hall and rooms.

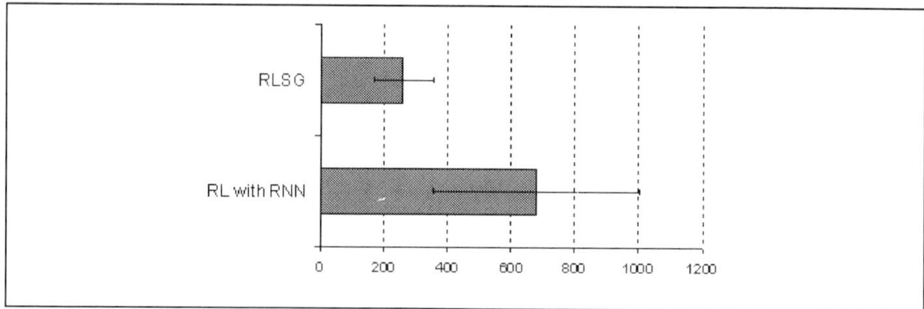

Fig. 8. Learning Performance in the Virtual Office Problem.

Results

In this experiment, all the states in the rights rooms, located near the goals, weren't considered as subgoals. Two doors were detected as subgoals. Again, all runs were convergent giving a good policy. Learning performance of two methods is shown in Fig. 8. The figure also shows RLSG outperforms RL with RNN.

5. Conclusion

In this chapter, we have proposed Reinforcement Learning using Automatic Discovery of Subgoals to accelerate learning of RL with RNN by profiting useful skills. Hidden units and their connections of RNNs, which are used by generated skills, are integrated into the RNN of the main policy. Experiment results of the E maze problem and the virtual office problem show the potential of this method.

6. References

Bakker, B. Reinforcement Learning with Long Short Term Memory, *Advances in Neural Information Processing Systems*, Vol. 14, pp. 1475-1482, 2002.

Barto, A. G. & S. Mahadevan. Recent Advances in Hierarchical Reinforcement Learning, *Discrete Event Systems, Special Issue on Reinforcement Learning*, Vol. 13, pp. 41-77, 2003.

Ballini, R., S. Soares & F. Gomide. A Recurrent Neurofuzzy Network Structure and Learning Procedure, *Proceedings of the IEEE International Conf. on Fuzzy Systems*, pp. 1408-1411, 2001.

Carroll, J. L. & T. S. Peterson. Fixed vs. Dynamic Sub-transfer in Reinforcement Learning, *Proceedings of the 2003 International Conference on Machine Learning and Applications*, 2002.

Carroll, J. L., T. S. Peterson & Nancy E. Owens. Memory-guided Exploration in Reinforcement Learning, *Proceedings of the International Joint Conference on Neural Networks*, 2001.

Champandard, A. J. *Reinforcement Learning*. Available at http://reinforcementlearning.ai-depot.com/Intro.html. Last access 9/25/2007.

Gers, F. A., J. Schmidhuber & F. Cummins. Learning to Forget: Continual Prediction with LSTM, *Neural Computation*, Vol. 12, pp. 2451-2471, 2000.

Gers, F., N. Schraudolph, J. Schmidhuber. Learning Precise Timing with LSTM Recurrent Networks, *Journal of Machine Learning Research*, Vol. 3, pp. 115-143, 2002.

Girgin S., F. Polat & R. Alhajj Learning by Automatic Option Discovery from Conditionally Terminating Sequences, *Proceedings of the 17th European Conference on Artificial Intelligence*, 2006

Gomez, F., J. Schmidhuber & R. Miikkulainen. Efficient Non-Linear Control through Neuroevolution, *Proceedings of the European Conference on Machine Learning*, Berlin, 2006.

Gomez, F. & J. Schmidhuber, Co-evolving Recurrent Neurons Learn Deep Memory POMDPs, *Proceedings of the Conference on Genetic and Evolutionary Computation*, Washington, D. C., pp. 1795-1802, 2005.

Hochreiter, S. and J. Schmidhuber. Long Short-Term Memory, *Neural Computation*, Vol. 9, pp. 1735-1780, 1997.

Ho, F. & Kamel, M. Reinforcement Learning using a Recurrent Neural Network, *Proceedings of the ICNN*, pp. 437-440, 1994.

Jordan, M. I. & Jacobs R. A. Hierarchical mixtures of experts and the EM algorithm, *Neural Computation*, Vol. 6, pp.181-214, 1994.

Kaelbling, L. P., M. L. Littman & A. W. Moore. Reinforcement learning: A survey, *Journal of Artificial Intelligence Research*, Vol. 4, pp. 237-285, 1996.

Kirschning, I., H. Tomabechi & J.I. Aoe. A Parallel Recurrent Cascade-Correlation Neural Network with Natural Connectionist Glue, *Proceedings of the IEEE ICNN*, pp. 953-956, Australia, 1995.

Le, T. D., T. Komeda & M. Takagi. Knowledge-Based Recurrent Neural Networks In Reinforcement Learning, *Proceedings of the 11th IASTED International Conference on Artificial Intelligence and Soft Computing*, pp. 179-184, Spain, 2007.

Le, T. D., T. Komeda & M. Takagi. Reinforcement Learning for POMDP Using State Classification, *Journal of Applied Artificial Intelligence*, 2008, in press.

Lin, L. J. Self-improving Reactive Agents based on Reinforcement Learning, Planning and Teaching, *Machine Learning*, Vol. 8, pp. 293-321, 1992.

Lin, L. J. and T. Mitchell. Reinforcement Learning with Hidden States, *Proceedings of the 2nd International Conference on Simulation of Adaptive Behavior*, 1993.

Lin, L. J. *Reinforcement Learning for Robots Using Neural Networks*, PhD. thesis, Carnegie Mellon, School of Computer Science, 1993.

Littman, M. Memoryless Policies: Theoretical Limitations and Practical Results, *From Animal to Animats 3: Proceedings of the 3rd International Conference on Simulation and Adaptive Behavior*, 1994.

McCallum, R. A. Instance-based State Identification for Reinforcement Learning, *Advances in Neural Information Processing Systems*, pp. 377-384, 1995.

McGovern, A. & A. G. Barto. Automatic Discovery of Subgoals in Reinforcement Learning using Diverse Density, *Proceedings of the 18th International Conference on Machine Learning*, pp. 361- 368, San Francisco, CA, USA, 2001.

Menache, I., Mannor, S. & Shimkin, N. Q-Cut Dynamic discovery of sub-goals in reinforcement learning, *Proceedings of the European Conference on Machine Learning*, pp. 295-306, 2002.

Ohta, M., Y. Kumada, I. Noda. Using Suitable Action Selection Rule in Reinforcement Learning, *Proceedings of the IEEE International Conference on Systems, Man & Cybernetics*, pp. 4358-4363, 2003.

Onat, A., H. Kita & Y. Nishikawa. Recurrent Neural Networks for Reinforcement Learning: Architecture, Learning Algorithms and Internal Representation, *Proceedings of the International Joint Conference on Neural Networks*, pp. 2010-2015, Anchorage, AK, USA, 1998.

Schafer, A. M. & S. Udluft. Solving Partially Observable Reinforcement Learning Problems with Recurrent Neural Networks, *Proceedings of the 16th European Conference on Machine Learning*, Portugal, 2005.

Schmidhuber, J., D. Wierstra, M. Gagliolo, F. Gomez. Training Recurrent Networks by Evolino, *Neural Computation*, Vol. 19, No. 3, pp. 757-779, 2007.

Simsek, O., A. & A. G. Barto. Identifying Useful Sub Goals in Reinforcement Learning by Local Graph Partitioning, *Proceedings of the 22nd International Conference on Machine Learning*, 2005.

Sutton, R. S., Precup, D. & Singh, S. P. Between MDPs and Semi-MDPs: A Framework For Temporal Abstraction in Reinforcement Learning, *Artificial Intelligence*, Vol. 112, pp. 181-211, 1999.

Sutton, R. & Andrew Barto. *Reinforcement Learning: An Introduction*, MIT Press, Cambridge, MA, 1998.

Taylor, M. E., P. Stone & Y. Liu. Value Functions for RL-based Behavior Transfer: A Comparative Study, *Proceedings of the 12th National Conference on Artificial Intelligence*, 2005.

Watkins, C. J. *Learning from Delayed Rewards*, PhD thesis, King's College, Cambridge, 1989.

Whitehead S. D., Lin L. J. Reinforcement Learning of Non-Markov Decision Processes, *Artificial Intelligence*, Vol. 73, pp. 271-306, 1995.

17

Anomaly-based Fault Detection with Interaction Analysis Using State Interface

Byoung Uk Kim
The University of Arizona
USA

1. Introduction

Fault detection, analysis, and recovery with effective monitoring in distributed systems is a challenging research problem due to the exponential growth in scale and complexity of system resources and applications, the continuous changes in software and hardware configurations, and the heterogeneous services being offered and deployed. In spite of enormous advances in hardware and software technology, there are many uncertainties and unpredictable operations in distributed systems that could be triggered by one or a combination of several events such as network failures, intermittent software failures, bugs in software and services, etc. Various distributed systems especially employed in safety-critical environments must work correctly in spite of the occurrence of faults.

The fault detection and analysis approach presented in this chapter is based on hardware/software fault tolerance techniques and data mining techniques including regression trees, neural networks, multivariate linear regression, fuzzy classification, logistic regression, classification tree, naïve bayes , and sequential minimal optimization.

In this chapter, we present an innovative approach to detect faults (hardware or software) and also identify the source of the faults. Our online monitoring mechanism collects significant interactions among system state components such as CPU, memory, I/O, and network interface in real-time between all the components of a distributed system. We record and trace these runtime properties and analyze all the interactions using data mining and supervised learning techniques to acquire the rules that can accurately model the normal interactions among these components. We have implemented an anomaly-based fault detection engine and used it to detect faults in a typical multi-tier web based ecommerce environment that implements ecommerce transactions based on the TPC-W web ecommerce benchmark (TPC-W, 2005).

The organization of the remaining sections of the chapter is as follows. In section 2, we review related work. In section 3, we explain theoretical framework including system presentation, normal and abnormal definition with system interfaces and attribute definitions. In section 4, we present anomaly analysis methodology to implement efficient fault detection and analysis. We discuss data sources, training and testing data and fault types used in our experiments and then present our experimental results and evaluation of our approach in section 5 and 6. In section 7, we summarize the chapter and discuss future research activities.

2. Related work

Fault detection and analysis has always been an active research area due to its importance to distributed systems and their applications. It is necessary for the system to be able to detect the faults and take the appropriate actions to avoid further degradations of the service. In this section, we classify fault detection techniques based on different categories such as hardware and software techniques and based on the detection schemes such as statistical methods, distance and model based methods and profiling methods.

2.1 Hardware based

(Reinhardt & Mukherjee, 2000) proposed Simultaneous and Redundant Threading (SRT) to provide transient fault coverage with high performance by taking advantage of the multiple hardware contexts of Simultaneous Multithreading (SMT). It provides high performance by using active scheduling of its hardware components among the redundant replicas and reduces the overhead of validation by eliminating cache misses. (Ray et al., 2001) proposed modern superscalar out-of-order datapath by modifying a superscalar processor's micro-architectural components and validating the redundant outcomes of actively duplicated threads of execution, while the fault recovery plan uses the branch-rewind mechanism to restart at a place which error happened. Commercial fault-tolerant systems combine several techniques such as error correcting codes, parity bits and replicated hardware. For example, Compaq Non-Stop Himalaya (Wood, 2004) employs *lockstepping* which runs the same program on two processors and compares the results by a checker circuit.

2.2 Software based

(Reis et al., Dec. 2005) introduced PROFiT technique regulating the stage of reliability at fine granularities by using software control. This profile-guided fault tolerance determines the weakness and performance trade-offs for each program region and decide where to turn on and off redundant by using a program profile. (Oh et al., 2002) proposed Error Detection by Duplicated Instructions (EDDI) which copies all instructions and inserts check instructions for validation. Software based mechanisms present high reliability gain at low hardware cost and high fault coverage. However the performance degradation and failure to directly check micro-architectural components result in another trend of fault detection, hybrid redundancy techniques (Reis et al., June. 2005) such as CompileR-Assisted Fault Tolerance (CRAFT).

We classify detection and analysis strategy based on the following approaches such as statistical, profiling, model-based, and distance-based methods.

2.3 Statistical methods

This method traces the system behavior or user activity by gauging variables over time such as event message between components, system resource consumption, login/out time of each session. It maintains averages of these variables and detects the anomaly behavior by making a decision whether thresholds are exceeded based on the standard deviation of the variables monitored. It also compares profiles of short/long term user activities using complex statistical models. (Ye & Chen, 2001) employs chi-square statistics to detect anomalies. In this approach, the activities on a system are monitored through a stream of events and they are distinguished by event type. For each event type, the normal data from audit events are categorized and then used to get chi-square for difference between the normal data and testing data. It considers large deviations as abnormal data.

2.4 Distance based methods

One of the limitations of statistical approaches is that it becomes inaccurate and hard to calculate approximately the multidimensional distributions of the data points when outlier detection exists in higher dimensional spaces (Lazarevic et al., 2006). Distance based methods try to overcome this limitation and identify outliers by computing distances among points. For example, (Cohen et al., 2005) presents an approach using usual clustering algorithms such as k-mean and k-median to get the system status. The difference with others focusing on clustering algorithm is that they use a signature and show the efficacy for clustering and connection based recovery by means of distinguished techniques such as pattern recognition and information retrieval.

2.5 Model based methods

This method describes the normal activity of the monitored system by using different types of models and identifies anomalies as divergence for the model that characterizes the normal activity. For example, (Maxion & Tan, 2002) obtains a sequential data streams from a monitored procedure and employs a Markov models to decide whether the states are normal or abnormal. It calculates the probabilities of transitions between the states using the training data set, and utilizes these probabilities to evaluate the transitions between states in test data set.

2.6 Profiling methods

It builds profiles of normal behavior for diverse types of systems, users, applications etc., and variations from them are regarded as anomalous behaviors. These profiling methods vary significantly different data mining techniques while others use various heuristic based approaches. In data mining methods, each case in training data set is configured as normal or abnormal and a data mining learning algorithm is trained over the configured data set. By using these methods, new kinds of anomalities can be detected in fault detection models with retraining (Lazarevic et al., 2006). (Lane & Brodley, 1999) uses a temporal sequence learning technique in profiling Unix user commands for normal and abnormal scenarios. It then uses these profiles to detect any anomalous user activity. Other algorithms for fault detection include regression trees, multivariate linear regression, logistic regression, fuzzy classification, neural networks and decision trees.

3. Theoretical framework

3.1 System presentation

Consider a general n input m output nonlinear dynamic system which can be expressed by the Nonlinear Auto Regressive Moving Average (NARMA) model (Chenand & Billings, 1994) as

$$y_\lambda(k) = f_\lambda(\bar{y},\ \bar{u},\theta)$$
$$\bar{y} = \{y(k-1), y(k-2),\ldots, y(k-n)\}$$
$$\bar{u} = \{u(k-\gamma-1), u(k-\gamma-2),\ldots, u(k-\gamma-m)\} \tag{1}$$

where $f : \Re^P \times \Re^Q \to \Re$, with $P = \sum_{i=1}^{m} p_i$, $Q = \sum_{j=1}^{n} q_j$ is the mathematical realization of the system dynamics for the λ_{th} output. $y(k) \in \Re$ is the output of the system at sample instant k, $u(k) \in \Re$ is the input to the system. p and q are the lengths of the regression vectors of $\bar{y}$ and $\bar{u}$, respectively. f is a recognized nonlinear function describing the dynamic characteristics of the system. γ is the relative degree of the system. n and m are known system structure orders. θ is the system parameter vector whose unanticipated changes are regarded as faults in the system. It represents all the potential faults in the nonlinear system such as sensors and processes.

In our research, we use available system input and output, respectively $\bar{u}$ and $\bar{y}$ to detect and predict any undesirable changes in θ. To simplify the presentation, we assume that during the initial stage $k \in [0, T]$, the normal and healthy values of these values are available and can be obtained from the system under consideration. There is a certain normal trajectory related with system interfaces. So, we can say the system parameter vector in normal activities is θ_N. It means that there is a known θ_N such that

$$\theta = \theta_N \tag{2}$$

To define the system abnormality, we may construct a redundant relation such that

$$m_\lambda(k) = | y_\lambda(k) - f_\lambda(\bar{y}, \bar{u}, \theta_N) | \tag{3}$$

If $m(k)$ is large enough by checking the values against a pre-specified threshold, we say there is abnormality in the system. Contrarily, if $m(k)$ is very small, the system is normal.

3.2 Normal and abnormal definition with system interfaces

We develop a systematic framework for identifying potential system abnormality. Ψ denote the system attributes, and $\Psi^{\lozenge}$ is the set of sequences over the alphabet Ψ. We say that system attributes $S \in \Psi^{\lozenge}$ is accepted by the detection system if executing the sequence S = $\{S_1, S_2, S_3, \dots\}$ does not trigger any alarm. Let $N \subseteq \Psi^{\lozenge}$ denote the set of system attributes allowed by the detection system, i.e.,

$$N \stackrel{def}{=} \left\{ S \in \Psi^{\lozenge} : S \text{ is accepted by the detection system} \right\} \tag{4}$$

Also, let $A \subseteq \Psi^{\lozenge}$ denote the set of system attributes that are not allowed by the detection system, i.e.,

$$A \stackrel{def}{=} \left\{ \begin{array}{l} S \in \Psi^{\lozenge} : S \text{ is an equivalent variant} \\ \text{on the given suspicious sequence} \end{array} \right\} \tag{5}$$

Now we can state the conditions for the existence of abnormality in distributed systems. The set $N \cap A$ is exactly the set of system attributes that give the suspicious or abnormal status to host without detection, and thus the abnormalities are possible if $N \cap A \neq \varnothing$.

3.3 Attribute definitions

We use the following attributes for the abnormality analysis: Attribute rate (AR) per target attribute, Component rate (CR) per target component, Aggregate System rate (ASR) per target system and Number of abnormal session (NAS)

Definition 1

AR per target address is used to find out the current flow rate for a given target IP address P_j as observed by a interface monitor and can be computed as in (1)

$$AR\ (A_i,\ P_j,\ t)\ =\ \{\sum_{t=T}^{2T} DT(t)\}\bigg/ \mathrm{T} \tag{6}$$

where DT denotes the number of data belonging to attribute A_i and to a target P_j within a given time T.

Definition 2

CR per target address is used to determine the current flow rate as observed by a Interface monitor for all the attributes A_i that go through the same interface (I_k) and have the same target IP address (P_j). This metric can be computed as in (2)

$$CR\ (I_k,\ P_j,\ t)\ =\ \sum_{\forall\ i} AR\ (A_i,\ P_j,\ t) \tag{7}$$

Definition 3

ASR per target address denotes the current flow rate for a given target IP address P_j as observed by Interface monitor

$$ASR\ (P_j,\ t)\ =\ \sum_{\forall\ k} CR\ (I_k,\ P_j,\ t) \tag{8}$$

Definition 4

NAS the number of abnormal sessions for a target P_j as observed by Interface monitor

$$NAS\ (P_j,\ t)\ =\ \sum_{\forall\ i} (1 - S_i) \tag{9}$$

where S_i is a binary variable that is equal to 1 when the session is successful and 0 and when it is not.

4. Abnormality analysis methodology

Our approach is based on autonomic computing paradigm that requires continuous monitoring and analysis of the system state, and then plan and execute the appropriate actions if it is determined that the system is deviating significantly from its expected normal behaviors as shown in Figure 1.

By monitoring the system state, we collect measurement attributes about the CPU, IO, memory, operating system, and network operations. The analysis of this data can reveal any anomalous behavior that might be triggered by failures.

Once a fault is detected, the next step is to identify the appropriate fault recovery strategy to bring the system back into a fault-free state. In this paper, we focus on monitoring and analyzing the interactions among these components to detect any hardware or software failures.

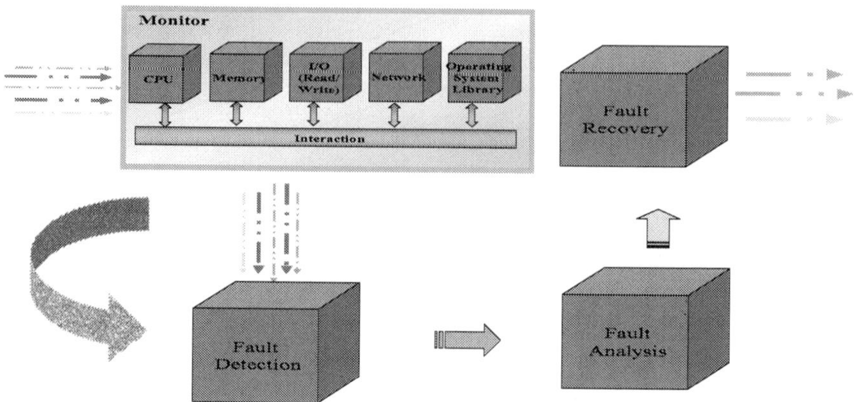

Fig. 1. Self-healing Engine

4.1 Monitoring and analysis of system component operations

The first step is to identify a set of measurement attributes that can be used to define the normal behaviors of these components as well as their interactions with other components within the distributed system. For example, when a user runs a QuickTime application, one can observe certain well defined CPU, Memory and I/O behaviors. These operations will be significantly different when the application experience un-expected failure that leads to application termination; one can observe that the application, although consuming CPU and memory resources, does not interact normally with its I/O components.

These monitored data are analyzed using two types of vector-based (VR) metrics (Wood, 2004): Local-VR (LVR) and Global-VR (GVR). The LVR is used to evaluate the interface interaction, detection, analysis and recovery measurements associated with a specific fault, f, in the set of faults in the fault hypothesis, F as shown in Equations 10-13:

$$\overrightarrow{LVR}_{\text{interfaces } f_i \in F} = (\text{ CPU,MEM,I/O,NET,OS}) \tag{10}$$

$$\overrightarrow{LVR}_{\text{detection } f_i \in F} = (\text{ AR, CR, ASR, NAS, Precision,} \\ \text{Recall, F-measure, False negative rate,} \\ \text{Fals positive rate, Time to detect, ... })\tag{11}$$

$$\overrightarrow{LVR}_{\text{analysis } f_i \in F} = (\text{ Accuracy, Time to analyze,} \\ \text{Analyzed or not? })\tag{12}$$

$$\overrightarrow{LVR}_{\text{recovery } f_i \in F} = (\text{ Accuracy, Time to recover,} \\ \text{Recovered or not? })\tag{13}$$

'CL' refers to metrics measured on the client, and 'DB' refers to metrics measured on the database server. Equation (10) is used to identify the measurement attributes associated with the interactions among system components. When a specific fault, e.g. application abnormal termination is generated in the system, $\overrightarrow{LVR}_{\text{interfaces } f_i \in F}$ is composed with the related measurement attributes. For example, $\overrightarrow{LVR}_{\text{interfaces } f_i \in F}$ in abnormal termination of QuickTime application will consist of measurements of user CPU, active memory in directory and I/O read activities as shown in Equation 10. Equation 11 describes several metrics used to find out the characteristic of interfaces explained in section 3.3 and evaluate the performance of the fault detection strategy using several metrics: 1) False negative rate is the percentage of abnormal flows incorrectly classified as normal 2) Precision is the proportion of correctly detected abnormal flows in the set of all normal flows returned by detection. 3) Recall is the number of correctly detected abnormal flows in retrieved as fraction of all abnormal flows. And 4) F-measure is used to quantify the trade-off between recall and precision. All these performance metrics were explained in (Kim & Hariri, 2007). Equation 12 and 13 evaluate the accuracy of our approach using several metrics such as: 1) Accuracy is used to estimate whether all actual faults are correctly identified. 2) Time to analyze/recovery is used for measuring the time taken the system to analyze/recovery from faults.

The global vector based metric GVR quantifies in a similar way to LVR the quality of the analysis, detection and recovery as shown in Equations 14-16.

$$\overrightarrow{GVR}_{\text{detection}} = (\text{ Throughput, Response time, Availability, Cost, Time }) \tag{14}$$

$$\overrightarrow{GVR}_{\text{analysis}} = (\text{ Throughput, Response time, Availability, Cost, Time }) \tag{15}$$

$$\overrightarrow{GVR}_{\text{recovery}} = (\text{ Throughput, Response time, Availability, Cost, Time }) \tag{16}$$

The main difference between LVR and GVR is in defining the target. That means LVR is used to evaluate the measurements associated with a specific fault in the set of faults but GVR is used to evaluate the role of the target system in a given environment. LVRs in each fault have an effect on the GVR. For example, if there is a memory related fault, we may see interface interactions in $\overrightarrow{LVR}_{\text{interfaces}}$ resulting in value changes in $\overrightarrow{LVR}_{\text{detection}}$. These changes also affect $\overrightarrow{GVR}_{\text{detection}}$ allowing us to evaluate the healthiness of the target system. This operation flow is depicted in Figure 2. We need this classification because our target system to detect the faults is in the domain of distributed system. Equations (14), (15), and (16) describe the metrics to measure the performance of the target system in detection, analysis, and recovery: 1) Throughput is the summation of data rates sent to all system nodes. 2) Response time means the time taken to react to a given goal such as 'detect' and 'recover' in the system. 3) Availability is the ratio of the total time through which the system is available to the overall total time.

Normal execution will have a certain trajectory with respect to system interfaces as shown in Figure 2. For example, if the disk is behaving normal without any fault, this can be recognized by obvious disk trajectory over time. In case of abnormal state, all information monitored in the normal state will have different trajectories. We capture and monitor this trajectory features, train this interface trajectory with $\overrightarrow{LVR}$ and $\overrightarrow{GVR}$ by using rules generated from the training data set and apply them at runtime. It shows normal trajectory drifting to suspicious trajectory by exemplifying one of $\overrightarrow{LVR}_{\text{interfaces } f_i \in F}$ and one of

Metric	Description
var_CL_CPUIF_KERNAL	variance of the number of kernel time spent on client received through cpu interface
var_CL_CPUIF_USER	variance of the number of user time spent on client received through cpu interface
val_CL_MEMIF_ACTIVE	value of number of memory hat has been used more recently and usually not reclaimed unless absolutely necessary received through memory interface on client
val_CL_MEMIF_IN_DIR	value of number of memory that takes more work to free on client
val_CL_MEMIF_IN_TARGET	value of number of memory that kernel uses for making sure there are enough inactive pages around on client
val_CL_IOIF_READ	value of IO load read received through IO interface on client
val_CL_IOIF_WRITE	value of IO load read received through IO interface on client
var_DB_IOIF_READ	value of IO load read received through IO interface on database server
val_CL_CON_SWITCHES	value of the number of context switches that counts the number of times one process was ``put to sleep'' and another was ``awakened'' on client

Table 1. A sample of metrics used to characterize the interaction among components

$\overrightarrow{GVR}_{\text{detection}}$ metrics over time. Rules can be formed of the interface metrics including states, events, state variables and time of transitions. These rules are generated to evaluate system healthiness as following:

Rule 1: $M_i \leq I_t \leq M_a \quad T \in (t_j, t_j + k)$

Interface I_t in some time k starting at time t_j is delimited by high value M_a and low value M_i when defined normal flow occurs.

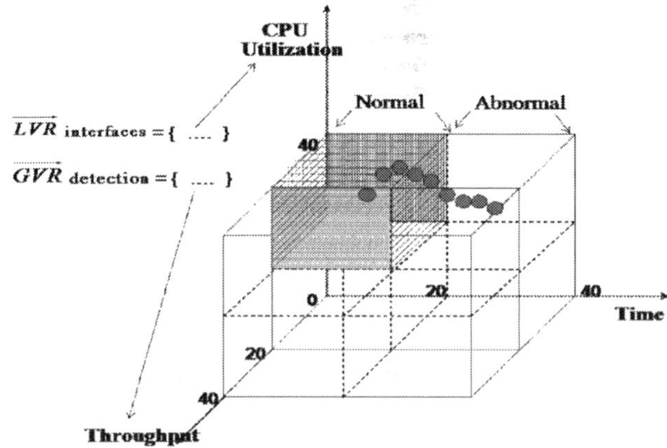

Fig. 2. Abnormality identification: LVR and GVR drift

Rule 2: $M_i \leq I_n \leq M_a \ \forall T \in (t_j, t_j + k) \Rightarrow M_i' \leq I_a \leq M_a' \ \forall T \in (t_g, t_g + r)$

Interface I_n delimited by high value M_a and low value M_i in time k will affect another interface I_a delimited by high value M_a' and low value M_i' and it will last some period r.

This rule is about interaction among interfaces and it needs higher latency than the previous rule because of matching more interfaces

We build a fault detection prototype to demonstrate the utility of VR metrics to detect faults. Figure 3 shows a sampling of metrics among more than 40 interfaces and real data monitored at the client side. For clarity, we pick a sample of metrics as shown in Table 1. All data monitored in the experiment with fault injections are stored in a database and the rules are generated during the training stage. In Figure 3, the set of data from time t_0 to the time before t_i is normal with respect to a given workload. The first injected fault at t_i shows the interaction with 5 interfaces such as var_CL_CPUIF_KERNAL, val_CL_MEMIF_ACTIVE, val_CL_MEMIF_IN_DIR, var_CL_CPUIF_USER, and val_CL_MEMIF_IN_TARGET.

Legend:
- → Major Interfaces
- → Minor Interfaces (Conditional)
- ⊘ → False Alarm Interface

	var_CL_CPUIF_KERNAL	var_CL_CPUIF_USER	val_CL_MEMIF_ACTIVE	val_CL_MEMIF_IN_DIR	val_CL_MEMIF_IN_TARGET	val_CL_IOIF_READ	val_CL_IOIF_WRITE
Time t_0	5.47264	16.418	135600	23	30612	398	654
	4.47761	35.323	135908	135	30608	423	234
	6.49751	10.995	134316	123	30612	478	432
	7.49254	20.995	134316	98	30612	222	311
	4.99503	25.995	134312	209	30612	209	309
	13.49751	18.995	134312	245	30612	390	512
	11.99503	31.493	134316	154	30612	312	265
Fault t_i	16.4479	83.582	126044	1556	31244	243	398
	18.408	81.592	126052	1620	31268	354	387
t_j	9.95025	5.4726	134796	58	30608	335	254
	4.47761	5.4726	134556	0	30612	512	401
Fault t_k	14.9254	38.075	126008	1680	31224	345	299
	17.9104	4.109	126016	1592	31220	478	289
t_l	22.607	15.6	133628	579	30612	391	312
	21.756	14.76	134248	1098	30608	326	308
Fault t_m	14.4279	85.582	126066	1680	31212	245	456
	16.4179	83.582	126056	1594	31296	1978	396
t_n	3.9801	6.4677	132956	2378	30624	349	299
	0.99503	1.9901	133044	1876	30612	431	364
Fault t_r	17.9104	83.09	126068	1556	31292	412	2994
	18.408	81.592	126084	1594	31296	477	2998

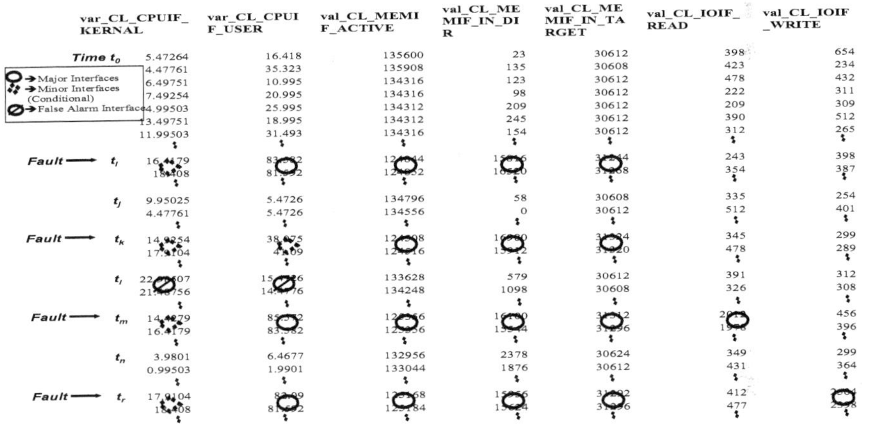

Fig. 3. A sampling of metrics and data monitored at a client side

We use these interfaces to catch the abnormality caused by the fault. All these 5 interfaces show significant difference when compared to normal value. The second injected fault is at t_k. In this case, there are three major interfaces and two minor interfaces. Major interfaces include val_CL_MEMIF_ACTIVE, val_CL_MEMIF_IN_DIR, and val_CL_MEMIF_IN_TARGET while minor interfaces include var_CL_CPUIF_KERNAL and var_CL_CPUIF_USER. At time t_l, if we consider only minor interfaces, it will cause false alarm because of the similarity of these states to normal states. The interfaces are used to form two types of significant rules that depend on injected faults. For example, the fault injected at t_m results in increase in read load that is related to IO but the fault at t_r results in the increase of write load. From the above, several types of rules can be generated as following:

- $20 \leq var\_CL\_CPUIF\_KERNAL_t \leq 40 \quad T \in (t_j, t_j + k)$

- $5 \leq ResponseTime \leq 40 \quad T \in (t_j, t_j + k)$

$$127845 \leq val\_CL\_MEMIF\_ACTIVE \leq 139821,$$

- $$5134 \leq val\_CL\_MEMIF\_IN\_DIR \leq 19321$$
  $$\text{and } 1395 \leq var\_CL\_IOIF\_READ \quad \forall T \in (t_j, t_j + k)$$

  $$0132 \leq val\_CL\_MEMIF\_IN\_DIR \leq 9846 \text{ and}$$

- $$20 \leq var\_CL\_CPUIF\_KERNAL_t \leq 40 \quad \forall T \in (t_j, t_j + k)$$

  $$\Rightarrow M_i' \leq Throughput \leq M_a' \quad \forall T \in (t_g, t_g + r)$$

The first rule explains that when the number of kernel time spent on client received through cpu interface is larger than and equal to 20 and less than and equal to 40 in time interval k, it is abnormal. The second and third rules are about response time, number of active memory and dirty memory and value of I/O load read. In Fourth rule, we didn't include it in our experiments but may classify the interactions more. It means that we can achieve high detection rate by revealing their behaviors and states by virtue of their interactions among interfaces. These kinds of rules are applied in the experiments to detect abnormal flows and increase the performance.

4.2 Abnormality analysis algorithm

Our approach for abnormality analysis to achieve self-healing system is anchored in behavior modeling and analysis of system component impact with rule based. Suppose we have λ system attributes (SA). Then, the flow behavior of SA can be represented as

$$SA_\lambda(t, R) = \{ SA_\lambda(t), SA_\lambda(t+1), \ldots, SA_\lambda(t+R) \} \qquad (17)$$

where R is preliminary block to acquire in-control data to determine the mean $\overline{SA}$ and covariance matrix S. These values are used to verify normal interactions with respect to the λ system attributes. The mean $\overline{SA}$ determines the normal region center and the sample covariance matrix S determines the shape of the normal region. We apply this idea to attribute definition such as AR, CR, and ASR explained in section 3.3 to quantify how close/far the current flow state of a component from the normal state for a given fault scenario which quantifies the current flow state of the system component based on the current values of one or more monitored attributes. The normalized abnormality extent degree (AED) with respect to each attribute is defined as

$$AED_\lambda(t, P_j) = \left[\frac{SA_\lambda(t, P_j) - AR_\lambda(P_j)}{\sigma_{SA_\lambda}(P_j)} \right]^2 \qquad (18)$$

where AR denotes attribute rates to find out the current flow rate for a given target IP address P_j as observed by a interface monitor and σ_{SA_λ} is the variance under the normal operation condition corresponding to flow. $SA_\lambda(t)$ is the current value of system attribute λ.

Figure 4 shows the rule-based analysis for abnormality detection algorithm used by our monitoring and analysis agents that compute and evaluate the attributed definition. During the training stage (line 2), we monitor and collect system attributes where R is the preliminary block to obtain in-control data (line 3). To acquire rule set (line 4), we input the data set into a rule engine (Cohen, 1995) that produce a rule set. After we get the rule set, we configure the key attributes to gauge attribute definition (line 5 and 6). Once the training stage is completed, process q is applied to real data (line 7). In this algorithm, K (line 9) denotes the number of observations and 15 is used for the number of observations. Attribute definition including abnormality extent degree will be computed for any new observation (line 11). If abnormality extent degree is beyond the normal thresholds and $SA(t)$ violates the rule set, then the system is assumed to be operating in an abnormal state, and then the recovery algorithm is activated to carry out the appropriate control actions such as restarting from the initial point and notifying the information to agents (line 12 and 13). Once accumulating K observations, the thresholds will be revised (line 14 and 15).

Process p:
1. Ruleset := 0
2. While (Training) do
3.   Monitor&Collect ($SA_1(t), SA_2(t), SA_3(t), ..., SA_R(t)$);
4. $RuleSet$ = Acquire_ $RuleSet$ (SA_λ);
5.   Configure_Important_Attributes ($RuleSet$);
6.   AED/AR/CR/ASR ← Gauge_Attribute_Definition;
7. EndWhile
Process q:
8. Repeat Forever
9. For (t = 1 ; t < K) do
10.   Monitor&Collect ($SA_1(t), SA_2(t), SA_3(t), ..., SA_P(t)$);
11.   D = Evaluate_Attribute_Definition($SA(t)$);
12.   If ((D > Threshold)&&($SA(t) \in RuleSet$))
13.   Anomaly_Analysis & Detection ($SA(t)$);
     apply rule and attribute definition both
14.   If (t = K)
15.   Revise_Threshold_Weights()
16. End For
17. End Repeat

Fig. 4. Rule-based analysis for abnormality detection algorithm

5. Problem definition

This section illustrates the fault detection problem, including the data source, abnormal loads, training data and testing data.

5.1 Data source

In our evaluation, we use TPC-W, an industry standard e-commerce application to emulate the complex environment of e-commerce application.

As shown in Figure 5, the system is used to run a typical end user e-commerce activity initiated through a web browser and consisting of several TPC-W transactions. It defines 3 types of traffic mixes such as browsing mix, shopping mix and ordering mix and specifies 14 unique web transactions. In our environments, the database is configured for 288,000 customers and 10,000 items. According to the TPC-W specification, the number of concurrent sessions is executed throughout the experiment to emulate concurrent users. The maximum number of Apache clients and maximum Tomcat threads are set to 90. The workloads are generated by the workload generator that varies the number of concurrent sessions and running time from 90 to 300 seconds. Also, we developed abnormal workload generator which will be defined later. It allows us to make and track the system abnormally behavior.

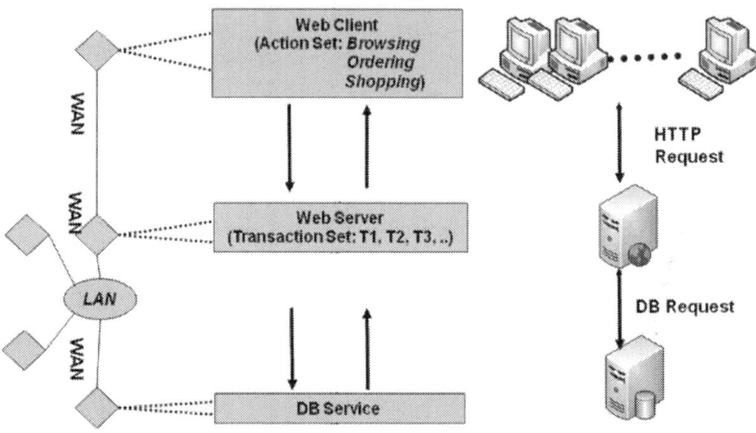

Fig. 5. TPC-W Benchmark E-commerce Application

While every components and workloads are given to the system, we monitor all system interactions and measure different lots of feature including the CPU, IO, memory, operating system, and network devices. The analysis of these features reveals any anomalous behavior that might be triggered by failures in any hardware or software component of the three-tier web based distributed system.

5.2 Abnormal loads

The abnormal loads used in this paper include generally accepted definition (Avizienis et al., 2000), fault and error. If we borrow the concepts, a fault is the cause generating the system corruption and an error that results in the failure is the system state corrupted. We both inject faults such as system corruption and errors such as directly throwing an exception. In our chapter, we usually call fault and error as fault or abnormal loads.

To enlighten our variety in abnormal loads, several papers (Oppenheimer et al., 2003) (Nagaraja et al., 2003) (Chen et al., 2002) are considered as a previous study in faults injected in their experiments. Some of them focus on triggering only application level failures; others inject the faults concentrated on problems that cause program crashes or byzantine faults. We believe that there are system interaction symptoms that characterize how system will respond to a fault injected. Thus, we have confidently decided to include software failures as well as hardware failures in complex distributed systems. Table 2 shows the types of fault classes to be used by our rule based fault detection scenarios. The fault classes can be broadly classified into two groups such as hardware and software. Each group is also divided into three types such as severe, intermittent and lenient.

In these experiments, we inject seven different types of faults explained in Table 2. We categorize and inject these faults by building three different categories. First category is application corruption regarding 3 different types of TPC-W traffic such as browsing, ordering, and shopping. We model faults that are triggered by the interfaces including interactions between an application and the operating system or between an application and other function libraries. These faults injected are from shared libraries into applications to

Fault class	Faults
Software, severe, intermittent	• TPC-W browsing – corruption (Segmentation Fault) • TPC-W ordering – corruption (Segmentation Fault) • TPC-W shopping – corruption (Segmentation Fault)
Hardware, lenient intermittent,	• Network disconnection
Software, severe or lenient, intermittent	• Declared exceptions and undeclared exceptions such as Unknown host Exception • Infinite loops interfering and stopping the application request from completing • DB failure – Access denied

Table 2. Fault cases injected

test the capability of applications to handle faults from library routines referring the fault injection technique [10]. We inject the faults using 3 different system calls such as read (), write (), and close () and observe the effect of injected faults related with interfaces. Hardware faults such as network failure are considered next. It allows us to isolate the node by removing the connection from the network interfaces. Third one is about database related failure such as access denial and application exceptions such as declared exceptions. Because java based e-commerce application engenders various different kinds of failures from programmer faults to IO faults, injection of exception faults are apposite to reveal the abnormal behavior of e-commerce application by tracking system interactions. Here, we injected declared exceptions which are often handled and masked by application itself such as unknown host exception and also infinite loops interfering and stopping the application request from completing. All these faults happen in the process of TPC-W transaction. We believe that the selected faults span the axes from expected to unexpected/undesirable behaviors and divulge the relationship of system interaction for the problems that can occur in a real life.

5.3 Training and testing data

In this study, we have several kinds of data set composed of different number of normal flows and abnormal flows. Our experiments are composed of four kinds of classes such as trustworthiness for fault, noise and data types and performance validation for testing data sets. These training data sets and testing data sets are gathered by tracing normal and abnormal activities. Normal activities and abnormal activities are emulated to produce these data sets by injecting our faults.

First experiment mentioned in section 6.1 is about trustworthiness and validation of our approach for each fault types. We implement and evaluate four scenarios. Fault scenario 1

(FS1) focuses on faults triggered by application corruption using three different types of TPC-W traffic such as browsing, ordering , and shopping. The data set used in scenario 1 consist of 23355 normal flows and 347 abnormal flows. Fault scenario 2 (FS2) considers hardware faults such as network disconnection. The data set consisting of 23355 normal flows and 70 abnormal flows. Fault scenario 3 (FS3) considers application and database faults such as declared exceptions, infinite loops, and database access denial. The data set of FS3 contains 23355 normal flows and 230 abnormal flows. Fault scenario all (FSA) includes all faults explained in section 5.2 and the data set consisting of same number of normal flows previously mentioned and 647 abnormal flows.

The data utilized in section 6.2 employs noise curves such as negative noise (NN) by varying the ratio of abnormal flows in the normal set from 10% to 90% incrementing by 10% each and positive noise (PN) by varying the ratio of nomral flows in the abnormal set from 10% to 90% incrementing by 10% each to evaluate the resilience of detecion algorithm and traced the error rate at each noise ratio points. Each NN and PN data set is consists of 650 abnormal flows and 23354 normal flows, respectively.

The experiment explained in section 6.3 reveals the impact of bulk training data set by composing data based on the specification supplied with the industry standard e-commere environments and includes the four scenarios. Data scenario 1 (DS1) consists of the abnormal set containing normal set containing 23354 flows and 650 flows that are using negative noise curves by varying the ratio of abnormal flows in the normal set from 10% to 90% with 10% increment. Data scenario 2 (DS2) also applies the negative noise curves to explore the correlation in trustworthiness with abnormal flows by building more abnormal flows. The data set is composed of the normal set containing 23354 flows and abnormal set containing 650 flows for data scenario 3 (DS3) and the normal set containing 46000 flows and abnormal set containing 650 flows for data scenario 4 (DS4). Both scenarios employ positive noise curves by varying the ratio of normal flows in the abnormal set to explore the correlation in trustworthiness. We use the testing data set consisting of 20144 flows for normal activities and 420 flows for abnormal activities in the validation of classifiers.

6. Experimental results and evaluation

In this section, we evaluated the detection capabilities of our approach using abnormality extent degree and rule-based fault detection algorithm. The failure data was collected through our distributed test environments shown in Figure 6. We can inject several faults that emulate failures in CPU modules, memory, the disk subsystem, and network modules.

To make the system behaviors as real as possible, we use the following six pairs of workload: TPC-W browsing, ordering, shopping, HTTP gif transfer, MPEG video stream, and HTTPS secure transactions. To generate the fault detection rules, we use a popular data mining tool, Repeated Incremental Pruning to Produce Error Reduction (RIPPER) rule learning technique (Cohen, 1995). The generated rules are based on the insight that abnormality can be captured from system interface flows. The comparisons between our detection approach and the other techniques such as SMO and Naive Bayes were showed and explained in our paper (Kim, 2007). In this approach, we train RIPPER to classify the normal and abnormal flows that occurred during the training period and then apply the generated rules to detect the faults that are injected during each experiment scenario.

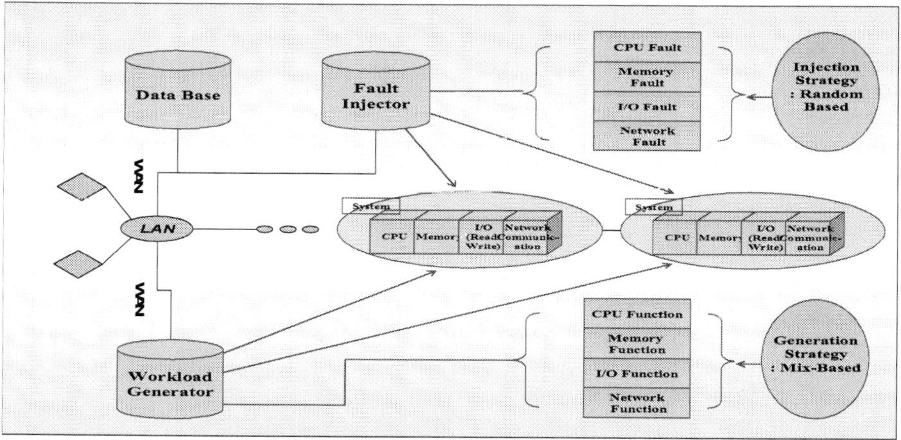

Fig. 6. Testing environments with fault injector and workload generator

6.1 Trustworthiness and validation of rule-based classifiers for fault types

In this experiment, we have three different fault scenarios explained in table 2 and section 5.3. We categorize and inject faults by building three different scenarios. In scenario 1, the faults injected are from shared libraries into applications to test the capability of applications to handle faults from library routines referring the fault injection technique (Avizienis et al., 2000). We injected the faults with three different system calls such as read (), write (), and close () and utilized TPC-W application with three different functions such as browsing, shopping and ordering to observe the effect of injected faults with interfaces. Hardware faults such as network failure are considered in scenario 2. It allows us to isolate the node by removing the connection from the network interfaces. In scenario 3, we chose to inject particular faults such as declared exceptions, infinite loops, and database access denied. For the three scenarios explained, we evaluate the cross-validated true positive rate (the percentage of abnormal flows correctly classified as abnormal) and false positive rate (the percentage of normal flows incorrectly classified as abnormal) to evaluate detection algorithm. To measure the accuracy of generated signatures, we calculated the values for F-measure. We utilized the C implementation of rule algorithm and employed noise curves (negative noise (NN)) by varying the ratio of abnormal flows in the normal set from 10% to 90% at 10% increments to evaluate the resilience of detection algorithm and traced the error rate at each noise ratio point.

Fault scenario 1 (FS1), fault scenario 2 (FS2), fault scenario 3 (FS3), and fault scenario all (FSA) that utilizes all previous three scenarios based on a random mix are given with the percentage of the noise in the abnormal set. Figure 7 shows the false positive rate, true positive rate and F-Measure for all studied scenarios. From the graphs, it is noticeable that FS1, FS2 and FS3 achieved the lowest false positive rate as well as the highest true positive rate. One might think that FSA would have the worst results compare to FS1, FS2, and FS3 since FSA has all of the generated faults that might result in complex and intricate interactions when compared to each fault type. But it is the other way around. Our results show that FSA has the highest false postitive rate, true positive rate, and F-Measure in many noise values such as false positive rate at 30 % and true positive rate at 20 %. (a) Use Custom Size Format, Width = 17cm, Height = 24cm, (b) top margin is set to 2,5 cm and bottom margin is set to 3,0 cm; left and right margins are set to 2,0 cm on the manuscript format 17x24 cm, (c) use the whole space of all pages, don't leave free space, (d) the text must finish exact at the bottom of the last page. The manuscript has to be submitted in MS Word (*.doc) and PDF format. If you use other word editors and can not transfer it in Word and PDF please contact us.

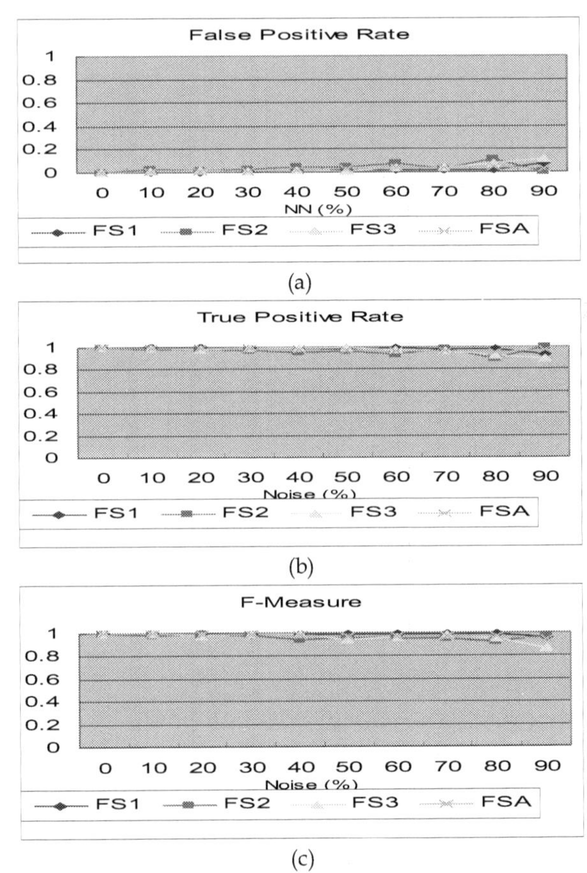

Fig. 7. (a) False Positive and (b) True Positive Rate (c) F-Measure for each fault scenario

6.2 Trustworthiness and validation of rule-based classifiers for noise types

We evaluated the true positive rate and false positive rate to evaluate the detection algorithm. To measure the accuracy of generated signatures, we calculated the values for precision rate.

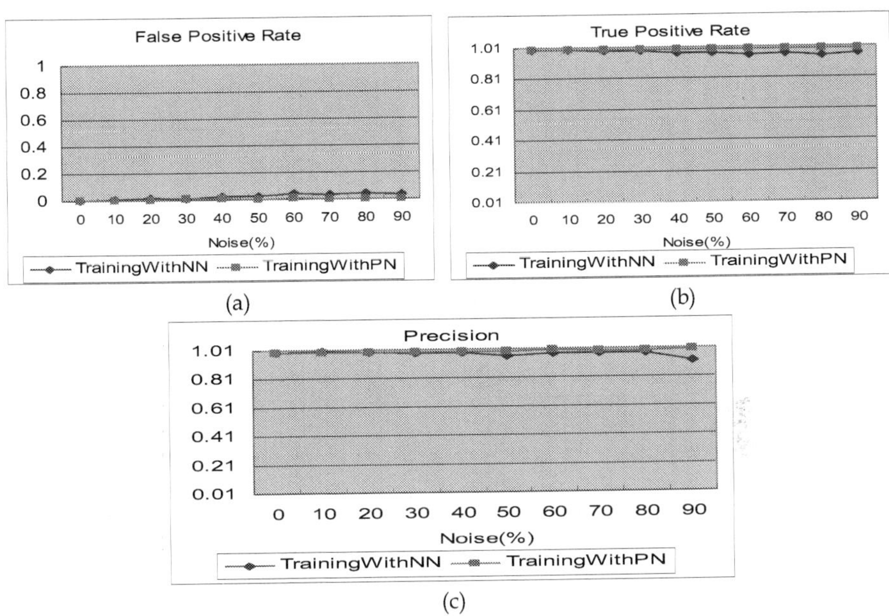

Fig. 8. (a) False Positive and (b) True Positive Rate (c) Precision under varying the noise percentage in the abnormal set and normal set

In this experiment, we employed noise curves (positive noise (PN) and negative noise (NN)) to evaluate the resilience of detection algorithm and traced the error rate at each noise ratio points. The detail description of data set was explained in section 5.3. The ratio of the normal flows in the abnormal set(TrainingWithNN) and abnormal flows in the normal set(TrainingWithPN) are given as the percentage of the noise in the normal set and abnormal set each. Figure 8 shows the true positive rates, false positive rates and precision rate for different noise percentage in the abnormal set and normal set. As shown in Figure 8, our rule based approach for abnormal detection is very reliable even in the nosiy flows. For example, the noise value of 50% produce 0.0265 (NN) and 0.03 (PN) for false positive rate, 0.9735 (NN) and 0.997 (PN) for true positive rate, and 0.959 (NN) and 0.998(PN) for precision rate. These results show that our detection approach is very trustworthy in the distributed computing environment. The performance of the detection algorithm that is trained with TraniningWithPN is more reliable in severe noisy flows. For example, the precision value that is trained with TraniningWithPN equals to 0.998 while the precision value that is trained with TrainingWithNN equals to 0.959 in 50% noise value. The difference between the two noisy environments results from the size of the training set which consists of 23354 normal flows and 650 abnormal flows. However, the 0.959 rate is superior when compared to the other algorithms.

6.3 Trustworthiness and validation of rule-based classifiers for data types

In this experiment, we classify and compose data based on the specification supplied with the multi-tier web benchmark by building four different scenarios. These four scenarios reveal the impact of bulk training data set. In scenario 1, the size of the training data set is 6,506k that consists of 650 abnormal flows and the 23354 normal flows that use negative noise curves by varying the ratio of abnormal flows in the normal set from 10% to 90% at 10% increments. We explore the correlation in trustworthiness with abnormal flows by building more abnormal flows, 1300 flows, in scenario 2. In scenario 3, the data set is made up of 23354 normal flows and 650 abnormal flows. In scenario 4, we explore the correlation in trustworthiness with normal flows in a data set that consists of 46000 normal flows and 650 abnormal flows.

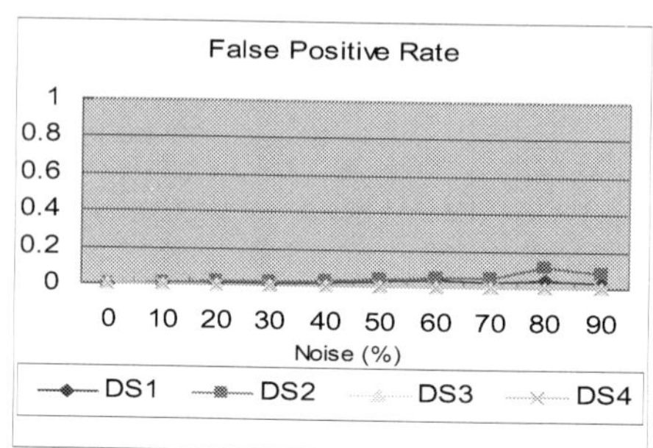
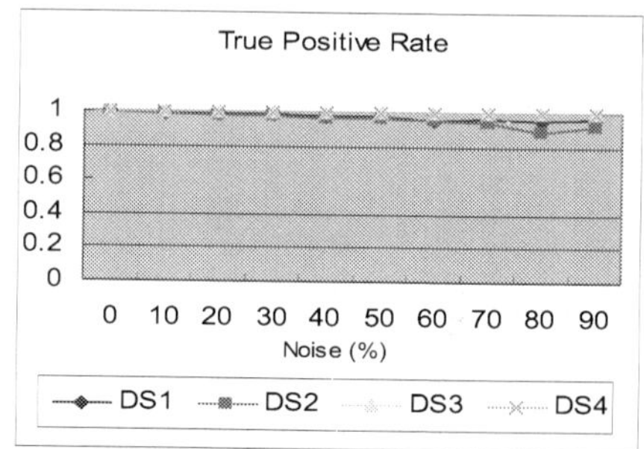

Fig. 9. (a) False Positive and (b) True Positive Rate for each data scenario

Data scenario 1 (DS1), data scenario 2 (DS2), data scenario 3 (DS3), and data scenario 4 (DS4) are given with the size of flows and the percentage of the noise in the abnormal set and normal set. The results are shown in Figure 9. One notable issue is in DS2. All scenarios have good results even in severe noisy flows. However, there is slight difference in DS2 when compared to the other scenarios because of the ratio of the abnormal flows in data set. DS2 has more abnormal noisy flows than the other scenarios. However, we still achieve the lowest false positive rate as well as the highest true positive rate even in DS2. As shown in Figure 9, our rule based approach is a trustworthy even with noisy flows and variance in data sizes.

6.4 Performance validation of rule-based classifiers for the testing data set

Based on the confidence about the results showed before, we tested each result obtained within the generated training data set for variation of the noise percentages, 0% and 10% to underscore the trustworthiness of the detection approach. The testing data set consisting of each abnormal set and normal set was explained in section 5.3. Table 3 shows the false alarm and missed alarm for all the scenarios for different noise percentage in each training data set. As expected, the false alarm and missed alarm rate were very good for fault scenarios such as FS1, FS2, and FS3. But FCA has a higher rate, but is still small. TrainingWithNN and TrainingWithPN achieved very low false alarm and missed alarm even in the noisy situation. Data scenarios also achieved very low false alarm and missed alarm. But the wrong rules generated in the traing stage because of the ratio of abnormal flows in the data result in the increase of missed alarm and false alarm in DS2 with noisy flows. Other than that, the missed alarm and false alarm rate is near 0%. It proves that our approach is superior in each fault scenario as well as the scenario with all faults.

	False Alarm (0% Noise)	Missed Alarm (0% Noise)	False Alarm (10% Noise)	Missed Alarm (10% Noise)
FS1	0 %	0 %	0 %	0 %
FS2	0 %	0 %	0 %	0 %
FS3	0 %	0 %	0 %	0 %
FSA	0.207952 %	0 %	0.399268 %	0 %
Training WithNN	0.207952 %	0 %	0.399268 %	0 %
Training WithPN	0.207952 %	0 %	0.399268 %	0.3 %
DS1	0.208 %	0 %	0.4 %	0 %
DS2	0.208 %	0 %	1.83 %	1.4 %
DS3	0.208 %	0 %	0.16 %	0.3 %
DS4	0.208 %	0 %	0.06 %	1.23 %

Table 3. False Alarm and Missed Alarm rate of all scenarios under applying the rules produced with varying the noise percentage in training data set

7. Conclusion

In this paper, we developed an effective rule-based fault detection algorithm to detect any type of faults for a distributed computing environment. And we evaluate the false alarm rates of our approach for four different fault scenarios and for different data sizes with varying levels of noise. Our analysis show that our approach is superior when compared to other techniques. For example, the precision value that is trained with Tranining with PN equals to 0.998 in 50% noise value and the missed alarm and false alarm rate is near 0%. We are currently extending our approach to not only detect the fault s once they occur, but also perform root-cause analysis and automatic fault recovery.

8. Referring

Avizienis, A.; Laprie, J.C. and Randell, B., Fundamental concepts of dependablility, *in Third Information Survivability Workshop*, Boston, MA, 2000

Chenand, S. & Billings, S.A., Neural networks for nonlinear system modeling and identification, *in "Advances in Intelligent Control"*, pp. 85- 112, Ed C. J. Harris, Taylor & Francis, London, 1994,

Chen, M.Y.; Kiciman, E.; Fratkin, E.; Fox, A. & Brewer, E. Pinpoint: problem determination in large, dynamic Internet services, *International Conference on Dependable Systems and Networks*, June 2002

Cohen, I.; Zhang, S.; Goldszmidt, M.; Symons, J.; Kelly, T. & Fox, A., Capturing, indexing, clustering, and retrieving system history, *ACM SOSP '2005*

Cohen, W. W., Fast effective rule induction, *in the Proceedings of the 12th International Conference on Machine Learning*, pp. 115-123, Morgan Kaufmann, July 9-12, 1995

Kim, B. & Hariri, S., Anomaly-based Fault Detection System in Distributed System, *in proceedings of the Fifth IEEE International Conference on Software Engineering Research, Management and Applications*, August 2007

Lane, T. & Brodley, C., Temporal Sequence Learning and Data Reduction for Anomaly Detection, *ACM Transactions on Information and System Security, vol. 2, 3*, pp. 295-331, 1999

Lazarevic, A. , Kumar, V. & Srivastava, J., *Intrusion Detection: A Survey, Springer US, Volume 5*, 2006

Maxion, R. & Tan, K., Anomaly Detection in Embedded Systems, *IEEE Transactions on Computers, vol. 51*, pp. 108-120, 2002

Nagaraja, K.; Li, X.; Bianchini, R.; Martin, R. P. & Nguyen, T. D., Using fault injection and modeling to evaluate the performability of cluster-based services, *in the proceedings of the 4th USENIX Symposium on Internet Technologies and Systems*, March 2003

Oh, N.; Shirvani, P. P., & Mccluskey, E. J.. Error detection by duplicated instructions in super-scalar processors. *In IEEE Transactions on Reliability*, pp. 63–75, 2002c

Oppenheimer, D.; Gananpathi, A. & Patterson, D., Why do internet services fail, and what can be done about it?, *in the proceedings of 4th USENIX Symposium on Internet Technologies and Systems*, 2003

Ray, J.; Hoe, J. C. & B. Falsafi. Dual use of superscalar datapath for transient-fault detection and recovery. *In Proceedings of the 34th annual ACM/IEEE international symposium on Microarchitecture*, pp. 214–224. IEEE Computer Society, 2001.

Reinhardt, S. K. & Mukherjee. S. S. Transient fault detection via simultaneous multithreading. *In Proceedings of the 27th annual international symposium on Computer architecture*, pp. 25–36. ACM Press, 2000.

Reis, G.A.; Chang, J.; Vachharajani, N.; Mukherjee, S.S. & Rangan, R.; Design and evaluation of hybrid fault-detection systems, *In the proceedings of the International Symposium on Computer Architecture*, pp. 148 – 159, June 2005

Reis, G. A.; Chang, J.; Vachharajani, N. & Mukherjee, S. S., Software - controlled fault tolerance, *ACM Transactions on Architecture and Code Optimization*, Vol. V, No. N, pp.1–28, December 2005.

TPC-W. http://www.tpc.org/tpcw, April 2005.

Wood, Alan, Data Integrity Concepts, Features, and Technology, *Tandem Division White paper*, Compaq Computer Corporation, 2004

Ye, N. & Chen, Q., An Anomaly Detection Technique Based on Chi-Square Statistic. *Quality and Reliablility Engineering International, vol. 17, 2*, pp. 105-112, 2001

18

Machine Learning Approaches for Music Information Retrieval

Tao Li[1], Mitsunori Ogihara[2], Bo Shao[3] and DingdingWang[4]
[1]*School of Computer Science, Florida International University*
[2]*Department of Computer Science, University of Miami*
[3]*School of Computer Science, Florida International University*
[4]*School of Computer Science, Florida International University*
USA

1. Introduction

The rapid growth of the Internet and the advancements of Internet technologies have made it possible for music listeners to have access to a large amount of on-line music data, including music sound signals, lyrics, biographies, and discographies. Music artists in the 21st century are promoted through various kinds of websites that are managed by themselves, by their fans, or by their record companies. Also, they are subjects of discussions in Internet newsgroups and bulletin boards.

This raises the question of whether computer programs can enrich the experience of music listeners by enabling the listeners to have access to such a large volume of on-line music data. Multimedia conferences, e.g. ISMIR (International Conference on Music Information Retrieval) and WEDELMUSIC (Web Delivery of Music), have a focus on the development of computational techniques for analyzing, summarizing, indexing, and classifying music data. In [Huron, 2000] Huron points out that since the preeminent functions of music are social and psychological, the most useful characterizationwould be based on four types of information: *genre, emotion, style,* and *similarity.* The four types of characteristics are strongly related to each other. Certain emotional labels prominently apply to music in particular genres, e.g., "angry" for punk music, "depressed" for slow blues, and "happy" for children music. A style is often defined within a genre, e.g., "hard-bop jazz" and "American rock." Similar music pieces are likely to be those in the same genre, of the same style, and with the same emotional labeling. However, there are traits that distinguish them from the rest. Emotional labeling is transient, in the sense that the labels can be dependent on the state of mind of the listener, and popular music styles are perhaps defined not just in terms of sound signals but in terms of the way the lyrics are written, which is likely beyond the reach of sound feature extraction algorithms.

In this chapter, we briefly discuss various machine learning approaches used for recognizing the above four types of features music information retrieval. In particular, we investigate the following approaches: (1) multi-class classification for music genre categorization; (2) multi-label classification for emotion detection; (3) clustering for music style identification; and (4) semi-supervised learning for music recommendation. Parts of the work presented in this chapter have appeared in [Li & Zhu, 2006, Li & Ogihara, 2006, Li & Ogihara, 2003, Li et al., 2003, Li & Tzanetakis, 2003, Shao et al., 2008].

The rest of the chapter is organized as follows: Section 2 briefly introduces the feature extraction from music audio signals and lyrics; Section 3 discusses the multi-class classification methods for music genre categorization; Section 4 presents multi-label classification methods for emotion detection; Section 5 studies the bi-modal clustering for music style identification; Section 6 proposes a graph-based semi-supervised learning method for music recommendation; and Finally Section 7 concludes.

2. Music feature extraction

Before applying machine learning approaches in music information retrieval, an important step is the determination of the features extracted from music data. All the machine learning methods discussed in this chapter make use of the content features extracted from music audio signals. In addition, for music style identification, we also make use of the text-based features from music lyrics.

2.1 Content feature extraction

There has been a considerable amount of work in extracting descriptive features from music signals for music genre classification and artist identification [Foote & Uchihashi, 2001, Tzanetakis & Cook, 2002a, Logan & Salomon, 2001, Li et al., 2003]. In our study, we use timbral features along with wavelet coefficient histograms.

2.1.1 Mel-Frequency Cepstral Coefficients (MFCC)

Mel-Frequency Cepstral Coefficients (MFCC) is a feature set that is highly popular in speech processing. It is designed to capture short-term spectral-based features. The features are computed as follows: First, for each frame, the logarithm of the amplitude spectrum based on short-term Fourier transform is calculated, where the frequencies are divided into thirteen bins using the Mel-frequency scaling. Next, this vector is then decorrelated using discrete cosine transform. This is the MFCC vector. In this work, we use the first five bins, and compute the mean and variance of each over the frames.

2.1.2 Short-Term Fourier Transform Features (STFT)

This is a set of features related to timbral textures and is not captured using MFCC. It consists of the following five types: Spectral Centroid, Spectral Rolloff, Spectral Flux, Zero Crossings, and Low Energy. More detailed descriptions of STFT can be found in [Tzanetakis & Cook, 2002a].

2.1.3 DaubechiesWavelet Coefficient Histograms (DWCH)

Daubechies wavelet filters are a set of filters that are popular in image retrieval (For more details, see [Daubechies, 1992]). The DaubechiesWavelet Coefficient Histograms, proposed in [Li et al., 2003], are features extracted in the following manner: First, the Daubechies-8 (db_8) filter with seven levels of decomposition (or seven subbands) is applied to 30 seconds of monaural audio signals. Then, the histogram of the wavelet coefficients is computed at each subband. Then the first three moments of a histogram, i.e., the average, the variance, and the skewness, are calculated from each subband. In addition, the subband energy, defined as the mean of the absolute value of the coefficients, is computed from each subband. More details of DWCH can be found in [Li et al., 2003].

2.2 Lyrics-based feature sets

To accommodate the characteristics of the lyrics, our text-based feature extraction consists of four components: bag-of-words features, Part-of-Speech statistics, lexical features and orthographic features.

- *Bag-of-words*: We compute the TF-IDF measure for each word and select top 200 words as our features. Stemming operations are not applied.
- *Part-of-Speech statistics*: We use the output of the part-of-speech (POS) tagger by Brill [Bill, 1994] as the basis for feature extraction. The POS statistics usually reflect the characteristics of writing. There are 36 POS features extracted from each document, one for each POS tag expressed as a percentage of the total number of words for the document.
- *Lexical Features*: By "lexical features" we mean the features of individual wordtokens in the text. The most basic lexical features are lists of 303 generic function words taken from [Mitton, 1987][1], which generally serve as proxies for choice in syntactic (e.g., preposition phrase modifiers vs. adjectives or adverbs), semantic (e.g., usage of passive voice indicated by auxiliary verbs), and pragmatic (e.g., first-person pronouns indicating personalization of a text) planes. Function words have been shown to be effective style markers.
- *Orthographic features*: We also use orthographic features of lexical items, such as capitalization, word placement, word length distribution as our features. Word orders and lengths are very useful since the writing of lyrics usually follows certain melody.

3. Music genre categorization

3.1 Problem overview

Here we study the problem of content-based music genre categorization, i.e., classification of music pieces into a single unique class based computational analysis of music feature representations. Automatic music genre classification is a fundamental component of music information retrieval systems. Once the content-based features have been extracted from music pieces, the problem of music genre categorization is reduced to a multi-class classification problem: identifying the genre labels for music pieces from a set of pre-defined genre categories based on the feature representation of music audio signals.

3.2 Method description

We test various classification algorithms for the actual classification: GMM (Gaussian Mixture Models) with three Gaussians, KNN (k-Nearest Neighbors) with $k = 5$, LDA (Linear Discriminant Analysis), and multi-class extensions of support vector machines (SVM). Support vector machines (SVM) [Vapnik, 1998] is a method that has shown superb performance in binary classification problems. Intuitively, it aims at searching for a hyperplane that separates the positive data points and the negative data points with maximum margin. The method was originally designed as a binary classification algorithm.

---

[1] See http://www.cse.unsw.edu.au/~min/ILLDATA/Function.word.htm.

Several binary decomposition techniques are known. We use one-againstthe-rest (denoted by S1) and pairwise (denoted by S2), which assemble judgments respectively of the classifiers for distinguishing one class from the rest and of the classifiers for distinguishing one class from another. We also use a multi-class objective function version of SVM, MPSVM [Fung & Mangasarian, 2001] (we use short-hand MPS to refer to this algorithm), which can directly deal with multi-class problems. For S1 and S2, our SVM implementation is based on the LIBSVM [Chang & Lin, 2001], a library for support vector classification and regression. For experiments involving SVM, we test linear, polynomial, and radius-based kernels. The results we show are the best of the three kernel functions.

K-Nearest Neighbors (KNN) is a non-parametric classifier. Theoretical results show that its error is asymptotically at most twice as large as the Bayesian error rate. KNN has been applied to various music sound analysis problems. Given K as a parameter, it finds the K nearest neighbors among training data and uses the categories of the K neighbors to determine the class of a given input. We use the parameter K to 5.

Gaussian Mixture Models (GMM) is a method that has been widely used in music information retrieval. The probability density function (pdf) for each class is assumed to consist of a mixture of a number of multidimensional Gaussian distributions. The iterative expectation-minimization (EM) algorithm is then used to estimate the parameters of each Gaussian component and the mixture weights.

Linear Discriminant Analysis (LDA) works by finding a linear transformation that best discriminates among classes. The classification is then performed in the transformed space using some metric such as Euclidean distances.

3.3 Experiments

We test the classification method on the dataset used in [Tzanetakis & Cook, 2002b], which consists of 1,000 30-second-long sound files covering ten genres with 100 files per genre. The ten genres are Blues, Classical, Country, Disco, Hiphop, Jazz, Metal, Pop, Reggae, and Rock. The files are collected from radio and CD's. The experimental results are presented in Figure 1. The average accuracy of the one-versus-the-rest classifiers over a ten-fold cross-validation test, as shown in Figure 2 is very high for all ten classes (ranging from 91 to 99 %).

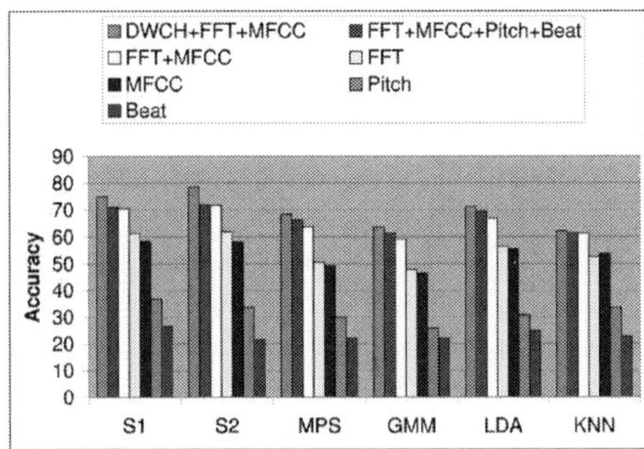

Fig. 1. The classification accuracy of the learning methods tested on the dataset using various combinations of features. The accuracy values are calculated via ten-fold cross validation.

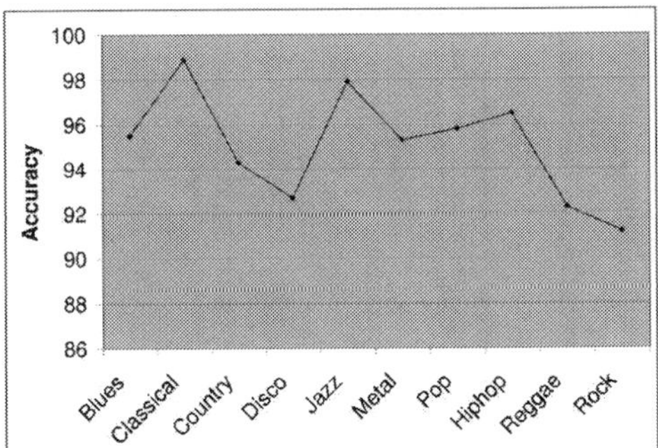

Fig. 2. The genre specific accuracy of the S1 method with DBCH, FFT and MFCC. The results are calculated via ten-fold cross validation.

Perrot and Gjerdingen [Perrot & Gjerdigen, 1999] report a human subject study in which college students were trained to learn a music company's genre classification on a ten-genre data collection, where the trained students achieved about 70% accuracy. Our results cannot be directly compared against their results because the datasets are different, but one can clearly say that the precision of the classification achieved here is satisfyingly high. The experiments demonstrate that music genre categorization can achieve good performances using machine learning techniques.

4. Emotion detection in music

4.1 Problem overview

Relations between musical sounds and their impact on the emotion of the listeners have been studied for decades. The celebrated paper of Hevner [Hevner, 1936] studied this relation through experiments in which the listeners are asked to write adjectives that came to their minds as the most descriptive of the music played. The experiments confirmed a hypothesis that music inherently carries emotional meaning. Hevner discovered the existence of clusters of descriptive adjectives and laid them out (there were eight of them) in a circle. She also discovered that the labeling is consistent within a group having a similar cultural background. The Hevner adjectives were refined and regrouped into ten adjective groups by Farnsworth [Farnsworth, 1958].

We cast the emotion detection problem as a *multi-label classification problem*, where the music sounds are classified into multiple classes simultaneously. That is a single music sound may be characterized by more than one label, e.g., both "dreamy" and "cheerful."

4.2 Method description

4.2.1 Multi-label classification

We resort to the scarcity of literature in multi-label classification by decomposing the problem into a set of binary classification problems. In this approach, for each binary problem a classifier is developed using the projection of the training data to the binary problem. To determine labels of a test data, the binary classifiers thus developed are run individually on the data and every label for which the output of the classifier exceeds a predetermined threshold is selected as a label of the data. See [Schapire & Singer, 2000] for similar treatments in the text classification domain. To build classifiers we used Support Vector Machines [Vapnik, 1998].

4.2.2 The dataset and emotional labeling

A dataset consisting of 235 instrumental jazz tracks is used for the experiment. The dataset was constructed by the authors from the CD collection of the second author. The files are labeled independently by two subjects: a 39 year old male (subject 1) and a 25 year old male (subject 2). Each track is labeled using a scale ranging from −4 to +4 on each of three bipolar adjective pairs: (Cheerful versus Depressing), (Relaxing versus Exciting), and (Comforting versus Disturbing), where 0 is thought of as neutral. Our early work on emotion labeling [Li & Ogihara, 2003] uses binary labels (existence versus non-existence) based on the adjective groups of Farnsworth. The classification accuracy is not very high (around 60%). The low accuracy can be attributed to the presence of many labels to choose from. The recent experiments conducted by Leman *et al.* [Leman et al., 2005] using scales on ten bipolar adjective pairs suggest that variations in emotional labeling can be approximated using only spanned three major principal components, which are hard to name. With these results in mind we decided to generate three bipolar adjective pairs based on the eight adjective groups of Hevner.

4.3 Experiments

The accuracy of the performance is presented in Table 1. Here the accuracy measure is the Hamming accuracy, that is, the ratio of the number of True Positives and TrueNegative against the total number of inputs. In each measure, the tracks labeled 0 are altogether put on either the positive side or the negative side. It is clear that the accuracy of detection was always at least 70% and sometimes more than 80%. Also, there is a large gap in the performance between the two subjects on the first two measures. We observe that this difference is coming from the difference in the cultural background of the subjects. To deal with labeling of a much larger group of listeners one should cluster them into groups depending on their labeling and train the emotion detection system for each group.

Subject	Cheerful vs. Depressing	Relaxing vs. Exciting	Comforting vs. Disturbing
1	83.3 (8.0)	70.4 (9.9)	72.4 (5.1)
2	69.6 (10.0)	83.7 (7.3)	70.9 (9.1)

Table 1. The accuracy (in %) of emotion detection. Within parentheses are standard deviations.

5. Music style identification

5.1 Problem overview

This section addresses the issue of music style identification. Ellis *et al.* point out that similarity between artists reflects personal tastes and suggest that different measures have to be combined together so as to achieve reasonable results in similar artist discovery [Ellis et al., 2002]. We focus our attention to singer-song-writers, i.e., those who sing their own compositions. We take the standpoint that the artistic style of a singer-song-writer is reflected both in the acoustic sounds and in the lyrics. We therefore hypothesize that the artistic styles of an artist can be captured better by combining acoustic features and linguistic features of songs than by using only one type of features. In this section, we describe our bi-modal clustering algorithms to group pop music pieces into groups with respect to the artists by using both acoustic features and linguistic features.

5.2 Method description

Our clustering algorithm is based on the basic principle of minimizing disagreement, i.e., minimizing the disagreement between two individual models could lead to the improvement of learning performance of individual models [Li & Ogihara, 2005]. The clustering algorithm is an extension of the EM method [Dempster et al., 1977]. In each iteration of algorithm, an EM type procedure is employed to bootstrap the model by starting with the cluster assignments obtained in the previous iteration. Upon convergence, the two individual models are used to construct the final cluster assignment. Table 2 lists the notions used for the algorithm and Figure 1 presents the algorithm procedure.

n	Number of Songs
$s_i = (s_i^1, s_i^2)$	A song s_i has two modes: content s_i^1 and lyrics s_i^2
$S = (s_1, \cdots, s_n)$	A collection of songs
K	Number of clusters
$\Lambda^1 = (\lambda_1^1, \cdots, \lambda_K^1)$	Modal 1 model parameters
$\Lambda^2 = (\lambda_1^2, \cdots, \lambda_K^2)$	Modal 2 model parameters
$Y = (y_1, ..., \cdots, y_n)$ $y_n \in \{1, \cdots, K\}$	Cluster assignment vector
$s \in S$	s represents a song from S
$y_s = k$	Song s is in k-th cluster

Table 2. The list of notations

We assume parameterized models, one for each cluster. Typically, all the models are from the same family, e.g., multivariate Gaussian. The algorithm described above is a variant of the EM algorithm. It performs an iterative optimization process for each data source by using the cluster assignments (possibly from another data source). Note that in each iteration, one data source is picked and every data point is reassigned to one of the clusters based on information from that data source and on its previous assignment. At the end of each iteration, the algorithm explicitly checks whether the agreement between two clusterings (one clustering from each data source) has been improved. If it is improved, the algorithm then continues to iterate. Otherwise, the algorithm will go back to the allocation step and hopefully get a new clustering.

5.3 Experiments
5.3.1 Data description

Our experiments are performed on the dataset consisting of 570 songs from 53 albums of a total of 41 artists. The sound recordings and the lyrics from them are obtained. To obtain the ground truth of song styles, we choose to use similarity information between artists available at All Music Guide artist pages (http://www.allmusic.com), assuming that this information is the reflection of multiple individual users. By examining All Music Guide artist pages, if the name of an artist X appears on the list of artists similar to Y, it is considered that X is similar to Y. The similarity graph of the 41 artists is shown in Figure 3.

Algorithm 1 : Bimodal Clustering

Input: S, K

Output: Cluster assignment Y as well as the trained model structure

1: **Initialization:** Initialize the model structure (Λ^1, Λ^2) as well as the cluster assignment Y

2: **while** the stopping criterion does not meet **do**

3:     **Step I:**
Randomly pick a different data source $i \in \{1, 2\}$

4:     **Step II:**
Model Re-estimation for source i: for each cluster k, the model parameters, λ_k^i, are re-estimated as

$$\lambda_k^i = \operatorname*{argmax}_{\lambda} \sum_{s:s \in S, y_s = k} \log P(s^i | \Lambda^i)$$

5:     **Step III:**
Sample re-assignment: for each data sample $s \in S$, set

$$y_s = \operatorname*{argmax}_{k} \log P(s^i | \lambda_k^i)$$

6:     **Step IV:**
Measure the agreement between two sources. If the agreement increases, goto Step I. Otherwise, goto Step II.

7: **end while**

8: Return Y as well as the trained models (Λ^1, Λ^2)

We select artists having a large number of neighbors. There are three of them, Fleetwood Mac, Yes, and Utopia. These three are neighbors to one another, so we select the neighbors of these three as a cluster. Of the remaining nodes we identify two other clusters in a similar

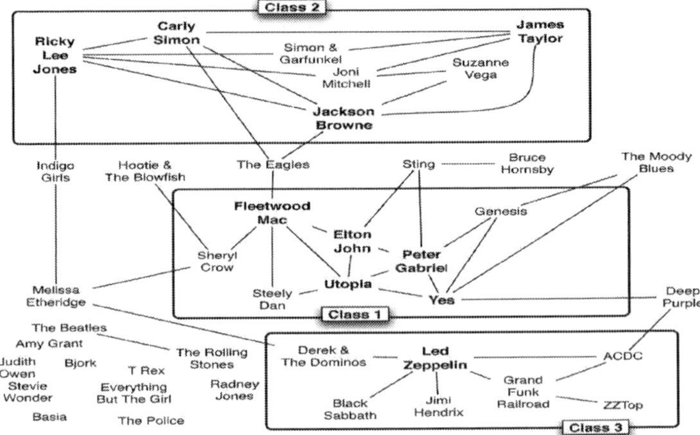

Fig. 3. The artist similarity graph. The names in bold are "core" nodes.

manner. All the remaining artists are in a separated cluster. The clusters are listed in Table 3. Our goal is to identify the song styles using both content and lyrics, i.e., cluster the 570 songs into the four different clusters. We use the cluster information of the artists as the labels for their songs.

Clusters	Members
No. 1	*{ Fleetwood Mac, Yes, Utopia, Elton John, Genesis, Steely Dan, Peter Gabriel }*
No. 2	*{ Carly Simon, Joni Mitchell, James Taylor, Suzanne Vega, Ricky Lee Jones, Simon & Garfunkel }*
No. 3	*{ AC/DC, Black Sabbath, ZZ Top, Led Zeppelin, Grand Funk Railroad, Derek & The Dominos }*
No. 4	All the remaining artists

Table 3. Cluster Memberships.

We use Purity and Accuracy [Zhao and Karypis, 2004, Ding et al., 2006] as our performance measures. Purity measures the extent to which each cluster contains data points from primarily one class [Zhao and Karypis, 2004]. In general, the larger the values of purity, the better the clustering solution is. Accuracy discovers the one-toone relationship between clusters and classes, therefore measure the extent to which each cluster contains data points from the corresponding class [Ding et al., 2006]. It sums up the whole matching degree between all pair class-clusters. The larger accuracy usually means the better clustering performance.

5.3.2 Result analysis

We compare the results of the bimodal clustering algorithm with the results obtained when the clustering is applied on the two sources of data separately. We also compare the bimodal clustering algorithm with the following clustering strategies on integrating different information sources: (1) Feature-Level Integration: Feature-level integration performs K-means clustering after simply concatenating the features obtained from the two data sources. (2) Cluster Integration: Cluster integration refers to the procedure of obtaining a combined clustering from multiple clusterings of a dataset [Strehl & Ghosh, 2003, Monti et al., 2003, Gionis et al., 2005]. Formally, let $C_1^1, ..., C_1^{k_1}$ denote the clusters obtained from source 1, and $C_2^1, ..., C_2^{k_2}$ denote the clusters obtained from source 2. Each point d_i can be represented as a $(k_1 + k_2)$- dimensional vector

$$d_i = (d_{i11}, \cdots, d_{i1k_1}, \cdots, d_{i21}, \cdots, d_{i2k_2})$$

$$d_{ijl} = \begin{cases} 1 & d_i \in C_j^{k_j} \\ 0 & \text{otherwise} \end{cases}, \text{ for } 1 \leq j \leq 2.$$

A combined clustering can be found by applying the K-means algorithm on the new representation. (3) Sequential Integration: Sequential integration is an intermediate approach of combining different information sources. It first performs clustering on one data source and obtains a clustering assignment, say, $C^1, ..., C^{k_1}$. We can represent each point d_i as a k_1-dimensional vector using the similar idea in cluster integration. Then we can combine the new representation with another data source using feature integration. Clustering can thus be performed on the new concatenated vectors. Depending on the order of the two sources, we have two sequential integration strategies:

a.   Sequential Integration I: firstly cluster based on content, then integrate with lyrics;

b.   Sequential Integration II: firstly cluster based on lyrics, then integrate with content.

We compare the results of bimodal clustering with the results obtained when clustering is applied on content and lyrics separately, and with the results of other integration strategies. Table 4 presents the experimental results. From the table, we observe the following: (1) The performance of purity and accuracy relative to the other is not always consistent in our comparison, i.e., higher purity values do not necessarily correspond to higher accuracy values. This is because different evaluation measures consider different aspects of the clustering results. (2) The purity and accuracy of feature-level integration are worse than those of content-only and lyric-only clustering methods. This shows that even though the joint feature space is often more informative than that available from individual sources, naive feature integration tends to generalize poorly [Wu et al., 1999]. (3) Cluster Integration: The cluster integration performs better than content-only and lyrics-only: cluster integration has higher purity and accuracy values than those of content-only and lyrics-only. This actually conforms to the results in [Gionis et al., 2005]: cluster aggregation would usually provide better clustering results. (4) Sequential Integration: the results of sequential integration are generally better than feature-level integration, and they are comparable with those of content-only and lyrics-only. (5) Our bimodal clustering outperforms all other methods in all three performance measures. The bimodal clustering algorithm can be thought as a kind of *semantic* integration of data from different information sources. The performance improvements show that bimodal clustering has advantages over cluster integration. The bimodal clustering aims to minimize the disagreements between different sources and it can implicitly learn the correlation structure between different sets of features.

Feature Set(s)	Purity	Accuracy
Content-only	0.436	0.438
Lyrics-only	0.444	0.402
Feature-Level Integration	0.425	0.380
Cluster Integration	0.465	0.423
Sequential Integration I	0.431	0.434
Sequential Integration II	0.438	0.407
bimodal Clustering	**0.471**	**0.453**

Table 4. Performance Comparison. The numbers are obtained by averaging over ten trials.

Experimental comparisons show that our bimodal clustering can efficiently identify song styles. For example, in our experiments, two songs from the album *Utopia / Anthology*: *Overture Mountain Top And Sunrise Communion With The Sun* and *The Very Last Time* would be put into two different clusters based on their contents or lyrics only. However, using both the content and lyrics, our bimodal clustering algorithm identifies them to be in the same cluster with similar styles. Similarly, bimodal clustering identifies two songs from the album *Peter-Gabriel / Peter Gabriel*: *Excuse Me* and *Solsbury hill* to be in the same cluster while other methods do not. In our experiments, we have identified around 50 such pairs and they give good anecdotal evidence that our bi-modal clustering algorithm can efficiently identify song styles.

6. Music recommendation

6.1 Problem overview

Music recommendation is the problem of delivering to a music listener a list of music pieces that he/she is likely to enjoy listening to. Music recommendation has been receiving a growing amount of attention recently [Uitdenbogerd & van Schyndel, 2002, Oliver & Kreger-Stickles, 2006, Pauws et al., 2006, Platt et al., 2002, Cai et al., 2007, Logan, 2004, Chen & Chen, 2001]. Our goal for music recommendation is to satisfy the following two requirements:

- *High recommendation accuracy.* A good recommendation system should output a relatively short list of songs in which many pieces are favored and few pieces are not favored.

- *High recommendation novelty.* Good novelty is defined as rich artist variety and well-balanced music content variety. Music content represents the information of genre, timbre, pitch, and rhythm, and so on [Tzanetakis & Cook, 2002a]. Well-balance means that the music content needs to be diversified and informative while not diverging much from the user preferences.

Various approaches for making music recommendations have been developed by utilizing the demographic information of the listeners, the contents of the music, the user listening history, and the discography (e.g., Last.fm, Goombah, and Pandora). These approaches can be generally divided into two types: collaborative-filtering methods and content-based methods. *Collaborative-filtering methods* recommend songs by identifying similar users or items based on ratings of items given by users [Cohen & Fan, 2000, Breese et al., 1998, Herlocker et al., 1999]. If the rating of an item by a user is unavailable, collaborative-filtering methods estimate it by computing a weighted average of known ratings of the item by similar users. *Content-based methods* provide recommendations based on the features extracted from audio signals of songs [Huang & Jenor, 2004, Knees et al., 2006, Li et al., 2004, Li a& Ogihara, 2004] and/or on the meta-data including genre, styles, artists, and lyrics [Pauws et al., 2006, Ragno et al., 2005, Yoshii et al., 2006]. That the contents are susceptible to feature extraction makes music recommendation different from movie recommendation, in which the meta-data is generally the only source of information available [Melville et al., 2002]. Recent proposals of probabilistic models and hybrid algorithms [Popescul et al., 2001, Jung et al., 2004, Yoshii et al., 2006] are designed by combining contents and user ratings [Popescul et al., 2001, Jung et al., 2004, Yoshii et al., 2006].

6.2 Method description

Here we introduce a strategy for music recommendation by way of mixing collaborative filtering and acoustic contents of music. The method proposed here uses a novel dynamic music similarity measurement that utilizes the access patterns from large numbers of users and uses an undirected graph as representation. Recommendation is calculated using the graph Laplacian and label propagation defined over the graph.

6.2.1 Dynamic music similarity measurement

The music features are vectors in a multi-dimensional space, and the distance between the representation vectors characterizes and quantifies the closeness between two pieces of music. Traditionally there are two popular distance functions for measuring similarity in multimedia retrieval [Foote et al., 2002, Logan & Salomon, 2001, Rui & Huang, 2000]: *Minkowski Distance Function* and *Weighted Minkowski Distance Function*. In the Minkowski distance measurement, every audio feature is assigned with the equal weight when determining the similarity of music. This could be inappropriate given that people are more sensitive to certain acoustic features than the others. In addition, it is well known that the perception of music is subjective to individual users. Different users can have totally different opinions for the same pieces of music. Using a fixed set of weights for acoustic features is likely to fail in accounting for the taste of individual users. It is thus important to design an automatic scheme for assigning weights to audio features based on the taste of individual users.

We propose a novel dynamic similarity measurement that utilizes the access patterns of music from a considerable number of users. Our measurement scheme is based on the assumption that two pieces of music are similar in human perception when they share similar access patterns across multiple users. Here we cast the problem of computing the appropriate similarity measures as a learning problem whose goal is to assign approximate weights to each feature [Wettschereck & Aha, 1995]. To determine automatically the weights for audio features, we explore the metric learning approach [He et al., 2004, Xing et al., 2003], which learns appropriate similarity metrics based on the correlation between acoustic features and user access patterns of music.

6.2.2 Label propagation on graph

Once we compute the similarities between pairs of songs, we can then construct the song graph. Once we obtain the song graph, music recommendation can be viewed as label propagation from labeled data (i.e., items with ratings) to unlabeled data.

In its simplest form, the label propagation is like a random walk on a song graph $\mathcal{G}$ [Szummer & Jaakkola, 2001, Kondor & Lafferty, 2002, Smola & Kondor, 2003, Zhu et al., 2003, Zhou et al., 2003]. Here we use the Green's function of the Laplace operator for music recommendation [Ding et al., 2007].

Given a graph with edge weights W, the *combinatorial Laplacian* is defined to be $L = D - W$, where D is the diagonal matrix consisting of the row sums of W; i.e., $D = \text{diag}(W\mathbf{e})$, $\mathbf{e} = (1 \cdots 1)^T$.

Green's function is defined on the generalized eigenvectors of the Laplacian matrix:

$$L\mathbf{u}_k = \zeta_k D\mathbf{u}_k, \quad \mathbf{u}_p^T D\mathbf{u}_q = \mathbf{z}_p^T \mathbf{z}_q = \delta_{pq}. \tag{1}$$

where $0 = \zeta_1 \leq \zeta_2 \leq \cdots \leq \zeta_n$ are the eigenvalues and the zero-mode is the first eigenvector $\mathbf{u}_1 = \mathbf{e}/\sqrt{n}$. Then we have

$$G = \frac{1}{(D - W)_+} = \sum_{k=2}^{n} \frac{\mathbf{u}_k \mathbf{u}_k^T}{\zeta_k}. \tag{2}$$

In practice, we truncate the expansion after some K terms and store the K vectors. Green's function is computed on the fly. So the storage requirement is $O(Kn)$.

Let $\mathbf{y}^T = (y_1, \ldots, y_n)$ be the rating for a user. Suppose we are Given an incomplete Rating $\mathbf{y}_0^T = (5, ?, ?, 4, 2, ?, ?, ?, 3)$ and the song graph illustrated in Figure 4.

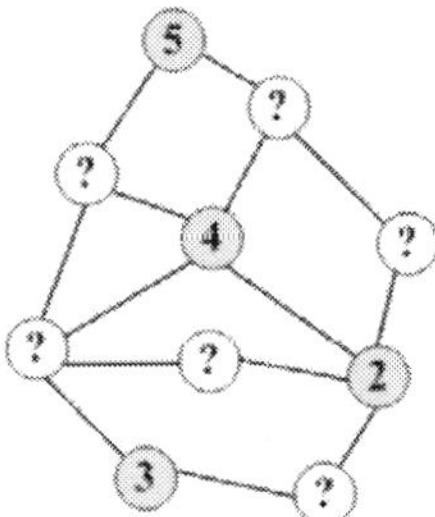

Fig. 4. An illustration of a recommendation task. The colored (shaded) nodes represent the rated items with their corresponding ratings. The others are the unrated items, whose ratings are unknown.

Our goal is to predict those missing values. Using Green's function, we initialize $\mathbf{y}_0^T = (5, 0, 0, 4, 2, 0, 0, 0, 3)$, and then compute the complete rating as the linear influence propagation

$$\mathbf{y} = G\mathbf{y}_0, \tag{3}$$

where G is the Green function built from the song graph.

6.2.3 Music ranking

After label propagation, we obtain the ratings for unrated songs and many of them might have the same rating. In practice, we might need a ranked list of the items to be recommended. The music ranking over a song graph G can be treated as the problem of finding the shortest path from the seed song node to the rest of the nodes in the song graph. The edges with low similarity have already been eliminated, so only the remaining edges can be used to construct shortest paths.

6.3 Experiments

The music data come from http://www.newwisdom.net. It is an educational and entertainment website in Chinese. It has about 4000 registered users visiting its forums regularly. They also listen songs and create playlists (called CDs on this website) as they prefer. Currently the website has a collection of more than 8,000 songs and hundreds of playlists.

By combining the user access pattern data with the content features of the songs, we generate the weight for each feature using the dynamic weighting scheme described above. Then we use the music ranking algorithm aforementioned to output the desired number of music pieces as our recommendations. In the experiments, the values of the ratings for the seed songs are set to be the same.

6.3.1 Comparison of different recommendation approaches

To demonstrate the performance of our music recommendation system, we compare the performance of the following five approaches:

1. **Content-based Approach (CBA)** This is solely based on acoustic content features extracted from the pieces of songs.
2. **Artist-based Approach (ABA)** This is solely based on artist, namely, it recommends songs only from the same artist.
3. **Access-pattern-based Approach (APA)** This is based on user access patterns. It selects the top songs with the highest co-occurrence frequency in the same playlists with the input song. This can also be thought as the item-based collaborative filtering method.
4. **Hybrid Approach (HA)** This is the approach explained in Section 1. It tries to integrate the collaborative filtering method and content-based method based on the algorithms described in [Jung et al., 2004].
5. **DWA** This is based on our approach, which first utilizes user access patterns to dynamically learn weights for each content features and then perform label propagation and ranking for music recommendation.

We conduct several sets of experiments to compare the performance of the listed approaches. The first comparison is designed to test the recommendation novelty and the playlist generation experiment is to examine the recommendation prediction ability, while the user study conducted is to assess the overall recommendation performance from the viewpoints of the end users.

6.3.2 Comparison on content variety

In this experiment, we evaluate if content variety as described in 1 are well balanced in different approaches. First of all, we cluster the 2829 songs using K-means algorithm according to their content features, and then, we study how many clusters the 10 songs recommended by each approach belong to. Also, we calculate the average distance among the 10 recommended songs of each of the 2829 seed songs using their content features. The more the clusters and/or the larger the distances, the more diverse the 10 songs, i.e. the more opportunity to get novel recommendation results.

Approach	Mean of Average Distance	Mean of Average Number of Clusters
CBA	2.55	2
ABA	8.74	5
APA	10.01	6
HA	5.28	4
DWA	5.88	4

Table 5. Results for content variety comparison.

From the experimental results listed in Table 5, we clearly observe that contentbased approach recommends songs with the highest content similarity, and the variety is very low. On the contrary, the access-pattern-based approach and the artist-based approach are diverse enough but lack of content similarity. Hybrid approach and our dynamic-weighting approach have comparable performance in well-balancing the content variety.

6.3.3 Comparison on playlist generation

Since playlists are generally a good means to reflect the interests of users, by comparing how accurate we can generate the whole original playlists from part of songs in them using different methods, we can analyze the ability of the approaches to predict the interests and preferences of the users.

In this set of experiments, we randomly select 200 playlists from the dataset of 274 playlists, and run hybrid approach and our dynamic-weighting approach on the data for the two approaches to learn. Then we randomly select 5 songs from each of the rest 74 playlists, and generate 74 new playlists, each of which contains 50 distinct songs based on the ordered recommendation lists of the these 5 songs. Then we check how many of the songs in the rest of each original playlists (the number of songs available for checking varies from 5 to 15) match the songs in the new larger playlists. Figure 5 lists the boxplot results of the comparison among content-based approach, hybrid approach, and our dynamic-weighting approach. From Figure 5 and Table 6, we observe that our approach outperforms content-based approach and the hybrid approach.

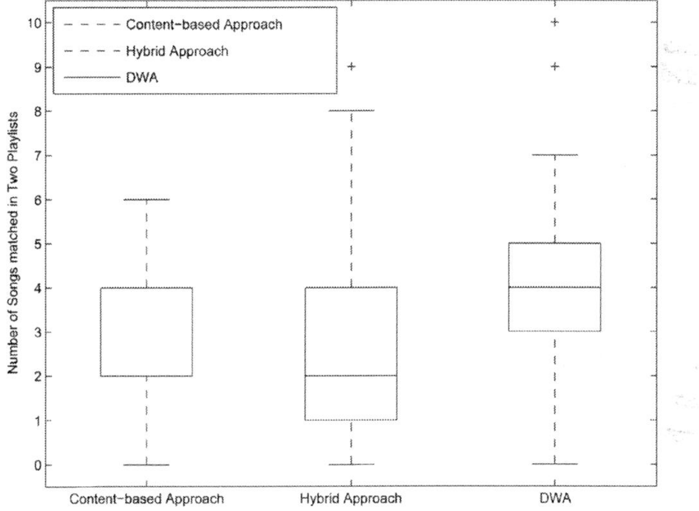

Fig. 5. Number of songs matched in user playlists and the playlists generated by different approaches

Approach	CBA	HA	DWA
Winning Rounds	8	20	37

Table 6. Times of one approach outperforms the other two by comparing the matches in two playlists

7. Conclusions

We discussed the following machine learning approaches used in music information retrieval: (1) multi-class classification methods for music genre categorization; (2) multi-label classification methods for emotion detection; (3) clustering methods for music style identification; and (4) semi-supervised learning methods for music recommendation. Experimental results are also presented to evaluate the approaches.

8. References

[Bill, 1994] Bill, E. (1994). Some advances in transformation-based parts of speech tagging. In *Proceedings of the twelfth national conference on Artificial intelligence (vol. 1)*, pages 722–727. American Association for Artificial Intelligence.

[Breese et al., 1998] Breese, J. S., Heckerman, D., and Kadie, C. (1998). Empirical analysis of predictive algorithms for collaborative filtering. In *Proceedings of the Fourteenth Annual Conference on Uncertainty in Artificial Intelligence*, pages 43–52.

[Cai et al., 2007] Cai, R., Zhang, C., Zhang, L., and Ma,W.-Y. (2007). Scalable music recommendation by search. In *MULTIMEDIA '07: Proceedings of the 15th international conference on Multimedia*, pages 1065–1074.

[Chang and Lin, 2001] Chang, C.-C. and Lin, C.-J. (2001). *LIBSVM: a library for support vector machines*. Software available at http://www.csie.ntu.edu.tw/~cjlin/libsvm.

[Chen and Chen, 2001] Chen, H.-C. and Chen, A. L. P. (2001). A music recommendation system based on music data grouping and user interests. In *CIKM '01: Proceedings of the tenth international conference on Information and knowledge management*, pages 231–238, New York, NY, USA. ACM.

[Cohen and Fan, 2000] Cohen,W.W. and Fan,W. (2000). Web-collaborative filtering: recommending music by crawling the web. *Comput. Networks*, 33(1-6):685–698.

[Daubechies, 1992] Daubechies, I. (1992). *Ten lectures on wavelets*. SIAM, Philadelphia.

[Dempster et al., 1977] Dempster, A., Laird, N., and Rubin, D. (1977). Maximum likelihood from incomplete data via the EM algorithm. *Journal of the Royal Statistical Society*, 39(1):1.

[Ding et al., 2007] Ding, C., Jin, R., Li, T., and Simon, H. D. (2007). A learning framework using green's function and kernel regularization with application to recommender system. In *KDD '07: Proceedings of the 13th ACM SIGKDD international conference on Knowledge discovery and data mining*, pages 260–269, New York, NY, USA. ACM.

[Ding et al., 2006] Ding, C., Li, T., Peng, W., and Park, H. (2006). Orthogonal nonnegative matrix t-factorizations for clustering. In *KDD '06: Proceedings of the 12th ACM SIGKDD international conference on Knowledge discovery and data mining*, pages 126–135, New York, NY, USA. ACM.

[Ellis et al., 2002] Ellis, D., Whitman, B., Berenzweig, A., and Lawrence, S. (2002). The quest for ground truth in musical artist similarity. In *Proceedings of 3rd International Conference on Music Information Retrieval*, pages 170–177.

[Farnsworth, 1958] Farnsworth, P. R. (1958). *The social psychology of music*. The Dryden Press.

[Foote et al., 2002] Foote, J., Cooper, M., and Nam, U. (2002). Audio retrieval by rhythmic similarity. pages 265–266.

[Foote and Uchihashi, 2001] Foote, J. and Uchihashi, S. (2001). The beat spectrum: a new approach to rhythm analysis. In *IEEE International Conference on Multimedia & Expo 2001*.

[Fung and Mangasarian, 2001] Fung, G. and Mangasarian, O. L. (2001). Multicategory proximal support vector machine classifiers. Technical Report 01-06, University of Wisconsin at Madison.

[Gionis et al., 2005] Gionis, A., Mannila, H., and Tsaparas, P. (2005). Clustering aggregation. In *ICDE*, pages 341–352.

[He et al., 2004] He, X., Ma, W.-Y., and Zhang, H.-J. (2004). Learning an image manifold for retrieval. In *Proceedings of ACM MM 2004*.

[Herlocker et al., 1999] Herlocker, J. L., Konstan, J. A., Borchers, A., and Riedl, J. (1999). An algorithmic framework for performing collaborative filtering. In *SIGIR'99: Proceedings of the 22nd annual international ACM SIGIR conference on Research and development in information retrieval*, pages 230–237.

[Hevner, 1936] Hevner, K. (1936). Experimental studies of the elements of expression in music. *American Journal of Psychology*, 48:246–268.

[Huang and Jenor, 2004] Huang, Y.-C. and Jenor, S.-K. (2004). An audio recommendation system based on audio signature description scheme in mpeg-7 audio. In *2004 IEEE International Conference on Multimedia and Expo*, volume 1, pages 639–642.

[Huron, 2000] Huron, D. (2000). Perceptual and cognitive applications in music information retrieval. In *Proceedings of International Symposium on Music Information Retrieval*.

[Jung et al., 2004] Jung, K.-Y., Park, D.-H., and Lee, J.-H. (2004). Hybrid collaborative filtering and content-based filtering for improved recommender system. In *Computational Science - ICCS 2004*, pages 295–302. Springer Berlin / Heidelberg.

[Knees et al., 2006] P. Knees, T. Pohle, M. Schedl, and G.Widmer. Combining audiobased similarity with web-based data to accelerate automatic music playlist generation. In *Proceedings of the Seventh ACM SIGMM International Workshop on Multimedia Information Retrieval*, pages 147–154, ACM Press, 2006.

[Kondor and Lafferty, 2002] Kondor, R. and Lafferty, J. (2002). Diffusion kernels on graphs and other discrete input spaces. In *Proceedings of the 2002 International Conference on Machine Learning (ICML)*.

[Li et al., 2004] Li, Q., Kim, B.-M., Guan, D.-H., and Oh, D.-W. (2004). A music recommender based on audio features. In *SIGIR '04: Proceedings of the 27th annual international ACM SIGIR conference on Research and development in information retrieval*, pages 532–533, New York, NY, USA. ACM.

[Li and Ogihara, 2003] Li, T. and Ogihara, M. (2003). Detecting emotion in music. In *Proceedings of the Fifth International Symposium on Music Information Retrieval (ISMIR2003)*, pages 239–240.

[Li and Ogihara, 2004] Li, T. and Ogihara, M. (2004). Content-based music similarity search and emotion detection. In *Proceedings of 2004 IEEE International Conference on Acoustics, Speech, and Signal Processing*, volume 5, pages 705–708.

[Li and Ogihara, 2005] Li, T. and Ogihara, M. (2005). Semi-supervised learning from different information sources. *Knowledge and Information Systems Journal*, 7(3):289–309.

[Li and Ogihara, 2006] Li, T. and Ogihara, M. (2006). Toward intelligent music information retrieval. *IEEE Transactions on Multimedia*, 8(3):564–574.

[Li et al., 2003] Li, T., Ogihara, M., and Li, Q. (2003). A comparative study on content-based music genre classification. In *Proceedings of SIGIR*, pages 282–289.

[Li and Tzanetakis, 2003] Li, T. and Tzanetakis, G. (2003). Factors in automatic musical genre classification of audio signals. In *Proceedings of 2003 IEEE Workshop on Applications of Signal Processing to Audio and Acoustics (WASPAA'03)*, pages 143–146. IEEE Computer Society.

[Li and Zhu, 2006] Li, T. and Zhu, M. O. S. (2006). Integrating features from different sources for music information retrieval. In *Proceedings of the Sixth IEEE International Conference on Data Mining (ICDM'06)*, pages 372–381.

[Logan, 2004] Logan, B. (2004). Music recommendation from song sets. In *Proceedings of ISMIR 2004*, pages 425–428.

[Logan and Salomon, 2001] Logan, B. and Salomon, A. (2001). A content-based music similarity function. Technical Report CRL 2001/02, Cambrige Research Laboratory.

[Melville et al., 2002] Melville, P., Mooney, R., and Nagarajan, R. (2002). Contentboosted collaborative filtering for improved recommendations. In *Proceedings of the Eighteenth National Conference on Artificial Intelligence (AAAI-02)*.

[Mitton, 1987] Mitton, R. (1987). Spelling checkers, spelling correctors and the misspellings of poor spellers. *Information Processing and Management*, 23(5):103–209.

[Leman et al., 2005] M. Leman, V. Vermeulen, L. De Voogdt, D. Moelants, and M. Lesaffre. Prediction of musical affect using a combination of acoustic structural cues. Journal of New Music Research, 34(1):39–67, 2005.

[Monti et al., 2003] Monti, S., Tamayo, P., Mesirov, J., and Gloub, T. (2003). Consensus clustering: A resampling-based method for class discovery and visualization of gene expression microarray data. *Machine Learning Journal*, 52(1-2):91–118.

[Oliver and Kreger-Stickles, 2006] Oliver, N. and Kreger-Stickles, L. (2006). Papa: Physiology and purpose-aware automatic playlist generation. In *Proceedings of the 7th International Conference on Music Information Retrieval*, pages 250–253.

[Pauws et al., 2006] Pauws, S., Verhaegh,W., and Vossen, M. (2006). Fast generation of optimal music playlists using local search. In *Proceedings of the 7th International Conference on Music Information Retrieval*, pages 138–143.

[Perrot and Gjerdigen, 1999] Perrot, D. and Gjerdigen, R. R. (1999). Scanning the dial: an exploration of factors in the identification of musical style. In *Proceedings of the 1999 Society for Music Perception and Cognition*, page 88.

[Platt et al., 2002] Platt, J. C., Burges, C. J. C., Swenson, S., Weare, C., and Zheng, A. (2002). Learning a gaussian process prior for automatically generating music playlists. In *Advances in Neural Information Processing Systems 14*, pages 1425–1432.

[Popescul et al., 2001] Popescul, A., Ungar, L., Pennock, D., and Lawrence, S. (2001). Probabilistic models for unified collaborative and content-based recommendation in sparse-data environments. In *17th Conference on Uncertainty in Artificial Intelligence*, pages 437–444, Seattle, Washington.

[Ragno et al., 2005] Ragno, R., Burges, C. J. C., and Herley, C. (2005). Inferring similarity between music objects with application to playlist generation. In *MIR'05: Proceedings of the 7th ACM SIGMM international workshop on Multimedia information retrieval*, pages 73–80, New York, NY, USA. ACM.

[Rui and Huang, 2000] Rui, Y. and Huang, T. S. (2000). Optimizing learning in image retrieval. In *Proceedings of IEEE Computer Vision and Pattern Recognition*, pages 236–243.

[Schapire and Singer, 2000] Schapire, R. E. and Singer, Y. (2000). Boostexter: A boosting-based system for text categorization. *Machine Learning*, 39(2/3):135–168.

[Shao et al., 2008] Shao, B., Wang, D., Li, T., and Ogihara., M. (2008). Music recommendation based on acoustic features and user access patterns. Manuscript in submission.

[Smola and Kondor, 2003] Smola, A. J. and Kondor, R. (2003). Kernels and regularization on graphs. In *Proceedings of the 16th Annual Conference on Learning Theory and 7th Kernel Workshop*, pages 144–158.

[Strehl and Ghosh, 2003] Strehl, A. and Ghosh, J. (2003). Cluster ensembles – a knowledge reuse framework for combining multiple partitions. *The Journal of Machine Learning Research*, 3:583–617.

[Szummer and Jaakkola, 2001] Szummer, M. and Jaakkola, T. (2001). Partially labeled classification with markov random walks. In *Advances in Neural Information Processing Systems*, volume 14.

[Tzanetakis and Cook, 2002a] Tzanetakis, G. and Cook, P. (2002a). Music genre classification of audio signals. *IEEE Transactions on Speech and Audio Processing*,10(5):293–302.

[Tzanetakis and Cook, 2002b] Tzanetakis, G. and Cook, P. (2002b). Musical genre classification of audio signals. *IEEE Transactions on Speech and Audio Processing*, 10(5).

[Uitdenbogerd and van Schyndel, 2002] Uitdenbogerd, A. and van Schyndel, R. (2002). A review of factors affecting music recommender success. In *Proceedings of ISMIR*.

[Vapnik, 1998] Vapnik, V. N. (1998). *Statistical learning theory*. John Wiley & Sons, New York.

[Wettschereck and Aha, 1995] Wettschereck, D. and Aha, D. W. (1995). Weighting features. In Veloso, M. and Aamodt, A., editors, *Case-Based Reasoning, Research and Development, First International Conference*, pages 347–358. Springer-Verlag, Berlin.

[Wu et al., 1999] Wu, L., Oviatt, S. L., and Cohen, P. R. (1999). Multimodal integration - a statistical view. *IEEE Transactions on Multimedia*, 1(4):334–341.

[Xing et al., 2003] Xing, E. P., Ng, A. Y., Jordan, M. I., and Russell, S. (2003). Distance metric learning, with application to clustering with side-information. In *Advances in Neural Information Processing Systems 15*, pages 505–512.

[Yoshii et al., 2006] Yoshii, K., Goto, M., Komatani, K., Ogata, T., , and Okuno, H. G. (2006). Hybrid collaborative and content-based music recommendation using probabilistic model with latent user preferences. In *Proceedings of ISMIR*.

[Zhao and Karypis, 2004] Zhao, Y. and Karypis, G. (2004). Empirical and theoretical comparisons of selected criterion functions for document clustering. *Machine Learning*, 55(3):311–331.

[Zhou et al., 2003] Zhou, D., Bousquet, O., Lal, T., Weston, J., and Sch¨olkopf, B. (2003). Learning with local and global consistency. In *In 18th Annual Conf. on Neural Information Processing Systems*.

[Zhu et al., 2003] Zhu, X., Ghahramani, Z., and Lafferty, J. (2003). Semi-supervised learning using gaussian fields and harmonic functions. In *ICML*.

19

LS-Draughts: Using Databases to Treat Endgame Loops in a Hybrid Evolutionary Learning System

Henrique Castro Neto, Rita Maria Silva Julia and Gutierrez Soares Caixeta
Computer Science Department, Federal University of Uberlândia
Brazil

1. Introduction

The Reinforcement Learning methods have been a subject of great interest in the machine learning area, since it does not require an intelligent "professor" to provide training examples. That is why it is a suitable tool for dealing with complex domains where it is hard or even impossible to obtain such examples (Russell & Norvig, 2003). Among the Reinforcement Learning methods, one can be stood out: the TD learning methods. They are widely used with highly efficient results, including in the construction of agents capable of learning to play Draughts, Chess, Backgammon, Othello, GO or other games (Samuel, 1959; Lynch, 1997; Lynch & Griffith, 1997; Neto & Julia, 2007; Schaeffer et al., 2001; Thrun, 1995; Tesauro, 1994; Leuski, 1995; Schraudolph et al., 2001 and Epstein, 2001). Such agents have demonstrated that the games are, undoubtedly, a very suitable domain to study and to check the efficiency of the main techniques of machine learning.

As an example of good automatic player agents, the LS-Draughts - (Neto & Julia, 2007) can be cited. It is a Draughts learning system based on Mark Lynch's NeuroDraughts player (Lynch & Griffith, 1997) which uses three important tools in machine leaning: Genetic Algorithms (AGs), Artificial Neural Network (ANN) and Temporal Differences (TD) Reinforcement Learning methods. It also adopts the NET-FEATUREMAP mapping technique to represent the game board states. This mapping represents the game board states by means of a set of functions – called features – that capture relevant knowledge about the domain of draughts and use this knowledge to map the game board in the input of an Artificial Neural Network. Using Genetic Algorithms, the LS-Draughts extends NeuroDraughts and automatically generates a concise and efficient set of features which is relevant to represent the game board states and to optimize the training of the draughts player agent (NeuroDraughts uses a fixed and manually defined set of features). The core of LS-Draughts consists of an Artificial Neural Network whose weights are updated by the Temporal Differences Reinforcement Learning methods. The Network output corresponds to a real number (prediction) that indicates to what extent the board sate represented by features in the Network input is favorable to the agent. The agent is trained by self-play coupled with a cloning technique. The minimax algorithm is used to choose the best action to be executed considering the current game board state. LS-Draughts shows that the GAs can be an important tool for improving the general performance of automatic players.

Furthermore, GAs presented a good performance along with another important machine learning technique: the Temporal Differences Reinforcement Learning methods. Despite of the fact that LS-Draughts improved the general performance of NeuroDraughts, it did not manage to lessen its endgame loop problems (Neto & Julia, 2007).

In order to attack this problem, here the authors present an extended version of LS-Draughts where the endgame databases of the exceptional automatic draughts player Chinook (Schaeffer et al., 1996; Schaeffer, 1997) have been added to.

The main purpose of including the endgame databases of Chinook into the extended LS-Draughts is to try to answer two important questions:

1. Will the addition of the endgame databases into the original LS-Draughts contribute, in fact, for improving its general performance?
2. Will the use of the endgame databases help to decrease the rate of endgame loops in the original LS-Draughts? (This problem occurs in NeuroDraughts as well).

Finally, a tournament was executed between the available player of NeuroDraughts, the best player of the original LS-Draughts and the best player generated by the extended version of LS-Draughts proposed here. Furthermore, the rates of endgame loops occurred during the training process of these three players were also estimated. The results obtained show that the insertion of endgame databases into LS-Draughts produced a much better player and decreased significantly the rate of endgame loops.

2. Temporal differences methods in games

This section explains how TD Reinforcement Learning methods can be used along with minimax search by a player Neural Network. First, the Network is rewarded for a good performance (that is, it receives from the environment a positive reinforcement corresponding to the endgame state, in case of victory) and it is punished for a bad performance (it receives from the environment a negative reinforcement corresponding to the endgame, in case of defeat). For all the intermediate game board states (between the starting board and the final board) represented in the input layer of the Network, as no specific reward is available, the TD mechanism calculates the prediction P of victory by means of the following equation:

$$P = g\left(in^{output}\right),\tag{1}$$

where g is the hyperbolic tangent function and in^{output} is the local induced field on the neuron of the Network output layer (Haykin, 1998; Lynch, 1997). It means that the value of P depends on the Network weights. Then, a prediction P corresponds to a real number belonging to the interval [-1,1] that indicates how much the game board state represented in the Network input is favorable to the agent. Each time the agent must move a piece, the minimax algorithm is used to build a depth n breadth-first search tree whose root S is the current state (resultant from the last opponent move), whose depth 1 nodes correspond to the states resultant from all possible moves available to the agent considering the state S, and so on for the depth 2, depth 3, ..., depth n, which correspond to all possible states resulting from the opponent's and agent's later moves up to the depth n level. The Network calculates, then, the predictions P for each depth n sate. Finally, these values will be returned to the minimax algorithm in order to allow it to indicate to the agent which is the best action to choose and to execute in S. Whenever the agent executes a move, the Network weights are updated according to equation 2 (Sutton, 1988):

$$\Delta w_t = \alpha \, (P_t - P_{t-1}) \sum_{k=1}^{t-1} \lambda^{(t-1)-k} \nabla_w P_k \,, \tag{2}$$

where P_t is the prediction corresponding to the current game board state, P_{t-1} is the prediction corresponding to the previous game board sate, each P_k represents the prediction corresponding to an earlier game board state, α is the learning rate (defined according to how fast the system will update the Network weights), λ is a constant defined according to how much the system will consider the impact of an earlier state P_k in the weight updating process and $\nabla_w P_k$ corresponds to the partial derivate of P_k with respect to the variable w (weight).

A small revolution in the field of Reinforcement Learning occurred when Gerald Tesauro presented his training results obtained by applying the TD methods to an evaluation function (Tesauro, 1992; Tesauro, 1995). Tesauro's program, TD-Gammon, is a backgammon player that, in spite of having very little knowledge about backgammon, is able to play as efficiently as the greatest world players (Tesauro, 1994). The principles of TD methods were first applied by Samuels, who pioneered the idea of updating evaluations based on successive predictions in a checker program (Samuel, 1959). Another very successful work with the TD methods is that proposed by Jonathan Schaeffer and other researchers (Schaeffer et al., 2001) that produced a detailed comparative study between an evaluation function trained manually by experts (which is the case of the current draught champion CHINOOK (Schaeffer et al., 1996)) and an evaluation function trained by the Temporal Differences methods. This analysis showed that the self-learning strategy along with the TD methods is an efficient tool to produce automatic agents able to play with a high level of performance.

Other works that obtained good results with the TD method are: Mark Lynch (Lynch, 1997), Neto and Julia (Neto & Julia, 2007), Thrun (Thrun, 1995), Leuski (Leuski, 1995), Schraudolph (Schraudolph et al., 2001), Baxter (Baxter et al., 1998) and Levinson and Weber (Levinson & Weber, 2002).

3. Evolutionary computation in games

Evolutionary Computation is an area of Computer Science which uses ideas from biological evolution to solve computational problems. Many such problems require searching through a huge space of possibilities for solutions, such as the classification task in data mining, the selection of a collection of rules (or actions) that will control a robot as it navigates in its environment, or the job-shop scheduling task. Such computational problems often require a system to be adaptive – that is, to continue to perform well in a changing environment.

The basis for Evolutionary Computation is the schema theory modeled mathematically by Holland (Holland, 1992). The schema theory is inspired on the principle of survival of the fittest individuals of the Darwin's theory of natural selection, where the fittest individuals are selected to produce offspring for the next generation. In the context of search, individuals are candidate solutions to a given search problem. Hence, reproduction of the fittest individuals means reproduction of the best current candidate solutions. Genetic operators such as selection, crossover and mutation generate offspring from the fittest individuals. One of the advantages of Evolutionary Computation over "traditional" search methods is that the former performs a kind of global search using a population of individuals, rather than performing a local search. The global search methods are more vigorous than the local search methods to avoid to be trapped into a local maximum. There are several approaches that have been followed in the field of Evolutionary Computation. The general term for such approaches is evolutionary algorithms. The most widely used form of evolutionary algorithms is Genetic Algorithms, which was the main focus of the original version of LS-Draughts (Neto & Julia, 2007). Other common forms of evolutionary algorithms are Evolution Strategies, Evolutionary Programming and Genetic Programming (Mitchell & Taylor, 1999).

The application of Evolutionary Computation in games has helped to produce very good player agents, principally as an alternative paradigm to the conventional training process. David Fogel, using evolutionary algorithms to update the weights of the chess player Multilayer Neural Network corresponding to his best chess player BLONDIE25 (Fogel et al., 2004), as well as to update the weights of the draught player Multilayer Neural Network corresponding to his best draught player ANACONDA (Fogel & Chellapilla, 2002), proved the usefulness of the evolutionary algorithms as a training tool, once BLONDIE25 and ANACONDA obtained the titles of master in chess and expert in draughts, respectively, due to their excellent performance in international tournaments.

Fogel also tested his player ANACONDA against an ancient good version of CHINOOK . The former obtained a better performance: 4 victories, 3 defeats and 3 draws.

4. Temporal differences x evolutionary computation

Paul Darwen demonstrates in (Darwen, 2001) that the TD methods are more efficient than Evolutionary Computation methods to train backgammon player agents implemented as nonlinear systems, since the former methods requires only a few hundred thousand training games to produce a good player, whereas the later ones would require billions of training games to obtain the same performance. On the other hand, Darwen showed that Evolutionary Computation is more efficient than TD methods to train backgammon player agents implemented as linear systems. The same seems to be also valid for draughts domain. For instance, ANACONDA needed 126.000 training games to present the same performance obtained by Schaeffer's world champion player CHINOOK – trained manually – after only 10.000 training games.

Inspired by Darwen's results, Neto and Julia demonstrated in (Neto & Julia, 2007) that GAs can be an important tool for improving the general performance of draughts player Neural Networks trained by the Temporal Differences methods. Their best draughts player obtained a better performance in relation to the Mark Lynch's NeuroDraughts player: 2 victories and 5 draws. However, despite of the fact LS-Draughts has improved the general performance of NeuroDraughts, it presented endgame loop problems. For example, analysing the 5 draws against NeuroDraughts, in 2 of them the best player of LS-Draughts could easily have won if it was able to detect endgame loops. In order to solve this problem, as mentioned above, the authors present, in the next section, the architecture and the implementation of the extended version of LS-Draughts (including the GA of the original version) where the endgame databases of the draughts player Chinook have been added to. Next, the problem of the endgame loops found in the original LS-Draughts will be shown. Finally, this chapter shows the results obtained by the extended version of LS-Draughts.

5. The LS-Draughts with endgame databases

The extended LS-Draughts is a learning system whose main objective is to generate a draught player agent able to play draughts on a high performance level. In order to cope with this objective, the LS-Draughts extends the Mark Lynch's NeuroDraughts player (Lynch, 1997; Lynch & Griffith, 1997) by the adiction of the following modules:

1. An automatic feature generation module whose purpose is to automatically generate, by means of Genetic Algorithms, a concise set of features which are essential for representing the game board states and to optimize the training of the LS-Draugths' player agents. More concisely, each agent consists of an Artificial Neural Network whose weights are updated by the Temporal Differences methods (Neto & Julia, 2007);

2. An endgame database module whose purpose is to anticipate the result of the game (victory, defeat or draw) for draughts board states with up to eight pieces on the board. By adding this endgame database, the extended LS-Draughts tries to improve the adjustment of the Neural Network weights through perfect information retrieved from the database indicating predictions of victory, defeat or draw (instead of using heuristic information). Indeed, this procedure tends to let the evaluation function of the extended LS-Draughts more efficienty and more accuraty, reducing, therefore, the rate of endgame loops.

The new architecture of LS-Draughts is indicated in figure 1. The figure shows, through a flowchart of arrows enumerated from 1 up to 14, an overview of total training process of LS-Draughts, including the six modules. The architecture and the flowchart are explained below.

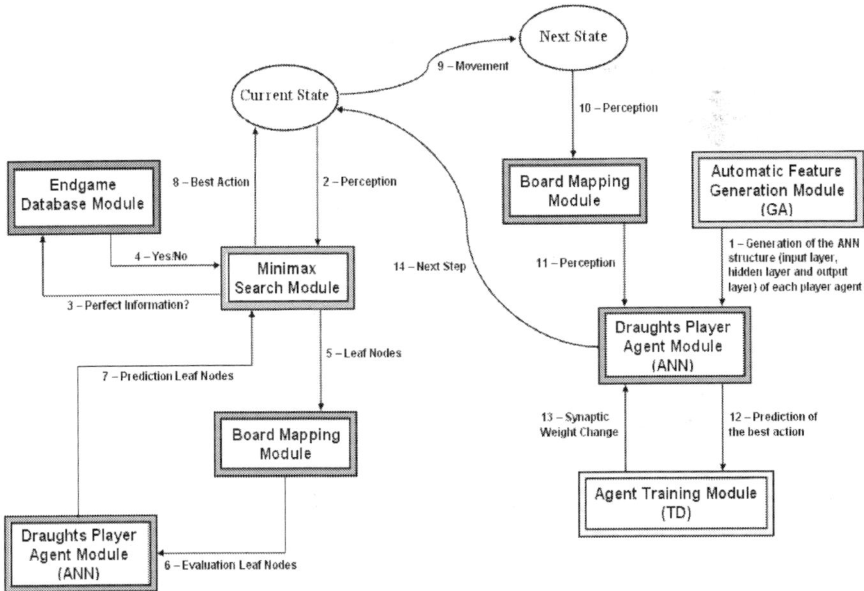

Fig. 1. LS-Draughts' new architecture, with endgame databases.

The system is composed of six main modules:

1. **The Automatic Feature Generation Module or GA:** corresponds to Genetic Algorithms that generate T_p individuals which represent subsets of every available features in the NET-FEATUREMAP mapping (the same mapping technique used by Lynch in NeuroDraughts);

2. **The Draughts Player Agent Module (ANN):** corresponds to a Multilayer Neural Network whose input layer represents a game board state. The Network output corresponds to a real number (prediction) that indicates to what extent the input state is favorable to the agent;

3. **The Board Mapping Module:** the draughts game board is implemented in an array of 32 positions, which each position represents a specific square of the draughts board. The mapping used by LS-Draughts is the NET-FEATUREMAP (more details about this kind of mapping can be found in (Lynch, 1997)). The role of this module is to represent a game board state (or array of 32 positions), in the Neural Network input, by means of a set of functions called features;

4. **The Minimax Search Module:** the role of this module is to select the best action to be executed by the agent according to the current game board state. The classical minimax algorithm can be found in (Russel & Norvig, 2003). Section 5.4.2 presents the pseudo-code corresponding to the search algorithm here proposed, which combines the minimax algorithm and the use of endgame databases;

5. **The Agent Training Module or TD:** corresponds to the learning process of the player agent or ANN. This module uses Temporal Differences Reinforcement Learning methods and self-play with cloning as training strategy;

6. **The Endgame Database Module:** the use of endgame database (Lake et al., 1994; Schaeffer et al., 1996) reduces the sequence of necessary moves, from the initial game board, in order to reach a position with defined theoretical value, that is, victory, defeat or draw. The endgame databases used by LS-Draughts are available on http://www.cs.ualberta.ca/~chinook/ and the library of functions that allows to access to these databases is available on http://pages.prodigy.net/ eyg/checkers/kingsrow.htm.

As cited in (Neto & Julia, 2007), the learning process of LS-Draughts is similar to the one performed by NeuroDraughts (this latter corresponds to second, third, fourth and fifth modules of the new architecture of LS-Draughts). However, the fifth module of LS-Draughts modifies the training process of NeuroDraughts in the following way: in the former, innumerous individuals – that is, innumerous sets of features – are trained, whereas in the latter, just one is trained. Furthermore, the first and sixth modules extend the Mark Lynch's player. The first module automatically generates, by means of GAs, feature sets that tend to represent, efficiently, the game board states in order to produce good draught players. The sixth module uses the endgame databases of Chinook in order to reduce endgame loop problems and to improve the learning of the individuals. Note that this new version of LS-Draughts extends the original version only by the addiction of the sixth module. The interaction between the second, fourth and fifth modules have already been described in the section 2. More details about these can be found in (Lynch, 1997).

An overview of the flowchart of arrows indicated in the figure 1 is presented as follow:

1. **Automatic Feature Generation Module (GA) → Generation of the ANN structure (input layer, hidden layer and output layer) of each player agent → Draughts Player Agent Module (ANN):** firstly, the GA generates T_p individuals which represent subsets of every available features in the NET-FEATUREMAP mapping. Next, each individual is introduced in the input of the Artificial Neural Network corresponding to it. Consequently, T_p draughts player Neural Networks (or draughts player agents) are produced here.

   Henceforth, the next steps of the flowchart of arrows (enumerated from 2 up to 14) will refer to the training process of the extended LS-Draughts considering only one individual, that is, just one player Neural Network. Therefore, in practice, during the training process of LS-Draughts, the next steps should be repeated for each individual associated to its player Neural Network, that is, T_p times;

2. **Current State → Perception → Minimax Search Module:** each time the player agent must move a piece, the minimax algorithm is used to build a depth n breadth-first search tree whose root S is the current state. So, the parameters of the Minimax Search Module are the depth n and the current state S;

3. **Minimax Search Module → Perfect Information? → Endgame Database Module:** before that the Minimax Search Module can build the game search tree for the current state S, it checks, through the Endgame Database Module, whether S belongs to the endgame databases;

4. **Endgame Database Module → Yes/No → Minimax Search Module:** if true, the Minimax Search Module goes to the step 8. Otherwise, it carries on next step;

5. **Minimax Search Module → Leaf Nodes → Board Mapping Module:** after building the game search tree, the Minimax Search Module checks whether all of the leaf nodes of this tree belong to the endgame databases. If true, then the Minimax Search Module can compute the game theoretic value (victory, defeat or draw) using the perfect knowledge of the endgame databases, instead of using the heuristic evaluation function. So, if all leaf nodes belong to the databases, the Minimax Search Module gets their corresponding theoretic values and goes to the step 8. Otherwise, for each leaf node that does not belong to the endgame databases, the Board Mapping Module is called for mapping the game board state associated to.

   Note that the theoretic value is obtained through the Endgame Database Module and the heuristic value is obtained through the ANN (Draughts Player Agent Module). The steps 6 and 7 below show the latter situation;

6. **Board Mapping Module → Evaluation Leaf Nodes → Draughts Player Agent Module (ANN):** the Board Mapping Module maps the game board states, associated to each leaf node of the game tree into the input layer of the player Neural Network;

7. **Draughts Player Agent Module (ANN) → Prediction Leaf Nodes → Minimax Search Module:** for each leaf node, represented in the input layer of the player Neural Network, a prediction P of victory is calculated. This prediction P corresponds to a real number belonging to the interval [-1,1] that indicates how much the game board state is favorable to the agent;

8. **Minimax Search Module → Best Action → Current State:** the values that are returned to the minimax algorithm (corresponding to the theoretic values of the endgame databases and/or corresponding to the heuristic values of the prediction of the player

Neural Network) are used in order to indicate to the agent which is the best action to choose and to execute in the current state S;

9. **Current State → Movement → Next State:** the best action is executed and the game board current state is changed to the next state S';

10. **Next State → Perception → Board Mapping Module:** the Board Mapping Module is called for mapping the game board state S' resultant of the best action executed by agent;

11. **Board Mapping Module → Perception → Draughts Player Agent Module (ANN):** the Board Mapping Module maps the new state S' in the input layer of the player Neural Network;

12. **Draughts Player Agent Module (ANN) → Prediction of the best action → Agent Training Module (TD):** the TD mechanism calculates the prediction P' of victory for the new state S' (represented in the input layer of the player Neural Network) by means of the equation 1 showed in the section 2;

13. **Agent Training Module (TD) → Synaptic Weight Change → Draughts Player Agent Module (ANN):** the new prediction P' calculated by TD mechanism is used for updating the synaptic weights of the player Neural Network according to equation 2 of the section 2;

14. **Draughts Player Agent Module (ANN) → Next Step → Current State:** the flowchart returns to the step 2 and repeats the whole flow until the end of the training game.

In the next subsections, the authors present the structures of the first and the sixth modules which characterize the LS-Draughts. As shown before, each individual generated by the first module will be attached to a neural network that will learn by means of training games guided by the TD methods.

5.1 Population and individual encoding in the LS-Draughts

Each individual in the population is encoded as a binary chromosome whose length is 15 genes. The binary representation indicates whether a determined feature F_i occurs or not in the gene G_i, where $i \in \{1, 2, 3, ..., 15\}$, as shown in figure 2.

F1	F2	F3	F4	F5	F6	F7		F14	F15
1	1	0	0	1	1	1	...	1	0
G1	G2	G3	G4	G5	G6	G7		G14	G15

Fig. 2. Example of an individual encoding in the population.

Table 1 shows the 15 features to be represented in the genes. Each integer number in column BITS corresponding to a feature F_i indicates the quantity of neurons that will be reserved to represent F_i in the input layer of the Network.

In this chapter, the GA population is composed of 50 individuals, that is, $T_p = 50$. Therefore, the population will be formed by 50 chromosome structures (or individuals) where each of them will be associated to a Neural Network. These 50 individuals will evolve within the GA along 50 generations (the original LS-Draughts evolved them along 30 generations).

FEATURES	BITS
F1: PieceAdvantage	4
F2: PieceDisadvantage	4
F3: PieceThreat	3
F4: PieceTake	3
F5: Advancement	3
F6: DoubleDiagonal	4
F7: Backrowbridge	1
F8: Centrecontrol	3
F9: XCentrecontrol	3
F10: TotalMobility	4
F11: Exposure	3
F12: KingCentreControl	3
F13: DiagonalMoment	3
F14: Threat	3
F15: Taken	3

Table 1. Set of features used by LS-Draughts.

The individuals will be generated according to the following steps:

1. All the 50 individuals of the first generation GE_0 are generated by a randomly binary activation (1 or 0) of their genes. Next, each of these individuals (which represents a game state) is introduced in the input of the Network that corresponds to it. The 50 Networks produced are trained (the training process will be discussed later). After this, LS-Draughts starts a tournament involving the 50 available trained Networks. At the end of the tournament, an evaluation (or fitness) is calculated for each individual based on its performance during the tournament (as detailed in the subsection 5.4). Next, the 50 individuals of GE_0 are passed as parents to the next generation (generation GE_1);

2. All the 50 individuals of the remaining 49 generations GE_i, where $1 \le i \le 49$, are generated as described below: 50 new individuals are generated by applying the genetic operators of crossover and mutation to 25 pairs of individuals chosen by a stochastic tournament selection process over the 50 parents received from the generation GE_{i-1}. Next, 50 new Networks associated to these 50 new individuals are trained. After this, LS-Draughts starts a tournament involving the 100 available trained Networks (50 corresponding to GE_{i-1} and 50 corresponding to GE_i). At the end of the tournament, an evaluation (or fitness) is calculated for each individual based on its performance during the tournament. The 50 individuals which present the best fitness will be passed as parents to the next generation GE_{i+1}, and so on.

5.2 Individual selection and application of genetic operators

The selection method used by LS-Draughts to select the parents in order to apply the genetic operators is the stochastic tournament whose tour is 3 (Mitchell & Taylor, 1999). For each 2 parents selected by the stochastic tournament selection, two new children are generated. The crossover method used is the simple crossing of genes (one-point crossover) with crossover probability = 100%. The mutation probability rate – P_{mut} – used is 0.3. Thus, in each individual, 5 genes are chosen randomly to be modified by mutation.

5.3 Neural Networks training

The multilayer Network associated with an individual I_i has N_A neurons in the input layer, where N_A represents the quantity of bits associated to the active genes (digit 1) in I_i. The hidden layer and the output layer have 20 neurons and 1 neuron, respectively. For example, in figure 3, the Network attached to the individual M will utilize only the features F_1, F_2 and F_{14} (corresponding to the 3 active genes) in order to represent the board state in the input Neural Network. Consequently, as shown in table 1, N_A is equal to 11 in the Network that represents the individual M. The initial weights of the Neural Network linked to individual I_i are generated randomly between -0.2 and +0.2 and the bias term is fixed as being 1. This process is repeated for every individual I_i, where $i \in \{1, 2, 3, ..., 50\}$.

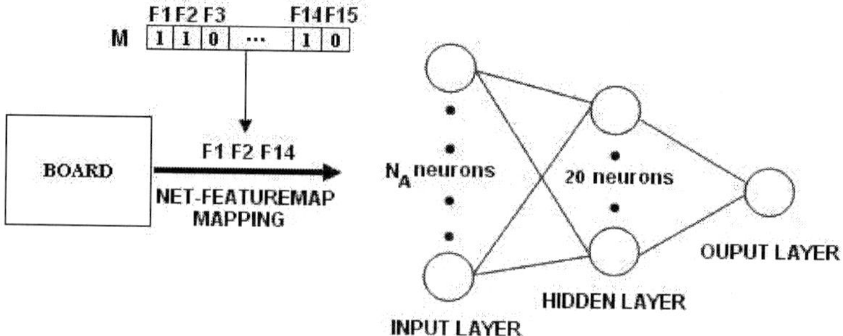

Fig. 3. Selection of active features of an individual M to define the NET-FEATUREMAP mapping which the attached neural network will use in the training.

After the generation of a Neural Network for each I_i, where $i \in \{1, 2, 3, ..., 50\}$, LS-Draughts starts the training phase of the 50 Neural Networks attached to the 50 generated individuals. In the training games, the Networks learn by reinforcement, as described in the section 2. The training of each Neural Network consists of a group of 4 sessions of 400 training games, where the Network plays a half of these 400 games as black player (black pieces) and the other 200 games as red player (red pieces). Such a strategy has the purpose of training the agent for diversified situations, once the features establish constraints that are related to the color of the pieces (for example: feature F_9 indicates the number of red pieces in the center of the game board).

Before starting the ten training session by self-play, a copy of the Neural Network net_i attached to the individual I_i is made, thus producing the clone Network $cnet_i$. Next, net_i and $cnet_i$ play the 200 games which correspond to the first session. During these games, only the weights of net_i are updated. At the end of the first session, two test-games are played to check whether the new Network net_i corresponding to the individual I_i (remember that the original weights of net_i were updated during the games) became better than its clone. If it is true, the $cnet_i$ weights are replaced by the net_i weights and the next session begins involving the players net_i and the modified $cnet_i$ (which are, in fact, equivalents). Otherwise, $cnet_i$ is not modified and the next session begins involving the players net_i and $cnet_i$. It is interesting to point out that in these test-games the strategy of changing the color corresponding to each player is adopted, that is, each network plays one game-test as red pieces and the other one as black pieces. This process is repeated until the end of the fourth session. Note that, in all these games, both player Networks use the same strategy to choose the best action described in the section 2.

Considering the possibility that it is not reasonable to guarantee that the best network obtained in the end of the fourth session is really the best one (in case it has been specialized to beat only its last clone during the training process), a small tournament is realized between the final network obtained and all its clones generated in the four sessions. Finally, the winner of this tournament is considered as being the best network corresponding to the individual I_i that has been trained.

The input parameters utilized to train an individual I_i are: a game board file containing the initial game board settings and the minimum score required to allow the replacement of the weights of a clone by the weights of the Network from which it originated; the learning rate α_1 corresponding to the first layer ($\alpha_1 = 1/N_A$); the learning rate α_2 corresponding to the hidden layer ($\alpha_2 = 1/20$); and, finally, the λ (see section 2) value ($\lambda = 0.1$).

5.4 Using endgame databases in the neural networks training

Considering the depth-first search algorithm, the time complexity is $O(b^m)$ for a state space with branching factor b and maximal depth m (Russell & Norvig, 2003). This means that the state space grows exponentially with depth. For large state spaces, a good solution for this problem consists of combining the depth-first search with retrograde analysis techniques based on information that is eventually stored in Databases (DBs). In other words, whenever the depth-firth search tries to evaluate a node N_1, before evaluating it, the algorithm will check whether the DB stores information about N_1. If it does, this piece of information will free the search algorithm from the burden of evaluating N_1. The state space of Draughts is approximately composed of $5*10^{20}$ distinct board states. Even considering recent computational resources, it is impracticable to traverse such a state space by adopting the depth-first search strategy. Therefore, the use of endgame DBs in Draughts strongly improves the general performance of player agents. In fact, even if the current board state S that is being evaluated is distant from endgame board states, some of its descendents may already be in the DB, what may limit the search depth to the level of these descendents. The great success and efficiency of Chinook, for example, is mainly based on its endgame DBs (Lake et al., 1994). Considering the large dimension of the Draughts state space, the construction of its endgame DBs is a hard task. In fact, in Chinook, the efforts to build the DBs have begun in 1989 and, since that year, almost continuously, several computers have worked exclusively to cope with this activity (Schaeffer et al., 2007). In 1992, there were more than 200 computers simultaneously working in the construction of these DBs.

Nowadays, they store information about all game board states that comprise 10 or less pieces. Particularly, for each of these states, the DBs indicate whether it corresponds to a win, a loss or a draw state. Considering the arguments above, in order to improve its search method, the extended LS-Draughts combines the minimax algorithm with a subset of endgame DBs of Chinook, which allows it to find the best movement spending much less time. During the search process, whenever a board state S is found in the DB, the extended LS-Draughts, instead of using its heuristic evaluation function to calculate the prediction corresponding to S, retrieves from the DB its exact value. In this case, the extended LS-Draughts does not need to evaluate any of the descendant nodes of S in the search tree, what correspond to a relevant simplification in the minimax search process. The combination between minimax and endgame DBs produces an efficient search method which simplifies the search tree and obtains more precise results, since the predictions of win, loss or draw retrieved from the DBs are exact (Schaeffer et al., 2002). The next subsections present how to construct endgame DBs and detail how the extended LS-Draughts uses them.

5.4.1. How to build endgame DBs

The previous section showed that retrograde analysis is an efficient tool to improve the search process. It has also been successfully applied in the construction of DBs for several games (Lake et al., 1994; Schaeffer et al., 2007; Gasser, 1990; Gasser, 1996; Romein & Bal, 2002; Romein & Bal, 2003). As the construction of DBs for games requires many resources of memory, execution time and input/output (I/O), the same techniques used to implement them can be also used to solve several problems in Mathematics and other related sciences where an optimal solution must be found in large state spaces. To construct DBs corresponding to Draughts board states with n pieces, the state space to be analysed will be a graph that may be a cyclic one (Diestel, 2000). The board states are represented in the nodes of the graph. The DBs for game boards composed of n pieces are calculated by means of an iterative algorithm which uses the results obtained for the DBs of $1, 2, ..., (n - 1)$ pieces previously calculated. Then, the DB for the board states with only 1 piece (terminal states) must be calculated first. Note that, in this case, according to the rules of Draughts, the player which owns the remaining piece is the winner. The algorithm must enumerate all the 120 possible terminal states and classify them as *win* or *loss*. Next, the DB corresponding to the board states with 2 pieces (6.972 distinct states) must be constructed based on the DB for the terminal nodes and so on. The following pseudo-code resumes the algorithm for constructing the DBs (Lake et al., 1994):

1.   Set all positions to *UNKNOWN*;
2.   Iterate and resolve all capture positions;
3.   Iterate and resolve non capture positions;
4.   Go to step 3 if any non-capture position was resolved;
5.   Set all remaining *UNKNOWN* to *DRAWs*.

First, every board state is classified as *unknown*. Next, the following considerations must be observed:

1.   Some board states may be classified as *win* or *loss*, according to the rules of the game. For example, a player without any piece or without any legal move available is in a *loss* terminal state;

2. All state nodes which have at least one child already classified in the DB as *win* will also be classified as *win* states;
3. All state nodes whose all children have already been classified as *loss* in the DB will also be classified as *loss* states;
4. Whenever there is no more information to modify the classification of any board state in the DB, all the board states that could not be classified (that is, which remained as *unknown* states), will be classified as *draw* states.

The execution of the first iterative module of the algorithm described above (step 2) takes into account one important rule of the Draughts game: a capture move must be executed before all the other ones. Therefore, the step 2 classifies all the capture states and postpones the classification of all the remaining ones for the next steps. Since a capture which has occurred in a state with n pieces takes to a board state with $(n - 1)$ pieces (or less), each capture state with n pieces is classified according to the BDs previously calculated. Near 50% of the states stored in the BDs correspond to capture states (Lake et al., 1994).

The execution of the second iterative module (step 3) tries to solve only the states S where no capture move is available. For each of them, all the legal moves are generated. Each legal move is executed and the values associated to the descendants of S are retrieved from the DB. The value *unknown* of S is only replaced when at least one of its children is classified as *win*, when all of them are classified as *loss*, or when all legal moves have already been solved. This procedure goes on until no board state can be solved anymore. At this point, all *unknown* states are classified as *draw* states.

In fact, there are two approaches to solve *unknown* states S:
1. **Forward Approach:** one generates the descendants of S and one tries to classify S according to them;
2. **Backward Approach:** one generates the ancestors of each solved state and one checks whether there is sufficient information to classify some of them.

The best choice depends on the proportion of solved and non solved nodes in a certain iteration process. In Chinook, it was performed a successfully combination of both approaches (Lake et al., 1994).

5.4.2. How LS-draughts uses endgame DBs

The endgame databases of Chinook that have been added to the extended LS-Draughts store information about victory, defeat or draw for:
1. All draughts board states with combination of 4 pieces x 4 pieces;
2. All draughts board states with combination of 4 pieces x 3 pieces;
3. All draughts board states involving 6 or less pieces on the board.

The main purpose of including the Chinook's endgame databases into the extended LS-Draughts is to try to answer two important questions:
1. Will the addition of the DBs into the original LS-Draughts contribute, in fact, for improving its general performance?
2. Will the use of the DBs help to decrease the rate of endgame loops in the original LS-Draughts? (This problem occurs in NeuroDraughts as well).

Next, it is presented the pseudo-code of the search algorithm of the extended LS-Draughts, followed by resuming of its main characteristics.

```
1. fun minimax (n:node, depth:int, bestmove:move) : float =
2.  if ((not isRoot(n)) and (isLookupBoard(n)))
```

```
3.          db_value := lookup_positions(n)
4.          if (db_value==1) and (n is a min node)
5.                  return -1.0
6.          if (db_value==1) and (n is a max node)
7.                  return +1.0
8.          if (db_value==2) and (n is a min node)
9.                  return +1.0
10.         if (db_value==2) and (n is a max node)
11.                 return -1.0
12.         if (db_value==3)
13.                 return 0.0
14.     if leaf(n) or depth=0 return evaluate(n)
    if n is a max node
        besteval := - infinity
        for each child of n
                v := minimax (child, d-1, bestmove)
                if v > besteval
                        besteval:= v
                        thebest := bestmove
                        bestmove := thebest
        return besteval
    if n is a min node
        besteval := + infinity
        for each child of n
                v := minimax (child, d-1, bestmove)
                if v < besteval
                        besteval:= v
                        thebest := bestmove
                        bestmove := thebest
        return besteval
```

Line 2: The function *isLookupBoard()* is used to check whether the current board state n satisfies the constraints that allow the access to the DBs (that is, it checks whether n owns the adequate quantity of pieces and respects the capture constraints). The function *not isRoot()* is used to guarantee that the states n to be consulted in the DB have, at least, one ancestor in the search graph;

Line 3: the function *lookup_positions()* consults the DB in order to try to retrieve the prediction corresponding to n;

Line 4: The result *db_value = 1* indicates that n corresponds to a victory for the next player to execute a move and, therefore, corresponds to a defeat for its opponent (the parent of n). Case n is a *min* node, its parent is a *max* node. Therefore, the value *-1.0* must be returned in **line 5** in order to guarantee that the parent of n only chooses this move in case there is no other choice for it;

Line 6: The result *db_value = 1* indicates that n corresponds to a victory for the next player to execute a move and, therefore, corresponds to a defeat for its opponent (the parent of n). Case n is a *max* node, its parent is a *min* node. Therefore, the value *+1.0* must be returned in **line 7** as an evident prevision that the parent of n, normally, will not choose that move;

Line 8: The result *db_value* = 2 indicates that n corresponds to a defeat for the next player to execute a move and, therefore, corresponds to a victory for its opponent (the parent of n). Case n is a *min* node, its parent is a *max* node. Therefore, the value *+1.0* must be returned in **line 9** in order to guarantee that the parent of n chooses this move whenever it is available;

Line 10: The result *db_value* = 2 indicates that n corresponds to a defeat for the next player to execute a move and, therefore, corresponds to a victory for its opponent (the parent of n). Case n is a *max* node, its parent is a *min* node. Therefore, the value *-1.0* must be returned in **line 11** as an evident prevision that the parent of n, normally, will choose that move;

Line 12: The result *db_value* = 3 indicates that n corresponds to a draw for the next player to execute a move and, therefore, corresponds to a draw for its opponent (the parent of n). In this case, the value *0.0* is returned in **line 13**, independently of the *min* or *max* situation of n;

Line 14: From this line, the classical minimax algorithm (see the Minimax Search Module presented in the beginning of the section 5) is presented. Note that it will be executed only when the current state n is not available in the DB.

5.5 Fitness calculus

In the tournament organized to calculate the fitness of the individuals in a given generation (cited in the subsection 5.1), each individual I_i plays 10 games against the remaining individual of that generation. The results of this tournament are used to calculate the I_i fitness in the following way: 2 points for each victory, 1 point for each draw and 0 point for each defeat.

6. Endgame loop problem in the original LS-Draughts

The original LS-Draughts was executed for 30 generations with a population of 50 individuals, as presented in (Neto & Julia, 2007). For each generation, the best individual was compared with the Mark Lynch's NeuroDraughts player, in a tournament composed of 7 games, in order to evaluate its performance in relation to the latter one. The best individuals of LS-Draughts that managed to beat NeuroDraughts were the best individual I_{B-9} of the 9th generation and the best individual I_{B-25} of the 25th generation. The scores of both individuals were: 1 victory and 6 draws for I_{B-9}; 2 victories and 5 draws for I_{B-25}. Despite of the good performance of I_{B-9} and I_{B-25} against NeuroDraughts, both individuals of LS-Draughts presented endgame loop problems. As shown in the section 4, by analysing the 5 draws of I_{B-25} against NeuroDraughts, one can conclude that, in 2 of them, the LS-Draughts could have won , since I_{B-25} counted on 3 checkers and 1 simple piece on the endgame board and NeuroDraughts only counted on 1 checker. Figure 4 shows this example of endgame loop problem which affected the individual I_{B-25} : from the game board position of the figure (4.a) , resultant of the NeuroDraughts' 43rd move, the game got up to the board position of the figure (4.b) after the 44th move of NeuroDraughts. Next, the game got back to the board position indicated in figure (4.a), as a result of the 45th move of NeuroDraughts. Finally, it occurred an alternate infinite loop between these two game board positions, that is, figure (4.a) and figure (4.b), respectively.

The same problem affected the individual I_{B-9}. Analysing the 6 draws of its tournament against NeuroDraughts, 3 of them it would easily have won if I_{B-9} was able to detect endgame loops. For example, in one of these 3 games, even though I_{B-9} counted on 2 checkers and 3 simple pieces, it was not able to beat NeuroDraughts, which only counted on 1 checker and 1 simple piece.

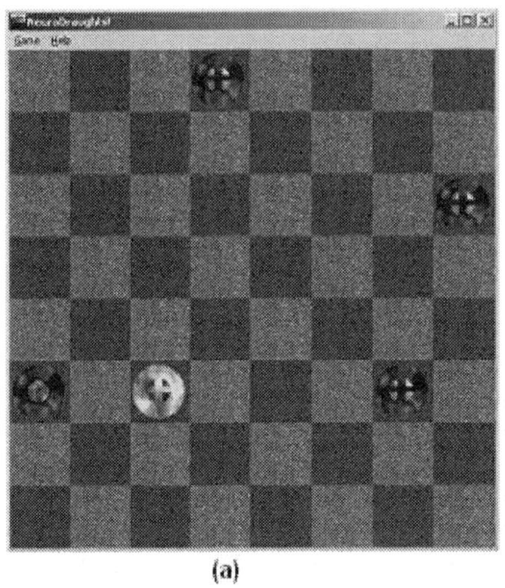

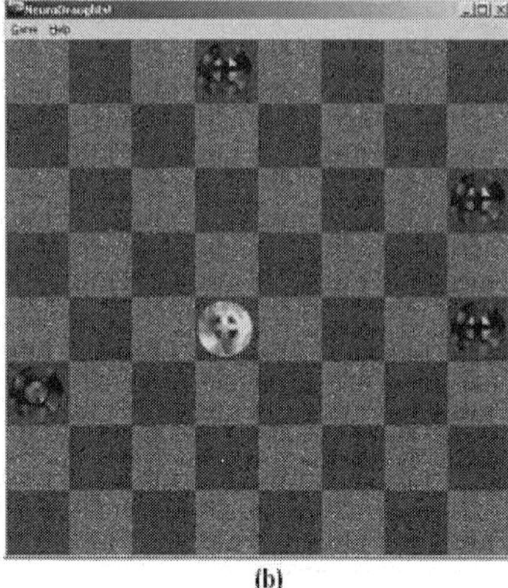

(a)   (b)

Fig. 4. Game between LS-Draughts' 25th best individual (black player) and the NeuroDraughts (red player). a) Position of the draughts game board state after the 43rd red player move; b) Position of the draughts game board state after the 44th red player move.

For many other individuals of the original LS-Draughts, the endgame loop problem came out.

7. Experimental results

The new version of LS-Draughts was executed for 50 generations with a population of 50 individuals. Differently from the original version presented in (Neto & Julia, 2007), the individuals here were trained using an endgame database module that allows to anticipate the result of the game (victory, defeat or draw) for draughts board states with, at most, 8 pieces.

As cited before, the main purpose of including the endgame databases of Chinook into the LS-Draughts was to try to answer two important questions:

1. Will the addition of the endgame databases into the original LS-Draughts contribute, in fact, for improving its general performance?
2. Will the use of the endgame databases help to decrease the rate of endgame loops in the original LS-Draughts? This problem was found by Neto and Julia in the players NeuroDraughts and original LS-Draughts (Neto & Julia, 2007).

In order to answer the first question, a tournament was executed between the available player of NeuroDraughts ($PLAYER\_1$), the best individual of the 50th generation of the original LS-Draughts ($PLAYER\_2$) and the best individual of the 50th generation of the extended version of LS-Draughts proposed here ($PLAYER\_3$):

1. FIRST MATCH: *PLAYER_1* x *PLAYER_2*
   - Number of victories of *PLAYER_2* : 5;
   - Number of defeats of *PLAYER_2* : 1;
   - Number of draws: 8 (6 real draws and 2 draws with endgame loop problem);
2. SECOND MATCH: *PLAYER_1* x *PLAYER_3*
   - Number of victories of *PLAYER_3* : 6;
   - Number of defeats of *PLAYER_3* : 0;
   - Number of draws: 8 (5 real draws and 3 draws with endgame loop problem);
3. THIRD MATCH: *PLAYER_2* x *PLAYER_3*
   - Number of victories of *PLAYER_3* : 3;
   - Number of defeats of *PLAYER_3* : 1;
   - Number of draws: 10 (3 real draws and 7 draws with endgame loop problem);

Furthermore, the rates of endgame loops occurred during the training process of *PLAYER_1*, *PLAYER_2* e *PLAYER_3* were also estimated in order to answer the second question raised above. However, to get these rates, the three players needed to be trained again, using the same training parameters, initial configuration and search, as follow:

- The player NeuroDraughts was trained using the set of features defined by Lynch in (Lynch, 1997; Lynch & Griffith, 1997), an Artificial Neural Network whose weights were generated randomly, search algorithm with depth 4 and a training strategy with 10 sessions of 200 training games. During the 2000 games, 1.045 games were finished with endgame loop problem;
- The best individual of the 50th generation of the original LS-Draughts also was trained using the following: an Artificial Neural Network whose weights were generated randomly, search algorithm with depth 4 and a training strategy with 10 sessions of 200 training games. During the 2000 games, 759 games were finished with endgame loop problem;
- Finally, the best individual of the 50th generation of the extended version of LS-Draughts was trained using an Artificial Neural Network whose weights were generated randomly, search algorithm with depth 4 and a training strategy with 10 sessions of 200 training games. During the 2000 games, 172 games were finished with endgame loop problem;

Figure 5 shows the rates of endgame loops obtained by three players during their 2000 training games. Note that que the extended version of LS-Draughts produced a rate of endgame loops corresponding to 16.46% of the one produced by NeuroDraughts, and cooresponding to 22.66% of the rate produced by the original LS-Draughts.

Games with endgame loop problems		
NeuroDraughts	**Original LS-Draughts**	**Extended LS-Draughts**
1045	759	172
100%	72.63%	16.46%
137.68%	100%	22.66%
607.56%	441.28%	100%

Fig. 5. Rates of endgame loops during 2000 training games

Theses results show that endgame DBs improved significantly the original LS-Draughts, introducing efficency and accuracy in its general performance and reducing, therefore, the rate of endgame loops.

8. Conclusion

This paper presented an extended version of LS-Draughts – a Learning System which, using endgame databases, GAs, TD methods, minimax algorithm and self-play with cloning strategy, generates a draught player much better than the original LS-Draughts. The results obtained show that:

1. The extended LS-Draughts was the best player of the tournament, with 6 victories, 8 draws and 0 defeat against NeuroDraughts and 3 victories, 10 draws and 1 defeat against the original LS-Draughts;
2. In relation to the rate of endgame loops, the extended LS-Draughts player decreased from 83% the rate of endgame loops produced by NeuroDraughts player and from 77% the rate of endgame loops produced by the original LS-Draughts player.

Therefore, the results confirm the improvement that was obtained in the original LS-Draughts with the insertion of the endgame databases module.

Nevertheless, the introduction of a search module more efficient than minimax algorithm can improve much more the performance of the extended version of LS-Draughts. That is why, as future work, the authors intend to substitute the alpha-beta algorithm combined with transposition table for the minimax algorithm of LS-Draughts.

9. References

Baxter, J.; Tridgell, A. & Weaver, L. (1998). Knightcap: a chess program that learns by combining TD(λ) with game-tree search, *Proceedings of the 15th International Conference on Machine Learning*, pp. 28-36

Darwen, P. J. (2001). Why co-evolution beats temporal difference learning at backgammon for a linear architecture, but not a non-linear architecture, *Proceedings of the 2001 Congress on Evolutionary Computation CEC2001*, IEEE Press, pp. 1003-1010

Diestel, R. (2000). *Graph Theory*, Springer-Verlag New York, Inc.

Epstein, S. (2001). *Learning to play expertly: a tutorial on hoyle*, Machines That Learn to Play Games, Nova Science Publishers, Huntington

Fogel, D. B. & Chellapilla, K. (2002). Verifying anaconda's expert rating by competing against Chinook: experiments in co-evolving a neural checkers player, *Neurocomputing*, Vol. 42, No. 1-4, pp. 69-86

Fogel, D. B.; Hays, T. J.; Hahn, S. L. & Quon, J. (2004). A self-learning evolutionary chess program, *Proceedings of the IEEE*, Vol. 92, No. 12, pp. 1947-1954

Gasser, R. (1990). *Applying Retrograde Analysis to Nine Men's Morris*. Available: http://citeseer.ist.psu.edu/gasser90applying.html

Gasser, R. (1996). Solving nine men's morris, *Computational Intelligence*, Vol. 12, pp. 24-41

Haykin, S. (1998). *Neural Networks: A Comprehensive Foundation*, Second Edition, Prentice Hall

Holland, J. H. (1992). *Adaptation in natural and artificial systems*, Second Edition, Cambridge, MA, USA, MIT Press

Lake, R.; Schaeffer, J.; LU, P (1994). *Solving Large Retrograde Analysis Problems Using a Network of Workstations,* Advances in Computer Chess VII, Maastricht, Netherlands, pp. 135-162

Leuski, A. (1995). *Learning of position evaluation in the game of Othello.* Available: http://people.ict.usc.edu/~leuski/publications

Levinson, R. & Weber, R. (2002). Chess neighborhoods, function combination, and reinforcement learning, *Revised Papers from the Second International Conference on Computers and Games,* Springer-Verlag, London, UK, pp. 133-150

Lynch, M. & Griffith, N. (1997). NeuroDraughts: the role of representation, search, training regime and architecture in a td draughts player, *Proceedings of Eighth Ireland Conference on Artificial Intelligence,* pp. 64-72. Available: http://iamlynch.com/nd.html

Lynch, M. (1997). *NeuroDraughts: An application of temporal difference learning to draughts.* Available: http://iamlynch.com/nd.html

Mitchell, M. & Taylor, C. E. (1999). Evolutionary Computation: An Overview, *In Annual Review of Ecology and Systematics,* Vol. 30, pp. 593-616

Neto, H. C. & Julia, R. M. S. (2007). LS-DRAUGHTS – A Draughts Learning System based on Genetic Algorithms, Neural Network and Temporal Differences, *Proceedings of 2007 IEEE Congress on Evolutionary Computation (CEC 2007),* Singapore, ISBN: 1424413400, pp. 2523-2529

Romein, J. & Bal, H. (2002). *Awari is Solved.* Available: http://citeseer.ist.psu.edu/romein02awari.html

Romein, J. & Bal, H. (2003). *Solving the Game of Awari using Parallel Retrograde Analysis.* Available: http://citeseer.ist.psu.edu/romein03solving.html

Russell, S. & Norvig, P. (2003). *Artificial Intelligence: A Modern Approach,* Prentice Hall, Ed. 2

Samuel, A. L. (1959). Some studies in machine learning using the game of checkers. *IBM Journal of Research and Development,* Vol. 3, No. 3, pp. 211-229

Schraudolph, N. N. ; Dayan, P. & Sejnowski, T. J. (2001). Learning to evaluate go positions via temporal difference methods, Computational Intelligence in Games Studies in Fuzziness and Soft Computing, Spring Verlag, Vol. 62

Schaeffer, J. ; Lake, R. ; Lu, P. & Bryant, M. (1996). CHINOOK: The world man-machine checkers champion, *AI Magazine,* Vol. 17, No. 1, pp. 21-29

Schaeffer, J. (1997). *One Jump Ahead: Challenging Human Supremacy in Checkers,* Springer-Verlag New York Inc

Schaeffer, J. ; Hlynka, M. & Jussila, V. (2001). Temporal difference learning applied to a high performance game-playing program, *Proceedings of the International Joint Conference on Artificial Intelligence (IJCAI),* pp. 529-534

Schaeffer, J. (2002). *Applying the Experience of Building a High Performance Search Engine for One Domain to Another*

Schaeffer, J. et al. (2007). Checkers is solved, *Science,* Vol. 317, No. 5844, pp. 1518-1522

Sutton, R. S. (1988). Learning to predict by the methods of temporal differences, *Machine Learning,* Vol. 3, No. 1, pp. 9-44

Tesauro, G. J. (1992). Practical issues in temporal difference learning, *Machine Learning,* Vol. 8, pp. 257-277

Tesauro, G. J. (1994). TD-Gammon, a self-teaching backgammon program, achieves master-level play, *Neural Computation*, Vol. 6, No. 2, pp. 215-219

Tesauro, G. J. (1995). Temporal difference learning and td-gammon, *Communications of the ACM*, Vol. 38, No. 3, pp. 58-68

Thrun, S. (1995). Learning to play the game of chess. *Advances in Neural Information Processing Systems 7*, The MIT Press, pp. 1069-1076

20

Blur Identification for Content Aware Processing in Images

Jérôme Da Rugna and Hubert Konik
Laboratoire LIGIV, Université Jean Monnet
France

1. Introduction

In many types of photographies, it is desirable to have the entire image sharp. And in the opposite occurrence, some techniques try to deblur them. Classically, the blur is modeled in image processing as $g(x) = (h * f)(x)$. With x a pixel, g the degraded image, f the true image, $*$ the operator of convolution and h the point spread function, noted PSF (Tao et al., 2005). The process of the image restoration is estimating the true image from the observed image (Savakis & Trussel, 1993). Many estimators like inverse filters or Wiener filters require a priori knowledge of the PSF. Nevertheless, PSF estimator gives more or less only information of smooth around a point but none information inside a specific zone. Another technique to extract blur information proposes to evaluate depth in image using in particular depth from focus or depth from defocus approaches (Ma & Staunton, 2005). We cannot confront these approaches to our problem as they require a bunch of images of the same scene obtained by combining different optic properties of the camera...where we consider only one image in this study.

Fig. 1. Illustrations: the sharp zones are the objects of interest

In fact, this paper addresses the problem of images where the blur is intrinsically on the contrary disable and more precisely perceptually powerful. Considering, for example classical holiday photographies or portraits or other any kinds of images as presented in figure 1, the blurry regions generally represent the background, otherwise speaking regions of no interest for the viewer. On the contrary, the sharp area can normally be seen as the interest part of the global image, at least for the one who took the picture... If a photographer decides to focus only on some objects in an image, he certainly considers that the rest of the image is not of the prime interest.

So our goal is to develop a computational approach that is broadly useful in order to achieve a detection of such sharp and blur zones in diversified images as illustrated in figure 2. Let notice some applications directly concerned: contrast enhancement (Chung et al., 2008) where different treatments permit to keep flat colors on blurry regions while increasing lively colors on sharp ones; assistance for visually impaired patients suffering notably from AMD (Bordier et al., 2005); auto-zooming to adapt the centering to the contents of the image (Taghva et al., 2003).

From now on let indicate that our approach will be decomposed first in a segmentation step and secondly in an identification step. In fact, an isolated pixel cannot be labeled as blur of sharp without taking into account its neighborhood. So, to identify blurry zones in an image, we assume that it requires a region approach directly based on human blur perception that does not consider point properties but zone aspects (Georgeson & Hammett, 2002).

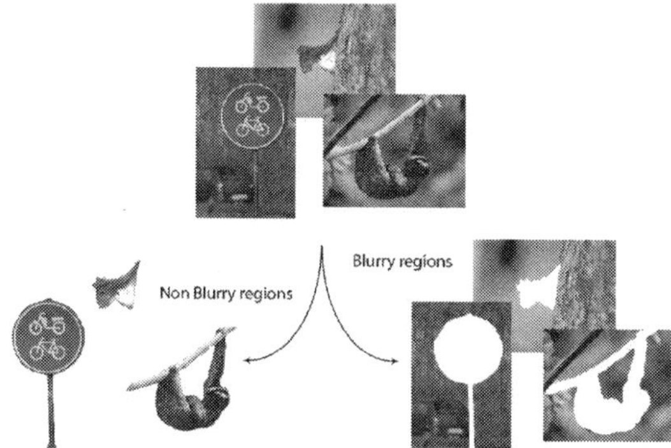

Fig. 2. Our goal: extracting blurry and sharp regions

This chapter is organized as follows: the outline of the identification process is briefly described. In the following section, the different steps are introduced. Section 3 presents the segmentation process; the evaluation of the ability of different approaches to well discriminate blurry and sharp zones and finally details the retained descriptors based on filtering and edge detection algorithms. Section 4 discusses about the learning step and compares several classifiers based on the previous descriptors in order to automatically classify each region. Section 5 illustrates the efficiency of the identification while putting the finger on the deficiencies of the mono-segmentation approach. The aim of the section 6 is to introduce a scheme turning to good account by combining classifiers built on several segmentations. The final section presents conclusion and future works.

2. Overall process

Let first specify the image domain covered by this work. Indeed, several kinds of blur are possible in an image, issue from optical lenses, motion or any image modification with specific software. In our research we consider only optical blur, id est the classical still image where the object of attention is salient. Finally, images we deal with may be described as follows:

- Made by a camera and gone through few image processing modifications
- Containing sharp zone and maybe a blurry one (camera focus was made on a specific zone of the scene). We do not restrict the position of the focused zone and this zone may be composed of several not connected areas
- Not containing any other kind of blur

In this study we then present a scheme that follows a region approach, where each of them is classified as blur or sharp. Regions are defined by a segmentation step, which is by definition a partition of an image into homogeneous regions according to a specific predicate. First, it supposes a ground truth dataset in order to qualify the classifier and then to measure the accuracy of such an approach.

Let first describe the training task presented in figure 3 where a training set of images is considered. For each image, we extract through an expertise 3 different zones as illustrated in figure 4: the blurry one called "B", the sharp one called "S" and a third one called "U" for undefined. This last zone is in fact the ambiguity one: it is clearly difficult to decide if it is blurry or not.

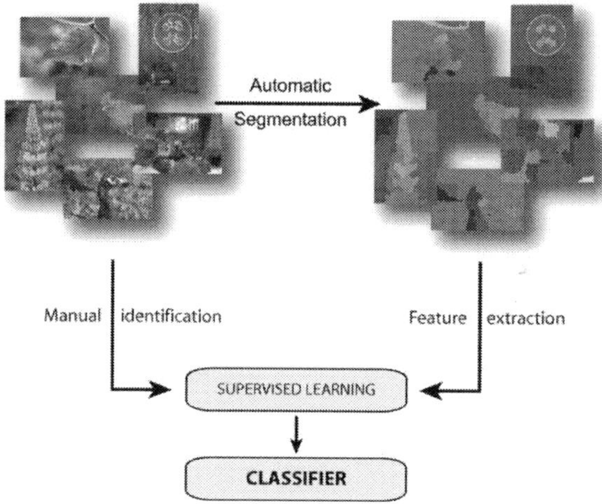

Fig. 3. Overall process of the classifier training

This identification on the training set is of course subjective as it was made using human judgment, in our case by image analysis specialists and amateur photographs. We may note that this decomposition is made without considering any segmentation: the expert has to draw using a precise pencil the three different zones.

Thus, considering the segmented image and its manual annotation, it is possible to specify for each region its label. A region is then set as blur if it is mainly recovered by the blur area. A numerical vector of region descriptors and a label are then obtained for each region. These data are the training data used during the supervised learning task, described in a next section.

Our training set is composed by 100 images containing, in average, around 63% of blur, 33% of sharp and 4% of undefined zones.

Fig. 4. Illustrations of the used labels to qualify the image (white for blur, black for sharp and gray for undefined)

Once the classifier computed, the identification task is divided in different steps, as illustrated in figure 5:
1.   Segmentation of the image.
2.   Computation, for each region, of numerical features.
3.   Decision, for each region, of label using the classifier.

Fig. 5. The identification process

We have described outlines of the blur identification; we now present the different steps, beginning by the segmentation task before focusing on the descriptors based principally on relative variations after filtering and edge density.

3. Image processing

3.1 Segmentation

The segmentation, when talking about image processing and computer vision, is one of its fundamental problems. Primary classified into four types: thresholding, boundary-based, region-based and hybrid techniques (Lukac & Plataniotis, 2007, Pal & Pal, 1993), published low level techniques are innumerable. Unfortunately, segmentation is still nowadays a very challenging task as no effective method has been developed so far. The best one will be, first of all, able to discriminate regions on the blur properties: segmented regions have to recover only one kind of label: S or B. We are also expecting the segmentation to get regions not too small– no decision can be taken on some few pixels – and to avoid agglomerate too much different zones (several color and/or textures) in the same region, which may produce numerical biased descriptors.

To that effect, we first have chosen four distinct classical methods covering a large panel of existing approaches:

- First, the pyramid model that allows simulating human focus at different scales. The weighted linked pyramid would be able to discriminate the blur property as this top-down link algorithm is based on homogeneity and dispersion criteria (Marfil et al., 2004).

- Secondly, two different algorithms: K-Means based on a split of the 3D color space (Da Rugna & Konik, 2008) using color clustering, and an histogram approach (Cheng, 2000) using homogeneity clustering on color image. In this last one uniform regions are identified via multilevel thresholding on a homogeneity histogram in preserving both local and global information. By segmenting images using properties homogeneity or color we expect that different hues and textures will not be merged.

- Finally, Graph-Based image segmentation (Felzenszwalb & Huttenlocher, 2004) that is chosen based on its ability to preserve details in low-variability image regions while ignoring detail in high-variability regions. This method applies a predicate for measuring the evidence for a boundary between two regionsn taking into account the visually difference between sharp and blur zones.

Our aim here is not to enter in a new segmentation debate but to concentrate our efforts on choosing the best segmentation algorithm. To evaluate segmentation process, the literature is plenty of segmentation evaluations (Zhang, 1997, Borsotti et al., 1998, Correia & Pereira, 2002) but it is difficult to adapt any protocol to our case: to get regions non biased. Thus, to evaluate if the algorithm merges too much blurry and sharp zone, it seems logical to use a measure of the way the blur and the sharp are mixed together. We do not integrate in this measure the undefined zones as merging blur and undefined or sharp and undefined is not, a priori, a bias.

Given segmentation $X = \bigcup_{j=1}^{m} X_j$ and $X = (B, S, U)$ the annotation of the image X and $\|A\|$ the surface in pixels of A let introduce for each region a merging measure δ_j:

$$\delta_j = \begin{cases} 1 \; if \; \dfrac{\min(\|X_j \cap B\|, \|X_j \cap S\|)}{\|X_j\|} \geq \alpha \\ 0 \; else \end{cases} \tag{1}$$

α is a threshold[1] that enables a region to be considered mixed only if the less represented label is at least present at a ratio of α. Then, the "mix coefficient" of one image is computed:

$$mix = \frac{\sum_{j=1}^{m} \delta_j}{m} \tag{2}$$

The mix value for one image expresses the ratio of regions that are potentially biased, in fact the ratio of n-tuple that would be able to disturb the supervised learning.

Also, we evaluate the confusion matrix C defined as follow:

---

[1] Set to 0.02 in this study

$$C^j_{(\Lambda,\Theta)} = \begin{cases} 0 \ if \ (\|X_j \cap \Lambda\| < \|X_j \cap \Theta\|) \\ \|X_j \cap \Theta\| \ else \end{cases} \qquad (3)$$

Λ and Θ take values in set {B,S}. $C^j_{(\Lambda,\Theta)}$ is 0 if the region X_j is mainly composed by pixels of class Θ and represents the number of pixels Θ otherwise. Then, the matrix C is defined by:

$$C_{(\Lambda,\Theta)} = \frac{\sum_{j=1}^{m} C^j_{(\Lambda,\Theta)}}{\|X\|} \qquad (4)$$

For example, $C_{(B,S)}$ represents the ratio of pixels of class S that are mixed with a region mainly composed by pixels of class B. Consequently, the value $C_{(B,S)} + C_{(S,B)}$ is the minimum error using the considered segmentation that an identification task may do.

Tables 1 and 2 present the mix coefficient and the confusion matrices for each segmentation algorithm. The mix coefficient varies from 0.07 for the K-Means method to 0.24 for the Graph-Based one. K-Means and Pyramid are, for this measure, the best algorithms as they produce less biased regions. This analysis is consolidated by the results of confusion matrices, in particular for the pyramidal method where less than 2% of pixels are confused in another class. The Graph-Based method still remains the less efficient one with about 18% of confused pixels. To explain these results, let notice that the Graph-Based method tends to create large regions on the contrary of K-Means one. K-Means gets the best mix coefficient but suffers from a lack considering the confusion matrix: in fact as it lies on only color homogeneity, some color similar regions are merged even if an edge separates them. It implies that some regions are extremely biased, a not present behavior concerning the pyramidal approach. Considering these two tables, it appears that pyramid segmentation is the most appropriate method to our goal, as a good compromise between the mix coefficient and confusion matrices.

Method	mix coefficient
Graph-Based	0.24
K-Means	0.07
Pyramid	0.11
Histogram	0.22

Table 1. Mix coefficient of segmentation algorithms. Parameters are optimized to get the best results, id est the lower values

Graph-Based	B	S
B	0,529	0.108
S	0.069	0.283

K-Means	B	S
B	0,600	0.037
S	0.0042	0.348

Pyramid	B	S
B	0.628	0.0097
S	0.0079	0.345

Histogram	B	S
B	0.604	0.033
S	0.0145	0.338

Table 2. Confusion Matrices of segmentation algorithms. Parameters are optimized to get the best results, id est the lower values

3.2 Region descriptors

We have to exhibit some descriptors sufficiently robust to discriminate blur and sharp regions. Among all literature texture descriptors we focused on those that seem to be more adapted to characterize local dispersions. In fact, these assumptions are used: blurry regions are more invariant according to low pass filtering; blurry regions contain fewer edges than sharp ones; pixels are more probably surrounded by similar ones in blurry regions; there are more high frequencies in sharp regions. We propose so to extract numerical features by globalizing at the region level, using average and standard deviation, local information and neighbourhood saliency around each pixel.

More precisely, exploiting the results of a previous study (Da Rugna & Konik, 2006), the following descriptors are computed:

- Evolution of statistical moments after different low-pass filterings
- Evolution of statistical moments after an anisotropic diffusion ((Sapiro & Ringach, 1996)
- Classical parameters using run-length matrices (Galloway, 1974)
- Edge density (Canny, 1986)
- Frequency parameters issued from Gabor wavelets (Song Goh et al., 2007)

4. Learning step

Given this set of observations we need at this point to introduce classifiers able to automatically discriminate the region labels. Classification by examples is one of the main machine learning problems (Mitchell, 1997). It is well known, there is no general rule to guide how to choose learner for a specific task. Intuitively we have selected 4 algorithms able to answer the request of blur identification:

- Decision Tree: C4.5 (Quinlan, 1996)
  This well-known classifier is easily converted to a set of production rules and does not have a priori assumptions about the nature of the data. This choice, and in particular the choice of C4.5, is so guided by the effective compromise between efficient results, rules size and learning time cost.
- Artificial Neural Network: Multi Layer Perceptron (Duda et al., 2001)
  We apply a classical back-propagation neural network to classify instances. This kind of classifier is often great at prediction and classification and, if it is slow compared to other learning algorithms, it is reasonable for a neural network.
- Support Vector Machines: Sequential Minimal Optimization (Keerthi et al., 2001)
  Support vector machines gave decisive results in numerous domains and for numerous studies: it is natural to select this linear classifier to reach our identification goal. We chose a SMO version using radial basis function.
- Decision Rules : Fast Effective Rule Induction (Cohen, 1995)
  To propose a very fast algorithm of learning, we implement a rule learner method. This method, an optimized version of IREP, repeat incremental pruning to produce error reduction.

To evaluate the ability of this identification in our context, it is necessary to introduce the classical measures of effectiveness. Let N the number of elements, f_i the classifier decision class and a_i the ground-truth class of i-th element. We will consider sharp label as the true instance and blur as the false. The overall efficiency, the precision and the recall of the classifier are then defined as $A = Accuracy = \frac{|\{i; f_i = a_i\}|}{N}$, $P = Precision = \frac{|\{i; f_i = a_i \,\&\, a_i = true\}|}{|\{i; f_i = true\}|}$

and $R = Recall = \frac{|\{i;f_i=a_i\ \&\ a_i=true\}|}{|\{i;a_i=true\}|}$. Thus, to estimate the final efficiency of our process, it requires an estimation method with low bias, low variance and handling over-fitting. Between well-known accuracy estimation methods, we choose cross-validation (Kohavi, 1995) as it is intelligible, simple to implement and efficient. We have selected a 10-Fold cross-validation.

Decision Tree	A	P	R
Graph-Based	0.782	0.843	0.845
K-Means	0.791	0.857	0.892
Pyramid	0.794	0.843	0.886
Histogram	0.823	0.852	0.870

Artificial Neural Network	A	P	R
Graph-Based	0.804	0.882	0.728
K-Means	0.829	0.835	0.966
Pyramid	0.824	0.848	0.922
Histogram	0.839	0.840	0.906

Decision Rules	A	P	R
Graph-Based	0.841	0.856	0.647
K-Means	0.816	0.827	0.958
Pyramid	0.814	0.829	0.926
Histogram	0.818	0.805	0.897

Support Vector Machines	A	P	R
Graph-Based	0.860	0.927	0.616
K-Means	0.819	0.831	0.957
Pyramid	0.814	0.842	0.914
Histogram	0.823	0.850	0.882

Table 3. Accuracy (A), Precision (P) and Recall (R) on segmentations using different classifiers

The table 3 presents the accuracy, precision and recall for each segmentation algorithm using previously introduced classifiers. Considering the segmentation methods, the main observation is the slight difference between the methods. Moreover, these results show similar efficiency for every classifier too, about 80-90 percent for accuracy, precision and recall. Despite these hopeful results it is necessary to affine the classifier behavior analysis, in particular to judge the influence of each kind of region label. To that effect, let present this study on tables 4-7, where the confusion matrices are given for each classifier and each segmentation method.

Graph-Based	S	B	U	M
S	14.41	1.51	0.87	0.47
B	2.34	62.31	1.89	3.01
U	1.02	2.54	1.56	0.21
M	0.89	6.58	0.70	0.01

K-Means	S	B	U	M
S	14.47	2.15	0.37	0.00
B	2.22	64.29	2.01	3.57
U	0.47	2.89	0.77	0.00
M	0.68	5.72	0.39	0.00

Pyramid	S	B	U	M
S	22.28	3.45	0.49	0.68
B	3.61	56.06	1.33	2.26
U	0.69	2.47	0.35	0.17
M	0.87	4.30	0.26	0.73

Histogram	S	B	U	M
S	35.89	2.86	0.49	0.87
B	3.04	43.86	0.98	2.55
U	0.57	1.34	0.70	0.20
M	1.09	3.43	0.24	1.88

Table 4. Confusion matrices obtained with the decision tree classifier

Graph-Based	S	B	U	M
S	18.95	3.78	0.00	1.18
B	0.83	69.04	0.15	1.52
U	0.03	0.10	0.12	0.23
M	0.78	0.11	2.44	0.84

K-Means	S	B	U	M
S	14.51	2.62	0.01	0.04
B	2.05	68.00	0.00	0.33
U	0.41	3.95	0.02	0.02
M	0.72	6.90	0.00	0.42

Pyramid	S	B	U	M
S	24.08	2.81	0.00	0.01
B	4.90	58.35	0.00	0.01
U	0.90	2.81	0.00	0.00
M	1.23	4.92	0.00	0.01

Histogram	S	B	U	M
S	37.23	2.57	0.09	0.22
B	4.08	45.69	0.03	0.64
U	0.73	1.93	0.11	0.04
M	1.57	4.24	0.02	0.82

Table 5. Confusion matrices obtained with the neural network classifier

Graph-Based	S	B	U	M
S	16.52	3.07	0.20	0.00
B	1.20	69.48	0.03	0.11
U	0.56	3.61	0.00	0.56
M	0.40	5.00	0.00	0.01

K-Means	S	B	U	M
S	14.15	2.99	0.02	0.03
B	2.80	67.45	0.02	0.11
U	0.54	3.83	0.02	0.01
M	0.57	7.25	0.00	0.01

Pyramid	S	B	U	M
S	22.78	4.11	0.00	0.00
B	4.64	58.61	0.00	0.01
U	0.81	2.87	0.00	0.00
M	1.04	5.12	0.00	0.00

Histogram	S	B	U	M
S	36.49	3.59	0.00	0.03
B	4.97	45.26	0.00	0.20
U	0.99	1.80	0.00	0.03
M	1.03	5.57	0.00	0.05

Table 6. Confusion matrices obtained with the decision rules classifier

Graph-Based	S	B	U	M
S	36.20	2.75	0.47	0.69
B	2.98	41.02	0.83	5.61
U	0.68	1.24	0.60	2.81
M	1.11	3.41	0.17	1.95

K-Means	S	B	U	M
S	14.52	2.65	0.00	0.00
B	3.03	67.35	0.00	0.00
U	0.56	3.84	0.00	0.00
M	0.88	7.17	0.00	0.00

Pyramid	S	B	U	M
S	23.62	3.28	0.00	0.00
B	5.47	57.79	0.00	0.00
U	0.90	2.77	0.00	0.00
M	1.38	4.78	0.00	0.00

Histogram	S	B	U	M
S	35.34	2.41	0.00	0.01
B	6.25	46.98	0.00	0.01
U	1.05	1.53	0.00	0.00
M	2.04	4.36	0.00	0.03

Table 7. Confusion matrices obtained with the support vector machines classifier

The results show first the lack of the classifier to learn the labels M and U, going sometimes as far as no learning at all these ones. And this behavior is similar whatever the segmentation method used. Let remind that the label M corresponds to the mixed regions, that is to say regions where several labels are included. As the characteristics are biased by definition, it seems logical that the classifier is not able to play its rule. Concerning the regions of label U, the regions where the expert is uncertain often represent the gradients between sharp and blurry zones. Undefined regions are few represented and descriptors are, a posteriori, unable to correctly characterize this kind of regions.

Considering the high recall (computed on S label) and the large majority of the blur regions in our test database, these two labels U and M are more often confused with B one instead of S one, as the superior values in the confusion matrices show it. All these results permit us to no more considering these two perturbing labels in the next results.

Table 8 presents performance measures for each classifier using the four segmentation algorithms. Obviously, the results are improved without taking into account undefined and mixed labels. Whatever the segmentation method used, the accuracy, the precision and the recall are always bigger than 0.90, except the recall for the couple SVM and Histogram. All the couples Segmentation-Classifiers rest nevertheless efficient enough to conclude the learning robustness. More precisely the Graph-Based method gives always the best results, just in front of respectively the K-Means, the histogram and finally the pyramid one. Let notice the method decision rules that gives another hierarchy, where K-Means seems to be more appropriated to this learning method.

Decision Tree

	A	P	R
Graph-Based	0.995	0.994	0.987
K-Means	0.947	0.965	0.969
Pyramid	0.917	0.939	0.943
Histogram	0.928	0.938	0.933

Artificial Neural Network

	A	P	R
Graph-Based	0.994	0.986	0.992
K-Means	0.947	0.967	0.967
Pyramid	0.915	0.950	0.927
Histogram	0.925	0.941	0.924

Decision Rules

	A	P	R
Graph-Based	0.910	0.896	0.728
K-Means	0.932	0.958	0.959
Pyramid	0.903	0.936	0.926
Histogram	0.905	0.927	0.901

Support Vector Machines

	A	P	R
Graph-Based	0.984	0.987	0.950
K-Means	0.935	0.962	0.957
Pyramid	0.903	0.946	0.914
Histogram	0.909	0.952	0.880

Table 8. Accuracy (A), Precision (P) and Recall (R) on segmentations using different classifiers without undefined and mixed regions

From now on, we can assume that the learning step is efficient and robust. That is to say the association descriptors-classifiers seems to be well-adapted to compute an automatic tool able to separate blur from sharp regions. Let then us now interest to its efficiency in the image application. More precisely, we have to judge the results on the entire image and not only on region labeling.

5. Blur identification in real images

We have retained the best approach to learn and decide labels from region descriptors, to classify regions using only blur and sharp labels. Let recall what it implies. Indeed, to classify correctly 95% of regions does not infer to classify correctly 95% of the image. First many regions include the two labels: sharp and blur, with one in majority, so to well classify this region will of course imply to miss classify the minority one. Also, it classifies only blur and sharp labels, as undefined and mixed labels are not learnable: these regions are necessarily going to engender bad classification.

To judge the identification task on images, it is necessary to qualify the accuracy on pixels and not on regions, as illustrated in figure 6. This basic example shows that even if all regions are well classified some pixels still remains miss classified.

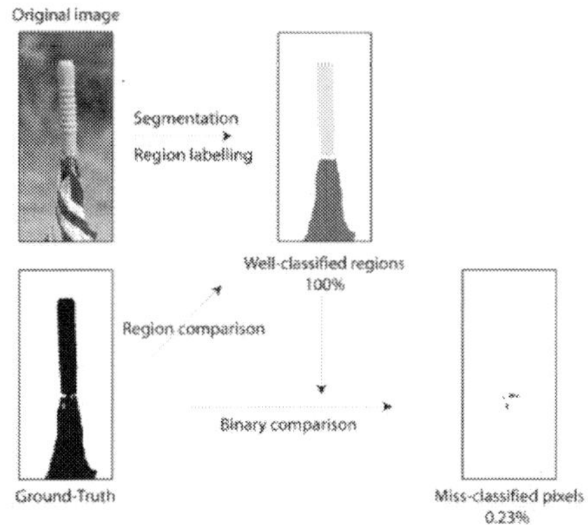

Fig. 6. Region accuracy is not pixel accuracy

The table 9 gives the ratio of well classified pixels.

Method	Graph-Based	K-Means	Pyramid	Histogram
Decision Tree	0.74	0.80	0.83	0.79
Artificial Neural Network	0.74	0.79	0.83	0.78
Decision Rules	0.71	0.74	0.79	0.75
Support Vector Machines	0.74	0.79	0.83	0.79

Table 9. Accuracy of blur identification, in pixels

Accuracy is varying from 0.74 to 0.83, whatever the choice of the pair segmentation and classifier. This slight diversity denotes the robustness of our method and its independence to the classifier, the deviation is mainly generated by the segmentation tool. Let notice that the pyramid seems to be the best whatever the learning tool. Nevertheless, the top result reached only 83%, which is far from the accuracies previously obtained on region classification. There is no better approach that is able to fully complete the identification task. Confronting these results to the previously obtained in sections 3.1 and 4, the main reason is clearly imputed to the segmentation step, this step tends to merge different labels in a same region. Also, the Graph-Based method is now the poorest one even so it was the best one considering region classification. In fact, the Graph-Based method highly suffers from its mix coefficient, the poorest one (0.24). Regions are well learned but are too much biased to reach a sufficient enough identification. In the opposite way the pyramid method is the best compromise between mix coefficient and region classification accuracy: this method gives the best final accuracy.

As a choice has to be made, from now on, we will consider the decision tree classifier as the reference one. None really suffers from some lacks but the C4.5 gives just slight higher values. Also, the C4.5 decision tree classifier naturally provides the distribution of the leaf classifying an unknown region. And, the more concentrated in one class the distribution is, the more the efficiency of the classification is expected to be. Figure 7 illustrates visually this property, using the pyramid segmentation. Original image and a blur map are shown. This map represents a continuum using the leaf distribution: the redder the region appears, the sharper the zone is expected to be.

We retrieve the numerical measures of accuracy obtained: the main majority of pixels and regions are well classified. Misclassified pixels are generally located on the borders between the blurry and the sharp zones. The more the "edge" between these two zones is smooth; the more the identification step is penalized. Logically, we can notice that identification is more difficult when focused objects are not clearly in a different depth than background elements. We may assume that, on this kind of images, the main problematic is the segmentation process itself.

These objective and visual results exhibit the difficulty to correctly segment images according to the blur properties. In fact, while region classification is very efficient, the accuracy in pixels is quite unsatisfactory and the segmentation is the step which intervenes most in these poor results. In fact, even if only one segmentation has been previously used to create the figure 7, the results for each segmentation were not extremely poorer. Our idea is then to use each of them hoping they will be complementary. In order to be convinced let present the different visual results obtained with the deer image in figure 8.

Fig. 7. Some illustrations of blur identification (the redder the region appears, the sharper the zone is)

Fig. 8. The complementarity of segmentation methods

Objectively, even if these several segmentations are very similar, the noticeable differences on some zones tend us to expect that combining each of them will improve the final identification.

6. Multi-Segmentations approach

Considering the set of blur maps issued from the selected segmentations, it produces, for each pixel, a set of labels. The figure 9 illustrates this approach using different segmentations, one unique classifier and combining the outputs to return the verdict. Among the many combination rules suggested in the literature "Sum" and "Vote" approaches are used the most frequently (Kittler & Alkoot, 2001). The Sum rule operates directly on a posteriori class probabilities and vote, on the other hand, operates on class labels assigned to each pattern. Many versions of Vote exist, such as unanimous voting, threshold voting, weighted voting and simple majority voting...
Let precise the 3 selected methods. The first algorithm (C1) is the simple majority voting. The second and third algorithms propose to use the leaf distribution of the tree classifier. The second method (C2) affects the label of segmentation with the highest value of class probability. By extrapolation, we may say that method C2 gives the label of the classifier the more certain of its decision. Finally, the third method (C3) is obtained by applying the maximum value selector to the class dependent averages.
The table 10 shows the results on our dataset using the 3 combining methods based on a decision Tree.

Method	Pyramid	C1	C2	C3
Accuracy	0.83	0.91	0.89	0.94

Table 10. Results with the 3 combination algorithms using decision tree classifier

The method combining segmentation results notably improves the global accuracy, from 0.83 from the best mono segmentation method to at least 0.89. The method C3 gives the best efficiency with a value of accuracy of 0.94, in second the C1 method and in last the C2 one. This hierarchy joins the analysis often done of a superiority of sum rule approaches (Kittler J. & Alkoot, 2001). The important gain (11 %) between the best mono method segmentation and the merger one C3 shows that this last one fills certain deficiencies of the segmentations and allows to best performing the blur identification task.
To visually confirm these behaviours, let introduce the figure 10 where combining results using the C3 method are proposed. Using the 4 blur maps issued from the 4 selected segmentations this combining rule provide quite complete blur identification.

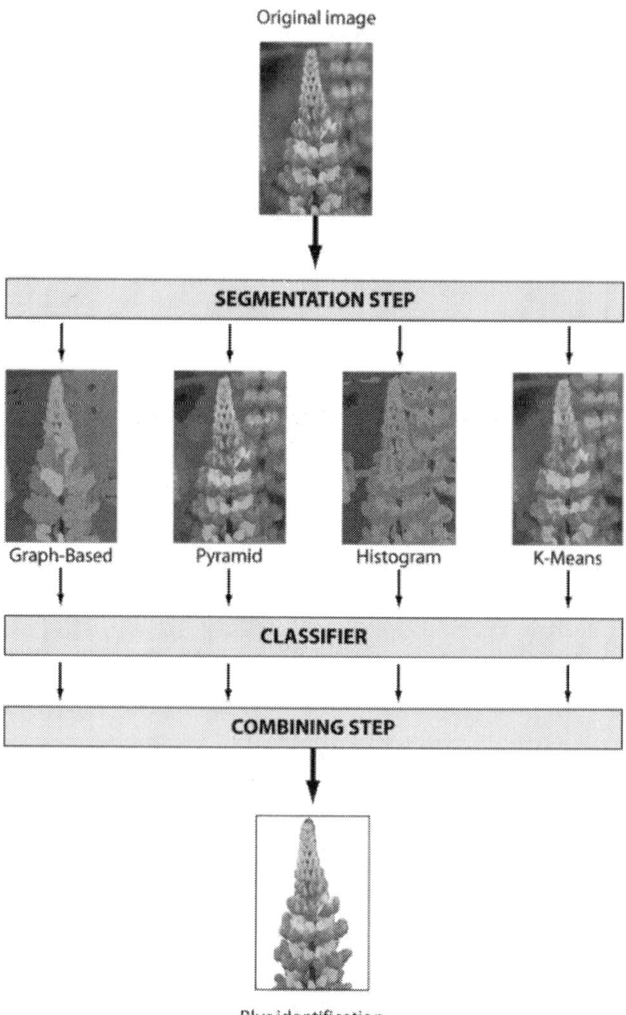

Fig. 9. Overall process of multi-segmentations approach

7. Conclusion and future work

This chapter proposes a new algorithm based on segmentation and texture descriptors that are common to many image processes. Robust learning methods well combined give an efficient blur identification tool for real images. After evaluating the efficiency of each tool

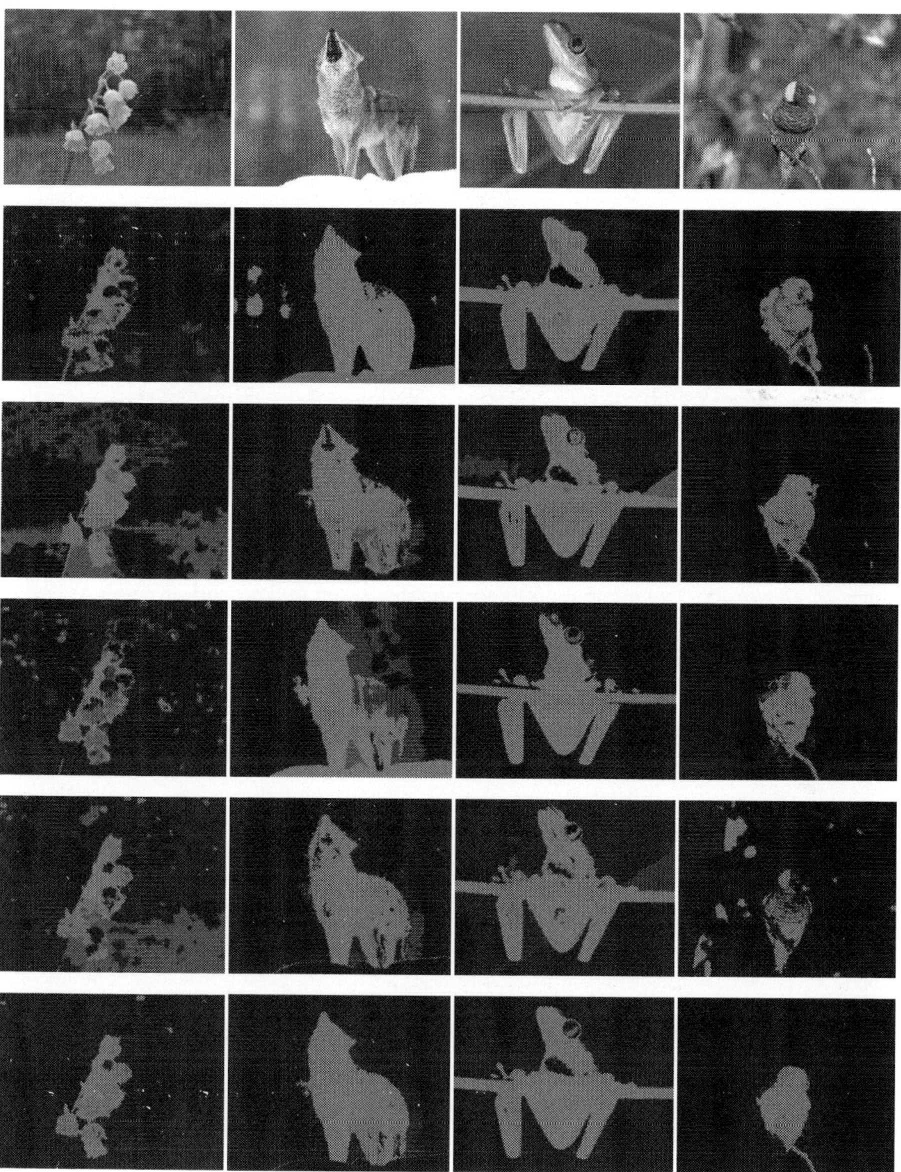

Fig. 10. Examples of multi-segmentation combining. From up to down, the original image; blur identification generated by Graph-Based, K-Means, Pyramid and Histogram segmentations; blur identification generated by C3

separately a final combining rule is proposed. Detection is successfully realized by the method, resulting in improved visual and objective qualities according to a ground-truth sufficient enough dataset. Although each tool taken independently suffers from some deficiencies, using four weak blur maps permits to create efficient blur detection, around 95% of well-classified pixels. Tools issued from pattern classification and machine learning permit to confront to image processing lacks and then to reach new visual intrinsic properties in images. It is not only necessary to develop better image processing methods to capture visually important features from the image, but also to develop them that they are simple, efficient and easily combinable using pattern classification approaches. At the conclusion of this work we possess a relatively good detector which is going to allow envisaging its use in algorithms of higher level treatments of images, what the community calls content aware processing. Without considering the low-level image processing is able to reach the semantic level in images, such a tool must be considered only as a link of a more global chain in charge to propose new services and usages around new multimedia technologies.

Experimental results presented in this chapter show that the segmentation is the crucial step of the method and future works based on the blur itself will be concluded in a new algorithm as required. To avoid the bias generated by the partition developing a supervised segmentation algorithm taking into account directly blur estimators must be reach. Moreover, the region neighborhood must be taking into account in order to decide the region label. Spatial relationship between regions would be certainly of any importance.

8. References

Bordier C.; Koenig-Supiot F; Vital-Durand F. & Knoblauch K. (2005). Quantitative Image processing to facilitate image identification by partially-sighted, Proceedings of Vision 2005, pp. 980-984

Borsotti M.; Campadelli P. & Schettini R. (1998). Quantitative evaluation of color image segmentation results, *Pattern Recognition Letters,* Vol. 19, pp. 741-747

Canny J. (1986). A Computational Approach To Edge Detection, *IEEE Trans. Pattern Analysis and Machine Intelligence,* Vol. 8, pp. 679-714

Cheng H. (2000). A hierarchical approach to color image segmentation using homogeneity, *IEEE Trans. on Image Processing,* Vol. 9, No. 12, pp. 2071–2082

Chung K.; Yang W. & Yan W. (2008). Efficient edge-preserving algorithm for color contrast enhancement with application to color image segmentation, *Journal of Visual Communication and Image Representation,* Vol. 19, No. 5, pp. 299–310

Cohen W. (1995). Fast Effective Rule Induction, *Proceedings of the Twelfth International Conference on Machine Learning,* pp. 115-123

Correia P. and Pereira F. (2002). Standalone objective segmentation quality evaluation, *Journal on Applied Signal Processing,* Vol. 2002, No. 4, pp. 389–400

Da Rugna J. & Konik H. (2006). Blur identification in image processing, *Proceedings of IEEE WCCI, International Joint Conference on Neural Network,* pp. 2536-2541

Da Rugna J. & Konik H. (2008). A robust approach to segment desired object based on salient colors, *EURASIP Journal on Image and Video Processing*, Vol. 2008, 11 pages, doi:10.1155/2008/489202

Duda R.O.; Hart P.E., & Stork D.G. (2001) Pattern classification, *2nd edition, Wiley*

Felzenszwalb P. & Huttenlocher D. (2004). Efficient Graph-Based Image Segmentation, *International Journal of Computer Vision*, Vol. 59, No. 2, pp. 167-181

Galloway M. (1974). Texture analysis using gray-level run length, Proceedings of *Computer graphics and image processing*, Vol. 4, pp. 172–199

Georgeson MA. & Hammett ST. (2002). Seeing blur: 'motion sharpening' without motion, *Proc Biol Sci*, Vol. 269, No. 1499, pp. 1429–1434

Keerthi S. ; Shevade S.K.; Bhattacharyya C. & Murthy K. (2001). Improvements to Platt's SMO Algorithm for SVM Classifier Design, *Neural Computation*, Vol. 13, No. 3, pp. 637-649

Kittler J. & Alkoot F. (2001). Relationship of Sum and Vote Fusion Strategies, *Lecture Notes in Computer Science, Multiple Classifier Systems*, pp. 339-348

Kohavi R. (1995). A study of cross-validation and bootstrap for accuracy estimation and model selection, Proceedings of *IJCAI*, pp. 1137–1145

Lukac R. & Plataniotis K. N. (2007) Color image processing: methods and applications, *CRC Press*

Ma L. & Staunton R. (2005). Integration of multiresolution image segmentation and neural networks for object depth recovery, *Pattern Recognition*, Vol. 38, No. 7, pp. 985-996

Marfil R; Rodriguez J.A.; Bandera A. & Sandoval F. (2007). Bounded irregular pyramid: a new structure for color image segmentation, *Pattern Recognition*, Vol. 37, No. 3 pp. 623-626

Mitchell Tom M. (1997). *Machine Learning*, McGraw-Hill, New York

Pal N. R. & Pal S. K. (1993). A review on image segmentation techniques, *Pattern Recognition*, Vol. 26, pp. 1277–1294

Quinlan J. R. (1996). Improved use of continuous attributes in C4.5, *Journal of Artificial Intelligence Research*, Vol. 4, pp. 77–90

Sapiro G. & Ringach D. L. (1996). Anisotropic diffusion of multivalued images to color filtering, *IEEE Transactions on Image Processing*, Vol. 5, pp. 1582–1585

Savakis, A. E. & Trussell, H. J. (1993). On the accuracy of psf representation in image restoration, *IEEE Trans. Image Processing*, Vol. 2, pp. 252– 259

Song Goh J. S.; Ron A. & Shen Z. (2007). Gabor & wavelet frames, *Lecture notes series, institute for mathematical sciences, national university of Singapore*, Vol. 10, 214 pages

Taghva K.; Borsack J.; Lumos S. & Condit A. (2003). A comparison of automatic and manual zoning, *International Journal on Document Analysis and Recognition*, Vol. 6, No. 4, pp. 230-235

Tao Q.; He X.; Deng H.; Liu Y. & Zhao J. (2005). Wavelet Transform Based Gaussian Point Spread Function Estimation, *Lecture Notes in Computer Science, Advances in Visual Computing, Springer Berlin*, pp. 396-405

Zhang Y.J. (1997). Evaluation and comparison of different segmentation algorithms, *Pattern Recognition Letters*, Vol. 18, pp. 963–974

21

An Adaptive Markov Game Model for Cyber Threat Intent Inference

Dan Shen[1], Genshe Chen[2], Jose B. Cruz, Jr.[3], Erik Blasch[4], and Khanh Pham[4]
[1]Intelligent Automation, Inc.,
[2]DCM Research Resources, LLC.
[3]The Ohio State University,
[4]The Air Force Research Laboratory,
USA

1. Introduction

Cyber attacks (CAs) have generally been one-dimensional, involving denial of service (DoS), computer viruses or worms, and unauthorized intrusion (hacking). Websites, mail servers, and client machines are the major targets. However, recent CAs have diversified to include multi-stage and multi-dimensional attacks with a variety of tools and technologies. Next-generation security will require network management and intrusion detection systems that combine short-term sensor information with long-term knowledge databases to provide decision support and cyberspace command and control. One of the important capabilities is to efficiently and promptly predict the threat's tactical intent from various network alerts generated by Intrusion Detection Sensors (IDSs) or Intrusion Prevention Sensors (IPSs).

Recent efforts to apply data fusion techniques to cyber situational awareness are promising (Salerno et al., 2005; Tadda et al., 2006), but assessing the potential impact of an attack and predicting intent, or high-level data fusion, continue to present substantive challenges. In this chapter, an adaptive Markov game approach is introduced to meet the challenge.

Game theory is not a new concept in the cyber defense domain. Current game theoretic approaches (Alpcan & Basar, 2003; Agah et al., 2004; Sallhammar et al., 2005) for cyber network intrusion detection and decision support are based on static matrix games and simple extensive games, which are usually solved by game trees. For example (see Fig. 1), red side (attacker) has five options while blue side (IDS) has two re-actions for information-set 1 (two blue bullets labeled as 1:1) about sub-system 1 and three possible actions for information-set 2 (three blue bullets labeled as 1:2) about sub-system 2 and 3. The payoffs of both sides are shown on the right side of each possible outcome (black bullets). A mixed Nash Strategy pair is shown with black lines. Attacker will choose action "Attack Sub-system 1" with probability 3/20, "Attack Sub-system 2" with probability 3/20, and "Do not attack sub-system 2/3" with probability 7/10. Blue side will set an alarm for sub-system 1 with probability 1, sub-system 2 with probability 5/12, sub-system 3 with probability 47/90, and ignore with probability 11/180. It is not difficult to see that these matrix game models lack the sophistication to study multi-players with relatively large actions spaces, and large planning horizons.

In this chapter, we propose a game theoretic situation awareness and impact assessment approach for cyber network defense system to consider the changes of threat intents during cyber conflict. From a perspective of data fusion and adaptive control, we use a Markov (stochastic) game method to estimate the belief of each possible cyber attack pattern. With the consideration that the parameters in each game player's cost function is not accessible to other players, we design an adaptation scheme, based on the concept of Fictitious Play (FP), for the piecewise linearized Markov game model. A software tool is developed to demonstrate the performance of the adaptive game theoretic high level information fusion approach for cyber network defense and a simulation example shows the enhanced understating of cyber-network defense.

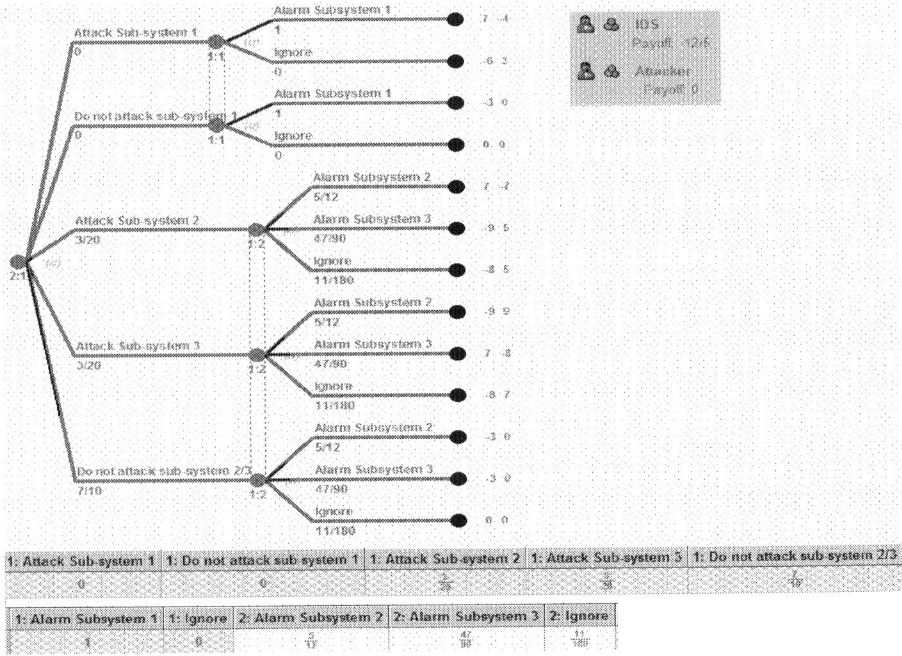

Fig. 1. An example of decision support based on static matrix game model

Our approach has the following advantages: (1) it is decentralized. Each network defense element or team makes decisions mostly based on local information. We put more autonomies in each group allowing for more flexibilities; (2) a Markov decision process (MDP) can effectively model the uncertainties in the noisy cyber environment; (3) it is a game model with two players: red force (network attackers) and blue force (cyber defense resources); and (4) FP learning concept is integrated. Each player presumes that his opponents are playing stable strategies (Nash equilibria). Each player starts with some initial beliefs and chooses a best response to those beliefs as a strategy in this round. Then, after observing their opponents' actions, the players update their beliefs. The process is then repeated. It is known that if it converges, then the point of convergence is a Nash equilibrium of the game.

The rest of the chapter is organized as follows. Section 2 describes our proposed framework. Section 3 presents a Markov model for cyber network defense. Then an adaptive design is described in Section 4. Section 5 discusses the simulation tool and simulation result, and Section 6 gives conclusions.

2. Framework for Cyber Threat Intent Inference

As indicated in Fig. 2, our cyberspace security framework has two fully coupled major parts: 1) *Data fusion module* (to refine primitive awareness and assessment, and to identify new cyber attacks); and 2) *Dynamic/adaptive feature recognition module* (to generate primitive estimations, and to learn new identified new or unknown cyber attacks).

The data fusion module permits refinement of primitive awareness and assessment to identification of new attacks while the dynamic/adaptive feature recognition module generates estimates and learns about them. The adaptive Markov game method, a stochastic approach, is used to evaluate the prospects of each potential attack. Game theory captures the nature of cyber conflict: determining the attacker's strategies is closely allied to decisions on defense and vice versa.

Fig. 2 also charts the data mining and fusion structure. For instance, detection of new attack patterns is linked to Level-1 (L1) data fusion results in dynamic learning, including deception reasoning, trend/variation identification, and multi-agent learning. Our approach to deception detection is heavily rooted in the application of pattern-recognition techniques to locate and diagnose anomalous conditions in the cyber environment. Dynamic learning and refinement can also enhance Level-2 (L2) and Level-3 (L3) data fusion.

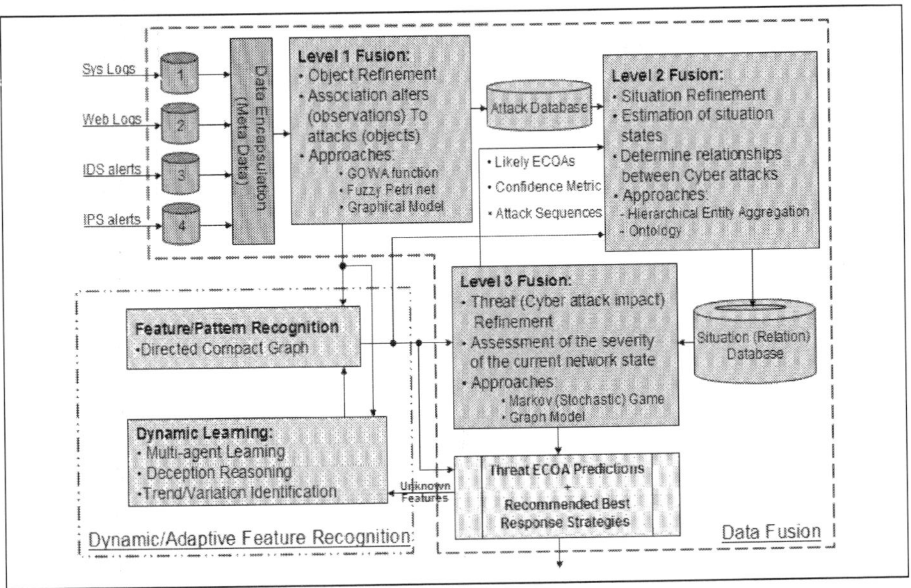

Fig. 2. Data Fusion Approach for Cyber Situation Awareness and Impact Assessment

Various logs and alerts generated by Intrusion Detection Sensors (IDSs) or Intrusion Prevention Sensors (IPSs) are fed into the L1 data fusion components. The fused objects and related pedigree information are used by a feature/pattern recognition module to generate primitive prediction of intents of cyber attackers. If the observed features are already associated with adversary intents, we can easily obtain them by pattern recognition. In some time-critical applications, the primitive prediction can be used before it is refined; because the high-level data fusion refinement operation is relatively time-consuming in the multiplicative of probability calculations.

High-level (L2 and L3) data fusion based on Markov game model is proposed to refine the primitive prediction generated in stage 1 and capture new or unknown cyber attacks. The adaptive Markov (Stochastic) game method (AMGM) is used to estimate the belief of each possible cyber attack graph. Game theory can capture the nature of cyber conflicts: the determination of the attacking-force strategies is tightly coupled to the determination of the defense-force strategies and vice versa. Also AMGM can deal with the uncertainty and incompleteness of the available information. We propose a graphical model to represent the structure and evolution of the above-mentioned Markov game model so that we can efficiently solve the graphical game problem.

The captured unknown or new cyber attack patterns will be associated to related L1 results in the dynamic learning block, which takes deception reasoning, trend/variation identification, and distribution models and calculations into account. Our approach to deception detection is heavily based on the application of pattern recognition techniques to detect and diagnose what we call out-of-normal (anomaly) conditions in the cyber environment. The results of dynamic learning or refinement shall also be used to enhance L2 and L3 data fusion. This adaptive process may be considered as level 4 data fusion (process refinement; see the 2004 DFIG model (Blasch & Plano, 2005)).

In this chapter, we will focus on the L3 data fusion (adaptive Markov game approach) part in the overall framework shown in Fig. 2.

3. Markov game model for cyber network defense

In general, a Markov (stochastic) game (Shapley, 1953) is specified by (i) a finite set of players N, (ii) a set of states S, (iii) for every player $i \in N$, a finite set of available actions D^i (we denote the overall action space $D = \times_{i \in N} D^i$), (iv) a transition rule $q : S \times D \rightarrow \Delta(S)$, (where $\Delta(S)$ is the space of all probability distributions over S), and (v) a payoff function $r : S \times D \rightarrow R^N$. For the cyber decision support and attacker intent inference problem, we obtain the following distributed discrete time Markov game (we revise the Markov game model (Chen et al., 2007) used for battle-space and focus on the cyber attack domain properties):

<u>Players (Decision Makers)</u> --- Cyber attackers and network defense system are two players of this Markov game model. We denote cyber attackers as "red team", and the network defense system (IDSs, Firewalls, Email-Filters, Encryption) as "blue team". The cooperation within the same team is also modeled so that the coordinated cyber network attacks can be captured and predicted.

<u>State Space</u> --- All the possible states of involved network nodes consist of the state space. For example, the web-server (IP = 26.134.3.125) is controlled by attackers. To determine the optimal IDS deployment, we include the defense status for each network nodes in the state space. So, for the ith network node, there is a state vector $s^i(k)$ at time k.

$$s^i(k) = (f, p, a)^T \tag{1}$$

where f is the working status of the ith network node, p is the protection status, a is the status of being attacked, and T is the transpose operator. "Normal" and "malfunction" are typical values of f with the meaning that the node is in the normal working status or malfunction (Recall that in battle space cases, the function status of any unit values can be "undestroyed", "damaged", or "destroyed"). p can be the defense unit/service (such as firewall, IDS and filter, with probability) assigned to the node and p = NULL means that the ith node is unprotected. The type of attacks will be specified in <u>Action Space</u>.

Remark 1: *It is not difficult to understand that the system states are determined by two factors: 1) previous states and 2) the current actions. So the whole system can be modelled by a first-order Markov decision process.*

The overall system state at time k is

$$s_k = [s^1(k), s^2(k), \cdots, s^M(k)] \tag{2}$$

where M is the number of nodes in the involved cyber network.

Remark 2: *The system states are updated based on the IDS and the control inputs from the decision makers. Our model does not require 100% accurate measurements from the IDS. The IDS can report several possible situations with the associated confidence vector. For example, one IDS can input "node 1 is damaged with the probability 0.85" and "node 1 is normal with probability 0.15".*

<u>Action Space</u> --- At every time step, each player chooses targets with associated actions based on its observed network information. For the red team (cyber network attackers), we consider the following types of network-based attacks:

Buffer overflow (web attack): it occurs when a program does not check to make sure the data it is putting into a space will actually fit into that space.

Semantic URL attack (web attack): In semantic URL attack, a client manually adjusts the parameters of its request by maintaining the URL's syntax but altering its semantic meaning. This attack is primarily used against Common Gateway Interface (CGI) driven websites.

E-mail Bombing (email attack): In Internet usage, an e-mail bomb is a form of net abuse consisting of sending huge e-mail volumes to an address in an attempt to overflow the mailbox or overwhelm the server.

E-mail spam (email attack): Spamming is the abuse of electronic messaging systems to send unsolicited, and/or undesired bulk messages.

MALware attachment (email attack): Malware is software designed to infiltrate or damage a computer system without the owner's informed consent. Some common MALware attacks are worms, viruses, Trojan horses, etc.

Denial-of-service (network attack): Denial-of-service (DoS) attack is an attempt to make a computer resource unavailable to its intended users. Typically the targets are high-profile web servers where the attack is aiming to cause the hosted web pages to be unavailable on the Internet. A distributed denial of service attack (DDoS) occurs when multiple compromised systems flood the bandwidth or resources of a targeted system, usually a web server(s). These systems are compromised by attackers using a variety of methods.

Remark 3: *Some attacks may be multi-stage. For example, e-mail spam and MALware are used first to gain control of several temporal network nodes, which are usually not well protected servers. Then a DoS attack will be triggered to a specified and ultimate target. Our dynamic Markov game model* *can handle these attacks from a planning perspective. Our mixed Nash strategy pair is based on a fixed finite planning horizon. See Strategies for details.*

For the blue team (network defense system), we consider the following defense actions:

IDS deployment: we assume that there are limited IDSs. IDS deployment is similar to resource allocation (target selection) problems in traditional battle-space situations. We try to find an optimal deployment strategy to maximize the chance of detecting all possible cyber network intrusions.

Firewall configuration: A firewall is an information technology (IT) security device which is configured to permit, deny or proxy data connections set and configured by the organization's security policy.

Email-filter configuration: Email filtering is the processing of organizing emails according to a specified criterion. Email filtering software inputs email and for its output, it might (a) pass the message through unchanged for delivery to the user's mailbox, (b) redirect the message for delivery elsewhere, or (c) throw the message away. Some e-mail filters are able to edit messages during processing.

Shut down or reset servers.

<u>Transition Rule</u> --- The objective of the transition rule is to calculate the probability distribution over the state space $q(s_{k+1}|s_k, u_k^B, u_k^R)$, where s_k, s_{k+1} are system states at time k and $k+1$ respectively, u_k^B, u_k^R are the overall decisions of the blue team (network defense system) and the red team (cyber attackers), respectively, at time step k. How to decide the overall actions for each team are specified in <u>Strategies</u>.

For each network node (server or workstation), the state of time $k+1$ is determined by three things: 1) state at time k; 2) control strategies of the two players; and 3) the attack/defense efficiency. If we compare part 3) to battle-space domain, the efficiency is the analogue of kill probability of weapons.

For example, if the state of node 1 at time k is ["normal", "NULL", "NULL"], one component of the red action is "email-bombing node 1", and one component of blue action is "email-filter–configuration-no-block for node 1", then the probability distribution of all possible next states of node 1 is: ["normal", "email-filter-configuration", "email-bombing"] with probability 0.4; ["slow response", "email-filter-configuration", "email-bombing"] with probability 0.3; and ["crashed", "email-filter-configuration", "email-bombing"] with probability 0.3. The actual probabilities depend on the efficiency of attacking and defending actions.

<u>Payoff Functions</u> --- In this Markov game model, there are two levels of payoff functions for each player (red or blue): lower-level (cooperative within each team) and higher-level (non-cooperative between teams) payoff functions. This hierarchical structure is important to model the coordinated cyber network attacks and specify optimal coordinated network defense strategies and IDS deployment.

The lower level payoff functions are used by each team (blue or red) to determine the cooperative team actions for each team member based on the available local information. For the jth unit of blue force, the payoff function at time k is defined as $\phi_j^B\left(\tilde{s}_j^B(k), u_j^B(k), W^B(k); k\right)$, where $\tilde{s}_j^B(k) \subseteq s_k$ is the local information obtained by the jth blue member, $u_j^B(k)$ is the action taken by the blue team member at time k, and $W^B(k)$, the weights for all possible action-target couples of blue force, is announced to all blue team members and determined according to the top level payoff functions from a team-optimal perspective.

$$\phi_j^B\left(\tilde{s}_j^B(k),u_j^B(k),W^B(k);k\right) = U\left(\tilde{s}_j^B(k)\right) - w\left(W^B(k),u_j^B(k)\right)C\left(u_j^B(k)\right) \tag{3}$$

where, $U\left(\tilde{s}_j^B(k)\right)$ is the utility or payoff of the current local network state. $C\left(u_j^B(k)\right)$ is the cost of action to be taken by the blue team member. Usually, $U(\cdot)$ is a negative value if a network node is in malfunction status due to a cyber attack. The specific value depends on the value of the network node. The counterpart in the battle-space domain is the target value of each platform. Function $w\left(W^B(k),u_j^B(k)\right)$ will calculate the weight for any specified action decision for the jth member of the blue team based on the received $W^B(k)$, which is determined on a team level and indicates the preference and trend of team defense strategies.

Similarly, we obtain the lower level payoff functions for the jth member of red player,

$$\phi_j^R\left(\tilde{s}_j^R(k),u_j^R(k),W^R(k);k\right) = U\left(\tilde{s}_j^R(k)\right) - w\left(W^R(k),u_j^R(k)\right)C\left(u_j^R(k)\right) \tag{4}$$

The top level payoff functions at time k are used to evaluate the overall performance, $V(\cdot)$, of each team.

$$V^B(\tilde{s}^B(k),u_k^B;k) = \sum_{j=1}^{M^B} \phi_j^B\left(\tilde{s}_j^B(k),u_j^B(k),W^B(k);k\right) \tag{5}$$

$$V^R(\tilde{s}^R(k),u_k^R;k) = \sum_{j=1}^{M^R} \phi_j^R\left(\tilde{s}_j^R(k),u_j^R(k),W^R(k);k\right) \tag{6}$$

In our approach, the lower level payoffs are calculated distributedly by each team member and sent back to network administrator via communication networks.

<u>Strategies</u> --- In game theory, the Nash equilibrium (Nash, 1951) is a kind of optimal collective strategy in a game involving two or more players, where no player has anything to gain by changing only his or her own strategy. If each player has chosen a strategy and no player can benefit by changing his or her strategy while the other players keep theirs unchanged, then the current set of strategy choices and the corresponding payoffs constitute a Nash equilibrium.

In our proposed approach, the sub-optimal Nash solution to the Markov game is obtained via a K time-step look-ahead approach, in which we only optimize the solution in the K time-step horizon. K usually takes 2, 3, 4, or 5. The suboptimal technique is used successfully for reasoning in games such as chess, backgammon, and monopoly. For our case, the objective of each team at time k is to find a serial of actions or course of action (COA) to maximize the following team level payoffs, $J(\cdot)$, respectively,

$$J_k^B(u_k^B,u_k^R,u_{k+1}^B,u_{k+1}^R,...,u_{k+K}^B,u_{k+K}^R) = \sum_{i=k}^{k+K} V^B(\tilde{s}^B(i),u_i^B;i) \tag{7}$$

$$J_k^R(u_k^B, u_k^R, u_{k+1}^B, u_{k+1}^R, ..., u_{k+K}^B, u_{k+K}^R) = \sum_{i=k}^{k+K} V^R(\tilde{s}^R(i), u_i^R; i) \tag{8}$$

Remark 4: *The K-step look-ahead (or moving window) approach well fits the situations in which multi-step cyber network attacks occurs since we evaluate the performance of each team based on the sum of payoffs during a period of K-time steps. With bigger K, the game model can predicate or detect more complicated network attackers with more stages. The cost is the increased computation complexity.*

In general, the system model is nonlinear. By the linearization transformation method (Sastry, 1999), the system dynamics can be approximately modeled by a linear system.

$$X_{k+1} = A_k X_k + D_k^B c_k^B + D_k^R c_k^R \tag{9}$$

where X_k is the state of network at time k. c_k^B and c_k^R are the action control of blue and red force, respectively, at time k. D_k^B and D_k^R are the related control gains.

The objective of each side is to minimize its cost function

$$J^B = \underbrace{\left(X_N\right)^T Q_N^{BR} X_N}_{\text{Gain of Red side}} - \underbrace{\left(X_N\right)^T Q_N^{BB} X_N}_{\text{Gain of Blue side}} - \underbrace{\sum_{k=1}^{N-1}\left(\left(c_k^B\right)^T P^B c_k^B\right)}_{\text{Cost of Blue Actions}} \tag{10}$$

$$J^R = \underbrace{\left(X_N\right)^T Q_N^{RB} X_N}_{\text{Gain of Blue side}} - \underbrace{\left(X_N\right)^T Q_N^{RR} X_N}_{\text{Gain of Red side}} - \underbrace{\sum_{k=1}^{N-1}\left(\left(c_k^R\right)^T P^R c_k^R\right)}_{\text{Cost of Red Actions}} \tag{11}$$

where Q_k^{BR}, Q_k^{BB}, Q_k^{RB}, and Q_k^{RR} are the gain matrices. Each player determines its gain matrix based on the network topology and its goals. P^B and P^R are the cost matrix of blue player and red player, respectively.

4. An adaptation design for linear quadratic games

With the consideration that the parameters in each side's cost function is not accessible to the other side, we propose to use an adaptation design based on the concept of Fictitious Play (FP) (Brown, 1951; Fudenberg & Levine, 1998) to learn these unknown properties. As a learning concept, FP was first introduced by G. W. Brown in 1951. Within the learning scheme, each player presumes that her opponents are playing stable (possibly mixed) strategies. Each player starts with some initial beliefs and chooses a best response to those beliefs as a strategy in this round. Then, after observing their opponents' actions, the players update their beliefs according to some learning rule (e.g. temporal-differencing, Q-learning, or Bayes' rule). The process is then repeated. It is known (Levine, 1998) that if it converges, then the point of convergence is a Nash equilibrium of the game.

4.1 Nash strategies of linear quadratic games

Let us first consider general two-person infinite-horizon simultaneous linear quadratic games

$$x_{k+1} = A_k x_k + B_k^1 u_k^1 + B_k^2 u_k^2 \tag{12}$$

with the cost functions

$$J^1 = \sum_{k=0}^{+\infty} (x_k^T Q^1 x_k + u_k^{1T} R^{11} u_k^1 + u_k^{2T} R^{12} u_k^2) \tag{13}$$

$$J^2 = \sum_{k=0}^{N-1} (x_k^T Q^2 x_k + u_k^{1T} R^{21} u_k^1 + u_k^{2T} R^{22} u_k^2) \tag{14}$$

where $x_k \in R^n$, $u_k^i \in R$, $Q^i > 0$, $R^{ij} > 0$, system (A, Bi) is stabilizable, (A, Ci) is detectable (where $C^{iT} C^i = Q^i$), and $\left| B^{iT} B^i \right| > 0$ for $i = 1, 2,$ and $k = 0, 1, 2, \ldots$. We assume that both players have perfect information structures, with which both players know the exact system dynamics $x_{k+1} = A_k x_k + B_k^1 u_k^1 + B_k^2 u_k^2$ and measure exact system states x_k. It is also assumed that the simultaneous game in (12) – (14) has a unique Nash strategy pair for both players. It is well known (Basar & Olsder, 1999) that the Nash strategy pair is specified by

$$u_k^{1*} \triangleq \arg\min_{u_k^1} J^1 = \gamma^1(x_k) = L^1 x_k \tag{15}$$

$$u_k^{2*} \triangleq \arg\min_{u_k^2} J^2 = \gamma^2(x_k) = L^2 x_k \tag{15}$$

where L1 and L2 are defined, respectively, by

$$L^1 = -[R^{11} + B^{1T} K^1 B^1]^{-1} B^{1T} K^1 [A + B^2 L^2] \tag{17}$$

$$L^2 = -[R^{22} + B^{2T} K^2 B^2]^{-1} B^{2T} K^2 [A + B^1 L^1] \tag{18}$$

K^1 and K^2 are specified in the following coupled discrete-time algebraic Riccati equations (DAREs) that, by assumption, have a unique positive semi-definite solution.

$$K^1 = Q^1 + L^{1T} R^{11} L^1 + L^{2T} R^{12} L^2 + \left(A + B^1 L^1 + B^2 L^2\right)^T K^1 \left(A + B^1 L^1 + B^2 L^2\right) \tag{19}$$

$$K^2 = Q^2 + L^{1T} R^{21} L^1 + L^{2T} R^{22} L^2 + \left(A + B^1 L^1 + B^2 L^2\right)^T K^2 \left(A + B^1 L^1 + B^2 L^2\right) \tag{20}$$

4.2 Adaptation schemes

In the one-side adaptation scheme, only one of the two players has perfect information of the cost functions of both players, i.e., the player knows exact Q^1, Q^2, R^{11}, R^{12}, R^{21}, R^{22}, while the other player only has access to its cost function and does not know the parameters of the cost function of its opponent. WLOG, we assume that player 1 knows exact Q^i, R^{ij}, A, B^i while player 2 has access to Q^2, R^{21}, R^{22}, A, B^i. We also assume that player 1 will apply its state feedback Nash strategies calculated based the information of system dynamics, system states and cost functions of both players. Player 2 knows in advance that its opponent will implement state feedback Nash strategies. Player 2 will estimate the control gain L^1 first, and then calculate/estimate its own control gain L^2.

We assume that player 1, who has perfect information structure, will apply its real state feedback Nash strategies $u^{1*} = L^1 x_k$, so we follow the convectional indirect adaptive control design method (Tao, 2003).

Consider the system defined in (12) with fixed controller (15) for player 1, let $\hat{L}_k^1$ be an estimate of the control gain L^1 of player 1, from the point view of player 2. The block diagram of indirect adaptive control system is shown in Fig. 3.

First, we have

$$\hat{x}_{k+1} = Ax_k + B^1 \hat{L}_k^1 x_k + B^2 u_k^2 \tag{21}$$

Since matrix $B^{1T} B^1$ is invertible, we obtain, from (14) and (21)

$$[B^{1T} B^1]^{-1} B^{1T} (\hat{x}_{k+1} - x_{k+1}) = (\hat{L}_k^1 - L^1) x_k \tag{22}$$

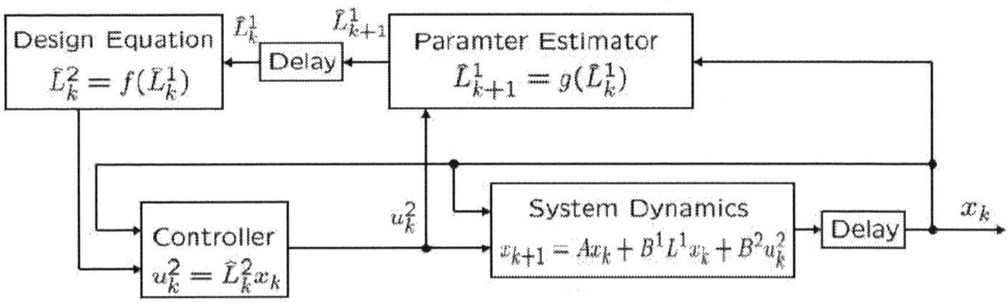

Fig. 3. Indirect adaptive control design for one-side adaptation scheme

We introduce the estimation error $e_k = [B^{1T} B^1]^{-1} B^{1T} (\hat{x}_k - x_k)$, ($e_k$ is a scalar), then

$$e_k = \tilde{L}_{k-1}^1 \phi_k \tag{23}$$

where $\tilde{L}_{k-1}^1 = \hat{L}_{k-1}^1 - L^1$ and $\phi_k = \frac{1}{z}[x]_k = x_{k-1}$. (Note that $\frac{1}{z}[x]_k$ denotes the output of the system with transfer function $\frac{1}{z}$ and input x_k.)

Choose the adaptive law for $\hat{L}_k^1$ as

$$\hat{L}_k^1 = \hat{L}_{k-1}^1 - \frac{e_k \phi_k^T \Gamma}{m_k^2} \tag{24}$$

where $0 < \Gamma = \Gamma^T < 2I_n$ is a gain matrix, and

$$m_k = \sqrt{\kappa + \phi_k^T \phi_k}, \quad \kappa > 0$$

As shown in Fig. 3, for any $\hat{L}_k^1$, a design function or mapping will be used to calculate $\hat{L}_k^2$. From (18) and (20), we have a best response strategy for player 2 given the estimated control gain $\hat{L}_k^1$ of player 1,

$$\hat{L}_k^2 = -[R^{22} + B^{2T} \hat{K}_k^2 B^2]^{-1} B^{2T} \hat{K}_k^2 [A + B^1 \hat{L}_k^1] \tag{25}$$

$$\hat{K}_k^2 = Q^2 + \hat{L}_k^{1T} R^{21} \hat{L}_k^1 + \hat{L}_k^{2T} R^{22} \hat{L}_k^2 + \left(A + B^1 \hat{L}_k^1 + B^2 \hat{L}_k^2\right)^T \hat{K}_k^2 \left(A + B^1 \hat{L}_k^1 + B^2 \hat{L}_k^2\right) \tag{26}$$

It is proved that the $\hat{K}_k^2$ specified in (25) and (26) is the solution to the DARE

$$\bar{A}^T X \bar{A} - X - \bar{A}^T X \bar{B} \left[\bar{B}^T X \bar{B} + \bar{R} \right]^{-1} \bar{B}^T X \bar{A} + \bar{Q} = 0 \tag{27}$$

where

$$\bar{A} = A + B^1 \hat{L}_k^1, \quad \bar{B} = B^2, \quad \bar{R} = R^{22} \text{ and } \bar{Q} = Q^2 + \hat{L}_k^{1T} R^{21} \hat{L}_k^1.$$

Remark 5: *We can easily obtain $\hat{K}_K^2$ by using commercial software such as MATLAB command dare ($\bar{A}, \bar{B}, \bar{Q}, \bar{R}$).*

Similar to the proof of Normalized Gradient algorithm (Tao, 2003, page 115-116), we define a parameter error measurement function $V(\tilde{L}_k^1) = \tilde{L}_k^1 \Gamma^{-1} \tilde{L}_k^{1T}$ for the adaptive law in (24). Then,

$$
\begin{aligned}
V(\tilde{L}_k^1) - V(\tilde{L}_{k-1}^1) &= \left[\tilde{L}_{k-1}^1 - \frac{e_k \phi_k^T \Gamma}{m_k^2} \right] \Gamma^{-1} \left[\tilde{L}_{k-1}^1 - \frac{e_k \phi_k^T \Gamma}{m_k^2} \right]^T \\
&= -\frac{1}{m_k^2} \left(\tilde{L}_{k-1}^1 \phi_k e_k + e_k \phi_k^T \tilde{L}_{k-1}^{1T} - \frac{\phi_k^T \Gamma \phi_k e_k^2}{m_k^2} \right) \\
&= -\frac{e_k^2}{m_k^2} \left(2 - \frac{\phi_k^T \Gamma \phi_k}{\kappa + \phi_k^T \phi_k} \right) \le -\alpha \frac{e_k^2}{m_k^2}
\end{aligned} \tag{28}
$$

where $\alpha=2-\lambda_{\max}[\Gamma]>0$. $\lambda_{\max}[\Gamma]\in(0,2)$ is the maximum eigenvalue of Γ which satisfies the condition $0<\Gamma<2I_n$. In the above, the equality in the first line comes from (24) and $\tilde{L}_k^1=\hat{L}_k^1-L^1$, so

$$\hat{L}_k^1 = \hat{L}_{k-1}^1 - \frac{e_k\phi_k^T\Gamma}{m_k^2} \quad\Rightarrow\quad \tilde{L}_k^1 = \tilde{L}_{k-1}^1 - \frac{e_k\phi_k^T\Gamma}{m_k^2} \tag{29}$$

Now let's testify the inequality in the last line. By the eigenvalue decomposition of Γ, we can obtain $\Gamma=W^T\Lambda W$ where $\Lambda=\mathrm{diag}(\lambda_1,\lambda_2,...,\lambda_n)$ is the eigenvalue matrix, and W contains the eigenvectors (and W satisfies the condition $W^T=W^{-1}$). Therefore,

$$\phi_k^T\Gamma\phi_k = \phi_k^TW^T\Lambda W\phi_k \leq \lambda_{\max}[\Gamma]\phi_k^TW^TW\phi_k = \lambda_{\max}[\Gamma]\phi_k^T\phi_k \tag{30}$$

Since $\kappa>0$, we have $\kappa+\phi_k^T\phi_k\geq\phi_k^T\phi_k$. Then

$$0\leq \frac{\phi_k^T\Gamma\phi_k}{\kappa+\phi_k^T\phi_k} \leq \lambda_{\max}[\Gamma] \tag{31}$$

This completes the verification of (28), from which we have

$$\alpha\sum_{k=1}^{N}\frac{e_k^2}{m_k^2} \leq V(\tilde{L}_0^1)-V(\tilde{L}_N^1) \leq V(\tilde{L}_0^1) \tag{32}$$

So $\lim\limits_{N\to+\infty}\sum_{k=1}^{N}\frac{e_k^2}{m_k^2}$ is bounded from above by $V(\tilde{L}_0^1)$. Since $m_k^2=\kappa+\phi_k^T\phi_k>0$, we obtain

$$\lim_{N\to+\infty}e_k = \lim_{N\to+\infty}\tilde{L}_{k-1}^1\phi_k = 0 \tag{33}$$

If ϕ_k is persistently exciting, then

$$\lim_{N\to+\infty}\tilde{L}_k^1 = 0 \quad\Rightarrow\quad \lim_{N\to+\infty}\hat{L}_k^1 = L^1 \tag{34}$$

We proposed two ways to satisfy the excitation conditions (AstrÄom & Wittenmark, 1995, page 63-67). The first one is a reference signal tracking method, and the other is called small system disturbance.

We also attend the adaptation design to two-side adaptation scheme (Fig. 4), in which each player needs to estimate the control gain of its opponent. We assume that each player has access to its own cost function as well as the system dynamics, and does not know the parameters of the cost function of its opponent. i.e., player 1 knows Q^1, R^{12}, R^{11}, A, B^1 and B^2 while player 2 has access to Q^2, R^{21}, R^{22}, A, B^1 and B^2. We also assume that each player knows in advance that its opponent will implement state feedback Nash strategies. So, as shown in Fig. 4, player 2 (or player 1) will estimate the control gain L^1 (or L^2) first, and then calculate/estimate its own control gain L^2 (or L^1). The convergence is proved (Shen, 2006) via two properties of "reaction-curve" like relations between control gains of two players.

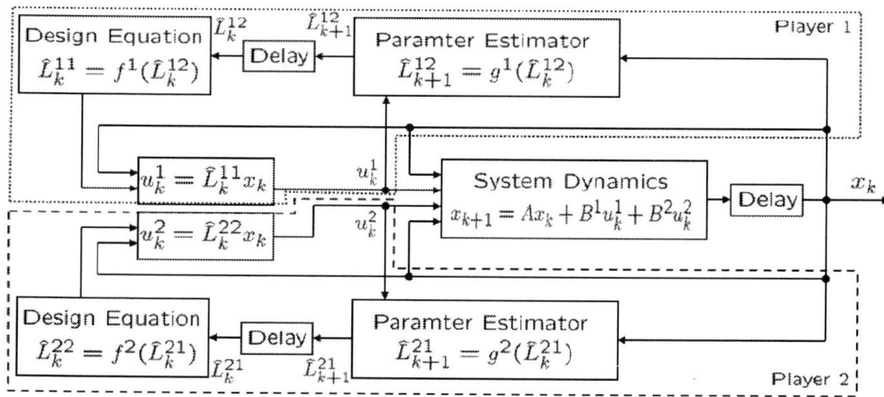

Fig. 4. Indirect adaptive control design for two-side adaptation scheme

5. Simulation and visualization tool

To evaluate our game theoretic approach for cyber attack prediction and mitigation, we have constructed a Cyber Game Simulation Platform (CGSP) (as shown in Fig. 5) based on an open-source network experiment specification and visualization tool kit (ESVT). Through this event-based, interactive and visual simulation environment, various attack strategies (single stage or multi-staged) and scenarios can be easily played out and the effect of game theoretic attack prediction and mitigation can be visually and quantitatively evaluated.

The implemented network components in this platform includes Computer (host), Switch, Open Shortest Path First (OSPF) Router or Firewall, Link (connection), and (Sub) Network (Simulated by a node).

Besides the ordinary network properties such as processing capacity, bandwidth, Pr{error}, and delay etc., CGSP components can be assigned a number of network attack containment or traffic mitigation properties to act as various defense roles, including smart IDS (intrusion detection systems), incoming traffic block, and outgoing traffic block. Additionally and more importantly, these defense roles or network defense properties can be deployed and re-deployed in real-time during a game simulation run-time based on the local intelligence and orders from higher-level command centers.

The color of a link represents the traffic volume on that link (in KBps and in Mbps). Light Gray: less than 1 percent of bandwidth; Green: more than 1 percent of bandwidth; Yellow: between green and red; Red: more than 30 percent of bandwidth. The color of a host indicates the host status. Red: Infected node; Green: Vulnerable node but not infected; Gray: Non-vulnerable node.

In the next run, we set the look-ahead step K=5. Then no network nodes are infected or hacked during the simulation of 2 hours. If a public server is infected, the defense side can foresee the enemy's next attacking internal server from the infected network node. Then a shut-down or reboot action will be taken to destroy the multi-stage attack at the first stage.

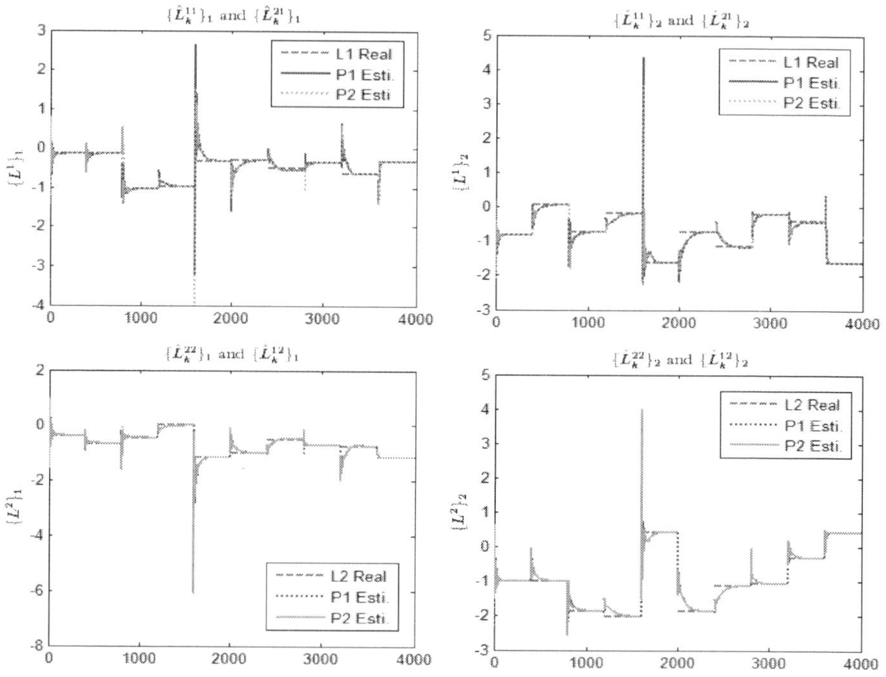

Fig. 8. Results of Adaptive Design

6. Conclusions

We implemented an adaptive Markov game theoretic situation awareness and adversary intent inference approach in a data-fusion/data-mining cyber attack and network defense framework (Fig. 2). The network security system was evaluated and protected from a perspective of data fusion and adaptive control. The goal of our approach was to examine the estimation of network states and projection of attack activities (similar to extended course of action (ECOA) in the warfare scenario). We used Markov game theory's ability to "step ahead" to infer possible adversary attack patterns. With the consideration that the parameters in each game player's cost function is not accessible to other players, we designed an adaptation scheme, based on the concept of Fictitious Play (FP), for the piecewise linearized Markov game model. A software tool was developed to demonstrate the performance of the adaptive game theoretic high level information fusion approach for cyber network defense and simulations were performed to verify and illustrate the benefits of this model.

7. References

Agah, A.; Das, S. K. & Basu, K. (2004). A non-cooperative game approach for intrusion detection in sensor networks, *Vehicular Technology Conference, 2004. VTC2004-Fall.* pp. 2902 – 2906, 2004.

Alpcan, T. & Basar, T. (2003). A game theoretic application to decision and analysis in Network Intrusion Detection, *42nd IEEE CDC 2003*, pp. 2595-2600, Maui, Hawaii, USA, 2003.

AstrÄom, K.J. & Wittenmark, B. (1995). *Adaptive Control.* Addison-Wesley Series in Electrical Engineering: Control Engineering, Addison-Wesley, second ed., 1995.

Basar, T. & Olsder, G. J. (1999). *Dynamic Noncooperative Game Theory*, SIAM Series in Classics in Applied Mathematics, second ed., January, 1999.

Blasch, E. & Plano, S. (2005). DFIG Level 5 (User Refinement) issues supporting Situational Awareness Reasoning, *7th International Conference on Information Fusion*, pp. xxxv-xliii, ISBN: 0-7803-9286-8, Philadelphia, PA, USA, July, 2005.

Brown, G. W. (1951). Iterative solutions of games by fictitious play, In: *Activity Analysis of Production and Allocation* (T. C. Koopmans, ed.), New York: Wiley, 1951.

Chen, G.; Shen, D.; Kwan, C.; Cruz, Jr., J. B.; Kruger, M. & Blasch, E. (2007). Game Theoretic Approach to Threat Prediction and Situation Awareness, *Journal of Advances in Information Fusion*, vol. 2, no. 1, pp. 35-48, June, 2007.

Fudenberg D. & Levine, D. K. (1998). *The Theory of Learning in Games*, Cambridge: MIT Press, 1998.

Nash, J. (1951). Noncooperative games, *Annals of Mathematics*, vol. 54, pp. 286-295, 1951.

Salerno, J.; Hinman, M. & Boulware, D. (2005). A Situation Awareness Model Applied To Multiple Domains, *Proc. Defense and Security Conference*, Orlando, FL, 2005.

Sallhammar, K.; Knapskog, S. J. & Helvik, B. E. (2005). Using Stochastic Game Theory to compute the expected Behavior of attackers, *Proceedings, 2005 Symposium on Applications and the Internet Workshops*, 2005.

Sastry, S. S. (1999). *Nonlinear Systems: Analysis, Stability and Control*, Springer-Verlag, New York, NY, 1999.

Shapley, L. S. (1953). Stochastic games, *Proc. National Academy of Sciences of the United States of America*, vol. 39, pp. 1095-1100, 1953.

Shen, D. (2006). *Nash strategies for dynamic noncooperative linear quadratic sequential games*, Ph.D. Dissertation, Adviser: Jose B. Cruz, Jr., Ohio State University, Electrical Engineering, 2006.

Tadda, G.; Salerno, J.; Boulware, D.; Hinman, M. & Gorton, S. (2006). Realizing Situation Awareness within a Cyber Environment, In: *Multisensor, Multisource Information Fusion: Architectures, Algorithms, and Applications 2006*, edited by B. V. Dasarathy, Proc. of SPIE Vol. 6242, SPIE, Bellingham, WA, 2006.

Tao, G. (2003). *Adaptive Control Design and Analysis*, Adaptive and Learning Systems for Signal Processing, Communications and Control Series, Hoboken, N.J.: Wiley-Interscience, 2003.

22

Life-long Learning Through Task Rehearsal and Selective Knowledge Transfer

Daniel L. Silver[1] and Robert E. Mercer[2]
[1]*Jodrey School of Computer Science, Acadia University*
[2]*Department of Computer Science, The University of Western Ontario*
Canada

1. Introduction

The majority of machine learning research has focused on the single task learning (STL) approach where an hypothesis for a single task is induced from a set of supervised training examples. In contrast, one of the key aspects of human learning is that individuals face a sequence of learning problems over a lifetime. Humans take advantage of this by transferring knowledge from previously learned tasks to facilitate the learning of a new task. *Life-long learning*, a relatively new area of machine learning research, is concerned with the persistent and cumulative nature of learning (Thrun, 1997). Life-long learning considers situations in which a learner faces a series of different tasks and develops methods of retaining and using prior knowledge to improve the effectiveness (more accurate hypotheses) and efficiency (shorter training times) of learning. Related names for life-long learning in the literature are *learning to learn* and *meta-learning*.

A challenge often faced by a life-long learning agent is a deficiency of training examples from which to develop accurate hypotheses. Machine learning theory tells us that this problem can be overcome with an appropriate *inductive bias* (Mitchell, 1997), one source being *prior task knowledge* (Baxter, 1995). Lacking a theory of knowledge transfer (Caruana, 1997, Thrun, 1997) that distinguishes knowledge from related and unrelated tasks, we have developed one and applied it to life-long learning problems, such as learning a more accurate medical diagnostic model from a small sample of patient data (Silver, 2000). The approach requires (1) a method of selectively transferring previously learned knowledge to a new task based on a measure of task relatedness and (2) a method of retaining learned task knowledge and its recall when learning a new task.

In (Silver & Mercer, 1996) we introduced ηMTL, a modified version of the multiple task learning (MTL) method of functional transfer to provide a solution to the first problem of selective transfer. Using a measure of previously learned secondary task to primary task relatedness, an ηMTL network can favourably bias the induction of a hypothesis for a primary task. Section 3 reviews the necessary aspects of ηMTL.

This paper focuses on the Task Rehearsal Method (TRM) to solve the second problem of retention and recall of learned task knowledge. TRM uses either the standard MTL or the ηMTL learning algorithms as the method of knowledge transfer and inductive bias. Task rehearsal is so named because previously learned tasks are relearned or *rehearsed* in parallel with the learning of each new task. It is through the rehearsal of previously learned tasks that the inductive bias of prior knowledge influences the hypothesis for the new task.

The contributions of this work is the demonstration that task knowledge can be effectively and efficiently retained within a neural network representation, that this knowledge can be selectively and accurately transferred using the TRM and ηMTL approach, and that a life-long sequential learning system can be developed based on the approach.

The following section provides appropriate background on knowledge based inductive learning, inductive bias, knowledge transfer with MTL neural networks and the origins of task rehearsal. Section 3 reviews selective knowledge transfer with ηMTL using a measure of task relatedness. Section 4 develops the TRM of life-long learning and discusses a prototype software system. Section 5 discusses the results of empirical studies using TRM and ηMTL on four domains of tasks. Section 6 presents the important findings made while implementing and testing the prototype system, reviews closely related work by other researchers and suggests future work in this area. Finally, Section 7 concludes with a summary of the paper.

2. Background

2.1 Knowledge based inductive learning

The constraint on a learning system's hypothesis space, beyond the criterion of consistency with the training examples, is called *inductive bias* (Mitchell, 1980). An inductive bias of a learning system can be expressed as the system's preference for one hypothesis over another, for example Occam's Razor suggests a bias for simple over more complex hypotheses. Inductive bias is essential for the development of a hypothesis with good generalization from a practical number of examples (Mitchell, 1997). Ideally, a life-long learning system can select its inductive bias to tailor the preference for hypotheses according to the task being learned (Utgoff, 1986). One type of inductive bias is knowledge of the task domain. The retention and use of domain knowledge as a source of inductive bias remains an unsolved problem in machine learning.

We define *knowledge based inductive learning* as a learning method which relies on prior knowledge of the problem domain to reduce the hypothesis space which must be searched. Figure 1 provides the framework for knowledge based inductive learning. *Domain knowledge* is a database of accumulated information which has been acquired from previously learned tasks. The intent is that this knowledge will bias a pure inductive learning system in a positive manner such that it trains in a shorter period of time and produces a more accurate hypothesis with a fewer number of training examples. In turn, new information is added to, or *consolidated* within the domain knowledge database following its discovery. Michalski refers to this as *constructive inductive learning* (Michalski, 1993). In the extreme, where the new classification task to be learned is exactly the same as one learned at some earlier time, the inductive bias should provide rapid convergence on the optimal hypothesis with very few examples. Formally, given a learning algorithm L and a domain knowledge inductive bias B_D, the problem becomes one of finding a hypothesis h, based on a set of examples $S = (x_i, t_i)$ from a concept space X, such that:

$$L \wedge B_D \wedge S \succ h$$

where $h(x_i) = t_i$ for all (x_i, t_i) in X and $\succ$ means inductive inference. The relation is not one of deductive inference because it is possible that B_D forms only a portion of all assumptions required to logically deduce h given S.

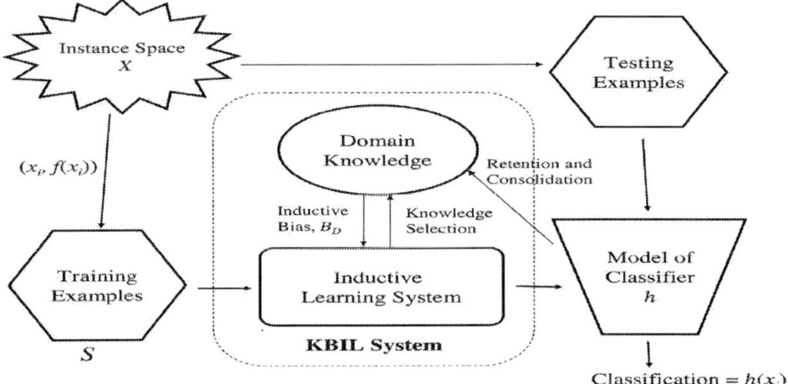

Fig. 1. The framework for knowledge based inductive learning.

When task domain knowledge is used to bias an inductive learner, a *transfer* of knowledge occurs from one or more *source* or *secondary* tasks to a *target* or *primary* task. Thus, the problem of selecting an appropriate bias is transformed into the problem of selecting the appropriate task knowledge for transfer.

The problem of knowledge transfer is an important aspect of life-long learning. For a good survey of knowledge transfer methods see (Pratt & Jennings, 1996), for a related survey on learning to learn read (Thrun & Pratt, 1997), and for a recent survey on metalearning see (Vilatlta & Drissi, 2002). Each of these surveys conclude that a significant problem in using prior knowledge is the selection of appropriate related knowledge when learning a new task.

2.2 Representational vs. functional transfer

In (Silver & Mercer, 1996) we define the difference between two forms of task knowledge transfer: *representational* and *functional*. The *representational* form of transfer involves the direct or indirect assignment of known task representation (weight values) to a new task. We consider this to be an explicit form of knowledge transfer from a source task to a target task. Since 1990 numerous authors have discussed methods of representational transfer (Fahlman & Lebiere, 1990, Pratt, 1993, Ring, 1993, Sharkey & Sharkey, 1992, Shavlik & Towell, 1990, Singh, 1992, Towell et al., 1990) which often results in substantially reduced training time with no loss in generalization performance.

In contrast to representational transfer is a form we define as *functional*. Functional transfer does not involve the explicit assignment of prior task representation to a new task, rather it employs the use of implicit *pressures* from supplemental training examples (Abu-Mostafa, 1995, Suddarth & Kergoisien, 1990), the parallel learning of related tasks constrained to use a common internal representation (Baxter, 1995, Caruana, 1997), or the use of historical training information (most commonly the learning rate or gradient of the error surface) to augment the standard weight update equations (Mitchell & Thrun, 1993, Naik & Mammone, 1993, Thrun, 1995). These pressures serve to reduce the effective hypothesis space in which the learning system performs its search. This form of transfer has its greatest value from the perspective of increased generalization performance. Certain methods of functional transfer have also been found to reduce training time (measured in number of training iterations). Chief among these methods is the parallel multiple task learning (MTL) paradigm which is discussed in the next subsection.

The form of knowledge transfer can be independent of the form of knowledge retention. For example, functional knowledge of a task can be retained in the form of training examples and later used to transfer knowledge when learning a new task. Alternatively, the representation of a task model can be retained and later used to generate training examples that can then be used for functional transfer.

2.3 Multiple Task Learning (MTL)

Psychological studies of human and animal learning conclude that besides the development of a specific discriminant function which satisfies the task at hand, there is the acquisition of general knowledge of the task domain. This general knowledge remains available for use in subsequent learning (Kehoe, 1988). This concept has been formalized by Baxter's work on learning internal representations (Baxter, 1995) and demonstrated by Caruana (Caruana, 1997) through a method called multiple task learning (MTL). We classify MTL as a functional form of knowledge transfer.

An MTL network uses a feed-forward multi-layer network with an output for each task to be learned. Figure 2 shows a simple MTL network containing a hidden layer of nodes, henceforth referred to as the *common feature layer*, that are shared by all tasks. The sharing of the *internal representation* (the weights of connections) below the common feature layer is the method by which inductive bias occurs within an MTL network. This is a powerful method of knowledge transfer. For example, a two output MTL network can learn the logical XOR and ¬XOR functions because they share a common internal representation. By comparison, it is not possible to learn these two tasks within the same single task learning (STL) network because their examples would conflict.

MTL training examples are composed of a set of input attributes as well as a target output for each task. The standard back-propagation of error learning algorithm is used to train all

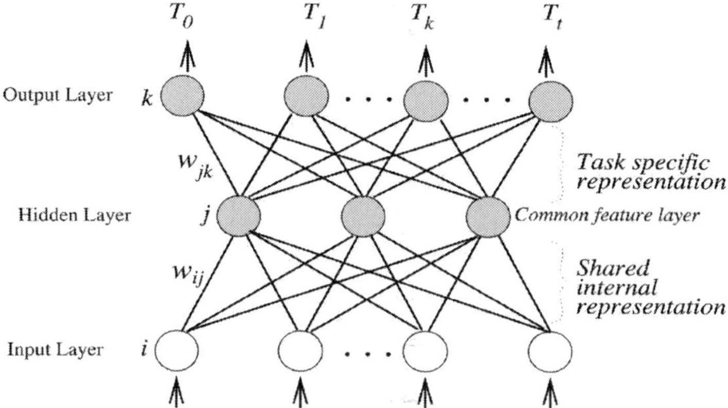

Fig. 2. A multiple task learning (MTL) network. There is an output node for each task being learned in parallel. The representation formed in the lower portion of the network is common to all tasks.

tasks in parallel. The weights, w_{jk}, affecting an output node k are adjusted according to the equation: $\Delta w_{jk} = \eta \frac{\partial E_k}{\partial w_{jk}}$; where η is the learning rate parameter, E_k is the error (or cost) function being minimized and $\frac{\partial E_k}{\partial w_{jk}}$ is the error signal that is propagated backward through the network. Under the standard back-propagation algorithm η is a constant, global parameter for all tasks. Consequently, the back-propagated error signal from any output node k is considered to be of equal value to all others. At the lowest training error, the back-propagation algorithm generates hypotheses that average the error across all of the output nodes. The averaging effect may not be beneficial for every task (Caruana, 1997).

Baxter has proven that the number of examples (sample complexity) required for learning any one task using an MTL network decreases as a function of the total number of related tasks being learned in parallel (Baxter, 1995). Baxter has also proven that the common internal representation acquired will facilitate the learning of subsequent related tasks sampled from the domain. In an MTL network this translates into a common representational component developed within the input to hidden weights for all tasks (see Figure 2). For any particular task the hidden to output weights constitute the task specific component. Since the number of weights in this section of the network is relatively small, the training of a new task from the domain can be accomplished with relatively few examples and with a smaller amount of effort compared with single task learning.

Functional transfer and positive inductive bias occurs in an MTL network due to the pressures of learning several related tasks under the constraint that the majority of the connection weights of each task are shared. Therefore, to ensure the functional transfer of knowledge from several secondary tasks to the primary task: (1) the MTL network should have a sufficient amount of internal representation (the sum of the hidden nodes required for learning each task under STL is suggested by (Caruana, 1997)), and (2) the secondary tasks should be as closely related to the primary task as possible.

2.4 Rehearsal of task examples

A fundamental problem with using back-propagation neural networks as the basis for a life-long learning system is the phenomenon of *catastrophic interference* (Grossberg, 1987, McCloskey & Cohen, 1989). Consider the problem of learning one set of randomly chosen input-output examples by an STL ANN and subsequently learning another set of examples using the same ANN. Catastrophic interference occurs as the hypothesis for the second set of examples interferes with the existing hidden node representation developed for the first set. The result is that knowledge of the first set of examples is "forgotten". Psychologists have long considered this a major failing of ANN models of long-term memory.

Rehearsal and *pseudo-rehearsal* of examples is presented as solutions to catastrophic interference in (Robins, 1995, 1996). Robins shows that the existing hidden node representation within an STL network can be maintained by relearning or rehearsing a subset of the previously learned examples while concurrently learning the new set of examples. Given sufficient internal representation (hidden nodes), an appropriate model will develop such that it satisfies the requirements of both set of examples to the extent to which the examples do not interfere. The *rehearsal* method requires that at least some portion of the training examples be retained indefinitely. The *pseudo-rehearsal* method overcomes this requirement by using the existing STL network to generate a random set of *pseudoitems* or *virtual examples* that can be rehearsed along along with the new examples.

Robins shows that pseudo-rehearsal is nearly as effective as rehearsal of retained examples. Although the work focuses on the integration of new examples into an STL network, Robins goes on to suggest that pseudo-rehearsal is a potential model for long-term memory consolidation in the mammalian neocortex. He relates this to a seminal neuroscience paper (McClelland et al., 1994) which discusses the complimentary roles of the hippocampus and the neocortex in human learning.

3. Selective knowledge transfer with ηMTL

The above background material has led to a theory of selective knowledge transfer in the context of back-propagation ANNs that can be used to develop a life-long learning system (Silver, 2000). The theory proposes (1) a method of retaining learned task knowledge and recalling it when learning a new task and (2) a method of selectively transferring previously learned knowledge to a new task based on a measure of task relatedness. This section summarizes those aspects of the theory that are concerned with selective transfer using a measure of task relatedness. In the following section we detail those aspects that cover the retention and recall of task knowledge; the major focus of this paper.

3.1 ηMTL: framework for a measure of task relatedness

To optimize the transfer of knowledge within an MTL network, the secondary tasks should be as closely related to the primary task as possible, else negative inductive bias can resultin a less accurate hypothesis. This suggests that tasks have degrees of relatedness to one another and that a measure of relatedness might be used to control the parallel learning of multiple tasks.

Abu-Mostafa develops the mathematics for learning a primary task from *hint* examples of several related tasks, within a single task learning (STL) network (Abu-Mostafa, 1995). Hints are a form of inductive bias that characterize properties of the primary task or task domain such as monotonicity or symmetry of the output with respect to the inputs. The theory states that minimizing the error across all hint examples will contribute toward the development of a more accurate hypothesis for the primary task. We adapt Abu-Mostafa's mathematics to an MTL network with multiple output nodes, one node for each secondary hint task. If a secondary task is related to the primary task, its examples act as hints for training the common feature layer shared by the primary task within the MTL network. If a secondary task is unrelated then its contribution to the MTL network for the primary task can be detrimental and therefore should be minimized.

Consider an objective function to be minimized by the BP algorithm across all task outputs that focuses on the development of the best hypothesis for the primary task:

$$\hat{E} = E_0 + E_1 + \ldots + E_k + \ldots + E_t$$

where E_k is the error on the training examples for hint tasks $k = 1, \ldots, t$ and E_0 is the error on the primary task training examples. By gradient descent the appropriate change to a weight w_{jk} at an output node k is given by $\Delta w_{jk} = -\eta \frac{\partial \hat{E}}{\partial E_k} \frac{\partial E_k}{\partial w_{jk}}$ where η is the learning rate.

Under these conditions, $\frac{\partial \hat{E}}{\partial E_k}$, the rate of change of the overall error with respect to the rate of change of the error for task k, can be consider the weight of importance of hint task k for learning the primary task. We define this weight of importance to be the *measure of relatedness*, R_k, between the primary and each of the secondary tasks; that is

$$R_k = \frac{\partial \hat{E}}{\partial E_k} \qquad \text{such that} \qquad \Delta w_{jk} = -\eta R_k \frac{\partial E_k}{\partial w_{jk}} = -\eta_k \frac{\partial E_k}{\partial w_{jk}}$$

Thus, an appropriate measure of relatedness, R_k, for a secondary source task, T_k, must regulate the impact of the task error, E_k, on the formation of shared internal representation. A separate learning rate, η_k, for each output node k can be considered and kept inside the backward propagated error signal $\frac{\partial E_k}{\partial w_{jk}}$. Thus, by varying η_k it is possible to adjust the amount of weight modification associated with any one task of the network[1]. This modified version of the standard back-propagation learning algorithm for MTL we have called the ηMTL algorithm.

Let the learning rate η_0 for the primary task, T_0, be the full value of the base learning rate η, that is, $\eta_0 = \eta$. Then let R_k vary $0 \le R_k \le 1$ for all tasks $k = 1, \ldots, t$, thereby constraining the learning rate for any parallel task to be at most η. Notice, that if $R_k = 1$ for all $k = 0, \ldots, t$, we have standard MTL. Alternatively, if $R_0 = 1$ and $R_k = 0$ for all $k = 1, \ldots, t$, we have standard single task learning (STL) of the primary function. In this way, the ηMTL framework generalizes over STL and MTL.

3.2 The nature of task relatedness

Critical to the transfer of knowledge from a pool of source tasks to a primary task is some measure of relatedness between those tasks (Thrun, 1996, Caruana, 1997, Vilatlta & Drissi, 2002). We define task relatedness in the context of functional transfer: *Let T_k be a secondary task and T_0 a primary task of the same domain with training examples S_k and S_0, respectfully. The relatedness of T_k with respect to T_0 in the context of learning system L, that uses functional knowledge transfer, is the utility of using S_k along with S_0 toward the development of an effective hypothesis for T_0. The relatedness of T_k can be expressed as a function of the efficiency and effectiveness of L using S_k to develop a hypothesis for T_0.*

The definition promotes the view that tasks have degrees of relatedness to one and another. Secondary tasks can be partially ordered from most related to least related such that the most related secondary task results in the most effective primary hypothesis, h_0, developed in the shortest period of time.

The definition suggests a brute force approach to determining the relatedness between two tasks. The learning system could learn T_0 in parallel with each secondary task and record the effectiveness of the resulting hypothesis. However, if combinations of secondary tasks are considered then the method would be impractical because of the factorial growth in time complexity. An *a prori* measure of task relatedness is needed.

We have developed and tested several *static, dynamic* and *hybrid* measures of task relatedness that are based on the principals of surface and structural similarity (Silver, 2000, Silver & Mercer, 2001). *Surface similarity* is defined as shallow, easily perceived, external similarity which is a measure of the external functional similarity based on the training

---

[1] The use of an adaptive or separate learning rate at the node or weight level is not a new concept. It has been used for various purposes, such as (Jacobs, 1988, Naik et al., 1992, Vogl et al., 1988).

examples available for each of the tasks. *Structural similarity* is defined as deep, often complex, internal feature similarity which is the degree to which two developing hypotheses utilize their shared internal representation (particularly, the common feature layer) to produce accurate approximations of tasks.

For the studies presented in this paper we use a hybrid measure that is composed of a static component based on the linear correlation of training set target values and a dynamic component based on the mutual information of hidden node features with respect to training set target values (Silver, 2000).

4. Sequential learning through task rehearsal

4.1 The task rehearsal method.

This section presents the Task Rehearsal Method (TRM) that extends the concept of pseudo-rehearsal (henceforth simply referred to as *rehearsal*) to MTL networks for learning sequences of tasks.

TRM, presented diagrammatically in Figure 3, is a knowledge based inductive learning system that relies on the rehearsal of previously learned tasks when learning a new task within an ηMTL network. After a task T_k has been successfully learned (to a specified level of generalization error), its hypothesis representation is saved in domain knowledge. This representation acts as a surrogate for the space of input-output examples that defines task T_k. Virtual examples of the input-output space for T_k can be produced (with the same level of generalization error) by passing inputs to the domain knowledge representation for T_k and recording the outputs. When learning a new task, T_0, the domain knowledge representations for tasks $T_1...T_k...T_t$ are used to generate corresponding *virtual* output values from the T_0 training examples. The resulting set of virtual examples is used to rehearse the domain knowledge tasks in parallel with the learning of T_0 in a new ηMTL network. The virtual examples can be considered *hints* (as discussed in Section 3.1) that are used to transfer knowledge (provide inductive bias) in a functional manner from $T_1...T_k...T_t$ to T_0.

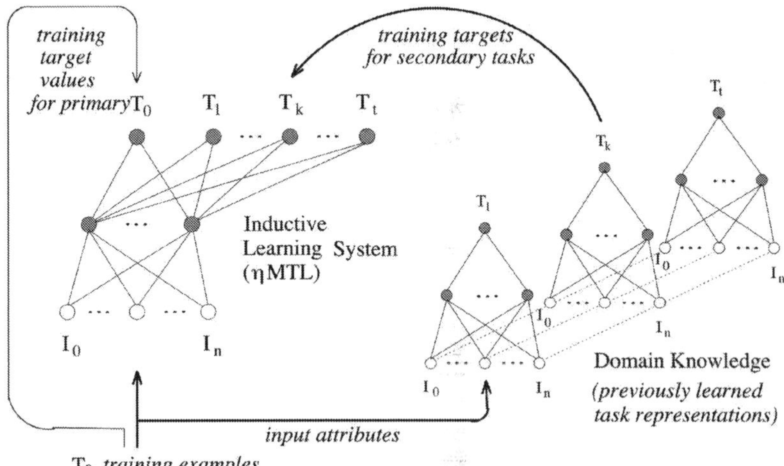

Fig. 3. A model of the Task Rehearsal Method.

The operationalization of TRM sees two sets of feed-forward neural networks interacting during two phases of operation. The following describes the networks and the phases of operation.

The Networks. The set of single output feed-forward networks, labelled *domain knowledge*, is the long-term storage area for the representation of tasks which have been successfully learned. Task representation consists of the network architecture (number of nodes in each layer) and the weights of the connections between the nodes.

The ηMTL back-propagation network, labelled *Inductive Learning System*, can be considered a short-term memory area for learning the new task while being influenced by the inductive bias provided by the domain knowledge networks. The architecture of the ηMTL network must contain enough representation (number of hidden nodes) to develop a sufficiently accurate hypothesis for at least the primary task and potentially for all secondary tasks. There is no requirement that the architecture of the ηMTL network be the same for each new task that is learned.

The major application of TRM is learning a new task from an impoverished training set. In this situation, the lack of training examples has the undesirable side effect of providing insufficient virtual examples for rehearsing accurate hypotheses for the domain knowledge tasks. Consequently, the system cannot provide appropriate inductive bias. To overcome this problem, additional virtual training examples are used with a special *unknown* target classification for the primary task. The back-propagation algorithm used in the Inductive Learning System recognizes these extra training examples and considers their contribution to primary task error to be zero. Consequently, for these examples, only the error of secondary tasks affect the development of the neural network's internal representation.

Phases of Operation. A new task is learned in the ηMTL network during the *knowledge recall and training phase*. Each training example for the primary task T_0 provides n input attributes and a target class value. The target values for secondary tasks $T_1...T_k...T_t$ are, of course, not part of this T_0 training data. These target values must be "recalled" from domain knowledge by feeding the n input attributes into each of the domain knowledge networks and appending the outputs to the original training example. The resulting virtual example is now acceptable to the the ηMTL network for training[2]. Training of the ηMTL network for all tasks begins from random initial weights. The error on a validation set is monitored so as to prevent over-fitting of the data to the network.

The *knowledge retention phase* follows the successful learning of a new task. If the hypothesis for the primary task is able to classify an independent test set of examples with an error rate below a user specified level, the task is considered successfully learned and its representation is saved in domain knowledge. The architectures of the stored networks can be completely different from one another. The fundamental requirement of domain knowledge is an ability to store and retrieve the representations of induced hypotheses and to use these representations to generate accurate virtual examples of the original tasks.

---

[2] The domain knowledge networks output continuous values, therefore, the virtual target values will range between 0 and 1. Continuous target values will more accurately convey the function of the domain knowledge networks and they provide the means by which dichotomous classification tasks may transfer knowledge from related continuous valued tasks in future research.

4.2 The prototype software.

A prototype software system has been developed that implements the TRM shown in Figure 3. The system uses enhanced back-propagation ANN software that is capable of single task learning (STL), MTL or ηMTL. The system employs a batch method of backpropagation of error that utilizes a momentum term in the weight update equation to speed the convergence of the network. A *save-best weights* method is used to save the representation of the network at minimum error on the validation set.

The prototype system uses a sequence table to control the order in which tasks will be learned. For each task in the table, the software moves through the two phases of operation described above. Before learning a new primary task, the examples for the primary task are used to generate the virtual examples for all secondary tasks. A domain knowledge table contains the names of previously learned secondary task representations. If so desired, the table can be populated with names of task representations learned during previous runs of the system.

After a minimum validation error hypothesis has been developed, the TRM software must determine if the hypothesis is sufficiently accurate to be stored within domain knowledge. If the accuracy criteria is met, the hypothesis representation is stored, and the task name is added to the domain knowledge table. If the accuracy criteria is not met, the hypothesis is rejected and no representation or record of the task is kept. A record of the task's name in the domain knowledge table ensures that the associated hypothesis will be considered during the learning of future tasks.

5. Empirical studies

5.1 The domains studied.

This section reports on the testing of TRM against four domains of tasks. The characteristics of an appropriate task domain for testing a life-long learning system is considered in (Silver, 2000). The most important factors are that (1) one or more primary tasks of interest have impoverished sets of training examples insufficient for developing accurate hypotheses under STL, and (2) the domain contain a mix of secondary tasks such that the majority of these tasks are unrelated to the primary task(s) so as to force the life-long learning system to overcome negative inductive bias.

The Band domain consists of seven synthetic tasks. Each task has a band of positive examples across a 2-dimensional input space. The tasks were synthesized so that the primary task T_0 would vary in its relatedness to the other tasks based on the band orientation. A preliminary study showed that T_4, T_5 and T_6 are the more related to T_0 when individually learned in parallel with T_0; they consistently resulted in the most accurate hypotheses for T_0.

The Logic domain consists of eight synthetic tasks. Each positive example is defined by a logical combination of 4 of the 11 input variables of the form, $T_0 : (A > 0.5 \vee B > 0.5) \wedge (C > 0.5 \vee D > 0.5)$. Tasks T_1, T_2 and T_3 are more related to T_0 with T_2 being the most related. The Band and Logic domains have been designed so that all tasks are non-linearly separable; each task requires the use of at least two hidden nodes of a neural network to form an accurate hypothesis.

The coronary artery disease (CAD) domain contains three real medical diagnostic tasks and four synthetic tasks. Each task has five input attributes (age, gender, resting blood pressure, level of chest pain, resting electrocardiogram results). Data for the real tasks were extracted from the heart disease database in the UCI machine learning repository (Detrano, 1989). The data were originally collected from three geographically different locations: the Cleveland Clinic Foundation, Cleveland (*clev*), the Hungarian Institute of Cardiology, Budapest (*hung*) and the V.A. Medical Centre, Long Beach, California (*vamc*). Predicting those patients with disease (50% stenosis of a coronary artery) from the *vamc* hospital is the primary task. Because of the relatively high degree of relatedness between these tasks, data for four additional tasks (*A, B, C,* and *D*) that vary in their relatedness to the real tasks were synthesized based on knowledge of general rules for predicting CAD.

The forest cover type (Cover) domain consists of six real tasks for predicting the type of tree cover from cartography information. The data concerns the Comanche Peak Wilderness Area of northern Colorado and was downloaded from the UCI repository (Blackard & Dean, 2000). Ten input variables were extracted from the original data (eg. elevation, slope, hillshade at noon, distance to waterway). Each task concerns the prediction of one cover type: Krummholtz, Douglas Fir, Aspen, Ponderosa Pine, Lodgepole Pine or Spruce/Fir. Each task required the use of two or more hidden nodes to produce the best STL models. The challenge is to develop models for Lodgepole Pine and Spruce/Fir from impoverished data sets after having developed models for the first four tasks.

Table 1 summarizes the size of the data sets used for training, validating, and testing each task of each domain under study. The tasks are presented in the order in which they are sequentially learned using TRM. Note that each training set is augmented with additional examples with *unknown* target values for the primary task. The number of additional examples varies for each task so as to ensure there are at least 50, 50, 100 and 126 training examples for the Band, Logic, CAD and Cover domain, respectfully. These additional examples are used by TRM to generate virtual examples for rehearsing the secondary tasks that have been previously learned (see Section 4.1).

Domain	Tasks and Size of Training Set								Val. Set	Test Set
Band	T_1	T_6	T_2	T_5	T_4	T_3	T_0			
	50	35	30	25	20	15	10		20	200
Logic	T_7	T_6	T_5	T_4	T_3	T_2	T_1	T_0		
	50	50	50	45	40	35	30	25	20	200
CAD	*A*	*B*	*C*	*D*	*clev*	*hung*	*vamc*			
	123	123	123	123	148	30	10		6–64	75–96
Cover	*krum*	*doug*	*aspen*	*pond*	*lodge*	*spruce*				
	126	126	80	70	60	50			64	6000

Table 1. Training, validation, and test set sizes for each task for the four domains.

5.2 Method.

The tasks for each domain are learned in the left-to-right order presented in Table 1 using the TRM system with each of the inductive learning methods: STL, MTL, and ηMTL. The neural networks used are all 3-layer architectures composed of an input layer of as many nodes as input attributes, a hidden layer of sufficient representation for all tasks in the domain and an output layer of as many nodes as there are tasks in the domain. A standard back-propagation learning approach is taken using validation sets to prevent over-fit of the network to the training data. Test sets are used to determine if the hypotheses that are learned are sufficiently accurate to be saved in domain knowledge. We consider an accuracy of 65% to be a minimum level of performance for the domains under study. Therefore, the maximum misclassification rate allowed on a test data set is 35%.

Analysis of the experimental results focuses on the performance of hypotheses developed for each task, particularly those at the end of the learning sequence for each domain. Table 1 shows that training sets for later tasks of each learning sequence have fewer examples than earlier ones. Our goal is to show that the TRM with ηMTL can overcome the impoverished training sets by selectively transferring knowledge from related tasks learned earlier in the sequence and saved in domain knowledge. The performance of the TRM system under each learning method is based on the accuracy of hypotheses against their respective test sets. The mean number of misclassifications from repeated experiments is the measure of performance. We also consider the true positive and true negative proportion statistics for those tasks where the ratio of positive and negative examples are unbalanced. The results shown below are based on 20 repetitions of sequential learning on each domain in which the random initial weights of the networks as well as the training, validation and test examples are resampled.

5.3 Results

Figures 4 and 5 and Table 2 present the test results for hypotheses developed for each task for each domain in the order in which they were learned. The STL results can be used as a baseline for comparison with the TRM results that used either MTL or ηMTL learning. In Table 2 hypotheses developed under MTL and ηMTL with mean percent misclassifications significantly less than STL hypotheses are indicated in bold (95% confidence based on difference of means t-test). Hypotheses developed under ηMTL with mean percent misclassifications significantly less than MTL hypotheses are shown in parentheses. The very best results are, therefore, in both bold and parentheses.

Domain	Mean Percent Misclassifications by Hypotheses							
Band	T_1	T_6	T_2	T_5	T_4	T_3	T_0	
STL	3.95	8.85	7.40	6.25	4.95	32.10	43.80	
MTL	3.95	11.55	6.90	12.85	22.75	30.65	**33.70**	
ηMTL	3.95	10.55	7.30	(7.85)	(9.65)	**26.80**	**(24.90)**	
Logic	T_7	T_6	T_5	T_4	T_3	T_2	T_1	T_0
STL	25.25	25.55	25.05	26.05	23.75	27.50	27.15	28.90
MTL	25.25	29.95	30.35	28.90	30.55	29.10	28.60	31.50
ηMTL	25.25	(27.00)	(26.35)	(26.00)	(26.30)	(25.60)	**(25.55)**	**(26.05)**
CAD	A	B	C	D	*clev*	*hung*	*vamc*	
STL	0.53	1.73	7.60	4.27	32.86	23.47	36.35	
MTL	0.53	1.47	5.20	2.40	33.96	**21.10**	**25.21**	
ηMTL	0.53	1.47	4.80	2.27	**(31.43)**	21.32	**(20.63)**	
Cover	*krum*	*doug*	*aspen*	*pond*	*lodge*	*spruce*		
STL	8.10	9.10	19.80	13.10	15.10	14.90		
MTL	8.10	8.90	**16.20**	**12.20**	22.20	16.40		
ηMTL	8.10	8.90	**16.00**	**12.10**	(21.20)	16.30		

Table 2. The mean percentage of misclassifications of test set examples by the hypotheses generated by the learning methods under TRM.

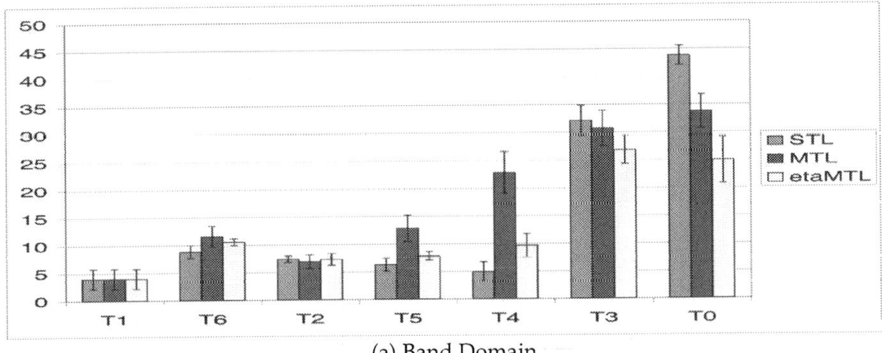

(a) Band Domain

(Mean Percentage of Misclassifications).

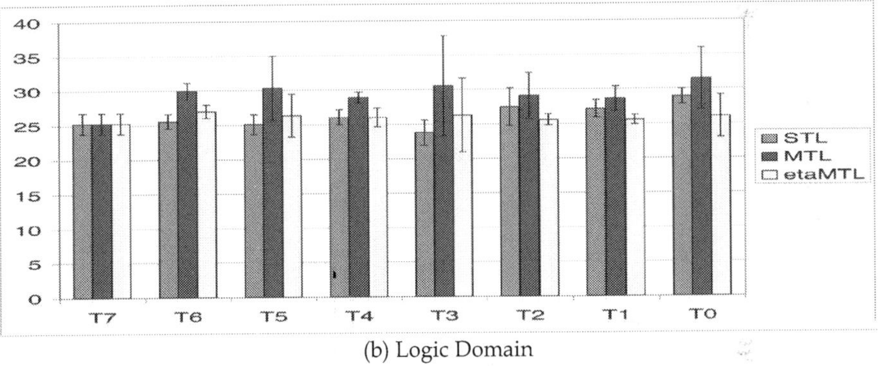

(b) Logic Domain

(Mean Percentage of Misclassifications).

Fig. 4. Performance results from sequential learning on the two synthetic task domains. Shown is the mean percentage of misclassifications by hypotheses generated by each learning method for each task. The results are presented in the order that the tasks were learned.

The results from the synthetic domains (Band, Logic) indicate that hypotheses developed under STL for tasks that have large numbers of training examples (the first four or five tasks) performed as well as or better than hypotheses developed under TRM. Those hypotheses developed under TRM using MTL as the learning method have misclassification rates that are, at times, significantly higher than that of STL hypotheses. The synthetic domains have more unrelated tasks than related ones, therefore, the arbitrary transfer of domain knowledge under this circumstance can have a detrimental effect on learning. This is most evident in the case of learning the Logic domain task T_3, where 40 training examples convey sufficient information to develop relatively accurate hypotheses under STL. Negative inductive bias from unrelated secondary tasks result in MTL hypotheses for T_3 having significantly higher error as compared with STL hypotheses. Inductive bias from secondary hypotheses will always have an effect on the internal representation developed

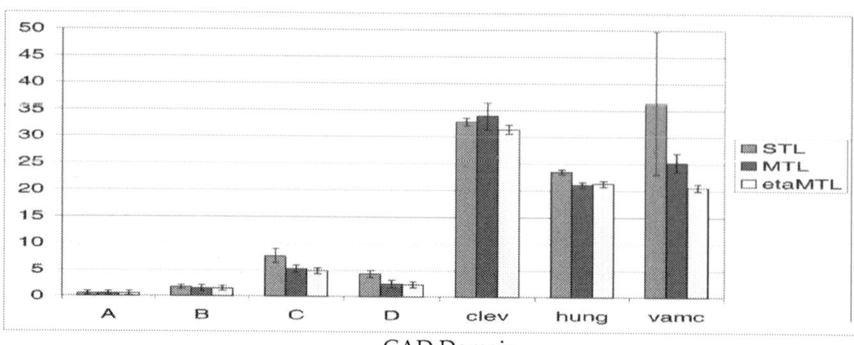

(Mean Percentage of Misclassifications).

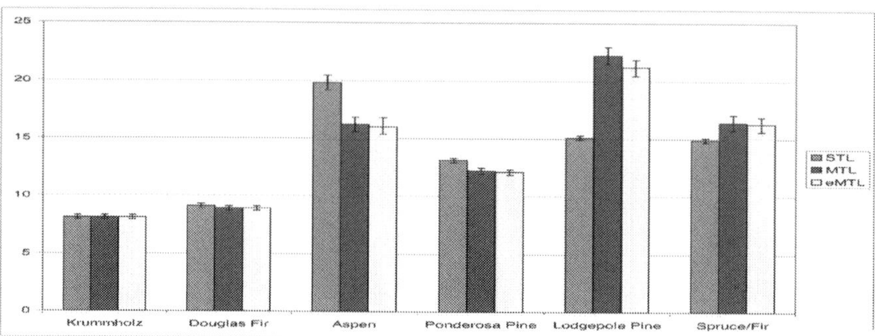

(b) Cover Domain

Domain (Mean Percentage of Misclassifications).

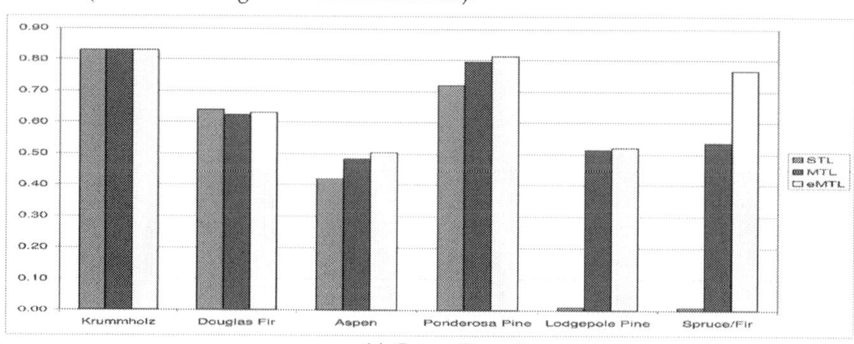

(c) Cover Domain

Domain (True Positive Proportion).

Fig. 5. Performance results from sequential learning on the two real task domains. Shown is the mean percentage of misclassifications by hypotheses generated by each learning method for each task. Also shown in graph (c) is the average true positive proportion for each task of the Cover domain. The results are presented in the order that the tasks were learned.

within the network. The challenge for a knowledge based inductive learning system is to filter out negative bias for the primary task. As shown in Table 2, TRM using ηMTL makes a significant improvement upon the MTL results for the synthetic tasks. The effect of negative inductive bias from unrelated tasks is mitigated by control over the individual learning rates for each of the secondary tasks. The error rate for the first four or five tasks under ηMTL are therefore closer to that of STL.

The results from the real domains (CAD, Cover) indicate that hypotheses developed using TRM with MTL and TRM with ηMTL consistently perform as well as or better than STL hypotheses for the first four or five tasks of each domain. Unlike the synthetic domains, the tasks of the real domains are more closely related to each other. Therefore, the knowledge transferred under MTL from prior tasks is almost always positive. Selective transfer under ηMTL produces only marginally better hypotheses. In interpreting the results of the Cover domain, it should be noted that the mean misclassification percentages for STL hypotheses for the last two tasks of the Cover domain are misleading. As shown by the True Positive Proportion graph of Figure 5, the low misclassification rates on LodgePole Pine and Spruce/Fir are because most of the STL hypotheses developed are naïve, that is, they classify all examples as negative.

The training data for the final two or three tasks of each synthetic and real domain are dramatically impoverished as compared to that of the first task in each learning sequence (see Table 1). STL has difficulty developing accurate hypotheses because the training data for these tasks provides so little information. The TRM with ηMTL augments the impoverished data with positive inductive bias from domain knowledge, resulting in better hypotheses for the last two tasks of all domains. The measure of relatedness reflected in each η_k is able to affect a selective transfer of knowledge from previously learned tasks. The TRM with MTL does not fare as well, particularly on the synthetic domains, because a mix of positive and negative inductive bias occurs from the domain knowledge tasks.

6. Discussion

The following summarizes the key observations that have been made while developing the TRM with ηMTL prototype system and conducting the experiments presented in this paper. A number of avenues for future work are suggested.

6.1 Retention and generation of task knowledge.

The experimental results demonstrate that TRM has the ability to retain accurate task knowledge in the form of neural network representations. The experiments also show that the TRM can generate virtual examples with the same level of accuracy as the retained network hypotheses.

Selective Retention of Accurate Task Knowledge. The TRM prototype system has demonstrated the ability to selectively retain only hypotheses which have met a pre-defined level of generalization accuracy based on the hypotheses classifying independent test sets of examples. This ensures that a level of domain knowledge accuracy is upheld.

Efficiency and Scalability of Task Knowledge Retention. The experiments demonstrated that TRM provides an efficient storage of task knowledge. The hypothesis representations saved in domain knowledge implicitly retain the information from the training examples in a compressed form. In the case of the Logic domain the 8 tasks have a total of 325 actual training examples composed of 12 values each. The total requirement is 3900 units of storage. This same information is retained within eight 11-6-1 network representations composed of 79 weights each. The total storage requirement in this case is 632 units. In general, the number of weights, W, in a 3-layer network can be computed as follows $W = (i+1)h+(h+1)o$; where i, h and o are the number of input, hidden and output nodes, respectfully. When learning a sequence of t tasks, the space requirement for saving all representations within domain knowledge is of $O(t(3+W))$; where 3 is the number of values (i, h, o) required to describe the network architecture. Therefore, the space requirements increase linearly with the number of tasks.

Accuracy and Value of Virtual Examples. The generation of accurate virtual examples from domain knowledge is essential to TRM because they are the means by which accurate knowledge is transferred from a secondary task to the primary hypothesis. The value of a virtual example can be measured by the difference in the mean performance of primary hypotheses developed with and without that example. Supplemental experiments have shown the value of more accurate virtual examples and the incremental value of additional virtual examples when developing hypotheses for related tasks (Silver, 2000). The more accurate the domain knowledge hypotheses (as recorded at the time of learning) the more accurate the virtual examples. This agrees with the reasonable expectation that the effort spent on accurately learning tasks early in life will benefit the learner later in life.

Importance of Input Attribute Range and Resolution. Supplemental experiments have also shown that the TRM can generate virtual examples with the same level of accuracy as the retained hypotheses, provided the input attributes of the virtual examples are within the same range and resolution of values as the examples used to develop the the domain knowledge hypotheses (Silver, 2000). One approach is to record the distribution of the original training and validation examples over the input space. For example the mean value and standard deviation of the original attributes could be computed and saved. These statistics could then be used to generate minimum and maximum boundaries for the input attribute values of virtual examples. Further research is needed into the best choice of attribute values for each new task.

Freedom to use Available Training Examples. TRM provides considerable freedom in the choice of training examples for a new task. Although an MTL method of knowledge transfer is used, there is no need to match specific examples of previously learned tasks. TRM will automatically generate matching virtual target values for the secondary tasks from the input attributes of new task examples. The ability to utilize all available training examples for a new task is a benefit for any life-long learning system.

Abundance of Virtual Examples. The source of inductive bias under TRM is the set of virtual examples generated from domain knowledge for relearning the secondary tasks. The larger the set of virtual examples, the richer the set of functional knowledge from each secondary task. When the number of primary task training examples is small, TRM can generate additional virtual examples for the secondary tasks through the use of primary examples that are marked with the *unknown* target value. These additional virtual examples should be selected bearing in mind the input attribute concerns expressed above. One must also be careful not to overwhelm the information provided in the actual training examples for the primary task with knowledge transferred from the virtual examples of the secondary tasks. Induction must be driven by a fair mix of information from the real examples and bias from the virtual examples. Further research is needed in this area.

Scalability of Virtual Example Generation. Generating virtual examples for TRM requires computational time and space resources. Two options are available. The target values for the secondary tasks can be computed on-line during learning at the cost of increased learning time. Alternatively, the target values can be generated in batch before learning begins at the cost of additional memory. Our current implementation uses the latter approach. The reader may consider that this conflicts with the benefit of efficient storage of training examples. However, because each training example has matching input attribute values, the additional memory cost is only for the storage of the target values of the secondary tasks. As the number of tasks within domain knowledge increases, one solution to this scaling problem is to only generate virtual examples for those domain knowledge tasks that are above a specified threshold of relatedness to the primary task. In this way the space or time complexity for generating the virtual examples would be held constant.

6.2 Selective transfer of task knowledge.

The experimental results show that the TRM with ηMTL can successfully transfer retained task knowledge to the benefit of tasks with impoverished training sets. The results on the last two tasks of each domain are particularly impressive with significantly lower mean number of misclassifications per task than hypotheses produced by either STL or the TRM with MTL.

Tasks having sufficient training examples. STL is able to produce comparatively accurate hypotheses for tasks that have sufficient training examples without needing additional inductive bias. Under MTL a negative transfer of knowledge occurs because of the interference at the common feature layer among unrelated tasks. ηMTL attempts to mitigate this interference but is not able to do so entirely. We are currently working on better measures of task relatedness to reduce the negative bias from unrelated tasks.

Scalability of ηMTL. Because the MTL and ηMTL methods uses the back-propagation algorithm, its time complexity is $O(W_3)$, where W is the number of weights in the ηMTL network (Mitchell, 1997). Naturally, W grows as a function of the number of tasks being learned in parallel. As suggested for the problem of generating virtual examples, a practical solution to lengthy training times is to reduce the number of weights in the network by eliminating secondary tasks that do not meet a predefined level of task relatedness to the primary task. In this way W and the time complexity can be kept constant.

6.3 An alternative explanation for the success of TRM

It could be argued that the reason for the development of more accurate hypotheses under TRM with ηMTL is due to the generation of stochastic noise either by the variation in η_k values during training or because of small errors introduced by the virtual examples for the secondary tasks. A number of authors have shown that stochastic noise can assist the backpropagation algorithm in escaping local minimum to find better hypotheses (Hanson, 1990, Heskes & Kappen, 1993, Wang & Principe, 1999). We have investigated this argument (Silver, 2000) and shown empirically using the Band and Logic domains that stochastic noise in the absence of related tasks cannot produce the same level of positive inductive bias.

6.4 Related work

Task Clustering (TC) Algorithm. Sequential learning, task relatedness and functional knowledge transfer in the context of a memory-based K-nearest neighbour learning system is discussed in (Thrun & O'Sullivan, 1995). The method partitions domain knowledge into clusters of related tasks based on a mutually beneficial Euclidean distance metric used by all tasks within each cluster. When a new task is to be learned, the system estimates the degree of relatedness between the primary task and each task cluster by using that cluster's distance metric to bias the nearest neighbour algorithm. The distance metric that produces the best generalization on the primary task's training examples selects the most related task cluster. The algorithm uses the chosen distance metric to classify future examples of the primary task. Based on experiments using object recognition data, the TC algorithm is shown to construct a meaningful hierarchy of related task clusters based on the distance metric.

In comparison to the TC algorithm, TRM with ηMTL has the advantage of being able to combine inductive bias from one or all domain knowledge tasks and not a predetermined cluster of tasks. The measure of task relatedness allows each new task to select an inductive bias unique to the training examples that are available and the domain knowledge that exists. The TC algorithm also has problems scaling up to a large number of tasks. TRM can overcome this problem by selecting *a priori* only those tasks most closely related to the primary task.

Life-Long Reinforcement Learning. Life-long learning and selective representation transfer is examined in the context of reinforcement learning in (Carroll et al., 2003). Knowledge transfer is recognized as being beneficial only when a source task is sufficiently related to the target task and that a measure of task relatedness is therefore necessary in the presence of multiple source tasks. The research focuses on more efficient learning and does not discuss generalization accuracy.

The TC algorithm, explained above, is extended to reinforcement learning and called the Reinforcement Learning Task Clustering (RLTC) method. RLTC uses a modified Q-learning algorithm that can have its state transition Q-values initialized to that of a related source task or the average of a cluster of related source tasks. Measures of task "similarity" are based on the vector of Q-values for each task. The paper explores methods of determining average Q-values and invariant Q-values within a cluster such that they can be used as the starting point for learning a new and potentially related task. Using a synthetic domain, experiments show that reinforcement tasks can be successfully clustered, and that the Qvalues of task clusters can be used to speed up the learning of a related task or slow down the learning of an unrelated task. The measure of task relatedness allows each new task to select an inductive bias unique to the training examples that are available and the domain knowledge that exists. The authors plan to investigate *a priori* measures of task similarity and the piecewise transfer of knowledge from various tasks in their future work.

Toward Continual Learning. In (Ring, 1997) a neural network based reinforcement learning agent called CHILD is introduced as a first step toward a system that is capable of continual, hierarchical, incremental learning and development. *Continual learning* is defined as "the constant development of increasingly complex behaviours; the process of building more complicated skills on top of those already developed". The system is capable of learning incrementally at each time step and hierarchically using what has been learned in the past to facilitate learning in the future. CHILD can only learn in restricted domains of finite automata tasks but exhibits the seven major characteristics of a continual learner defined in the paper. The system combines Q-learning and temporal transition hierarchies learning and utilizes a novel learning rule to create *higher-order* network units and associated connection weights when needed to overcome network error. Representational knowledge transfer occurs through the use of the weights of previously learned tasks. This can make for rapid learning of related tasks that increase in complexity. Test results on a domain of maze problems demonstrates CHILD's ability to accumulate and use knowledge from related tasks. However, the system shows some difficulty overcoming negative inductive bias from recently learned and unrelated tasks. Catastrophic interference reduces the system's ability to develop an accurate model of a previously learned task.

Knowledge-Based Cascade-Correlation. The Cascade Correlation algorithm (Fahlman and Lebiere, 1990) is extended to the Knowledge Based Cascade Correlation (KBCC) method in (Rivest, 2003, Shultz and Rivest, 2003). KBCC allows previously-learned source networks to compete with each other and with single hidden nodes for recruitment into a target network when learning a new task. The representation of source networks are temporarily connected to the target network and the new connection weights are trained so as to increase the correlation of the source networks' output with the target network's error. The best correlating source network is installed permanently into the target network and its surrounding weights trained to produce a hypothesis for the target task.

Experiments on families of Cartesian input tasks similar to the Band Domain demostrate that the KBCC is able to recruit and use prior task knowledge to quickly develop hypotheses for new tasks. The analysis of the experiments focuses on efficiency of learning and does not examine generalization accuracy. Tasks vary in their shape (rectangles, circles), orientation and size. Although the concept of task "relevance" is discussed and the effect of using different prior tasks on learning is examined the term is not formally defined. A link must be made between the relatedness of prior tasks and the reasons behind recruiting the best correlating prior task. We anticipate that the authors will address these issues in future work.

7. Summary

This paper reviews the importance of inductive bias to learning and discusses the relationship between inductive bias and knowledge transfer. A general model of knowledge-based inductive learning is presented that promotes the retention and use of task knowledge when learning a new task from the same domain. The difference between the representation and functional forms of task knowledge is defined along with the recognition that knowledge retention and transfer can take either form.

An approach to life-long learning is presented in the context of back propagation neural networks. The approach requires (1) a method of selectively transferring previously learned knowledge to a new task and (2) a method of retaining learned task knowledge and its recall. This paper reviews our approach to selective transfer based on a measure of task relatedness, but focuses on the second problem of knowledge retention and recall and presents the Task Rehearsal Method (TRM) as a solution.

TRM, is a knowledge-based inductive learning approach. It is able to retain task knowledge and use that knowledge to bias the induction of hypotheses for new tasks. TRM saves the representation of previously learned neural network hypotheses within a domain knowledge storage area. Domain knowledge is used to generate functional task knowledge in the form of virtual examples at the time of learning a new task. The virtual examples are rehearsed as secondary tasks in parallel with the learning of a new (primary) task using the ηMTL neural network algorithm, a variant of multiple task learning (MTL). The ηMTL algorithm uses a measure of task relatedness to selectively transfer knowledge from the the most related secondary tasks to the hypothesis for a new task. In this way positive inductive bias from prior knowledge is obtained.

The results of repeated experiments on two synthetic and two real domains of tasks demonstrate that TRM with ηMTL produces hypotheses of significantly greater accuracy than either STL or TRM with MTL for tasks with impoverished training data. The success can be attributed to the functional knowledge within the virtual examples generated by the TRM and to the effective use of that knowledge through ηMTL's ability to select the more related secondary tasks. In a similar manner, the TRM with ηMTL is able to mitigate but not eliminate the effect of the negative inductive bias on tasks that have sufficient training examples. Further work on the generation and use of virtual examples as well as the development of better measures of task relatedness are required in order to improve upon selection of inductive bias.

TRM is attractive because of the scalability of its method of task knowledge retention and virtual example generation. Furthermore, TRM provides the freedom to use available training examples for new tasks and the ability to generate additional virtual examples for secondary task rehearsal.

Perhaps of greatest importance, the work on TRM has confirmed the importance and complexity of adding background knowledge to machine learning systems. If inductive bias is a function of stored domain knowledge and a measure of task relatedness, then inductive bias is always relative to the frame of reference created by the previously learned tasks. This requires that domain knowledge be carefully managed; for example, we have observed that redundant task knowledge and task error must be minimized. We are now of the opinion that a consolidated representation of domain knowledge tasks would have a number of benefits over the independent task representations that were used in the experiments of this paper. Consolidated domain knowledge would provide the potential for more efficient learning through representation transfer. It would also allow the use of better measures of task relatedness based on structural similarity of shared representation. More recent research has explored the consolidation of domain knowledge and its use within the TRM (Silver & McCracken, 2003, O'Quinn et al., 2005, Silver & Poirier, 2004).

8. Acknowledgments

The authors wish to express their gratitude for funding provided by the Government of Canada through NSERC.

9. References

Yaser S. Abu-Mostafa. Hints. *Neural Computation*, 7:639–671, 1995.

Jonathan Baxter. Learning internal representations. *Proceedings of the Eighth International Conference on Computational Learning Theory*, 1995.

Jock A. Blackard and Denis J. Dean. Comparative accuracies of artificial neural networks and discriminant analysis in predicting forest cover types from cartographic variables. *Computers and Electronics in Agriculture*, 24(3):131–151, 2000.

James L. Carroll, Todd Peterson, and Kevin Seppi. Reinforcement learning task clustering. In M. Arif Wani, editor, *Proceedings of the Internation Conference on Machine Learning and Applications (ICMLA'03)*, pages 66–72, Los Angeles, CA, 2003.

Richard A. Caruana. Multitask learning. *Machine Learning*, 28:41–75, 1997.

Janosi-A. SteinbrunnW. Pfisterer M. Schmid J. Sandhu S. Guppy K. Lee S. & Froelicher V. Detrano, R. International application of a new probability algorithm for the diagnosis of coronary artery disease. *American Journal of Cardiology*, 64:304–310, 1989.

S.E. Fahlman and C. Lebiere. The cascade-correlation learning architecture. *Advances in Neural Information Processing Systems 2*, 2:524–532, 1990. ed. D.S. Touretsky.

Stephen Grossberg. Competitive learning: From interactive activation to adaptive resonance. *Cognitive Science*, 11:23–64, 1987.

S. J. Hanson. A stochastic version of the delta rule. *Physica D*, 42:265–272, 1990.

Thomas Heskes and Bert Kappen. On-line learning processes in artificial neural networks. In J. Taylor, editor, *Mathematical Foundations of Neural Networks*. Elsevier, Amsterdam, Netherlands, 1993.

R.A. Jacobs. Increased rates of convergence through learning rate adaptation. *Neural Networks*, 1:295–307, 1988.

E. James Kehoe. A layered network model of associative learning: Learning to learn and configuration. *Psychological Review*, 95(4):411–433, 1988.

James L. McClelland, Bruce L. McNaughton, and Randall C. O'Reilly. Why there are complementary learning systems in the hippocampus and neocortex: Insights from the successes and failures of connectionist models of learning and memory. *Technical Report PDP.CNS.94.1*, 1994.

Michael McCloskey and Neal J. Cohen. Catastrophic interference in connectionist networks: the sequential learning problem. *The Psychology of Learning and Motivation*, 24:109–165, 1989.

R.S. Michalski. Learning = inferencing + memorizing. *Foundations of Knowledge Acquistion: Machine Learning*, pages 1–41, 1993.

Tom Mitchell and Sebastian Thrun. Explanation based neural network learning for robot control. *Advances in Neural Information Processing Systems 5*, 5:287–294, 1993. ed. C. L. Giles and S. J. Hanson and J.D. Cowan.

Tom. M. Mitchell. The need for biases in learning generalizations. *Readings in Machine Learning*, pages 184–191, 1980. ed. Jude W. Shavlik and Thomas G. Dietterich.

Tom M. Mitchell. *Machine Learning*. McGraw Hill, New York, NY, 1997.

D.K. Naik, R. J. Mammone, and A. Agarwal. Meta-neural network approach to learning by learning. *Intelligence Engineering Systems through Artificial Neural Networks*, 2:245–252, 1992.

D.K. Naik and Richard J. Mammone. Learning by learning in neural networks. *Artificial Neural Networks for Speech and Vision*, 1993.

Robert O'Quinn, Daniel L. Silver, and Ryan Poirier. Continued practice and consolidation of a learning task. In *Proceedings of the Meta-Learning Workshop, 22nd International Conference on Machine Learning (ICML 2005)*, Bonn, Germany, 2005.

Lorien Pratt and Barbara Jennings. A survey of transfer between connectionist networks. *Connection Science Special Issue: Transfer in Inductive Systems*, 8(2):163–184, 1996.

Lorien Y. Pratt. Discriminability-based transfer between neural networks. *Advances in Neural Information Processing Systems 5*, 5:204–211, 1993. ed. C. L. Giles and S. J. Hanson and J.D. Cowan.

Mark Ring. Learning sequential tasks by incrementally adding higher orders. *Advances in Neural Information Processing Systems 5*, 5:155–122, 1993. ed. C. L. Giles and S. J. Hanson and J.D. Cowan.

Mark Ring. Child: A first step towards continual learning. *Machine Learning*, 28(1):77–109, 1997.

Francois Rivest. *Knowledge-Transfer in Neural Network: Knowledge-Based Cascade-Correlation*. PhD Thesis, School of Computer Science, McGill University, Montreal, PQ, 2003.

Anthony V. Robins. Catastrophic forgetting, rehearsal, and pseudorehearsal. *Connection Science*, 7:123–146, 1995.

Anthony V. Robins. Consolidation in neural metworks and in the sleeping brain. *Connection Science Special Issue: Transfer in Inductive Systems*, 8(2):259–275, 1996.

Noel E. Sharkey and Amanda J.C. Sharkey. Adaptive generalization and the transfer of knowledge. *Working paper - Center for Connection Science*, 1992.

Jude W. Shavlik and Geoffrey G. Towell. An appraoch to combining explanation-based and neural learning algorithms. *Readings in Machine Learning*, pages 828–839, 1990. ed. Jude W. Shavlik and Thomas G. Dietterich.

Thomas R. Shultz and Francois Rivest. Knowledge-based cascade-correlation: Varying the size and shape of relevant prior knowledge. *New Developments in Psychometrics*, pages 631–638, 2003.

Daniel L. Silver. *Selective Transfer of Neural Network Task Knowledge*. PhD Thesis, Dept. of Computer Science, University of Western Ontario, London, Canada, 2000.

Daniel L. Silver and Peter McCracken. The consolidation of neural network task knowledge. In M. ArifWani, editor, *Proceedings of the International Conference on Machine Learning and Applications (ICMLA'03)*, pages 185–192, Los Angeles, CA, 2003.

Daniel L. Silver and Robert E. Mercer. The parallel transfer of task knowledge using dynamic learning rates based on a measure of relatedness. *Connection Science Special Issue: Transfer in Inductive Systems*, 8(2):277–294, 1996.

Daniel L. Silver and Robert E. Mercer. Selective functional transfer: Inductive bias from related tasks. *Proceedings of the International Conference on Artificial Intelligence and Soft Computing (ASC2001)*, pages 182–189, 2001.

Daniel L. Silver and Ryan Poirier. Sequential consolidation of learned task knowledge. *Lecture Notes in Artificial Intelligence, 17th Conference of the Canadian Society for Computational Studies of Intelligence* (AI'2004), pages 217–232, 2004.

Satinder P. Singh. Transfer of learning by composing solutions for elemental sequential tasks. *Machine Learning*, 1992.

Steven Suddarth and Y Kergoisien. Rule injection hints as a means of improving network performance and learning time. Proceedings of the EURASIP workshop on Neural Networks, 1990.

Sebastian Thrun. Lifelong learning: A case study. *Technical Report CMU-CS-95-208*, Nov 1995.

Sebastian Thrun. Is learning the nth thing any easier than learning the first? *Advances in Neural Information Processing Systems 8*, 8, 1996.

Sebastian Thrun. Lifelong learning algorithms. *Learning to Learn*, pages 181–209, 1997.

Sebastian Thrun and J. O'Sullivan. Clustering learning tasks and the selective cross-task transfer of knowledge. *Technical Report CMU-CS-95-209*, Nov 1995.

Sebastian Thrun and Lorien Pratt. Learning to learn: Introduction and overview. *Learning to Learn*, pages 3–17, 1997.

Geoffrey G. Towell, Jude W. Shavlik, and Michiel O. Noordewier. Refinement of approximate domain theories by knowledge-based neural networks. *Proceedings of the Eighth National Conference on Artificial Intelligence (AAAI-90)*, 2:861–866, 1990.

Paul E. Utgoff. *Machine Learning of Inductive Bias*. Kluwer Academc Publisher, Boston, MA, 1986.

Ricardo Vilatlta and Youssef Drissi. A prespective view and survey of meta-learning. *Artificial Intelligence Review*, 18(2):77–95, 2002.

T.P. Vogl, J.K. Mangis, A.K. Rigler, W.T. Zink, and D.L. Alkon. Accelerating the convergence of the back-propagation method. *Biological Cybernetics*, 59:257–263, 1988.

C. Wang and J. C. Principe. Training neural networks with additive noise in the desired signal. *IEEE Transactions on Neural Networks*, 10(6):1511, 1999.

23

Machine Learning for Video Repeat Mining

Xianfeng Yang[1] and Qi Tian[2]
[1]*Academy of Broadcasting Science,*
[2]*Institute for Infocomm Research,*
[1]*China*
[2]*Singapore*

1. Introduction

An incommensurable amount of digital audiovisual information is becoming available in digital archives, on the World Wide Web, in broadcast data streams and in personal and professional databases, and this amount is only growing. Mining short video repeats is just providing an effective way to extract useful information from fast growing video data and exploit the reuse value of video archives. Short video clips, ranging from a few seconds to a few minutes, are widely used in many types of video production, including news video, sports video, education program where they serve as program logo, station logo, sports reply flying logo or as commercials. These short video clips are repeated many times in these video programs because of the nature of their usages in video production. Identifying these short video repeats based on their contents has great value in many media applications. First it can be used to monitor commercials and detect infringement of copyrighted content in broadcast videos or web videos (Agnihotri et al., 2003; Cheung et al., 2005; Lienhart et al., 1997; Snchez et al., 2002; Kashino et al., 2003; Yuan et al., 2004), and this content based video identification approach is an important complementary method to other media copyright protection techniques such as watermarking. Second, short video repeat mining is very useful in video structure analysis task. By detecting video repeats in unlabeled raw video data, we can discover correlation of different video parts and structural video elements used for syntactic segmentation purpose, thus video structure model can be effectively constructed and applied to video syntactical segmentation (Yang & Tian et al., 2007). Structure analysis by finding repeat objects has also been extensively employed in DNA data mining domain (Kurtz & Schleiermacher, 1999; Bao & Eddy, 2002). Video repeat mining also has many other applications, such as content summary, personalization as well as lossless video compression (Pua & Gauch, 2004).

Video repeats are defined as those video clips having the same video contents, but low level signal distortions are allowed, such as noises, image quality reduction, frame size change et al. Video repeat mining problem can be classified into two categories: one problem is to identify known video repeats. In this case we have a model of a sample video in advance, then use this model to detect its repeated instances in video archives, which is treated as a pattern recognition problem; The second problem is to identify unknown video repeats. In this case we do not have prior knowledge about the video repeats including their frame content, length and location. What we do is to define some rules to discover these video repeats through machine learning techniques, which is treated as a data mining problem.

To identify known short video repeats, we propose a novel representation scheme for short video clips based on composite HMM. HMM is a powerful statistical model for time-series data and composite HMM is a network of single HMM. Composite HMM has been successfully applied to speech recognition (Rabiner, 1989; Young et al., 2000), and we will show it also has good performance on video sequence recognition. Compared to single HMM approach proposed by Kulesh et al. (2002), composite HMM approach is more robust to temporal editing of video clip (Yang et al., 2003).

To solve unknown video repeat mining problem, we propose a novel approach which combines with video segmentation, self-similarity analysis, cascaded detection, LSH indexing and reinforcement learning (Yang et al., 2005; Yang & Xue et al., 2007; Yang & Tian et al., 2007). Video self-similarity was used by Cooper & Foote (2001) to detect scene boundary, and we applied this approach to repeat sequence detection. Compared to other media repeat pattern identification methods (Cheung et al., 2005; Herley, 2006; Pua & Gauch, 2004), our approach can detect very short repeats (e.g. those less than 1 second) along with long ones, and high accuracy has been achieved in our experiments. Methods by Cheung et al. (2005) and Herley (2006) both use a fixed time window to do feature extraction and comparison, so those repeats significantly shorter than the window are very likely be missed. The method by Pua et al. (2004) is able to identify repeated shots but can not identify partially repeated shots, while our approach can identify even small portion of a shot or clip by adopting segmentation with granularity smaller than the shot. Another novelty of our approach is that a reinforcement learning approach is adopted to train the video repeat detectors, and this approach demonstrates effectiveness and efficiency in parameter learning, which makes the repeat mining system manageable and easy to train.

The remainder of this chapter is arranged as follows: In section 2, we present the HMM based video repeat identification approach. In section 3, we present the unknown video repeat mining method, and concluding remarks are presented in section 4.

2. Short video clip recognition by composite HMM

In this section we propose a composite HMM approach to represent known short video clips and recognize their repeated instances. This approach is not only robust to video feature distorion but also robust to temporal editing. Details of this approach are presented in the following.

2.1 Short video clip modeling

The modeling process is divided into two levels. The first level is the clip level modeling based on video shots, and the second level is shot modeling using HMM. A video clip is composed of a series of shots, and the reproduction of the clip is often based on shot editing, so it is meaningful to exploit the clip structure based on shots. In this approach, a video clip is firstly segmented into shots, and a directed graph G is used to represent the temporal constraints of the shots. Each shot is a node of the graph G. If shot 1 precedes shot 2, then shot 2 is a child node of shot 1, and there is a directed edge from shot 1 to shot 2. It is assumed that a shot can reach any of its child nodes. Besides all the shots, two other null nodes are added into the graph, namely entry node and exit node. Entry node is the parent node of any other node, and exit node is the child node of any other node. These two nodes will not occupy any time. The clip graph with 4 shot nodes is shown as Fig. 1 in which shot 1 precedes shot2, shot 2 precedes shot3, and shot3 precedes shot 4. In the clip graph, not only the temporal constraints of the shots of sample video clip are preserved, but also the possible structure variations of the clip are also included. For example, because the entry node can reach any child node, the sequence can start from any shot, and end at any shot. This graph representation is suitable for short video clips because the number of shots in them is generally within 20, so the graph will not be complex.

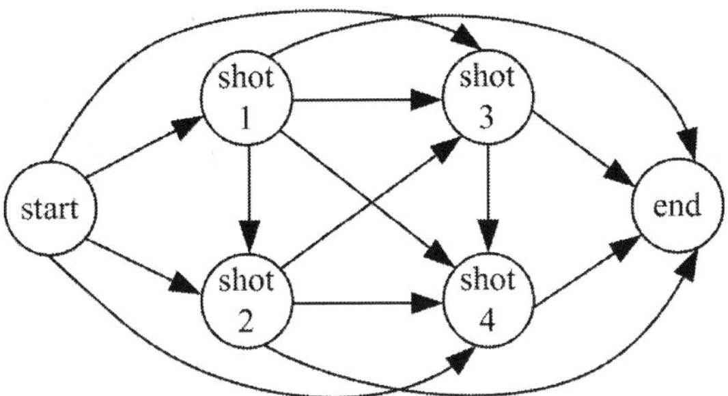

Fig. 1. Clip graph with 4 shots

For each shot node, one HMM is used to represent the color feature distribution within the shot, so the clip graph G becomes as a composite HMM. The RGB histogram of a frame is chosen as the color feature vector, and all the frame features constitute the feature sequence. Each color channel is quantized into 8 bins, resulting in a 512 dimensional feature vector. To reduce the dimensionality of the feature, the feature vectors are mapped to symbols by vector quantization, so the color feature sequence is transformed to a symbol sequence which is used for model training and testing. The symbol values do not represent real feature values, and adjacent symbol values do not mean that their underlying real feature values are close to each other.

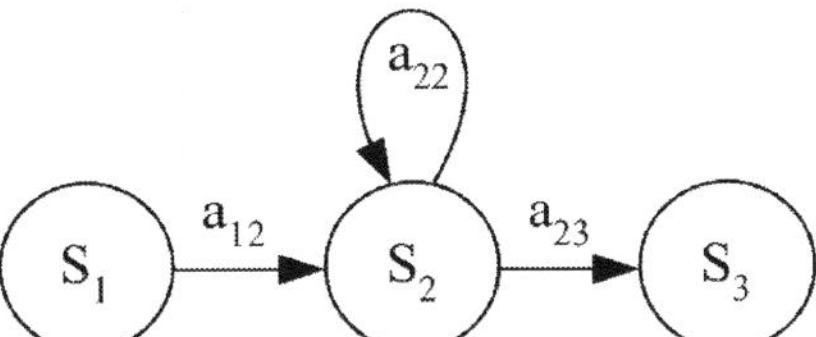

Fig. 2. One state HMM for a shot

Because in many cases the color within one shot is homogeneous, so we choose one state HMM to represent the color statistics. In order to connect to other models in recognition networks, one entry and one exit state are added to the model, as shown in Fig.2. S_1 and S_3 are entry and exit state of the model. The self transition probabilities of S_1 and S_3 are both zeros, and a_{12} equals to one. S_2 is the state that actually captures the color statistics of the shot. The output probability distribution, as well as the state transition probabilities a_{22} and a_{23}, is estimated by Bum-Welch algorithm (Rabiner, 1989). Each model is trained by symbol sequences of sample videos. The learning results show that parameter a_{22} is generally a large value close to 1, while a_{23} is a small value close to 0. The output probability of the state is the discrete probability of the symbols.

2.2 Video repeat recognition using composite HMM

After the video clip model was built, recognition of a test video sequence is to compute the likelihood of the test sequence generated from this model. Given a composite HMM G and the test video's symbol sequence $o_1 o_2 \cdots o_n$, the log probability of $o_1 o_2 \cdots o_n$ generated from G is computed by maximizing the following conditional probability:

$$\log P(O_1 O_2 \cdots O_n | G) \approx$$
$$\max \sum_{i=1}^{m} \log P(O_{starti} O_{starti+1} \cdots O_{endi} | N_i \in G) \tag{1}$$

where m is the total number of nodes the test sequence passes through, N_i represents one node of G, and N_i is a child node of N_{i-1}, for $2 \leq i \leq m$. $\log P(O|N_i)$ is the logarithm probability of sequence O belonging to shot model N_i. o_{starti} is the first observed feature assigned to node N_i, and o_{endi} is the last observed feature assigned to node N_i. The maximum score can be efficiently computed by Viterbi algorithm.

Because the testing sequence may have variable length, the score should be normalized by the sequence length. The average log probability per frame is used to make decision. If there are multiple video models, the test sequence will be match against each model. If the highest score is above a threshold, then the title of the model is determined as the title of the test video.

2.3 Results

In the experiment, 100 different advertisement clips ranging from 10 to 60 seconds are collected for model building. The video format is: MPEG-1, CIF, frame rate 30fps, bit-rate 242 kbits/s. The average number of the shot per clip is 11. Several clips have more than 20 shots, but some have less than 5 shots. The color features of all the shots are extracted and used to construct the codebook of vector quantization. The codebook size is set to 128.

To test this method's robustness against feature distortion, the clips for modeling are transformed by the following operations: Frame rate is reduced to 8fps; bit-rate is reduced to 121 kbits/s. To test the recognition performance on shorter version of the video clips, we remove nearly half of the shots from each clip and join the rest shots together. The shots are removed by this way: shot 1,3,5,... are retained, while shot 2,4,6,... are removed. The transcoding and cut version clips are considered as true positive samples. In addition, another 100 clips which do not belong to any of the 100 advertisement clips are used as negative test samples. So there are totally 300 test samples.

As a performance comparison, each clip is also modeld by with single HMM approach proposed by Kulesh et al. (2002). The number of the states of HMM is set as the number of shots of the clip. The ROC curves of our approach and single HMM is shown in Fig.3. As is shown the ROC curve of composite HMM is closer to the origin than single HMM approach. The performance comparison of two approaches is also shown in Table 1.

From Table 1 we can see that the composite HMM outperforms single HMM when recognizing clip's cut versions. Even though nearly half of the shots are missing in the cut version, composite HMM approach can correctly recognize them and the error is just about 1%. This result coincides with our expectation that composite HMM would more accurately model the video clip and its variations. The results also show that composite HMM is robust to transcoding operations which severely change the quality of the image and the frame rate.

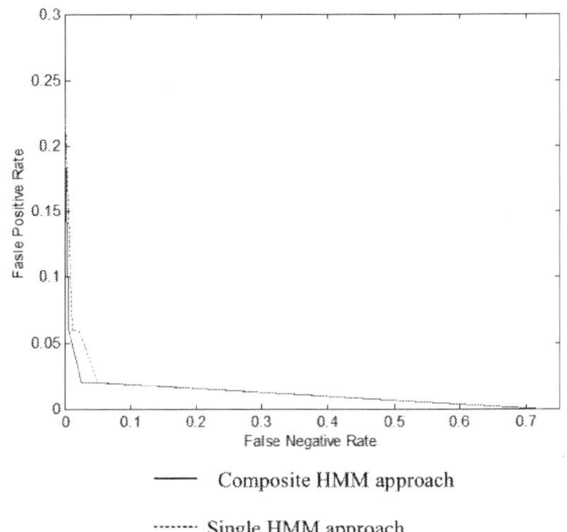

Fig. 3. Receiver Operating Curve: FNR vs FPR

Accuracy	Transcoded version	Cut version
Composite HMM	98.0%	99.0%
single HMM	98.0%	96.0%

Table 1. Recognition performance comparison

3. Unknown video repeat mining

This section we propose a novel approach for unknown repeat repeats mining. Two detectors in a cascade structure are employed to achieve fast and accurate detection, and a reinforcement learning approach is adopted to efficiently maximize detection accuracy. In this approach very short video repeats (< 1s) and long ones can be detected by a single process, while overall accuracy remains high. Since video segmentation is essential for repeat detection, performance analysis is also conducted for several segmentation methods.

3.1 Method overview

The proposed repeat mining framework is shown as Fig. 4. It contains the following main components: 1) video abstraction and feature extraction function; 2) two stage detectors in cascade. The first stage detector performs similarity analysis on abstracted form of video to efficiently detect most true repeats with a reasonable size of errors, while the second stage detector performs more accurate classification on candidate repeat clips based on their full frames; 3) two detection modes: stand-alone and reference mode. The stand-alone mode is detecting unknown repeats from one input video through self-similarity analysis, while reference mode is detecting repeats between two videos by cross-similarity analysis, and this mode can be used to search known video clips in video stream; 4) locality-sensitive hashing (LSH) of video unit features used to reduce repeat searching complexity; 5) repeat instance extraction and labeling.

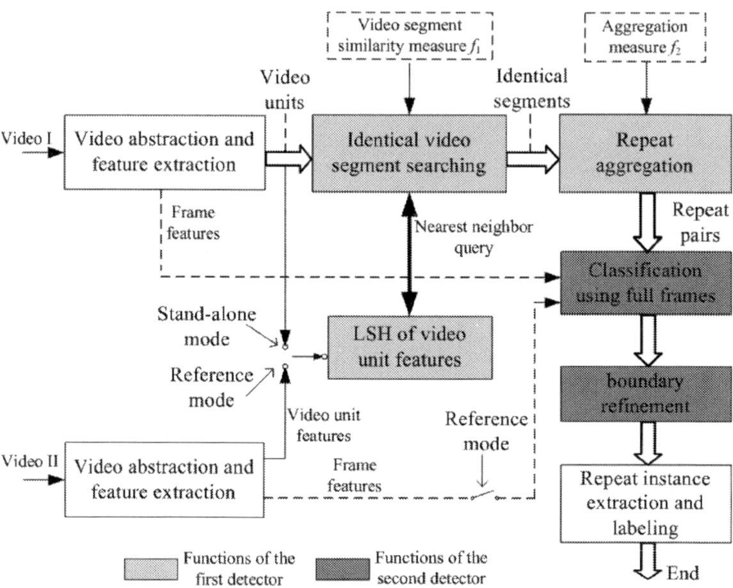

Fig. 4. Framework of repeat clip mining

The first step in this framework is video data reduction and feature extraction. Raw video data is sampled or segmented into a sequence of basic video units (VU) and their features are calculated to feed into the first detector. Meanwhile feature of each frame is computed for the second detector.

The first stage detector discovers unknown repeats through two steps. Firstly W neighbor video units are bunched into bigger size video segments (VS), e.g. two units as one group. Then time-indexed segments are compared with each other using a binary similarity measure f_1 to find identical segment pairs. The set of identical segment pairs is denoted as

$$\omega : \{(VS_{i_1}, VS'_{j_1}), (VS_{i_2}, VS'_{j_2}), \cdots, (VS_{i_n}, VS'_{j_n})\},$$ where $i_1, \ldots, i_n$ and $j_1, \ldots, j_n$ are time indexes, and VS_i, VS'_j represents the ith and jth video segment. If in stand-alone mode VS_i and VS'_j will belong to the same video, but in reference mode they will lie in two input videos respectively. Secondly identical segment pairs are aggregated into repeat clips by aggregation measure $f_2 : \omega' \subset \omega \mapsto (VC, VC')$, where (VC, VC') is a repeat clip pair, and in

reference mode VC, VC' will lie in two input videos respectively. If binary similarity values between time-indexed video segments are embedded into a binary matrix S in which '1' represents one identical segment pair, then repeat clips will correspond to diagonal tracks of '1'. Under stand-alone mode S is a self-similarity matrix, so diagonal tracks should offset from the main diagonal by a certain time.

The first detector also contains an LSH function to reduce complexity of identical segment searching. Suppose similarity measure f_1 is based on distance in feature space, each video segment only needs to compare with those within a distance to find its identical ones, which would be a small portion of the total segments. LSH is such a method that can efficiently perform approximate nearest neighbor search even in high dimensional space. In stand-alone mode all video units of the input video will both be indexed by LSH and used as queries, but in reference mode only one video's units are indexed, while the other's act as queries.

To improve detection accuracy the second cascaded detector employs full frames matching to further classify candidate repeat pairs obtained from the first detector. Once a repeat pair is verified a boundary refinement is followed to extend their boundaries to the maximum ones.

The last step of this framework is to extract repeat instances from repeat pairs and group them into multiple categories each of which represents an independent repeat pattern.

3.2 Video representation

The two stage detectors adopt different video representations. The first stage detector performs video abstraction to reduce detection complexity. However, data loss by abstraction will downgrade the detection accuracy. Therefore it is important to choose suitable abstraction strategy to balance detection efficiency and accuracy, and we are especially interested in that for short video repeats detection.

3.2.1 Video abstraction strategy

Video abstraction methods usually depend on frame sampling. Uniform sampling is simple, but it disregards video characteristic, so content redundancy can not be well removed. Moreover, this method is not robust to boundary shift between two repeat objects. Content-based keyframe selection is more effective for video abstraction. It can well remove video redundancy while capturing significance of video sequence (Zhang et al., 1997). Generally it can achieve more than ten times frame reduction. Shot based video representation is also widely used in video analysis. However, its granularity is probably too big to effectively detect many short video repeats.

Content-based keyframes is the first choice for video abstraction in our approach. Keyframe selection can be based on color or motion criterions. The interval between two consecutive keyframes is treated as the basic video unit (VU), as is shown in Fig. 5, and its average granularity should be smaller than that of shots. This video unit representation can also compensate temporal information loss of simple keyframes sampling because temporal and motion features can be extracted from the unit. The second level video representation (VS) is formed by grouping two neighbor units, e.g. the ith unit and $(i+1)th$ unit forming the ith video segment. Compared to the first level, the second level has almost the same number of video samples, but its discriminative ability will improve a lot, thus providing a less noisy platform to build higher repeat clip level.

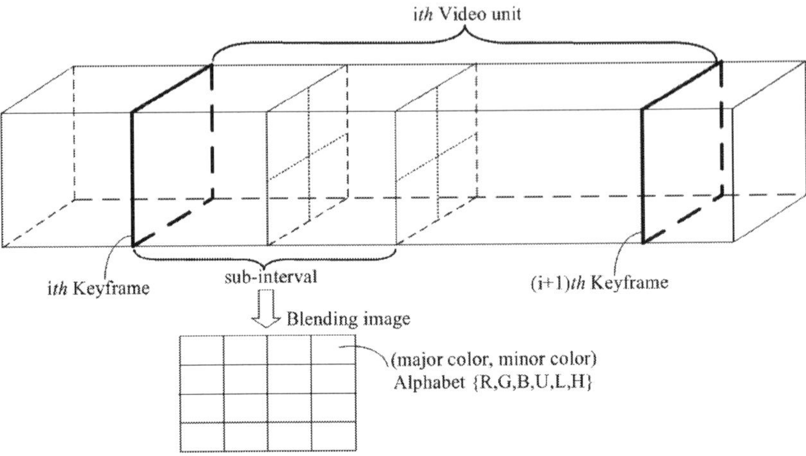

Fig. 5. Illustration of video segmentation and feature extraction

3.2.2 Video features

Two types of video features are extracted. The first one is video unit (VU) feature used by the first stage detector, and the second one is frame feature for the second stage detector.

1.   Video unit feature

Video unit feature includes interval length and color fingerprint proposed by Yang et. al (2004). A video unit is partitioned into K sub-intervals, and represented by K blending images formed by averaging frames within each sub-interval along time direction. Each blending image is then divided into $M{\times}N$ equal size blocks each of which is represented by the major and minor color components among RGB, as illustrated in Fig. 5. Color fingerprint is the ordered catenation of these block features. If $\overline{R}$, $\overline{G}$, $\overline{B}$ are the average color values of a block, and their descending order is (V_1, V_2, V_3), then the major color and minor color are determined by the following rules:

Rule 1: if $V_1 > V_3$,

$$\text{Major Color} = \begin{cases} \arg\max(\overline{R},\overline{G},\overline{B}) & \text{if } (V_1 - V_3) > \tau \\ \text{Uncertain} & \text{if } (V_1 - V_3) \le \tau \end{cases}$$

$$\text{Minor Color} = \begin{cases} \arg\min(\overline{R},\overline{G},\overline{B}) & \text{if } (V_2 - V_3) > \tau \\ \text{Uncertain} & \text{if } (V_2 - V_3) \le \tau \end{cases}$$

Where τ is the parameter that controls the robustness to color distortion and discriminative ability of this feature.

Rule 2: if $V_1 = V_3$ (gray image),

$$\text{Major Color} = \text{Minor Color} = \begin{cases} \text{bright} & \text{if } V_1 > \tau_1 \\ \text{dark} & \text{if } V_1 \le \tau_1 \end{cases}$$

Major and minor color patterns have six possible symbol values from alphabet {R, G, B, U, L, H}, where U, L and H stand for uncertain, dark and bright respectively. In this work one blending image ($K=1$) is used for each unit, and divided into 8x8 blocks ($M=N=8$), thus the color feature is a 128 dimensional symbol vector. Parameter τ is set to 3.0 to achieve good balance between robustness and discriminative ability, while τ_1 is set to 127.

2.   Frame feature

Each frame is divided into 4 sub-frames, and RGB color histogram(8x8x8 bins) of each sub-frame is quantized to a symbol by VQ, so each frame is represented by 4 symbols.

3.3 Detector functions
3.3.1 Video segment similarity measure

Given two video units vu_i and vu_j, their distance $D(vu_i, vu_j)$ is defined as

$$D(vu_i, vu_j) = \sqrt{d^2(F_i, F_j) + \left[len(vu_i) - len(vu_j) \right]^2}$$
(2)

where F_i, F_j are color fingerprint vectors of vu_i and vu_j, $d(F_i, F_j)$ is color fingerprint distance function (Yang et. al, 2004), $len(\cdot)$ is length feature. Similarity measure f_1 between the ith segment and jth segment $VS_j : \{vu_j, vu_{j+1}\}$ is defined as:

$$f_1(VS_i, VS_j) = \begin{cases} 1 & \text{if } D(vu_i, vu_j) < \varepsilon_1, D(vu_{i+1}, vu_{j+1}) < \varepsilon_1 \\ 0 & \text{otherwise} \end{cases}$$
(3)

where ε_1 is distance threshold.

3.3.2 Complexity reduction by LSH indexing

We apply LSH indexing on the color fingerprint to efficiently retrieve nearest neighbors of a video unit. LSH can perform $(\lambda;\varepsilon)$-NN similarity search in sub-linear time (Indyk and Motwani, 1998). For a query point $\mathbf{q}$ in d-dimensional space, if we want to retrieve its nearest neighbors in distance ε, LSH can return indexed points within a distance $(1+\lambda)\cdot\varepsilon$ ($\lambda>0$) with high probability, while those beyond this distance with low probability, and its efficiency is related to λ. Similarity search is realized by designing a set of hash functions that can make hash collision probability for two points be related to their distance. If two points are close, their hash collision probability should be high; otherwise it should be low. By using multiple such hash functions with different parameters in parallel, LSH can reduce the false negative rates.

LSH algorithm proposed by Gionis $et\ al.$(1999) transforms a feature vector into a bit string, and selects a subset of bits that satisfies locality-sensitive property. The color fingerprint can be easily converted to bit vector without incurring extra errors. The hashing algorithm is described in Table 2. According to this hash function, the hash collision probability of two points with p percent bit difference can be estimated as $1 - \left[1 - (1-p)^k \right]^l$. The two parameters k and l should be tuned to balance NN search accuracy and efficiency. Increasing k can improve recall but result in more non-nearest neighbors at mean time.

Select parameters k, l, and a hash table size M;
For i=1 to l,

Produce k different random integers $\{I_1^i,...,I_k^i\}$ within $[1, n]$
End

Produce k random integer hash coefficients $\{h_1,...,h_k\}$

Given a binary vector $B=\{b_1,...,b_n\}$
For i=1 to l,
Select subset of bits of B $\{b_{I_1^i},...,b_{I_k^i}\}$,

$$sum = b_{I_1^i} \cdot h_1 + \cdots + b_{I_k^i} \cdot h_k$$

$res = sum$ mod M;
Insert time index of B and partition number i into bucket res.
End

Table 2. LSH algorithm

3.3.3 Repeat aggregation algorithm

Repeat clips will appear as diagonals in similarity matrix. However, due to segmentation errors, the line will not be the integrated one. Moreover those line fragments will not be collinear if non-uniform partition is used. Fig. 6 shows part of a similarity matrix computed in our experiment. As we can see, diagonal tracks are fragmented and contaminated by noises. To get the whole repeat clip correctly we design a hierarchical aggregation algorithm purely based on temporal boundaries of repeat segments.

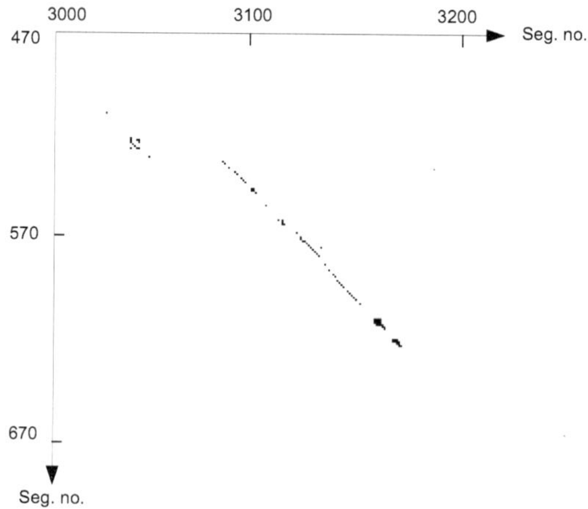

Fig. 6. Example of diagonal tracks for repeat sequences

This algorithm is described as follows:

Step 1.   First link strong diagonal tracks whose length exceeds one. The start and end time of two pairs of repeat sequences (I,I′) and (II,II′) corresponding to two diagonal lines are represented by $(T1_{start}, T1_{end})$, $(T1'_{start}, T1'_{end})$ and $(T2_{start}, T2_{end})$, $(T2'_{start}, T2'_{end})$ respectively, which is illustrated in Fig. 7.

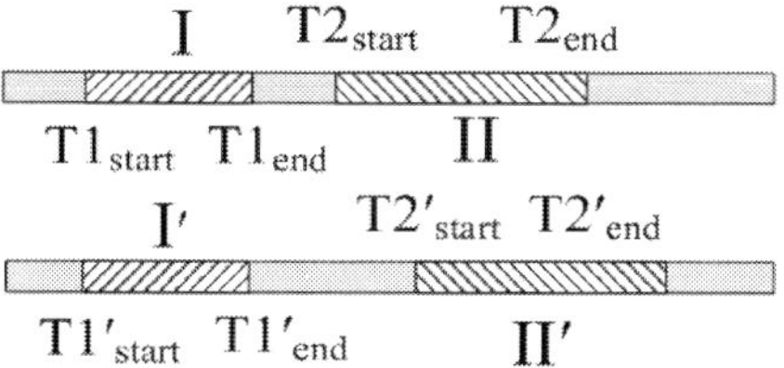

Fig. 7. Illustration of two pairs of adjacent repeat segments

If one of the two conditions in (4) is satisfied, (I,I') and (II,II') will be merged into one repeat pair.

a. Overlap: $T1_{start} \leq T2_{start} \leq T1_{end}$, $T1'_{start} \leq T2'_{start} \leq T1'_{end}$

b. Adjacency: $|T2_{start} - T1_{end}| < \mu_1$, $|T2'_{start} - T1'_{end}| < \mu_1$, $|(T2_{start} - T1_{end}) - (T2'_{start} - T1'_{end})| < \varepsilon_2$ (4)

where μ_1 defines neighborhood distance, ε_2 is displacement allowed for neighbor repeat segments, thus controls temporal variations of the whole repeat clip.

Boundaries of merged repeat pair are computed as:

$$T_{start} = \min(T1_{start}, T2_{start}), \quad T_{end} = \max(T1_{end}, T2_{end}) ;$$

$$T'_{start} = \min(T1'_{start}, T2'_{start}), \quad T'_{end} = \max(T1'_{end}, T2'_{end}).$$

This new repeat pair will be put into the repeats list to replace originals, and the above process is iterated till no change of the list.

Step 2. Connecting single dots based on results of step 1 with the same merging criterion as step 1.

Step 3. The connected sequences after above two steps are further connected and merged until there is no change.

By the above aggregation algorithm the whole image of repeat clips can be well constructed from their local repeat segments, thus providing good foundation for further similarity analysis and boundary refinement. Moreover, this algorithm only needs to store boundaries of repeat segments but not similarity matrix, which can have efficient implementation for even large video data mining.

3.3.4 Second stage matching

In this stage the repeat pairs obtained from the first stage detection are further matched using their full frames in order to remove false positives. If a repeat pair only has minor length variation, simple frame by frame matching method can be used; otherwise, dynamic programming should be used to align two symbol sequences with different length. The total number of identical symbols of aligned frames is normalized by the average sequence length to get the similarity score. A repeat pair is classified as true one if the following condition is satisfied,

$$score > (1 + e^{-L})\varepsilon_3 \tag{5}$$

by gray codes corresponding to the outputs of n Bernoulli quasilinear units. After receiving a reinforcement r, the weights of Bernoulli quasilinear units are updated by

$$\Delta w_i = \alpha(r - b)(y_i - p_i) \tag{7}$$

where α is a positive learning rate, b serves as a reinforcement baseline, y_i is the output of the ith Bernoulli quasilinear unit, and p_i is the Bernoulli distribution parameter. It has been shown by Williams (1992) that this learning algorithm statistically climbs the gradient of expected reinforcement in weight space, which means that the detector parameters will change in the direction along which the sum of recall and precision increases.

3.5 Results

This section presents experimental results of repeat detection accuracy and efficiency, performance comparison for different segmentation methods, and news video structure analysis results. Experiments are mainly conducted on news videos, but several hour movies and commercials are also included. CNN and ABC news videos from TRECVID data are chosen to form two video collections each of which contains 12 day programs with 6 hours around. The CNN news videos contain a lot of repeated commercials and program logos, such as headline news logo, health program and sports program logo etc, with length ranging from less than 1s to 60s. ABC news videos contain few program logos, but still contain many repeated commercials. It is also observed that there exist non-trivial distortions between many repeat clips especially for those short program logos, and distortions include color distortion, caption overlay, length truncation etc. So the two video collections provide a very good platform to test the robustness of a detection approach on variable length short video repeats.

A. Ground truth setting

To calculate recall of repeat clips, we manually inspect the two collections to find short repeats. Since manual identification of unknown repeats is quite difficult, we first boost a repeat detector with empirical parameters to get initial results based on which we further search interesting repeated program logos and commercials, but miss still scenes, such as anchor shots, black frames. By this approach we found 34 kinds of repeated clips with totally 186 repeat instances from CNN collection. Among the 34 repeat types 14 are program logos, while the rest are commercials. From ABC collection we found 35 kinds of repeated clips that have totally 116 instances, but only two types are program lead-in and lead-out, while the rest are all commercials.

B. Detector training

Parameters of the two detectors are learned by the approach presented in section 3.4. Three hour CNN news videos are randomly chosen for training. Videos are segmented by content based keyframes which are selected by the following criterion,

$$\left|1 - \text{inter}(H_1, H_0)\right| > \eta \tag{8}$$

where H_1 and H_0 are color histograms(RGB 8x8x8bins) of current decoded frame and the last keyframe respectively, $\text{inter}(\cdot, \cdot)$ is histogram intersection, η is threshold set to 0.15. Video unit feature is 128 dimensional color fingerprint plus unit length. Frame feature is 4 symbols, and codebook size of LBG VQ is 128. The vector quantizer is trained by histogram features of 5000 frames randomly chosen from a collection of commercials.

The reinforcement learning rate α in (7) is set to 0.01 and reinforcement baseline b set to 0.7. Parameters ε_1, ε_2 and ε_3 are each encoded by 5 bit gray code, so there are totally 15 Bernoulli units in this network. Parameter value range is set to [0,1]. Initial parameters are set to empirical values, and initial weights are all zeros. During each learning round we manually check the detection results to compute recall and precision, then feed their sum as reinforcement of the learning network. Recall and precision are calculated as (9).

$$recall = \frac{number\ of\ correct\ repeat\ instances}{number\ of\ all\ true\ repeat\ instances}$$

$$precision = \frac{number\ of\ correct\ repeat\ instances}{number\ of\ all\ detected\ instances} \tag{9}$$

In experiment recall and precision in the first round learning are 74% and 100%, but after ten rounds of learning, recall and precision already climb to 94.2% and 96% respectively. Since the next several rounds of learning do not lead to reinforcement increase, we then stop the learning.

C. Testing results

The trained detectors are tested on the rest 3 hour CNN videos and 6 hour ABC videos. Recall and precision on CNN videos are 92.3% and 96%, while 90.1% and 90% those for ABC videos. This accuracy is obtained without setting a minimum sequence length to filter errors, so most of the errors come from those very short clips. The shortest correct repeat detected is just 0.26s (partial of "play of the day" logo in CNN video), while the longest one is 75 seconds long. Our results also show that partial repeats can be effectively detected. In some repeat categories the shortest instance is less than half of the longest one.

Fig. 10 shows temporal distribution of short video repeats identified from CNN news videos of six days. Those repeat instances linked by curves are chosen as marker instances. From this map we can clearly see that the whole program is segmented into several layers each of which contains certain topics, such as health program, top stories, financial news, sports news, commercials et al.

We also measure how accurately the detected boundaries of repeat pairs approach their maximum boundaries which are manually chosen. We selected 300 repeated pairs that cover almost all repeat patterns and checked their boundary shift before boundary refinement. The smallest shift is 0 s, while the largest one is 16.4s. The average shift is 0.47s. Around 80% of the shifts are within 0.2 seconds. After frame by frame boundary refinement those large shifts can be effectively reduced to 0~1 second.

D. Performance analysis of segmentation methods

Video segmentation is essential for this approach, so experiments are conducted to compare performances by proposed keyframe based segmentation, uniform segmentation and shot segmentation. The video data are 3 hour CNN videos used in Section 3.5-B. Two keyframe based segmentations are implemented with η=0.15, 0.30 respectively. Uniform segmentation utilizes I frames (every 12 frames). Shot detection includes cuts, fades in-outs and dissolves. Video unit features for all segmentations are color fingerprint and length. The video segment (VS) size W for shot segmentation is set to 1, and the minimum number of diagonal points in repeat aggregation is also set to 1. Thus this method can not only detect single repeat shots, but also repeat clips beyond shots. Detectors are separately trained for each segmentation to achieve their nearly optimal performance, and training results are shown in Table 3.

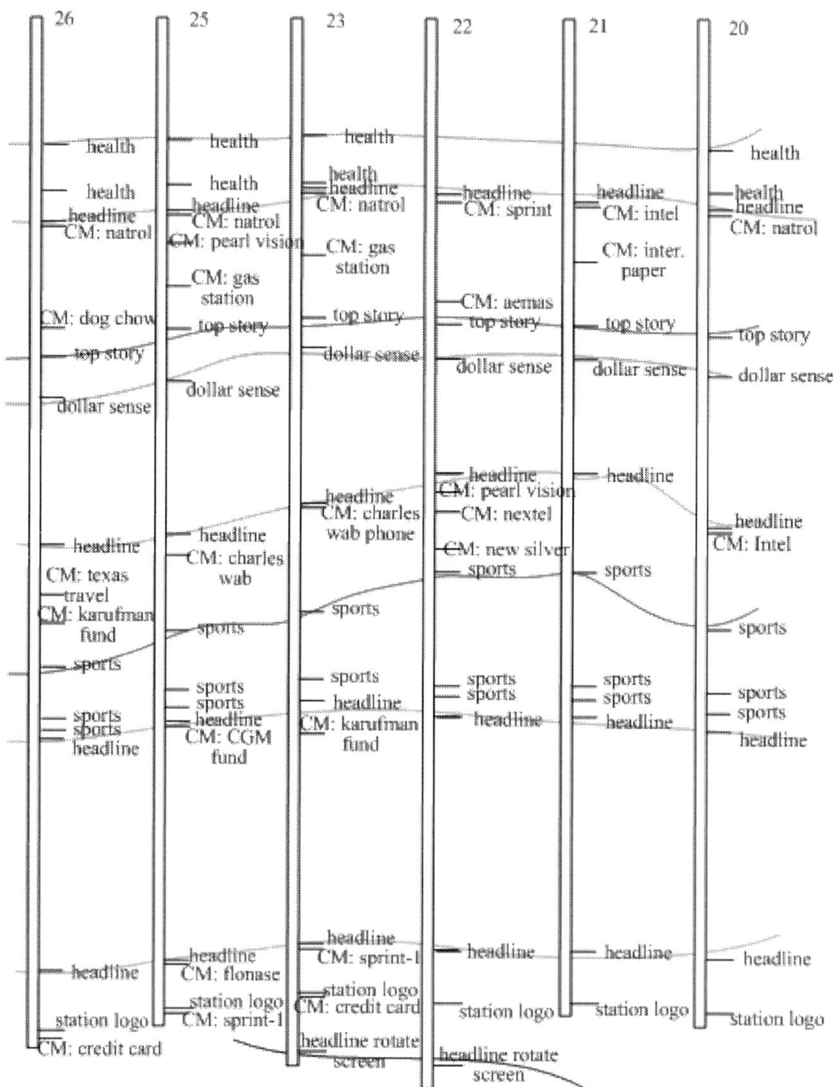

Fig. 10. CNN news video structure analysis by video repeats

	Uniform sampling	Keyframe (η =0.15)	Keyframe (η =0.30)	Shot based
recall	87.8%	94.2%	90.7%	66.7%
precision	95.9%	96.0%	86.0%	84.7%
Video units	26344	14872	6316	1911

Table 3. Performance comparison of video segmentation methods

From Table 3 we know that keyframe based segmentation achieves best performance. The uniform segmentation results in several times more video units than keyframes, but still gets lower recall on program logos and commercials. Uniform segmentation also detects quite many stationary scenes, such as anchor shots and black frames which occupy nearly 74% of the whole detected repeat clips pool thus overwhelm other interesting repeat patterns like program logos and commercials. Under keyframe based segmentation these still scenes are all filtered, program logos and commercials are main body of detected repeats. Shot based segmentation results in much fewer video units, but its total accuracy is much lower and many fast changing program logos are missed. When granularity of keyframe based segmentation becomes bigger, its performance will also drop because of heavier data loss.

E. Efficiency evaluation

1) **Speed**

In experiment LSH parameters are set as: k=50 and l=30, thereby the average number of retrieved units for a query unit of CNN collection (totally 629,380frames and 31496 units) is 320, and the number of color feature comparisons are further reduced to 20 by pre-filtering one dimension length feature at trained distance threshold ε_1 =0.1, thus speedup factor is about 1575 compared to pair-wise searching. For ABC collections (totally 616,780 frames and 29838 units), the average number of retrieved units for a query unit is 1026, and further reduced to 56 by length filtering, thus speedup factor is 533. On PC with Pentium-4 2.5GHz processor the two stage detections on 6 hour CNN videos can be finished in 22 seconds, while 40 seconds for ABC videos.

It is found that adjusting LSH parameters to shrink nearest neighbor distance would significantly reduce feature comparison complexity, but final recall almost does not change. For instance, when k =50 and l=30, recall of video units at distance threshold 0.1 for a query unit is roughly 37.4%, which is estimated from the hash collision probability. When k = 70 and l = 30, recall of video units at distance threshold 0.1 decreases to 8.4%. The average number of retrieved units for a query decreases from 320 to 186 for CNN collection, and from 1026 to 773 for ABC collection, but final recall of repeats does not drop, while precision even increases a bit. The main reason includes robust color fingerprint and repeat aggregation algorithm that is quite robust to loss of identical video segments on diagonal tracks. This property gives this approach much space to pursue speed without compromising accuracy.

When this approach works on reference mode to search one-minute video clip against 12 hour video database, the whole detection can be finished in 1 second after video features are extracted.

2) Storage requirement

In our implementation the color fingerprint is a 128-byte string, and length feature is a 4-byte float number. Frame feature is represented by four bytes. In our approach similarity matrix is not needed to be created, but only temporal boundaries of repeat segments should be stored, which usually occupy small memory and can be ignored. The storage requirements for 24 hours video database are as follows:

Color fingerprint + length feature: 15.5 Mega-bytes
Frame feature: 9.9 M; Hash table: 150 M
Total: 175 M

4. Conclusion

In this chapter we have proposed two methods to identify known and unknown video repeats respectively, and different machine learning approaches are used in the two methods. Composite HMM approach used for known short video repeat identification models the probabilistic temporal relation of the clip's shots as well as their frame feature distributions, and the model is trained by statistical learning approach. Although the model building process appears somewhat complex, the reward is that this approach can resist severe video content tamper, such as random shots removal. The color histogram used as observed feature in HMM shows robustness to feature distortion induced by transcoding.

The proposed unknown video repeat mining method achieves high accuracy on arbitrary length video repeats detection by cascaded detectors that employ different features and similarity measures. The detectors' performance can be efficiently optimized in a few rounds of reinforcement learning, which makes our approach easily adapt to different video data. Repeat searching complexity is largely reduced through video abstraction and LSH indexing. Moreover, the robust color fingerprint feature and repeat aggregation measure enable much space to pursue speed without compromising final detection accuracy. Video segmentation utilizing content-based keyframes achieves best balance between detection accuracy and efficiency on short video repeats compared to uniform and shot based segmentation. Results also show that short video repeats mining is an effective way to discover syntactic structure of news videos.

5. References

Agnihotri, L; Dimitrova, N; McGee, T; Jeannin, S; Schaffer, D& Nesvadba, J (2003). Evolvable visual commercial detector. *Proc. IEEE Int. Conf. Computer Vision and Pattern Recognition*, 2003.

Bao, Z; Eddy, S.R. Automated deno vo identification of repeat sequence families in sequenced genomes. Genome Research, 2002, 12 (8): 1269-1276.

Cheung, S-C. & Ngueyen, T P. (2005). Mining Arbitrary-length Repeated Patterns in Television Broadcast. *Proc. IEEE Int. Conf. on Image Processing*, 2005.

Cooper, M & Foote, J (2001). Scene Boundary Detection via Video Self-Similarity Analysis. *Proc. IEEE Int. Conf. Image Processing, 2001.*

Gionis, A; Indyky, P & Motwaniz, R (1999). Similarity Search in High Dimensions via Hashing. *Proc. Int. Conf. Very Large Data Bases*, pp. 518–529, 1999.

Herley, C (2006). ARGOS: Automatically Extracting Repeating Objects From Multimedia Streams. *IEEE Trans. Multimedia*, vol. 8, no. 1, pp. 113-129, Feb. 2006.

Indyk, P & Motwani, R (1998). Approximate Nearest Neighbor - Towards Removing the Curse of Dimensionality. in *Proc. the 30th Symposium on Theory of Computing*, 1998, pp. 604-613.

Kashino, K; Kurozumi, T & Murase H (2003). A quick search method for audio and video signals based on histogram pruning. *IEEE Trans. Multimedia*, vol. 5, no. 3, pp. 348–357, Sep. 2003.

Kulesh, V; Petrushin, V & Sethi, I (2002). Video Clip Recognition Using Joint Audio-Visual Processing Model. *Proc. Int. Conf. on Pattern Recognition* , August 2002, Quebec City, Canada.

Lienhart, R; Kuhmunch, C & Effelsberg, W (1997). On the detection and Recognition of Television Commercials. *Proc. IEEE Int. Conf. Multimedia Computing and Systems*, 1997.

Oostveen, J.C; Kalker, A.A.C & Haitsma, J.A (2001). Visual hashing of digital Video: applications and techniques. *Proc. SPIE applications of digital image processing XXIV*, July/August 2001, San Diego, USA.

Pua, K.M & Gauch, J.M (2004). Real time repeated video sequence identification. *Computer Vision and Image Understanding* 93 (2004) pp.310-327.

Rabiner, L.R (1989). A tutorial on hidden Markov model and selected application in speech recognition. *Proceedings of the IEEE*, 77 (2), 257-286, Feb. 1989.

Snchez, J.M; Binefa, X & Vitri, J (2002). Shot partitioning based recognition of TV commercials. *Multimedia Tools and Applications* 18 (2002), pp. 233–247.

Kurtz, S; Schleiermacher, C. REPuter: Fast computation of maximal repeats in complete genomes. Bioinformatics, 1999, 15 (5): 426-427.

Williams, R.J (1992). Simple Statistical Gradient-Following Algorithms for Connectionist Reinforcement Learning. *Machine Learning*, vol. 8, pp. 229-256, 1992.

Yang, X; Tian, Q & Gao, S (2003). Video clip representation and recognition using composite shot models. *Proc. IEEE Pacific Rim Conf. Multimedia 2003*, Singapore, Dec. 2003.

Yuan, J; Duan, L.-Y; Tian, Q & Xu, C (2004). Fast and robust short video clip search using an index structure. *Proc. ACM Multimedia's Multimedia Information Retrieval Workshop*, 2004.

Yang, X; Tian, Q & Chang, E.C (2004). A Color Fingerprint of Video Shot for Content Identification. *Proc. ACM Multimedia* 2004, NY, USA, 2004.

Yang, X; Xue, P & Tian, Q (2007). Automatically Discovering Unknown Short Video Repeats. *Proc. Inter. Conf. on Accoustic, Speech and Signal Processing (ICASSP)*, Hawaii, USA, 2007.

Yang, X; Xue, P & Tian, Q (2005). A repeated video clip identification system. in *Proc. ACM Multimedia*, Singapore, 2005.

Yang, X; Tian, Q & Xue, P (2007). Efficient Short Video Repeat Identification With Application to News Video Structure Analysis. *IEEE Trans. Multimedia*, vol.9, pp: 600 – 609, April 2007.

Young, S et al. (2000). "The HTK Book ver. 3.0", Cambridge University 2000.

Zhang, H. J; Wu, J; Zhong, D & Somaliar, S.W (1997). An integrated system for content-based video retrieval and browsing. *Pattern Recognition* 30 (1997), no. 4, pp. 643–658.